THE COMPLETE BOOK
OF
RETIREMENT
SECRETS

The Insider's Guide To A Happier
Healthier·Wealthier·Retirement

BOARDROOM CLASSICS
55 Railroad Ave., Greenwich, CT 06830

First Printing
10 9 8 7 6 5 4 3 2 1

Boardroom® Classics publishes the advice of expert authorities in
many fields. But the use of this material is not a substitute for
legal, accounting, or other professional services. Consult a
competent professional for answers to your specific questions.

Library of Congress Cataloging-in-Publication Data
Complete Book of Retirement Secrets
    p.cm.
    Includes index.
    ISBN 0-88723-121-7

Boardroom® Classics is a registered trademark of
Boardroom,® Inc.
55 Railroad Ave., Greenwich, CT 06830

Printed in the United States of America

Contents

4 • BANKING SAVVY

5 • ESTATE PLANNING STRATEGIES

6 • INSURANCE INFORMATION

7 • A HEALTHIER YOU

8 • YOUR EMOTIONAL HEALTH

9 • SECRETS OF SUCCESS

10 • MEDICAL PROBLEMS AND SOLUTIONS

11 • DOCTORS, HOSPITALS AND MEDICINES

15 • ENJOYING YOUR TRAVEL AND LEISURE

16 • SELF-DEFENSE

17 • RETIREMENT OPTIONS

1

Smart Ways to Save Money

How the Prudent Penny-Pincher Pinches Pennies

I am not a penny-pincher by nature. But four years ago I didn't have a choice. That's when my husband, Alan, was forced to take a new job with a decrease in salary of $25,000.

Almost overnight, a strict budget became essential for us and our four children, then ages 5, 11, 13 and 16. At first it was tough—but the more I learned, the more I enjoyed trying to save money without compromising our lifestyle too much.

Now it's a thrill to get a great deal—like finding a designer suit for $12 or cutting my grocery bill by one-third. Here's how I do it—and how anyone can cut costs without sacrificing too much…

Food…

• *Plan your food shopping.* Though I love to save money, I do not visit 10 different super-markets looking for the best price on each item. I don't have the time.

I shop only once every two weeks. That cuts down on impulse purchases. This is important because a lot of people bust their budgets with impulse buys. The more you shop, the greater the risk that you'll make an unplanned purchase.

I also do not clip dozens of coupons each week, though I use a few of them. My main strategy is to pick up the supermarket's circular the day before I do my marketing. That gives me a chance to plan menus around items that are on sale.

Savings: A recent bill for 10 bags of groceries was $141.60. It would have been $72.98 higher if I hadn't bought sale items. And it would have run an additional $21.39 more if I hadn't used coupons.

• *Buy in bulk.* When a staple product is on sale, I stock up and store goods on shelves in the basement. I also buy from a food co-op at wholesale prices. The minimum purchase at our co-op is $400, so we only do this occasionally, pooling our order with another large family.

1

We used to combine orders with a dozen families, but splitting up the food took hours and became a time-consuming chore. After all, time is money.

• *What you choose to eat can dramatically affect your food budget.*

Meat: For both health and money reasons, we eat very little meat. But we enjoy the taste of it, so sometimes I use small amounts to add flavor to pot pies, soups and stir-fry dishes.

Produce: I get the best deal by using store scales to weigh prepackaged fruits and vegetables. I buy the heaviest package and wind up with additional food worth about $3 per supermarket visit.

I also never buy produce out of season. Asparagus, for example, is three times as expensive during the winter as it is during the spring.

• *Try growing your own.* We maintain a 45-foot by 45-foot garden. We grow berries, grapes, vegetables and lettuces. It saves us about $1,000 a year in produce.

Utilities...

I used to think I was very careful about electricity—turning off lights and appliances when they weren't in use. Then I made some changes and cut my utility bills by $100 per month...

• *Lights.* We use fluorescent bulbs almost exclusively. They are more expensive—$6 to $20 apiece—but they last 14 times longer than incandescent bulbs and use 75% less electricity. Fluorescent bulbs cut our electric bills by $40 per month.

• *Refrigerator.* To further reduce electricity costs, I use a ZTI Power Saver* plug for the refrigerator.

To use: Plug the ZTI Power Saver into the outlet and then plug the refrigerator into the Power Saver. It reduces the amount of electricity that your appliance needs without compromising its performance or causing damage. Each one costs $49 and, when used with a refrigerator, washer or dryer, it should pay for itself within a year.

• *Dryer.* Two years ago, when our dryer broke, I began hanging clothes to dry. I soon

*For information, contact Zemos Technologies, Inc., 43260 Christy St., Fremont, California 94538. 510-657-0278.

saw our electric bill drop by $50 a month... and I never fixed the dryer.

Insurance...

I've slashed our annual insurance costs by $1,200.

• *Homeowner's insurance.* When my homeowner's policy was mailed to me for renewal three-and-a-half years ago, I took the time to read it. This wasn't easy—but it sure has been lucrative.

All the riders were listed in codes, which were explained at the back of the policy. I found that I was insured for furs and jewelry, which didn't make sense since I only owned a $100 wedding band. So I eliminated that rider.

I also found that the insurance company assumed the value of my home was increasing by more than it actually was. The replacement cost of my home was inflated in another way as well. The replacement cost included the $30,000 value of my one-third-acre lot and the $15,000 value of my foundation. Even if the house were gutted by fire, those parts would still remain. So I reduced the replacement value of my home by $45,000.

• *Auto insurance.* I've raised the deductible on my two cars from $200 to $500—which reduced the premium by 15%. I also dropped the collision coverage on one car, since it was over five years old. This saved us $512 per year.

Both policies have also been cut by having homeowner's and auto coverage with the same company. They were reduced even further when my husband took a defensive driving course. I am planning to take one, too.

Clothing...

• *Fancy clothes.* I like designer labels and good clothes. When I appear on local TV, as I often do, I care about how I look. But I don't love to shop, and I refuse to pay full price for these clothes.

I buy most of my clothing at thrift shops. I just bought five suits for a total of $35. For my dressy clothes, I go to outlets or a nearby resale shop that won't sell any item that is more than two years old. Prices are 70% to 75% below retail.

I focus on colors that look best on me— fuchsia, royal blue and purple. This makes it easier to mix and match clothes, and I keep my wardrobe fresh without having to own as many clothes.

• *Everyday clothes.* I take my family to end-of-season bag sales at a local thrift shop. At these sales, you get to fill a 14-gallon plastic bag with as much clothes as will fit inside. Prices around the country range from $6 to $22 per bag.

College…

Our oldest daughter just finished her second year of college in Maryland. We encouraged her to get a work-study job to help pay the bills. As luck would have it, she landed a job in the financial aid office. This has helped us learn several money-saving strategies. *They include…*

• If you're applying for financial aid, file your tax returns early. Aid is often dispensed on a first-come, first-served basis, and you'll need to include a copy of your tax return with the aid forms.

• If you think you're entitled to more financial aid, appeal and explain your case. We did so on the basis of our $25,000 income shortfall and major medical expenses. As a result, we received an additional $4,000 in financial aid.

• Whenever possible, avoid having your children live in dormitories, which are often cramped and expensive. Our daughter rents an 8,000-square-foot apartment and sublets part to other students. This covers her rent and groceries and really helps us out.

Source: Jackie Iglehart, editor, *The Penny Pincher,* a newsletter specializing in money-saving strategies, 2 Hilltop Rd., Mendham, NJ 07945. 800-41-PENNY.

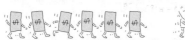

20 Easy Ways to Save Hard Dollars… Year in…Year Out

Small changes in your lifestyle can add up to significant savings over the course of a year. If you adopt just half of these suggestions, you'll save over $1,000 a year…

• Switch from a bank to a credit union. The average checking account now costs $185 a year in service charges to maintain. Credit unions are nonprofit organizations that return surplus funds to members in the form of low-cost services. Larger credit unions offer free checking, low or no annual fees on credit cards and excellent rates on car loans.

Disadvantages: Fewer branch offices, and the branches may not have automatic teller machines. But, remember, not very long ago, we all survived without ATMs.

• Buy your home heating oil in the summer. In my area, prices drop 20¢ a gallon during the off-season, so filling a 275-gallon tank in the summer saves $55. If you are a do-it-yourselfer with extra space, you can buy a used second tank, so you'll have two tanks that can be filled in the off-season. Check local laws about installation and inspection of the second tank. You will have to monitor prices for some weeks to get the best deal in your area, but the bottom should hit some time between July and early September.

Caution: Don't wait until November, when prices go back up, to get your first fill-up.

• Change the oil in your car yourself.

• Review your insurance policies. Take higher deductibles where you can afford them, and eliminate coverage you don't need for your lifestyle.

Examples: Many people past childbearing age are still paying for maternity benefits. Most car insurance policies cover car rental reimbursement when the car is in the shop—but will you use this? Maybe you have a second car or friends who will help out. Are there extra drivers listed on your insurance who no longer live with you? Many home owners' policies cover furs, jewelry, computers or other items you may not own.

Also, check with your agent to make sure you are getting any discounts you qualify for.

Examples: Nonsmoking on health insurance, alarm systems or safe driving records on car insurance, owning multiple policies with one company.

• Make your own popcorn. A family that pops two batches of traditional generic popcorn a week instead of an equivalent amount of microwave popcorn will save $100 in a year. And it can take less time to make popcorn in a hot-air popper than in a microwave.

• Reduce your smoking by three cigarettes a day. (Or give up smoking altogether and save even more.)

• Rent videos instead of going to the movies. Even better, check them out of the library.

• Make pizza from scratch instead of having it delivered.

• Give personal services rather than store-bought presents. Offer to garden, clean bathrooms or baby-sit for your friend in the hospital. Bring your hostess potted herbs from your kitchen or a homemade casserole. Give the new graduate "free résumé service" or 100 pages of thesis typing. Fill out change-of-address forms for your friend who just moved. Refinish a chest of drawers for newlyweds. And don't forget to make your own greeting cards.

• Share a newspaper subscription with your neighbor. Are you finished with the paper before you leave for work in the morning? Does your neighbor read the paper before supper? Share magazine subscriptions, too. Many public libraries microfilm, then discard magazines every six months. Request the outdated issues be held for you. Raid recycling bins.

• Hang four loads of laundry a week instead of running the dryer.

• Drink four fewer cans of soda per week—saves $100 a year.

• Tape ten pieces of music from the radio rather than buying commercially recorded audiotapes.

• Cut your family's hair yourself. A child's haircut costs as much as $8 to $10 every six weeks. An adult haircut at $25 every six weeks adds up to $217 a year. If you learn to trim it yourself you will only need to have a professional job at the hairdresser half the time. This will save you $100.

• Bake one batch of bread (two loaves) once a week.

• Write one good letter a month instead of making an $8 long distance telephone call.

• Use half your usual amount of cleaning and personal care products. Find the minimum effective level of shampoo, conditioner, laundry detergent, bleach, dishwasher detergent, toothpaste, shaving cream, lotion, perfume, etc.

You may find you can make do with less than half your usual amount.

• Buy articles of clothing from thrift shops and yard sales rather than paying store prices. This is also a fun way to shop.

• Barter for one regular service. Handy with graphics? Arrange to make fliers and do an advertising layout for your massage therapist in return for monthly sessions. Want help cleaning? Offer to take your cleaning person's kids for a weekly activity in return for two hours of housecleaning. Are you an accountant? Trade tax preparation for lawn care or TV repair.

Consider three-party trades to get what you need.

Example: You want ten $10 computer lessons, the computer instructor needs a $100 repair on her car, so you prepare the mechanic's tax return in exchange for fixing the car, in exchange for your lessons.

Be creative!

• Use dry milk. A gallon of whole milk costs up to $2.59 per gallon. Dry milk, purchased in the 20-quart store-brand box, costs $1.60 per gallon. Dry milk is 100% fat-free, while whole milk contains 4% fat. By mixing the two kinds of milk half and half, you can make your own 2% milk. If you use a gallon of milk every three days, you will easily save $100 in a year by substituting dry milk in cooking, homemade cocoa mix and in using the half-and-half mixture for drinking.

Source: Amy Dacyczyn—"The Frugal Zealot." She is the author of *The Tightwad Gazette,* a book of excerpts from her newsletter of the same name. Villard Books. *The Tightwad Gazette* is published monthly. RR1, Box 3570, Leeds, ME 04263.

Saving Money With Coupons

Most of us pay more than we should for groceries, household products, and other goods and services. The biggest mistake we make is failing to take full advantage of cents-off coupons, refund offers, two-for-one deals, and other money-saving offers. Of the record 314 billion coupons issued last year, fewer than eight billion were redeemed.

Reasons: Many shoppers are too embarrassed to present coupons to checkout clerks. Others are not aware or interested in the available deals, or feel that clipping coupons is too time-consuming.

Today, however, more consumers are looking to cut weekly costs and stay on a budget. There are several ways to clip coupons and save up to 25% on your supermarket bill. *How I do it...*

•Set up a system. Spend a few minutes each week looking over newspaper inserts and other likely sources of coupons. Clip the ones you think you might use and toss them into a shoe box, then separate them by category. Mark each grouping of coupons with its own labeled note card. Be as general or as specific as you like with your categories.

Just prior to each trip to the grocery store, review your shopping list. Transfer the coupons you plan to use from the storage box to an envelope labeled unused. Take this envelope and a second, empty one (labeled used) along to the store. As you toss each item on your list into your shopping cart, transfer its coupon from the first envelope to the second.

•Be choosy. Coupons should be used to buy only two types of products—those you use regularly and those you'd like to try. Don't let coupons entice you to buy products you neither need nor truly want. Don't be trapped by brand loyalty. Buy whatever brand you have coupons for.

•Accumulate as many coupons as possible. Today coupons are available from a wide variety of sources, including product labels and cartons, supermarket ads, inserts in your Sunday newspaper, and displays placed along supermarket shelves. Recently, coupons have been distributed directly through the mail, on airline flights, and at movie theaters.

•Save unused coupons. Take them along to the supermarket. *Reason:* Some markets maintain informal coupon-exchange bins where customers can exchange coupons they don't want for those they do.

•Join a coupon-exchange club. There are several large clubs to choose from, all offering the same basic service.

How they work: Upon joining, members fill out a form specifying which products they use. Periodically, members mail in coupons they don't need...and the club mails back coupons they do.

•Shop at "coupon-friendly" supermarkets. Some markets accept coupons only grudgingly. Others not only accept them, but will give you twice their face value.

•Use coupons in conjunction with other savings offers. When reading through your local newspaper's supermarket ads, watch for "double plays"—items discounted by both coupons and special sale prices.

Even better: Triple plays. These occur when prices are reduced not only by coupons and specials, but also by a mail-in refund offer.

To keep track of the thousands of refunds being offered at any given time, there are now refunding newsletters. They not only list all the offers, but also detail the often Byzantine regulations governing how to obtain the refunds.

My favorite: Refundle Bundle, Box 141, Centuck Station, Yonkers, New York 10710.

•Bank your savings. Because coupons net you only a few dollars each time you shop, it's easy to squander the money saved by using them. *Solution:* Open a savings account specifically for your coupon savings. Decide on a particular item to save for. Don't dip into the account until you've accumulated enough to make the purchase.

Source: Linda Bowman, a devoted coupon-clipper and the author of six books on money-saving hints, including *Free Food...& More*. Probus Publishing Corp.

How to Use Coupons to Cut Your Supermarket Bill By as Much as 80%

Most people use grocery coupons at least occasionally. Over 75% of all multiperson households regularly redeem one to five coupons a week. But while most people save 50¢ here and $1 there, I routinely save at least 70% on my shopping trips—and often more.

Key: Organization. Over 20 years, I have developed a system that cuts my grocery bills in half from the use of coupons alone.

In addition, I've sent for as much as $1,800 a year in cash refunds. For the past 10 years, I've deposited these manufacturers' rebates in a separate bank account. With accrued interest, it's now worth more than $35,000.

You don't have to become a "professional shopper" to realize substantial savings from coupons and rebates. Even a moderate commitment to systematic shopping can easily cut every grocery bill by 20%. *The basics:*

• See couponing as an enjoyable hobby. The more routine your system becomes, the less the hassle. You needn't invest more than a few hours a week to get organized.

• Give up brand and store loyalty. Shop at the stores and purchase the brands that provide the best deals.

• Collect coupons of all types. You can trade those you don't want.

Sources for coupons…

• In-store promotions, including aisle-dispensers, hangtags on the necks of bottles, peel-off coupons on packages and supermarket bulletin boards.

• Inserts in Sunday newspapers. Collect multiples from recycling bins.

• Local newspapers on "food day."

• Stores' advertising circulars.

• Women's magazines—raid those at doctor's and dentist's offices.

• Product packaging.

• Set up a portable filing system. Most couponers use envelopes, coupon wallets or index-card file boxes. I use heavy, accordion-style, business-size envelopes secured with rubber bands. Arrange coupons by product category, not by brand.

Examples: Breakfast cereals, canned goods, dairy products, frozen foods, etc. Use index cards as dividers.

Helpful: Tailor categories to your personal shopping patterns. Give some thought to the categories you choose, as most people find it hard to change their system once it's in place.

File coupons alphabetically within product categories. Place those with the earliest expiration dates first.

Helpful: Do this right before making your shopping list.

• Plan shopping trips. Code the items on your list for which you have coupons. Take your entire coupon file with you to the supermarket for unexpected bargains.

Key to maximum return: Skillful combining. Shop in stores that double the face value of coupons. Combine doubled manufacturer's coupons with store coupons or store sales to get the best values. Buy in quantity when you can. If a store runs out of a sale item, always request a raincheck.

Example: A name brand toilet paper recently went on sale for 77¢ per four-roll package. The regular price is $1.29. I had saved eight 25¢ coupons, good off the purchase of two packages. The store doubled my coupons to 50¢ off, and I bought 16 packages. *My savings:* $12.32.

• Buy brand names and small sizes. Leading brands are cheaper than store brands when purchased on sale with doubled coupons. Small sizes are often cheaper when you calculate the per-ounce savings.

• Send for refunds and rebates. Rebate offers include cash refunds, coupons toward future purchases and free merchandise or premiums. You must pay for the cost of envelopes and postage to take advantage of refund offers, but while the value of coupons averages 50¢, refunds are commonly worth $2 to $5 or more.

Added value: Refund money is tax-free. The IRS considers it simply a reduction in the price of a purchase you already paid for with your taxed income.

Refunding involves some paperwork. *Here's what you'll need…*

• Forms. Manufacturers distribute forms describing offers and how you can qualify. Forms can be found where coupons are found and are common on tear-off pads on supermarket bulletin boards or shelves. If the forms are gone, the back of the pad will list instructions.

• "Qualifiers." Most people don't want to save every box top, plastic wrapper or paper label from the products they buy. But about

80% of all refund offers ask for Proof of Purchase seals, UPC symbols and/or net weight statements.These easy-to-collect seals are printed on packaging. Save them, label and file them and pull them as offers become available.

•Cash register tapes. Save them, review them to find the purchases you need to complete, fulfill the qualifications and cut the piece you need. Write the store name and date on the receipt before sending it as a rebate qualifier. Save the remaining register tape for future offers.

Alternative: Request a "rebate receipt" from a store where you've made multiple purchases. These forms are rarely refused and easy to fill out.

•Look for "triple plays"—sale items you buy with double coupons, for which you can also get a refund. It's a fine feeling when you realize you've *made* money on a product!

•Subscribe to a refunding newsletter. While refund offers are good nationally, most are only advertised regionally. Refunding newsletters publish listings of hundreds of offers, so you can send for forms for those that interest you. My newsletter, *Refundle Bundle,* also runs a form and qualifier exchange, and gives general information on refunding, filing, etc. A typical issue has about 400 offers.

•Network with other couponers and refunders. Many people enjoy coupon clubs and conventions for trading and information. Check supermarket bulletin boards and local shoppers' guides to find one in your area.

• *For advanced couponers:* Buy and sell coupons. The Select Coupon Program catalogs coupons for more than 1,000 brand name products, which are offered on monthly selection lists. A one-year membership is $19.95, and you get $20 worth of free coupons for joining. Thereafter you pay $6 for each $18 in coupons you order.

For $7.50, you can purchase a trial Need List from the Official Coupon Supplier Program. Program members collect hundreds of coupons for products on the Need List. Different face values are accepted, but there must be at least five coupons per product, neatly sorted. The company pays a commission of 5% to 15% on the face value of the coupons you supply. Annual membership is $22.50, with lists $2.50 thereafter.

For more information: Select Coupon Program or Official Coupon Supplier Program, 66 S. Central Ave., Elmsford, New York 10523.

Legality of selling coupons...

It is true some cash-offs contain a statement claiming the coupon is void if transferred.

Now, transferring occurs constantly (between friends and relatives and through exchange boxes maintained by supermarkets and libraries, for example), and I've never heard of such transferred coupons failing to be honored.

Additionally, I have no knowledge of any federal or state statute that prohibits the transfer of coupons in a free market society.

However, the statement may give manufacturers the right to refuse redemption of transferred coupons. Shoppers concerned about this should simply not use transferred coupons that contain such statements.

In the end, selling coupons appears to be perfectly legitimate. Probably all, and certainly most, coupons are simply commodities whose values are determined by the prices individuals are willing to pay for them in the free marketplace.

Source: Susan Samtur, author of *The Super Coupon Shopping System,* Hyperion. She also edits the shoppers' newsletter *Refundle Bundle,* Box 140, Centuck Station, Yonkers, NY 10710.

Better Car-Rental Rates

Quote the advertised discount directly from the company's ad when calling the reservation number. *Problem:* Reservation agents often will not volunteer the best available price up front. *Helpful:*

Mention the promotion's discount code, usually listed in small print beneath the boldly displayed rate, or in the description of the terms and conditions of the rental.

Source: Ed Perkins, editor, *Consumer Reports Travel Letter,* 101 Truman Ave., Yonkers, NY 10703.

Wintertime Money Savers

Winter is the season of higher electricity and gas bills, car maintenance and repair bills, bills for cold and flu medications and so on. But there are several ways that you can cut down on expenses without sacrificing great comfort.

Avoid costly car repairs...

• Keep your gas free of water. The most frequent problems mechanics see in winter are caused by water in the gas. To prevent problems, add a drier (such as Prestone Gas-Drier or Heet) to your gas every few fill-ups.

• Check your radiator fluid and the condition of the radiator hoses. If the fluid is low, add a 50/50 mixture of antifreeze and water. In the coldest parts of the country or when an extreme cold snap strikes, you may want to alter this by using more antifreeze. *Best:* Use a mixture of 70% antifreeze and 30% water. Muddy-looking fluid should be changed. Make sure that the rubber hoses leading from the radiator to the engine are not cracked, brittle, bulging, or mushy when they are squeezed.

• Keep your battery terminals clean to avoid starting problems (and costly towing bills). Clean the battery terminals occasionally with baking soda and then reduce the corrosion problem by smearing them with a thin coating of petroleum jelly.

• Promptly repair any nicks in your windshield. Stop those smaller than a quarter from spawning spider legs and ruining the windshield by covering them on both sides with transparent tape (duct tape works too). Then get the car to a windshield-repair specialist. Cost for a nick ranges from $30 to $50, compared to the $300 to over $600 it can cost to replace the whole windshield.

• Check tire inflation every few weeks with an accurate gauge. Changes in temperature alter tire pressure, and under-inflation increases tire wear and gas consumption by as much as 5%. *Important:* Check the pressure while tires are cold. Know how many pounds of pressure they require. Then check them again at the gas station (after they've warmed from being driven on) and add the pounds of pressure that were needed when they were cold.

Save on heating...

• Put on an extra sweater and modify your heating habits. Keep the daytime thermostat at 65 degrees Fahrenheit (rather than 70) and the nighttime temperature at 55 degrees Fahrenheit (rather than 60 or 65). This can reduce your heating bill 15% or more. And turn down the heat when you leave to run errands.

• Keep fireplace dampers closed when not in use. Install glass fireplace doors. Then heat won't escape through the chimney.

• Have your home's insulation checked by your utility company. Many utilities perform this inspection service free or for a nominal fee. Make sure your home's insulation meets the US Department of Energy's recommendations.

• Wrap fiberglass insulation around heating ducts and hot water pipes in basement, attic and crawl space. Putting 2½ inches of insulation around these ducts and pipes will pay for itself in one season.

Save on lighting...

• Replace incandescent lights with fluorescent lights in areas that need light for hours each day. Today's fluorescent tubes produce warmer hues that won't make your home feel like a factory, and they're three to four times more efficient. If you don't want to install the tubes, use compact fluorescent bulbs. They screw into standard sockets.

• Use outdoor light fixtures that turn on and off by means of built-in heat/motion detectors and timers. They're far more economical than those that burn nonstop.

• Don't turn lights on and off frequently. Turning the lights out every time you leave the room for a few minutes may seem like it's doing good, but it shortens the life of the bulbs. So don't turn out the light unless leaving for more than a few minutes.

Grandma's remedies...

• Get an annual flu shot if you're 65 or older or suffer from cardiac or respiratory problems. It's cheap insurance against the major problems a flu can precipitate.

•Have prescriptions filled at a discount drugstore. It is much cheaper than using your hospital's pharmacy.

Miscellaneous money savers...

•Freeze your credit. This is a good idea any time of year, but works especially well around the holiday season. Put your credit cards in a bowl of water and place them in the freezer. It sounds crazy, but by the time the ice melts enough to retrieve the cards, the urge to buy may have passed. And writing checks or paying cash for items forces you to do a "reality check" on how much you really have to spend.

•Put rubber half-soles on the bottom of your shoes. In damp or wet weather, the leather soles of your shoes are constantly absorbing water, which slowly damages the leather and reshapes the shoe. Half-soles cost $12 to $15 and add years of life to your shoes. *Also:* Alternate the shoes you wear each day. Having a day to dry and air between uses greatly extends shoe life.

Source: Andy Dappen, author of *Cheap Tricks: 100s of Ways You Can Save 1000s of Dollars*. Brier Books.

Secrets of BigTime Food-Bill Savings

Most of us have had the thought, "I can't believe I'm paying this much for one bag of stuff," as the supermarket cashier finishes ringing up the "few things" we ran to the store for.

"Did I really buy that much?" we wonder. Usually, we haven't bought that much—just paid too much. Here are some ways to save big on the family food bill.

Supermarket savings...

•Shop with a list...or you'll spend more than you save.

•Clip coupons—and keep them organized. Don't throw money away with the garbage. Coupons can easily save you $1,000 a year.

Be willing to give up brand loyalty in favor of a meaningful discount. One brand of tomato paste or dish detergent is much like another.

File coupons in envelopes by category—canned goods, cereals, pet foods, paper prod-

ucts, etc. Put coupons you plan to use right away and those with short expiration dates in the front. Take them with you to the store, along with an empty envelope to put coupons in for the items you select, so you don't have to sort them at the checkout counter.

Shop at a supermarket that honors double the value on the face of coupons. You can also increase your savings by combining in-store sales with coupons. Be sure to calculate the per-unit price of products when using coupons.

Example: A 6-ounce jar of instant coffee may cost $3.29, or 55¢ an ounce, and a 10-ounce jar $4.99, or 50¢ an ounce. Normally, the larger size is the better buy. But with a 75¢ coupon, at a double-coupon store, the 6-ounce jar costs $1.79, or 30¢ an ounce, while the 10-ounce jar is $3.49, or 35¢ an ounce.

•Companion product offers. Companies and supermarkets often issue coupons for a free item, with the purchase of a companion item.

Examples: A free gallon of milk with the purchase of a breakfast cereal...a free box of pasta with the purchase of spaghetti sauce.

•Refund and rebate offers. You may need to clip UPC symbols or save register receipts as "proof of purchase" to send for these offers. They are worth the trouble—and can be very lucrative, whether you get a cash rebate, additional coupons or free products.

•Senior discounts. Many large chain stores and some independent markets issue senior discount cards that allow cashiers to subtract as much as 5% to 10% off the final bill.

•Generic brands. Not only are they here to stay, they are growing and growing. Generics can provide substantial savings, especially on grooming products, cereals and canned goods.

•Track savings. Most supermarkets total the amount saved with coupons at the bottom of the register receipt. You can deposit monthly savings from coupons, refunds, etc., in an account earmarked toward a goal.

Supermarket alternatives...

•Join a wholesale or warehouse shopping club. These huge operations are springing up in metropolitan areas nationwide. Shopping is a no-frills enterprise, and products must often be purchased in bulk or large sizes. Brand selection may be limited and may change at any given time. But savings can be excellent. *Key:* Know your prices. Some warehouse club prices are not significantly better than prices at the discounters.

• Shop at farmers' markets, where vegetables and fruits are fresher, tastier and cheaper. Buy in bulk in-season, then can or preserve.

• Shop at bakery outlets and "thrift stores." Thrift stores are one-brand outlets for companies such as Entenmann's, Pepperidge Farm, Arnold's Bakery, Sunbeam Bread and Wonder-Bread/Hostess. Prices run 30% to 50% off retail for day-old goods.

• Food co-ops and buying clubs. Consumer cooperatives are run by members and usually buy food in bulk and then repackage it for buyers. Members can save 15% to 50% on most items, because brokers, middlemen and costly packaging are eliminated from the exchange.

• Do it yourself. Grow a vegetable garden, make your own frozen dinners from leftovers.

Restaurant savings…

• Happy hour buffets. Between 4 pm and 6 pm, for the price of a drink—not necessarily alcoholic— many restaurants provide free buffets. If you don't mind eating early, many people find these feasts to be filling, fun dinners and a change in daily routine.

• Early bird specials. Many restaurants offer much lower prices for those who order dinner between 4 pm and 6 pm. You get the same food as on the dinner menu, often with dessert and beverage included, for less than you'd pay for the entrée alone during peak hours. To find specials, check local newspapers or call the restaurants that you are interested in.

• Senior menus. Some restaurants, particularly large chains, have senior menus, which offer smaller portions at lower prices. Carry your identification.

• Two-for-one or free item coupons. Check newspapers and circulars for coupons from area restaurants for "buy one entrée, get the second of equal or lesser value free" or "free wine or dessert with entrée" offers.

• Restaurant discount books.

Examples: Entertainment Publications publishes regional guides for about $35, with about 200 coupons for 2-for-1 meals and discounts at restaurants, fast food chains and specialty shops. 2125 Butterfield Rd., Troy, Michigan 48084, 313-637-8400. The Premier Dining Club qualifies you for 2-for-1 or other discounts at member restaurants nationwide. 831 Greencrest Dr., Westerville, Ohio 43081, 800-346-3241.

Invest in savings…

Other companies publish local or regional discount books as well. These can be a wise investment if you like to dine out a lot—but shop around. Prices and services vary substantially.

Key: Make sure the book contains enough discounts you will really use to pay for itself.

Source: Linda Bowman, professional bargain hunter and author of *The More for Your Money* series of guides, including *Free Food & More and Freebies (and More) for Folks Over 50.* Probus Publishing Co.

Great Buys by Mail and Phone

Why settle for the best deal in town when you can get the best deal in the United States? You can save big, big bucks off the price of major appliances, top-of-the-line furniture and large equipment by telephoning a price-quote company.

For a broad spectrum of items—lingerie, high-quality art supplies and name-brand sporting goods, you can thumb through a wide variety of very attractive specialized direct mail catalogs, mail or phone in your order and save.

Big-ticket items…

The average consumer doesn't know much about price-quote companies because they don't spend a great deal of money advertising—but their salespeople are eager to receive your call. They require that you know what you want, the name of the manufacturer, model number and other descriptive details of the item you intend to buy. Here's a sampling of the kind of merchandise offered by price-quote companies handling calls from around the country:

• Furniture. Cedar Rock Furniture carries all major brands of furniture at up to 50% below retail.

Cedar Rock Furniture, Box 515, Hudson, North Carolina 28638.

• Appliances. EBA Wholesale offers dozens of products from more than 50 top-name manufacturers, including Admiral, Panasonic, Litton, KitchenAid, Westinghouse and General Electric at up to 60% less than list price.

EBA Wholesale, 2361 Nostrand Ave., Brooklyn 11210.

• Automobiles. Nationwide Auto Brokers will send you a form ($9.95) showing all the operational equipment available for the car you want and then arrange delivery with a local dealer. You save from $150 to $4,000 by allowing the broker to negotiate a dealer-to-dealer price break that eliminates the salesperson's commission.

Nationwide Auto Brokers, 17517 W. 10 Mile Rd., Southfield, Michigan 48075.

• Computers. CMO offers name-brand computers like IBM, Epson and Hewlett-Packard as well as systems and software at savings as great as 40% off retail.

CMO, 2400 Reach Rd., Williamsport, Pennsylvania 11701.

• Fitness equipment. Better Health and Fitness will help you complete your fitness center with name-brand equipment at savings of up to 25%.

Better Health and Fitness, 5302 New Utrecht Ave., Brooklyn 11219.

To locate a price-quote firm in your area, turn to the *Yellow Pages,* for the type of item you're looking for, but understand that there are tiers of discounters, with those who do the highest volume buying getting the best prices. Your best bet by phone will be a company with nationwide delivery. But shop discounters, too.

Example: If you want a new stove, look in the *Yellow Pages* under a major heading such as:

Appliances…

• Household

• Major dealers

You often will find promotions touting "top brand names" at "wholesale prices to the consumer."

Smaller items…

There are hundreds and hundreds of fabulous catalogs you'll never know about unless you watch for their rare ads in the back of newspapers or magazines or you learn about them through word of mouth.

Yet, these catalogs offer you the opportunity to buy your favorite brand of merchandise at a great price without spending money on gasoline and sacrificing hours out of your day to trek to the mall.

There are catalogs for just about anything you might want—from the mundane to the exotic. *Here's a sampling of nontraditional catalog types:*

• Art supplies. Cheap Joe's Art Stuff. Save 30% on paint, canvas, brushes, mat cutters, books on art. Free catalog.

Cheap Joe's Art Stuff, 300A Industrial Park Rd., Boone, North Carolina 28607.

• Fragrances. Essential Products Company lets you save up to 90% on perfumes. Essential Products buys them from a company that copies designer scents. Free brochure.

Essential Products Company, 90 Water St., New York 10005.

• Bed and bath. Harris Levy, Inc. Save up to 50% on Wamsutta, J.P. Stevens, Springmaid and Fieldcrest, etc. Free catalog.

Harris Levy, Inc., 278 Grand St., New York 10002.

• Collectibles. Quilts Unlimited. Save 20% to 30% by buying from "America's largest antique quilt shop." *Catalog:* $5.

Quilts Unlimited, 440-A Duke of Gloucester St., Williamsburg, Virginia 23185.

• Boating supplies. Goldberg's Marine Distributors. Save up to 60% on boating equipment and nautical clothing, and receive your shipment in three to seven days. Free seasonal catalog.

Goldberg's Marine Distributors, 201 Meadow Rd., Edison, New Jersey 08818.

• Camera equipment. Porter's Camera Stores. Save up to 35% on equipment, cameras. Free catalog.

Porter's Camera Stores, Box 628, Cedar Falls, Iowa 50613.

• China. Greater New York Trading Co. Save up to 60% on Lenox, Waterford, Wedgwood and just about every other major manufacturer of fine china. Free brochure.

Greater New York Trading Co., 81 Canal St., New York 10002.

Basics...

•Whether you are calling a price-quote company or a direct mail marketer, always understand the return policy before you make a commitment—sometimes there is a restocking charge for returned items.

•Use a credit card so you have recourse if you need to return an item.

•Keep records of your transaction by noting the date the order was placed and name of the order-taker.

•Save your receipts.

•If you ask for a price quote through the mail, it will help to send a business-sized self-addressed, stamped envelope to speed the response.

Armchair shopping pays off...

Not only do you get great convenience by checking with price-quote firms and ordering through direct mail catalogs, but you get big savings. Sometimes those calls are free with the 800 number, and with high-ticket items or quantity purchases, shipping charges may be waived.

Source: Sue Goldstein, author of *Great Buys by Mail (And Phone!).* Penguin Books.

How to Take Back Anything You've Bought... Or Been Given

Most shoppers would like to return many more purchases than they actually do—for many reasons...

The single biggest reason people avoid returning items they don't want is that they are afraid someone will say "no."

But why tie your money up in useless possessions?

Here's how to take back almost any unwanted purchase or gift—even when rude sales clerks insist you can't.

•Have a valid reason for making the return. There are many valid reasons for making returns, including "I just don't like it."

You do not need to invent a complicated story to return an item, nor must you justify yourself to a sales clerk. But for people who are uncomfortable making returns, it helps to be clear on your reason ahead of time. The clerk will probably ask for a reason to fill in on the store's return form. In most cases, this is not a challenge to your right to make the return. It is simply the clerk's job.

Common valid reasons for returns:

•Item doesn't fit well.

•Item faded, bled, shrank.

•Color is wrong.

•Item is defective.

•Item does not perform as promised.

•Item arrived too late.

•Parts are missing.

•Item was an unwanted gift.

•Changed mind, don't like it.

•Ordered two, want to return one.

•Have one just like it.

•Found one for a lower price.

•No longer need it.

•Toy/item is dangerous.

•Save proof of purchases. It is always easier to make returns if you have the sales receipt. But a credit card slip or statement is usually enough to prove where you bought an item and how much you paid for it. *Good policy:* Staple tags or credit card slips to sales receipts and keep them for a while after making purchases.

•Charge your major purchases. Charging allows you more "return leverage" because you have a record of your purchase, even if you lose the receipt. If a store refuses to honor a reasonable return request, you can threaten to withhold payment.

Caution: The store may use such action to file a negative credit report against you, so be sure to consult the credit reporting company's rules before doing this.

•Shop at stores that have favorable returns policies. Generally, large department stores are matter-of-fact about returns. Small shops and boutiques are likely to have more conservative return policies. We have found a wide disparity in store policies. *Common variable factors:* Window of time allowed for returns…whether cash refunds or store credits are issued.

Caution: Always ask about the return policies at small businesses.

•Return merchandise promptly—in good condition. If you know you want to return something, do it promptly, as some stores limit the amount of time from the date of purchase they will accept returns. Whenever possible, return merchandise in the original box or bag, clean, refolded or polished.

•Deal with the person in charge. Often, store clerks do not have the authority to accept a return. If you meet with a reluctant or rude store clerk—always ask to speak with the manager. Most stores want their customers to be satisfied, and will try to please you—so don't take no for an answer.

•Be prepared to compromise. In the event you have exceeded a store's returns policy, be flexible. You may not get exactly what you want—a cash refund—but you may be able to negotiate for a store credit, partial refund or exchange.

•Don't feel—or act—guilty. Returning merchandise is neither immoral nor illegal—so don't keep unwanted items.

Stores can resell merchandise returned in good condition…stores can usually return used or damaged merchandise to their suppliers for credit…losses incurred for merchandise that can't be returned are a legitimate cost of doing business that stores build into their prices.

You are already paying for your right to return—so use it!

•Know your legal rights. Manufacturer's warranties generally provide for repairs at no charge if an item doesn't work. Most merchants will exchange defective items for new ones. But even if an item you purchase has no warranty, all merchandise is sold by law under an "implied warranty."

This unwritten warranty provides that the product you buy will do what you bought it for, for a reasonable amount of time.

Example: A shirt is made to be washed or dry cleaned. If it shreds, bleeds or shrinks, it is not performing as a shirt.

•Know your recourse. Most minor and major problems with consumer products can be resolved by speaking to the store manager. When this approach fails, you should write a letter of complaint both to the retailer and to the manufacturer.

Helpful: Call the Better Business Bureau, a local action line, hot line or consumer action panel or your state consumer protection agency.

If a substantial amount of money is at stake, you may wish to file a claim in Small Claims Court. Finally, you may wish to complain to a federal agency, such as the Consumer Product Safety Commission.

• *Don't fall for these myths:*

•*Myth:* I've already worn it, so I can't return it. Not true. While you can't return something because you ruined it yourself, you can certainly return any item that does not do what it is supposed to do.

Example: A popcorn maker that doesn't pop.

•*Myth:* I can't return it—it was a gift. Even if you don't have a receipt, most stores will accept returns of gifts that can be identified as theirs from a label or packaging.

•*Myth:* The receipt says "All sales final." Could be—but it's always worth a try. You may be able to exchange the item for store credit.

Exception: Personal items, such as bathing suits or underwear, are generally not returnable unless the original packaging is undisturbed.

•*Myth:* I can't return it—I bought it months ago. A defect may not appear for some time, but this doesn't mean that you can't ask to have it repaired or replaced at no charge.

Example: I bought a VCR which broke down after four months. Even though the 90-day warranty had expired, the store replaced it anyway, because it contained a defective part.

•*Myth:* I can't return food. Most supermarkets will gladly accept returns of unopened canned foods or foods that are spoiled or defective.

Example: After my cat went on a "diet," I returned several cans of a brand of cat food I no longer wanted.

• *Myth:* It's my tough luck if I found one cheaper after I already bought this one. If an item goes on sale soon after you bought it for the regular price, or if you find the same item elsewhere for a lower price, by all means, take it back! Many stores will refund the difference.

Source: Arlene Singer, a professional buyer in the advertising field, and coauthor, with Karen Parmet, of *Take It Back! The Art of Returning Almost Anything,* National Press Books.

Run Personal Finances Like a Business

Most executives neglect their personal finances because they are too busy with their jobs or businesses. That's a serious mistake. *Stay alert for opportunities to save and profit:*

• Pension plans. Business owners and the self-employed can take advantage of special pension options open to them. If you are making $100,000 a year, you could easily put away $30,000 pre-tax into a defined-benefit pension plan. Greater earnings may justify even larger contributions. Compounding tax-free dollars gives an enormous investment edge.

• A favorite tax-planning tactic is to have a minor child work for the family-owned business. The first $3,700 earned by the child is tax-free, and further income is taxed at low rates. In addition, the company gets a deduction for the child's salary. Now, a dramatic taxpayer victory shows just how effective this tactic can be:

The taxpayers owned a mobile-home park and hired their three children, aged 7, 11, and 12, to work there. The children cleaned the grounds, did landscaping work, maintained the swimming pool, answered phones, and did minor repair work. The taxpayers deducted over $17,000 that they paid to the children during a three-year period. But the IRS objected, and the case went to trial. *Court's decision:* Over $15,000 of deductions were approved. Most of the deductions that were disallowed were attributable to the 7-year-old. But even $1,200 of his earnings were approved by the court.

Key: The children actually performed the work for which they were paid. And the work was necessary for the business. The taxpayers demonstrated that if their children had not done the work, they would have had to hire someone else to do it.

Types of jobs children could do: Write checks or send out bills for your business, do simple maintenance and painting for investment real estate you own, etc.

• Set a spouse up in business. Most male executives don't realize the tax benefits they could get from encouraging their wives to start a business. *Some of the benefits:*

• As long as the business shows a profit for three of the first five years, the IRS generally won't challenge the right to deduct losses in the other two years. These losses can be offset directly against the high-earner's high-tax-bracket income.

• If the wife's business travel plans coincide with those of her husband, she can travel with him, all fully deductible. (Of course, a business trip can also coincide with vacation travel. But be sure it's predominantly business travel.)

• The wife can invest up to $2,000 of earned income in an IRA. (The full $2,000 is deductible only if neither you nor your spouse is an active participant in an employer-sponsored retirement plan or, if you are, your adjusted gross income on a joint form is less than $40,000.)

• Three-generation financial planning. Consider asking your parents to transfer some of their wealth directly to your children. (*Easiest way to skip a generation:* Each grandparent gives each grandchild $10,000 a year in tax-free gifts.)

• Supporting elderly parents. If you are self-employed, consider employing your parent in the business. *Opportunities:* Write the monthly checks. Manage a piece of real estate. Investigate any investment you are considering.

Special concern: If your parent is under 70 and receives Social Security benefits, he or she will lose $2 of Social Security for every dollar earned over a certain amount. *One way around this:* Set up an S corporation with the parent as stockholder. The dividends paid out of the S corporation do not diminish Social Security payments. Of course, once the parent reaches 70, no earnings affect Social Security payments.

Caution: The Social Security Administration has authority under the law to look beyond the facade of a business enterprise and determine the true situation. It is possible that it can, if it finds the corporation was established solely to avoid deduction of Social Security benefits, impose deductions against benefits.

All About Cash

When financial experts talk about putting your assets in *cash*, they usually mean cash equivalents such as certificates of deposit, bank money market accounts and passbook savings accounts. Risk-free investments can include taxable and tax-free money market funds.

These cash equivalents can be liquidated quickly and will return your principal plus interest. Most risk-free cash equivalents now offer annualized returns of between 3% and 4%.

That's fine when you need a place to put your money for a few months. But if you intend to park your cash for a year or longer, there are more profitable places to put it.

Here are my favorite places for cash now, depending on your needs and tolerance for some risk.

• Pay down your outstanding credit card balances. This may seem like an odd suggestion for cash. But if you have money to spare and have an unpaid balance on your credit card, paying off that balance is the best use of cash.

The interest you pay on such debts can be as high as 19%. Eliminating this non-deductible debt is the equivalent of making an investment that yields 30%. No investment today can beat that rate…without subjecting your investment to great risk.

• Put money in a money market fund—*for virtually no risk*. If you find the current stock market too scary and don't expect to invest for a while, put your money in a good money market fund.

• Stay away from bond funds. Bond holders are in for a rough ride as interest rates rise… and bond prices sink. The only exception is junk bond funds, which are not really interest rate-sensitive.

Be especially wary of *insured* municipal bonds, which are only as good as the insurance companies that back them. A study of these insurance companies indicates that the companies are grossly overrated. If the insurance companies are overrated, the bonds that rely on their ratings for credibility are overpriced. A realistic valuation by the marketplace could cause investors to lose market value. Many insurance companies would have a mediocre rating of BBB if they were rated realistically.

With three million bond issuers out there, it's difficult to get accurate information on each one. There is also no reliable secondary market if you want to sell before your insured municipal bonds mature. It will be especially difficult to sell if the bonds' ratings are lowered.

• Try a high-yield (junk) bond fund—*if you can stomach a bit more volatility*. Not only do junk bond issues pay decent returns, they appreciate as the economy recovers because their credit quality improves. Even though junk bonds were not immune to the recent correction in the markets, I think they've been through the worst of it.

Source: William E. Donoghue, publisher of *Donoghue On-Line*, an electronic service that provides mutual fund performance charts, 11754F S. Harrell's Ferry, Baton Rouge 70816. He is author of *William E. Donoghue's Mutual Fund Superstars: Invest with the Best, Forget About the Rest.* Elliott & James.

Rules for Keeping More of Your Money

• Any investment that pays more than a bank involves risk.

• If it doesn't make sense to you, don't do it. Investments that actually work should be simple to understand.

• If you have a choice, take the money now.

• Pay off debt. Saving and being in debt at the same time works only if the interest you *earn* is more than the interest you *pay*.

• Never spend principal. The purpose of your nest egg is to produce income.

• Avoid anything irrevocable. The combination of unknown future inflation, lengthening life spans and increasing health care costs should make explanations unnecessary.

• Invest only risk capital in speculative investments. "Risk capital" is money that remains after you've done everything you must do. This includes preparing for emergencies, buying insurance, saving for kids' educations and your retirement, and paying off debt. "Speculative" means any investment for which the outcome is unknown.

• Don't mess with the IRS. To begin with, they've got you outnumbered.

Source: H.W. "Skip" Weldon, ChFC, CLU, a fee-only financial planner, Box 61185, Columbia, SC 29260.

Shrewder Computing

Purchase of used PCs is now a viable option —offering substantial savings with little or no risk. *Important:* "Used" doesn't mean the PC was used by someone else, sold and then resold. In many cases, it could be a demo, refurbished, discontinued, a factory repack or part of a closeout. The latter machines come in unopened factory-sealed cartons and a 30 to 90-day warranty by the original manufacturer or supplier is typical.

Source: Jim Morgan, editor, *Purchasing Magazine,* 275 Washington St., Newton, Massachusetts 02158.

Premium Gasoline

Premium gasoline may decrease engine performance. *Reason:* Many premium gasolines are refined from lower-volatility feedstocks. The average car engine may have difficulty vaporizing these heavier gasolines, a situation that can result in poor combustion, vehicle hesitations and stalls, and higher emissions. *Result:* Poorer

driving performance and increased tailpipe pollution. *Helpful:* Stick with the octane rating recommended by your car's owner's manual.

Source: Jim Spearot, General Motors Research and Development Center, Warren, MI.

Checkbook Checklist

Your check register is a good record of deposits and spending if you record all transactions in it. Be sure to include date, check number, name and invoice number or date of invoice. *More ideas...*

• Keep a spare check or two in your wallet.

• Paper clip the checkbook on the page you are working.

• Write check numbers in the register ahead of time.

• Color code in the register. Use red for tax-deductible items.

• Round up check amounts to the nearest dollar.

• Cut addresses off extra deposit slips for address labels.

• Keep a small, thin calculator in your register.

• Use black or blue ink. Light colored ink doesn't copy as well.

• Keep track of monthly expenses at the back of the book.

Source: Heloise, whose syndicated column *Hints from Heloise* appears in more than 500 newspapers internationally. She is the author of a number of books, including *Heloise: Household Hints for Singles,* Perigee Books.

How to Get the Government Aid that You Are Entitled to For Health Care and Medical Bills

Given the skyrocketing costs of medical care and health insurance, it is particularly important to make sure you receive the benefits you're entitled to…and to minimize the expenses for which you are liable.

The primary federal health-care programs are Medicare…and Medicaid—for the needy.

Other government programs, for which fewer people are eligible, include Veterans Administration (VA) benefits and Supplemental Security Income (SSI), which assists the low-income aged, the blind, and the severely disabled.

Medicare and Medicaid aren't charity programs. They are tax-funded insurance programs you have paid annual premiums for—through Social Security—and that you are entitled to. Most beneficiaries of Medicaid, which now covers half of the US nursing-home population, have paid premiums for most of their working lives.

Even with an employer-provided health insurance plan—and we recommend you keep any plan you have—you should enroll in Medicare Part A (hospital insurance), when you turn 65…and purchase Part B (doctor insurance) within three months of your 65th birthday. Otherwise you will have to pay an additional 10% premium for every year you wait. Enrolling keeps that cost to your employer down and maximizes the benefits of your existing plan.

Medicare was never intended to cover all of its beneficiaries' health costs. Everyone's share is rising. Today, the elderly spend up to 20% of their income on health care, even with Medicare. The Medicare premium rises every year, and in 1988, the Part B section rose a staggering 35%—and is still rising.

Money-saving solutions: Make the most of Medicare. Make sure you have supplemental private insurance ("Medigap" coverage)…and try to keep all medical costs as low as possible.

How to get the most from Medicare…

Maximize your coverage by tuning into Medicare's best-kept secrets…

• Doctors' fees are very negotiable. A doctor who accepts Medicare assignments agrees to accept the fee that it pays for the procedure or treatments provided, and handles the paperwork. You remain responsible for your deductible and 20% co-payment.

Only 40% of doctors accept assignments for all of their Medicare patients. But 70% accept assignments for some of their patients or for some services. So it is up to you to persuade your doctor to accept Medicare assignments on all of your bills.

Helpful approach: "I believe that Medicare pays a fair rate, and I hope you will respect my request, as I cannot afford more than the 20% co-payment. However, if you do not accept assignments, perhaps you could refer me to another practitioner who does." Doctors do not like to lose clients. Most people who take the trouble to negotiate assignments are successful.

• You never have to pay more than the Maximum Allowable Actual Charge (MAAC) for any service, even if your doctor does not take assignments.

Medicare has set a maximum fee (MAAC) for all services that doctors who do not take assignments may charge Medicare patients. To find out a specific MAAC, call the Medicare carrier in your area. If your doctor bills you for more than the MAAC, neither you nor your insurance company has to pay the difference.

Example: Your doctor charges $3,000 for a procedure. Medicare pays $2,000 for the same procedure, and has set the MAAC at $2,500. Medicare will pay 80% of the $2,000 "reasonable cost," or $1,600. If your doctor accepts assignments, you would only have to pay the 20% co-payment, or $400. If the doctor does not take assignments, you must pay the difference between $1,600 and the $2,500 MAAC, or $900, and the doctor must absorb the other $500. But if you haven't bothered to check the MAAC, you may be billed for the full $3,000, less Medicare's $1,600, and unknowingly pay the $1,400 difference.

• The fact that Medicare refuses payment does not necessarily mean that you must pay. You are not responsible for any medical bill that you could not reasonably have been expected to know wasn't covered. You must be informed in writing from an official source, such as a Medicare notice or pamphlet, that a service isn't covered. If your doctor tells you something is covered by Medicare and it isn't, then the doctor —neither you nor your insurer —is responsible.

•You cannot be discharged from the hospital before you are medically able to go. You cannot be discharged because your Medicare payments or "DRG" (Diagnosis-Related Group system) days have been used up. When you are admitted to the hospital, you will be issued a form outlining your rights as a Medicare patient. If you think you are being discharged too soon, request a review by your state's PRO (Peer Review Organization), a group of doctors who review Medicare cases. The PRO will decide if your Medicare coverage can be extended, based on medical necessity.

Shopping for "Medigap" insurance...

Employer-provided retiree health insurance is usually as good as the available high-option Medigap policies, and often better. But more than five million older Americans are paying for unnecessary, duplicative insurance that they mistakenly believe supplements their Medicare coverage. If you have an employer-sponsored plan, you may not need more coverage. If you do not, consider supplemental insurance. *What to look for:*

The federal government certifies "Medigap" policies as meeting minimum standards for Medicare supplemental insurance if the company requests it. To check on an individual policy, call your state insurance office.

Under Part A, supplemental policies are required to cover $78.50 per day co-insurance for care in a skilled nursing facility through the hundredth day, when Medicare stops paying. A generous policy will provide coverage past the hundredth day.

Under Part B, supplemental policies must pay the 20% co-payment not covered by Medicare, but only up to $5,000 total, and only after you have paid the $100 deductible and the first $100 of co-payment.

Key: A good policy will cover doctors' fees in excess of Medicare-approved amounts.

It is against the law for a policy that calls itself a Medicare supplement to exclude any pre-existing conditions for more than six months.

Choose a policy that has a stop-loss provision, or ask your agent to add a rider (usually for a small extra fee).

Make sure the policy is automatically adjusted to increases in Medicare deductibles and co-payments.

Saving on out-of-pocket expenses...

You can minimize your co-payments and keep premiums down by trying to keep your medical expenses as low as possible.

•Take advantage of low-cost or free health services offered by counties, organizations, or health fairs.

Examples: Inoculations, screenings.

•Make sure you are aware of your health plan's limits and exclusions.

Example: Number of chiropractic visits.

•Shop around for prescription prices, and buy generic drugs when possible.

•Guard against unnecessary or excessive testing. Many physicians have adopted new, costly tests while continuing to administer the old ones —often less expensive, and as effective.

•Avoid hospitalization and surgery unless absolutely necessary. Avoid for-profit hospitals —they're up to 23% more costly. Avoid weekend admission.

•Bring your own food, vitamins, and drugs.

•Specify in writing that surgery or invasive procedures must be done by the person you are paying, i.e., your fully-trained physician, not a resident or intern.

•Keep track of all bills and services while hospitalized.

Common errors to check for: Type of room... number of days (look for an extra day on checkout day)...tests actually received, medications actually taken, physician's visits that actually occurred, as opposed to those routinely billed.

Source: Charles B. Inlander, president of the People's Medical Society, a nonprofit consumers' health organization, 462 Walnut St., Allentown, PA 18102. His new book, co-authored with Karla Morales, is *Getting the Most for Your Medical Dollar*. Pantheon.

2

Investment Opportunities

Bill Donoghue's Investment Strategies Under the New Tax Law

Changes in the new tax law threaten everyone building a retirement nest egg. *Checklist to re-think retirement planning:*

1. Build your investment strategy on capital gains. The new rates for higher-bracket taxpayers make income a "punishable offense." Keeping the capital gains rate at 28% favors retirement investments that offer long-term capital gains over high current income.

Invest retirement funds more aggressively. The further from retirement you are, the more aggressive you can be. Growth stock funds seem riskier than funds that generate income. But income will be taxed at the new, higher rates. Gains from growth stocks will be taxed at the 28% capital gains rate.

Caution: Beware of mutual funds with lots of unrealized capital gains. In a correction, they might take those gains—hitting you with unexpected tax. Morningstar Mutual Funds, a mutual fund tracking and ranking service, now calculates unrealized capital gains for funds. Ask funds about their tax situations before investing.

2. Capture capital gains in fixed-income investments. Investors have built up big gains in most long-term bonds—including CMOs (collateralized mortgage obligations) and zero-coupon bonds—and in bond funds and unit trusts. When interest rates inevitably go up, much of your appreciation will vanish. So—consider selling now. Be wary of new fixed-income investments.

Caution: Capital gains are seen as a benefit for the rich, so today's 28% rate may go up in the future—another reason to take gains now.

3. Consider taking capital losses now. Dump losing investments as part of restructuring your portfolio. Use your losses to offset long-term capital gains, so you don't pay taxes on at least part of the gains. Large capital losses can be carried forward to offset long-term capital gains in future years.

4. Invest the maximum in all tax-sheltered accounts. IRAs and 401(k) plans let you trade in your portfolio without worrying about tax consequences. You should invest retirement savings more aggressively than non-sheltered savings. Higher tax rates make it more advantageous than ever to invest in an IRA or Keogh. Keep transaction costs low by investing in mutual funds that waive loads and transaction fees for tax-sheltered accounts.

5. Contribute the maximum to your employer-sponsored retirement savings plan. Such plans let you invest more than the $2,000-a-year limit for IRAs, are fully deductible and often provide for employer matching contributions. Invest to the maximum in your plan before you invest in an IRA.

6. Ask for more choices in your 401(k). The investment option most frequently missing is an international stock fund. That is exactly what you need now. You can invest in an old bull market in the US or in a young bull market internationally. Ask your employer for a wider, more sophisticated choice of investment options. It is to your employer's benefit for you to take responsibility for your retirement plan.

7. Explore variable insurance products. Variable annuities are a way to shelter unlimited amounts of money for retirement. But given their current structure—up-front load and high expenses—they can be an expensive way to turn long-term gains into ordinary income. You pay taxes on money when you withdraw it. When you die, taxes are due on unrealized gains before anything goes to your heirs.

If you want a variable annuity, go for the lowest costs. Vanguard and Fidelity offer no-load variable annuities. Look for a wide range of investment choices. An investment with a good recent track record may not be good in the future.

Alternative: Consider variable universal life insurance. If you fund it properly—through four substantial equal payments over a seven-year period—you can borrow out the cash value tax-free. Whatever value is left when you die passes to your heirs—also tax-free. As with variable

annuities, go for the lowest fees and a wide array of investment choices.

8. Don't overpay your state taxes. It isn't just federal taxes that are going up. State taxes are, too. Don't pass up ways to cut your state tax bill. Income from federal government obligations—including Treasury bills, bonds and notes and Savings Bonds—is exempt from most state and local taxes. Report the income on your federal return, but not on your state return. Mutual funds holding US government issues will tell you what portion of your income came from sources exempt from state taxes.

9. Take advantage of any taxes paid by a mutual fund to foreign governments. Taxes paid by global and international mutual funds can reduce both your federal and state tax bills. Expect the fund to report any foreign tax credits on your 1099. If you have foreign tax credits, don't take them as deductions. Take them as credits, where each $1 of credit cuts your tax bill by $1.

10. Don't let your tax situation steer you to unsound investments. Even with the new law, tax considerations come second to sound investment choices. Tax-exempt securities—municipal bond funds and tax-exempt money market funds—do generate tax-free income. Using only tax considerations as your guide, tax-exempt bond and money market funds will seem to be a top choice.

But long-term municipal bonds are extremely interest-rate sensitive, and bond prices have risen dramatically. If interest rates rise, the values of municipal bond funds will go down. It could become a bloodbath, if funds have to sell bonds at fire sale prices.

The small advantage you get from tax-free income isn't worth the risk. Invest in taxable investments. Pick a money market fund that invests 100% in US government securities. Given the exemption from state and local taxes, you'll make as much as in a tax-free money fund—in a higher-quality investment.

Source: William E. Donoghue, publisher of *Donoghue's Moneyletter,* 290 Eliot St., Box 9104, Ashland, MA 01721.

Playing the Stock Market Now

As a fund manager and investor, I try not to be swayed by day-to-day news and activity in the economy. Instead, I'm a long-term optimist. *Here's why...*

Productivity in the US is increasing. We are now globally competitive, beating back the Japanese in areas such as computer microchips and international banking.

The dollar is cheap when compared with other currencies, putting our export industries in better shape than they've been in for decades. The North American Free Trade Agreement (NAFTA) and the General Agreement on Tariffs and Trade (GATT) make the prospects for expanding trade even brighter. Of course, I'm cautious in the current environment—with stock market growth being restrained by the Federal Reserve Board.

If the Fed raised short-term rates from 6% to 6.5% and the prime rate from 9% to 9.5% or 9.75%, the Dow Jones Industrial Average (DJIA) would likely slip from around 3,980 to 3,500 or 3,600. That wouldn't be too bad. But if we had *two* more tightenings, it could drop to 3,200 or 3,000.

Here's where I believe the economy and the stock market are headed and what you should do to protect yourself...

The big picture...

We're in a market that is similar to the one of the 1960s, when the trading range for the DJIA was between 600 and 1,000. It went up and down a few times during that decade, but a lot of money was made by investors who owned the right stocks.

I think the range for the 1990s will be between 3,000 and 5,000. As a result, investors will be able to make money by buying on dips ...and by making their selections carefully. This time the opportunities are global—and not just in foreign markets but in America's multinational companies, too. In the 1990s, we will be worrying about inflation—even though inflation will probably never really become a big problem. Such fear keeps the Fed on its toes and holds the economy in check. This fear and

economic reaction occurred in the 1960s, when interest rates increased, holding back inflationary pressure.

Important: Bonds won't make you wealthy in today's world. You need stocks that are outgrowing the increase in interest rates.

What to do now...

An unsettled market should not trouble a long-term investor or convince that investor to sell his/her stocks. There are ways to invest in such an environment...

• *Be more careful about the quality side.* Sell off your worst positions—companies that have lots of debt or whose prospects are built on hopes without much in the way of earnings. I almost never buy any company whose debt-to-equity ratio is more than 50%. You can figure this ratio by dividing the company's total liabilities by its total debt plus shareholders' equity. Or you can call the company's investor relations department for the data.

• *Keep some money on the sidelines*, and invest it slowly by dollar-cost averaging. That's the successful way to invest in an unsettled market. Invest a fixed amount of dollars in the stock market at fixed intervals—monthly, quarterly, semiannually—no matter how it is doing.

• *Consider declines in the DJIA as opportunities* to buy more shares of stocks that you already own and new stocks at bargain prices.

Hot industries...

Financial services. The 1990s will be the decade of financial services stocks. Interest rates will rise...inflation will be moderate... and baby boomers will be saving big for their retirements.

Now the financial services sector is performing badly, having suffered decreased earnings.

This is the perfect time to buy the stocks of these companies. Prices are low, and mergers and acquisitions will continue through the 1990s.

Banks. Banks are also selling at huge discounts to the market's average price/earnings ratio of 15. Banks have not done well because people are borrowing less as interest rates have climbed.

Yet banks have good growth prospects with higher yields than average and the potential for handsome dividend increases. America's investment banking companies lead the world and will likely become global financial superpowers. They will serve as conduits for raising capital, giving advice, feeding mergers and acquisitions—all of which will be on the rise in the new free-market world.

Insurance. The insurance industry continues to consolidate as companies merge or buy other companies. Stronger companies are emerging.

Technology. Driving the economy for job creation, productivity and growth, it's a hard area in which to invest because everything changes so fast. Yet every investor should have a stake here.

Source: Shelby Davis, who has managed the New York Venture Fund for the past 25 years, Box 1688, 124 E. Marcy St., Santa Fe 87504.

Answers to Commonly Asked Questions about Money and Investing

During the many speeches that I give around the country each year, I'm asked hundreds of questions about money and investing. *Here are the answers to the questions that I'm asked most frequently…*

Should I take my retirement money as a lump sum? Annuity?

Many pensions offer retirees two forms of payment—a little at a time through an annuity or as a lump sum. This decision could be the most important financial decision of your life—but it is very hard to get an objective opinion.

Reason: The annuity is an insurance-industry product, so people in the insurance business are likely to tell you to take your pension as an annuity. People in the investment management business will tell you to take it as a lump sum and roll the money over into an investment account.

The answer to this question draws attention to an important lesson. There are few all-or-nothing decisions in personal finance. People who are willing to sacrifice some potential

income for the assurance that they will receive steady payments are best served by taking part of the money as a lump sum and part as an annuity.

Strategy: If you retire at or before the normal retirement age, you generally should take the lump sum. Then when you are older, there is nothing to prevent you from investing in an annuity.

There are some very innovative annuity products being developed, such as immediate payment variable annuities. Your money is invested in mutual funds, and you begin receiving investment payments immediately.

In a few years, you probably will have a better choice of annuity products. If you can't wait, shop around. Don't just take the annuity your employer or broker offers. This is a competitive business, and once you buy, it's difficult to change your mind.

Important: If you or your spouse go into a nursing home, your lump sum distribution would have to be used to help pay nursing home costs. A lot of people in that situation wish they had chosen an annuity for part of their savings because nursing-home care has wiped out their long-term savings. An annuity at least assures a continuing income—for your spouse and for you if you leave the nursing home.

If you made just one investment today, what would it be?

There are two candidates…

• A 20-year zero-coupon Treasury bond. These bonds sell at discounts to their face values, so you receive the full amount when they reach maturity. If you buy a 20-year zero-coupon bond now, your money will grow at an annual rate of around 8%. In 20 years, it will almost quintuple with no risk. But you should buy zero-coupon bonds only for your tax-deferred retirement account. Otherwise, you will have to pay income taxes on "imputed interest"—interest you don't receive in cash until the bond matures but that the IRS requires you to pay each year you own the bond.

• A fund that invests exclusively in science and technology stocks. Our economy is in a fundamental period of transition. The old blue chip manufacturers have had their day. A new generation of blue chip stocks is emerging—and, of course, many of them will be science and technology companies.

How much should I invest in stocks vs. bonds?

Rule of thumb: Multiply your age times 80% (0.8). The result will give you the maximum percentage that you should invest in bonds for the long term.

Example: At age 50, you should have at most 40% of your portfolio in bonds (0.8 times 50). I would put 50% of that money in highly rated municipal bonds, 25% in corporate bonds and 25% in Treasury bonds of different maturities—or in mutual funds that invest in those bonds.

Right now, municipal bonds—particularly those in your home state—are providing a significant yield advantage over Treasuries for investors in the 28% tax bracket and higher.

Example: A 10-year Treasury bond currently yields 8%, while a 10-year municipal bond yields about 6.6%. But once you take federal income tax out of the Treasury bond interest, its yield drops to 5.52%. If you're in the 31% or higher federal tax bracket, the municipal advantage is even greater.

The rest of a sound long-term portfolio would go into growth investments—particularly stocks. That strategy may strike some investors as dangerous. But you can reduce your risk by spreading your equity holdings among different sectors of the stock market. When one or more sectors decline temporarily, your other sectors will rise.

Right now, I advise my clients to put 40% of their portfolios into *income-producing* stocks or funds that hold these stocks.

I also advise my clients to divide the rest of their portfolios evenly among three other types of funds—specifically growth, foreign stock funds and small-cap funds.

What kind of estate planning do I need?

At the very least, you should have three documents…

• *Will.* Make sure that it is valid and up-to-date.

• *Living will.* This tells doctors that you don't want to be kept on a life-support system if you're terminally ill.

• *Durable power of attorney.* This appoints someone to run your finances if you become incapacitated. If you neglect to draw up one, the court will decide who will look after your finances…and the court's choice is not always best.

Important: If you or your spouse have an estate that is valued at more than $600,000, you will need a credit shelter trust. It allows each spouse to take advantage of the $600,000 exemption from estate taxes. By creating such a credit shelter trust, an estate of $1.2 million or more will avoid paying more than $200,000 in taxes when the surviving spouse dies.

Should I pay-down my mortgage early?

Many people argue against doing this. They believe that the money you use to pay-down your mortgage at a faster rate could be invested elsewhere at a higher return.

They also point out that mortgage payments are tax deductible. Even so, I am strongly in favor of reducing the time it takes to pay off a home loan.

Reasons: Your return on other investments will rarely be much higher than the interest payments you'll save by paying down the mortgage. They most certainly weren't in 1994. Also, one of the most important things for investors is the ability to sleep well at night. I think there is a major psychological benefit to knowing that you are paying down your mortgage at a rapid rate.

It is great to enter your retirement mortgage-free. Even an extra $100 a month can make a big difference.

How much life insurance do I need?

Start out by considering two numbers…

• *Minimum amount of coverage:* Five times your annual spending, including taxes.

Example: If you earn $50,000 and save $5,000 annually, you should have five times $45,000 in coverage. That amount will provide your family with time to get on firmer financial footing if something happens to you.

• *Maximum amount:* Ask an insurance agent to provide an estimate. Believe me, he/she won't leave much out.

For most people, the best amount lies between the minimum and the maximum.

Example: If you have children who are not in college yet, you might insure your life for five times your annual spending—*plus* a sufficient amount to pay off your mortgage and fund the children's college educations.

When should I sell a mutual fund?

Let's assume that you bought a mutual fund because it had a solid long-term record, and nothing has changed about the management of the fund.

A fund has to perform below the average for funds in its category for two consecutive years before I will consider selling it. For instance, a growth fund must trail other growth funds...a small-company fund must trail other small-company funds, etc.

You can find category averages in *Barron's* every week under "Lipper Mutual Fund Performance Reports."

My approach means you have to be patient —but it will probably be rewarding. When a good fund underperforms for a year, it often snaps back and does very well afterward.

Source: Jonathan Pond, president of Financial Planning Information Inc., 9 Galen St., Watertown, MA 02172, and author of *The New Century Family Money Book.* Dell.

IRA Trap

Don't have your IRA invest in tax-exempt state or municipal bonds. *Why:* Any amount withdrawn from an IRA is taxable income, even if the withdrawn amount was earned from a tax-exempt bond. So, by having the IRA invest in tax-exempt bonds, you forfeit the tax exemption for them that would have been available had they been held outside the IRA.

You Can Crash-Proof Your Retirement Investments

Your retirement money has to last the rest of your life—unless you're prepared to risk doing

without, or sponging on the kids. That means building the right mix of retirement assets to begin with, and shuffling them around when changing circumstances dictate.

That's not so easy in a time of constant change and uncertainty in the economy and in the financial markets. But you can do it, if you follow this eight-step guide...

Don't forget your rainy-day fund. You can get so absorbed with planning for retirement you forget to keep money set aside against the unexpected, like illness or job loss.

The first step in crash-proofing is to keep at least three months' living expenses safe—and readily accessible. Many people now keep a higher cash reserve than they used to because they're worried about job stability. If you're 50, and planning to retire at 60, consider a higher cash reserve because if you lose a job, it may not be so easy to find another.

The problem, given today's low interest rates, is where to put the money so that it earns money and is safe. I favor a money market mutual fund, or a credit union which may pay a little more than a bank. For anyone above the lowest tax brackets, you'll earn a higher after-tax return from a tax-exempt money fund.

Retiree Alert I: The cash reserve rule may not apply to you if you are retired and have a steady income stream from Social Security, a pension or regular withdrawals from an IRA.

Alert II: Even if you are retired, you may be in a high enough tax bracket that a tax-exempt money fund makes sense for what cash you do keep.

Don't put all your investment eggs in one basket. Don't put all your money into bonds or stocks or money in the bank. If you spread your retirement money over a wide array of assets, a setback in one market won't wipe you out.

Our current asset allocation model for someone who wants the best blend of risk and return ...40% stocks, 30% fixed-income investments, 20% real estate, 5% cash, 5% "other" investments. Adapt that model to your own circumstances—and be sure to diversify.

Go for growth over fixed income. The worst mistake for someone who is retired, or about to retire, is to invest money only to earn income. Many retirees invest for income because they think that this strategy is safe. Crash-proof your retirement money by investing it for total return—dividends plus capital appreciation—for as long as you can. You want the principal to grow and the income stream to grow so you are able to combat both inflation and taxes adequately.

You must invest your retirement money with the idea that it is going to last another 40 to 50 years. If you invest only for income, and not for growth, it may not.

Retiree Alert: Keep investing for total return, rather than for income alone, even after retirement. You should find that your need for current income diminishes in retirement. After age 65, most people don't spend money as they did earlier.

Balance stocks vs stock mutual funds. There's a lot to be said for picking the best mix of common stocks—as opposed to putting all your funds into mutual funds. Mutual funds distribute gains yearly—hitting you with an annual tax liability. You don't pay taxes when individual stocks appreciate until you sell the stocks. And the right mix of individual stocks will usually out-perform a mutual fund. High performance and low taxes is a wonderful way to crash-proof your retirement money.

But, with communication as rapid as it is today, I think many mutual funds get information—and act on it—faster than investment advisers, stockbrokers or individual investors. Also, there are over 4,000 mutual funds around today. I think putting together portfolios of mutual funds makes sense. *Bottom line:* Invest in mutual funds over stocks unless you are in a position to lose money.

Finally, too many individuals get emotionally attached to stocks. They say, "I can't sell my IBM" or "I can't sell my Philip Morris," and they don't sell when they should. Mutual fund managers can sell at the optimum time because they don't have the same affection for a stock.

Build a defensive mutual fund mix. Consider "hybrid" funds—which invest in a range of securities—for crash-proofing at least part of your mutual fund investing. For instance, there are bond funds which invest in a mix of US corporate bonds, high yield bonds and international bonds.

"Balanced" funds split pretty evenly between stocks and bonds. Asset allocation funds shift among stocks, bonds and cash—seeking the best combination of risk and reward for given market conditions.

In every case, diversification is your most important crash-proofing tool. With these funds, you're buying a lot of diversification in one fund, since it's rare for both stocks and bonds to lose in a single year.

You could build a total portfolio around income, balanced and asset allocation funds. *But I still favor dividing your fund investments three ways:*

- One-third in bond funds.

- One-third in balanced funds.

- One-third in good quality growth stock funds.

Follow a low-risk bond strategy. Too many people—retirees and those planning for retirement—are being sold bonds based on the record of the past 10 years, which saw rates steadily falling and prices steadily rising.

Things are likely to be different in the future, with rates going back up and bond prices coming down. Crash-proof your retirement funds by taking those changing market forces into account. As a general rule, the shorter the maturity of a bond, the less the price that bond will fall when rates move up.

Exactly how you apply that depends on how much money you have. With a portfolio of good size, look into a "ladder" of maturities—have a series of individual bonds—with another bond maturing every couple of years. Prices of your other bonds may be down, but you can invest money from the maturing bond at the new, higher interest rate.

With less money, go with a mix of bond funds—split 50-50 between intermediate term and short term. You can use taxable bonds if they're for a tax-shielded account, such as an Individual Retirement Account. Consider tax-exempt bonds if they're in your own name. Tax-exempt bonds now return 85% of what taxable bonds return, and you pay no federal taxes on the income. Single-state tax-exempt bond funds free you from state and local taxes.

Send some money on an overseas vacation. I think it's important to have some of your retirement money in international investments outside the United States. That may not sound like a conservative tactic, but I think it's a good hedge if you're concerned, as I am, about the high level of prices in the US stock market. International securities do pose more risk than US stocks or bonds. But you can find better values in international markets today, and interest rates are higher overseas than they are in the US.

I recommend that 10% to 20% of your total portfolio be internationally oriented. It would be in international stock or bond mutual funds according to your investment objectives and your tax bracket.

Don't put your stocks away and never look at them again. Market timers try to pick the ideal time to buy an investment and the ideal time to sell. If you could do that perfectly, you wouldn't have to worry about crash-proofing your retirement money.

Unfortunately, trying to time your investments seldom works out, except for very short periods. Usually, you can do a better crash-proofing job if you concentrate on choosing investments wisely, invest on a regular basis, and hold on for the long term. That's because, in a growing economy, most investments show gains over time. What you hope, in selecting a mutual fund, is that the portfolio manager will make wise investment decisions for you.

This doesn't mean you can buy stocks or mutual funds for your retirement fund, and never think about them again.

Look at IBM and Philip Morris. Investors are so nervous it seems that every day, they take out another stock and shoot it. One company recently reported earnings down by only four cents a share and the stock immediately lost 20% of its value.

Don't neglect your investments. You can't say "I've taken care of all contingencies," and go happily about your life. You must review your investments regularly yourself, or you must sit down with an adviser at least twice a year just to check that you're on the right track. There are too many things that are changing, that have to be watched.

Source: Alexandra Armstrong, certified financial planner, and chairman of Armstrong, Welch & MacIntyre, Inc., 1155 Connecticut Ave. NW, Suite 250, Washington, DC 20036.

Answers to the Most-Asked Questions About Money And Retirement

It's not easy building a strong, well-rounded retirement portfolio, given today's high stock prices and low bond yields. Each step of your planning raises questions about how and when to invest.

Here are answers to 10 of the questions that retirees—and those saving for retirement—are asking most often today:

• *What's the best overall allocation of assets for a retirement portfolio—stocks vs. bonds vs. cash?* My rule of thumb is that your age equals the percentage of your portfolio you should be putting in bonds. Reasonably affluent people planning for retirement should have half to 60% of their assets in stocks, the rest in bonds. Whatever the split is, I recommend you further break down your retirement portfolio this way:

Stocks or stock mutual funds…
- 30% income
- 20% growth
- 20% small cap
- 30% international.

Bonds or bond mutual funds:
- 40% municipals
- 20% treasuries
- 20% corporate
- 20% mortgage-backed.

Obviously, keep the municipals outside the tax-sheltering of your retirement funds (they're already tax-free).

• *What's the best allocation of assets in a 401(k) plan for someone over 50?* Follow the same rule-of-thumb as above, your age equals the percentage of 401(k) assets that should be in bonds. Again, affluent people can put 50% to 60% of their 401(k) assets in stock.

But don't put any of your 401(k) money into the stock of your own company. I don't care how optimistic you are about that company's future, you never know what's going to happen to that stock. It's just too risky. I would also avoid money market funds and Guaranteed Investment Contracts (GICs). Over time, bond funds will probably outperform GICs.

The range of choices in a 401(k) tends to be abysmally narrow. That's why it's important to coordinate your 401(k) plan with your other investments.

• *Are utility stocks still good retirement investments?* As a long-term investment, utilities do have a role in a portfolio. Just don't go too heavily into them. The past few months have shown that utility stocks, while often perceived as being fairly insulated from downturns, really aren't. And at current valuations they aren't providing a lot of income. Putting more than 20% of your wealth into utility stocks is placing too much of a bet on a sector that is reasonable but not spectacular.

• *Is it wise to invest in Real Estate Investment Trusts (REITs) today?* REITs have been very hot lately. But I think the people who are getting into them lack a sense of history, because REITs have gone through protracted periods of grievous downturns. I think they're trading at very high values, given the fact that there's nothing that suggests that our national real estate outlook is ebullient. REITs could play a role in a portfolio, but it should fall on the speculative side.

• *Is there one type of mutual fund that you particularly favor for retirement planning?* I refer to balanced funds as the one fund to own if you own only one fund. A balanced fund requires the manager more or less to stay within a fairly narrow parameter of stocks and bonds. Almost universally that is 60% stocks, 40% bonds.

Maintaining that balance forces the manager to do the right thing. If stock prices have risen, he/she is forced to sell stocks. If stock prices drop, he's forced to buy stocks. It's that en-

forced discipline that has given balanced funds, over the long term, just about as good a performance as the aggressive stock funds with considerably less risk.

• *How much of someone's retirement savings should be invested overseas?* I think 30% of the stock side of your portfolio could be invested overseas. I think there's an opportunity in the international bond market. I could see as much as 20% of the bond side of a portfolio going into the foreign bond sector.

If you're going to invest in foreign stocks, invest in an international fund that only invests overseas, not in a global fund that can invest in the US stock market as well. Avoid single country or single region funds. When you invest in an international fund, you're paying the manager not only to pick good stocks, but to decide which countries those stocks should be in.

• *What role should a variable annuity play in retirement planning?* It's certainly a vehicle to put money aside for retirement in a tax-advantaged form. But only buy a variable annuity after you've contributed the maximum to a 401(k) or 403(b) plan—and only after you've contributed the maximum to an IRA or to a Keogh plan if you have self-employment income.

The higher the fees on a variable annuity, the more your return will be reduced. You probably can save some money by going to one of three major no-load mutual fund companies that offer variable annuities. In alphabetical order, they are Fidelity, Scudder and Vanguard.

They have good underlying funds, and their fees aren't as onerous as the fees of many of the annuities that are sold by insurance salespeople. Weigh the allocations in favor of stocks, because you're going to need a big return to offset those annual fees you're paying.

• *How much of a retirement portfolio should be in bonds—and what are the rules for buying bonds today?* The way to play bonds is to "ladder" maturities—spreading your money over different maturities. That's easy to do with bond funds because you have short-term funds, intermediate-term funds and long-term funds. Intermediate bonds, or intermediate bond funds, give you 85% of the yield of a long-term bond with a lot less volatility.

Interest rates in real terms aren't that low because inflation is quite low.

But you can't let bonds play a major role in your retirement portfolio, even with low inflation, or you're going to run out of purchasing power before you die. Even in retirement, you need to keep investing for growth.

In lieu of bonds, I would look for stocks that have a good record of increasing their dividends over the years. There are plenty out there.

• *Should you try to invest for life in your retirement portfolio—or should you actively manage this money?* It's crucial to actively manage a portfolio, even when it's a retirement portfolio. After all, you're still a long-term investor when you're 65 or 75. The world changes and you have to be alert to that. In retirement you have the time to do it.

• *What can help someone overcome inertia and fear—and start actively saving for retirement?* You have to face reality, and the reality is that you've got to beat inflation by 3% after taxes in order to provide an income that's going to just keep up with inflation.

People have to realize how important this is —and that's the stick. The carrot is obviously that the more preparation you do for retirement, the more you are preparing a financially comfortable, worry-free retirement.

Source: Jonathan Pond, author of *The New Century Family Money Book,* Dell. He is president of Financial Planning Information, Inc., 9 Galen St., Watertown, MA 02172.

Avoiding the Biggest Mistakes Investors Make

The ever-continuing changes in the tax laws are making it more and more difficult for investors to retain their investment gains.

And the changes of recent years—particularly the elimination of the favorable tax rate on long-term capital gains—are about to be compounded by new higher tax rates. In this environment, it is essential to plan ahead to make the most of investment returns and to avoid the tax traps investors commonly fall into.

Basic mistakes...

• *Mistake:* Not considering taxes until you begin preparing tax returns. By then it's often too late to adopt strategies that could have cut the tax bill. Monitor the tax implications of your investments throughout the year, and periodically consult with your accountant.

• *Mistake:* Failing to take responsibility for tax and investment strategies. Some investors rely completely on accountants, brokers, lawyers, or other advisers. Of course, you should seek advice from tax and investment professionals, and use their expertise when implementing the strategies you decide upon. But it's important to remember that you are the person who will have to live with the results, so take responsibility and begin planning ahead now to make the most of your investments.

• *Mistake:* Not quantifying tax consequences when comparing investment options. This means looking at the dollar numbers earned after taxes from investments that receive different tax treatment.

Example: Consider the after-tax returns paid out over 10 years by a 10% taxable investment and an 8% tax-free or tax-deferred one. Let's assume the investments were made by a person paying both a 31% federal tax rate and a 15% local rate in a high-tax area like New York City...

	Before taxes		After taxes	
	10%	8%	10%	8%
Starting value	$10,000	$10,000	$10,000	$10,000
After 10 yrs.	$25,937	$21,589	$17,690	$21,589
Net return	$15,937	$11,589	$17,690	$11,589

Without working through the numbers, you are likely to be surprised that taxes cut the return from the higher-yielding investment by more than half (from $15,937 to $7,690)—and that the "lower" yielding investment in fact pays over 50% more after taxes ($11,589 vs. $7,690).

This example is simpler than most real cases. Some investments are partially taxable—for example, US Treasury issues are exempt from state tax but not from federal tax. Also, your own tax bracket will vary according to local law, income level, and the deductions and credits available to you. Although this calculation appears to be complicated, it is made simple with the worksheets I provide in my book.

In some cases, it may pay to increase tax exposure.

Example: If you live in a low- or no-tax state, it may pay to move funds from Treasury bonds to a portfolio of AAA-grade corporate bonds, to receive more income after taxes with almost the same safety, even though more total tax will be due.

The way to know which investment plan is best for you is to work through the numbers illustrating different options.

• *Mistake:* Not making full use of retirement plans. Tax-favored retirement programs let you obtain the higher returns offered by taxable investments in a tax-deferred environment. Today, personal retirement accounts such as IRAs, Keoghs, and Simplified Employee Plans (SEPs) can invest in almost anything except collectibles, mortgaged rental properties, or a business in which you own an interest of 5% or more. Many employer-provided 401(k) savings plans also offer self-directed investment options.

Common mistake: Thinking the main tax benefit from a retirement-plan contribution is the deduction for it, and making contributions at the last minute each year. In fact, over the long run, the tax-deferral obtained for compound retirement-plan earnings can be more valuable than the contribution deduction.

Example: A $2,000 IRA contribution saves $800 for a person in a 40% combined federal and state tax bracket. But a contribution made early in the year will also earn tax-deferred income within the account during the year. If the IRA earns 10%, $2,000 contributed a year before the deadline for just one year will earn $200, and over 30 years this $200 will compound to $3,490—all of which is forfeited if you make your contribution at the last minute instead. If this contribution is made early each year, the increase in total retirement funds available is significant.

Make plan contributions as early in the year as possible. Also consider making nondeductible contributions—in addition to your deductible ones—to an IRA to obtain the benefit of long-term tax deferral.

Estate-planning mistake...

Not averting estate taxes is a big mistake. Many people put off estate planning simply because thinking about death is not pleasant. Others underestimate the cost of estate taxes because they believe the $600,000 unified credit will protect them, or because they know they can pass assets tax-free to a spouse. *Traps:*

• Your estate may be pushed far over the $600,000 amount by assets that you don't think of—such as life-insurance proceeds, the value of retirement accounts, or appreciation in the value of your home.

• Passing all your assets to your spouse can be a costly mistake, because he/she will be able to pass no more than $600,000 to the next generation tax-free—while the two of you could plan together to pass a combined $1.2 million.

• *Self-defense:* Have the insurance on your life owned by your spouse, a child, or a trust benefiting family members. You can provide the money needed to pay the premiums through annual tax-free gifts. When you die, the insurance proceeds will not be part of your taxable estate.

• *Self-defense:* If your assets exceed $600,000, make double use of the $600,000 unified estate- and gift-tax credit by passing up to $600,000 of your assets to children directly. Alternative: Use a trust that pays income to your spouse for life and then distributes its assets to your children, while leaving the remainder of your assets to your spouse. The $600,000 credit will be available both for your disposition of property, and for your spouse's disposition of property inherited from you.

• *Self-defense:* Use gifts to cut your estate. You can make gifts of up to $10,000 each to as many separate recipients as you wish annually, free of gift tax. The limit is $20,000 if the gift is made jointly with your spouse. You can also make larger tax-free gifts by using part of your unified credit. Although this will reduce the amount of the credit that will be available to your estate, it can pay off if you expect the gift assets to appreciate in value before you die.

Gifts of income-producing assets to family members in lower income-tax brackets, such as children over age 14, can cut family income taxes as well. And gifts of appreciated assets to low-bracket family members can be cashed in by these family members with less gains tax resulting.

Strategy: When older family members have less than $600,000 in assets, a reverse gift can save big taxes. You can make gifts to them of assets that have appreciated in value. When they die, the assets will pass back to you or to other family members with stepped-up basis— revalued for tax purposes at market value—so potential gains tax on their appreciation is eliminated.

More tax-cutting ideas…

• Earmark stock and mutual fund shares to maximize the tax advantage when shares are sold.

Example: Say you bought shares in a stock or mutual fund at different times at different prices, and now wish to sell some. If you have price records for specific shares, you can sell the particular shares that produce the optimal gain or loss—perhaps to minimize taxable gain, or to maximize a capital loss that will protect other gains from tax. If you do not have price records, the IRS will treat the first shares bought as the first sold.

• Get the IRS to absorb part of the sales load on a mutual fund. Do this by buying shares in a money fund offered by a family of funds. After three months or more, transfer out of the money fund and into one of the other fund options (stocks, bonds, etc.). The sales load will produce a loss on the sale of the money fund shares, which you can deduct or use to shelter other gains from tax.

• Look for losses in your portfolio that can be used to offset gains or generate deductions.

Tactic: Use tax swaps to produce paper losses that can shelter gains from tax. *How:* Sell a security to produce a loss, then immediately buy back a similar security.

Example: You can sell a bond and then buy back a bond from a different issuer that pays the same interest and has the same maturity date and credit rating. You get a loss deduction while maintaining your investment position. You cannot buy back the same security within 30 days to produce a tax loss.

The 30-day time limit does not apply if you sell a security to produce a gain. So if you already have a loss, you can sell a security at a gain, shelter the gain with the loss, then immediately buy back the same security, avoiding future tax that would otherwise have been due on its appreciation.

• Consider "trader" status. If you actively manage your portfolio to profit from market swings—instead of profiting from appreciation, and dividend and interest payments—you may qualify as a professional stock trader and become eligible to deduct investment costs on Schedule C as business expenses. This enables you to fully deduct items which provide only limited deductions to investors, such as interest and investment expenses.

Although you cannot make deductible contributions to Keogh or SEP retirement plans from trading gains, trading gains are not subject to self-employment taxes either. Consult your tax adviser about how the rules may apply to your situation.

Source: Ted Tesser, CPA, 30 Waterside Plaza #9G, New York 10010. His firm, Waterside Financial Services, assists clients with tax, investment, and retirement-plan strategies. He is author of *The Serious Investor's Tax Survival Guide*, which includes a free tax update, *Maximizing Profit Under the Clinton Administration*, Traders' Library.

How to Get Out of a Guaranteed Investment Contract Trap

The troubled condition of several large insurance companies has suddenly raised concern among many conservative, long-term investors in annuities and guaranteed investment contracts (GICs) about the safety of those holdings.

GICs and annuities written by insurance companies have been heavily used to fund retirement accounts.

• GICs. These contracts between an employer and an insurance company to pay a fixed rate of return for a set number of years, have attracted more than two-thirds of the estimated $125 billion in company 401(k) savings plans.

• Deferred annuities. Deferred annuities have been aggressively marketed by insurance companies to individuals in recent years as tax-deferred retirement investment accounts.

Takeover trap: Thousands of employees found their long-standing company pensions converted into annuities when their companies were taken over. New, financially slick managements identified hidden assets in "overfunded" pension accounts, took out the surplus, terminated conventional pension plans and bought annuities to cover remaining pension liabilities.

The problems that GIC and annuity investors suddenly became aware of this year...

• GICs are not very guaranteed. The "guarantee" by the insurance company applies to the rate of interest—not the investment itself. Protection of principal is dependent on the financial condition of the insurance company. Executive Life Insurance Co., seized by California insurance regulators in April 1991, had sold about $3 billion in GICs. Thus far the company's conservators have not paid anything on these contracts—though they are fully paying out death benefits on Executive Life's life insurance policies.

• Annuity trap. The Pension Guaranty Corporation, created under the Employee Retirement Income Security Act (ERISA) to insure pension plans, does not guarantee the annuities employees may be left with once a company terminates the pension plan.

• No GIC defender. The life insurance industry's guarantee programs, organized on a state-by-state basis to protect policy holders when an insurance company gets into financial trouble, show little eagerness to cover GICs.

• Annuity defense. Many—but not all—insurance industry guarantee programs cover annuities. So far, the California State Insurance Department is paying only 70 cents on the $1 to Executive Life annuity holders.

GIC options...

What individuals who have substantial savings in GICs can do:

• Immediately ask the company benefit manager which insurance companies are behind the GICs in your company's 401(k) plan. (Except for the very smallest plans, most compa-

nies negotiated contracts with more than one insurance company to diversify risk.)

• Ask the company benefit manager what the most current rating of those insurance companies is. *Least risk for you:* The companies that are top rated—A+ for the A. M. Best rating service and A+ for Weiss Research...AAA for Standard & Poor's and Duff & Phelps...Aaa for Moody's.

• If the insurers are not top-rated by at least two—preferably three—of these rating agencies, express your concern and ask what the company is doing to move to a less risky carrier.

Ask specifically: Does the GIC contract have a liquidity feature?

This would enable the company to get out of the contract—usually at a penalty. That would reduce the value of the invested funds—a loss for the employees invested in the GIC. And a new GIC contract would probably pay a lower rate of interest.

• If you have a substantial sum invested in the GIC option of your company savings plan and find it is "guaranteed" by an insurance company that is not top-rated, seriously consider diversifying your investment into other plan options. Likely limitation: Many company savings plans that offer a GIC option do not have another fixed-income option, such as a money-market fund or a bond fund. Your only other option may be a stock fund or company stock. You will have to assess whether a move to equities opens the door to more risk than you potentially face in the GIC.

Annuity options...

Individuals who have purchased annuities should also ask their brokers to provide specific ratings information on the insurance company behind the annuity.

Anthony Amodeo, vice president of Metropolitan Life, a top-rated insurance company, tells us what options individuals with substantial investments in annuities backed by low-rated insurers have.

Unfortunately, if you are one of those whose company pension has been transferred to an annuity, there's nothing that you can do to move to another company.

And your options are nil, too, if you made a major lump-sum investment in an immediate annuity—one that pays you a set amount until death.

But you probably don't have to lose too much sleep over these accounts.

State insurance guarantee associations either cover annuities of failed insurance companies or are showing a disposition to cover them when a problem surfaces, even if their regulations don't yet require it.

Deferred annuities: You do have options with deferred annuities. Look at the plan's surrender charges. Typically, such plans have a maximum surrender charge—say about 7% of the total value of the annuity—if you cancel the annuity in the first, second or third years. After that the surrender charge diminishes, eventually to zero for most. Factors you must balance in deciding whether or not to withdraw from such an annuity:

•Surrender penalty, if any.

•Income tax liability, if any, on the withdrawn funds.

It might be possible to defer taxes by transferring to another annuity.

But IRS rules on annuity withdrawals are tricky. Make sure you get professional tax advice.

•The possible loss of a tax-deferred investment.

•Opportunities that you perceive in putting your money into an alternative investment.

Source: Several insurance industry insiders.

Investment Lessons

There's no shortage of financial advice on Wall Street. The problem is that much of this financial advice is conflicting and leaves individuals confused or stuck in bad investments. So what's an investor to do?

Decisions/decisions...

•"Buy low and sell high" is sound financial advice—but there are actually four decisions to make. Stock-market experts like to say that timing is everything, and most investors strive to sell at the top of a market and buy at the bottom.

This strategy is also known as the "contrary opinion"—doing the opposite of what most other investors are doing at a given time.

But moving successfully against the crowd is very difficult.

Trap: Market cycles contain many small, deceptive movements—so the buy-sell phases aren't always clear. *Here are four decisions a contrarian investor must make...*

•When the market is approaching the bottom of a cycle, sellers no longer have the stomach to buy. This creates an opportunity for bargain hunters. To determine when the market has reached this point, you can evaluate stocks using historically low valuations of revenues, earnings, and dividends. Or you can wait for an uptrend before buying.

•After you buy, don't sell immediately after the bull trend becomes obvious to everyone. Let the crowd join you as the movement upward progresses.

•When serious overvaluation is reached, go against the majority and sell. Determine this moment by setting a price objective beforehand. Or base your timing on the heat of the market. Wait for the first sign of market weakness.

•As the downward cycle advances, resist the temptation to buy back your stock at a lower price. Wait until the market approaches the bottom again before buying.

•Don't confuse portfolio activity with progress toward investment goals. A common mistake made by many investors is rapid portfolio activity. They regard time as the enemy and believe that if they wait too long, that is an invitation for something to go wrong.

It's unrealistic, however, to expect that instant profits are easy to grab. When too much attention is focused on achieving short-term goals, the real opportunity—which is long-term—is forgotten. Think of time as an ally, not as an enemy.

•Beware of the company that offers creative excuses for underachievement. Some companies have a talent for making excuses for problems. Be especially wary of companies that wrap bad news in good news. *Danger signs:*

•When shortfalls and disappointments come with good-news announcements, such as the introduction of a new product or overhead-reduction programs.

•When you find your mailbox jammed with "We love you, shareholder" letters from the company.

•When bad news is accompanied by an announcement of a management shake-up. Did the company also say what took so long for them to clean up the problem? If not, incompetents may still be in charge.

Once credibility has been destroyed, it takes a long time for a company to win it back. When management repeatedly says, "Things will be better next year," it's time to sell.

•Focus on essentials…skip the merely interesting. Experienced investors are humble. They've learned that they can't possibly know everything. Less seasoned investors, on the other hand, may feel that if they had only a few more hours to do research, their investment returns would be considerably better. Usually this is hogwash.

Save time by not seeking out the opinions of yet another expert. Formulating intelligent questions that you then go out and seek answers to is much more valuable than collecting opinions.

Focus on an industry's prospects, the strength and track record of a company, and the long-term implications of a new development.

•Good corporate news can lead to a dangerous sense of euphoria. When there's good news, companies can't wait to circulate it. Many ladle it out in advance, tipping off key stock-market analysts. The result is that these stocks often rise before the news hits the media and afterward rise only slightly—or even fall.

Reasons: Many pros "sell on the news"—or take profits as the news becomes widely known and the price rises—and companies often use good news as an opportunity to seek more equity financing.

Similarly, beware of remarkably upbeat presentations at investment conferences. Instead, wait a few weeks or a month, and you'll almost always be able to buy the stock cheaper.

Opportunity: Look at the volume in the weeks before an "announcement." If it's high, this tells you that you may be late in getting the word.

•Study the composition of a company's board of directors. The role of a company's board of directors is to represent the interests of all stockholders. One way to determine whether the directors are representing your interests is to look at the people who make up the board. *How to tell a good board from a bad one…*

•Determine how many directors come from the company and how many are from the outside. If most are from the inside, the board may not be independent enough to resist undue pressure from top management.

•Examine the credentials of the outsiders. If they are not particularly distinguished, they may have been chosen as "good buddies."

•If the board is small—fewer than five members—it's likely that outside directors were chosen for their cooperative attitude toward management preferences. On the other hand, a large board—more than 10—is probably too unwieldy to support much independence on the part of outside directors.

•The company's proxy statement will reveal the extent of each director's stock ownership and options and interest in the future of the company. Token holdings are danger signs.

•Learn to distinguish the truly underappreciated stock from the real losers. *Key question:* Is the stock misunderstood by Wall Street or is it more likely that management misunderstands what's happened to its market?

Don't be fooled by a company's aura or unduly impressed by its past glories. "What have you done for me lately?" is a legitimate question to ask. "What do you plan to do tomorrow?" is an even better one.

Don't jettison a stock simply because it's the biggest loser in your portfolio. That's a short-term balm that usually turns into a long-term mistake.

Source: George Stasen, a venture-capital expert and chief operating officer of Supra Medical Corp., and Robert Metz, a financial journalist. They are coauthors of *It's a Sure Thing: A Wry Look at Investing, Investors, and the World of Wall Street*, McGraw-Hill.

Loopholes for Investors

One type of income that is taxed at beneficial rates is long-term capital-gain income. This income is taxed at a top rate of 28% today—three percentage points less than the top rate on other income.

The Clinton tax changes keep the capital gains rate at 28% while raising the top tax rate on other types of income.

• *Loophole:* Make full use of capital losses. Losses on the sale of securities are fully deductible against gains. If your losses exceed your gains, up to $3,000 of those excess losses are deductible each year against your salary and other income. Unused losses that you can't deduct because of the $3,000 limit can be carried forward to future tax years until they are used up.

• *Loophole:* Buy stock in a mutual fund before it makes a capital gain distribution. This is a way of "creating" capital gains. The distribution to you is capital-gain income. You can offset that income with losses you've accumulated from other sales. That way you won't pay tax on the distribution.

• *Loophole:* Give appreciated securities to your children instead of selling the securities and giving the children cash. This is a tax-wise way to come up with money for education expenses for a child who is older than 13. If you sell the securities yourself, you'll pay tax on any long-term gains at the 28% rate. But if you give the securities to the child and let him/her sell them, the gain will be taxed at the child's low rate. Children are in the 15% tax bracket in 1993 until their income goes above $22,100.

• *Loophole:* Give appreciated securities to charity. When you do this, you get an income-tax deduction for the full fair-market value of the securities at the time of the gift, and you don't pay tax on the gain that has built up since the time you bought the securities.

• *Loophole:* Be prepared to specifically identify the shares of stock you want your broker to sell. This is important when you've purchased different lots of a company's stock at different prices and you're selling less than your total holding.

If you don't tell your broker which shares you want to sell, the IRS requires you to use the first-in, first-out (FIFO) method. The shares you sell are considered the first ones you purchased. But if you can specifically identify which shares you want to sell, you can tell your broker to sell those.

Example: You can tell your broker to sell the ones you paid the most for to minimize your taxable gain on the sale. Tell him/her to sell the 200 shares of XYZ Company that you bought on October 4 for $13 a share. *Key:* Keep detailed records of your purchases—the number of shares you bought, the amount you paid per share, the date of each purchase, and the total dollar amount of the purchase, including such items as commissions and fees.

• *Loophole:* Swap bonds for tax losses to use against capital gains. Review your portfolio and look for bonds that have declined substantially in price since the time you bought them. Sell them and reinvest the proceeds in similar but not identical bonds—for instance, a bond of a different municipality that has the same rating as the bond you sold.

The sales will generate capital losses, which can be used to offset capital gains that you've already taken. The swap can also be used to improve your portfolio by replacing bonds that are performing badly with others that have greater income or profit potential.

• *Loophole:* Create capital losses. You may want to create losses that can be used to offset capital gains and shelter up to $3,000 of other taxable income.

As long as you are careful to avoid the wash-sale rule, you can lock in losses on securities that have dropped in value while substantially retaining your current investment position.

You can do this by doubling up—that is, buying a matching lot of the same securities as the ones you own, holding the new lot for 31 days, then selling the old one at a loss. Or you can lock in losses by selling first and buying back the same securities after waiting the required 31 days.

• *Loophole:* Deduct losses on the sale of Section 1244 stock. Only $3,000 of net capital losses are deductible each year against salary and other income. But losses on the sale of stock in a small business company (no more than $1 million of paid-in capital) may be deductible as ordinary losses far in excess of the $3,000 capital-loss limitation.

The company's stock may qualify as Section 1244 stock. If it does, you can deduct up to $50,000 of losses ($100,000 on a joint return). Have your tax adviser see whether the stock is Section 1244 stock.

• *Loophole:* Write off worthless securities. Losses from the worthlessness of stock or other securities are deductible in the year in which the security becomes worthless. They're deductible as capital losses. One way to establish the loss is to sell the security to a friend for a nominal amount—say, a dollar.

Alternative way of establishing worthlessness: Get a letter from your broker saying that the cost of selling the security will be more than the amount realized in the sale.

Source: Edward Mendlowitz, partner, Mendlowitz Weitsen, CPAs, Two Pennsylvania Plaza, New York 10121. Mr. Mendlowitz is the author of *New Tax Traps, New Opportunities*, Boardroom Special Reports.

How to Get Money Out of A Mutual Fund...Quickly

Most mutual fund investors don't think about getting their money out of a fund when they put it in. Too often, when financial markets dip and they want to redeem their shares, they find that getting their money back is time-consuming, frustrating, and sometimes costly.

Reasons:

• The phones are tied up. Mutual fund offices can be so inundated with orders to buy and sell shares that their switchboards may be busy at critical times. When you call requesting information about how to redeem shares, you may have to let the telephone ring for a few minutes before someone answers.

• The procedures for redeeming shares are bureaucratic. With most funds you must not only write a redemption letter requesting a check for the value of your investment, but you

must also have your signature guaranteed by a commercial bank or by your broker. That can be time consuming, especially if you bought your shares directly from the fund instead of through a broker, and you don't happen to have an account with a commercial bank. Notarized signatures aren't acceptable and most funds will refuse to accept guarantees from savings-and-loan institutions. If your personal bank is an S&L, you'll have to go to a commercial bank that your bank has established a relationship with to have your signature guaranteed.

To avoid these obstacles:

• Make a copy of the section of the fund prospectus that refers to redemption procedures—and keep it handy. That way you won't have to make a phone call to get information on redemption procedures.

• Prepare a redemption letter in advance. Have your signature guaranteed by your broker or commercial bank so you can simply date the letter whenever you decide to pull out of the fund. Follow prospectus instructions for writing a redemption letter (usually, all you need to do is request that a check be sent to your home address, and give the number of shares owned, and your account number).

• Consider buying shares only in stock or bond funds managed by firms that also have money market funds to which you can switch part of or all of your account by telephone. That way you have access to the money via money market account checks, usually within two days. *Caution:* It's always a good idea to call in a switch as early in the day as possible, because after 3 pm on heavy-volume days, many fund offices can be especially busy.

• When you fill out the forms to purchase fund shares, complete the section for authorizing wire transfers of redemptions to your bank. That service allows you to have shares redeemed and the proceeds deposited directly in your checking or savings account, usually on the same day you make the request. If you need the money fast and you have trouble getting through by phone, you can request a bank transfer in a redemption letter sent by overnight mail.

Source: Sheldon Jacobs, publisher, *The No-Load Fund Investor*, Box 283, Hastings-on-Hudson, NY 10706.

How to Make the Most of the Rally in Small-Cap Stocks

After more than seven years of under-performance, stocks of smaller secondary companies surged ahead recently, significantly outperforming large company stocks.

The NASDAQ* composite has gained 53% since the market hit bottom in October 1990—compared with a 21% gain for the S&P 500. That's more than four times the gain it achieved from October 1985 to October 1990. Does this herald the arrival of another sustained rally in small-cap stocks—or merely another false start?

We believe the stage is set for a period of sustained but more selective good performance by smaller companies. Unlike the 1970s—when it was difficult to be wrong—and the 1980s, when it was difficult to be right, the 1990s will be markedly different for small-cap stocks.

Strategy: Concentrate on small undervalued companies in niche markets with the potential for superior earnings growth.

Perspective…

Historically, small-cap stocks perform best during, and coming out of, a recession. These small company stocks have outperformed large company stocks for periods lasting from two to seven years, so selected small companies should still have far to go.

But success in the small-cap area during the coming decade will not be determined by size alone. Because of their recent run-up in prices, secondary stocks are neither cheap…nor expensive. Nor do they offer unparalleled opportunity across the board.

Rather, their future performance is likely to be much more in line with that of the market in general. Only those companies with low relative market values and the potential for superior earnings growth are apt to outperform the market during the coming decade.

*National Association of Securities Dealers Automated Quotation.

Tricky times…

Indeed, the soft recovery and slow recovery scenario for the 1990s will be perilous for many small companies.

Large companies will be scrambling to exploit new markets. They'll be unwilling to relinquish these opportunities to smaller companies. And if large companies resort to price wars to gain market share, the impact could be devastating for their smaller competitors.

Furthermore, large companies have a strong advantage operating and raising capital overseas, where much of US firms' future growth will come from.

Good news: Smaller companies are not burdened by the huge debt that many large companies took on during the restructuring binge of the 1980s. As a result, they are much more flexible than their larger counterparts. Savvy investors who concentrate on the basics should be able to find some standouts.

Strategy: Look for companies with a strong franchise that can protect them from competitive threats. Those companies with a niche in the marketplace, with patent protection, or with a unique product that can command premium prices are those most likely to be able to turn in strong earnings growth.

Source: Mary Farrell, strategist with a special interest in small company stocks for PaineWebber, and a frequent panelist on *Wall Street Week* with Louis Rukeyser.

Shift Investments from Stocks to Bonds

Shift investments from stocks to bonds at a gradual rate as you grow older. *Rule of thumb:* The percentage of your portfolio invested in stocks should equal 100 minus your age. So if you are 55, you should be 45% invested in stocks and 55% invested in bonds or cash. *Rationale:* Stocks are risky in the short run, but over the long run they consistently outperform bonds. You'll need this extra income for retirement. The money you keep in bonds will meet your short- and medium-term cash needs, letting you maintain your stock investments long enough for them to recover from any short-term market drop and protecting you from ever having to cash in your stocks while the market is low.

Source: *It's Never Too Late to Get Rich* by James Jorgensen, editor, *It's Your Money* newsletter. Dearborn Financial Publishing, Chicago.

Adding International Stocks to Your Portfolio Reduces Risk

Every monitored investment newsletter that recommends a blend of US and international investment has increased its return and lowered its risk by doing so. *Why:* International stock markets do not move in lockstep with US markets, so when US markets are down foreign ones are likely to be up and vice versa. Thus, buying international stocks reduces the risk that your whole portfolio will decline in value at one time. And international markets have equaled or surpassed the performance of the US market in recent years. Investments in interntional stocks are easily made through high- quality mutual funds.

Source: Mark Hulbert, editor, *Hulbert Financial Digest*, 316 Commerce St., Alexandria, VA 22314.

Bond Investment Trap

Before investing in bonds check to see if they are subject to a call provision that lets the issuer pay them off before maturity. *Key:* Bonds go up in value when interest rates go down. But if bonds are subject to a call provision when interest rates decline, you can expect the issuer to redeem them and refinance at a lower rate. Thus, the call provision limits the potential for gain from a bond while leaving you with the full downside risk of loss if interest rates go up. *Point:* While a call provision is onerous on bonds, it is especially so on high-yield "junk"

bonds because of the greater risk involved in owning them.

Source: Ben Weberman, financial columnist, *Forbes,* 60 Fifth Ave., New York 10011.

Taking Money Out of an IRA

Is it true that one can take money out of an IRA before age 59½ without paying the 10% premature-distribution penalty if payments are received in the form of a lifetime annuity?

Yes, and this opens tax-planning opportunities. *Example:* In one case, a person took early annuity payments from an IRA and used them to make mortgage payments on a new house. The mortgage-interest deduction sheltered the annuity payments from income tax. The undistributed funds that remained in the IRA continued to earn tax-deferred income that could be used to make future mortgage payments.

Thus, the individual had found a tax-favored way to finance his new home. In a private ruling, the IRS held that the arrangement was proper.

How to Save a Million Dollars on An Inherited IRA

A married couple must plan ahead so they'll know in advance how to handle an IRA that one spouse inherits from the other.

Vital: There are choices to make about the IRA. Make the wrong choice and the IRA dies with the surviving spouse. Make the right choice and the IRA can continue for decades, accumulating tax-deferred income. A modest sum can easily grow from a few hundred thousand to a million dollars or more.

Trap: Many otherwise well-informed taxpayers don't know even the basics of how to handle an inherited IRA.

The basics: A person who inherits an IRA from a spouse has the choice of treating it in one of two ways:

- Take the inherited account as a beneficiary.

- Treat the inherited fund as your own, and roll it over into a new account in your own name.

The choice made can have huge consequences if, as is usually the case, the deceased spouse was over age 70½ when he/she died. The law requires the IRA owner to begin taking distributions by April 1 following the year in which he attains age 70½. After required distributions have begun…

- When the spouse takes the inherited IRA as a beneficiary, distributions must continue at least as rapidly as under the method being used before the IRA owner's death. When the surviving spouse dies, amounts remaining in the account are distributed and subject to income tax.

- When a spouse takes the inherited IRA as his/her own, distributions can be made over the combined life expectancies of the spouse and a newly named beneficiary.

Key: Because the beneficiary may be much younger than the inheriting spouse—40 or 50 years younger in the case of a grandchild—a huge tax-deferral can result, producing an extra 40 or 50 years of compound tax-deferred income in the account before it is fully distributed.

Payoff: In the fairly common case where an inherited IRA contains a few hundred thousand dollars—which may represent a lifetime of retirement savings rolled over from a company pension plan—several extra decades of tax-deferred compound earnings can easily amount to a million dollars or more.

An example of how the rules work:

Say that a husband is 78 and his wife is 74 in 1993, and they have a nine-year-old grandchild. The husband and wife are required to make IRA withdrawals over their joint life expectancy, which is 15.9 years according to IRS tables if they use the recalculation method. (This assumes that the taxpayers by error or design used the recalculation method instead of the term-certain method.) Thus, they must withdraw 6.3% ($\frac{1}{15.9}$) of their account in 1993.

Assume the husband dies after taking this distribution. The wife must choose how to treat the inherited IRA. She can take it as a beneficiary and continue to receive payments based upon her single life expectancy, since the recalculation method is in effect. By taking the IRA as her own and naming her grandchild as her beneficiary, she can greatly lengthen the payout schedule.

The grandchild, now age 10, and the grandmother, age 75, have a true combined life expectancy of 71.7 years. But for purposes of computing required IRA withdrawals, a non-spouse beneficiary is treated as being no more than 10 years younger than the IRA owner while the owner lives.

Thus, under IRS tables, the combined life expectancy in 1994 of the now 75-year-old grandmother and the grandchild is considered to be 21.8 years under a special rule. The required annual withdrawal the grandmother must make is reduced to 4.6% ($\frac{1}{21.8}$). This smaller withdrawal leaves more money in the account earning tax-deferred income. During the next two years under the special rule, IRS tables give a combined life expectancy for grandmother and grandchild of 20.9 and 20.1 years, requiring annual distributions of 4.8% and 5%.

Assume the grandmother dies in 1996. If she had taken the IRA as a beneficiary, the money remaining in it would be distributed to her estate during the calendar year after her death —and that would have been the end of the IRA.

But because she took the account as her own, the IRA passes to the now 12-year-old grandchild—who can base his/her required withdrawals starting in 1997, at age 13, on the remaining period that is left in the 71.7 year initial true combined life expectancy period, which is 68.7 years. The grandchild need withdraw only 1.5% ($\frac{1}{68.7}$) of the account for the year as his required minimum distribution. This withdrawal is so small that the account can be expected to start growing again as a result of investment earnings, and the grandchild can expect to reap tax-deferred earnings in it for the next 68 years!

Bottom line: A person who inherits an IRA from a spouse may elect to treat it as his/her own and may select a beneficiary in order to take advantage of the extended payout rules.

The IRS gives an example in which the surviving spouse claims the IRA as her own in the year that the IRA owner dies. In that case, the surviving spouse must select a beneficiary and commence payments by no later than December 31 of the following year. The surviving spouse must create a brand-new IRA and not consolidate it with an old IRA.

Note: The election cannot be made by an executor on behalf of a person who dies before making the election.

Consult with an adviser who is an expert in IRA tax planning for details. Refer the adviser to *IRS Letter Ruling 9311037*, the most recent ruling on this type of arrangement.

Source: Seymour Goldberg, professor of law and taxation at Long Island University and senior partner in the law firm of Goldberg & Ingber, PC, 666 Old Country Rd., Garden City, NY 11530. Mr. Goldberg is the author of *A Professional's Guide to the IRA Distribution Rules*, Field Services, New York State Society of Certified Public Accountants.

Build Retirement Wealth In 10 Years with A Defined-Benefit Keogh Plan

Anyone with self-employment income from personal services, including sideline business income, consultant's fees, freelance income, and director's fees, can have a Keogh plan. Keogh plans are retirement plans for self-employed taxpayers.

They're approved by the IRS and their tax benefits weren't cut back by tax reform. *Main benefits…*

• Contributions to the plan are tax-deductible.

• Earnings on contributions are not taxed while in the plan.

• Taxes are deferred until retirement, when you are likely to be in a lower tax bracket than you are now.

Problem: Defined-contribution Keogh plans —the most common kind of Keogh—won't work for someone who is 50-plus because the most you can put away each year is 13.04% of self-employment income, up to $30,000. This is enough for people who have many years to save before retiring, but not for people who are closer to retirement.

Solution: A defined-benefit Keogh plan. With defined-benefit Keoghs you can put away a much bigger percentage of your income. That's because you are funding an account that is designed to pay you a fixed monthly amount when you retire. So the older you are, the more you can contribute to the plan each year.

They're perfect for someone who has 10 to 15 years to go before retirement.

Opportunity: Because contributions are deducted on your tax return each year, you can shelter large amounts of income during your peak earning years. Money in the account builds up tax-free until withdrawals begin.

How defined-benefit Keogh plans work: The size of your annual retirement payment is based on a percentage of your salary and the number of years that you have remaining to work before retirement. Next, actuarial tables are used to calculate how much money must be contributed to the defined-benefit plan every year.

In 1996 you can set aside enough money in a defined benefit plan to pay you as much as $115,641 a year when you retire. The limit is indexed annually for inflation.

Example: A self-employed 55-year-old sets up a defined-benefit plan to provide annual payments of $115,641, the legal maximum, starting at age 65. The first year's contribution is $51,893. That rises each year, to $95,403 by year 10. Assuming the investment earns 7% a year, the account would be worth $954,038 at retirement.

Caution: The $115,641 annual limit is reduced if you retire before the Social Security retirement age, from 65 years old to 67 years old depending on the year you were born. Also, the benefit cannot exceed 100% of your average compensation for your highest three consecutive years' earnings.

Drawback: Tax rules are much stricter for defined-benefit plans than for defined-contribution plans. You must make minimum contributions every year or face a 10% underfunding penalty.

Cost: The defined-benefit plan must be custom-made for you by a pension specialist. Expect to pay between $1,000 and $2,000 a year to administer the plan.

Source: Richard A. Imperato, principal, KPMG Peat Marwick, 345 Park Ave., New York 10154.

The Biggest Traps in Retirement Planning

To make the most of your retirement years, start planning now. The earlier you start, the more you will be able to achieve.

Set goals...

The first mistake of retirement planning is not having goals. When you don't know what you want, you are *un*likely to attain it. *Helpful:* Draw up a "dream list" for your retirement years. *Consider...*

•Where you will want to live.

•Your desired lifestyle.

•The income you will need.

•The specific steps required to turn as much of the list as possible into reality.

Goal-setting requires you to...

...take action. By having a goal of a certain amount of savings by a fixed date, you know how much you must save each year starting now. This also shows you how costly it is to delay saving, giving a greater incentive to start saving right away.

Example: Put away just $50 a month starting at age 25 and, assuming an average 5% after-tax annual return, you'll have $76,619 saved by age 65—at $100 a month, your nest egg will be $153,238. By contrast, put away the same $50 a month starting at age 55, and you'll have just $7,796 by age 65...$100 a month will yield only $15,593.

...be realistic. Everybody wants many things, but goal-setting makes you decide what's most important. Once you decide this, you can begin to assess how much money you're going to need. But more than finances are involved here. You're more likely to be happy in your retirement years if you've achieved what's important

to you than if you've left your dreams too vague to be realized.

...be consistent. People typically want two things from their retirement investments—safety for their savings and big returns to fund a comfortable retirement lifestyle. But, of course, there's an inherent conflict here.

A sound investment plan designed to meet specific goals will make the most of the trade-off between risk and opportunity and enable you to avoid the costly and common mistakes of investing either too riskily or with too much caution.

Example: You might invest in aggressive growth stocks while retirement is still years away, knowing that if the stock market falls there will be plenty of time for your portfolio to recover. Then, as retirement nears, you can shift money gradually into safer investments. With a specific financial target, you will know how much to shift each year to guarantee security. Excess funds can remain invested aggressively in the hope of hitting a financial "home run." The chance of big gains remains while risk is minimized.

Key: The target retirement date you set will have a big impact on planning strategies and the amount you must save each year.

Pick a date that is sooner rather than later. If you work beyond your planned retirement date, the extra income will simply make you even better off. But if you are forced to retire early, you will be glad to have planned for it. And it will always be pleasant to have the option of retiring early if you want to.

To avoid other common mistakes...

•Understand your company's retirement plan. Most people don't. *Ask:*

•How do benefits differ if you are terminated, take early retirement, or leave at the normal retirement age?

•What would happen if you left the company today?

•Is there a vesting schedule that requires you to stay with the company a set number of years in order to receive full benefits?

•Will you receive a fixed pension with a dollar value you can estimate now? Or does the company have a profit-sharing plan under which its contribution to your account varies each year, making your final benefit an uncertain amount?

• Are plan benefits adjusted in line with inflation? Danger: If inflation continues at the 5% rate of recent years, a fixed pension will lose half its value in 14 years. You may need extra income.

• How and when will you get paid? Plan payouts may not occur until months after you retire. And if a company has more than one plan, they may make payouts at different times. This can drastically affect personal cash flow, so anticipate a retirement plan's red tape.

Warning: Beware of plan modifications. Many firms are cutting back retirement benefits to save costs. Employees must be notified when their retirement plan is modified, so pay attention and be sure you understand changes that affect you.

• Understand Social Security. Figure your expected benefit in advance. *Helpful:* Contact your local Social Security office and ask them to compute your expected benefit for you.

Big trap: Most people expect that they will receive their pension and Social Security. But many companies have "integrated" plans under which the designated pension amount includes Social Security—the company's contribution toward your pension is reduced by the amount of Social Security you receive. Find out whether your company's plan is integrated or not.

Social Security options: Some firms allow workers to retire early—before they are eligible to receive Social Security. Those companies increase early pension payments by the amount of the monthly Social Security that the retiree will ultimately receive. When Social Security payments start, pension payments are reduced accordingly. The result is an even flow of income to the employee that can facilitate early-retirement planning.

Consider taking Social Security benefits early, at age 62, instead of at age 65. While waiting until 65 provides a larger monthly benefit, you also miss three full years of payments in the meantime, and it can take many years of increased monthly payments to make up this difference.

If you work past retirement age, your benefits remain the same—they don't increase—so there's no monetary advantage in not taking them at 65.

• Make full use of company life insurance. Some companies have group policies that allow departing employees to convert their term insurance into whole life coverage without going through a physical examination. If your company offers this benefit, don't overlook it. If this benefit isn't offered, be aware that when you are older it may be more difficult to pass a required physical to get insurance. If you will need coverage then, take steps to secure it now.

• Consider health insurance. Figure out in advance what the cost of insurance will be after you retire. Ask if your company provides retirement health benefits, and what are the plan limits. If you will have to pay for your own coverage, figure it in as a cost of retirement and start saving for it now.

Ask now about nursing-home insurance and Medigap insurance for expenses not covered by Medicare, so that if the day comes in retirement that you need to obtain such coverage you will be familiar with it. Don't make the mistake of thinking, "It won't happen to me."

• Protect yourself as a spouse. *Ask:* What are your rights under your spouse's retirement program? Has your spouse selected a survivorship option, so benefits will continue to be paid to you should he/she die first? Do you know where all necessary documents are located in the event your spouse dies or becomes incapacitated? What will happen to benefits in the event of divorce?

Note: Alimony is considered compensation and can be used to make deductible IRA contributions.

Important: The worst time to make serious financial decisions is while experiencing the trauma of the loss of a spouse. Do financial planning beforehand so you will know what to do if or when the day comes.

• Diversify wealth. It's dangerous to keep all your wealth in one investment as retirement nears. Yet many people do so, especially sole proprietors and executives who keep their money in their own businesses.

Better: As retirement draws near, spread funds among several investments so that your retirement position won't be endangered by a loss suffered in any one area.

• Consider a lump-sum distribution. When you retire, it may be advantageous to take your benefit in the form of a lump-sum payment, rather than through annual pension or annuity payments. This gives you investment control over your money. A lump-sum distribution may be rolled over into an IRA tax-free if deposited within 60 days of receipt. The money must be transferred directly from the company plan to the IRA to avoid a 20% withholding tax on the payout.

If you were born before 1936, the IRS provides a tax break for a lump-sum distribution in the form of income averaging—treating it as if it were received over a period of years. The result is that much of the distribution avoids being taxed at top-bracket rates. Technical rules apply, so consult with your tax adviser about making the right choices.

• Consider taking money out of an IRA before age 59½ without paying an early withdrawal penalty. This is possible if payouts are taken in the form of an annuity—that is, in even payments over your life expectancy.

• Do the paperwork. Make sure, for example, that all beneficiaries are properly designated or survivor benefits may not be paid out according to your wishes.

• Get qualified advice. Both investment advice and tax advice are absolute musts. Remember, you're planning your future and managing your life savings, so seek out the most qualified experts that you can find.

Source: Anna Polizzi-Keller, tax partner in the financial counseling and expatriate (citizens based outside the country of their citizenship) areas, Ernst & Young, 701 Market St., St. Louis 63101.

Pension Benefits

The bottom line in retirement planning today: Don't count benefits that you've been counting on. With general restructuring and cost-cutting efforts, many companies have been finding ways to terminate or reduce their pension obligations. *Changes to watch out for:* Companies often take workers' Social Security payments into account when figuring pension benefits. They reason that since they paid half of those premiums, they're entitled to reduce their share of your defined benefits by half of whatever you'll be receiving from Social Security.

Problem: Most employees think of their pension benefits as separate from Social Security. *Somewhat helpful:* The Tax Act of 1986 specified that in most cases employers can't subtract more than 50% of your pension benefits, regardless of how much you receive from Social Security.

Protection: Ask your employer annually for a benefits statement showing how much you would receive at retirement if you left the company now or at various points in the future. You'll find, for example, that if you were to retire at 55 instead of at 65, most companies would cut your pension benefits in half. Be sure to ask for the figures with and without salary increases, since those are, of course, not guaranteed.

Never assume that pension benefit projections will hold up 100%. Often they turn out to have been too optimistic. *Goal:* To replace at least 50%–70% of your final salary. That's considered a minimum for living in relative comfort during retirement.

Source: Kenneth P. Shapiro, president, Hay/Huggins Co., Inc., the benefits and actuarial consulting subsidiary of Hay Group, 229 S. 18 St., Philadelphia 19103.

How Safe Is Your Pension?

More and more people are discovering—to their horror—that they can't rely solely on their company defined-benefit pension plan for retirement security. Some companies have even terminated plans. And sometimes plans fail because of a company's financial problems or problems with an insurance company that provided a guaranteed income contract.

What can you do? Not much, if a pension-plan failure catches you unprepared. You could write to the US Department of Labor, but in practice it can't be counted on to do much unless you're with a large company. Nor is the IRS likely to provide much help. The Pension Benefits Guaranty Corporation is supposed to pay when defined-benefit plans fail, but it has payout caps that could be much less than what you were counting on, and some observers claim the organization is overextended. Nearly all lawyers with pension- plan expertise work for plan sponsors, not individual participants.

Avoid bad surprises...

Keep yourself informed about your company's pension plan. Ask yourself fundamental questions (some of these can be answered by your pension plan's annual report)...

• What's the pension plan invested in?

• Is the pension portfolio heavily loaded with your company's stocks?

• Is the pension plan in sound condition?

• If your company offers a guaranteed income contract portfolio, is it provided by a single insurer? If just one, how solid is it?

• How sound is your company? Monitor annual reports, quarterly reports, and business news affecting your company.

• What are the ratings of insurance companies involved with your guaranteed income contract portfolio? Consider a B- (or lower) rating from A.M. Best, Moody's, or Standard & Poor's as a warning flag.

Self-defense...

• Consider a pension plan as one part of an overall portfolio. Don't rely on a company pension plan to provide the bulk of your retirement assets. Put eligible funds into an IRA. Buy an annuity. Build your own portfolio of savings and investments.

Your portfolio should be properly diversified, enabling you to survive in the event that something goes awry. Diversification is especially important for the millions of people who acquired large chunks of their company's stock through employee stock-ownership plans. If you have more than 5% to 10% of your assets in a single stock, look to diversify your portfolio.

• Think ahead about healthcare. Because costs are escalating dramatically, more and more companies are curtailing dollar payouts in many ways. You might not be able to use the doctor or hospital of your choice unless you pay out-of-pocket. Set aside additional savings for adequate healthcare protection or consider other forms of health insurance appropriate for your circumstances.

Source: George E. L. Barbee, executive director, Client Services, Price Waterhouse, 1251 Avenue of the Americas, New York 10020. He is a contributor to the *Price Waterhouse Retirement Adviser*, Pocket Books.

Pension Traps— Annuity Opportunities

Before collecting checks from your company pension plan or a single-premium deferred annuity, it pays to investigate your options.

By choosing an immediate annuity, you may wind up with hundreds of dollars more per month in your pocket—at no additional risk.

An immediate annuity is an insurance contract that, in return for a one-time payment, starts paying a fixed sum for your lifetime or for some other period right away.

A single-life annuity, for example, pays the agreed-upon sum every month until the purchaser dies. The payment doesn't have to stop at the first death. It depends on the option you select: Joint and two-thirds survivor, joint and 50% survivor, and joint and 100% survivor. A joint-and-survivor annuity for a married couple, by contrast, pays one larger sum while both spouses are alive, and a lesser amount after the first spouse dies. Payments continue at the lower level during the lifetime of the surviving spouse and end only when that person dies.

It pays to shop...

Comparison shopping in the immediate annuity market can pay off quite nicely.

Example: Recently, I checked out rates—which are expressed as monthly income per $10,000 of premium—for a 65-year-old woman. For a $100,000 investment, the monthly income ranged from a high of $915 to a low of $716—a difference of almost $200, or about 28%.

Trap: Don't automatically go for the highest monthly income figure. Given all the turmoil in the insurance industry these days, and the recent failure of Executive Life, in the example above I decided not even to consider the seven companies paying the top rates because I had reservations about their soundness. Bear in mind that you are purchasing something that you intend to last for the rest of your life.

I wound up recommending my client purchase an annuity that ranked 20th out 100. It was offered by Northwestern Mutual, the solid, conservative, and well-run Minnesota company. The annuity provided monthly income of $839. The median income figure was $809 a month.

Compare carefully…

Two common situations in which investigating what you'd receive with an immediate annuity makes sense…

•When you're retiring from your company. Before you automatically accept the monthly pension check your company plan offers, ask if the plan permits a lump-sum distribution instead. Many, but not all, plans do.

See what you can get in monthly income by purchasing an immediate annuity with some of that money. You may be surprised to discover that you'll get a much larger payment with the annuity than with your company pension.

•When you're ready to start annuitizing, or receiving distributions, from a single-premium deferred annuity that you purchased years ago. Just because you purchased the annuity from Company A, don't assume that it now offers the best deal in terms of monthly income. You may do better by switching to Company B or C.

Caution: In either case, don't sink all your money into an immediate annuity all at once. You may be purchasing at a trough, and annuity rates may subsequently shoot up. I recommend that people purchase several contracts over time and that they not annuitize more than 50% of their total investable assets.

It's vital that you do your comparative shopping right at the point when you are ready to make your purchase.

Reason: The immediate annuity market is a very fluid one, and rates can fluctuate widely, even within a given company, depending upon the details of your individual situation.

Example: A particular company may post attractive payouts one month, but not the next. Or, it may be competitive at some ages but unattractive at others.

To check on the different rates offered by different companies, consult *Best's Retirement Income Guide.* It's published twice a year and is available in many public libraries. The guide contains comparative information on many different types of annuities, both fixed and variable, offered by hundreds of different companies. To find out the annuity rate for an immediate annuity, you must consult the tables in the back, which give the monthly income you would receive if you pay a set sum to different insurance companies queried.

It's also possible to deal with a reputable broker who maintains a broad database of annuity rates paid by different companies. *Sources:*

•The Annuity Network, a subsidiary of the Laughlin Group in Beaverton, Oregon (800-547-3257). The parent company evaluates the safety and stability of insurance companies. The Annuity Network works with about 300 insurance companies. The network is compensated on a commission basis from companies whose policies it sells.

•United States Annuities, Englishtown, New Jersey (800-872-6684). An insurance-brokerage and research firm that specializes in immediate annuities. It also works on a commission basis. The firm publishes the *Annuity Shopper,* a bimonthly newsletter that compares different insurers' ratings, rates, and charges. US Annuities, 98 Hoffman Rd., Englishtown, New Jersey 07726.

Of course, there are some drawbacks to opting for an immediate annuity, rather than for your company pension. Rejecting your pension might be unwise, for example, if your company has a history of increasing its pension payouts from time to time in order to offset inflation. The annuity check you get the first month is the same amount you'll receive 20 years from now—assuming you're still alive to collect.

And—pensions are insured by the Pension Board Guaranty Corporation, while immediate annuities are only as good as the company that issues them.

Before you jump at the highest available rate, you should always very carefully investigate the issuing company's financial health.

Aim: To be reasonably sure it will be able to make those payouts as long as you live.

Caution: Some, but not all, insurers require annuity buyers to pay upfront policy fees or other charges, which can range from $150 to $500. And about 10 states impose premium taxes that amount to 1% to 3% of the amount invested.

Source: Glenn Daily, a fee-only insurance consultant and author of *The Individual Investor's Guide to Low-Load Insurance Products*, International Publishing Corp.

Borrow from Your Pension Plan

Did you know that you can usually borrow from your pension plan? You must have a good reason for the borrowing and definite repayment arrangements. Also, you must pay interest on the loan at the going rate.

There are limitations on the maximum amounts that can be borrowed as follows:

Vested Portion in Pension Plan	Maximum Amount of Borrowing
Up to $100,000	50% of amount of plan
Over $100,000	$50,000 maximum amount

Source: *New Tax Traps/New Opportunities* by Edward Mendlowitz, CPA, Boardroom Special Reports.

Benefits of Early Retirement

Collecting Social Security early can pay off. Even though benefits are reduced, they'll usually add up to more in the long run.

Example:

If full benefits are $750 per month for retiring at age 65, you can get reduced benefits of $600 a month by retiring at age 62. You'd have to collect full benefits for 12 years to make up

the $21,600 you'd receive during the three years of early payments.

Source: *Changing Times*, Washington, DC.

IRAs...to Consolidate... Or Not Consolidate?

Taxpayers who have set up a number of IRAs over the years may be tempted to gather them together into one big IRA. There are definite advantages to consolidating accounts:

•Save on trustees' fees. Instead of paying separate administration fees for each account, you'll be paying only one.

•Simplify paperwork.

•Accumulate larger balances for investment. You get a greater rate of return on a $10,000 Certificate of Deposit (CD) than on a $1,000 CD.

Main disadvantage in consolidating IRA accounts: Problems with early withdrawals. When you consolidate accounts, you lose flexibility in making penalty-free early withdrawals.

Source: Deborah Walker, partner, KPMG Peat Marwick, 2001 M St. NW, Washington, DC 20036.

Price Earnings Ratios

Price earnings (P/E) ratios have little to do with whether a stock is a good or bad buy. Many analysts recommend stocks with low P/Es as "cheap" and warn that stocks with high P/Es are "expensive." But history shows otherwise. *Study:* During the 33 years from 1953 to 1985, the stock market had an average P/E of 15. But the top-performing stocks of this period started their market run-ups with an average P/E of 20 and ended with an average P/E of 45. *Reality:* Firms with low P/Es often have them simply because they are poor stocks, while firms with high P/Es usually have demonstrated superior prospects. The simple truth is that most firms have P/Es that fairly reflect their value.

Source: *How to Make Money in Stocks: A Winning System in Good Times or Bad* by William J. O'Neil, publisher, *Investor's Business Daily*. McGraw Hill.

Hard Ways to Take Money Out of Your 401(k) Plan

401(k) plans can have a special feature that allows money to be withdrawn in case of hardship.

To qualify as a hardship, a distribution must be...

•For an immediate and heavy financial need of the employee.

•Sufficient to satisfy the need (plus penalties and taxes), but not more than that amount.

The taxpayer must first exhaust all means of borrowing from other retirement plans...make no contributions to the 401(k) plan for the following 12 months...and reduce any contributions for the taxable year after the year of the hardship by the amount contributed during the year of the hardship.

Expenditures that qualify as hardship include...

•Medical expenses for the employee and his/her dependents.

•The purchase of a principal residence for the employee.

•Tuition payments for postsecondary education for the employee and his dependents.

•Expenditures to keep the employee from being evicted from his principal residence.

Caution: Hardship withdrawals are subject to income tax and the 10% early withdrawal penalty if you're under age 59½.

Source: David J. Clark, attorney, Joseph Clare & Company, CPAs, 200 California St., San Francisco 94111.

3

Tax Savvy

The Big Bad Retirement Tax Traps

People who are charting retirement finances better watch out for the minefield of tricky IRS rules. Here are the ones that are apt to trip you up and strategies to help you negotiate around them.

• *Trap:* Mandatory withholding on retirement plan distributions. Plan sponsors must withhold 20% of any money that is not directly rolled over into an IRA or another company's plan. *Double trouble:* The IRS views the withheld amounts as premature withdrawals if you're under 59½, so you owe a 10% penalty plus income tax on those amounts.

Example: You take $10,000 from your company plan when you leave the firm, but the plan sponsor only gives you $8,000 in cash. You owe a $200 penalty plus tax on $2,000.

Avoidance: If you replace the $2,000 with your own money and roll this amount over

within 60 days of receipt into an IRA or other qualified plan, you can sidestep the penalty and tax. That money is returned to you by the IRS at tax time in the form of a tax refund. But there can be a significant delay. If you withdraw money from the plan in February, you won't receive the refund until April of the following year, or 14 months later.

Better: Ask the plan sponsor to roll the money directly into another qualified plan or into an IRA. That way, no money will be withheld and no penalties will apply.

Strategy: If you're not sure which investment is best for your plan money, or you haven't found another job yet, have the plan sponsor roll the money into an IRA money market fund.

Strategy: If you need to use part of the money, have your company directly roll the entire sum into an IRA first. That way, you avoid withholding on the entire amount and just owe the early withdrawal penalties of 10% plus tax on the money that you take out. If you

47

replace the money in 60 days, you won't owe anything at all.

• *Trap:* Failing to take the required minimum distributions from retirement plans. You must begin withdrawing money from your retirement plans by April 1 following the year in which you turn 70½. The penalty for people who fail to do so is steep—50% of the amount that should have been distributed, but wasn't. When these amounts are ultimately distributed they are subject to income tax. Some banks and mutual funds alert their investors when distributions must begin, but the final responsibility rests with you.

The minimum required to be withdrawn is based on your life expectancy, or the lives of you plus a beneficiary. To prevent excess deferrals of tax on retirement plan money, the IRS deems the age of any beneficiary (other than your spouse) who is more than 10 years younger than you to be only 10 years.

Example: You are 72 and your beneficiary is your grandson, who is 12. The IRS minimum is based on joint life expectancies of 62 and 72 years.

• *Trap:* The excess distribution penalty. You will be hit with a 15% excise tax if you withdraw more than $150,000 from your retirement plans in one calendar year (that amount is indexed for inflation). *Caution:* When you figure the $150,000, remember to include distributions from a 401(k), IRA, company pension, and all other types of qualified plans.

Strategy: If you need a large sum, say, $300,000, you can take out $150,000 on December 29 and the balance on January 2.

• *Trap:* Not making the most of tax-free compounding. When you retire, use your investments and other money held outside retirement plans first. That way, you defer taxes on the money inside the plans longer.

Example: You have a large sum inside an IRA and smaller amount in other investments. If you had used the after-tax money to cover living expenses for two years, your IRA would have grown at the rate of return you invested it, with the additional benefit of tax-free compounding.

• *Trap:* Paying too much tax on retirement plan distributions. You can elect more favorable tax treatment called five- or 10-year forward averaging when you take a lump sum from a retirement plan. This method treats the money as if it had been taken in five or 10 equal installments rather than all at once, thus taxing more of the money in the lowest tax brackets.

Who is eligible? You may elect 10-year averaging if you were age 50 or older on January 1, 1986. Otherwise, you must elect five-year averaging. An averaging election can be made only once in a lifetime. Either method usually gives you a smaller tax bill than you would have had if you paid ordinary income tax rates.

Exceptions: If the distribution is bigger than approximately $450,000, five-year averaging is usually better than 10-year averaging because the tax rates used for 10-year averaging (in the 1986 tables) begin to exceed today's rates.

Caution: Remember to factor in the impact of state taxes when you do the calculations.

Caution: Generally, as the lump-sum distribution is larger, rolling the money into an IRA and delaying distributions is more beneficial than averaging.

• *Trap:* Failing to qualify for averaging. You can use the averaging methods only if you have been an active plan participant for more than five years before you retire.

Strategy: Job-skippers should make sure to stay at least five years before the year they receive the distribution with one company before they retire.

Caution: Money in any IRA, including a rollover IRA, doesn't qualify for averaging—something to keep in mind when you are deciding whether to roll plan money into an IRA or the new company's plan when you switch jobs.

• *Trap:* Making your estate, not your spouse, the beneficiary of your retirement plan. If you do, your estate may owe a 15% excise tax on the assets in excess of the $150,000 annual limit multiplied by a factor based on your life expectancy. But by electing your spouse as beneficiary of the plan, you may avoid the excise tax or at least delay it.

• *Trap:* By having your estate as the beneficiary, you cannot use a joint life expectancy for calculating the minimum distribution.

Source: Stephen Pennacchio, partner, KPMG Peat Marwick LLP, 345 Park Ave., New York 10154.

Tax Strategies for Tough Times

Tax planning is more important than ever when times are tough. The money that can be saved in taxes is much more meaningful. *Helpful:* Withholding and estimated payments.

• Check withholding early in the year. Make sure the IRS is not getting more than is absolutely necessary. The aim should be to come out even with the IRS on April 15. Get a new W-4 form and carefully work through the calculations. Withholding allowances can be claimed for anticipated itemized deductions in addition to dependents.

• Base estimated tax payments on this year's tax—rather than last year's—if this year's income will be less than last year's. This will minimize estimated payments. To avoid penalties, estimated payments must total 90% of the tax that is owed for 1995. Starting in 1994, estimated payments must total 100% of last year's tax if your adjusted gross income is $150,000 or less or 110% of last year's tax if your adjusted gross income exceeds $150,000.

If you can't pay your taxes…

• File your tax return on time—even though you can't pay the tax you owe. This way you'll avoid late-filing penalties. You will, however, be required to pay late-payment penalties plus interest on the tax you owe.

• Negotiate an installment-payment agreement with the IRS—if you can't pay your tax bill in full. Discuss your financial situation with the IRS collection people and present them with a reasonable plan for paying off your debt.

• Make an offer in compromise—if your tax debt is so big that you won't ever be able to pay it. Under this IRS procedure, a taxpayer offers to settle the debt for less than the total amount involved. If the IRS is convinced that that's the most they'll get, they'll take the offer. In some cases they'll settle for a certain amount down and a percentage of the taxpayer's future income.

For taxpayers who are seriously strapped, an offer in compromise may be the only way to avoid bankruptcy. Sometimes the mere threat of bankruptcy will convince the IRS to accept an offer in compromise.

Hidden money sources…

In troubled times, all sources of financing must be considered.

• *Home-equity borrowing:* Individuals who own a house may be able to take out a home-equity loan. There's a tax benefit in doing this —interest on up to $100,000 of home-equity borrowing is fully tax-deductible, no matter how the loan proceeds are spent.

Caution: If your income is low this year, the interest deduction may be meaningless.

• Retirement plans can be a source of cash in an emergency. The problem with taking money out of plans is that you have to pay income tax on the funds plus a 10% penalty if you're under age 59½. But for those whose income is low this year, the tax and penalty won't total that much because of the low tax bracket.

Tax-advantaged ways to tap into your retirement plans…

• Get short-term use of IRA funds. You can't borrow from an IRA, but you can get the use of the money for a very brief period. The tax law allows you to withdraw money from an IRA without tax consequences as long as you redeposit the funds into the IRA—or another one—within 60 days of taking them out. This is called an "IRA-to-IRA rollover." There are no restrictions on what you can do with the money. As long as you meet the 60-day recontribution deadline, you can use the money for personal purposes—tax-free and interest-free.

Limitation: You can make only one rollover a year from an IRA.

Caution: If you miss the 60-day deadline, the money you withdraw is subject to income tax …and a 10% penalty tax if you're under the age of 59½.

• Withdraw voluntary contributions you've made to your company's pension plan. If you put after-tax money into the plan, you can take it out and most of it will be non-taxable. You will, however, pay income tax on that portion of the withdrawal that represents the interest income your money has earned while in the plan. You'll also have to pay a 10% penalty tax on the income portion if you're under age 59½.

• Terminate your Keogh plan and roll the money over into an IRA. You must deposit the Keogh funds into an IRA within 60 days of receiving them or you'll pay income tax and penalties on the Keogh. But you'll have the use of the money tax-free and interest-free for 60 days. Once you set up the IRA you could do an IRA-to-IRA rollover and get the use of the money for another 60 days.

• Borrow from your 401(k) plan. Most 401(k)s and some Keoghs and pension plans permit borrowing. The tax law limits the amount you can borrow to the greater of $10,000—or one-half of your account balance, with a maximum of $50,000. (If you have a balance of $150,000, you can only borrow $50,000. If your balance is $10,000, you can borrow $10,000.)

Drawbacks: Interest you pay on the borrowed money is not usually deductible, regardless of how you use the money. If you leave your job with a 401(k) loan outstanding, you may have to repay it immediately or the IRS will treat the loan as a distribution. This means you will have to pay taxes on the amount of the distribution as well as possibly be subject to the 10% early withdrawal penalty if you're under age 59½.

• Take a hardship distribution from your 401(k) plan. Employees can take money out of many 401(k) plans in the case of hardship. This is defined in the tax law as "immediate and heavy financial need." The rules are very strict —but vary from plan to plan. Usual needs that justify a hardship withdrawal are medical expenses, college tuition, and payments to a bank to prevent foreclosure on a mortgage.

Problem: Hardship withdrawals are subject to tax and to the 10% early withdrawal penalty if you're under age 59½.

• Roll over 401(k) money into an IRA. If you lose your job, you can take the money that's in your 401(k) plan. You can keep the money and pay tax on it (plus the early distribution penalty) or roll it over into an IRA within 60 days, in which case you'll avoid tax and penalties. Or, you may wish to keep some of the money and pay tax on it and roll the balance over into an IRA. In either case, you'll have the use of the full amount of the 401(k) distribution for 60 days.

Bankruptcy and taxes...

The general rule is tax debts aren't wiped out by filing for bankruptcy.

Exception: Unpaid tax on returns that have a due date, or extended due date, that is more than three years prior to the bankruptcy filing can be discharged. This three-year rule is less beneficial than it might seem, however.

Exceptions to the exception: If a tax debt is still under dispute within the IRS or in the courts, it doesn't get discharged in bankruptcy even though the return is more than three years old.

And if the taxpayer has given the IRS a waiver of the statute of limitations on assessing tax, the debt isn't discharged even though three years have passed since the return was due.

Chapter 13. Tax debts may be discharged in whole or in part if the bankruptcy filing is under Chapter 13 of the Bankruptcy Code. This is for those wage earners who have steep liabilities and no assets. Generally, the court works out a payment plan by directing that a percentage of the taxpayer's salary go to creditors—and the IRS is one of the creditors. To the extent that the liabilities are greater than what the payment plan can ever pay off, they are discharged.

Limitation: Chapter 13 cannot be used where the liabilities are very substantial. To use Chapter 13, an individual must have a regular income— and owe less than $100,000 of unsecured debts and less than $350,000 of secured debts.

Source: Michael F. Klein, Jr., senior tax partner, national director of tax consulting services, Price Waterhouse, 1251 Avenue of the Americas, New York 10020.

Tax Shelter Loopholes

The way taxes are structured now, with phaseouts, surcharges, and state and local taxes thrown in, it's not hard to find yourself in the 50% bracket. That's where tax shelters come in.

Though not the hot topic they used to be, there are still enough left to save the taxpayer a few dollars.

• *IRAs, Keoghs, SEPs, and 401(k)s.* You get a current deduction for money you put into these plans. In addition, the income your money earns in the plan is income-tax deferred. You don't pay tax until you withdraw money from the plan.

• *Oil and gas drilling.* Losses incurred in working interests in oil and gas wells are deductible directly from your salary and other income, without regard to the passive loss rules. The deductions shelter other income from tax. The passive loss rules limit deductions for activities you don't materially participate in, but they don't apply to oil and gas drilling.

This kind of investment is generally in the form of a share in the mine and the costs are deductible on Schedule C—*Profit or Loss from Business.*

• *Rental real estate.* Up to $25,000 of losses on rental property that you actively manage are deductible against your salary and other income if your Adjusted Gross Income (AGI) is below $100,000. The rental loss deduction is reduced by $1 for each $2 of AGI above $100,000. Once your AGI reaches $150,000, you get no deduction for rental losses.

Loophole: A husband and wife filing a joint return meet the eligibility requirement for deductible rental losses if, during the tax year, one spouse performs more than 750 hours in a real estate trade or business. So, if one spouse puts in 750 hours selling real estate, say, no matter how much that spouse earns, the other spouse's real estate losses would be deductible against the couple's salary and other income.

• *US savings bonds.* The US government is the biggest seller of tax shelters. Interest on US savings bonds is tax sheltered in that it is tax deferred. You don't have to pay tax on the interest until you cash in the bonds.

Loophole: Interest on US savings bonds is exempt from state and local income tax.

Loophole: You can, if you wish, elect to pay the tax each year on savings bond interest. This makes savings bonds an ideal investment for children under the age of 14, since the interest may escape tax entirely because of the child's standard deduction ($650 for investment income in 1995).

Loophole: The interest on savings bonds issued after December 31, 1989 is tax free for certain taxpayers if the bonds are used to pay for education expenses. To get the full benefit though, your income in the year you redeem the bonds can't exceed $93,450 (if married) or $57,300 (single).

• *Charitable remainder trusts.* This is a trust that pays you an income for life, and on your death the assets in the trust go to a charity you have named. To maximize the benefits of such an arrangement, put into the trust greatly appreciated assets that are paying a low dividend. The trustee will sell the assets, reinvest the proceeds, and pay you a higher income—for life. You get a charitable deduction at the time the assets are put into the trust. (The deduction will be the present value of the interest the charity will get on your death.)

Loophole: You avoid paying capital gains tax on the assets that go into the trust.

• *Life insurance.* The income earned on investment-oriented life insurance, such as universal life, is tax deferred. If you hold the policy until the time of your death, and the income is paid out in the form of a death benefit, that income will escape tax entirely.

Loophole: If you withdraw money from the insurance policy before death, the withdrawal isn't taxed unless it exceeds the total amount of premiums you've paid over the years. Then, only the amount that exceeds the premiums is taxed. Withdrawals up to the amount of premiums are considered a return of capital and are not taxed.

Single Premium Deferred Annuities are still available from insurance companies and they're taxed in the same way as universal life insurance.

Catch: Most policies prohibit you from making withdrawals in the first few years.

Loophole: In split-dollar life insurance, where your employer pays the bulk of the premiums and receives back from the death benefit the money it paid in premiums, the insured's estate receives the balance of the death benefit income tax free (and possibly estate tax free).

• *Like-kind exchanges.* If you trade a business asset—say land, or a building—for similar property, you don't have to pay tax on the exchange. Tax is deferred until you sell the asset you receive.

• *A home of your own.* This is the ideal tax shelter because…

• Mortgage interest and property taxes are deductible.

• Interest on up to $100,000 of home-equity borrowing is tax deductible no matter what you spend the loan proceeds on.

• Appreciation isn't taxed until you sell the home.

• If you are 55 or older when you sell, up to $125,000 of your profit is tax free.

• When you sell, you can defer tax on your gain if you buy a more expensive replacement home within two years of the sale.

• If you own the home when you die, the appreciation escapes tax entirely.

• *Investment in a business.* If the business is set up as an S corporation, and you participate in running it, your share of the losses is deductible on your tax return against your salary and other income provided you have basis.

• *Child on the payroll.* The salary is deductible by the business. In 1995, a child can earn up to $3,900 in wages without owing any federal income tax. An additional $2,000 of salary will escape tax if the money is put into an IRA.

Loophole: Wages paid to a child under the age of 18 from a parent's unincorporated business are not subject to Social Security tax.

• *Incentive stock options* issued by an employer are not taxed when the options or the stock are issued, but only when the stock is sold.

Trap: The untaxed profit when the options are exercised might be subject to the Alternative Minimum Tax (AMT).

• *Regulated futures or foreign currency contracts.* Inventory positions using the mark-to-market system are treated as if they were sold on the last day of the year, with 60% of the gains or losses treated as long-term capital gain (or loss) and 40% treated as short-term capital gain, irrespective of the actual holding period.

Source: Edward Mendlowitz, partner, Mendlowitz Weitsen, CPAs, Two Pennsylvania Plaza, New York 10121.

How to Negotiate With the IRS…and Win

When you have a tax problem, don't presume that the IRS holds all the cards. While there are mountains of tax rules and regulations, there's also some *wiggle room* built into the system. Taxpayers always have some room to maneuver. You just have to know where that is and how far the IRS can go.

Taxpayers can represent themselves or use professionals to negotiate for them.

Caution: Always use a professional in criminal matters. Penalties may include going to jail.

Trap: You run the risk—by representing yourself—of making incriminating statements.

The ins and outs of negotiating with the IRS depend upon the type of issue at hand. *Among these are…*

Audits and appeals…

In the initial stages of an audit, you are contacted by an IRS agent. His/her job is to gather all the facts and apply these to the IRS interpretation of the law and regulations.

At this stage, you can tussle with the agent over the facts.

Example: If the agent finds that your documentation of an expense is inadequate, the expense will be disallowed.

The law requires that taxpayers keep adequate records. *Reality:* Few taxpayers' records meet this high standard, something that the IRS recognizes.

Negotiating strategy: Maximize deductions. Show the auditor that you have made a good faith attempt to keep adequate records, even if you cannot document every penny. The auditor can use his discretion to accept other, less well-documented deductions.

How: Before the audit, organize your receipts and canceled checks by type of deduction. Then attach an adding machine tape that shows how you came up with the figure claimed on your tax return.

Negotiating strategy: Make mutual concessions. Let's say that you have a very strong issue on your return, one for which you have almost all of the necessary documentation. You also have an issue that is much weaker. *One solution:* You concede the weaker issue in return for the IRS dropping the stronger one entirely.

Negotiating strategy: Ask to see the auditor's supervisor. When you cannot work satisfactorily with the IRS agent assigned to your case, you have the right to see the agent's supervisor. This right is listed in IRS Publication 1, *Your Rights as a Taxpayer.* If the supervisor is more fair and open-minded than the agent, you may have a better chance of resolving your case at this level.

When you get nowhere with the supervisor, the next step is to take your case to the IRS Appeals Division.

Caution: You have only 30 days after the revenue agent's report is issued to file your appeal.

Negotiating strategy: Take into account the "hazards of litigation." The appeals officer is allowed to negotiate with taxpayers based on the hazards of litigation. This means the odds are that the IRS will prevail if your case goes to court.

Example: If the IRS decides that you have a 50% chance of success in court, it can settle for one-half of the disputed amount.

The odds of settling your case in the appeals division are very high. Appeals court settles nine out of 10 cases without litigation.

Negotiating strategy: Handling the meeting. Present your case *in writing* to the appeals officer before your face-to-face meeting.

That way, he has a chance to think about it and the meeting can be devoted to discussing the differences between your positions.

Include all relevant information. There's nothing to be gained by holding back essential information as a "bargaining chip." Be professional in your presentation, not emotional. If your case moves to litigation, you may have another chance to negotiate a settlement with the IRS attorney assigned to direct the case.

Exception: Some IRS attorneys take the position that you had a chance to settle with the appeals officers and that their job is only to litigate.

Collections...

Negotiating strategy: Make early initial contact. Contact the IRS collections division as soon as you know that you will not be able to pay your tax bill. Being up front about your financial situation helps build credibility that shores up your negotiating position.

Let's say that you can't pay your taxes immediately when you file your return on April 15. You can request an extension to pay the taxes due. These are short-term deferrals of up to six months.

If that is too short, you can negotiate an installment agreement that lets you defer paying taxes for up to several years. But—the IRS doesn't make it too easy for taxpayers to do this.

How to negotiate an installment agreement: Submit Form 9465 with your tax return or immediately afterwards. The form asks for information such as how much tax is due and how much you propose to pay monthly. Send it to the IRS service center where your return was filed.

How much should you pay monthly? While deferring the tax bill as long as possible seems to make sense, try to pay off the total as soon as you are able. *Reason:* Penalties plus interest

---

of about 9% will greatly increase the amount you owe. (This figure fluctuates from quarter to quarter.)

The IRS will ask you to complete Form 433, *Collections Information Statement.* That asks you to des-cribe your monthly income and expenses, plus your assets and liabilities. The agency uses this to determine how much it can reasonably ask you to pay.

Negotiating strategy: Make installment agreements. The IRS is much more likely to accept installment agreements now than it was one year ago.

Reason: The agency is under severe pressure to collect as much of its accounts receivables as possible from the general public.

Another option: You can negotiate an offer in compromise. This lets you pay a reduced amount to the IRS in full payment of your debt.

How to do it: Submit your request using Form 656, which lays out information such as all of your assets and liabilities and prospects for future income.

Odds of acceptance: The IRS received 29,087 offers in compromise last year. It accepted 14,047.

Source: Howard Berman, director, tax controversies practice for the northeast region, Arthur Andersen, LLP, 1345 Avenue of the Americas, New York 10105.

The Biggest Traps in Dealing With The IRS

Knowing how to deal effectively with the IRS can prevent little problems from escalating into tax nightmares. Here are the biggest traps taxpayers fall into…

Trap: Failing to respond promptly to IRS notices. Most IRS communication with taxpayers is in the form of a series of notices and/or demands. All too often, taxpayers fail to treat these notices with the sense of urgency that is required. Before they know it, they're facing a big problem—a simple request for information has become a demand for more tax.

The IRS provides a timetable for responding to notices. Usually the deadline is 30 days from the date of the notice. (In some instances it's 60 days.) *Problem:* If it takes the notice a week to get to you, then you have only three weeks to respond.

*If you don't respond in time…*The next notice you get from the IRS could be a statutory notice of deficiency. This requires you to pay the tax or file a petition with the Tax Court contesting the assessment. That can be a costly proposition, and certainly not necessary since in most instances the problem that prompted the notice can be resolved by correspondence. How you respond to an IRS notice is important. *For an effective response…*

• Mail it by certified mail, return receipt requested, so that you'll have proof that the IRS received it.

• Enclose a copy of the notice you received from the IRS. There are symbols on the notice that will direct it to the right person at the IRS.

• Send your response in the envelope the IRS provides. The envelope is bar-coded so that it will get to the correct IRS destination.

• If you can't accumulate the information requested by the deadline, write a letter asking for more time. Enclose the documents you have collected and ask for an additional 60 days. Usually the Service is receptive to these requests.

Trap: Ignoring incorrect notices from the collection division. The notice you get from the IRS may be based on wildly incorrect information. For instance, I have a client who got a notice saying he had failed to file a Form 942 remitting employment tax for a domestic employee. But the client didn't have a domestic employee. A lot of people would be tempted to ignore a notice of this kind because it was so off-the-wall. But these notices must be answered, too.

If you don't respond to such a notice the IRS will assume that it's right. It will file a return for you and assess your tax. It has the power to do that under Section 6020(b) of the Tax Code.

Bottom line: Never ignore an IRS notice even if it's wrong.

Trap: Getting stuck in the system. It's a mistake to keep writing to the same IRS location over and over again. If, despite your response, you continue to get computer-generated notices from the IRS, contact the IRS's Problem Resolution Office (PRO). The job of the PRO is to sort out administrative problems taxpayers are having with the IRS.

Every IRS Service Center and District Office has a PRO. A complete listing of addresses and phone numbers for the PRO can be found in IRS Publication 1320, *Operation Link.* This publication is available free from the IRS by calling 800-829-FORM. The PRO is also in the government listings in the phone book.

Before the PRO will take your case: If your problem is notices...you must have responded to two notices and have received a third notice on the same issue which does not acknowledge your earlier replies.

It's usually better to write than call, because the PRO will need to see documentation before it accepts the case. *Include...*

• Copies of all IRS notices together with copies of your responses.

• Copies of documentation you've sent with your replies.

• A concise explanation of the history of the problem you're having.

Cases accepted by the PRO are assigned to individual case officers, so you'll no longer be dealing with the nameless IRS bureaucracy. The case officer will keep you informed about the progress of the case. Experience shows that the PRO is very effective at resolving administrative tax problems.

Trap: Representing yourself at an audit where the issues are complex. If the audit is simply a matter of presenting receipts for your deductions, you can handle it yourself. But if the audit is more involved, and the issues are not simple, you should consider having somebody represent you. *Types of issues you may need help on:*

• Issues of valuation.

• Whether something is a business expense.

• Whether an expense is job-related.

• Deductions for volunteer work for charity.

• Sophisticated stock transactions.

Trap: Most taxpayers who handle complex issues themselves are too talkative at the audit.

That can only lead to other issues being raised by the auditor. An audit that was intended to be limited to one or two items on the return may become an across-the-board audit.

Trap: Not reporting miscellaneous income. Companies that pay "miscellaneous income," such as income for freelancing, are required to report it to the IRS on a 1099 if the amount is more than $600. But sometimes the companies don't file a 1099 for items less than $600.

That doesn't mean you can get away with not reporting the income on your tax return. If the IRS later audits the company—and they're doing a lot of auditing in this area—they'll discover that you didn't report income that you were supposed to report. They'll tax you on the income and impose a 20% negligence penalty on the tax you didn't pay.

If the unreported amount is substantial in relation to your earnings, and if the non-reporting continued for a number of years, there's always the chance the IRS will deem the unreporting to have been fraudulent. The penalty for fraud can be jail.

Some people simply don't report miscellaneous income even though they receive a 1099 for it. That's a mistake. The IRS is matching more and more 1099-MISC information forms with taxpayers' income tax returns—and catching more and more non-reporting. It's clear that the era of not reporting miscellaneous income is quickly winding down.

Source: Pete J. Medina, tax consultant on practice and procedure before the IRS, Ernst & Young, CPAs, 787 Seventh Ave., New York 10019. Mr. Medina is former District Director of the IRS Manhattan District.

The Biggest Tax Mistakes People Make with IRAs

An IRA is one of the best ways for Americans to save for retirement, but many people fail to make the *best* use of these tax-advantaged accounts. Below are some of the most common mistakes people make with their IRAs.

Mistake: Not understanding the rules for making deductible contributions. These can be complicated if you're married, and if one spouse participates in a tax-qualified retirement plan at work.

The law says that if you, or your spouse, is an active participant in a plan such as a company pension or a 401(k) plan, then *neither* of you can have a deductible IRA if your adjusted gross income exceeds $50,000.

On the other hand, if *neither* of you participates in a company plan, you could make $1 million and still have a deductible IRA.

Mistake: Failing to realize that making nondeductible contributions to your IRA is a smart move. It's wrong to assume that just because your company has a pension plan that you can't contribute to an IRA.

You can still contribute to the IRA, you just can't claim a deduction for that contribution.

It pays to do so because interest builds up tax-free. First, make maximum use of pretax savings opportunities, such as 401(k) plans (or Keogh plans if you're self-employed). Then, if you have money to spare, make a nondeductible IRA contribution.

Reason: Your IRA earnings will grow tax-free —and at a faster rate than outside the IRA—until you withdraw the money, presumably at retirement, when you may be in a lower tax bracket.

One drawback of nondeductible IRAs is the extra paperwork involved. You must file IRS Form 8606, *Nondeductible IRAs, Contributions, Distributions and Basis* each year that you make a nondeductible contribution and each year that you withdraw funds.

Also, once you begin distributions, you must combine your nondeductible IRA with your deductible IRA (if you have one), and then calculate what portion of each payout is taxable and what portion is nontaxable.

Since a nondeductible contribution is made with money that was taxed the year it was earned, the portion of your withdrawal representing the nondeductible contribution is not subject to tax for a second time. Only the portion of your withdrawal representing a deductible contribution or earnings within the IRA is taxable.

Mistake: Not understanding the rules for spousal IRAs. If you are married to someone who does not work outside the home, and if you do not exceed the income limit, you are allowed to establish a special spousal IRA for your nonworking partner and to make a deductible IRA contribution of up to $2,250 a year.

Many people mistakenly believe that they can contribute the entire $2,250 to just one spouse's IRA. But the $2,250 is an aggregate amount and no more than $2,000 can be contributed to either spouse's IRA. You could put $2,000 in your IRA and $250 into your non-working spouse's IRA. Or, you could split the $2,250 contribution equally and put $1,125 into each separate account.

Mistake: Not understanding the IRA rollover rules. The general rule is that once you have transferred the assets in—or rolled over—your IRA from one bank or brokerage firm to another —you cannot do it again for another 12 months. You have 60 days from the date you receive the distribution to place it with another bank or brokerage house without penalty.

Any subsequent distributions you receive within one year of that first distribution are subject to regular income tax. This assumes you directly receive the IRA proceeds—typically in the form of a check made payable to you— before sending the money to the new bank or brokerage.

If instead you do a trustee-to-trustee transfer and arrange for the old trustee to send the IRA proceeds to the new trustee (and never get your hands on the money), you can do as many of these transfers as you wish within a year without becoming subject to tax.

Mistake: Not understanding the new withholding rules. A recent change in the tax law requires that when you receive a distribution from a pension or profit-sharing plan, and roll it over into an IRA, the plan trustee must withhold a tax of 20% from the distribution unless you ask that payment be made directly to the trustee of the new IRA.

With more people receiving large distributions from their 401(k) plans because of continuing corporate downsizings, this is becoming a major issue. Withholding will be taken out even if you intend to roll over the distribution before the 60-day deadline. The only way to avoid withholding is to arrange for a direct rollover from your company to your IRA trustee. Otherwise, you'll receive only 80% of what you had been expecting.

Example: You receive a $100,000 distribution from your company profit-sharing plan when you decide to retire at age 60. Because you take the distribution in the form of a check written to you personally, you receive only $80,000. (The $20,000 is treated as witholdings.)

You should roll over the distribution directly from the company plan trustee into a separate "conduit" or "rollover" IRA. That way, you'll receive the full $100,000 that is in your account. If you later decide to take a part-time job and your new employer's plan accepts rollover contributions, you can then roll over the distribution from the conduit IRA into this new plan. When you finally begin taking distributions, you may be able to use favorable five-year or 10-year averaging to minimize the tax bite on your withdrawals.

Mistake: Not understanding the premature distribution rules for IRAs. Unless you are disabled, if you begin withdrawing funds from your retirement account before age 59½, you'll become subject to an early withdrawal penalty of 10% of the amount of the distribution. On top of that, you must pay ordinary income tax on the distribution.

One way to avoid the 10% penalty (but not income tax) is to stretch out distributions by taking them in the form of a series of substantially equal payments made at least once a year over your life (or life expectancy)—or the joint life (or joint life expectancy) of you and the person you designate as your beneficiary (typically your spouse). This works especially well if you're married to someone considerably younger than you are.

Example: Say you want to retire at age 45, are married to someone 35 and have accumulated a few million dollars in your IRA. By withdrawing a modest portion of your IRA each year, you get a steady source of income while the bulk of your retirement account keeps on generating tax-free earnings.

Mistake: Naming the wrong beneficiary. As long as you are happily married, naming your spouse as beneficiary of your IRA is generally the smartest move.

Reason: Special tax rules allow your spouse to treat the IRA as his/her own and to delay distributions so the funds can continue to grow tax-free as long as possible.

If you name your children or someone else as beneficiary, they must begin withdrawals from the account within five years of the date of your death—if you had already started distributions, they must continue the distribution schedule that you had begun.

The freedom of your spouse to delay distributions is especially beneficial if you're married to someone much younger than you, since your partner will be able to keep the assets within the tax-sheltered IRA for many years.

Mistake: Taking distributions that are too big. If your withdrawals from all your tax-qualified retirement accounts exceed $150,000 in any one year, you must pay an "excess distribution penalty" of 15% of the amount over the limit.

Trap: Many people think their IRA withdrawals are in a separate category and thus not subject to this excess distribution penalty. But distributions from all your qualified accounts must be added together for purposes of this rule.

Example: You want to take $200,000 from your IRA rollover account (into which you put your 401(k) account proceeds when you retired) to buy a condo in Florida. But you also receive a pension of $30,000 a year. You must add the $30,000 pension to the $200,000 IRA withdrawal. That means your total distributions for the year are $230,000…or $80,000 over the limit. The penalty you must pay on the excess is $12,000. A better approach would be to take the $80,000 from some other account.

Mistake: Failing to take distributions early enough. Some people who don't need the income from their IRAs forget to begin taking withdrawals by the time they're 70½. Otherwise, they must pay a 50% excise tax on the amount they should have taken out, but didn't. The law says you must begin taking minimum distributions by April 1 of the year after you turn age 70½.. The minimum distribution is determined by taking the balance in your IRA as of the end of the previous year and dividing it by your life expectancy (or the joint life expectancy of you and your beneficiary).

Example: You had $500,000 in your IRA as of year-end 1993 and turned 70½ in April of that year. Your life expectancy would be 12.1 years. You must begin taking minimum distributions by April 1, 1994. (Divide $500,000 by 12.1, which means your minimum annual withdrawals will be about $41,322.)

Trap: You must double up on your distributions in the year you begin your initial distributions, since you will be combining distributions for the previous year and the current year in the same 12-month period.

Source: Stephen Pennacchio, a tax partner who specializes in retirement planning and employee benefits in the New York office of KPMG Peat Marwick, 345 Park Ave., New York 10154.

The Right Way to Take Money Out of Your IRA

IRA owners who reach age 70½ are required to begin taking money out of their accounts—or be penalized for not doing so.

The law provides a choice of one of two methods for making the required annual withdrawals. Unfortunately, *IRS Publication 590, Individual Retirement Arrangements (IRAs),* does not clearly tell people how to exercise this choice.

Result: The more favorable method for calculating withdrawals is often overlooked.

The two methods permitted are the *recalculation method* and the *term-certain method.* Both are based on life expectancy, using IRS tables. The IRA account balance at the beginning of the year (technically, it's December 31 of the preceding year) is divided by the person's life expectancy to determine the minimum amount that must be withdrawn from the account.

• *The recalculation method:* This method takes into account the fact that as a person survives each year, his/her life expectancy moves a bit further into the future. Under the recalculation method, life expectancy is recalculated every year.

Example: The life expectancy of a single person who turned 70½ in 1993 would be 16 years in 1993, 15.3 years in 1994, 14.6 years in 1995, and so on. The life expectancy drops by less than one year each year, so the time over which you can take the distributions is increased. This makes this withdrawal method initially appealing.

Problem with the recalculation method: When you die, your estate must receive all the money from the account and pay income tax on it one year after your death.

If your surviving spouse is the beneficiary of the account, and doesn't roll the account over into an IRA of his/her own, then all the money in the IRA is taxable in the estate of the spouse one year after the spouse's death.

If your beneficiary dies before you, all the money is taxable in your estate one year after your death. In each of these situations, the IRA abruptly comes to an end.

That is not the case with the term-certain method.

• *The term-certain method:* Under this method, the money is paid out over a fixed number of years based on the life expectancy of the IRA owner in the year he/she attains age 70½, regardless of how long the account holder actually lives. The IRA survives the account holder's death.

If the account holder dies two years after payments begin, his estate can continue to receive annual payments from the IRA account for the duration of the fixed term. If a surviving spouse is beneficiary of the IRA account as of the IRA owner's required beginning date, which is April 1 of the year after the year in which he/she turns 70½, then both life expectancies can be used in determining the term-certain period. Both life expectancies are determined based upon the spouses' ages in the year the IRA owner attains age 70½. Upon the death of either the IRA owner or his spouse, payments to the survivor may continue for the balance of the fixed term and then to the estate of the second to die until the end of the fixed term.

Impact: Taxes are lower because only a small part of the account is subject to tax each year.

And…the IRA continues to earn tax-deferred income until the end of the term of years.

• *How to make the election:* By law, you have until April 1 of the year after you turn age 70½ to make the election of which method to use, and to begin making withdrawals.

Life expectancy tables are in *IRS Publication 590, Individual Retirement Arrangements (IRAs).* This publication, though it's not very clear, does indicate that you have a choice of withdrawal methods. It doesn't say how you are supposed to make that choice. Suppose you want to choose the term-certain method instead of the recalculation method. How do you do that?

Many accountants and financial planners are not familiar with the mechanics of making the election. Obviously, a written election has to be made. Some banks have an election form on which you tell the bank whether you want the term-certain method or the recalculation method. But many brokerage companies don't have such a form. If your IRA is with a brokerage firm, or a bank that doesn't have an election form, you are likely to be placed, by default, into the recalculation method.

To make an election of the term-certain method, write a letter to the firm that holds your IRA saying:

"I, John Smith, the IRA owner, hereby elect the term-certain method of making withdrawals from my IRA based on my life expectancy and my spouse's life expectancy. I elect the term-certain method, and I don't wish the recalculation method to be used. The term-certain period that I elect is ___ years, which period does not exceed our joint life expectancies as determined in the year that I, John Smith, attain age 70½."

Mail the letter to the IRA department of the firm. Send it by certified mail, return-receipt requested, so you can prove you made the appropriate election. You should consult with your attorney in making the election.

If you elect the term-certain method, you have to determine how much you must take from the IRA each year. Each year you calculate this by taking your account balance at the beginning of the year (technically it's December 31 of the preceding year) and dividing it by the number of years remaining in the term-certain period. You then tell the IRA company how much to distribute to you.

Adjustment: If you take your first distribution on April 1 for the preceding year, you can reduce your beginning-of-the-year account balance by the amount of the distribution in calculating your second distribution. This adjustment is only available in the first distribution year.

• *Bottom line:* In the event of the death of the IRA owner and his spouse in their late seventies or early eighties, the recalculation method will force beneficiaries to pay taxes on the IRA accounts far too soon.

IRAs are being distributed— and taxed— much earlier than they need to be if death takes place in the periods described above.

Worse: Taxpayers' money is being lost on the tax-deferred earnings the accounts could have accumulated had they not been distributed early if death takes place in the time described above.

Safe haven: If the spouse survives the IRA owner, then he/she may use a spousal rollover approach to break the recalculation method. The spouse may not roll over any minimum required distributions that the IRA owner was required to take in the year of the owner's death.

Source: Seymour Goldberg, author of *A Professional's Guide to the IRA Distribution Rules.* Mr. Goldberg is a professor of law and taxation at Long Island University and a senior partner in the law firm of Goldberg & Ingber, 666 Old Country Rd., Garden City, NY 11530. Mr. Goldberg's book may be obtained from Field Services, Foundation for Accounting Education of the New York State Society of Certified Public Accountants, 200 Park Ave., New York 10166. 212-973-8373.

Best Places to Retire to Tax-Wise

Few people decide to retire to a particular state solely because of tax reasons. Most people select a retirement community because of friendships, relatives, or lifestyle—a warm climate, a slower pace, etc. But you can combine taxes and other reasons if you do a little planning.

Trap: People often forget to factor in estate taxes in thinking about a retirement state.

Minimizing estate tax...

The best states to retire to are those that have what is known as a *pick-up tax* for estate-tax purposes. This is the lowest amount of death tax a state imposes.

Pick-up tax credit runs from 0.8% of the federal taxable estate to 16%, which is the maximum amount of credit the federal government gives for state death taxes.

High-tax states go beyond the maximum credit. New York, for example, imposes an estate tax that runs as high as 21% of the federal taxable estate; therefore, it is actually 5% over the credit amount.

The low-tax states which impose a pick-up tax are...

•Alabama, Alaska, Arizona, Arkansas, California, Colorado, District of Columbia, Florida, Georgia, Hawaii, Idaho, Illinois, Maine, Minnesota, Missouri, Nevada, New Mexico, North Dakota, Oregon, Rhode Island, South Carolina, Texas, Utah, Vermont, Virginia, Washington, West Virginia, Wisconsin, Wyoming.

The generation-skipping tax...

Some states that have a pick-up tax impose a *generation-skipping tax,* similar but in addition to the federal generation-skipping tax. A generation-skipping tax taxes gifts and bequests that bypass a generation of heirs.

A gift that goes from a grandparent to his/her grandchild is a generation-skipping gift because it bypasses the parent's generation. The government is deprived of the tax in the parent's generation, so it taxes the original gift to make up for this.

Most states have an exemption from the generation-skipping tax for a certain amount of generation-skipping gifts. The federal exemption is $1 million. In some states the generation-skipping exemption is that high, but in others it is not.

The states that impose a generation-skipping tax are...

•Alabama, Arizona, California, Colorado, Florida, Illinois, Missouri, Nevada, Rhode Island, South Carolina, Texas, Virginia, Washington.

If you're planning to make very large gifts directly to your grandchildren, you might want to avoid a generation-skipping-tax state.

Income tax...

Some of the favorable states that impose only a pick-up tax do not have an income tax. *Those states are...*

•Alaska, Florida, Nevada, Texas, Washington, Wyoming.

Caution: Some of the states that don't impose an income tax have other taxes. *Example:* Florida, which imposes an *intangibles tax*—a tax on stock and other intangible assets.

Switching states...

When you decide on a state in which you want to retire, make sure that you affirmatively change your domicile so your old state cannot come back and tax you as a resident as well. *Prudent steps...*

•Spend a greater portion of each year in your new domicile state.

•Execute and file a declaration of domicile with the appropriate office in your new domicile state.

•Dispose of your home in your old domicile state.

•Register and vote in your new domicile state.

•File all tax forms at the IRS Service Center for your new domicile state.

•Register cars, boats, etc., in your new domicile state.

•Sign a new will in your new domicile state.

•Obtain a driver's license in the new state and surrender your old license to your previous domicile state.

•File a final resident tax return in the old domicile state.

Tax checklist...

Become familiar with all of the various taxes in the state to which you are planning to move. Income tax is important, but it's not the only consideration. *Also...*

Sales tax:

•What is the rate?

•What does the state tax?

•Is there a county sales tax?

Gift tax:

•Does the state you are moving to impose a gift tax?

•What is the rate?

•Is there a minimum exempt amount?

Estate tax:

•Which assets are subject to tax?

•What is the tax rate?

•Does your state have the marital deduction?

Income tax:

•Which assets are taxed?

•How are retirement-plan distributions taxed?

•What is the tax rate?

•If there is no income tax, is there an intangibles tax?

•What is the rate of the intangibles tax?

Source: Tamara G. Telesko, vice president, manager of the financial and estate-planning departments, Chase Manhattan Bank, US Private Banking, 1211 Avenue of the Americas, New York 10036.

Summertime Tax Deductions

You'll get extra enjoyment from summer travel or a vacation home when you take advantage of opportunities to deduct their cost. *Here's how...*

Domestic travel...

By combining business with pleasure, you are able to get business deductions for a trip that has a large element of pleasure.

The basic rule for travel within the United States is that if your primary motive for making a trip is business, you can deduct the full cost of travel to and from your destination—along with the cost of lodging and 50% of the cost of meals incurred there.

This remains true even if you spend a substantial amount of time engaged in activities not related to business, such as visiting friends or relatives or going to entertainment events.

Spouse's travel break: When you bring your spouse along on a trip for nonbusiness pur-

poses, you do not have to limit your travel deduction to half of your combined costs. You can still deduct the full cost you would have incurred traveling by yourself.

Example: You can deduct the full cost of a single hotel room even if a double room costs only a few dollars more. And you can deduct the full cost of a single air fare even if a family-fare discount obtained by traveling together gets your spouse a ticket at little extra cost.

The result is that you may be able to deduct most of your combined costs when your spouse accompanies you for pleasure purposes on a business trip.

You cannot deduct extra expenses incurred during nonbusiness side trips or during an extension of your stay for nonbusiness purposes. Unless there is a bona fide purpose for the spouse's presence, you cannot deduct the separate nonbusiness expenses of your spouse, such as those for meals, entertainment, and the like.

Foreign travel...

The rules are tougher for deducting travel outside the United States. Under special rules, you can deduct all of your business-related foreign travel expenses only if...

•The trip lasts seven days or less, not counting the day you leave but counting the day you come back, or...

•You spend less than 25% of your time outside the US in nonbusiness activities, or...

•You are an employee and did not have substantial control over the trip, or...

•You can otherwise establish that a personal vacation was not a major consideration for the trip.

The percentage of time spent on business activity is figured by dividing the number of "business days" on the trip by the total number of travel days. Business days include...

•Days spent traveling directly to or from your business destination—or, if you take a side trip, the number of days it would otherwise take to get to or from your destination.

•Days on which your presence is necessary at a specific location for a business purpose, even if most of the day is spent on nonbusiness activity.

• Days on which your principal activity during working hours is business.

• Weekends and holidays that occur between business days. *Example:* You travel to Canada to work on Friday and Monday, and sightsee over the weekend. All four days are business days. If you worked only on Friday or Monday, you would have only one business day.

When a foreign trip is primarily motivated by business, but you spend 25% or more of your time on nonbusiness activity, you can deduct only the percentage of travel costs that correspond to the percentage of trip days that are business days.

More business-travel rules...

• Conventions. Attendance at a convention for business purposes qualifies a trip as a business trip. If you go to the convention for investment, political, or social purposes, you may not deduct your travel expenses.

The cost of attending a business convention held outside the United States is deductible if the meeting is directly related to the conduct of your business and it is as reasonable for the meeting to be held outside the US as in it.

• Cruise ships. If you travel to your business destination by ocean liner, your travel deduction is limited to twice the highest per diem travel allowance provided to employees in the executive branch of the federal government. Currently this is $348.

You can deduct the cost of attending a business convention on a cruise ship if the ship is registered in the US and all ports of call are located in the US or its possessions. There's a deduction limit of $2,000 per person annually.

• Charity trips. You can deduct the cost of attending a convention of a charitable organization if you attend as a chosen representative, but not if you attend simply as a member of the organization.

You can also deduct travel costs incurred while away from home performing services for a charitable organization, but only if there is no significant element of personal pleasure, recreation, or vacation in such travel. This rule eliminates any deduction, for example, for working on an archaeological dig in a vacation locale.

When you travel, keep a diary that documents the amount of time spent on business or charitable activity.

Vacation homes...

The vacation homes that people enjoy during the summer can also be a source of valuable tax breaks. *Opportunities:*

• Tax-free income. If you rent your vacation home out to others for 14 days or fewer during the year, your rental income is completely tax-free. You don't even have to report it on your tax return.

• Deductible expenses. If you rent out your vacation home for 15 days or more, your rental income is taxable, but you can deduct expenses related to your rental activity. These may include home ownership costs that otherwise would not be deductible, such as depreciation, maintenance expenses, utilities, and insurance. The portion of such expenses that is deductible depends on the relative amount of personal and rental use.

Example: If you rent out a house for 90 days during a year and use it 10 days yourself, you can deduct 90% of the home-related costs.

Limit: You will not be able to deduct costs that exceed your rental income if you make personal use of the house for more than the greater of 14 days, or 10% of the number of days it is rented to others. Use by members of your family is counted as personal use.

If you do not exceed this personal-use limit, you can deduct up to $25,000 of net rental losses against your income from other sources (such as salary). This deduction phases out as your Adjusted Gross Income increases from $100,000 to $150,000.

• Mortgage interest. If your vacation home qualifies as a second residence, mortgage interest payments on it are fully deductible and it can be used to secure up to $100,000 of home-equity borrowing (against both your homes), which produces deductible interest.

To qualify a vacation home as a residence, you must use it yourself during the year for more than 14 days and at least 10% of the number of days you rent it out to others.

Note: A boat with living quarters can qualify as a second residence.

Source: Nadine Gordon Lee, partner in the personal tax and financial-planning departments, Ernst & Young, 277 Park Ave., New York 10172.

Out-of-State Tax Trap

Retirees who relocate may find that their pensions remain taxable in the state they've moved from. *Examples:* California and New Jersey take income tax on pension benefits regardless of the recipient's current residence. *Rationale:* Pension benefits were accrued during working years, and income earned in a particular state should be taxed in that state. Two bills have been proposed in Congress to end this practice.

Source: *Medical Economics,* 680 Kinderkamack Rd., Oradell, NJ 07649.

Medical Deductions for Nursing-Home Expenses

Deductions for nursing-home care fall into a gray area of the tax law. The types of expenses that can be taken as medical deductions depend on the reasons for being in the nursing home.

Guidelines:

•Fully deductible. The entire cost for nursing-home care—including meals and lodging —is deductible if a principal reason for being in the home is to receive continual medical services.

•Partly deductible. In situations where medical need is not a principal reason for being in a nursing home, expenses attributable only to medical care can be deducted.

Example: If your grandmother were in a nursing home because she was too frail to care for herself, she would not be able to deduct the cost of meals and lodging at the home. However, she could deduct the cost of any medical services received while in the home. Ask the nursing home operator to break the bills down into medical and non-medical care.

•Lump-sum payments. In some cases, a lump-sum fee is paid for lifetime care in a nursing home. The home should be able to provide you with a statement detailing the portion of the fee that will be required for the patient's future medical care, based on the nursing home's past experience. This amount is generally deductible in the year it is paid—even though it is for future medical care.

•Dependents' medical expenses. You may deduct medical expenses that you pay for your spouse or a qualifying dependent. Your parents or other relatives generally qualify as your dependents if you could claim a personal exemption for them on your tax return.

Note: The gross income test, which says that a dependent must earn less than $2,500 for 1995, does not apply when claiming a dependent's medical expenses. The person must be your dependent either at the time care was received or when the expenses were paid.

•Nature of services. Whether or not an expense is deductible is determined by the nature of the services provided, not by the qualifications or experience of the provider.

Example: Assume you broke your hip and hired domestic help. If that person also helped with your in-home physical therapy, you could claim as a medical expense the charges for the time spent on your exercises. It wouldn't matter if the provider were not a qualified medical professional, as long as the physical therapy program was for legitimate medical reasons and was prescribed by a doctor. However, the cost of having the same person do housework would not be deductible. The fact that your injury made you unable to do the housework yourself is irrelevant.

Reminder: Medical expenses are only deductible to the extent that they have not been reimbursed by insurance and exceed 7.5% of your Adjusted Gross Income.

Source: William G. Brennan, partner, Ernst & Young, CPAs, 1225 Connecticut Ave. NW, Washington, DC 20036. Mr. Brennan is the editor of the *Ernst & Young Financial Planning Reporter.*

Sideline Business Or Hobby?

A favorite technique of tax auditors is to disallow a deduction claimed for a sideline business on the grounds that the activity is really just a hobby. The auditors try to establish their case by asking the taxpayer for copies of returns for the past four or five years. If the activity has produced a loss each year, the auditor will summarily conclude that the current loss is a nondeductible loss.

Helpful: Avoid falling into this trap by not taking copies of previous years' tax returns to the audit. The taxpayer, in general, has no obligation to provide copies of returns that have already been filed with the IRS. *Also helpful:* Ask the auditor where in the law it says that you must actually show a profit on a sideline business—ever. All that's required is that you intend to make a profit.

Motheraid

A son paid his mother's medical expenses with money he withdrew from her bank account under a power of attorney. The IRS disallowed the son's deduction for these expenses, saying the money was really the mother's. But the Court of Appeals allowed the deduction. The money was legally his—a gift from his mother to him.

Source: *John M. Ruch*, CA-5, 82-4463.

Future Income to Grandchildren— No Taxes Now

"Grandfather trust" is a term used to describe a trust set up by an individual for the benefit of someone he is not legally obligated to support, even though the income is in fact used for support purposes. Thus, when a trust's income is used to provide support for a grantor's grand-

child, whom he is not legally obliged to support, trust income is not taxed to the grantor.

The trust principal would not be included in the grandfather's estate when he dies, so his tax situation benefits from such an arrangement in another respect.

The grandchild also benefits, receiving support he otherwise might not receive. And so does the grantor's son, who has been relieved of the obligation of providing support for his child.

If an individual sets up a trust with a third party, such as a bank serving as trustee, and the trustee has the authority in its sole discretion to use trust income for the support of a person that the grantor must support, such as his wife or minor child, the grantor is not regarded as the owner of the trust fund.

Source: *Estate Planning: The New Golden Opportunities* by Robert S. Holzman. Boardroom Books.

Private Foundations Are a Plus

Private foundations make sense for entrepreneurs who have sold a business or otherwise have an unusually large amount of taxable income. Immediate tax deductions can be taken up to a limit of 30% of Adjusted Gross Income, and the excess can be carried forward for five years. The founder can maintain absolute control over the foundation's operations. *Caution:* At least 5% of total assets must be given to charities or charitable activities each year. And there's a 23% federal tax on the investment income of the foundation (less administrative expenses).

Source: *Legacies*, Baylor University, Box 98011, Waco, TX 76798.

IRA Trap

Don't have your IRA invest in tax-exempt state or municipal bonds. *Why:* Any amount withdrawn from an IRA is taxable income, even if the withdrawn amount was earned from a tax-exempt bond. So, by having the IRA invest in tax-exempt bonds, you forfeit the tax exemption for them that would have been available had they been held outside the IRA.

Joint/Separate Returns

Married couples can file a joint return or separate returns. Usually, a joint return works out better, especially if one spouse has appreciably higher income than the other.

Nevertheless, filing separately can be advantageous in some situations:

•Deductions for casualty losses must be reduced by 10% of adjusted gross income (AGI). On a joint return, combined AGI is reduced even if only one spouse suffered the loss. If separate returns are filed, the loss is reduced by only 10% of that spouse's income.

Example: A husband has AGI of $70,000; his wife, $20,000. The wife's jewelry, worth $25,000, is stolen. On a joint return, the loss must be reduced by $9,000 (10% of combined income); on a separate return, by only $2,000 (10% of wife's income).

•The same considerations apply if one spouse, but not the other, has heavy medical expenses, since you can deduct only expenses in excess of 7.5% of AGI—or heavy miscellaneous expenses, which can only be deducted to the extent they exceed 2% of AGI.

Other options: If married persons live apart for the entire year, either spouse may file as head-of-household (with reduced rates) if he or she has an unmarried child or dependent living with him or her for the entire year. The other spouse would then have to file separately (higher rates) unless that spouse also had a child or dependent in his or her household. *Or:* They could file jointly, if that works out better.

Caution: The only way to tell for sure whether it's better to file jointly or separately is to take pencil and paper and figure the tax both ways.

Source: Mahoney, Cohen & Co., 111 W. 40 St., New York 10018.

Benefits Loopholes

Here are some ways to get the most mileage from the noncash benefits your company provides.

•Pension and profit-sharing plans. Your employer contributes money on your behalf and the money accumulates on a tax-deferred basis. You don't pay tax on the money until you withdraw it. These are the basic tax advantages, but there's more…

Loophole: Take a tax-free loan from the pension or profit-sharing plan. You can do this if the plan permits borrowing—not all do. Plans that allow borrowing usually make it easy on the participant—no need to justify why the loan is needed.

Tax law limits: The amount you can borrow is limited to your vested balance up to the greater of $10,000 or one-half of your vested account balance, with a maximum of $50,000.

Loophole: Put some of your own money into the plan—many plans allow employees to make voluntary contributions. Such contributions are not tax-deductible, but the money accumulates income on a tax-deferred basis.

Loophole: If your company's plan is inactive, in that no additions are being made and no benefits are accruing on your behalf, you are eligible to contribute to an IRA.

•401(k) plans. You contribute part of your salary to a company-sponsored savings program. You pay no income tax on the dollars you contribute until they're withdrawn. Interest, dividends, and other earnings accumulate tax-deferred until you take them out.

Loophole: Though the amount you can contribute each year is limited by the tax law, it's far more than you could put into an IRA. *Maximum 401(k) contribution for 1995:* $9,240.

•Company-paid life insurance. As long as the coverage doesn't exceed $50,000, you are not taxed on the premiums the employer pays. But if it is more than $50,000, you are taxed on part of the premiums.

Loophole: The taxable amount is figured from IRS tables and is less than the actual premiums the employer pays. You pay some tax for the extra coverage, but it is far less than it would cost you to buy similar life-insurance coverage outside the company.

Loophole: The first $5,000 of death benefits paid by an employer to an employee's beneficiaries are tax-free to the beneficiaries.

• Medical and disability insurance. Company-paid insurance is not taxable to the employee.

Loophole: Even if the employee's dependents are covered by the insurance, the employee does not have to pay tax on the premiums.

Drawback: Disability payments received are taxable income to the employee.

• Cafeteria plans allow employees to choose between cash and a shopping list of benefits, including group medical insurance, disability, child care, and the like. The employees choose their own menu of benefits. The benefits do not have to be included in the employee's taxable income.

Loophole: These plans are very easy to set up and administer.

• Employee loans. Employers can make interest-free loans of up to $10,000 to their employees. The employee does not have to report the foregone interest as taxable income.

• Use of an apartment by an employee. This is taxable to the employee at fair market rent.

Loophole: Fair market rent for this purpose is a price that is consistent with the apartment's value to the employee. If an employer puts an employee up in a three bedroom apartment, but the employee only needs a one bedroom apartment, the employee would only have to pay tax on the value of a one bedroom apartment.

• Stock with cash in tandem. If a company gives stock to an employee as an incentive or bonus, the fair market value of the stock is taxable to the employee in the year it is received. The tax cuts deeply into the true value of the bonus. But the company gets a tax deduction for the stock's full value.

Loophole: In addition to the stock, the company gives the employee cash to cover his tax liability on the stock and the cash together. Assuming the company and the employee are in roughly the same tax bracket, the transaction will be a wash. The amount the company saves in taxes will be about equal to the amount the employee owes.

• Incentive stock options. When a company gives an employee what are known as "non-qualified stock options," the employee must pay tax when he exercises the options. But if the company gives "incentive stock options," tax does not have to be paid until the employee sells the stock. No taxable income is recognized by the employee when the option is granted or exercised.

Trap: The difference between the option price and the fair market value at the time an incentive stock option is exercised must be included in calculations for the Alternative Minimum Tax. It's complicated, so look into it with your tax advisor.

Loophole: The employee can, if he chooses, elect to pay tax on the value of the stock in the year that he gets the stock, not in the year it becomes available to sell. This is an election made under Section 83(b) of the Tax Code. In many instances, if the company is expected to grow very rapidly, it would be advantageous to make this election.

• Phantom stock, also called "stock appreciation rights," are sometimes issued to employees. No actual stock is given, but payments are made as if actual stock had been issued. If any dividends are paid to stockholders, they are also paid to the phantom stockholders. This money is taxed as compensation, rather than as dividends.

Loophole: The employee doesn't pay tax until there is an actual payment to him as a phantom stock holder. No tax is payable when he first receives the phantom stock.

• Secular trusts. These trusts have been developed to ensure that companies pay employees the deferred compensation that has been promised them. *How they work:*

The company puts money into an irrevocable trust for the employee and gets an immediate deduction for the contributions. The employee is taxed currently on all contributions credited to the trust. But, the company makes a payment to the employee to cover his tax liability. When benefits are eventually paid, the employee gets them tax-free.

Loophole: A secular trust is less expensive for a company to establish than its relative, the Rabbi trust.

Source: Edward Mendlowitz, partner, Mendlowitz Weitsen, CPAs, Two Pennsylvania Plaza, New York 10121. Mr. Mendlowitz is the author of several books including his latest, *Aggressive Tax Strategies*, Macmillan Publishing Company.

How to Cut Taxes on Retirement-Plan Payouts...with a Sub-Trust

Most professionals, key executives, and company owners put away as much as possible in retirement plans to reap the tax savings. But putting too much into a retirement plan can backfire and siphon away up to 80% of your retirement-plan wealth.

Problem: Every dollar above $750,000 is subject to estate tax, income tax, and excise tax. A 15% excise tax is levied when all types of retirement-plan accounts are worth more than $750,000.

You can avoid much of the tax liability on a substantial part of your retirement assets by setting up a network of trusts that include a "sub-trust."

Key: Use life insurance as the funding vehicle for the trusts. *How to do it:*

• Create a sub-trust within your retirement plan. It's called a sub-trust because your retirement plan is itself a trust.

• Create another trust outside of your retirement plan—an irrevocable life-insurance trust. Designate a trusted individual or a financial institution as the trustee of this trust—not yourself.

• Have the trustee of the sub-trust buy a life-insurance policy on your life. Name the sub-trust as the beneficiary of the life-insurance policy. Name the irrevocable life-insurance trust as the beneficiary of the sub-trust. Name your children as the beneficiaries of the life-insurance trust, with your spouse to get income from the trust assets for life.

• When you die, the life insurance proceeds are paid first to the sub-trust. Then they are paid over to the life-insurance trust, and from there they go to your beneficiaries.

• Have the premiums on the life insurance paid out of your retirement-plan contributions.

Tax impact: Your retirement plan pays the insurance premiums out of your contributions to the plan. Thus, what you have is a tax-deductible life-insurance policy—since retirement-plan contributions, within certain limits, are tax-deductible. *Impact:*

• Income tax is avoided because life insurance proceeds, payable on your death, aren't subject to income tax.

• Estate taxes are avoided because neither the sub-trust nor the irrevocable life-insurance trust are part of your estate.

• Excise taxes are avoided if this arrangement keeps your official retirement-plan assets under $750,000.

Rich example: By adding a $1 million insurance policy, plus these trusts, to a $1 million retirement plan, your beneficiaries will get $1.5 million instead of $500,000 after taxes. The trust arrangement triples your beneficiaries' after-tax return.

Watch out: Skilled drafting of the sub-trust and the life-insurance trust is imperative. So is fine-tuning the mechanics of the transaction, including paying the insurance premiums to the retirement plan.

The IRS has allowed sub-trusts without challenge so far. However, the technique has not yet withstood a challenge in court. But even if the sub-trust was disallowed by a judge, you would be no worse off tax-wise than you would otherwise be.

Source: Alan Nadolna, president, Associates in Financial Planning, 100 S. Wacker Dr., Suite 1650, Chicago 60606.

Delaying Marriage

Delaying marriage until after year-end may pay. The "marriage tax" can significantly increase the tax bill of two-earner couples. Your marital status as of December 31 determines your filing status for the entire year. *Flip side:* If one spouse will earn almost *all* the couple's income for the year, you probably can cut your tax bill by marrying *before* year-end.

Source: Ed Mendlowitz, partner, Mendlowitz Weitsen, CPAs, in New York.

New Charitable Tax Rule

New tax rules are in effect for charitable giving. For 1995 returns you must get a receipt for each contribution of $250 or more. The IRS will not accept a canceled check as proof of a deduction of this size. A second new rule says that when charities give gifts in return for contributions exceeding $75, the charities must issue statements of value.

Source: Laurence I. Foster, a tax partner in the personal financial planning practice of KPMG Peat Marwick, 345 Park Ave., New York 10154.

Your Health and Your Taxes

Medical deductions have been allowed for the following items…

•Apartment rent when the apartment was rented for an ailing dependent, because it was cheaper than hospitalization.
Sidney J. Ungar, TC Memo 1963-159.

•Elastic stockings recommended by a doctor for a person with varicose veins.
Bessie Cohen, TC Memo 1/21/51.

•Fluoridation device installed at home on the recommendation of a dentist.
Revenue Ruling 64-267.

•Hair removal through electrolysis performed by a licensed technician.
Revenue Ruling 82-111.

•Mattresses and boards bought solely to alleviate an arthritic condition.
Revenue Ruling 55-261.

•Mobile phone installed in a car to enable a person who has heart disease to immediately call a doctor in an emergency.
George M. Womack, TC Memo 1975-232.

•Telephone calls made long-distance to a therapist for psychological counseling.
Letter Ruling 8034087.

•Reclining chair bought on a doctor's advice to alleviate a heart condition.
Revenue Ruling 58-155.

•Transportation to AA meetings.
Revenue Ruling 63-273.

Source: Robert S. Holzman, PhD, professor emeritus of taxation, New York University.

Deductible Eyeglasses

Prescription eyeglasses are tax-deductible if you need them to do your job. To qualify for the deduction, the glasses must have been customized for the workplace and unsuitable for general use. *Helpful:* Have the optometrist write "occupational use only" on the lens prescription. The deduction is taken as a miscellaneous expense and is subject to the 2% miscellaneous itemization deduction limits on Schedule A.

Source: American Optometric Association, 243 N. Lindbergh Blvd., St. Louis 63141.

How to Deduct Nondeductible Expenses

The tax law imposes strict limits on personal deductions. But creative tax planners have found ways to get around these limits.

With a little careful planning, you can turn nondeductible expenses into tax deductions.

• *Take interest deductions.* Interest on personal debt is not deductible. This includes interest on car loans, college loans, credit cards, revolving charge accounts, installment purchases, and late-paid taxes. But interest on home-equity loans of up to $100,000 is fully deductible.

Loophole: Take out a home-equity loan on your first or second home…and use the proceeds to pay off personal debt. Your interest payments will then be deductible. You will have converted nondeductible personal interest payments into deductible mortgage interest.

• *Hire your kids.* Instead of paying your child a nondeductible allowance, put him/her to work as a bona fide employee in your business. The wages are a deductible business expense.

Loophole: If your business is unincorporated, you don't have to pay Social Security tax on wages paid to a child who is under 18.

• *Buy a vacation home if you can.* It can be a source of personal pleasure and valuable tax breaks. When you rent a vacation home for *fewer* than 15 days, the rental income is tax free. This is one of the few instances in the Tax Code where income is considered nontaxable. You are not even required to report it on your tax return. You are still entitled to full deductions for mortgage interest and property taxes. When you rent your vacation home to others for *15 days or more*, the income you receive is taxable. But expenses related to the property rental (including depreciation) are deductible, subject to certain limitations depending on the number of days you personally use the place.

To get the full deduction, you yourself cannot use the place for more than the *greater* of 14 days or…10% of the number of days it is rented to others.

Loophole: Days spent fixing or maintaining the house are not counted as personal use.

• *Deduct medical expenses of dependents.* Even though you may not be able to claim a personal exemption for your contribution to the support of relatives because they had a gross income of $2,500 or more, you can still deduct any medical expenses that you pay on their behalf. *Key:* You must provide more than one-half of the relative's support.

Loophole: Instead of giving your relative cash to pay medical bills, pay the bills yourself. This may give you a deduction.

Whoever is claiming a dependency exemption for a parent under a *multiple* support agreement (Form 2120) with other relatives should also pay the dependent's medical expenses. *Reason:* In determining qualification for the exemption, the payment of medical expenses is treated as part of the dependent's support. The payment is also deductible as a medical expense.

Impact: You get a *double* tax benefit for the same payment…a dependency exemption and a tax deduction.

Another way to get a double benefit is to make a charitable contribution on your parents' behalf. The payment is included in calculating support. You get a charitable deduction.

• *Turn hobby losses into deductions.* Expenses for activities that are primarily sport, hobby, or recreation are not deductible. To convert these nondeductible expenses into allowable deductions, the activity must be changed to an activity carried on for the production or collection of income. This is not hard to do if you keep accurate records. Factors that the IRS considers include the following…

• You had a profit in at least three of the immediately preceding five years.

• The nature of the activity is considered businesslike.

• The extent of your knowledge and expertise and the manner in which you use them in the activity.

• Your success in conducting other types of activities.

• *Take employee business-expense deductions.* As an employee, you can deduct unreimbursed expenses for business-related travel, transportation, meals, entertainment, and gifts.

Trap: Most unreimbursed employee business expenses come under the category of "miscellaneous itemized deductions" and as such, can only be deducted to the extent that they exceed 2% of your Adjusted Gross Income (AGI). If your expenses don't reach this floor, you get no deduction for them.

Loophole I: Have your employer reduce your salary by the amount you normally spend during the year on business expenses—say $1,000. Then have your employer reimburse you directly for the $1,000 of expenses. *Impact:* You no longer have to worry about the 2% floor. You get a deduction for the full $1,000 of expenses through the salary reduction.

Caution: The salary reduction may affect your pension contributions.

Important: Be sure to adequately account for the expenses to your employer. If you don't, you could be required to pick up the entire amount of the reimbursement as ordinary income.

Loophole II: Impairment-related work expenses (for anyone who is physically or mentally handicapped) are not subject to the 2%-of-AGI limit on miscellaneous itemized deductions.

Loophole III: Beat the 2% floor on deductibility of employee business expenses by filing Schedule C, *Profit of Loss from Business,* where there is no such limitation.

To qualify for reporting your expenses on Schedule C, you must fit into one of the following categories...

• *Self-employed individual...*or independent contractor.

• *Statutory employee.* This is a category of worker that includes full-time outside sales-people or life insurance agents, commission drivers, and home workers. Statutory employees are entitled to file Schedule C even though Social Security tax has been withheld from their paychecks and they have been issued W-2 forms.

• *Qualified performing artist.* To qualify in this category, a taxpayer must have performed services in the performing arts for at least two employers in the tax year...and had performing-arts-related business expenses in excess of 10% of performing arts gross income...and had AGI of $16,000 or less. Performing arts expenses can be deducted even though deductions are not itemized.

• *Deduct passive losses.* The passive loss rules generally limit the deductibility of losses from passive activities to the amount of income derived from such activities. Passive activities are defined as those activities involving the conduct of a trade or business in which the taxpayer does not materially participate. Material participation in a trade or business activity means satisfying any one of a variety of tests.

Loophole I: If you or your spouse actively participate in real estate activities for at least 750 hours a year, then losses from your total real estate activities can be deducted against other income without limitation.

Loophole II: IRS regulations for self-charged interest permit the matching of interest income (normally portfolio income) directly against passive losses to the extent that the loss includes self-interest charged through the entity by an S corporation shareholder or partner.

Source: Edward Mendlowitz, partner, Mendlowitz Weitsen, CPAs, Two Pennsylvania Plaza, New York 10121.

Cars Help Kidneys

The National Kidney Foundation of New York/New Jersey will cart away older and late model cars, whether or not they are in working condition. Proceeds benefit the foundation's programs. The foundation sends a letter acknowledging each gift. Donors may be entitled to a tax deduction equal to a car's fair market value. *More information:* 800-633-6628.

4

Banking Savvy

How Not to Be Outsmarted By Your Bank

I'm always amazed at how people go out of their way to get an extra eighth of one percent on a CD…and then pay their banks much more than that in fees they have been told are unavoidable.

Reality: Banks don't want you to know their fees and interest rates *are* negotiable. Often all you have to do is ask.

Example: Most banks will give senior citizens, the disabled and students *free* checking accounts. *But you have to ask.*

Strategy: Learn the chain of command at your bank. If you encounter a bank employee who won't negotiate fees, ask to speak with his/her boss. Most senior personnel would prefer you to be happy with the bank, especially if you are a good customer.

Here is how to minimize your ATM fees, your overdraft charges and the penalties for falling below minimum balance requirements…

• *Use a small bank.* Your bank should be one of the smallest in your area. A big bank won't go the extra mile for you because it doesn't feel it needs your business. A small bank will be flexible because it needs satisfied customers in order to attract new customers and to grow.

• *Don't use ATMs*—except in emergencies. Not only can they be costly, they prevent you from establishing important personal relationships with bank officers. Those cordial relationships can help you get better rates and terms on bank loans and services.

• *Avoid overdraft charges.* Ask your bank to electronically monitor and "red flag" your checking account…and telephone you if it is overdrawn. Most community banks will give you until 3 pm the same day to come in with a deposit before they bounce a check—saving you a $15 to $25 overdraft charge and the embarrassment of a returned check.

• *Ask for minimum balance requirements to be waived.* Many banks will waive these requirements if you insist. If your bank won't, consider a credit union, which usually is cheaper and offers better service. For more information, call the Credit Union National Association at 800-358-5710.

• *Plan before you borrow.* Go into the bank and update your personal financial statement every six months or so—even if you don't need a loan. Strike up conversations with the people who help you.

Reason: You want at least one teller, one loan officer and one bookkeeper to know your face. Anyone can borrow if they have good collateral. But if you need a loan based only on collateral, you're much more likely to get it if you—and your credit history—are familiar to the bank's employees.

• *Refuse unnecessary products.* Banks are intimidating to average consumers, who are afraid to question what is put in front of them.

Example: Most people are so happy to get a car loan, they're afraid to refuse the hugely overpriced credit life and disability insurance the bank often adds to the loan. Even worse—they don't realize that because the insurance cost has been added to the loan, the premium is subject to a finance charge.

Source: Edward F. Mrkvicka, Jr., president of Reliance Enterprises, Inc., a national financial consulting firm. A former CEO of an Illinois bank, he is editor of *Money Insider* newsletter and author of *The Bank Book: How to Revoke Your Bank's "License to Steal"—and Save Up to $100,000.* Harper Perennial.

How to Protect Yourself From Your Banker

Reality: While there are certainly some smart and some honest bankers in the United States, as an industry, bankers have not run their business at all well. In the past seven years…

…more than 1,100 banks have failed. Taxpayers may have to bail out savings and loans to the tune of up to $500 billion or more before it's over. And many individuals have lost all of their life's savings.

…bank insurance reserves have dwindled from $18 billion to virtually nothing.

Self-defense: Ask questions and look out for your own interests in any dealings with your bank.

Comparison shop…

No matter how convenient your bank may be or how long you've done business there, it's important today to at least call around and see what's available from other banks in the area.

Example: All banks today are trying to increase their earnings through added fees. Just the fees for an average checking account can cost you several hundred dollars annually, net of any interest you may earn on that account. So, it pays to shop around for the bank with the lowest fees.

Bargains: If you qualify as a senior citizen by whatever standards a given bank uses, it will often give you free checking. But most banks don't advertise this. You must ask for it. If your bank doesn't offer free checking, it may pay to switch to another bank.

Ask around, too, to see whether other banks have senior citizen clubs that offer discounts on local restaurant meals, transportation, travel, etc.

What's really insured?…

Of course it's comforting to know that your deposits are insured for up to $100,000, but don't make the mistake of thinking that just because there's an FDIC symbol on the door, all transactions with your bank are protected. They're not… and often bank employees don't know (or don't tell you) that.

Safe-deposit box contents, for example, aren't considered deposits and may or may not be insured by the bank.

Any IRA accounts or mutual funds that you may have with a bank's broker don't fall under FDIC insurance either.

At best, they're covered by the Securities Investor Protection Corporation (SIPC), which protects brokerage accounts against fraud, but not market declines.

Rule: If a bank tries to sell you anything other than a Certificate of Deposit, which is covered under FDIC protection, find out whether it is insured. What happened in the notorious Charles Keating (Lincoln Savings & Loan) bank failure was that investors had been switched out of CDs and into bank bonds that were not insured.

Don't simply take the word of bank employees. They may have been told that bank products are insured in order to sell them.

Better: Verify the information with the FDIC
in your region, the state banking authority or—
for banks with "National" in their names—the
US comptroller of the currency. If investments
are not insured and the bank gets into trouble,
it could take years to get your money back, if
you ever do.

Form a relationship...

It's important for everyone—especially
seniors—to get to know their banker by name.
When your banker knows you, he/she can be
helpful if an emergency arises.

Many banks are now charging $15 to $25 per
bounced check, for example, and it can cost
even more for overdraft protection. Once you're
known, instead of buying expensive overdraft
protection, ask to speak to the bookkeeper and
request that he/she red flag your account and
call you immediately if there's an overdraft.
Then, at no cost, you have until the end of the
business day to add funds. Again, if your bank
won't do this, find one that will.

Don't trust trust departments: If you must deal
with a bank trust department, pick a big bank. I
have real reservations about using bank trust
departments, especially when you don't have
enough money to command adequate attention
from senior officers. Banks are known more for
their mismanagement of trust moneys than for
astute investment advice. You can probably do
better with a smart trust accountant, trust attorney or trust company.

What to avoid...

• ATMs. Young people may swear by them,
but most seniors are not comfortable with automatic teller machines (ATMs). That's fine because it's becoming more and more costly to
use the machines and, since they can be a mag-
net for criminals, elderly people could easily
become victimized.

• Bank-sponsored mutual funds. Many banks
are now pushing to sell mutual funds to deposi-
tors. But you should be aware that almost all of
what they sell are load funds that carry a sales
commission of up to 8%. And most banks offer
a very limited universe of funds with only one

or two selections in each category. By doing a
little research at your library and reading financial publications, you can easily find many well-
managed funds with good histories and invest
in them directly without paying a sales load.

• Reverse mortgages. With so much current
emphasis on getting the equity out of your
home, more banks can be expected to offer
some form of reverse mortgage financing—an
annuity-like upside-down mortgage—to seniors.
I don't recommend it because essentially you're
giving away your home—at least a big share of
the equity you've built up over the years—to the
bank in order to stay there. Diluting your (and
your heirs') hard-earned equity in your home
should be a last resort.

For younger seniors with a longer life expectancy, the monthly income from a reverse mortgage probably won't be enough to make much
difference and, because the interest compounds
over a long period, it becomes a very expensive
way to borrow.

Better: Sell your home to your children and
let them pay you $300 to $400 a month. Or sell
to an outsider under an arrangement that allows
you to live there as long as you wish.

Check with your state information office.
There are many programs to help with real-
estate taxes, repairs and maintenance, and assistance for health reasons. These programs may
be enough to ensure you don't have to move.

Source: Edward F. Mrkvicka, Jr., former bank president
and now president of Reliance Enterprises, a financial
consulting firm, and publisher of *Money Insider,* 1206
Alsace Way, Lafayette, CO 80026. He is also author of *The
Bank Book: How to Revoke Your Bank's "License to Steal"
—and Save Up to $100,000,* HarperCollins.

How to Protect Your Money from The People Who Protect The Places That Protect Your Money

Most of us who have accounts at banks or
savings-and-loan institutions know little about

Federal Deposit Insurance Corporation (FDIC) protection.

This lack of knowledge can be costly if your bank or savings-and-loan goes under—for part of your money may not be insured. Answers to the most common questions about FDIC coverage…

• *Are all banks and savings-and-loans protected by the FDIC?* Most banks are protected, but some private banks are not. Be sure to look for the FDIC label on your bank's door or at the tellers' windows.

• *Are all individual accounts covered separately by the FDIC? Up to how much?* Most people know that the FDIC covers individual accounts up to $100,000. What they don't know is that an individual account is determined by adding up each account held under a common name or Social Security number.

Example: If a person has a savings account with $50,000 in it and a certificate of deposit for $60,000 at the same bank, $10,000 is uninsured.

Accounts set up under the Uniform Gifts to Minors Act are considered to be the child's account, even though the parent has control over it.

• *What about joint accounts? Are they fully protected?* Joint accounts held by the same combination of persons at the same bank are only protected up to $100,000, regardless of whose Social Security number appears on them.

Example: A husband and wife with two joint accounts of $100,000 each are insured only up to $100,000, not $200,000.

Avoid this restriction by using both individual and joint accounts.

Example: If you have an individual savings account of $100,000 and a joint savings account with your spouse of $100,000 at the same bank, each account has full protection. Your spouse can have an individual savings account of $100,000 and receive full coverage on it as well.

• *Are all deposits covered by the FDIC?* Mutual funds and other investments made through a bank are not protected. If you have any questions concerning FDIC insurance, call the FDIC at 800-934-3342.

• *Are trust accounts treated separately by the FDIC?* Yes, but only if the trusts are for members of your immediate family—a spouse, child, or grandchild. But, if you set up an account in trust for your father, for example, it is treated as part of your account.

Trust accounts for a spouse, child, or grandchild (including step- and adopted children) enjoy separate coverage, even if you have both an individual and a joint account.

Example: If you have an individual account with $100,000, a joint account with your spouse of $100,000, and a trust account for your spouse of $100,000, the accounts are all fully insured.

• *Can an individual open accounts at several branches of the same bank and receive full protection for each?* You cannot increase the limit of coverage by depositing funds in different branches of the same bank.

Self-defense: Diversify your funds among several banks.

• *Are IRAs and Keoghs fully protected?* At the moment, each retirement account is treated separately from individual accounts and receives full coverage.

Example: If you have an individual account of $100,000, an IRA of $100,000, and a Keogh of $100,000 at the same bank, each account is fully insured.

Important: After December 19, 1993, IRA and Keogh accounts became lumped together for purposes of coverage limits. But transitional rules afford some protection for existing accounts.

Self-defense: As IRA or Keogh CDs mature, roll over sufficient amounts to other institutions to maximize FDIC coverage.

Source: Cody Buck, a former executive of the FDIC and author of *The ABCs of FDIC: How to Save Your Assets From Liquidation*, CoSTARR Publications.

Safer than Banks

Investors suffering from high anxiety are turning more and more to the safest investment there is: US Treasury securities.

Treasury bills (maturing within one year), notes (maturing in two to 10 years), and bonds (maturing after 10 years) are actually safer than government-insured bank accounts. *Trap:* There's only 1¢ in government insurance for every dollar of insured bank accounts. *Even worse:* Some of the insurance funds aren't in cash, but in illiquid receivables accepted from troubled banks.

By contrast, every penny of a T-bill is guaranteed by the full faith and credit of the federal government. And the government has never failed to pay its obligations.

Bonus: Liquidity, especially if they're purchased through a mutual fund that offers check-writing privileges. *Special tax status:* T-bills, notes, and bonds bought by individuals aren't subject to state income taxes. When these securities are purchased through a mutual fund, 25 of the 40 income-tax states levy a tax.

Source: James M. Benham, chairman, Benham Capital Management Group, 755 Page Mill Rd., Palo Alto, CA 94304.

How to Protect Yourself From Banks' New Services

Banks are offering an avalanche of "new" services that are just old services—repackaged. And, they are charging you for them.

Charges for some bank services have gone up 400% since the banking industry's deregulation in the mid-1980s.

How your bank may be squeezing you...

• Controlled dispersement services—your ability to transfer money electronically to cover checks. This used to take only a call to your bank. Now many banks charge customers $1 or more for these offsite transactions.

• Overdraft service. In the good old days, you could call your bank and ask to be notified if a check came in that your funds couldn't cover. Then, they would give you a chance to deposit money that day to cover the check.

Now, overdraft services cost consumers a hefty service fee—plus, if you have overdraft "protection," interest on the "borrowed" funds.

• Automatic Teller Machines (ATMs) used to be a free service—but now many banks charge 50 cents to $1 for each transaction.

• Calling in for balances—and a record of checks cashed. You once could call your friendly teller for this service, free of charge—but it now may be costly.

• Home-equity lines of credit are just repackaged second mortgages...with a bundle of additional service fees tacked on.

Self-defense...

When you shop for a bank—compare the fees on new services. Go with the bank that has the lowest fees for the services you use most ...and stay away from the routine use of ATMs.

Don't immediately opt for the checking and savings account packages that have a lot of services attached.

If you only write a few checks a month, ask the bank for its low-cost, minimum standard checking account. And if you're a student, or disabled or a senior citizen, ask for a service-charge-free checking account. Most banks make these available, although few promote this service.

Get to know your banker...

If you know your banker, go to the bank and ask him/her to phone you to let you know when an overdraft occurs—instead of paying for an overdraft "service." And, if you know your banker, you are much more likely to get a loan...be able to negotiate service charges, fees, and loan interest rates...or get a dispute with the bank solved quickly and favorably.

You should know at least one teller, a loan officer, and a vice-president at your bank. These are the people that can solve virtually every banking problem you encounter. I call this preventive maintenance.

Source: Ed F. Mrkvicka, Jr., author of *The Bank Book: How to Revoke Your Bank's License to Steal*, HarperCollins. He is also publisher of *Money Insider*, a financial newsletter for consumers, Reliance Enterprises, Inc., Box 413, Marengo, IL 60152.

Don't Pay Too Much

Nearly three out of four mortgage holders pay too much into escrow accounts—set up by lenders with a borrower's money to pay real-estate taxes and home-insurance costs. *Self-defense:* Check monthly payments carefully against copies of all tax and insurance bills. If what's due in taxes is less than the funds in escrow—seek a refund immediately. *Bottom line:* While you pay monthly, the lender might pay only quarterly—or even annually. Any funds held in escrow until those payments come due are the equivalent of giving the lender a no- or low-interest loan.

Source: Edward F. Mrkvicka, Jr., Reliance Enterprises, Inc., Box 413, Marengo, IL 60152.

Bank-Failure Loophole

If your bank fails and your deposits exceed $100,000 (the maximum amount insured by the FDIC), you can still use the uninsured portion to pay off any outstanding debt to the bank you may have. *Self-defense:* Request a "voluntary offset" from the bank's claims agent. *Example:* Someone with $120,000 in deposits and a $50,000 bank loan can ask that the $20,000 not covered by the FDIC be used to pay down the loan. *Rationale:* You probably won't see the $20,000 for some time, and when you do, you aren't likely to receive the full amount. Meanwhile, your debt would be reduced by the amount offset, dollar for dollar.

Source: Cody Buck, former senior executive of the FDIC's division of liquidation. He is author of *The ABCs of FDIC: How to Save Your Assets from Liquidation*, CoStarr Publications.

Bank Safe-Deposit-Box Trap

In effect, many banks don't insure safe-deposit boxes for theft. If there is insurance, it is very difficult to collect because you can't prove the box's contents. You could have a bank officer sign a safekeeping receipt each time you visit to confirm the contents...but this sacrifices your confidentiality and doesn't guarantee coverage. *Best:* A home safe. Models that exceed the fire safety of a bank vault cost less than $250 and losses are covered by your homeowner's insurance. List each item in a policy rider.

Source: Edward F. Mrkvicka, Jr., author of *The Bank Book: How to Revoke Your Bank's "License to Steal" and Save Up to $100,000*, HarperCollins.

ATM Self-Defense

Discarding your ATM receipt at the bank may help thieves loot your account. High-tech bandits are using video cameras to observe/record customers punching in ID numbers at teller machines. Then they match it to the account numbers on receipts left behind. *Self-defense:* Guard your PIN number...retain receipts to match up against monthly bank statements. If there's a withdrawal discrepancy, report it immediately to the bank.

Source: Edward F. Mrkvicka, Jr., financial consultant and former bank president, is author of *The Bank Book*, HarperCollins.

Beware of Bank IRAs

Retirement planning: One cannot overstate the importance of it. And...in investigating all of your Individual Retirement Account (IRA) options, I believe you'll find that a bank IRA is the least acceptable alternative.

In fact, a bank IRA could be the most unrewarding investment you ever make.

Some banks advertise how you can "easily" accumulate a million dollars in your IRA.

Unfortunately, a Government Accounting Office study revealed that if inflation continues at its historical pace, your million dollars may be worth, in buying power, only $50,000. In other words, you'll be lucky to get back exactly what you put in.

There are other investments that could return much more for your retirement—even if you have to pay taxes on them.

Problem: Banks like IRAs for one reason and one reason only—they are cheap money for the banks. Bank IRA interest rates are historically one to three percentage points below those of other market IRA vehicles available from brokers and mutual-fund families. In later years, when your IRA balance is substantial, that could mean tens of thousands of dollars in interest lost every year.

Bigger problem: The banks' below-market IRA interest rates can be even more unfavorable, depending on how the bank calculates interest. *Target:* Day-of-deposit-to-day-of-withdrawal, compounded and paid daily.

Under some plans, the bank also maintains the right to change the basis on which it pays interest, at its own discretion.

The insurance trap: Too many older investors say to me, "Never mind that I may be sacrificing some interest—at least I know that my retirement funds are insured by the full faith and credit of the US government."

For many years investors could have confidence in government insurance, at least up to the maximum insured limit—currently $100,000 (IRA balances in excess of $100,000 are not insured). But in the past 10 years, everything has changed.

We should have learned from the savings-and-loan disaster about the questionable value of government-backed deposit insurance. The Federal Deposit Insurance Corporation (FDIC) is severely stretched now because there have been so many bank failures. Over a hundred commercial banks have been failing each year—the government insurance fund can't keep bailing banks out forever. Recent giant bank mergers are a "solution" that is just buying time.

Sooner or later there will be failures of major money-center banks—banks that have been getting away with privatizing their profits—and socializing their losses by claiming they're "too big to fail."

As with the savings-and-loan bailout, this means that US taxpayers—you and I—are paying for those bank losses caused by illegal behavior, greed, incompetent regulatory agencies, and a Congress that looks the other way.

Don't invest in a bank IRA because of bank insurance that is coming right out of your pocket.

Source: Ed F. Mrkvicka, Jr., author of *The Bank Book: How to Revoke Your Bank's License to Steal*, HarperCollins. He is also publisher of *Money Insider*, a financial newsletter for consumers, Reliance Enterprises, Inc., Box 413, Marengo, IL.

Cosigner's Trap

To obtain credit for their children, parents often cosign credit cards or other loans for them. But parents should be aware that creditors in most states are not required to notify cosigners when a borrower exceeds a credit limit or falls behind on loan payments. So a cosigning parent can become liable for overdue payments and penalties without ever knowing there is a problem. The parent's credit rating may be harmed as well. *Defense:* If you cosign a child's borrowings, monitor payments and monthly statements closely. *Better:* Consider having the child cosign *your* credit card. That way, the child will have access to the credit line and build a credit history while monthly statements come directly to you.

Source: Gerri Detweiler, consumer advocate and author of *The Ultimate Credit Handbook*, Good Advice Press.

Auto Financing

Those who have to take out a five-year car loan in order to afford the payments probably can't afford the car.

Better: A less expensive model that can be paid off in three or four years.

Source: *The Guide to Managing Credit: How to Stretch Your Dollars Through Wise Credit Management* by David L. Scott, PhD, professor of accounting and finance, Valdosta State University, Georgia. The Globe Pequot Press.

Instant Mortgage Approvals

Instant mortgage approvals with lower fees will soon be available through a computerized application process being tested by the Federal Home Loan Mortgage Corporation. *How:* The application is entered into a computer that electronically checks the applicant's files at all major credit agencies, evaluates the applicant's risk, assesses appraisal data on the property to be bought and gives a *yes* or *no* in two to four minutes. Also, loan funds are made available in two to five days. Appraisal charges, title search and insurance costs are expected to be cut, as are credit report fees.

Source: Peter Maselli, vice president for automated underwriting, Federal Home Loan Mortgage Corporation, McLean, VA.

Smarter Home Loans

You'll find that when applying for a home-equity loan, home appraisals are almost always lower than the *market-value* appraisal of a home. The bank does this for protection in case of a default on the loan. If you want a larger loan than the original appraisal would allow, there is recourse. Have your home independently appraised—this can usually be done through a real estate agent. Ask for a *Comparative Market Analysis,* which reports on your home in relation to others in your area, and for an estimate of your home's fair market value. Then call the bank with the new information and ask it to reconsider. If the bank is still uncooperative, go to a new bank with your appraisal. The second bank will likely be more flexible than the first because its appraiser won't feel comfortable deviating

greatly from the information you provided prior to his appraisal.

Source: Edward F. Mrkvicka, Jr., president, Reliance Enterprises, a financial consulting firm in Marengo, IL, and author of *The Bank Book.* HarperCollins.

Fight Rising Bank Fees

To fight rising bank fees, inquire about getting a "linked" account that combines balances of both checking and savings accounts when figuring daily balances…inquire about a no-frills account—often available to those who limit check writing to *no more than* 10 checks per month…ask for fee waivers when paychecks are directly deposited and/or you opt for a monthly summary of your paid checks, rather than receiving back the canceled checks …read any insert that comes with your monthly bank statement—this is where fee hikes are first announced.

Source: Chris Lewis, director, Banking and Housing Policy for the Consumer Federation of America, Washington, DC.

Credit Card Smarts

Competition has become so hot in the credit card business that it is foolish to pay 18% interest—or an annual fee. Many card issuers now charge 12% for conventional cards (purchases only, not advances)—and a few credit cards are under 8%. AT&T's Universal card stimulated the no-annual-fee trend, and new cards introduced since then have gone beyond no fees to offering users extra incentives such as free air travel, gas-purchase rebates and credits toward the purchase of a new car.

Source: Robert Heady, publisher, *Bank Rate Monitor,* Box 088888, N. Palm Beach, FL 33408.

5

Estate Planning Strategies

Pass Your IRA on to Your Heirs

Most people leave their Individual Retirement Accounts (IRAs) to their spouse. But if your spouse is adequately provided for, you may want to leave some or all of your IRA money to your children or grandchildren. You get the greatest mileage from an IRA that you leave to your grandchildren, or other beneficiaries who are much younger than you. *Benefits of leaving an IRA to a grandchild...*

•The IRA will continue for a long period of time—50, 60, or even 70 years, depending on the grandchild's age and the payout method selected.

•IRA earnings will accumulate on a tax-deferred basis for that period of time. This can add hundreds of thousands of dollars to an IRA.

•There's a substantial income-tax saving in leaving money to a low-bracket grandchild rather than to a spouse. A spouse will pay income tax on IRA payouts at the 31% rate or more. But once a grandchild reaches age 14, income is taxed at his/her rate, not the parents'.

•There's an estate-tax saving. The IRA assets and their growth over the years will not be included in your spouse's estate.

•The IRA assets avoid probate.

Caution: The most you can give to your grandchildren is $1 million. After that, gifts to grandchildren are subject to the generation-skipping tax, which is a 55% tax on gifts that pass over a generation of heirs—usually the parents' generation.

Problem: Few professionals know how to keep an IRA alive for a person's grandchildren. Some consultants may advise nonspouse beneficiaries to take all the money and pay tax on it the year after the account holder dies.

Solution: Understand how IRA distribution rules work. Do the paperwork now to keep the IRA alive long after you are gone.

Distribution rules...

IRA owners are required to begin taking money out of their account by April 1 of the year after they reach age 70½. But the distribution rules for beneficiaries are different.

• If you die before reaching your required beginning date, which is April 1 after the calendar year in which you attain age 70½, and you've named a grandchild as beneficiary, your grandchild has two options...

• *Option 1:* Take all the money in the account by the end of the year following the fifth anniversary of your death, or

• *Option 2:* Begin taking annual distributions based on his/her life expectancy in the year following your death. *Example:* A grandchild who was 20 at this time would have a life expectancy of 61 years. To satisfy the minimum distribution rules for IRAs, he/she would have to take only ⅟₆₁ out of the IRA in the first year. If there was $200,000 in the IRA at the end of the year in which you died, the required distribution would be $3,278.69 (⅟₆₁ of $200,000). The IRA would continue for another 60 years.

To use the life expectancy method (option 2), your grandchild or his trustee will have to file a written election with the IRA institution by no later than December 31 of the year after the year you die, saying the IRA money is to be paid out over the grandchild's life expectancy —61 years in the above example. Payments from the IRA must commence no later than December 31 of the year after you die.

If these requirements aren't met, your grandchild will default into option 1, and all the money in the IRA will have to be paid out to your grandchild five years after your death.

• If you reach your required beginning date, the rules are different. You must begin taking money from the IRA by April 1 of the year following the year you reach 70½. The amount you withdraw each year can be based on the joint life expectancy of you and your beneficiary.

If your beneficiary is your grandchild and he is more than 10 years younger than you, the withdrawals must be based on what is called the Minimum Distribution Incidental Benefit (MDIB) table that is found in *IRS Publication 590, Indi-*

vidual Retirement Arrangements, in Appendix E. The table calculates the withdrawals as if your beneficiary were only 10 years younger than you. This is required by the tax law.

Example: You are 71 and your grandchild, your beneficiary, is 12 in the year you attain age 70½. (If you are born in the first half of the year, you are 70 instead of 71.) Your joint life expectancy is 69.8 years. But the MDIB tables say you must use 25.3 years and take out ⅟₂₅.₃ as your first withdrawal. Each year thereafter, the period is adjusted based upon the MDIB table.

Surprising: When you die, your beneficiary can pick up the original joint life expectancy— 69.8 years in the above example minus the number of annual withdrawals that have been made—to calculate future annual withdrawals. The MDIB tables have to be used only while you're alive.

Example: You die at 74 after taking out four annual payments. Your grandchild would be able to withdraw the remaining money over 65.8 years, starting the next year (your joint life expectancy of 69.8 years minus the four years you've taken money out).

Letter to your IRA custodian: To make this all perfectly clear, you should write a letter to your IRA custodian spelling out the distribution methods you're using...

"I hereby elect to take the money out of my IRA based on my life expectancy and my grandchild's life expectancy determined in the year I attained age 70½. (69.8 years in the above example.) However, while I'm alive, the MDIB rule is operative and that table shall be used. Upon my death, payouts shall be based on the original joint life expectancy of me and my grandchild, reduced by all years that have passed since I was 70½."

Trust required...

If your grandchild is a minor, you'll need an irrevocable trust for the benefit of your grandchild to handle the money being paid from the IRA. You can name a family member as trustee.

Bank accounts: On the death of the grandfather, the trustee would open up a bank account in the name of the trust. He/she would also open a custodial account for the grandchild at a bank or brokerage firm.

The trust says that money goes from the IRA to the trust, and then from the trust to the custodial account, until the grandchild reaches the age of majority—18 or 21, depending on state law. After your grandchild turns 21, the money goes directly to him. Under appropriate circumstances, the custodian could use the money to pay your grandchild's college expenses.

There's no tax to the trust because the money is going right out—the trust is just a conduit. The money is taxed to the grandchild, but at the grandchild's tax rates.

One of the advantages of having a trust is that the assets will be protected from the child's creditors, should the child have an accident or become involved in other legal problems—such as bankruptcy, divorce, etc.

Note: The fact that the trust is irrevocable doesn't mean that you can't change beneficiaries if circumstances dictate a change. You can make beneficiary substitutions until you die.

Best: A separate trust for each grandchild to whom you leave IRA money. *Cost:* $3,500 to set up the trust (or multiple trusts for a number of grandchildren) and an annual fee of $200 or $300 to prepare and file tax returns for the trust after you die.

Practical use: This is a good way to develop a college fund for a grandchild at low tax cost.

Source: Seymour Goldberg, professor of law and taxation at Long Island University and senior partner in the law firm of Goldberg & Ingber, 666 Old Country Rd., Garden City, NY 11530. Mr. Goldberg is the author of *A Professional's Guide to the IRS Distribution Rules*, Field Services, New York State Society of Certified Public Accountants, 200 Park Ave., New York 10166. 212-973-8373.

Who Is the Spendthrift?

A grantor may not be concerned so much that his son or daughter has spendthrift tendencies, but that this person's spouse is the one who is likely to be wildly extravagant or gullible. The grantor may provide that anything he gives or leaves to his son or daughter is to be in the form of a life income from a trust, so that the principal cannot get into the hands of the spouse. The remainderman or remaindermen will be specified as the grantor sees fit—often the grandchildren are named, rather than the prodigal spouse.

How to Avoid the Naming Of an Administrator

To ensure that an executor of your selection will serve, this is what you should do:

1. Sound out your designated executor to see whether he will actually serve if named in your will. Do this periodically. Is his health still satisfactory? Has he taken on full-time responsibilities elsewhere? Is he still interested in you and your beneficiaries? If not, replace him.

2. Seek to ensure your designated executor's agreement to serve by recommending to him knowledgeable and able attorneys, accountants, and (where appropriate) appraisers and brokers who can help him to carry out his responsibilities without excessive detail work with which he isn't familiar.

3. Name one or more successor or contingent executors, so that if the person of your choice doesn't serve, at least it will be your second or third choice, rather than an administrator that you would never have engaged.

4. Name a trust company as co-executor. This virtually assures the permanence and continuity of an executor you have seen fit to name.

5. Make certain that your will is valid so that the executor chosen by you will qualify. Have an attorney familiar with state law check such requirements as the minimum number of witnesses required. State laws vary as to the technicalities to be met.

6. Be sure that your will can be found when the time comes to have it probated. A perfectly executed and technically correct will is useless if nobody knows where it is. Have your will in your attorney's office, or with your federal income tax workpapers.

Source: *Encyclopedia of Estate Planning*, Boardroom Books, Greenwich, CT 06830.

Using Disclaimers to Save Estate Taxes

Despite the way it seems in the movies, the instructions in a person's will are not necessarily the last word on how assets are distributed.

After death, those named in the will can alter a decedent's estate plans—and save taxes—by filing what is known as a disclaimer.

A disclaimer is a legal document in which a person refuses to accept some or all of the benefits that result from a decedent's death.

The heir making the disclaimer cannot say who will inherit in his/her place. Under the terms of the will, the property passes as if that heir had died before the decedent.

Example: A decedent's will leaves $1 million to his adult child who is already wealthy and planning his/her own estate. The adult child does not wish to add to his estate these additional funds, so he executes a disclaimer refusing to accept the bequest. The disclaimed amount passes, as if the child had predeceased his father, to the grandchildren or other beneficiaries named in the father's will. If the disclaimer is properly executed, there will be no additional gift or estate tax.

Trap: A disclaimer must be signed within nine months of a decedent's death. Failure to act promptly can mean that the person disclaiming will be treated as making a gift, subject to gift tax, to the person who inherits as a result of the disclaimer.

Caution: Before signing a disclaimer, check to see who will inherit under the terms of the will as a result of the disclaimer. Make sure the property does not pass to someone who might not benefit from the disclaimer, such as a relative in a nursing home who is on Medicaid and can't own any property.

A disclaimer is an important after-death estate-planning tool since it is, in effect, a second chance to rework a decedent's will. This does not necessarily mean that the will is faulty. It can simply mean that since making the will, tax laws or family economic circumstances have changed.

There are certain key situations in which to consider using a disclaimer:

• To save taxes. Suppose a will provides that all property is to go directly to a surviving spouse. There will be no tax in the first estate because of the unlimited marital deduction. But the survivor's estate will be taxable. Tax in the survivor's estate could have been reduced had the decedent left $600,000 worth of property to persons other than the survivor. The survivor can, in effect, create this tax break by disclaiming up to $600,000 worth of benefits provided under the will. This $600,000 will then pass to other beneficiaries. It will be tax-exempt because of the $600,000 exemption every estate is entitled to. *Impact:* Less tax on the death of the surviving spouse.

• To bring a pre-1981 will up to date. Some married couples may not have redone their wills since the laws on the marital deduction where changed in 1981 to allow an unlimited amount of property to pass to a spouse tax-free.

Their wills may still specify that only 50% of the estate go to the surviving spouse, with the balance in trust. That trust may provide for other beneficiaries besides the surviving spouse and would not be eligible for the marital deduction. If those other beneficiaries disclaim, it may be possible to have the trust qualify for the marital deduction. *Impact:* Less tax on the death of the first spouse.

The use of disclaimers is not necessarily limited to property passing under a will. Disclaimers can be applied to assets that pass automatically as a result of the decedent's death. For example, an individual can disclaim the inheritance of an IRA or other pension benefits.

When making a will, keep in mind the possibility of an heir disclaiming. Check that the "fall-back position," the terms that apply if the named beneficiaries are out of the picture, are conducive to disclaiming.

Example: A grandfather with successful children may not want to disinherit them. But the grandfather should be mindful of the fact that the children may choose to disclaim in order to avoid additions to their own estates. If the grandfather's will provides that bequests to minors will be distributed outright at age 18 or even 21, the children may be reluctant to disclaim for fear that their children will dissipate the property. On the other hand, if the grandfather's will provides an extensive trust arrangement for minors with distributions spread out to age 35 or 40, the children can disclaim without worry.

Source: David S. Rhine, tax partner, BDO Seidman, 15 Columbus Circle, New York 10023.

Is It Worthwhile to Avoid Probate?

It's possible to avoid probate for a good portion of your estate by establishing a living trust …or a revocable trust that directs how your assets will be managed and administered after your death.

But is a trust worth the effort?

Advantages of trusts…

•Cost savings. You may save probate fees, which in some states are a percentage of an estate's total value. You also save court costs and attorney's and accountant's fees which may be incurred in probate court.

•Privacy. Court records of probate proceedings are public. But the terms of a trust are private.

•Protection. Trusts generally are tougher to challenge than wills. Trusts aren't frozen during a probate period, so the trustee can distribute assets immediately, making it more difficult for a disgruntled heir to raise a challenge.

Drawbacks to trusts…

•You still need a will. It's unlikely you'll be able to handle all your assets through a trust. And you'll need a will to handle any unforeseen contingencies that might arise. A will is also necessary to name a guardian for your minor children.

•Cost. In addition to the cost of drawing up the trust, you'll have to pay annual trustee fees.

•Estate taxes. You do not save estate taxes by avoiding probate. Your estate-tax bill will be the same whether you use a trust or a will.

•Income tax. While you're alive, having a trust will not save you any income tax. After your death, it's beneficial to have your property pass under your will rather than through a trust. Estates, but not trusts, can pick a beneficial tax year for as long as the estate is in the administration process. Additionally, an estate can continue to deduct, for the first two years, $25,000 of real-estate passive-activity losses. A trust can't.

Source: David S. Rhine, partner, BDO Seidman, 15 Columbus Circle, New York 10023. He specializes in estate planning.

Leaving-the-Company Trap

If you take the money out of your firm's tax-sheltered 401(k), you will owe taxes on everything except the after-tax contributions.

To preserve tax benefits: Leave the money in your former firm's plans, if permitted…or transfer it to the 401(k) of your new employer…or set up a rollover IRA. *Caution:* With the IRA option, have funds transferred directly to the rollover account.

If you take the money out and personally roll it over, 20% will be withheld under IRS rules.

Source: David Ellis, editor, *Tax Hotline*, 55 Railroad Ave., Greenwich, CT 06830.

Liquidating Your Business

Distributions in excess of your original cost are subject to capital gains tax.

Loophole: If you are near retirement, consider selling the operating assets of the business at book value, but keep the corporation intact as a personal holding company. Do not distribute the cash from the sale, but keep it in the corporation, invested in tax-exempt municipal bonds. When you die, the assets will pass to your heirs at their stepped-up, date-of-death value, and income tax on any gain will be avoided.

Source: Edward Mendlowitz, partner, Mendlowitz Weitsen CPAs, Two Pennsylvania Plaza, New York 10121.

Lump-Sum Distributions

Most of my clients first come to me because they've just received their lump-sum distributions. These distributions are one-time cash payments that many people receive from their former employers in lieu of monthly pension checks upon retirement. For most of these people, these lump-sum distributions represent the largest single amount of money they have ever received.

Problem: Too often, people who receive these distributions don't handle this money correctly. They squander the money on expensive cars and extravagant vacations, at the gaming tables, make bad investments that gobble up their retirement nest eggs...or they retire too soon and don't have enough money to support themselves during their golden years.

The most common mistakes...

Mistake: Taking a lump-sum distribution when you shouldn't. There are many advantages that a lump sum offers—most importantly, the opportunity to create a new source of wealth that you can leave to your family. But receiving a lump sum also makes your financial life more complicated...

• You must make decisions on investment and tax matters.

• You must deal with investment risk and, in many cases, rely on other people—a financial planner or an accountant, for example—for help.

If you are a poor money manager or are heavily in debt, you should probably take your pension in the form of an annuity. By doing this, you will receive a piece of the pension each month.

Mistake: Not planning your retirement before planning your lump-sum investments. Most people are so dazzled by the size of the lump-sum distributions that they focus on how much money they will earn. Instead, you need to first deal with some important issues...

• Where you are going to live during your retirement years.

• Whether you're going to work part-time, start a business or take it easy.

• Whether you're going to travel or buy that boat you've always wanted.

Lifestyle decisions should come before investment decisions.

Mistake: Not knowing your tax position. The biggest single obstacle to preserving your distribution and watching it grow is taxes—not investments.

Many people will rake themselves and their advisers over the coals because of a $3,000 investment loss. Yet these same people are often unaware that poor planning could cost them hundreds of thousands of dollars in unnecessary taxes.

Trap I: If you roll over the lump sum into an IRA but fail to start taking large enough withdrawals after age 70½, you face a 50% penalty on the amount you should have withdrawn but didn't.

Trap II: If you begin withdrawals before age 59½, you face a 10% early withdrawal penalty, unless you structure the payout properly.

Trap III: If your withdrawals are large and exceed a certain threshold, you are subject to a 15% excess-distribution penalty—and your heirs may face estate tax problems after you die.

The larger the lump sum, the more important it is that you consult a financial planner or an accountant who can help you preserve your newfound wealth.

Mistake: Reaching for the reward without considering the risk. People constantly ask me, *How have your investment returns been over the past year or two?* Then they compare those numbers with various benchmarks.

This is a dangerous strategy because the comparison is always made to yesterday's winners. People who ask instead, *How do you manage risk?* will always fare better.

Key: The best way to approach investing your lump sum is to look first at risk and then at reward.

Example: If a client comes in with a $400,000 lump sum, I'll ask how he/she would feel if he lost $40,000 in the stock market during the first year. If the client squirms and flinches, I know that investing in the market is not for him.

But if he acts unconcerned and says he's in the market for the long term and has lost that much—and more—before, I know I'm safe taking a more aggressive investment stance.

Mistake: Avoiding risk without considering lower returns. Some people are so afraid of losing even one penny of their lump sum that they opt for totally riskless investments. These investments have much lower yields than do comparable investments that carry very little risk. Therefore, these people are needlessly sacrificing their earning power because of the risk.

Example: Instead of buying 10-year AAA corporate bonds that yield nearly 8% and have very little downside risk, they buy 10-year Treasury notes that yield only 7% and miss the extra income.

Mistake: Not considering the impact of inflation. After taxes, nothing chews up a lump sum faster than the rising cost of living—otherwise known as inflation.

Over the past two decades, annual inflation has averaged 5.9%. But even a modest 3% or 4% annual inflation rate can erode a nest egg.

Example: Over 10 years, a 4% annual inflation rate can whittle down the value of a $100,000 lump-sum distribution to about $66,500. Over 15 years, a 6% annual inflation rate can reduce the value of the lump sum to less than $40,000.

Mistake: Not planning your estate. Typically, the mere act of receiving a lump sum of money can create an estate tax problem.

Reason: The lump sum swells the value of your estate—which previously may not have been large enough to trigger federal estate taxes. Your heirs must now worry about how much the government will take after your death.

Example: Take the case of someone who has $600,000 in assets from the family house and some investments. This amount would not be subject to federal estate tax. But if the person now receives a $400,000 lump-sum distribution, the value of that individual's estate increases to $1 million. After the person's death and the death of his/her spouse, estate taxes could amount to as much as $200,000.

Solution: Create a trust, especially if the assets will pass to a beneficiary who is not capable of handling large sums of money.

Mistake: Not reevaluating your retirement plan regularly. Most people find the whole process of creating a plan for their retirement years so difficult that they never want to discuss the topic again. It is just too stressful. But everyone needs to give their retirement plans annual checkups.

Circumstances can change. You may be widowed, divorced or remarried. You may have sold your family home in the snowy North and replaced it with a condominium in the balmy South. Your holdings may have tripled in value—or declined by 50%.

All of these changes can affect your finances. It's always better to proceed from a vantage point of knowledge rather than from ignorance. By periodically monitoring your retirement plan, you may discover that you're needlessly skimping...or find that it's easy to make your expenses match your income by making a few modest adjustments.

Mistake: Not enjoying some of the money from your lump-sum distribution. I find that the older people get, the more they tend to hoard money, even if they have plenty of it. They seem to develop an increasing sense of financial insecurity.

I tell my clients who are already in their 60s to enjoy themselves—that now is the time to celebrate their lifetime of hard work and achievements.

The point is that if you've got the financial resources, you should relax and have a good time while you are in your 60s. You should take that big vacation you've always dreamed of and let yourself enjoy some of the luxuries you denied yourself previously.

If you wait, you may never have the opportunity to do so again.

Source: Anthony Gallea, senior vice president and portfolio manager with Smith Barney, 71 Monroe Ave., Pittsford, NY 14534. He is author of *The Lump Sum Handbook: Investment and Tax Strategies for a Secure Retirement*, Prentice Hall.

Durable Power Of Attorney

A durable power of attorney gives a trusted adviser the power to handle your financial affairs during any period in which you are incapacitated. *Important:* The power of attorney should include *specific authority* for that person to deal with the Internal Revenue Service on your behalf. This is often overlooked but may prove vital if your adviser must take responsibility for your tax affairs.

Source: Martin M. Shenkman, attorney, New York.

Better Estate Planning

To ensure that your estate's taxes will be as low as possible, add a sentence to your *durable power of attorney* authorizing the person who will handle your affairs if you become incapacitated to make gifts on your behalf. Without this, the Internal Revenue Service may ignore the gifts made by your designee—and tax them as part of your estate upon your death. *Important:* You can also specify who is to receive the gifts.

Source: Michael Insel, partner and the head of the trust and estate department at the New York City law firm of Kelley Drye & Warren, 101 Park Ave., New York 10178.

6

Insurance Information

How to Get Your Health Insurance Company to Pay Up

Don't give up if you have trouble getting a fair claims settlement from your health insurance company. There are a number of steps you can take to fight the insurer's decision to refuse your claim.

First: Resubmit another medical insurance claim form about 30 days after the refusal. Very often, a company randomly denies a claim... and just as randomly approves the same claim when it comes in again. It does no harm to try for reimbursement of a doctor's bill by submitting your insurance forms a second time.

Second: If that does not work, contact the insurer and request, in writing, a full explanation of the refusal to pay. Sometimes the denial-of-benefits statement is filled with numeric or alphabetic codes that are undecipherable by a layperson. Request a clear explanation. There should be no ambiguity as to why a health insurer will not pay the benefits that you think are called for in the contract.

Third: Once you are given the insurance company's rationale for turning you down, you have a couple of other weapons in your arsenal...

...the insurer cannot give you an alternative reason for the refusal after you refute the initial one.

...when the refusal is based on a rule against paying for experimental treatment, you can marshal evidence from your doctor and others that the treatment was, in fact, the treatment of choice—and therefore should be covered by the policy.

Fourth: If it becomes necessary to appeal, start within the company. Write directly to the president—whose name can be found in insurance directories at your local library...or call the company and ask.

Enclose copies of all relevant documents... claims forms, medical receipts, responses from the insurer, notes of telephone conversations and any backup materials.

Caution: Never send any originals, since you may need them for future action.

Fifth: If you get nowhere at the company level, write to your State Insurance Department. Every state now has a section set up to assist consumers with complaints. You can reach them by checking directory assistance for a toll-free number.

With the correct department and address, again mail copies of the relevant documents and ask for a response. The Insurance Department won't take your side in every dispute, but it can obtain an answer from your insurance company in situations where you have been stonewalled or treated unfairly.

Ultimate weapon: File a suit against the insurer in Small Claims Court, or in a regular court if the amount at stake is too large to be handled by the Small Claims Court. If you go to regular court you'll need a lawyer, preferably one who takes the case on a contingency basis, where the fee is a percentage of what you recover. You can handle a small claims case yourself. If the insurer's behavior is particularly abusive, you may be able to collect punitive damages from such a suit.

Real case: A man was conned into trading in his health policy for another on the basis that the second policy was substantially improved. Yet when he filed a claim, he found the new policy paid 40% less in benefits than the old one. He sued the insurance company for fraud …and wound up collecting over $1 million in punitive damages.

Bottom line…

Carefully review your policy before filing claims for illness or injury.

Go to your corporate benefits manager or insurance agent with any questions about coverage and costs. By knowing exactly what you can expect from your policy, you won't be surprised when the reimbursement check arrives. And in the event that the insurer sends you the wrong amount, you will be ready to take whatever action is necessary to obtain the money you deserve.

Source: Robert Hunter, former president, National Insurance Consumer Organization, Box 15492, Alexandria, VA 22309.

Protect Yourself From Your Insurance Company

What is this world coming to? Institutions that we were taught to trust implicitly have broken their solemn promises and squandered our hard-earned money.

So far, six major life insurance companies have failed, and in most cases customers with annuities or whole-life policies have been unable to withdraw the full value of their policies.

Even when a failed insurer is on the mend, as in the case of Executive Life of California and Mutual Benefit Life, policyholders have few rights.

Though both companies are currently in rehabilitation and are meeting the majority of their contractual obligations, the courts have prohibited customers from transferring money to stronger companies, taking out policy loans, or cashing in policies until further notice.

Both are expected to agree in principal to pay about 55 cents on the dollar to policyholders who want their money now. Settlements on the full amount, however, are not final and there is no firm date yet for distribution. *The new challenge:* Know what happens if your insurer fails—and what you can do now—to protect yourself.

Not at risk…

•Variable annuities and variable life policies. Policyholders with these investments at any insurer are never denied access to annuities or the full benefits of their polices as promised, even if the insurer fails.

Reason: Your money is never commingled with the general account of the life-insurance company. Instead, it is invested in separate accounts, which are not available to the insurer's creditors.

•Death benefits. It is the avowed intention of the insurer and/or its regulators and rehabilitators to pay death benefits in full.

What is at risk, however, is your access to and the eventual return of the full cash value of your policy while you're still alive.

What about state guarantee funds?

These are funds set up by the states to protect policyholders when life insurers fail.

In the case of Mutual Benefit Life and Executive Life, most state guarantee funds are taking the position that they are not obligated to make up the principal losses of policyholders who accept the early settlement offers.

Example I: Colorado will pay nothing to policyholders of these insurance companies because it says they were in trouble before the state established its guarantee association in 1991.

Example II: In Minnesota, the state guarantee association agreed to make up the shortfall but won't pay out, however, until the insurance companies' final settlement, which could come in five to seven years or more.

What you can do...

If your insurer fails, consult with your insurance agent, accountant, lawyer, and/or financial planner to fully understand your options and determine the following...

•If you have taken out loans against the policy over the years, how much cash value is left in the policy?

•Will you be able to qualify for a new life-insurance policy?

•Do you still need the full insurance-policy coverage or do you need even more?

Do not pay the insurer any new money. Instead, take out an automatic premium loan from the company against the cash value of your policy. Use it to pay the interest or principal payments on policy loans and/or premium payments. In most cases it won't significantly erode your death benefits.

Executive Life or Mutual Benefit Life Policyholders: Be wary of an offer of a cash discount for cash payments. It's unlikely to be worth it. Remember, you'll only get about 55 cents on the dollar now, while it may take years before you get the full value of your policy. You are dealing with insurers that have failed to keep their promises and are financially impaired. Treat them suspiciously.

If you are insurable elsewhere...

If you qualify, apply for a hardship withdrawal from the failed insurer. *You may qualify if...*

•You can prove the money is needed for college tuition bills.

•You are permanently disabled or have a terminal illness.

•You have medical bills but no health insurance.

•You are being evicted from a hospital or nursing home.

That way you will get 100 cents on the dollar rather than 55 cents on the dollar for the amount you withdraw. If you win a hardship agreement, you'll receive up to $30,000 at Executive Life, and up to $50,000 at Mutual Benefit Life.

Though the criteria are extremely demanding, especially at Executive Life, thousands of hardship cases have been granted.

Call the companies for details on their policies on hardship withdrawals. Mutual Benefit Life/800-821-7887, Executive Life of California/800-444-3542.

If you are denied a hardship withdrawal, take the early-settlement deal, file a claim with the state guarantee fund, hope you don't have to sue to get paid, and get on with your life.

The next step...

When you buy new insurance, investigate no-load and low-load insurance policies—as well as full-loaded insurance for the best buy. And be choosy. Buy new insurance only from strong companies rated C+ or above by Weiss Research (800) 289-9222.

It's also important to diversify. Don't put all your eggs in what may very well turn out to be one surprisingly fragile basket. Where practical, spread your total insurance needs among a few strong companies.

If you are uninsurable...

Review your current needs for life insurance. If they are less than they were originally, you may want to reduce the size of your insurance benefits so the money you have already paid will cover the policy.

Important: If you don't have enough cash value, do not stop making payments, which would cause your policy to lapse. While you may not have immediate access to the cash value at 100 cents on the dollar, you are still insured. Remember why you bought the policy in the first place.

Source: William E. Donoghue, publisher of *Donoghue's MONEYLETTER* and the new audiocassette service Money-Talk.

Life Insurance If You Can't Pass a Physical

Can't pass the life insurance physical? Don't give up—there may be a way.

Find an agent who knows his way with insurance companies. Their standards vary on overweight, blood pressure, smoking, and other medical conditions. *Example:* Six-foot middle-aged man weighing 270—many companies would add a big surcharge premium for his age. But one company will insure him with no surcharge at all.

The agent's job is to find the exceptional company and know how to present the application in the most favorable light. Few agents do this well. You've got to insist the agent shop for you.

If an individual policy isn't available (or only at very high cost), group policies can be found in clubs, fraternal orders, religious orders, volunteer firemen. It may pay to join a club just for the group insurance. The saving on the premium is usually more than the dues.

Source: Frank J. Crisona, attorney and principal of the Crisona Agency, Box 130, Carle Place, NY 11514.

Medicare: What It Doesn't Cover

Don't fool yourself that all your old-age medical needs will be taken care of by Medicare. This program is riddled with coverage gaps. Be aware of what not to expect from Medicare.

What is Medicare?

Medicare must be distinguished from Medicaid, which is the federal program providing medical coverage for the indigent of all ages. Most elderly people wind up on Medicaid when their assets are exhausted paying for what Medicare doesn't cover. This can be a tragedy for people who had hoped to leave something to their children.

Medicare is an insurance program for people over 65. It is subsidized by the federal government through the Social Security Administration. Each month, elderly people pay premiums to private insurance companies (Blue Cross/Blue Shield or companies like them), which act as fiscal intermediaries for Medicare. The program is overseen by a watchdog agency, Professional Standards Review Organization (PSRO), which makes sure hospitals are not used improperly. *Drawbacks:* Private insurance companies, acting in their own best interests, tend to deny benefits whenever possible. PSRO interprets Medicare regulations restrictively, since they must save government money.

Major problems with Medicare...

• Congress passed much of the Medicare legislation with the intention of helping the elderly by keeping them out of institutions. However, the local agencies administer Medicare restrictively in a misguided attempt to save money. Actually, money is being wasted by forcing the elderly into nursing homes unnecessarily. *Result:* Benefits we thought would go to the elderly simply don't materialize.

• Medicare does not deal with the problem of custodial care. It is geared toward rehabilitation, which is hardly realistic for the population it serves.

• Medicare is part of an overall supply-and-demand problem. There are simply more and more old people every year, as modern medicine enables us to live longer. While the over-65 population expands, nursing homes are filled to capacity and have long waiting lists, and Social Security benefits and services to the elderly are being cut back. *Fear for the future:* Some see the frightening possibility that euthanasia may be discussed.

Hospital cutoffs...

Hospital cutoffs are the biggest problem with Medicare today. *Example:* An elderly woman goes into the hospital with a broken hip. After surgery, she cannot go home because she can't take care of herself. She needs nursing-home rehabilitation or an around-the-clock companion at home. Because of the shortage of these long-term-care alternatives, she has to remain in the hospital, though everyone agrees she is ready to leave. But Medicare cuts off hospitalization benefits, claiming that she no longer needs hospitalization. The family gets a threatening letter from the hospital—if she isn't out in 24 hours, the family will have to pay privately. At approximately $300 per day for a hospital bed, the family's assets will be wiped out very quickly.

The appeal process...

The only way to deal with such unfair (and inhumane) bureaucratic decisions is to appeal them aggressively. Appeal is a long and costly process, but a $300-per-day hospital bill is even more costly. Also, as good citizens, we must make our government accountable for benefits promised but not delivered.

Chances on appeal: Very good. At the highest level, Federal Court, the reversal rate on Medicare cases is extremely high.

There are four levels of appeal:

• *Reconsideration* is a paper review by a bureaucrat. You can request this when Medicare is first denied. Some 95% of reconsiderations confirm the original denial of benefits.

• An *administrative law judge* will review the case after the reconsideration is denied. You present evidence at this hearing, and a lawyer is recommended. Some of these judges are competent and sympathetic. However, many judges fail to understand the issue.

• The *Appeals Council* in Washington is the next step. They will usually rubber-stamp the decision of the administrative law judge.

• *Federal Court* is your final crack. You do stand a good chance of winning here because judges at the federal level are not employees of the Social Security Administration. They tend to be less sympathetic to the agency's viewpoint.

At this level, a lawyer is necessary. *Important:* No new evidence can be presented in Federal Court, so be sure all your facts are presented to the administrative law judge.

Medicare and nursing homes...

Under the law, up to 100 days of skilled nursing care in a nursing home are to be paid for by Medicare. In fact, Medicare pays for an average of only five days, claiming that nursing homes do not provide skilled care. This is another patently unfair decision that must be appealed on an individual basis.

Beyond 100 days, you're on your own as far as nursing-home care is concerned. Medicaid will take over only after your assets are totally exhausted. At an average cost of $30,000 per year, few families can afford long-term nursing-home care. *Important:* Plan ahead for this possibility well before a nursing home becomes necessary. Transfer your assets to your children or set up a trust fund that the government can't invade. *Be aware:* You may be liable for payment if your assets have been transferred within less than an average of two and a half years before entering a home, depending on the state.

Recommended: Consultation with a specialist in elder law. Ask your lawyer or a social worker in a local hospital or nursing home to recommend one.

Home care...

The home care situation under Medicare is also dismal. Medicare will pay for a skilled person to come into the home occasionally on a doctor's orders to perform tasks such as giving injections or physical therapy. There is virtually no coverage for the kind of help most elderly people need—a housekeeper/companion to help with personal and household tasks. Many senior-citizen groups are currently lobbying for this type of home custodial care to be provided by Medicare.

Assignment rate:

As far as general healthcare is concerned, Medicare supposedly pays 80% of the "reasonable rate" for medical care as determined by a board of doctors in the community. In reality, the "reasonable rate" is usually set so low that most doctors will not accept it. So, instead of paying 20% of their doctor bills, the elderly frequently wind up paying 50% or even more.

Suggestions:

•Don't drop your major medical insurance when you retire. If you keep it up, it will cover the gaps in your Medicare insurance. It is extremely difficult to buy such coverage after you reach 65.

•Be wary of insurance-company policies that supplement Medicare. You must be extremely careful when you buy one. Be sure it complements rather than duplicates Medicare coverage.

•Get together with other senior citizens to create consumer leverage. If a group of 50 seniors go to a doctor and all promise to patronize him providing he accepts the Medicare assigned rate, it might be worth his while.

Source: Charles Robert, an attorney specializing in elder law, Hempstead, NY.

If You Don't Need Medigap Insurance

Medigap insurance may not be needed. If you are enrolled in a health maintenance organization or competitive medical plan that has a contract with Medicare, extra coverage is not necessary. And individuals who qualify for Medicaid do not need—or qualify for—supplemental insurance.

Source: *Your Parent's Financial Security* by Barbara Weltman, John Wiley & Sons, 605 Third Ave., New York 10158.

Social Security and You... And Your Family

The Social Security system, including Medicare, has become too complicated for anyone but an expert to understand in full.

But you can—and should—know at least your basic rights, how to protect them, and how to make sure you get all the benefits you're entitled to.

To get a record of earnings credited to your account, just send in Form 7004, *Request for Earnings and Estimated Benefits Statement.*

Check your records tegularly...

You can get the form from any Social Security office. Check the record at least once every three years.

Reason: In most cases, the statute of limitations prevents correcting the records after three years, three months, and 15 days.

The Statement will also include an estimate of the benefits you'll receive if you retire at age 62, age 65, or age 70, as well as the benefits payable in the event of your disability or death. The figures are based on your earnings record and your own estimate of future earnings.

This statement is indispensable for financial planning—regardless of your age. Social Security isn't just a retirement system. It also provides benefits for survivors if you should die. Your children, for example, could receive benefits until they reach age 18 (19...if attending high school ...or permanently if the child is disabled before age 22). Total family benefits could exceed $20,000 a year.

Other survivors who might qualify: Widows, widowers, grandchildren, dependent parents, divorced spouses.

When to file...

It's best to file a few months before you retire, but you don't have to. Retroactive benefits can be paid for six months back from the month of filing.

Important exception: If you retire before age 65, no retroactive benefits are payable. Benefits can start no earlier than the month you file. So don't delay.

You're eligible for Medicare at age 65, even if you don't retire, so you should file at that time.

For Part A hospital insurance: You can also file at any time afterwards.

For Part B medical insurance: The rules are more complicated...

You can file during a seven-month initial enrollment period—the month you reach age 65 ...three months before...and three months after.

If you don't file during that time period, you can file only during general enrollment periods—January 1 to March 31 of each year. If you wait more than a year, you'll be charged an extra premium—10% higher for each 12 months delay.

Exception: If you work past age 65 and are covered by your company's health plan, there's no penalty if you wait until retirement to enroll. If you're covered by your spouse's company plan, you can enroll when your spouse retires.

Delaying retirement...

If you reach age 65 in 1993, your monthly benefit will be increased by 7/24 of 1% for each month you delay retirement. If you reach age 65 in later years, the increase will be even greater, reaching two-thirds of 1% per month in 2010.

Continuing to work can increase your benefit in another way. Benefits depend on your average monthly earnings in work covered by Social Security, figured all the way back to the 1950s. Continuing to work can increase this average in two ways...

•The amount of wages covered by Social Security has increased faster than inflation. In the early 1950s, only $3,600 a year was subject to Social Security tax. Even after adjusting for inflation (as the law requires), this comes to only a little over $20,000—compared with the current maximum of $57,600.

•You're probably nearer the maximum end of the scale than you were in your younger years.

Taxation of benefits...

Up to 50% of your benefits may be taxable if your "income" exceeds $32,000 (joint returns) or $25,000 (all other individuals). "Income" includes taxable income plus tax-exempt municipal-bond interest. Some investments, however, produce returns which do not count as income.

•Annuity payments are partly income and partly a tax-free return of your capital investments. Ginnie Mae securities also provide regular payments that are partly a tax-free return of capital. Many utility stocks pay tax-free dividends that are considered return of capital.

•US Savings bonds. Interest on Series EE bonds doesn't have to be reported as income until the bonds are cashed.

•Growth stocks often pay no dividends. Instead, they use the profits to expand the business. Stockholders have no taxable income until they sell the stock.

•Rental real estate often produces a positive cash flow, but no taxable income, because of deductions for depreciation. (It may even show a tax loss.)

Caution: Some of these investments (real estate, especially) may tie up your cash. Don't consider them unless you're sure you have enough to live on.

Medicare...

•Long-term care. The most common—and most serious—misconception about Medicare is that it provides for long-term nursing-home care. It does not. It covers only short-term stays (up to 100 days a year) in a skilled nursing-care facility.

I would urge everyone to consider buying long-term care insurance. Look for a policy that covers custodial care as well as skilled care, does not require a prior hospital stay, and provides for home care without requiring a prior nursing-home stay.

•Know your appeal rights. You can't learn all the complex Medicare rules, but you should know that you have the right to appeal from any adverse decisions. Don't hesitate to exercise this right. *Prime examples:*

•Hospital stays. If Medicare decides hospitalization is no longer necessary, you must be notified in writing. At that point, you'll either have to go home...or pay all costs if you remain in the hospital. Appeal at once.

Your Medicare coverage is automatically extended while the appeal is pending...plus 24 hours. Even if you lose, you can remain in the hospital at Medicare's expense while the appeal is processed.

You also have appeal rights from the denial of nursing-home stays or home care.

•Doctor's bills. If Medicare denies payment of a doctor's bill, or does not pay what you regard as enough, don't hesitate to appeal. About 75% of such appeals have resulted in higher payment.

Source: Peter J. Strauss, Esq., partner, Fink Weinberger, PC, 420 Lexington Ave., New York 10170.

You Can Fight Insurance Companies…and Win

I hear horror stories every day from families whose insurance companies refused to make timely payments on legitimate claims. Individuals are inhumanely hounded by collection agencies because their insurance companies haven't paid the bills they are legally obligated to pay. The disabled are forced to go on welfare. Some people have even been driven to attempt suicide.

Very few people—fewer than 1% of those with insurance claims—question claim denials. By not questioning a denied claim, there's a good chance your insurance company is cheating you out of money that rightfully belongs to you.

Good news: Most of those who do challenge insurers either win their cases or significantly improve their positions.

What it takes to win…

•Positive attitude. Don't assume "they" must be right and take the first no for a final answer. Insurance companies count on the fact that most people simply accept their decisions.

•Persistence. The adage, "a squeaky wheel gets the grease," is true when it comes to dealing with a claim denial.

•Knowledge. Educate yourself on specific issues and the tools available to help you fight a large insurance company.

You be the judge…

On any claim refusal, exercise your rights as a consumer…

•Insist on a written explanation. Most state laws require an insurance company to give you one.

•Compare the explanation you get from the company with the language of the policy. Insurers notoriously write policies that are difficult to understand and then interpret them to their own advantage. But in court, where language is unclear, the meaning is construed against the insurance company. Some courts have even held that the reasonable expectation of the policyholder governs the meaning of policy language.

•Rely on your own common sense. Judge for yourself "what is fair" and "what you expected." If what the insurance company offers doesn't seem fair, there is a good chance that it isn't.

•Don't be put off if your claim is denied for technical reasons. An insurer cannot deny benefits because you filed late or filled out a form improperly unless the company can show it has been harmed by your failure. That's very, very rarely the case.

•Use intermediaries to press your claim. The agent who sold you the policy, or if you have a group policy, the administrator who handles claims for your company, can often give a decisive nudge to the insurer.

•Always put your claim in writing. Arm yourself with supporting evidence. One of the most common reasons insurers give for rejections is that a bill exceeds regular and customary charges. But some companies use outdated fee schedules or averages that don't apply to your case. Get written estimates from other doctors for the same treatment to prove your point.

Example: One woman who received much less than she expected for a Cesarean delivery called 27 doctors in her area and asked what they charged for a C-section. Only three charged less than her gynecologist, 10 charged more. Faced with these figures, the insurer paid up.

•Pursue your claim up the company's chain of command. Keep written notes of every conversation—who you talked to, his/her telephone extension, what was said.

Go the extra mile…

If the insurer continues to stonewall, seek outside help. *Sources:*

•States' department of insurance. Most try to identify and prevent unfair claims practices. Strong ones—like California, New York, and Illinois—will even act as a referee between you and your insurance company.

•Small-claims court. Sue the insurer yourself if the claim does not exceed the maximum recovery amount for small-claims court, usually between $1,000 and $2,500. Rather than spending their time and money to defend themselves against you, the company may well settle.

•Lawyer. It isn't hard to find one who will work on a contingency basis if you have a really strong case. You may end up collecting not just the claim amount, but additional sums for economic loss, emotional distress, and—if the company has been really unscrupulous—punitive damages for wrongful conduct.* *Example:* A client of mine had a $48 gripe against his insurance company, which refused to pay for medicine. After we proved the company had fraudulently changed its basic policy coverage, the jury awarded him $70,000 in compensatory damages—and $4.5 million in punitive damages.

Whichever routes you take, the important thing is to keep pushing to get the benefits you rightfully deserve. Don't be a victim.

Source: William M. Shernoff, a consumer-rights lawyer who practices in Claremont, California. He is the author of *How to Make Insurance Companies Pay Your Claims and What to Do If They Don't,* Hastings House, 141 Halstead Ave., Mamaroneck, NY 10543.

Mistakes When Filing Insurance Claims

Failure to accurately calculate losses. It's hard to believe, but many people can't accurately determine their losses—whether by damage or theft. *Reason:* They fail to maintain effective accounting and record-retention procedures to document the losses. It's not uncommon to hear of a situation in which a theft loss amounted to $250,000 but the claimant could substantiate only $100,000 of the loss. It's important to plan ahead with your accountant to determine the best procedures for demonstrating what you own in case you have to make a claim.

Overstating the loss. This is a subtle problem. If a claimant purposely overstates the loss to the point where the insurance company could question his integrity, the latter will take a hard line. Generally, if the claimant takes a fair position, the insurer will still bargain over the loss claim but will be more reasonable.

Underestimating the loss. This sounds like a contradiction of the above, but it's not. Immedi-

*Group policyholders governed by Employee Retirement and Income Security Act (ERISA) regulations can recover only policy benefits from successful lawsuits.

ately after losses are claimed, the adjuster will ask the claimant for an estimate of the damage, not an accurate, justified number. The insurer requires such a rough estimate, but be wary of providing a number before taking the time to get a reliable estimate. If the adjuster reports a number that's too low and then must go back later to the insurer and restate it much higher, both his credibility and yours are hurt. He looks foolish. Those hurt feelings can make future loss negotiations tricky. So tell the adjuster about any problems you have in coming up with a number.

Health Insurance: How to Determine Adequate Coverage

Most of the shortcomings in medical insurance occur because buyers are unfamiliar with what is available in the market. They don't have a checklist of questions to ask. Even many brokers are unaware of the pitfalls in some policies. So read the terms of the contract before you buy. Once you have a policy, fighting for additional payments is very frustrating. Therefore, have the right policy in the first place.

Many hospitalization and surgical policies do not cover the entire cost of a hospital stay or surgery. *Example:* Many plans only cover a semiprivate room up to $200 a day. Many surgical plans, such as Blue Shield, insure operation costs on a national average basis. Therefore, if you have an operation in New York, Boston, or San Francisco, you are apt to have significant out-of-pocket expenses, since doctors there charge considerably more than in, say, Kansas City.

To supplement such plans, get a major medical with a sizable deductible that "wraps around" your primary hospitalization and surgical coverage. These policies can enable you to have a private nurse or specialized care in many cases.

In areas where Blue Cross/Blue Shield is noncompetitive in price or benefits, and there is no prepaid group plan such as a Kaiser-Permanente or Health Insurance Plan (HIP), get a comprehensive major medical plan from a private insurer.

Read the terms of the insurance contract to determine what the insurance company will pay for each situation. Private insurers often use the phrase "reasonable and customary charge" to limit what they will pay for operations and doctors' services. *Reasons:* The insurer wants to discourage victims of illness from visiting very expensive specialists for any minor complaint. However, "reasonable and customary" falls within a fairly wide spectrum and is negotiable up to a point. Limitations are not absolute.

Example: A New York resident flew across the border to Montreal for a gallbladder operation. He was able to prove that the operation with the cost of the flight was cheaper in Canada than a doctor and hospital in New York. The insurance company found the case convincing and paid air fare and all bills.

However, some insurance firms establish inside limits or scheduled benefits for various operations. Each situation is described with the sum the insurance company gives for room, board, and the surgery. Read these carefully. Check out how these limits compare with actual practices in your region. If possible, avoid these policies and stick to the reasonable and customary policies. Obviously, you get what you pay for. Policies with inner limits are cheaper, but the cost differential is minimal.

Look into the limits of major medical insurance. Are they lifetime or per cause limits? *How they work:* If you have a $250,000 lifetime limit and get cancer treatments that use up the $250,000, you are not able to collect money for treatments when you get a heart ailment the next year. But if you have a per cause limitation of $250,000, the insurer will pay up to the limit, $250,000, for the heart ailment after you use up $250,000 for cancer. If you get any other disease, then you can obtain still another $250,000 for treatment.

Check out the extent of coinsurance. Few companies will pay 100% of all medical treatment. They want the consumer to undertake some of the payments, partly to avoid malingering. Therefore, they make you pay 20% of the second $2,000, $5,000, $10,000, $50,000, or even an unlimited amount. The insurance company picks up the other 80%. Naturally, you want to avoid policies with large coinsurance clauses. With extensive hospitalization for a major illness, you could wind up being $10,000 or even more out of pocket. If your 80/20 coinsurance is limited to $2,000, you will only be a maximum of $400 out of pocket.

Source: Leon Sicular, president, Leon Sicular Associates, benefit consultants, 22 Sintsink Drive East, Port Washington, NY 11050.

Safest and Weakest Insurers... Now

Highest rated insurers...

Country Life Insurance	A+
Guardian Life Insurance	A+
Jefferson-Pilot Life Insurance	A+
Northwestern Mutual Life Insurance	A+
State Farm Life Insurance	A+
United Insurance Company of America	A+
American General Life Insurance	A-
Chubb Life Insurance	A-
Farm Bureau Life Insurance	A-
Franklin Life Insurance	A-
Guardian Life & Annuity	A-
Massachusetts Mutual Life Insurance	A-
Metropolitan Life Insurance	A-
Minnesota Mutual Life Insurance	A-
Mutual of Omaha Insurance	A-
New York Life Insurance & Annuity Corp.	A-
Southern Farm Bureau Life Insurance	A-
USAA Life Insurance	A-
Western & Southern Life Insurance	A-
New York Life Insurance	A

Lowest rated...

Blue Cross & Blue Shield of Mass.	D+
Union Labor Life	D+
American Skandia LI ASR	D
Aurora National Life ASR	D
Empire Blue Cross/Blue Shield	D
London Pacific Life	D
MBL Life ASR	D
Pacific Corinthian Life	D

Southwestern Life ....D-

National Heritage ....E

Source: Martin Weiss, President of Weiss Research and editor of *Safe Money Report.* Safety ratings on insurance companies are available starting at $15 per company. Weiss Companies, 4176 Burns Road, Palm Beach Gardens, FL 33410.

Disability Insurance Confidential

When disability strikes, you have to replace your income with something or face losing your house, your lifestyle, savings, and investments. Ironically, most people routinely buy life insurance to protect their families in case they die, but they neglect to buy disability insurance. *Fact:* Chances of being disabled during your working years are four to five times greater than chances of dying during the same period.

Comparing policies:

• *Concern #1:* How the policy defines disability. You want the broadest definition you can find and/or afford. Some policies, for example, define disability as inability to perform any of the duties required by your occupation. *Be careful:* Under many definitions, including that of Social Security, disability is the inability to perform any occupation. Under that definition, you get no payment as long as you can work at something, even if the job you can perform after being disabled is low paying.

A split definition of disability that's often used: Strict for a specific period of time and broad for the duration of the benefit period.

• *Concern #2:* The length of the benefit period. Will the policy continue to pay you after age 65? Many policies stop paying then and you may still need funds. Unless another retirement fund kicks in, you'd have an income gap.

Also: Check the waiting period, the time between the start of the disability and the actual beginning of payment of benefits. If you can wait 90 days before you need income, the premiums will be significantly lower than if you wait only 30 days.

Example: A person who is 45 years old wants a disability policy that will protect his income of $55,000 a year. Yearly premiums with a 30-day waiting period will cost $1,900—with a 60-day wait, $1,700—and for a 90-day waiting period, $1,550.

Source: Karen P. Schaeffer, Schaeffer Financial, Greenbelt, MD.

The New Problem... Aged Parents Needing Very Expensive Care

There's nothing underhanded about making an effort to conserve aging parents' assets to pass along to children, while using Medicaid or, under the new Medicare Catastrophe Act, Medicare to pick up much of the cost of home care or nursing-home care. In fact, Congress has made clear that it doesn't want middle-class families to deplete all their assets for such care.

The key legal device to conserve an elderly parent's assets is the Medicaid Qualifying Trust. The parents divest their assets into the trust and receive annual interest payments. Those interest payments are then used to meet the bills of home and nursing-home care with Medicaid picking up qualifying expenses over that amount. The principal in the trust would remain intact, to be inherited by designated beneficiaries.

Until the beginning of this year, when the Medicare Catastrophe Act became law, this divestiture had to be made at least two years before a family applied for help from Medicaid. Under the new Act, 2½ years is the requisite period.

It is essential, however, to get expert legal advice on how this law works now in your particular state. Ask your local bar association to recommend lawyers who specialize in legal counseling on problems of the aged.

Source: Lewis Kamin, partner, Cappa, Kamin, and Goldberg, 244-14 Jericho Turnpike, Floral Park, NY 11001, a law firm that works with Corporate Consultations in Aging, Inc.

Whole Life Insurance

A typical whole life, or ordinary life, policy covers you for your entire life and offers a guaranteed death benefit—a fixed sum payable to your heirs when you die. Some whole life policies pay dividends, which can:

- Reduce your premiums.
- Buy paid-up additions to your life insurance policy to increase your death benefit.
- Be returned to you in cash.
- Be deposited with the insurance company, where it will earn interest and serve as an additional savings account.

When you purchase a whole life policy, part of the premium pays the actual cost of the insurance risk, part pays the insurer's expenses and part goes into a reserve fund known as cash value.

This cash value, which allows the premiums to remain level during your lifetime, builds up annually and grows in value on a tax-deferred basis. Insurance companies are not obligated to tell you how your premium dollar is divided.

Because of the conservative nature of life insurance, various state regulations and the desire of insurers to fulfill their obligations, these guarantees are very low. But your actual cash available is usually higher than that which is guaranteed in the policy, if your dividends are used to purchase more insurance or are left in savings accounts with the company.

The most widely used whole life contract insures one life and pays a death benefit to the beneficiary upon his/her death. A newer variation is called second-to-die insurance, which insures two lives and pays the death benefit when the second person dies. The cost of a second-to-die policy is lower than that of two individual policies.

Whole Life drawback I: The premiums for a whole life policy are higher than those for a term policy because some of the money goes toward cash value.

Whole Life drawback II: Not all whole life policies pay dividends. And even when dividends are paid, they are not guaranteed...but rather reflect the insurance company's earnings, net of expenses.

Ideal candidates: Individuals with estates of more than $600,000, or couples with a combined estate of more than $1.2 million, who will be hit with estate taxes upon the death of the surviving spouse.

Source: Virginia Applegarth, president of Applegarth Advisory Group Inc., a Boston-based fee-only financial insurance advisory firm. She is author of *How to Protect Your Family with Insurance.* Lee Simmons Associates, Inc., 40 Richards Rd., Port Washington, NY 11050.

Disability Insurance Considerations

You're five times less likely to die than you are to become disabled—if you are single or married, younger than 45 and childless. *Self-defense:* Consider a disability insurance policy that replaces some or all of your lost income, should you be unable to work due to illness or accident.

Source: *Bill Staton's Money Advisory,* 300 E. Boulevard, B-4, Charlotte 28203.

Term Insurance Demystified

Term life insurance is relatively simple to understand. Unlike a cash-value insurance policy—which has complicated savings or investment components—a term insurance policy merely provides protection for an agreed-upon period of time.

Buying the *right* term policy, however, is a little more difficult. Thanks to different cost structures and options, comparison shopping among different term policies can be confusing and tricky. Here's how to minimize these difficulties and find the best policy for you and your family...

- Determine whether term life insurance is right for you. Term insurance is ideal for someone who requires financial protection for a defined period of time but does not want to spend a lot of money for it each year.

In many cases, a family's need for life insurance is highest when the children are young—and then decreases or disappears when the children graduate from college, the mortgage is paid off and other financial hurdles are passed.

Important: You—not an insurance agent—are the best judge of how long your family's insurance protection needs will last. Until you've charted your projected time frame, you won't be able to comparison shop for the lowest total policy cost. *Key questions:*

• What is the present value of the money needed to accomplish your after-death goals?

• What is the present value of the money you now have available?

The difference between these answers is the amount of life insurance you need.

• Understand the two types of term policies. Consider both when shopping for the best overall deal...

• *Annual renewable term,* also known as *yearly renewable term,* charges premiums that increase yearly. To sweeten the package, some companies offer fixed rates for the first two or three years. Annual renewable term policies typically charge bargain-basement rates during their earliest years so you can buy protection at a minimal cost. Once you've qualified, you'll never have to take another medical exam to qualify for extended coverage.

Drawback: Over time, you spend more than for other types of term policies because annual renewable rates increase each year.

• *Level premium term policies* charge fixed premiums for set periods—typically five, 10, 15 or 20 years. It's easier to project your total insurance costs over this period, especially when you can time your insurance needs to the policy's rate guarantee.

Example: You could cancel the policy after 10 years, just before your rate rises.

Although the rates on these policies run higher in early years than those charged on annual renewable term policies, total costs over the long run are usually lower.

Drawback: Once the guaranteed-rate period expires, you'll have to take another medical exam to requalify for a new fixed-rate schedule ...or you can choose to be charged premiums

that rise annually. Rate increases on level premium term policies often occur at a much faster clip than do those for regular annual renewable term policies.

• Compare option features. Each term life insurance policy can be quite different from other term policies. In some cases, you may want to pay more for other features. While it is certainly true that not every option will matter to every potential policyholder, here are some points to ask about...

• *Accelerated death benefit.* An option offered by some insurers, it promises policyholders that in the event of terminal illness, they may receive, say, 50% of their death benefit during their final year of life. While this may be an appealing option, there are risks to consider.

Example: The benefits may be taxable income...people who receive these benefits may be disqualified from a variety of government-subsidized programs.

• *Convertibility.* This gives policyholders the right to convert term policies into cash-value policies—without having to provide evidence of medical insurability at that point.

Strategy: If you anticipate a cash-value conversion, be sure the insurer will permit a conversion over a long period, ideally until you reach age 60. You should look at the quality of the cash-value policies. Low-load term policies are usually convertible to low-load cash-value policies that don't charge commissions.

• *Flexibility.* Many insurers let you reduce your coverage and premium without having to apply for a new policy or pay additional fees. This may be useful if you anticipate that your insurance needs will shrink gradually before finally disappearing. As your needs decline, you may want to reduce your coverage to cut down on your premium.

With term policies, it pays to reevaluate the face value of your life insurance coverage every few years—to make certain that you're not paying for more protection than your family actually needs.

• Compare the widest possible range of policies. If you want to find the lowest price and best package of features, you'll have to shop around.

Look at both low-load products, which are purchased directly from insurers, and agent-sold products to find a policy that best suits your needs.

The quickest way to narrow your search is to make two phone calls:

• *Quotesmith* (800-556-9393), a free service that provides price-comparison reports of 150 term life policies sold by agents and brokers.

• *The Wholesale Insurance Network* (800-808-5810), which provides quotes for low-load policies.

The insurer's financial stability is somewhat less important when you are buying a term life insurance policy than when you are buying cash-value insurance. That's because you're not making a long-term investment commitment. But that's no reason to completely disregard insurer ratings when choosing between policies.

• Compare carefully. Make no decision to buy without comparing the present value of projected premiums during the entire anticipated period of your coverage. If your insurance agent won't help you work through these numbers, retain a financial adviser who can.

Helpful: Project worst-case scenarios. If you're considering a 10-year level-premium term policy but expect to need coverage for an additional five to 10 years, project your costs as if you would not medically qualify for another guaranteed rate and then would have to pay for annual renewable term coverage.

Key: Choose the policy that looks cheapest over the long run and offers options that matter most to your family.

Source: Glenn S. Daily, a fee-only insurance consultant, 234 E. 84 St., New York 10028. He is author of *The Individual Investor's Guide to Low-Load Insurance Products* (International Publishing Corp.) and *Life Insurance Sense and Nonsense*, available from the author.

Common HMO Traps And How to Escape Them

As more than 11 million Americans are already aware, joining an HMO can be an excellent way to save money on medical bills.

But HMOs can end up costing you money and providing less than optimum health care. *Here's how to avoid the most common HMO traps...*

Trap: Feeling uncared for. Today's HMO doctors are sometimes so strapped for time that they often leave the simple tasks such as taking blood pressure for nurses and assistants. They pop in for a brief evaluation, then rush off to the next patient.

While nurses and assistants generally are capable of performing these tasks without problem, this division of services causes some patients to feel neglected by their doctor.

If you feel that way, don't hesitate to speak up. Tell your doctor that you would prefer that he/she take your blood pressure and perform other similar tasks. Surprisingly, most doctors are willing to oblige—if you ask nicely.

Trap: Getting "stuck" with a doctor you don't like. Most HMOs let you pick a doctor from a list of practitioners affiliated with the HMO. To make sure you select a doctor with whom you can develop a good rapport, schedule a preliminary appointment.

Ask about his medical training...his approach to illness prevention...and his general philosophy regarding medical care. If the doctor's responses don't reassure you, schedule an appointment with another doctor. Even if the doctor you select turns out to be a dud, however, you're far from "stuck." Contact the HMO administrator and ask to find a new doctor.

In an effort to minimize administrative work, most HMOs are reluctant to talk about switching doctors...but they will generally let you switch if you insist.

Trap: Assuming an HMO will cover you while traveling. Most HMOs refuse to pay for care rendered out of town or by doctors outside the organization. *Exception:* Genuine emergencies, such as a heart attack, automobile accident, etc.

If you spend a considerable amount of time away from home, find out in advance exactly what medical expenses your HMO will cover. It may be necessary to purchase conventional fee-for-service health insurance instead of your HMO coverage.

Trap: Getting a second opinion that's biased. When getting a second opinion, it's important to find a doctor who has no significant relationship with the doctor who provided the first opinion. A doctor who is a friend or close colleague of the first doctor is not a good bet.

Problem: In an HMO, the doctor who provides the second opinion belongs to the same HMO as your primary doctor. He may be hesitant to give you an honest, unbiased opinion—simply because he fears offending his colleague.

Solution: Check whether the HMO permits you to get a second opinion from a doctor outside the HMO. If not, consider going outside the HMO network for the second opinion anyway—even if it means you must pay for it.

Source: Arthur R. Pell, PhD, a human resources consultant based in Hempstead, NY. Dr. Pell is the author of 37 books on health and human resources management, including *Diagnosing Your Doctor: A Straightforward Guide to Asking the Right Questions and Getting the Health Care You Deserve,* DCI/Chronimed Publishing.

7

A Healthier You

How We Can Slow Our Aging Processes

Today, people are living longer, but enjoying it less. Many of us fear old age as a period of declining powers and failing health. But if we learn to replace that fear by a positive attitude, an enhanced physical and spiritual awareness of our bodies, and a sensible pattern of activity, we can expect to enjoy the blessings of a vigorous and healthy old age.

A century ago, less than one person in 10 reached the age of 65. Most of those who did live that long had been worn out by a lifetime of inadequate nutrition…widespread disease …backbreaking physical labor. Their remaining years were difficult not because they were old, but because their bodies were in a state of breakdown.

Today, relieved of those harsh external pressures, most of us will live well into our 60s and 70s…and the physical disease and mental breakdown we fear in old age is largely a result of internal stress we can learn to avoid.

People age differently…

Your well-being depends far less on your chronological age—how old you are according to the calendar—than on two other indicators…

• Biological age tells how old your body is in terms of critical life signs and cellular processes.

Every individual is affected differently by time…in fact, every cell and organ in your body ages on its own timetable.

Example: A middle-aged marathon runner may have leg muscles, heart and lungs of someone half his age, highly stressed knees and kidneys that are aging rapidly and eyesight and hearing declining on their own individual paths.

Most 20-year-olds look alike to a physiologist …but at 70, no two people have bodies that are remotely alike.

• Psychological age indicates how old you feel. Depending on what is happening in your life and your attitude to it, your psychological age can change dramatically within a very short period.

Examples: An old woman recalling her first love can suddenly look and sound as if she has just turned 18…a middle-aged man who loses his beloved wife can become a lonely old man within a few weeks.

Aging is reversible…

It is not news that psychological age can decrease. *We all know the old proverb:* You are as old as you feel. And—now scientists have learned that biological aging can be reversed.

Example: Muscle mass is a key factor in the body's overall vitality…and it was believed until recently that it inevitably declined with increasing age. But Tufts University researchers discovered that isn't so. They put 12 men, aged 60–72, on a weight-training program. After three months, the men could lift heavier boxes than the 25-year-old workers in the lab…and milder weight-training programs proved equally successful for people over 95!

That's not all the good news for aging bodies. The Tufts team found that regular physical exercise also reverses nine other typical effects of biological age…

- Reduced strength
- Lower metabolic rate
- Excess body fat
- Reduced aerobic capacity
- Higher blood pressure
- Lower blood-sugar tolerance
- Higher cholesterol/HDL ratio
- Reduced bone density
- Poorer body temperature regulation.

To get optimum benefits from exercise, the type and amount have to be expertly tailored to your individual constitution. You don't have to be a fitness freak to gain from exercise…just 20 minutes of walking three times a week improves the cholesterol/HDL ratio. No expert advice is needed to benefit from another important route to longevity…a balanced lifestyle.

A study of 7,000 Southern Californians found that the longest-lived followed seven simple rules:

- Sleep seven to eight hours a night.
- Eat breakfast.
- Don't eat between meals.
- Don't be significantly over- or underweight.
- Engage in regular physical activity…sports …gardening…long walks.
- Drink moderately…not more than two alcoholic drinks a day.
- Don't smoke.

The study found that a 45-year-old man who followed these rules could expect to live another 33 years…but if he followed only three of them or less, he would probably die within 22 years.

Role of stress…

The human body reacts to stress by pumping adrenaline and other powerful hormones into the bloodstream. This "fight or flight" response provides energy for taking rapid action and is vital when you are actually faced with pressing external danger.

But it makes your metabolism work in the direction of breaking your body down instead of building it up.

If it occurs too often or continues too long it produces lasting harmful effects including muscle wasting…diabetes…fatigue…osteoporosis…hypertension…effects typical of aging.

That is why a major contribution to the aging process in modern life comes from situations that do not present real physical dangers but produce dangerous levels of stress.

Example: Our cities are full of unavoidable noise, a serious source of stress. Studies have shown increased levels of mental disorder in people who live under the flight paths near airports…elevated blood pressure in children who live near the Los Angeles airport…more violent behavior in noisy work environments.

Fortunately, we have discovered a number of measures that can reduce the aging effects of stress and other hazards of modern life.

To reduce stress and slow the aging process…

- Experience silence. Research has shown that people who meditate have higher levels of DHEA, a hormone that protects against stress and decreases with age. Spending 20 minutes twice a day in calm silence pays great benefits in detaching you from the mad bustle of the world and finding your true self.

•Avoid toxics...not only foods and drinks that stress your system, but relationships that produce anger and tension.

•Shed the need for approval by others...it's a sign of fear, another stress factor that promotes aging.

•Use relationships with others to learn your own self. People we love provide something we need...those we hate have something we need to get rid of.

•Change your inner dialogue. Change from What's in it for me? to How can I help others? Selfishness is bad for you. Psychologist Larry Scherwitz found that people who used the words "I," "me," "mine" most often in their conversations had the highest risk of heart disease.

•Be aware of your body's needs. The body only recognizes two signals...comfort and discomfort. You will be healthier if you learn to respond to its signals.

Example: Don't eat by the clock...eat when you're hungry...stop when you're full.

•Live in the moment. Much stress comes from living in the past or the future instead of the present.

Example: If you're angry at something that already happened...or fearful of something that may happen...your stress can't produce any useful result now. When those feelings occur, bring yourself back to the present.

•Become less judgmental. Don't get stressed by other people's decisions...your viewpoint may not be right for them.

•Stay in contact with nature. It will make you feel you want to stay around to enjoy it longer...and your body will respond.

Source: Deepak Chopra, MD, executive director for the Institute for Mind/Body Medicine, San Diego, CA. He is the author of *Ageless Body, Timeless Mind: The Quantum Alternative to Growing Old.* Harmony Books.

You Can Reverse The Aging Process

Many of our assumptions about aging and its effects on health and well-being aren't true.

Muscle weakness, loss of energy, greater susceptibility to illness, difficulty in getting around —much of this decline is due not to aging itself, but to inactivity and poor nutrition.

Study after study shows that regular exercise and a healthy diet can slow—or even reverse— the deterioration in fitness, vitality and independence that we associate with age. Even if you haven't been health conscious in the past, you can still reap benefits by changing your lifestyle now...whether you're 50, 60—or 90.

Biomarkers...

In our laboratory research, we've singled out 10 biomarkers—biological signs of aging—that are highly responsive to changes in exercise and/or diet.

The first four are closely related—and they affect the remaining six. *The four key biomarkers...*

•Muscle mass.

•Strength.

•Basal metabolic rate.

•Percentage of body fat.

But, as muscle is lost with age and inactivity, there's a corresponding loss of strength. The body's metabolic rate also decreases, so that it takes fewer calories to maintain the same weight. The likely result is an increase in body fat. These changes can, in turn, lead to problems ranging from diabetes to heart attack. All four key biomarkers can be controlled with exercise. *The other six biomarkers...*

•Aerobic fitness. The ability of heart, lungs and circulatory system to collect and distribute oxygen. Aerobic capacity is greater among regular exercisers.

•Blood sugar tolerance. Ten percent to 15% of people age 50 and older have Type II diabetes, and another 15% are considered to be at high risk for developing the disease. It has serious complications if left untreated. A low-fat diet and regular exercise can control symptoms—and better—prevent the disease.

•Cholesterol/HDL ratio. Even more important than a low total cholesterol count (which should be under 200) is the ratio of total cholesterol to "good" cholesterol, or HDL. That ratio should be 4.5 or lower to help protect against heart disease...and diet and exercise can help keep it there.

•Blood pressure—if it's high, you're at greater risk of heart attack and stroke. Exercise and a low-fat diet can help to keep it under control.

•Bone density. A decline in bone mineral content can lead to osteoporosis—the condition in which bones become porous, brittle and vulnerable to breaking. Increasing the intake of calcium may play a role in strengthening bones. Weight-bearing exercise (running, cycling, weight training—but not swimming) is possibly even more important.

•Internal temperature. As the older body loses its ability to regulate temperature and fluids, heat stroke becomes a serious danger. Older people in good physical shape adjust better to heat. Their bodies hold more water, and they sweat more—the body's natural cooling mechanism.

Because the sense of thirst decreases with age, older people need to make a point of drinking plenty of fluids in order to prevent dehydration.

Reverse aging through exercise...

Our thinking about exercise has changed in the years since the fitness boom began. We now know that significant benefits can be gained from even small amounts of exercise, if done regularly and consistently.

Of course, it's even better if you have the motivation and commitment to work out vigorously at least four times a week. But anything you do to move your body is better than no exercise at all. The key is to keep it up—or you'll lose the gains you've made. For many people, the simplest way to work more activity into the day is by walking.

Examples: Parking at the far end of the grocery store parking lot, instead of hunting for a parking space near the entrance...walking around the golf course instead of riding in the cart...walking up one or two flights of stairs instead of using the elevator... going for at least a five-minute walk around the block every morning and evening.

Once mild exercise has become a habit, you may be inspired to begin a more formal fitness program. Of course, you should check with your doctor first. *The ideal exercise program will include:*

•Strength training—to build muscle mass and increase your metabolic rate. This will make aerobic exercise easier.

Strength conditioning works the muscles against resistance—either with weights or by using the body's own weight against gravity, as with push-ups or pull-ups. For cheap hand weights, fill gallon containers of milk with water or sand.

Weight training isn't just for muscle-bound kids. People in their 90s have successfully started working with weights...and increased their muscle mass as a result.

Workouts should be about 20 minutes each, two to three days a week. The weight should be heavy enough to tire your muscles in 10 repetitions. Rest when you've reached your limit and then do another 10. Increase the weight as you grow stronger. The only limit is however strong you want to become.

You can learn an all-around series of resistance exercises from books (the instructions are in my book, among others) or classes. Be sure to use correct form—both to avoid injury and to work the muscles as efficiently as possible. Your local Y or health club should have instructors who can help you learn correct technique.

•Aerobic exercise. This is the kind of workout that leaves you slightly out of breath for a sustained period of time—and keeps your circulatory system in shape.

Examples: Running, swimming, cycling, brisk walking.

The American College of Sports Medicine recommends a minimum of 30 minutes of aerobic exercise, three days a week. That's a good guideline...but I don't want to discourage people from doing less if this schedule seems too difficult.

Large studies conducted by Steven Blair at the Cooper Institute in Dallas indicate that even shorter exercise sessions may slightly increase life expectancy. If you take a 15-minute walk every day, that's terrific—keep up the good work.

•Stretching—to increase flexibility and prevent injury. Begin and end every exercise session with five to 10 minutes of gentle stretching. This warm-up and cool-down time will help prevent injury, and increase flexibility in muscles. For people with arthritis, stretching can greatly increase range of motion.

Reverse aging through diet…

If we continue our usual eating habits while calorie needs decline, the muscle-to-fat ratio will continue to shift in favor of fat.

Eat nutrient-dense foods—foods that supply more nutrients for fewer calories. This means shifting away from the traditional American high-fat diet to one that emphasizes carbohydrates—fruits, vegetables, grains and beans—and is low in fat. Learn which kinds of food are higher in fat calories and then make simple, logical choices until they become routine.

Examples: Substitute a low-fat muffin for your morning croissant or doughnut. Get most of your protein from lower-fat sources—skinless chicken, fish, beans—rather than high-fat beef and pork. For calcium, drink skim milk.

You don't have to calculate the fat percentage of everything you eat, but you should certainly start reading labels to find out what proportion of a food's calories are from fat, carbohydrate or protein.

Formula: One gram of fat equals nine calories…one gram of protein or carbohydrate equals four calories.

Supplements…

The one vitamin supplement I recommend is vitamin E, 200 to 400 International Units per day. There's good evidence that this vitamin can strengthen immune function—which may become compromised with age—and protect against heart disease. It's also an antioxidant—it acts against the oxidation of fats in the body that may contribute to aging.

Source: William Evans, PhD, director of the Noll Laboratory for Human Performance Research at Pennsylvania State University. He is coauthor of *Biomarkers: The 10 Keys to Prolonging Vitality.* Fireside Books.

Predicting Longevity

Childhood personality predicts longevity. Children described as being conscientious and dependable were 35% more likely to live to age 70 than those described as being optimistic and having a sense of humor. The reason for this difference in longevity is unknown.

Source: Howard Friedman, PhD, professor of psychology, University of California, Riverside. His review of data from a study of 1,178 children begun in the early 1920s was published in the *Journal of Personality and Social Psychology,* 750 First St. NE, Washington, DC 20002.

Most Common Time of Day for Heart Attacks

Most heart attacks occur during the morning or late evening. In a recent poll of heart attack sufferers, 25% said they were awakened by heart attack symptoms in the early morning. Another 25% said their heart attacks occurred within four hours of waking…and 20% said their attacks came 11 to 12 hours later—often following a heavy supper.

Source: Robert W. Peters, MD, chief of cardiology, Veterans Affairs Medical Center, Baltimore. His study of more than 3,000 heart attack patients was published in the *Journal of the American College of Cardiology,* 9111 Old Georgetown Rd., Bethesda, MD 20814.

How Doctors Shop For Toiletries

If you're confused by the vast selection of soaps, shampoos and other toiletries lining supermarket shelves, remember this—inexpensive products usually work just as well as costly ones.

Skin cleansers…

All cleansers are capable of dissolving dirt and oils. The challenge is selecting one that's appropriate for your skin type.

•Very dry skin. Use cold cream, "milk cleanser" or another lipid cleanser. These products clean while adding moisture to your skin.

•Dry skin. Use a soap with added fat or oil. *Example:* Oilatum soap.

•Normal skin. Use oil-free soap or detergent bars. *Examples:* Glycerine soaps like Purpose or Neutrogena.

•Oily or acne-prone skin. Use a soap with strong drying properties, such as Ivory or a deodorant soap. Antibacterial agents in deodorant soaps kill bacteria that promote acne growth.

•Very oily skin. Use an oil-cutting astringent like Sea Breeze or Propa pH.

If you live in an area with "hard" water, it may be difficult to rinse off soap completely... and soap left on the skin is irritating. In such areas, use detergent cleansers instead of soaps (which contain sodium or potassium tallowate or sodium or potassium cocoate).

Shampoos and conditioners...

•Normal hair. Experiment with several different types of shampoo until you find one that you like. Use just enough shampoo to work up a lather. More than that, and you risk drying your hair and scalp.

•Dandruff. Wash your hair every day, alternating between two different dandruff shampoos (with different active ingredients). *Reason:* Different active ingredients fight dandruff in different ways. Using two shampoos will work better than using a single one.

For very severe dandruff, see a dermatologist. Ask about Nizoral shampoo. This prescription product contains a compound that kills dandruff-promoting fungi that live on the scalp.

•Itchy scalp. Use shampoo containing coal tar. *Examples:* Denorex, Tegrin, Pentrax.

Whatever shampoo you use, follow up with a conditioner to remoisturize your hair. To make thinning or flat hair appear thicker, select a protein conditioner.

Moisturizing lotions...

Vaseline and other oil-based products are very effective at keeping hands moisturized. Except for people with extremely dry skin, however, they're too greasy for everyday use.

Better: Lotions containing urea or another humectant. These oil-free ingredients help the skin retain moisture without making it feel greasy.

Best: Moisturizers containing glycolic acid, lactic acid (also listed as *lactates* on product labels). These alpha-hydroxy acids (AHAs) act more like drugs than cosmetics. They make the layers of skin more compact so that they hold water better.

Sunscreens...

Look for a sun protection factor (SPF) of at least 15. But don't make the mistake of thinking that such a product will enable you to sunbathe indefinitely. It won't.

Most sunscreens block ultraviolet B (UVB) light only. To block the full spectrum of sunlight—both UVB and the deeper-penetrating ultraviolet A (UVA)—pick a sunscreen containing *avobenzone* or *titanium dioxide*. While ordinary sunscreen is okay for most people, those who have had skin cancer may be better off with a full-spectrum preparation.

Always apply sunscreen before going into the sun. Reapply it immediately after bathing or perspiring heavily—even if it's labeled waterproof.

Antiperspirants and deodorants...

Antiperspirants prevent wetness by temporarily plugging pores. Deodorants don't prevent wetness, only odor.

To avoid possible skin irritation, try deodorant first. If you perspire heavily or have an odor problem, switch to an antiperspirant containing *aluminum chlorhydrate* or *zirconium chlorhydrate*. These ingredients cause less irritation than those used in other antiperspirants. Any moisture will keep antiperspirant from getting into pores. To make sure your skin is completely dry before using, use a hair dryer for a few seconds.

Source: Andrew Scheman, MD, assistant clinical professor of dermatology, Northwestern University School of Medicine, Chicago. He is coauthor of *Cosmetics Buying Guide.* Consumer Reports Books.

For Indigestion and Heartburn Sufferers

Catnip tea soothes indigestion and heartburn by helping to relax digestive-tract muscles. *Recipe:* Pour one cup of boiling water over one to two teaspoons of catnip, then steep in a covered pot for 20 minutes. Add sweetener or lemon if desired. Catnip is available at health food stores.

Source: Elson M. Haas, MD, director of the Preventive Medical Center of Marin, San Rafael, CA, and author of *Staying Healthy with Nutrition.* Celestial Arts.

For Better Vision

Vision-enhancement "goggles" improve vision dramatically in those with very poor eyesight. The Low-Vision Enhancement System (abbreviated LVES and pronounced "Elvis") contains three separate black-and-white video cameras. A control unit worn on the belt allows the user to adjust contrast and magnify images from three to 10 times. LVES is available to individuals who have experience using low-vision devices or who have previously been in a low-vision program. *Cost:* $5,200. *Information:* Call the Lion's Vision Center at Johns Hopkins Wilmer Eye Institute, 410-955-5033.

Source: Robert W. Massoff, PhD, professor of ophthalmology, Johns Hopkins Wilmer Eye Institute, Baltimore.

Single Shoes for Amputees

Single shoes for amputees and "mismatched" pairs for people whose feet are of different sizes are available through the National Odd Shoe Exchange (NOSE). This not-for-profit membership organization maintains a list of 19,000 potential shoe mates.

Source: NOSE, 7102 N. 35 Ave., Phoenix 85051. 602-841-6691. *Dues:* $25, plus a $15 annual fee, for adults...$15, plus a $10 annual fee, for children six to 18 years of age...$10 for seniors older than 62. Free membership for children younger than five.

Pneumonia Warning

Pneumonia kills more than 40,000 people a year. That number could be cut in half if doctors were more vigilant about immunizing their patients. The Centers for Disease Control and Prevention recommends pneumonia vaccinations for all adults 65 and older. But less than 20% of those get the vaccine, usually when prompted by some underlying medical condition. *Self-defense:* If you are older than 65 and your doctor hasn't mentioned the pneumonia vaccine, bring the subject up.

Source: Raymond Strikas, MD, medical epidemiologist, national immunization program, Centers for Disease Control and Prevention, Atlanta.

Caffeine and Recovery

A caffeine pill before surgery helps coffee drinkers recover faster. In a recent test, coffee drinkers were given either a caffeine pill (equivalent to one cup of coffee) or a placebo one hour before outpatient surgery. *Result:* Those who received caffeine were released from the recovery room 40 minutes earlier than those who received the placebo. *Theory:* The presurgical caffeine prevents symptoms of caffeine withdrawal—fatigue, muscle pain and clouded thinking—making patients more alert and aware.

Source: Joseph Weber, MD, fellow, department of anesthesiology, Mayo Clinic, Rochester, MN.

Most Causes of Death Are Preventable

Officially, the top 10 causes of death in the US, in order, are heart disease, cancer, stroke, accidental injury, lung disease, pneumonia/influenza, diabetes, suicide, liver disease and AIDS.

But these categories camouflage the true, underlying causes of death—most of which are preventable.

In a single year...

...tobacco kills 400,000 people. Causes cancer, heart disease and stroke.

...diet/inactivity kills 300,000 people. Causes high blood pressure, diabetes and cancer of the colon, breast and prostate.

...alcohol kills 100,000. Causes cirrhosis of the liver, cancer and unintentional injury from car wrecks and other mishaps.

...infections kill 90,000. Includes meningitis, encephalitis and other parasitic diseases.

...toxic agents kill 60,000. Includes contaminated food and water, chemical additives, asbestos, lead and radon.

...motor vehicles kill 47,000. Using seat belts, air bags, child car seats and motorcycle helmets would halve this number.

...firearms kill 36,000.

...sexual transmitted diseases kill 30,000. Includes AIDS, hepatitis and cervical cancer.

...illegal drugs kill 20,000. Drugs account for a large portion of the deaths officially attributed to suicide, homicide, car accidents, AIDS and more.

Source: J. Michael McGinnis, MD, deputy assistant secretary for health (disease prevention and health promotion), US Department of Health and Human Services, Washington, DC. His research on the actual causes of death was published in the *Journal of the American Medical Association.*

Death-from-Heart-Disease Predictor

The *ankle/arm blood pressure index (AAI)* is a fast, noninvasive test that compares blood pressure in the upper and lower extremities. A reading of 0.9 or lower suggests an increased risk of death—even in persons who seem healthy.

Finding: Women 65 and older with low AAI values were five times more likely to die of heart disease than women of the same age with higher values. A separate study yielded similar results for men.

Self-defense: Periodic measurement of AAI in a physician's office or screening center may be

appropriate to identify older men and women at high risk of premature death.

Source: Molly T. Vogt, PhD, assistant professor of epidemiology, Graduate School of Public Health, University of Pittsburgh. Her four-year study of almost 1,500 women was published in the *Journal of the American Medical Association.*

Comfort and Health In the Sky

Planning before air travel and care while in the air can help avoid some common travelers' ills.

• Make yourself comfortable. Pick an aisle seat so you can get up. Raise feet, but don't cross legs.

• Avoid dehydration. Drink water, bottled if hygiene is in doubt. Avoid caffeine and alcohol. Use eyedrops and moisturizer.

• Protect your ears. Try using a decongestant and chewing gum to help keep your Eustachian tubes open.

• Choose good food. Order low-salt, low-fat or vegetarian meals ahead of time. Bring your own healthy snacks.

Do Your Own Medical Research

A doctor's advice is usually accepted at face value. Yet when it comes to treating a serious illness, that advice should be given close scrutiny.

Reason: Even the most caring, compassionate physician is ultimately performing a job. He/she has less at stake than the person who's sick—and whose life may be on the line. In a world where medical breakthroughs occur on an almost daily basis, no doctor can be expected to be up-to-date on every new treatment for every illness.

If you assume that your doctor has all the pertinent information, and accept his suggestions about the "best" course of action without providing any input of your own, you're behaving dangerously.

When your well-being is at stake, you must be your own best advocate. To do that, you must educate yourself about your condition—the various treatment options…and what the latest research reveals about new and possibly experimental treatments. You must then work with your care-givers to assure optimal care.

How I saved my life…

Four years ago my doctor told me I had a rare and incurable form of leukemia. What he did not know—and what my own research revealed—was that a new anti-leukemia drug had become available three months before my grim diagnosis.

This new drug was especially effective against the rare form of leukemia I was suffering from—80% of those treated achieved a complete and lasting remission. Because of that new treatment I am alive and cancer-free today. *Here is how you or a loved one can learn what you need to know about a serious illness…*

Second opinions…

If you heed no other advice in this article, be sure to get a second opinion. It can literally spell the difference between life and death.

Example: Six years ago, a friend of mine was diagnosed with advanced liver cancer. My friend's doctor offered him no treatment and gave him only months to live. But on the advice of his brother-in-law, a hospital administrator, Frank sought a second opinion from a major cancer research center. The doctors there recommended a new type of surgery. Frank got the surgery—and he is now healthy and cancer-free.

Moral of this story: Medicine is an inexact and rapidly evolving science. Doctors vary widely in their knowledge. Some are diligent about keeping up with advances in their field. Others aren't. By seeking out a second or perhaps even a third or fourth opinion, you boost your odds of finding a practitioner knowledgeable about every form of therapy that might prove beneficial to you.

Caution: The choices garnered from multiple opinions aren't always clearly black or white,

right or wrong. One doctor might recommend a treatment that has an 80% cure rate—but a 20% risk of serious long-term adverse effects. Another might recommend a treatment with a 50% cure rate—but with only a 5% chance of serious side effects. Which is the better option? It's up to the patient to decide.

Using a medical library…

Medical information—including information on the latest developments in treatment for virtually every illness, is readily available. The key is knowing how—and where—to find it.

Libraries affiliated with medical schools or major hospitals tend to have the most complete information.

If you're already hospitalized, federal law requires that you be given access to the hospital library—and that the hospital librarian respond to your requests for help in doing research.

If you're not hospitalized, call the library and find out if it's open to the public. If not, ask which local medical libraries are. If none are, ask about exceptions to the restricted access policies. In most states, at least one health library is open to the public.

In addition, at least two medical libraries in the US are geared specifically to lay people…

•Center for Medical Consumers, 237 Thompson St., New York 10012.

•Planetree Health Resource Center, 2040 Webster St., San Francisco 94115.

Pinpointing information…

Pinpointing information in a medical library can be a daunting task to the uninitiated.

To start, ask the librarian to help look up relevant studies in the *Index Medicus*, the master index of medical information. Copy down the names of relevant articles in respected medical journals—such as *The New England Journal of Medicine, the Journal of the American Medical Association* and *The Lancet,* a British periodical.

What are you looking for? A general overview of your illness, plus details of the latest research. In particular, you'll want to know different methods of treatment—including their success rates and their possible complications—and whether there's been any recent development that your primary physician may not yet know about.

You also want to know about clinical trials —experiments that test new treatments at the cutting edge of medicine. Participating in these experiments carries some risk, but it also offers hope where previously none existed. Despite the risks, far more people have been helped than hurt by clinical trials in this country.

If you find an article that details a promising new treatment, call the author of the article— or ask your doctor to call for you. Some researchers prefer talking to other medical professionals rather than to patients.

On-line medical databases...

Thanks to powerful computers and high-speed modems, medical information is now readily available from large medical databases held on government and private computers.

Benefit: Research that might take days of labor in a library can now be compiled in a matter of minutes using on-line databases.

Many medical libraries now provide access to these computer databases. To do on-line searching on your own, you'll need a modem, communications software and an account with a database provider. *Useful resource: Grateful Med,** a program designed to provide easy, user-friendly access to Medline, a vast compilation of medical articles, as well as many other important medical databases.

Via the popular on-line service Compu-Serve,† you can gain limited access not only to Medline but also to Physician's Data Query (PDQ), a database that provides detailed information about new drugs and other treatments for all types of cancer.

Through CompuServe or by mail you can also check out the database maintained by the National Organization for Rare Disorders (NORD), Box 8923, New Fairfield, Connecticut 06812. 203-746-6518. By mail, the first report is free. Additional reports cost $3.25 apiece.

Caution: As efficient as they are, on-line databases are neither user-friendly nor cheap. If you're not familiar with the arcane search

*Grateful Med is available from the US Commerce Department, National Technical Information Service, Springfield, VA 22161. 703-487-4650.

†To sign up for CompuServe, call 800-848-8199.

techniques required to access these databases, consider hiring a medical research firm to do the research for you. *Three excellent services:*

• *The Health Resource*, 564 Locust St., Conway, AK 72032. 501-329-5272.

• *Planetree* (see above for address). 415-923-3581.

• *Schine On-Line*, 39 Brenton Ave., Providence, RI 02906. 800-346-3287 or 401-751-0120.

Source: Gary Schine, president of the medical research agency Schine On-Line, Providence, RI. He is the author of *If the President Had Cancer....* Sandra Publications.

Polio Vaccinations Still Necessary

Polio has been eliminated from the Western Hemisphere. The last reported case occurred in Peru in 1991. Since then, the Americas have been free of the disease. But polio vaccinations are still necessary for all children—to prevent the virus from returning to this hemisphere from the other. The vaccine is also recommended for any person not previously vaccinated...and anyone who plans to live or work in a county where the virus is known to be present.

Source: Frederick Robbins, MD, chairman, International Commission for the Certification of Poliomyelitis Eradication, Pan American Health Organization, 525 23 St. NW, Washington, DC 20037.

Why You Should Brush Your Gums

Brushing the gums with a soft toothbrush can help reduce inflammation from wearing full dentures. *Best method:* Circular brushing for two and a half minutes twice a day.

Source: *Special Care in Dentistry,* American Dental Association, Chicago.

Tip for Denture Wearers

Removing dentures at night can lead to aching jaws, headaches, and insomnia. *Reason:* Jaws adapt to closing over teeth. If you sleep without your dentures, you may "overclose"—which strains the jaw joint and muscles. *Recommended:* If you have morning-after pain, try leaving dentures in at night (but remove them for four hours during the day).

Source: An Army study of 200 denture wearers, cited in *American Health*, New York.

Japanese Women vs. American Women

Japanese women have fewer hot flashes and other menopausal symptoms than American women.

Possible reason: They eat about two ounces a day of foods made from soybeans, such as tofu (bean curd) and miso (soybean paste). Soybeans are rich in isoflavinoids, which are converted during digestion to estrogen-like substances that can help prevent hot flashes.

Source: Barry Goldin, PhD, and Sherwood Gorbach, MD, Tufts University School of Medicine, and Herman Adlercreutz, MD, Helsinki University, Finland.

Scalding Self-Defense

Water at 140 degrees can scald a child in as little as three seconds, though it may feel only moderately hot to an adult. *Important:*

•Never leave a child alone in a bathroom or kitchen.

•Set your home's water heater at 120 degrees, or the "low" setting (depending on your thermostat).

•Always check bathwater before placing your child in the tub.

•Place cooking pots on back burners, and turn pot handles toward the back of the stove.

•Place hot foods and drinks far back from table and counter edges.

•Keep appliance cords—especially those for appliances that might contain hot food or drinks—out of children's reach.

•Never nurse or hold a baby while drinking a hot beverage.

•Never let children remove food from a microwave oven.

Source: Martin R. Eichelberger, MD, director of emergency trauma service and the burn unit of Children's National Medical Center, Washington, DC, and president of the National SAFE KIDS Campaign, Washington, DC.

Plastic Surgery Problems

Whether it's an ordinary nose job or the removal of a rib to achieve a smaller waistline, cosmetic surgery performed by a qualified surgeon is usually safe and effective.

As with any medical procedure, however, cosmetic surgery occasionally results in complications—in a small portion of all procedures. And when complications occur, the results can be devastating.

Cosmetic surgery risks...

•Persistent infection. The most common complication—and usually the easiest to correct. Antibiotics are effective in most cases, although implants sometimes have to be removed.

Exception: Cartilage infections, especially those following a nose job (rhinoplasty), rarely may persist for a year or longer even with aggressive antibiotic treatment...and they can destroy the nose's shape.

Self-defense: Choose a qualified surgeon—one who has performed the same procedure dozens of times.

•Silicone granulomas. Silicone gel implants are generally safe, although some experts contend that in the case of breast augmentation, they make mammography more difficult.

When large amounts of liquid silicone are injected into the breasts or other parts of the body, however, silicone granulomas sometimes develop. These lumpy, oozing lesions distort the shape of surrounding skin…and they sometimes progress to open, draining wounds.

Self-defense: Injected silicone should be used only for small, superficial defects—not large ones.

•Nubbin nose. Nose jobs involving excessive cartilage removal can cause big trouble later in life. As the patient ages, the skin thins, and the nose appears to shrink—sometimes to little more than a tiny nubbin.

In extreme cases, a nubbin nose causes not only acute embarrassment, but also breathing difficulties. The only way to correct the problem is to transplant cartilage taken from elsewhere in the body.

Self-defense: The less tissue removed during any cosmetic surgery, the safer.

•Lumpy skin. Surgeons performing liposuction must wield the cannula (fat-sucking instrument) very deftly, since uneven removal of fat results in lumpy or rippled skin. These defects are difficult or impossible to fix, even with additional liposuction or fat transplantation.

In very rare cases, fat cells liberated during liposuction cut off the supply of blood to the heart or brain. Although rare, some fat embolisms are fatal.

Also in rare cases, liposuction can result in inadvertent damage to the spleen or other internal organs. A ruptured spleen usually necessitates emergency surgery to control bleeding.

Self-defense: Use an experienced surgeon. Check out the doctor's reputation, enlist word-of-mouth recommendations, and directly ask the doctor questions about his/her background.

•Barbie Doll hair. Hair transplantation is safe and effective, but the process takes months or even years to complete. Impatient patients who fail to see it through to the end often wind up with obvious plugs of hair arrayed in regular rows across the scalp.

Self-defense: Start hair transplants only if you intend to see them through.

•Distorted eyes. Surgeons performing eye tucks (blepharoplasties) must be careful to remove just the right amount of tissue around the eyes. Otherwise, the patient may be left with eyes that seem to turn downward or outward, or with an exposed mucous membrane around the eyes.

Sometimes the eyelids are stretched so tight by surgery that the eyes cannot fully close. Botched eye jobs can also result in acute glaucoma…even blindness.

Self-defense: Choose a highly experienced surgeon.

•Lopsided face. In rare instances, face lifts damage the facial nerve. *Result:* Diminished muscle tone or even partial paralysis. The patient may develop a crooked smile, sagging cheeks or may have difficulty blinking.

Similarly, implants in the chin, cheeks and other parts of the face must be firmly attached to bone, or over time they may be mobile. More than an annoyance, mobile facial implants can result in a lopsided appearance.

Self-defense: Make sure the surgeon plans the implants so they are placed on bone.

•Rashes and redness. Collagen used to fill in acne scars and other skin defects can cause severe rashes and persistent redness. Theoretically, collagen injected directly into a blood vessel rather than just under the skin could interrupt the flow of blood to an eye—resulting in blindness.

Self-defense: The doctor should make sure the patient is not allergic to collagen before large quantities are injected. This can be done by test injections, introducing a small amount of collagen into the body in an inconspicuous place.

•Bad nose job. The problem of rhinoplasty is that the removal of too much bone or cartilage can result in the collapse of the tip of the nose which impairs breathing and gives an artificial looking nose.

Self-defense: The patient must emphasize that they want a natural looking nose with a minimal amount of bone and cartilage removed. An experienced surgeon would already be aware of this.

•Too-tight face lift. This usually occurs on repeat face lifts and strictly skin lifts. Newer face lifts include both deeper layers and skin and give a more natural look.

Self-defense: Ask what technique the surgeon uses and how much experience he/she has with the procedure. Ask to see other patients …or their photographs.

Source: Linton A. Whitaker, MD, chief of the division of plastic surgery, the Hospital of the University of Pennsylvania, and professor of surgery, University of Pennsylvania School of Medicine. Dr. Whitaker specializes in facial surgery.

It's Important to Take Charge of Old Age Now...

It's no longer news that more Americans are living longer—the 75-plus and 85-plus age groups are the fastest growing segments of the US population. But for the first time, we can benefit from studies that tell us not only who is living longer, but why—and what we can do to enrich and lengthen our lives.

Recent research consistently shows that there is more to healthful aging than just staying physically fit. Maintaining strong social ties plays an essential role. And a third factor, less frequently discussed, is also important…a sense of personal purpose. *Bottom line:* People who lead purposeful lives live longer than those who do not.

Physical health: Basic life-extenders...

•Eliminate tobacco, regardless of your present age and health status.

•Drink alcohol in moderation, if at all. If you are one of the nation's 10 million alcoholics, get help. There are very, very few elderly alcoholics.

•Lower the amount of fat in your diet. Most Americans get up to 40% of their calories from fat. *Better:* 10% to 20%.

•Mediate the effects of stress with exercise and other techniques.

•Exercise for a half-hour daily, five days a week. Choose a solid cardiopulmonary program. Fast-walking is inexpensive and effective.

Caution: Golf is not recommended. It is useless as exercise, and can be stressful if combined with business.

Mental health and abilities...

Contrary to popular belief (and barring disease), intelligence does not decline with age. While reaction speed does slow, some abilities such as judgment, accuracy and general knowledge may actually increase as learning continues. Important: Ongoing stimulation.

In terms of human development, one of the essential tasks of old age is to find ways to understand and use the lessons of one's lifetime. This entails learning to apportion one's strengths and resources, and to adapt to changes and losses as they occur.

Key: People must continue to adapt to stay healthy, both mentally and physically. Failure to adapt to changing circumstances can result in physical or mental illness at any age.

A comprehensive Seattle study found wide variation in intellectual changes among individuals as they aged. A large number showed little decline, even in their eighties. What they had in common: These people had no cardiovascular disease, were not poor, were actively involved in life…and their attitudes and behavior were already flexible in mid-life, and remained so.

Expect some emotional changes with aging. Most common: Family authority roles begin to reverse, usually in the mid-fifties. Women tend to grow more active and assertive, while men tend to become more engendering or nurturant. This pattern occurs in many cultures, and should be supported, as each sex explores potentials that may have been neglected in earlier life.

Recommended: Encourage men to share and network, women to be more self-determining and active in the world beyond their families.

Helpful to men: Beginning to recognize and develop your nurturant side now, whatever your age, can help to prevent or alleviate the common syndrome of stress, coronary disease and shortened life expectancy associated with overidentification with work and subsequent "retirement shock."

Other changes to expect—and support...

•Desire to leave a legacy. This can take many forms: Artwork, fortune, grandchildren, possessions, family recipes, memories in the minds of others. Many older people find the role of "elder" (counselor, mentor, teacher) to be particularly enriching.

• Altered sense of time. Older people tend to lose both "time panic" and boredom, in favor of a sense of time based on the appreciation of the truly important things in life… human relationships, nature, etc. *Result:* An ability to live in the moment that can make old age a richly enjoyable time, filled with emotional and sensory awareness. Older people also experience a personal sense of the cycle of life and one's place in the cycle…for many, a deepening of spiritual beliefs.

• Creativity and curiosity. Most older people stay productive and active their entire lives, barring ill health or social problems, such as poverty. *Less well known:* Many older people become creative for the first time in their lives. *Keys:* An attitude of curiosity and the ability to be surprised throughout one's lifetime.

• Feelings of serenity, wisdom, fulfillment. As older people come to accept the inevitability of death, feelings of satisfaction with one's life, of having done one's best, of having survived life's challenges, are more common than generally believed—though not as common as possible. The process of reminiscence that characterizes old age is essential to the emotional well-being of older people, as they work to resolve past conflicts and find significance in their life history.

Recommended: Pay attention to examining personal conflicts and reviewing one's life as a lifetime habit. Listen and support the process in the elderly. It can be hurtful, even devastating, for an older person to be told his/her life story is boring or unimportant.

Social health…

People who have healthy social networks have less disease and live longer than those who do not. A study of men and women over age 65 conducted at Duke University Medical Center found the risk of mortality to be four times greater in people who had little social support, even when other factors, such as gender, health, smoking, economic status, depression, etc. were considered.

A Swedish study found that social isolation is one of the best predictors of mortality from all causes. Other studies have found that individuals who are "self-starters," able to initiate new social contacts and activities, have the least disease and the longest survival rates.

Researchers are just starting to appreciate the importance of friendship at all phases of life. In addition to immediate family, friends are seen as "family" by many older persons, and they lend important support in times of need.

Studies are beginning to show that one reason women may outlive men is their greater skill in seeking and maintaining friendships. Mortality following the loss of a spouse is also lower in women, due in part to their better social networks.

Recommended: Use the telephone, write letters and cards, attend reunions. Nurture friendships with people of all ages throughout your lifetime. While many consider retirement communities to be artificially segregated environments, studies show older people who live among other older people make more friends than those who live among the young.

Caution: American cultural beliefs about independence and "doing for oneself" can foster a sense of isolation in people who resist help when it is needed. By contrast, people in group-oriented societies (Israeli kibbutzim, for example) can accept the support of others with no loss of self-esteem or feelings of dependence.

Recommended: Make use of support groups in the times of grief, stress or loss that are an inevitable part of life: Illness, widowhood, family crisis. *Also very useful:* Humor, a healing mechanism and coping skill that is underused in the elderly.

A sense of purpose…

One's goal or purpose in later life (or any other time) need not be lofty. A sense of purpose can be derived from volunteer work, one's role as a grandparent or an attachment to the New York Yankees. Retirees who organize their daily lives to accommodate their goals live longer than those who do not.

Example: A University of Michigan study found that men who did volunteer work at least once a week were two-and-a-half times less likely to die than those who did none.

Caution: The highest suicide rate in America is among white men in their eighties. *Reason:* This group suffers the greatest loss of power, influence and status, and can therefore experience the greatest sense of helplessness and impotence.

Essential: Maintaining the deep sense of self-esteem that is derived from inner purpose.

Recommended: Begin now to make good use of your time...tutor, fund-raise, work for a cause you admire. *Key:* Choose a regularized activity that is outside yourself.

Source: Robert N. Butler, MD, chairman of the department of geriatrics at Mount Sinai School of Medicine, Mount Sinai Hospital, in New York City. Dr. Butler is co-author of *Aging and Mental Health*, Macmillan.

How to Have a Healthier Heart

Because cardiovascular disease is so familiar to all of us, we tend to think we know all about it. In fact, many ideas about heart disease commonly held by laypeople and physicians alike are nothing more than myths. *Included:*

• *Myth:* That an aspirin a day prevents heart attacks. *Reality:* A daily aspirin tablet does seem to help people who have had one heart attack from having another—but there's very little benefit for those without pre-existing heart disease.

Recent study: For every 1,000 otherwise healthy people who took a daily aspirin tablet, heart attacks were prevented in only eight people. In contrast, 991 people experienced neither harm nor benefit...and one person suffered bleeding into the brain from the aspirin.

Aspirin has also been linked to stomach ulcers. And there is no evidence that taking a daily aspirin boosts life expectancy—people simply die from something other than a heart attack.

Self-defense: Do not take aspirin if your heart is healthy. If you have had a heart attack, take no more than one aspirin tablet a day—preferably children's aspirin.

• *Myth:* That we should all try to lower our cholesterol levels. *Reality:* Special diets and cholesterol-lowering medications make sense only for certain people—hypertensives, smokers, diabetics, people with cholesterol levels 280 or above...and those already diagnosed with heart disease.

Others who try to lower their cholesterol readings may be wasting their effort. Lowering your cholesterol level does nothing to increase your longevity, even if it does reduce your risk of heart attack.

Note: Elevated cholesterol readings should be of little concern in healthy people aged 65 or older. Studies have shown that these elderly people are no longer at increased risk for heart attacks—if cholesterol hasn't led to heart disease by this age, it is probably no longer a threat.

• *Myth:* That a prudent lifestyle prevents heart attacks. *Reality:* Adopting a healthy diet, losing weight and giving up smoking help prevent heart attacks, but nothing can guarantee a healthy heart.

Despite all kinds of precautions, some people wind up suffering a heart attack...just as others eat all the wrong foods and never exercise and remain healthy.

Bottom line: There is no way to eliminate your risk of heart disease entirely, even with the most aggressive preventive measures.

This does not mean a healthy lifestyle is of no value. I am a strong advocate of exercise and sensible diets, but primarily from the standpoint of improved self-image. Odds are your lifestyle will have little effect on your overall risk of heart disease.

• *Myth:* That all hypertensives should avoid salt. *Reality:* Only about half of all cases of hypertension respond strongly to salt reduction. About 30% respond weakly. In about 20% of all cases, salt intake plays no role at all.

• *Myth:* That a normal electrocardiogram (EKG) means a healthy heart. *Reality:* The EKG is an imperfect tool.

Although it's highly effective at pinpointing electrical disturbances in the heart and whether the patient is having or has ever had a heart attack, it reveals little about the health of the coronary arteries (the ones that sometimes clog and cause heart attacks).

Even hearts with severe blockages often appear normal on an EKG. I've had patients who had severe heart attacks within a week after having a normal EKG.

Alternative: The stress test. In this procedure, EKG readings are made during rigorous exercise on a treadmill. Stress tests are more likely to uncover potentially serious heart problems than are standard EKG's. However, even stress tests are not fail-safe.

•*Myth:* That heart murmurs are always dangerous. *Reality:* Although heart murmurs can be symptomatic of potentially deadly heart valve defects, they're often harmless.

In fact, a murmur means only that a physician using a stethoscope can hear blood rushing through the heart. This could mean a defective valve, but it's more likely the result of some other factor—a thin chest wall, pregnancy or even a highly conditioned heart.

If you are diagnosed with a heart murmur, make sure your doctor explains its nature—and whether or not you need to curtail physical activity.

•*Myth:* That a normal blood-pressure reading means a healthy heart. *Reality:* There is no such thing as normal blood pressure. The lower your blood pressure, the lower your risk of stroke and heart disease. So even a very low blood pressure reading is generally a good thing.

But blood pressure readings are notoriously inaccurate. They can be thrown off by many things, including illness, anxiety, medications... even posture.

Doctors should always take several readings before confirming a case of hypertension. In some cases, the physician may ask the patient to wear a 24-hour blood-pressure monitor for a day.

•*Myth:* That bypass surgery restores the heart to good health. *Reality:* All it does is restore blood flow to parts of the heart that had been blood-deprived.

Bypass surgery may lower the risk of subsequent heart attacks and increase life expectancy. It cannot undo the effects of a previous heart attack. Damaged heart muscle remains damaged.

And unfortunately, the effects of bypass surgery do not last forever. Grafted blood vessels tend to clog back up within five to 10 years after surgery. Second and even third bypass operations are sometimes necessary.

If your physician recommends bypass surgery, find out how many blood vessels are diseased. If there are three or more, odds are you can benefit from bypass. For blockages in one or two coronary arteries, however, nonsurgical intervention is usually just as beneficial—and safer and less expensive.

Source: Bruce Charash, MD, assistant professor of medicine, Cornell University Medical College. A frequent lecturer on heart disease, Dr. Charash is the author of *Heart Myths*, Viking Penguin.

Tobacco Dangers

By now, most Americans are well aware that smoking causes lung cancer. But tobacco is a far bigger villain than most of us could ever imagine. Cigarettes, pipes, cigars, snuff and chewing tobacco kill more than 434,000 Americans each year—accounting for almost one out of five premature deaths in this country.

Lung cancer is just the first in a long and harrowing litany of tobacco-related problems.

Other tobacco dangers...

•Addictiveness. While some people have likened the addictive potential of nicotine to that of heroin, the good news is that tens of millions of people have been trying to quit smoking.

•Back pain. Smoking is probably a major risk factor in recovery from back pain (the leading cause of worker disability in the US) because poor oxygen levels of those who smoke prevent lumbar disks from being adequately oxygenated.

•Bladder cancer. Smoking causes 40% of all cases of bladder cancer, accounting for more than 4,000 new cases annually.

•Breast cancer. Women who smoked heavily, more than one pack per day, and who started smoking at an early age are 75% more likely to develop breast cancer than nonsmoking women.

- Cervical cancer. Up to one-third of all cases of cervical cancer—12,000 new cases a year—are directly attributable to smoking. Women who smoke are four times more likely to develop the disease than are nonsmoking women.

- Childhood respiratory ailments. Youngsters exposed to parents' tobacco smoke have six times as many respiratory infections as kids of nonsmoking parents. Smokers' children also face an increased risk of cough, chronic bronchitis and pneumonia.

- Diabetes. Smoking decreases the body's absorption of insulin. *Also:* Smoking exacerbates the damage of small blood vessels in the eyes, ears and feet of diabetics.

- Drug interactions. Smokers need higher than normal dosages of certain drugs, including theophylline (asthma medication), heparin (used to prevent blood clotting), propranolol (used for angina and high blood pressure) and medications for depression and anxiety.

- Ear infections. Children of smokers face an increased risk of otitis media (middle ear infection).

- Emphysema. Smoking accounts for up to 85% of all deaths attributable to emphysema.

- Esophageal cancer. Smoking accounts for 80% of all cases of esophageal cancer, which kills 15,000 Americans yearly.

- Financial woes. A pack of cigarettes (which costs the manufacturer less than 20¢!! to make) sells for about $2.50 a pack—nearly $1,000 a year for a pack a day user.

- Fires. Smoking is the leading cause of fires in homes, hotels and hospitals.

- Gastrointestinal cancer. Preliminary research indicates that smoking at least doubles the risk of cancer of the stomach and duodenum—the portion of the small intestine just downstream from the stomach.

- Heart disease. Smokers are up to four times more likely to develop cardiovascular disease than nonsmokers. Mechanism: Carbon monoxide and other poisonous gases in tobacco smoke replace oxygen in the blood cells, pro-

mote coronary spasm and cause accumulation of clot-producing platelets.

- Infertility. Couples in which at least one member smokes are more than three times as likely to have trouble conceiving than nonsmoking couples.

Explanation: Tobacco smoke interferes with the implantation of a fertilized egg within the uterus. It reduces the number and quality of sperm cells in a man's ejaculate and raises the number of abnormal sperm cells...and increases a man's risk of penile cancer. Women who smoke are more likely to miscarry or deliver prematurely than nonsmoking women. Some scientists now theorize that toxins in the bloodstream of pregnant smokers pass through the placenta to the fetus, sowing the seeds for future cancers.

- Kidney cancer. Smoking causes 40% of all cases of kidney cancer.

- Laryngeal cancer. Smokers who smoke more than 25 cigarettes a day are 25 to 30 times more likely to develop cancer of the larynx than nonsmokers.

- Leukemia. In addition to tobacco smoke condensate, better known as tar, tobacco smoke contains several powerful carcinogens, including the organic chemical benzene and a radioactive form of the element polonium, both of which can cause leukemia.

- Low birth weight. Women who smoke as few as five cigarettes daily during pregnancy face a significantly greater risk of giving birth to an unnaturally small, lightweight infant.

- Mouth cancer. Tobacco causes the vast majority of all cancers of the mouth, lips, cheek, tongue, salivary glands and even tonsils. Men who smoke, dip snuff or chew tobacco face a 27-fold risk of these cancers. Women smokers—because women have tended to use less tobacco—face a six-fold risk.

- Nutrition. People who smoke tend to have poorer nutrition than do nonsmokers. Smokers also have lower levels of HDL (good cholesterol).

- Occupational lung cancer. Although a nonsmoker's risk of lung cancer increases six times due to prolonged occupational exposure to asbestos, that risk jumps to 92 times in an asbestos worker who smokes.

• Osteoporosis. Women who smoke experience menopause on an average of five to 10 years earlier than nonsmokers, causing a decline in estrogen production—and thinning bones—at an earlier age.

• Pharyngeal (throat) cancer. Last year, cancer of the pharynx killed 3,650 Americans—the majority of these deaths resulted directly from smoking.

• Premature aging. Constant exposure to tobacco smoke prematurely wrinkles facial skin and yellows the teeth and fingernails.

• Recovery from injury or surgery. Wound and bone injuries of smokers take a longer period of time to heal. Smokers also have a greater risk of complications from surgery, including pneumonia (due to weaker lungs), and remain in the hospital for longer periods.

• Stroke. Smoking increases the risk of stroke two-fold both among men and women.

Special danger: For women who smoke and use oral contraceptives, the risk of stroke is ten-fold.

• Tooth loss. Use of snuff or chewing tobacco causes gum recession and tooth abrasion, two frequent contributors to tooth loss.

Source: Alan Blum, MD, family physician, Department of Family Medicine, Baylor College of Medicine, Houston. Dr. Blum is the founder and president of Doctors Ought to Care (DOC), c/o Department of Family Medicine, Baylor College of Medicine, 5510 Greenbriar, Houston 77005, an antismoking group long-recognized for its service to public health.

When Chest Pain Means Heart Attack and When It Doesn't

Chest pain is psychosomatic almost half the time, according to a recent study. *Key:* If the pain is sharp and stabbing, or it's on the left side of the chest, it's likely caused by psychological stress. But a heavy, gripping sensation in the central chest is a typical heart attack symptom, especially if it lasts five to six minutes. Consult your doctor in either case.

Source: Study by Dr. Christopher Bass, King's College Hospital, London.

How to Handle the Catastrophic Health-Care Problem Now

Amazing as it seems, two-thirds of all people since the beginning of time who have ever lived beyond age 65 are alive today.

What's more, the average person who lives to be 65 today will live to be 87. *Staggering implication:* That person will have to finance 22 years of retirement in sickness or in health. It's estimated that 30 million Americans—15 million of them now working—have no medical insurance at all. And, many others are seriously underprotected. *New realities in health care:*

• Hospital and medical costs are going up at an alarming rate because of expensive new medical technology, inflation, and high medical malpractice insurance rates that doctors must pay.

• Strained by the budget deficit, the government has been reducing its role in health care. It has toughened Medicare payment standards, raised premiums for people over 65, and tightened eligibility requirements for Medicaid coverage of the poor. It's also trying to shift some of the burden for health-care costs to the private sector by, for example, requiring employer health plans to pay benefits to any employees before Medicare kicks in.

• Companies, trying desperately to cut costs and remain globally competitive, are trying to shift health costs to their employees by means of higher deductibles, co-payments, and shared premiums. Most vulnerable: Retirement health benefits for current employees. Some companies simply won't offer them. Others will make employees pay a big share of the cost.

• Insurers, faced with the spectre of such catastrophic illnesses as AIDS, which now costs about $250,000 per patient, will surely toughen underwriting standards as much as allowed by law. Where they're permitted to give applicants blood tests, they'll not only screen out those carrying the AIDS virus, but may also uncover other medical conditions that will cause them to refuse coverage or charge extra premiums.

•Due to an organized campaign by senior citizens groups who objected to paying up to $800 in supplemental premiums based on their tax liabilities, Congress just repealed the much-misunderstood Medicare Catastrophic Coverage Act it enacted in 1987. Now, some are predicting a Congressional backlash against the elderly.

What to do now...

Put health insurance at the top of your priority list. If you don't have it through an employer, talk to your insurance agent and select a comprehensive health-care policy from a strong (rated A+ excellent by A. M. Best) company with a good reputation for paying claims. Having a respected agent behind you can often help in getting insurance and claims service.

Costs: For an individual in his or her late 30s, good medical comprehensive coverage can be had for $1,500–$2,000. For a family of four, with the parents in their 40s, it will cost closer to $6,000.

Coverage everyone needs:

•Basic hospital insurance. The Blue Cross program is the best-known hospital insurer nationally, but it really consists of local entities that vary in service from place to place. What *you'll want covered:* A semi-private hospital room with meals, general nursing services, in-hospital lab and x-ray fees, operating room costs, in-hospital medications, and various other in-hospital expenses.

Trap: The average hospital stay right now is only about nine days. Thus, it's a mistake to pay for insurance only on the basis of how many hospital days it will reimburse you for. Also, find out what the insurance company's definition of "in-hospital" is because many procedures are now performed on an outpatient basis and you'll need coverage for these, too.

•Surgical medical coverage. This covers visits to doctors, including any necessary opera-

tions. Again, Blue Shield is the best known nationally, but many other companies offer similar policies. Blue Cross and Blue Shield can be somewhat cheaper because they are non-profit companies, but some of their tax advantage was removed by tax reform so they don't have as great a cost advantage as they used to.

•Major medical. This is critical because it picks up after the relatively low limits on the first two types of insurance and acts as a kind of umbrella coverage to protect you if you are struck by a major illness or injury, such as cancer or a heart attack. Look for a policy that pays up to $1 million or more because any major problem these days can run into thousands of dollars.

Use big deductibles...

The best way to get the most protection for the least premium dollar is to take big deductibles. Ask yourself how much of the initial cost of an illness or hospitalization you can afford to bear without creating a severe long-term financial hardship. Most people could probably afford a deductible of $750 on a major medical policy, for example. After the deductible, look for coverage that pays at least 80% of expenses up to a level of, say, $2,000–$5,000 and then 100% thereafter.

Important: Find out whether the deductible is a "per-cause" or "calendar-year" or "benefit-year" type. An all-cause calendar-year or benefit-year deductible is preferable because you would then be reimbursed at any point when your total covered medical expenses for the year reached the deductible. In the following year, you would be responsible for another deductible.

Medigap insurance...

Those over 65 on Medicare need supplemental private insurance called Medigap. This generally covers the basic Medicare in-hospital deductible plus some portion of the many extras that Medicare doesn't cover or covers to only a limited extent, e.g., doctor's bills that are above Medicare's limits. One of the best Medigap policies is offered by the American Association of Retired Persons (AARP). The company has already announced that its Medicare Supplement Plans will probably adjust benefits (and premiums) to make up for cutbacks in Medicare. No doubt it will continue to fill those gaps. And if not, other companies will.

Nursing-home care…

The most frightening aspect of growing older is the possibility of having to spend many months or years in a nursing home or an extended-care facility. Current statistics show that 40% of people over 65 will need care in a nursing home at some time in the future. In 1988, the average cost for long-term nursing home care was $70–$115 per day ($25,510–$42,000 a year). Costs for long-term care at home ranged from $5,000–$10,000 per year depending on the area and level of care received.

Depressing: A recent study estimated that 80% of single people and 55% of married people over 65 in nursing homes will have impoverished themselves. After two years, the number rises to nearly 90% for both groups. But Medicare basically doesn't cover long-term nursing-home or at-home care. Even Medicaid, the joint federal and state program to provide a safety net for those with low incomes or high medical bills, will pick up the tab only after you've exhausted nearly all of your own assets (except your home) and those of your spouse.

Result: Some 100 companies are now marketing nursing- home or long-term care insurance. It's one of the hottest insurance products today, although it's not cheap.

What to look for: Get a policy that is guaranteed renewable for life, with a grace period of seven to 31 days in case premiums are paid late. Some offer an inflation protection option. Ask on what basis premiums will be increased.

Try to find a policy that does not require prior hospitalization and that does provide coverage for skilled, intermediate, or custodial care without requiring licensed medical professionals. That's key for getting help caring for Alzheimer's patients, for example. *Trap:* Make sure that Alzheimer's is covered. It's called an organically based mental condition and if that's not mentioned, it may not be covered.

Leading companies offering this insurance: Aetna, American Express, Continental Casualty, and Travelers.

When to buy: Not before your 50s, but if you buy then you may be able to get a more favorable premium later on. Certainly consider it when you're 60. Then you can rest assured that if serious or prolonged illness strikes, it won't bankrupt your family.

Source: Sam E. Beller, CLU, ChFC, is president of Diversified Programs, Inc., 450 Seventh Ave., New York 10123. He is an insurance agent and a financial planner and is the author of *The Great Insurance Secret*, William Morrow.

Fat Removal Technique

Liposuction—surgery performed to remove excess fat from various parts of the body—is now the most popular cosmetic operation in the United States. The doctor inserts a thin tube called a cannula through a small incision in the skin and moves it back and forth to break up a fatty deposit. The dislodged fat is then evacuated through this tubing by strong suction.

In cases where a person has good skin elasticity—up into their early 40s for most people—a double chin can be fixed without undergoing a face-lift. Liposuction can remove fat from a full neck, giving the patient a clean jawline and only a tiny scar. *Cost:* $2,500.

Source: Dr. Henry Zackin, a plastic and reconstructive surgeon in private practice in New York City.

Harmful Denture Adhesives

Denture adhesives can actually be more harmful than helpful to users. Karaya gum, a common ingredient, is highly acidic and eats away the enamel of natural teeth. Constant use may dissolve bone tissue and promote fungus infections in the mouth. *The good news:* Properly fitting dentures don't require adhesives in the first place.

Source: Dr. George Murrell, University of Southern California, Los Angeles 90007.

How to Change Your Biological Age

Gray hair, wrinkled skin, growing flabbiness, loss of vitality and reduced resistance to injury and disease…

To most Americans, these are harbingers of old age, unwelcome but inevitable milestones along a path that leads inexorably to the grave.

In fact, recent research suggests something quite different—that the body's gradual decline stems not from the passing of years but from the combined effects of inactivity and poor nutrition. So no matter what your present health status or your chronological age, regular exercise and improved eating habits will lower your biological age.

Benefits: Reduced body fat…increased muscle mass…strength increases of 200% to 300% …increases in aerobic capacity by 20% or more …and reduced risk of heart disease, diabetes, osteoporosis and other age-related ailments.

To lose fat and gain muscle: Be sure to combine a low-fat diet with regular exercise.

• Aerobic capacity. To gauge fitness, doctors often measure the body's ability to process oxygen during exercise. The greater this aerobic capacity, the faster oxygen is pumped throughout the body—and the fitter the individual. Like other biomarkers, aerobic capacity often declines with age. Typically, by age 65 it is 30% to 40% below its level in young adulthood.

• Blood-sugar tolerance. For most Americans, aging brings about a gradual decline in the body's ability to metabolize blood sugar (glucose). So common is this problem that by age 70, 20% of men and 30% of women are at an increased risk of diabetes, a potential killer.

At special risk for problems: The overweight, the sedentary and those who eat a fatty diet.

Good news: A low-fat, high-fiber diet, combined with regular exercise, will cut your diabetes risk. Be sure to include both strength-building and aerobic exercise in your routine.

• Cholesterol ratio. As most of us already know, a high cholesterol level boosts your risk of heart disease. But total cholesterol isn't the only thing that counts.

Very important: The ratio of total cholesterol to HDL (good cholesterol). For older people, the ideal ratio is 4.5 or lower. A person whose total cholesterol is 200 and whose HDL is 50, for example, has a ratio of 200/50, or 4.0.

To lower your ratio: Stop smoking, lose weight, reduce your intake of fatty, cholesterol-rich foods (especially animal products) and exercise regularly. Exercise is the only way to boost HDL levels.

• Blood pressure. In many parts of the world, advancing age brings little if any change in blood pressure. In the US, however, where older people tend to be both overweight and sedentary, blood pressure does rise with age, often spiralling far above the maximum "safe" level of 145/80.

To keep pressure in check: Stay slim, don't smoke, get regular exercise and limit your consumption of fat, salt and alcohol. If these steps fail to regulate pressure, pressure-lowering drugs may be necessary.

• Bone density. As we age, our skeletons slowly become weaker and more brittle. While some mineral loss is inevitable, the severe and potentially deadly condition known as osteoporosis is not.

Prevention: Although consuming at least 800 milligrams of calcium a day will retard the loss of bone, that alone rarely does the trick. *Also needed:* Weight-bearing exercise, such as walking, running or cycling.

Not helpful: Swimming and other forms of exercise that do not subject the long bones to the stress of gravity.

• Body temperature regulation. Compared with young people, old people sweat less, get less thirsty and excrete more water in their urine. These seemingly minor changes, which are a part of aging—plus the loss of muscle tissue needed for efficient shivering—hinder the body's ability to regulate its internal temperature, which raises our risk of dehydration in summer and hypothermia in winter.

Source: William J. Evans, PhD, chief of the human physiology lab at the Human Nutrition Research Center on Aging, a Boston-based facility operated jointly by the US Department of Agriculture and Tufts University. Dr. Evans is the coauthor of *Biomarkers: The 10 Keys for Prolonging Vitality.* Fireside Books.

Leg-Pain Warning

Pain that causes limping may be a sign of poor blood supply to the legs—caused by hardening or clogging of the arteries in the lower body. This condition is often associated with narrowed arteries to the heart and brain. Untreated, clogged arteries can lead to heart attack or stroke. *Self-defense:* See your doctor if you feel any cramping, fatigue or tightness when walking that disappears when you stop walking.

Source: John Cooke, MD, cardiologist and director, vascular medicine section, Stanford University Clinic, Palo Alto, CA.

Inhaling Steam Doesn't Help Get Rid of a Cold

Previous studies suggested that steam inhalation kills the cold-causing rhinovirus in the respiratory tract. But in a new study, volunteers who breathed steam long enough to raise the temperature inside their nostrils to 109° Fahrenheit—the minimum needed to inactivate the virus—reported no differences in their symptoms compared to those who simply inhaled warm air.

Source: G.J. Forstall, MD, assistant professor of medicine and staff physician, department of infectious disease, McLaren Regional Medical Center, Flint, MI.

How to Overcome Headaches, Arthritis, Backache and Other Common Sources of Chronic Pain

Our brains are programmed to interpret pain as a sign of acute injury. Almost instinctively, we stop what we're doing...we limit our movement...and we get help. When pain is chronic, however, these instincts are counterproductive. Inactivity won't heal a bad back, constant headaches or arthritis—it just creates more problems.*

People come to our pain center seeking total relief. But that isn't always possible. What they must really learn is to *manage* their pain, to focus on quality of life. That way, they can learn to live happily, even with pain.

Overreacting to pain...

One of the first things I ask new patients to do is to describe their pain. More often than not, they describe not the sensation of pain, but what the pain means to them.

Typical responses: "Pain makes my life miserable...pain drives away my friends...it means that something is terribly wrong...it consumes my whole life...it makes me irritable and angry."

Such negative thoughts can be more devastating than the pain itself. This "pain-button thinking" turns every twinge into a catastrophe. Do any of these "catastrophizing" thoughts sound familiar?

- Things are bad and getting worse.
- This pain will destroy me.
- My body is falling apart.
- Poor me.

Thinking that severe pain must mean some dreadful disease adds mental anguish to physical discomfort. Many people experience pain as a form of punishment—like being spanked as a child. That only makes it worse.

None of these negative thoughts makes sense. Becoming aware of your pain-button thinking is the first step to getting rid of it.

Enduring discomfort...

One of the most important strategies for coping with chronic pain is to develop a capacity to endure discomfort.

Modern Americans are so accustomed to comfort and convenience that we expect it. As a result, we're less able to withstand pain than people were a century ago. A minor ache that our ancestors might not have given a second thought to can debilitate us.

To have a full life, you must be willing to tolerate some discomfort.

The real cause of chronic pain...

Although few pain sufferers are aware of it, chronic pain usually goes hand in hand with tense, weak muscles.

Example I: Most chronic headaches are the result of muscular ten-sion. You may feel the pain in the front of your head, but it's really coming from tight muscles in your neck and shoulders.

Example II: Pain blamed on osteoarthritis sometimes comes not from the joints them-selves but from stiff muscles around the joints. Exercising to strengthen those muscles and make them more limber will diminish your pain—even if your joints remain stiff.

Example III: Weakened or tense muscles are responsible for at least 80% of chronic back pain. Even when a high-tech test like magnetic resonance imaging (MRI) shows evidence of herniated disks, there's no proof that these are causing the pain. In fact, 40% of people who display spinal abnormalities on an MRI (includ-ing herniated disks) have no pain.

Perhaps the most effective way to tame chronic pain is to relax, stretch and strengthen your muscles.

Pain-relief strategies...

•Breathe from your belly. Most people move their chests in and out when they breathe. *Problem:* This type of breathing places constant strain on the muscles of your neck and shoul-ders, exacerbating headaches and back pain.

Better way: Place your hands on your belly or over your head and relax your shoulders. Breathe so that your abdomen goes in and out while your chest remains still. Once you get the hang of it, practice belly breathing without using your hands—and try to breathe that way all the time.

•Get regular exercise. If your pain is too severe to permit aerobics classes, jogging or weight-lifting, try walking or swimming. They will increase the flow of blood and oxygen to muscle cells without causing more pain.

Pacing is essential. Plan to finish your walk or swim before you become tired. If necessary, start off by going only a very short distance. Increase the distance gradually. Concentrate on gentle, stress-free motions.

•Reduce psychological stress. Stress intensi-fies pain by restricting blood flow and tighten-ing muscles. And negative feelings speed the transmission of pain impulses from the body to the brain. Pleasant emotions help block the transmission of pain signals.

Learn to recognize the links between tension and pain. Notice the situations that cause back pain or headache to flare up. Consider what role might be played by your thoughts and emotions. Once you've tuned in to the triggers, look for better ways to solve problems and eliminate hassles.

Helpful: Keep a "pain diary" that details what you're doing and thinking when pain strikes.

If you notice that you can sit for 45 minutes before your back starts to hurt, for example, you can then make it a point to get up before that time is up.

Once you break the association between a specific activity and pain, you'll avoid the anti-cipation that makes pain a self-fulfilling pro-phecy. This way, you'll gradually increase your endurance.

•Be more assertive. If chronic pain limits your energy, you must learn how to set limits— to say "no" in a reasonable way, without anger or guilt.

Also important: Good planning skills. Each morning, make a list of what needs to be done that day. Recognize that focusing wisely on the top 20% of your list will fulfill 80% of your needs. Intelligent management of your time prevents the fall behind/catch-up spiral that exacerbates chronic pain.

•Get enough sleep. Go to bed and get up at the same time every day...and avoid caffeine, alcohol, sleeping pills and naps. Use your bed for sleeping and sex only.

If you're not sleepy—or if you wake up in the middle of the night—get out of bed. Read or listen to music until you're drowsy.

Essential: A firm mattress. If your body "gels" into position on a soft mattress, you'll wake up in more pain than if you had moved around throughout the night.

•Steer clear of painkillers. While they're help-ful for acute pain, long-term use often causes severe side effects. Regular use of painkillers can actually *cause* some forms of chronic pain.

As your ability to tolerate discomfort grows, cut back gradually—under your doctor's supervision, of course.

Source: Norman J. Marcus, MD, president, International Foundation for Pain Relief, and medical director of the New York Pain Treatment Program at Lenox Hill Hospital, both in New York City. He is the author of *Freedom from Chronic Pain,* Simon & Schuster.

Smoking and Death

Forty-eight million Americans still smoke. Each year, about 24 billion packs of cigarettes are sold...and 400,000 Americans die as a result of smoking-induced illness.

Source: Centers for Disease Control and Prevention, 1600 Clifton Rd., Atlanta 30333.

How Well Can You Smell?

Although the sense of smell is usually viewed as a source of pleasure, it also plays a key role in protecting us from environmental hazards. *An inability to smell (anosmia) makes you vulnerable to...*

• Fires and gas leaks. People who cannot smell lack the ability to detect gas leaks and smoke. Equipping your home with smoke detectors will protect you against fire. Natural gas monitors are available from Lab Safety Supply, 800-356-0783. *Cost:* $300-400.

Self-defense: If your home has gas ranges or gas heat, keep it well ventilated—especially during the winter. Periodically open an outside door or crack a window. If you're moving, consider buying a home that has electric cooking and heating rather than gas.

• Food poisoning. Because they cannot smell rancid, moldy food, people with anosmia must use extreme caution when eating leftovers.

Self-defense: Eyeball everything you eat before you eat it. If there's any doubt about a food's freshness, have a friend check it—or throw it out.

• Workplace hazards. For most occupations, a poor sense of smell is of little consequence. But it is often a dangerous liability for firefighters, chemists, certain factory workers, etc.

Self-defense: Talk to your boss about making arrangements with a colleague to alert you to any dangers—including fires. If it's impossible to use a "buddy system," you may have to find other work.

Anosmia can also hinder your ability to taste and enjoy food. *Reason:* What we think of as taste is actually a combination of taste and smell.

Coping strategy: Select foods that are strongly sweet, sour, bitter or salty. Those four flavors alone can be detected by the taste buds on your tongue. You can taste them even if you cannot smell.

If you notice a decline in your ability to smell, consult a specialist in sensory disorders. Usually, the best choice is an ear, nose and throat specialist certified by the American Academy of Otolaryngology. Ask your primary doctor to refer you to one.

The otolaryngologist will use a variety of tests to determine the cause of your anosmia. Frequently, anosmia is simply the result of sinus congestion caused by an allergy or a severe cold.

Congestion prevents odor molecules from reaching the delicate odor-sensitive cells lining the roof or top of the sinuses (the olfactory epithelium). Fortunately, congestion-related anosmia usually goes away on its own in a few days or weeks.

But colds aren't the only cause of anosmia. *Other causes include...*

• Advancing age. Men typically start to lose their ability to smell around age 65, women about 70. Most age-related anosmia is irreversible.

• Chronic sinusitis. Even a small amount of sinus inflammation can prevent odor molecules from reaching the olfactory bulb.

Fortunately, oral and topical steroids, along with antibiotics in case of infection, usually resolve the problem. If drugs fail, minor outpatient surgery may be necessary to widen narrowed nasal passages.

•Head trauma. About 5% of people who sustain a severe head injury (typically in a car accident) develop anosmia. Even without treatment, one-third of these people gradually regain their sense of smell. But about two-thirds of the time, scar tissue or damage to the olfactory bulb renders the anosmia permanent. There is no effective treatment for such cases of anosmia.

Source: Heather J. Duncan, PhD, research assistant professor of otolaryngology, University of Cincinnati College of Medicine, Cincinnati, OH.

Elderly People May Need More Protein

Elderly people may need more protein—25% to 50% more—than the familiar recommended dietary allowance (RDA). Current guidelines call for 0.36 gram of protein per pound of body weight per day (equalling 63 grams for a 170-pound person and 50 grams for a 143-pound person). But in a recent study, healthy subjects 56 to 80 years of age who ate a diet containing the RDA for protein excreted more protein than they ate. Inadequate protein intake may result in muscle mass loss, which can lead to frailty. *Self-defense:* Elderly men of average build should consume at least 93 grams of protein a day, elderly women at least 78 grams.

Food	Grams of protein
One cup of 1% fat milk	8
One cup of lowfat yogurt	10
One cup of cooked lentils	39
Three ounces of tuna	24

Source: Wayne Campbell, PhD, research associate, Noll Physiological Research Center, Pennsylvania State University, University Park.

Premature Gray Hair And Osteoporosis

Premature gray hair is an early predictor of low bone density. Individuals whose hair was more than half gray by age 40 were 4.5 times more likely to suffer osteoporosis. *Theory:* Genes responsible for bone density may somehow be linked to early loss of hair color. *Self-defense:* If you're more than half gray by 40 and have a family history of osteoporosis, ask your doctor about having a bone-density test.

Source: Clifford J. Rosen, MD, chief of medicine, St. Joseph Hospital, Bangor, ME. His study of 59 women and four men referred to an osteoporosis clinic was reported in *Internal Medicine News & Cardiology News,* 12230 Wilkins Ave., Rockville, MD 20852.

The Taoist Principles of Preventive Medicine

Many Chinese follow a way of life called *Taoism.* Its goals are to promote balance and harmony…in both the immediate environment and the universe. Taoists believe that anyone can reach a state of enlightenment called *hsing ming shuang hsiu,* the balance of mind and body. *Required:* Great self-discipline and personal effort, including the cultivation of health and longevity.

Interesting: The Taoist emphasis on preventive medicine is so strong that in old China people paid their physician only when they were well. If they got sick, the treatment was free.

The breath of life…

Taoists believe in an internal energy called *Chi,* the breath of life. Chi corresponds closely to western concepts of bioelectricity, the body's electrical program. By changing this inner program, people can influence their metabolism in a way that actually strengthens the immune system.

Taoists believe that Chi flows through a system of subtle veins, called meridians. If the Chi is blocked anywhere in the body, you'll have too much Chi—too much energy—on one side of the blockage, and too little on the other.

To open the blocked areas along the meridians so the Chi can flow freely, the Chinese use a series of exercises that involve breathing, gentle movement, and visualization.

Called *Chi kung*, these exercises are based on five animals—the crane, bear, monkey, deer, and tiger. Each exercise affects a specific internal organ and bodily system. Chi kung, which resemble tai chi exercises, are easy to learn.

The three treasures...

In addition to the meridian system, Taoists believe that the human body contains three basic forms of energy that create health when they are in balance with each other.

• *Chi* is breath energy. It resides in the chest and lungs.

The three sources of Chi are the air we breathe, the food we eat, and the energy and strength of the immune system that we inherit from our parents. The more Chi you accumulate, the greater your vitality and better your health.

Exercise: Stand with your feet about shoulder-width apart, legs slightly bent, back straight but not stiff, chest relaxed, abdomen loose, with your palms at waist height, facing downward. Inhale and allow the lower abdomen and back to expand as though you were filling a balloon. When you exhale, the lower abdomen and back should contract. Continue to do this exercise as long as you can comfortably. If there's pain there's no gain.

This exercises the diaphragm, gently massaging the internal organs. And because the lower lobes of the lungs are stretched downward, the body can take in more air...and more Chi.

• *Jing* is sexual energy, which is believed to be stored in the lower abdomen and cultivated through balanced sexual relationships.

Exercise: To enhance Jing, stimulate the endocrine system, and improve sexual health, men should contract the muscles of the perineum (the soft band of muscles located between the scrotum and anus) when they inhale and release when they exhale. Women should contract and release the anal and vaginal muscles while continuing to breathe naturally. These exercises, known in the West as Kegel exercises, also help solve sexual problems, including prostate enlargement in men and irregular menstruation in women.

• *Shen* is spiritual or intuitive energy. Shen, which means clarity of mind, requires the ability to temporarily shut off the interference of constant thinking. Most people's minds are like a TV that they can't turn off. Without the clarity and fullness of Shen, which is developed through meditation, none of the other techniques are possible.

Exercise: Sit upright in a chair and breathe at a natural pace. At the same time, observe any thoughts that pass by, as if you were watching passing clouds. Make no judgments and don't try to control or manipulate your thoughts. I call this being an open window of awareness. And although it may sound quite easy, it is very difficult for most westerners, who always have to be doing something.

Basic Taoist principles...

There are two underlying principles of Taoist philosophy that tell us how to live in a manner that promotes health and well-being.

• *Tzu jan* involves things that grow from the inside out rather than being created outside. *Translation:* Spontaneity, which shouldn't be confused with impulsiveness. Spontaneity means sensing what is coming from inside you and allowing it to express itself.

• *Wu wei*, or effortlessness, involves going with the flow, lacking artifice, using only those muscles needed for the task at hand.

Taoists think that these two principles should be applied consistently on every level—lifestyle, relationships, exercise, movement, etc.

Example: Unless sexual partners surrender completely to the experience, there can be no exchange of energy. *Result:* None of the elaborate Taoist sex techniques will work until both partners are willing to go with the flow of the experience and express whatever they feel.

Source: Kenneth S. Cohen, MA in psychology, a master scholar of Chinese healing arts. A former faculty member of Boulder Graduate School psychology department, he is currently director of the Taoist Mountain Retreat in Nederland, CO.

8

Your Emotional Health

The Amazing Power Of Writing to Yourself

Keeping a diary or a journal has been recommended for years by therapists because most of us aren't aware of our feelings except when they are extreme.

Journal-writing is an antidote to our culture's excessive emphasis on the denial of feelings that is required to be successful. No matter what you do for a living, writing provides a soothing, relaxing way to get in touch with the feelings of the day.

Why be in touch?...

Many achievement-oriented people work very hard to get where they are. However, most kinds of work that lead to achievement require effort that isn't in time with our natural rhythms. In order to tolerate the pain of working when we don't feel like it, we suppress our negative feelings and keep working. The price, however, is steep. Unexpressed feelings are the cause of

most psychosomatic illnesses, including some life-threatening ones.

Feelings are the greatest source of a person's motivation. So people who are not in touch with their feelings don't know why they're doing what they're doing and often don't know why they're going through conflicts or pain.

Why keep a journal?...

Expressing your feelings in the haven of your own journal not only reduces stress and promotes good health, but enables you to understand yourself and make better decisions in business, personal life and relationships. Each time you write you have the opportunity to get to know yourself better.

Journal-writing gives you an opportunity to reflect on positive as well as negative things that you may be ignoring. You may start to become more sensitive and notice people who would like to become your friends...and people you've been at odds with who want to reconcile.

If you have a place to reflect and feel your feelings, it's more likely you'll be aware of dangerous situations in which people are trying to undermine or manipulate you. Sometimes both positive and negative signals are so low in the static of everyday noise that they're only discoverable in the quiet of journal-writing.

Since so much of our time with people involves doing things together rather than sharing feelings, we often have feelings, positive and negative, that we're afraid to express with friends, lovers, spouses, relatives. There's a comfort in acknowledging and affirming that you really have these feelings. This is especially true for men, who often have trouble expressing feelings. They can benefit most from journal-writing.

The most popular relaxation tool is the television. But TV distracts us from our feelings. Journal-writing may be the only way for chronic television addicts to find out who they really are.

Another issue has to do with trust. These are paranoid times. Urban living crowds us and the general level of trust among people is low. Telling your problems to your journal is even more safely anonymous than telling them to a bartender.

In a hectic lifestyle, journal-writing is like meditation or taking long walks, one of the few sources of solitude. It's safe, available and you can do it on a rainy day. Journal-writing may be the only solitude a high-achieving person or working parent gets.

The final advantage is a personal record. Very often people's problems escape them because they don't have an adequate perspective. I've often found that when people do journal-writing over time they can look back and discover very important things about themselves.

Common: Discovering that you've been having the same problems and feelings over and over and getting nowhere. Or alternatively, that you're making progress. It's a different perspective from memory, which is quite unreliable.

With more and more of us becoming cosmopolitan and living far from the culture and geography we grew up in, many of us are like refugees to other countries. We develop divided personalities to adjust to new circumstances.

The city-dweller behaves differently with different people throughout the day, in ways that are different from how he/she grew up. Also, we have fewer lifelong friends that can help us maintain a sense of continuity.

Journal-writing enables the divided self to note how many people he/she has to be today and what all their thoughts and feelings and opinions are about whatever is going on.

Example: An internal conflict between your vulgar, risk-taking, obnoxious self and your careful, conservative, bean-counting self.

Suggested: Use multiple colors for journal-writing. The risk-taker might write in red, the conservative self in black and the romantic in purple. *Result:* You'll get a sense of how many people are on "your committee," who they are, and what they agree and disagree about. As the chairperson of your personality, you can make better choices taking into account all the aspects of yourself.

Example: Changing jobs. The conservative self might write about how scary it is and how he doesn't like change. The risk-taker might write that he'd rather go into business for himself and get rich. The romantic might write about wanting to chuck work altogether to become a beach bum. Becoming aware of these aspects of your personality makes it more likely that you'll make a decision you can live with.

How to keep a journal…

Don't just list events in your life. Share your feelings, concerns, opinions and reflections on the meaning of actions.

To avoid list-making: Just write down events that elicited strong feelings. You don't have to make an entry of anything that didn't have an impact in terms of feelings, negative or positive.

To get to your feelings: Write down fantasies. Write a review of how a performance related to your life. Write about other people's lives and how they're similar or dissimilar to yours. Read a compelling novel and write about it. Do volunteer work with children or sick people—and write about it.

Pick a comfortable place to write. It should be a place where you feel safe to express yourself.

You don't have to write every day, though that probably is the most effective way to tune into the fine details of feelings. Some people do more journal-writing during a single weekend at the beach than they did in the entire three weeks before.

Find the kind of journal you want to write in. I like a highly tactile book with a corduroy cover. I always look forward to touching it. Other people like silk, velvet or the kind of black-and-white speckled notebook they used in the first grade. Some people prefer a computer. *Also:* Pick up something you like to write with, whether it's a felt tip or a fountain pen… or a pencil.

Important: Take appropriate security measures to make sure that what you write will be private.

Source: Martin G. Groder, MD, a psychiatrist and business consultant in Chapel Hill, NC. His book, *Business Games: How to Recognize the Players and Deal With Them,* is available from Boardroom Books.

Healing and the Mind-Body Connection

Over the past century, physicians have learned much about the workings of the various organs in the human body…and have also found effective treatments for many diseases.

This focus on the machine-like aspects of the human body has led many doctors to ignore the many natural ways people can heal themselves when they are aware of the connection between the mind and the body.

The mind-body connection…

The human body is a complex mechanism that regulates itself using naturally occurring chemical substances. When something is wrong in one organ, messenger molecules of various kinds flow through the body and instruct other chemicals to correct the situation.

Example: When you cut your finger, your body reacts by releasing chemical clotting factors, which thicken the blood in the vicinity of the cut, preventing you from bleeding to death from a cut.

Blood clotting occurs unconsciously, but every process that happens in our bodies, including thought, involves chemical reactions.

In recent years, scientists have learned about important chemicals such as peptides—chains of amino acids that transmit chemical messages. And they've learned about endorphins—proteins that are powerful natural painkillers.

Peptides are found throughout the body, not just in the brain. It has become evident that there is no clear distinction between mind and body.

Since antiquity, we have known that chemicals like drugs and alcohol affect both the mind and the body. Changes in the balance of the chemicals in our bodies also affect the way we feel.

Example: When we have a problem in just one part of the body…like a toothache…our whole self tends to feel down.

More surprisingly, the mind-body connection also works the other way. We are finding more evidence every day that the way we feel about life does not simply reflect the state of our health—it also affects it.

Doctors long ago observed that about 30% of patients respond positively even when given a placebo—an inert pill with no curative properties.

The placebo effect occurs because those patients believe that they are being given a useful medicine…and their bodies follow that belief by fighting their sickness better than they would have otherwise.

Unfortunately, many doctors themselves encourage a reverse placebo effect. By emphasizing that a certain treatment has only a small statistical chance of success, they encourage patients to expect failure…and their bodies are likely to get the message.

Better way: Doctors should discuss procedures more positively, encouraging patients to adopt a hopeful attitude, so their bodies will be more likely to react favorably. Patients should not let themselves be convinced by statistics… because every person is a unique human being, not a statistic.

The body's natural wisdom…

Today, a growing number of physicians recognize that their patients have an ally in the body's natural wisdom. Sensitivity to signals sent by our bodies helps us detect emerging health problems before standard medical tests reveal them.

Example: Journalist Mark Barasch had a terrifying dream that he was being tortured by hot coals beneath his chin and thought he had cancer in his throat. Months later, he felt symptoms and went to a doctor, but his blood tests were normal. However, during a later and more complete examination, a thyroid tumor was found.

And, conversely, by sending hopeful signals back to the body, we encourage our bodies to respond with their surprising self-healing capabilities.

Example: In December, Mary was told she had only a few weeks to live. Her daughter, Jane, tried to cheer her up by buying her a new winter nightgown. Mary, who had always been very frugal, said she didn't want the gown, but would like a new summer purse.

This reaction surprised Jane until she interpreted it as a signal that her mother thought she could survive another six months. Jane demonstrated that she shared that belief. Mary recovered enough not only to enjoy her new purse but was active enough to wear it out... and a half dozen more.

One of the most striking examples of the mind-body connection is susceptibility to disease. About 40 years ago, researchers at the University of Rochester found that people who adopted an attitude of helplessness and hopelessness were those most likely to contract a variety of diseases.

Other studies have found that people who repress their emotions because of unhappy childhood relationships with their parents are prone to suffer heart disease, hypertension, mental illness and cancer.

Mental attitudes also affect the ability to overcome disease.

Patients who take an active part in treatment ask doctors and nurses many questions, insist on finding out what lies behind every request before complying and want to be given a choice between a variety of treatment options. They want to be told what the choices and the priorities are for each. But a Yale study showed that the most "difficult" patients were those with the most active immune systems. They survived longer than "good" patients who were quiet and submissive.

How to survive...

You are most likely to survive serious illness if you can answer "yes" to the following questions:

• Does your life have meaning?

• Do you express your anger appropriately— in defense of yourself?

• Are you willing to say no?

• Do you make your own choices?

• Are you able to ask for help?

• Do you have enough play in your life?

People who answer yes are survivors because their minds give their bodies a good reason to fight for survival. Everyone is eventually going to die. I see life as a labor pain. But like a mother willing to suffer labor pains to give birth to a child, survivors accept the pain of fighting back against disease as part of giving birth to their own renewed life.

Source: Bernie S. Siegel, MD, a surgeon and writer. His latest book is *How to Live Between Office Visits: A Guide to Life, Love and Health,* HarperCollins.

The Astounding Healing Power of Pets

Animals, like babies, can do wonders for the image, which is why politicians try to be photographed with both as often as possible. Every American president in living memory has exploited his pet's electoral appeal.

Millie Bush, the last president's Spaniel, wrote a best-seller and Socks Clinton, current First Cat of the White House, has his own newsletter. But are companion animals as good for your health as they are for the profile?

Public health experts have long been skeptical. After all, dogs bite and pass on parasites, pigeons and parrots cause lung disease, cats can provoke asthma and tortoises can transmit salmonella. Yet animal lovers should take heart from recent findings.

In 1991, researchers at the University of Cambridge discovered that just months after acquiring a cat or a dog, some Britons suffer less from perennial health problems such as headache, backache and flu. And it was announced last year that Australians who keep pets tend to have less cholesterol in their blood than non-pet owners with comparable lifestyles, making them less likely to develop heart disease.

For the time being, these findings are little more than puzzling correlations. Why should owning a pet make you less likely to suffer from backache? Why should it reduce your cholesterol level? Many researchers suspect that answers will be found in the subtle links between mental and physical well-being. If the newly discovered correlations between human health and pet ownership can be confirmed, they are likely to trigger fresh research on the psychological and physiological effects of keeping pets.

Pets and longevity...

The first hint that pets could help some people to live longer came from a discovery made over a decade ago. Erica Friedmann, who was then a graduate student at the University of Maryland and is now at the City University of New York, investigated whether a person's social life and degree of social isolation might influence his/her ability to survive a heart attack.

Friedmann interviewed 92 convalescing male patients and quizzed them in detail about their lifestyle, a few questions touching upon pets. A year later 14 of the 92 men had died. Friedmann went back to her data to look for differences between those who had and those who had not survived. She found that socially isolated people were more likely to succumb, and that those who had pets were more likely to recover.

So unexpected was this finding that Friedmann began to look for other explanations. Perhaps the benefits came from the extra exercise dog owners took walking their pets. Yet she found that people with other sorts of pets that needed no exercise were also more likely to survive. She then investigated the possibility that pet owners were healthier to start with and so had less severe heart attacks. This theory also proved to be false.

Nor did pet owners appear to have different psychological make-ups from those without pets, at least judging from their responses to a wide range of standard psychological tests. Friedmann concluded that owning a pet really did help people to recover after a heart attack.

The benefit she found was small: A 3% fall in the probability of death. But given that more than a million people in the US die of heart disease every year, that means that pets could help 30,000 Americans to survive in any given year.

In a recent study by Warwick Anderson at the Baker Medical Research Institute in Prahran, Australia, 5,741 people attending a heart disease risk clinic were questioned about their lifestyle and whether they had any pets. Researchers found that the average cholesterol level of the 784 patients who owned pets was 2% lower than those who did not own pets. Epidemiologists estimate this might lower the risk of heart attack by 4%. Pet owners also had lower levels of triglyceride fats in their blood and lower blood pressure, which indicated that owning a pet was as efficient at reducing blood pressure as eating a low-salt diet or cutting down on alcohol.

Fishy experience...

No one has yet suggested a mechanism by which pets could lower levels of cholesterol or triglyceride fats. But Friedmann and her team have at least established that people sometimes produce physiological responses to animals. They measured the blood pressure of volunteers who were either resting, talking, reading out loud or greeting their dogs. As expected, blood pressure levels rose as the volunteers performed the slightly stressful tasks of talking or reading to the experimenters. But when the volunteers talked to their dogs, their blood pressure fell to resting levels or below.

What's more, it seems that such responses do not necessarily depend on stroking or talking to a pet. In various tests involving psychological questionnaires and standard observational checks of anxiety levels, adults and children proved to be more relaxed simply in the presence of a friendly dog. Aaron Katcher, a psychiatrist at the University of Pennsylvania, showed that people who watch an aquarium full of tropical fish experience a fall in blood pressure greater than those who merely stare at a blank wall.

Yet such studies do not prove there is anything special about our reactions to animals. It has long been known that anything that distracts our attention from our preoccupations has a calming effect on the body. In a recent experiment, also by Katcher, watching a videotape of tropical fish proved more absorbing and relaxing than watching a tankful of real fish, judging from measurements of blood pressure. Could pets improve human health simply by distracting and absorbing us?

Many researchers think this is unlikely. According to advocates of "pet therapy," animals can also make us feel better indirectly, by making strange settings or people seem less threatening. It is hard to design experiments to test this theory rigorously, but anecdotal evidence abounds. In the late 1960s, for example, Boris Levinson, an American psychiatrist, noticed that severely withdrawn children who were afraid to communicate with people made rapid contact with his dog Jingles. By carefully insinuating himself into the child-dog relationship, Levinson found he was able to reach his child patients.

Animals can even promote social contact between strangers. Peter Messent, a British zoologist, spent days hanging around public parks watching people strolling through. Those with dogs were much more likely to experience positive encounters with other people, including prolonged conversations with people who were alone or with children.

Pets may thus be "confirming cultural symbols of harmless respectability," says James Serpell, formerly director of the Companion Animal Research Group at the University of Cambridge who is now at the University of Pennsylvania. But his research shows that they are far more than this. According to questionnaire responses, pet owners value their pets "as distinctive personalities with whom they have affectionate relationships." And it is here, in friendship, argues Serpell, that we find the real explanation for pets' beneficial effects on our health.

Study after study has shown that people who feel isolated and depressed are more likely to succumb to illness than people who claim to be contented. And last year, Serpell and his colleagues showed for the first time that pets could improve an ordinary person's general health. They recruited three groups of people. At the start, there was no significant difference between their scores on a questionnaire monitoring minor health problems. Then one group of people were given dogs, another cats.

A month later, they filled in the questionnaire again. Those who owned new pets reported a marked improvement in their general health, which lasted throughout the 10-month study. In contrast to Friedmann's earlier study, dog owners fared slightly better than cat owners, perhaps partly because they also increased the amount of exercise they took. Serpell is now repeating the study over 18 months, with three times as many people, all of who have the same socioeconomic status. He also has access to doctors' assessments of their patients' health. Halfway through the experiment, results bear out the earlier study.

Good listeners...

Part of the explanation, argues Serpell, is that pets can provide owners "with a special kind of emotional support which is lacking or at least uncommon in relationships between people." He claims that an animal's muteness is a boon, not a burden. The problem with language is that although we use it to communicate our deepest thoughts and emotions, we also use it to deceive, misinform, criticize and insult others. The fact that pets listen and seem to understand but do not question or evaluate may be one of their most endearing assets as companions, says Serpell. It resembles the relationships some psychotherapists try to build.

Dogs and cats are the most cherished animal companions, largely because they are adept at feeding us with nonverbal signs of affection, argues Serpell. They make us feel respected, admired and wanted. The typical feline expression of slightly detached contentment is enormously appealing to humans, while the way dogs' facial muscles are arranged enables them to express a wide range of human-looking emotions.

"Our confidence, self-esteem, ability to cope with the stresses of life and, ultimately, our physical health depend on this sense of belonging," says Serpell. The sense of responsibility involved in caring for an animal is especially significant. Such nurturing gives meaning to our lives, a sense of being needed that can deeply sustain an ability to set personal goals. "Far from being perverted, extravagant or the victims of misplaced parental instincts, most owners are normal rational people who make use of animals to augment their existing social relationships," says Serpell.

Childhood experiences...

Why, then, doesn't everyone keep pets? Serpell has found that childhood experiences with pets are the key. Children brought up with pets are much more likely to have them as adults. Those who went without pets as children seem to remain indifferent to companion animals throughout their lives.

Childhood experience also seems to direct preferences for animals in specific ways. People brought up with dogs remain dog lovers, those with cats, cat lovers. Only those who had both as children remain fond of both. No one has yet found consistent personality differences between cat and dog lovers, nor between pet owners and nonpet owners.

Yet people who have, or have had, pets do tend to have something distinctive about them. In a survey of undergraduates, Serpell's colleague Elizabeth Paul has found that people with experience of pets tend to have a more positive and humane attitude to animals, the environment and a tendency to greater "emotional empathy" for people, too.

Pet ownership has its disadvantages, however, not least the risk of catching something from your companion animal. Britain's canine population deposits about 4.5 million liters of urine and 1 million kilograms of feces every day, some of it in public places where it can be a health hazard. Dogs can transmit *toxocariasis* —infection by a roundworm parasite—which can cause blindness in children. But the condition remains rare—about 10 cases of toxocariasis are reported each year in England and Wales

—and can be prevented by giving puppies and nursing bitches antiworm drugs.

More common is *toxoplasmosis*, with symptoms like glandular fever, caused by a parasitic protozoan. About 700 cases are reported each year in Britain, and most people catch it by eating undercooked meat from sheep, goats and pigs, or by coming into contact with cat feces. The parasite can be avoided by wearing gloves when gardening or handling cat litter, and washing hands after handling raw meat. Bird-fanciers need to be on guard for *psittacosis*, caused by a viruslike organism inhaled in the dust from the droppings or feathers of infected birds. The flulike symptoms can be treated with antibiotics.

Pet animals also cause significant injury to people: In Britain alone, more than a quarter of a million dog bites are registered each year. Yet many of these problems could be minimized by public education and restrictions on dogs in recreation areas, according to the report of a working party on companion animals in society, set up by the Council for Science and Society in London and chaired by Lawson Soulsby, head of the department of clinical veterinary medicine at the University of Cambridge.

There are more grounds for concern, perhaps, from the pets' point of view—not all pet owners are good for their animal's health. Every summer, animal shelters run by charities fill up with pets abandoned as their owners go on holiday. New forms of human exploitation may emerge if the health benefits of keeping pets become widely accepted. According to Nicholas Tucker, a psychologist at the University of Sussex, "pet burnout" (tiredness and irritability) has been recorded among some of the dogs and cats acting as four-footed therapists among the mentally ill or socially deprived. In the US, castrated, de-toothed monkeys have been trained to act as domestic servants to paraplegic patients. "Being de-clawed or un-voiced may be fairer on the furniture or the neighbors," Tucker says, "but what might it be doing to the pets?"

Source: Gail Vines, PhD, a science journalist based in Cambridge, England, and author of *Raging Hormones*, University of California Press.

Secrets of Better Living With a Terminal Illness

In June of 1990, my doctor told me that the excruciating back pain that had plagued me for six months was caused by *multiple myeloma*, a rare bone marrow cancer that was attacking my spine and ribs.

Multiple myeloma accounts for only 1% of all cancers—and it's incurable. I was 53 years old, and I knew it was unlikely that I would survive more than a few years.

I hate the cancer, and there have been times that I railed against it. But I decided early on to try to put my disease in its place and go about my business.

Today is the only day I have. I'm going to enjoy it. This philosophy can benefit not only people with terminal or chronic illness, but also those who are healthy. *Here are some of the other lessons I've learned...*

• View terminal illness as the key that opens the vault to unknown treasures. Since I got sick, I've experienced more love, concern, compassion and care on a single day than I used to experience in an entire year.

Even though I know my days are numbered, I really enjoy life. I have a good time with my family and friends. I realize that I am one of the richest people in the world.

• Accept help. My close friends and relatives all felt powerless when I told them I had cancer. They wanted to help, but there wasn't much they could do. So they did what they could. Some came and did yard work for me. My brother-in-law put up a banister. A friend dropped by once a week to have dinner with me.

They couldn't cure my cancer or take away my pain, but they could help in other ways. And their help has helped me not only in practical terms, but also emotionally.

My friends all say, "You'll beat this." Of course, I won't. They're in denial, but I don't let that bother me. It's their way of coping. It's also their way of trying to be kind to me.

• Don't worry about the things you can no longer do. Instead, try to focus on what you still can do.

My cancer has caused my bones to deteriorate. As a result, I now have severe osteoporosis. If I attempt heavy physical labor or try to lift more than 20 pounds, I risk a fracture.

It would be easy to feel sorry for myself. But I'm not in pain, and I've been able to resume gardening and biking—two pleasures I'd thought were history—so I'm content. Sure, it would be safer to avoid these activities, too, but I refuse to wrap myself in a protective sheath.

• Don't view yourself as a patient. When you do, you see yourself sick, lying in a hospital bed with tubes sticking out of your body. That's not a pleasant concept, and it's certainly not one you have to dwell on.

Although I might be a bit more physically flawed now than I used to be, I'm really not too different from you or anyone else. We're all flawed. It's the daily struggle to better ourselves physically, spiritually, intellectually and emotionally that makes life interesting and challenging. Illness is just another imperfection that we can strive to overcome.

• Take charge of your health care. If you're used to being "in control" of your life, suddenly being diagnosed with an uncontrollable illness can be overwhelming.

I've always been a take-charge person. While I can't control the course of my illness, I refuse to give up power over the one thing that I do have control of—my treatment.

I've become a partner in my health care. My doctor and I decide on all treatments together. I stay on top of the latest medical advances. I read medical journals and use Medline, an on-line computer database that gives me access to the articles in the National Library Medicine.* I discuss the things I read about with my doctor.

If you or a close friend or family member has a serious illness, you should do the same. Hospital libraries are an excellent place to start your search for helpful information.

• Decide what you want in a hospital. Many of us have a choice between teaching hospitals and community hospitals. Teaching hospitals tend to offer the most up-to-date care, but they have certain drawbacks...

*National Library of Medicine, 8600 Rockville Pike, Bethesda, MD 20894. 301-496-6095.

• You'll often be seen by a medical resident instead of your regular doctor.

• You may have to wait a long time before you're seen.

• You may have to commute to get to the hospital.

I decided to go to a local four-doctor practice because I wanted to get individualized care. Each of these doctors knows who I am and what my condition is. I don't have to reeducate them each time I come in for a checkup.

• Practice positive thinking. The latest research shows that the mind has at least some control over the body. And how you feel can control the mind. To keep myself optimistic, I focus on all the great things in my life—especially my family and close friends.

When my cancer was diagnosed, one of my greatest disappointments was that I wouldn't live to see my twenty-fifth wedding anniversary. But I did! Joy is great medicine.

• Decide whether the side effects of treatment are worth its benefits. For cancer that's curable, you go ahead with chemotherapy or radiation regardless of the side effects. But some people with incurable cancer decide against chemo and radiation because they don't want to suffer the nausea, fatigue and other side effects that often accompany these treatments.

I take chemotherapy treatments that don't abuse my body terribly but suppress the cancer sufficiently to give me some more and better days.

I know that eventually my cancer may destroy my kidneys. But I've decided not to go on dialysis. Getting hooked up to a machine three times a week and knowing I'll never quite feel well again is not the sort of life I can bear to live. If you want to maintain your quality of life, you must know when to say no to treatment.

• Root your hope in reality. People living with terminal illness need hope, but a hope that denies reality is a false one. It makes you prey to charlatans who seek to profit off your suffering.

I know that I'm going to die in a few years. I can't keep thinking that maybe there's something out there to cure me. If my bones start breaking, if I get pneumonia and my kidneys are going…then it's time to say good-bye.

• Join a support group. I've always hated meetings. And I never thought I needed any psychological counseling. But support groups are different. They let you share your concerns and feelings with others who are just like you.

Midway through the first meeting of my support group, I realized something very powerful—that I was able to help everyone in the room—and that everyone was helping me. Some people say they don't feel comfortable opening up. If you're one of them, realize that in a support group, nobody forces you to talk.

If you'd like information on cancer support groups in your area, contact a hospital social worker or the American Cancer Society at 800-227-2345.

• Plan for your future. Tending to the business of dying is not easy. But it's something that we must do—both for ourselves and for our loved ones. I've made a living will. It says that when I'm near the end and I can no longer express myself, I want to die as quickly as possible.

I also have a durable power of attorney, which gives another person—my wife—the right to carry out my wishes. If you don't get your affairs in order, hospitals and doctors are liable to use mechanical marvels to keep you alive—even if you'd simply prefer to die.

• Appreciate the spirituality of illness. A terminal illness forces you to look inward and find what's important in your life. It's comforting to know that if your priorities have been misplaced, you can correct them for whatever days remain.

Those of us who believe in God can make ourselves fit for the journey to come. That might mean squaring ourselves with people with whom we've quarreled in the past.

Those who do not believe in a divinity probably feel even more strongly about leaving behind favorable and healing memories.

• Seize the day. My motto is the Latin phrase *carpe diem* (literally "seize the day"). I think of it as "enjoy today." Those of us with terminal illness have had life's brevity impressed upon us. Yet because our tomorrows are limited, our todays become much more important. In reality, of course, we all have a limited number of days. We should enjoy each one as if it were our last.

My wife and I are very much living in the moment. Recently, after dreaming of seeing Rome for years and years, we finally made the trip. We also visited Nova Scotia, where my maternal grandparents were born.

I'm storing up great memories, not so much for myself but for my wife and daughter. My attitude is, *Let's get on with the good times.* You may not be able to have them later.

Source: Ed Madden, a columnist for the *Dorchester Reporter*, a weekly newspaper in Dorchester, MA, and author of *Carpe Diem: Enjoying Every Day with a Terminal Illness*, Jones and Bartlett Publishers.

 # You & Your Brain— Your Brain & You

We've all been taught to take care of our bodies so we can live longer, healthier lives. But mere physical survival does not guarantee quality of life. A meaningful life requires the use of a healthy brain.

Although today's Americans live longer than ever, we fill nursing homes at a record rate. *Reason:* It's not loss of physical function that conscripts most people to a nursing home…it's the loss of mental faculties.

Good news: Barring severe injury or progressive disease—Alzheimer's, Parkinson's, etc.—much loss of brain function is preventable.

Aging and the brain…

Failing brain function is not normal. It is a sign of disease, injury, or neglect.

Although we lose brain cells as we age, maturing brains compensate for cell loss in ways that increase brain function.

How: The sheath around the nerve fibers grows thicker, improving the transmission of electrical signals in the brain. And the nerve fibers, or dendrites, grow new branches. *Result:* More interconnections for richer, deeper thinking.

Certain kinds of intelligence, however, do decline as we age.

Example: People slowly lose their ability to work out complex problems in theoretical mathematics…although their ability to do simple calculations isn't impaired.

Applied skills—law, medicine, engineering, architecture, etc.—do not deteriorate with age. And areas that depend on interpretation—art, music, drama, etc.—are actually enhanced as wisdom and judgment deepen. The ability to speak and write also improves from age 50 to 70. And philosophers don't hit their stride until they reach 70 or 80.

Preventable brain drains…

For every patient I see with Alzheimer's or another serious brain disorder, I see 20 who are impaired by something that is preventable or treatable. *Common culprits:*

•Depression. The number-one reversible cause of memory loss in the elderly.

People who are depressed enough to warrant professional attention suffer from reduced attention span and poor concentration. *Result:* Impaired performance and a loss of the ability to form new memories.

In severe cases, depressed brain function lessens a person's ability to retrieve old memories. In the elderly, depression can mimic Alzheimer's disease.

•Medication. Many of the medicines that a lot of older people take—for high blood pressure, sleep disorders, anxiety, emotional problems, etc.—have side effects, some of which can impair the brain.

Older people are often overmedicated, a result of seeking relief from pain and other problems. Most do not tolerate drugs in the same doses they once did. And certain medications—which are perfectly safe on their own—can cause trouble when combined with others.

•Alcohol. The number-one brain poison in our society, it's abused by six million Americans. Alcohol breaks down the blood-brain barrier—a built-in defense that normally protects our brain cells from poisons that enter the bloodstream. A person who is alcohol-poisoned can suffer as much disability as a person with a stroke, tumor, or brain injury. The difference is in duration, not degree.

Alcohol abusers run a 30% greater risk of suicide than the general population. *Other risks:* Memory loss, vitamin B1 deficiency, seizures, Korsakoff's psychosis (a brain disorder with severe memory loss).

• Cocaine and other illicit drugs. Opiates, stimulants, depressants, and hallucinogens all penetrate the blood-brain barrier and alter brain function. Cocaine can cause convulsions, stroke, and outbursts of violence.

• Lack of stimulation. This alone can seriously depress brain function.

Example: A partially blind stroke victim spent two years in a bed positioned so her sighted side faced a blank wall. It appeared her mental faculties were failing, until she was turned to face the world. *Result:* Remarkable improvement.

An interesting, challenging environment promotes increased brain function. Lacking stimulation, brain function and development are interrupted.

• Other potential brain drains. Physical illness, including stroke, pain, stress, head injury, and poor nutrition.

Build a better brain...

Our brains improve with stimulation. We can enrich our thinking, sharpen our response time, and improve our memory with simple techniques of diet and exercise.

• Diet. For optimum brain efficiency, avoid excessive salt, saturated fats, and sugar. Breakfast should be the big meal of the day. Eat a full breakfast high in protein such as fish, chicken, turkey, or soy products. The last meal of the day should be light, and several hours before bed.

Although many doctors do not think that vitamin/mineral supplements are necessary, I do recommend them. *Reason:* Most recommendations are based on what our body needs to avoid vitamin-deficiency-induced diseases, such as scurvy, rickets, and pellagra. That's not enough to keep the brain healthy. Various studies correlate increased vitamin intake with improved verbal and non-verbal intelligence, behavior, memory, and visual acuity. *Note:* Check with your doctor before you take any supplements.

• Exercise. The brain benefits from mental exercise the same way the body does from physical activity. *Suggested:*

• Balance your checkbook without using a calculator. The mathematical centers atrophy with disuse. Math exercises maintain skills and improve concentration and attention.

• Practice printing with your nondominant hand. Start by making large letters. Don't worry if they're not perfect. *Goal:* To develop speech abilities in the nondominant side of your brain. This will facilitate quicker recovery in the event of a stroke.

• Draw geometric figures and designs. You can do this while you're on the phone. Then copy the drawings with your nondominant hand. *Goal:* Improved perception of complex spatial relations and integration of both brain hemispheres.

• Put information you want to remember in a verse or song. Melody and versification are generated in the nondominant hemisphere. Combining melody with lyrics employs the whole brain and improves retrieval.

• Read challenging material. Good choices include histories, technical information, biographies, quality novels by writers with a good grasp of language (Proust, Austen, Stout, etc.). Read aloud. Listen to books on tape.

• Punctuate brain activity with brain rest. Brain rest is not the same as napping or watching TV. Brain rest requires temporarily shutting down some brain function.

Example: Sit quietly, close your eyes, and progressively relax the parts of your body that use the brain most—the lips, tongue, thumbs, index fingers, and big toes. Learn this exercise when you are not stressed.

• Avert inaction. Doing is more rewarding and enriching than watching. Sensory stimulation in its active rather than passive forms is terrific brain food. *Suggested:* Don't just look at art...paint...don't just listen to music—play an instrument...don't just read—write.

Source: Neurosurgeon Vernon H. Mark, MD, FACS. He is co-author, with Jeffrey P. Mark, MS, of *Brain Power*, Houghton Mifflin.

Mental Fitness Made Easy…Almost

Just as it takes energy and attention to stay physically healthy, it takes time and effort for us to keep fit mentally. And, just as we've learned to exercise and watch our diets, we can learn to "think like a shrink" for optimal mental health.

What is mental fitness?

Mental fitness is the ability to overcome self-pity, anger, guilt and emotional isolation in favor of self-esteem, usefulness, wonder, intimacy…and the other joyful feelings that give life meaning.

Therapists who focus on solving problems quickly use an active, systematic approach to help patients identify and resolve troubling issues and emotional problems. They are called short-term therapists. We can use their techniques in our daily lives as ongoing strategies to maintain mental fitness.

How a therapist thinks…

An effective therapist helps the patient address the universal issues with which we all struggle…

- Dependence versus independence.
- Inappropriate attachment versus the ability to separate.
- Self-sabotage versus self-actualization.
- Chronic grief versus acceptance of loss.
- Emotional isolation versus the ability to feel one's feelings.
- Distancing versus intimacy.

All of us have developed ways to avoid examining our most troublesome behaviors and feelings. The short-term therapist takes an "observant posture" to identify the patient's defenses —the common techniques we all use to shield ourselves from painful truths about our present or past experiences.

Defenses always conceal hidden feelings. So the therapist intervenes when the patient makes a defensive statement, and pursues the defense rather than the content of the statement.

Here is a sample session, greatly condensed. A hypothetical patient, Mr. J, age 52, has been laid off from his job and is very depressed.

Therapist: How did you feel when you lost your job?

Mr. J: Well, the economy is bad, and they needed to make cut-backs, so…

Therapist…hears Mr. J rationalizing: Yes, but how did you feel?

Mr. J: Like there's nothing I can do about it. I'm too old to start again.

Therapist…challenging defense of helplessness: You're taking a helpless posture here. How did you feel?

Mr. J: Angry, lousy. After all I had done for that company!

Therapist…hears defensive anger: What was underneath the anger?

Mr. J: I felt betrayed, and foolish for having expected the company to protect me, to be loyal. And I was scared. Where would I find another job? What would happen to my family?

Therapist: Anything else?

Mr. J: I felt ashamed. I felt that I was a failure.

Therapist: What do these feelings bring to mind?

Mr. J: My father, telling me I will never amount to anything, and letting me down when I needed his help.

Therapist…after further exploring the association with Mr. J's father: Were there any positive feelings the day you lost your job?

Mr. J: I felt relief, like I was suddenly free, and a strange sort of excitement that I might get to start over again doing something new.

Therapist: Anything in particular?

Mr. J: Well, I've always wanted to teach French cooking classes.

Therapist: That doesn't seem like a viable occupation now. Are you going to put your energy into proving your father right? What are you going to do about solving this problem?

By actively challenging a patient's defenses, the therapist helps him/her to recognize the underlying emotions and associations.

After this process, the therapist can then issue a call to action—What are you going to do about remedying your problem?

The "work" of therapy involves learning to take inventory of our mixed emotions. We can learn to do this on our own.

Required: A sensitivity to—and understanding of—common defenses…and unrelenting honesty.

The aim: To reach a sense of emotional balance. This lets us see our options clearly…let go of our anxiety or fear of intimacy…take action on our own behalf…change our self-defeating behaviors…and move forward.

The defenses…

Each of us favors certain defenses over others. When you notice yourself being defensive, challenge yourself to search for the emotions and associations beneath the defense. *There are three types of defenses:* Helpless, emotional and intellectual.

•The defenses of helplessness often reflect a lack of self-esteem.

•Vagueness. I guess I feel…Maybe, I don't know…I suppose.

•Passivity and helplessness. I can't do anything about it…really means, I won't do anything, I won't change.

•The emotional defenses are used to mask underlying pain.

•Crying is an appropriate response to sadness or loss. But often it masks anger, hurt or guilt. I got so frustrated I cried.

•Depression is also an appropriate response to grief. But defensive depression usually has a self-devaluing quality, and tends to come and go. My life is worthless.

•Anger is an appropriate response to an attack or threat. Defensive anger is a way to feel powerful and to mask feelings of hurt, insecurity, inadequacy, or powerlessness.

•The intellectual defenses are used to avoid dealing with the emotions.

•Rationalization. Explaining or making excuses to hide feelings. She only said that because she was under a lot of stress.

•Intellectualization. Retreating into philosophy to avoid taking action. Man was meant to be alone.

•Avoidance. Distancing from situations that are painful or intimate. Leaving the room to avoid conflict, avoiding social situations, using sarcasm to keep people away, being bossy or controlling to avoid feeling out of control.

•Denial. Denying that feelings or behaviors exist. I wasn't drunk, the cop was a jerk. I wasn't upset at all.

•Projection. Attributing one's own unacceptable feelings or qualities to another.

Example: A man who is afraid to admit he is attracted to a woman who is not his wife says, All these young guys want to do is chase girls.

Society's defenses…

Defenses work on a community level as well as a personal one. The more we understand how defenses work in our own lives, the better we can understand the greater issues that trouble us.

Example: Many Americans responded defensively to the Japanese accusation that American workers are lazy and illiterate, angrily Japan-bashing and smashing cars. If we were mentally fit, we would have accepted the comment in a spirit of challenge, rather than in rage. *Underlying truth:* Faced with a rather long, demoralizing recession, we have lost faith in ourselves. Our anger is a shield against the pain of believing the Japanese message.

Balance yields wisdom…

The therapeutic process produces a growing awareness that an array of conflicting feelings usually lies beneath our defenses…that among them are positive feelings that can help balance the negative ones. (I am angry at my father's coldness, I feel the hurt of wanting intimacy, and I also feel love and gratitude for the lessons he taught me and our moments of tenderness.)

In taking responsibility for our own contributions to our problems, we learn to stop searching for outside solutions and are no longer hostages to situations.

The quest for balance—pro and con…yin and yang—yields wisdom: Understanding of the world's complexity.

Source: Christ Zois, MD, co-author of *Think Like A Shrink: Solve Your Problems Yourself with Short-Term Therapy Techniques.* Warner Books. Dr. Zois is director of the New York Center for Short-Term Dynamic Psychotherapy, 350 E. 54 St., New York 10022.

Self-Talk/Personality Link

Almost all of us talk to ourselves. There are two kinds of self-talk —silent inner speech and vocalized private speech. Both serve the function of self-regulation…but the method varies by personality. In those who have high self-esteem, such self-talk is positive and self-congratulatory. Those with lower self-images rehearse future conversations with others and wish they could transform previous conversations.

Source: Thomas Brinthaupt, PhD, assistant professor of psychology, Middle Tennessee State University, Murfreesboro, TN.

Optimists Live Longer

Healthy elderly people living in the community who rated their health as "poor" were two to six times more likely to die within the next four years than those who said their health was "excellent."

Source: Study of individuals 65 and older, and a review of earlier studies by Ellen L. Idler, PhD, associate professor, Institute for Health, Health Care Policy and Aging Research, Rutgers University, New Brunswick, NJ.

 # Stress Reliever

Proper breathing reduces stress and helps you relax. It slows your heart rate and lowers blood pressure. *Technique:* Rapidly blow out all the air in your lungs…*slowly* breathe in through your nose. *Helpful:* Think of it as caressing your lungs with air…relax your stomach muscles… when lungs are full and without stopping to hold your breath, breathe out slowly and completely…repeat six times.

Source: *Sexual Pleasure: Reaching New Heights of Sexual Arousal and Intimacy* by Barbara Keesling, PhD, sex therapist and teacher at Pepperdine University, Malibu, CA. Hunter House, Inc..

Master Your Moods

Despite the popular belief that our behavior and emotions are solely the product of our upbringing and immediate environment, new research suggests that we are *born* with many of these traits.

That doesn't mean we're sentenced to feel and behave in particular ways for the rest of our lives. But it does imply that trying to *change* our personalities may be less effective than learning to understand and work with our inborn set of emotions.

Behavior myths…

A number of popular myths have made us strangers to our emotions. By encouraging us to fight our natural feelings and inclinations, these myths often lead to discouragement, shame and self-loathing when our efforts fail to result in change.

Myth of uniformity: All well-adjusted, normal people should respond to life circumstances in the same way.

Myth of good and bad: Pleasant feelings are somehow "better" or "healthier" than unpleasant feelings, and unpleasant feelings should be eliminated.

Myth of control: Emotions are like unruly children who should be subdued…and we can—and should—tame them.

Myth of perfectibility: Psychological perfection exists and is attainable.

Myth of emotional illness: Extreme emotionality is a symptom of serious emotional disturbance that must be "cured."

Myth of positive thinking: Unpleasant feelings are a sign of faulty thinking, and if we just change our thoughts, our feelings will change.

Instead of treating our emotions as enemies, we should try to better understand them…and use that understanding to manage our reactions. Each of us can do this by learning more about our personality or temperament type.

Four types:

The sensor…

A sensor is highly sensitive to stimuli, from noise, movement, challenging situations or his/her own thoughts. Because a sensor feels emotionally aroused much of the time, he tends to avoid additional stimulation—such as social contact—that might raise his arousal further.

A sensor is usually highly intuitive, empathetic, compassionate and sensual—as well as anxious and easily hurt.

Task for sensors: Instead of perceiving arousal as a danger sign, familiarize yourself with the experience. Learn to think of discomfort not as a signal to stop but as a signal to go on.

Start with imagery. Visualize yourself in situations that produce anxiety and picture yourself dealing with them competently, successfully and calmly. Then expose yourself to challenging real-life situations—gradually.

The focuser...

A focuser's low innate arousal level creates a sense of boredom and numbness. To alleviate these emotions, focusers look inward, ruminating about their dilemmas and feelings, which often include sadness or emptiness.

Focusers are good at completing tasks that require concentration and follow-through... but they are also prone to obsessiveness and depression.

Task for focusers: Problem solving can be useful, but obsessive analyzing is not. Focusers must learn to break the cycle of rumination by switching to enjoyable, equally absorbing activities.

Make a list of your favorite distractions such as movies, mystery novels, physical exercise. Turn to one of these activities whenever you're about to get caught up in the self-focusing cycle. When you've successfully broken that pattern through distraction, you'll have energy available for more productive problem solving.

The discharger...

Dischargers express their overarousal outwardly, in passionate and often volatile ways. They may be charismatic, dynamic, intense... as well as irritable, hostile and likely to alienate others.

Task for dischargers: Benign release. Dischargers shouldn't try to suppress their volatile emotions—it does not help and may even lead to physical problems, such as ulcers. If you're a discharger, accept your volatility instead of judging it. Then you can learn to shift your reaction away from the original target.

Instead of yelling at your spouse, go for a vigorous walk, stomping and growling and swinging your arms—whatever helps release your anger. Rather than blowing up at your boss, clench your fists under the table while you count to 10...and plan to yell what you're thinking as soon as you reach the privacy of your home.

The seeker...

Seekers attempt to raise characteristically low arousal levels by engaging in stimulating, high-risk activities. They welcome challenges, initiate projects, make exciting discoveries...but may find commitment difficult. Of the four types, they are the most likely to turn to the self-defeating sensation-seeking of substance abuse.

Task for seekers: Although seekers risk burn-out from excessive sensation-seeking, too much rest may create feelings of boredom and emptiness. Seekers need to balance rest and stimulation.

Learn to enjoy passive pursuits in small doses. Spend a half-hour each evening reading the paper or walking around the neighborhood. (Working out at the gym doesn't qualify as rest.) Instead of filling every minute of the weekend with challenging proj-ects, set aside an hour to read or chat with your spouse. Knowing that each period of relaxation will soon be followed by activity frees seekers from the rest-induced fear that they'll never be energized again.

Caution: Don't use drinking as a way to slow down. Find other, more constructive forms of relaxation.

Source: Melvyn Kinder, PhD, a clinical psychologist in private practice who also conducts workshops on workplace stress, 521 N. La Cienega Blvd., Suite 209, Los Angeles 90048. The codirector of Westridge Psychiatric Medical Group in Los Angeles, he is also author of *Mastering Your Moods: Temperament Types, Comfort Zones, and the Psychobiology of Emotions,* Simon & Schuster.

Career Booster

Unlike bragging, which can be annoying, *self-promotion* is a subtle skill that can help keep your career on track. *Helpful:* Relay your successes to coworkers and supervisors casually—but enthusiastically—when the opportunity arises. Send memos to the appropriate people to keep them up-to-date on your progress. Mention achievements to friends in the industry—and particularly to trade journals so word gets out and around. *Key:* Use humor, optimism and enthusiasm when promoting yourself. *Remember:* Share the credit with those who have helped you.

Source: *Career Strategies for the Working Woman* by New York-based career strategist Adele Scheele, PhD. Fireside Books.

How to Deal with Difficult People at Work

Nearly every business operation has its share of difficult people. In many cases, you can ignore them. But ignoring is impossible when they are your coworkers or managers.

Though you can't change a difficult colleague's personality, you can control your own reaction to that person. By keeping your temper in check, refusing to act like a victim and building alliances, you'll earn points as an effective manager and will be more self-confident when you see how effective you can be.

Best of all, the skills you use to handle difficult coworkers can help you stop being victimized by people throughout your life.

What is your reaction style?

Most people have one of three responses to a problem colleague…

•Rationalization and denial. You excuse the person's behavior…tell yourself it doesn't matter…or pretend the situation isn't happening at all.

This is the most common strategy—but it's likely to lead to chronic anxiety, back pain, upset stomach or other stress-related symptoms that remind you that this is not an effective style.

•Burning bridges. You blow up, make a scene…seek revenge…and come across as unprofessional and out of control. This type of

response is never appropriate in a work environment—in fact, you may end up with a reputation as bad as that of the person who provoked you.

•Finding the opportunity for growth. You collect your thoughts…explore your emotional reactions…and use the situation to learn more about yourself, your workplace and difficult people in general. You are creative in searching for a way to defuse the situation while also standing up for yourself. This is the most effective response—and the response that is most likely to win you respect as a manager.

Creative power…

Here's how the creative approach works with five of the most common types of difficult people…

•The Angry Screamer. This person intimidates others by throwing temper tantrums. You never know when he/she is going to explode …but you can be pretty sure it will be soon.

Effective response: Instead of yelling back or cowering in fear, your task is to enhance your sense of control and competence by staying *awake, alert, creative* and *professional.* This can be hard to maintain when someone is attacking you—so try the following steps:

•Calm yourself by focusing on your breathing. Repeat silently, *His anger isn't about me.*

•Create emotional distance by asking yourself, *Is there anything valuable in what this person is saying?* Listen to the useful information, and ignore the rest.

•Prepare an effective comeback. Rehearse it beforehand—so you'll be able to remember and deliver it during the heat of battle. *Effective comeback lines…*

•*Please stop! I don't appreciate being spoken to like this.* This is nondefensive, unthreatening…and very clear.

•*Time out! I want to hear what you're saying, but I must ask you to slow down a little bit.* Suggesting that you want to listen may calm the attacker. Asking him to slow down rather than quiet down sounds less like a criticism—an important point, since any perceived criticism may send this person into another rage.

•*Let's talk about this. You go first, and I won't*

144

interrupt. Then when you're done, I'll see if I have any questions. This response establishes you as a facilitator, manager and respectful listener. An angry person will often raise his voice louder if he thinks he's being interrupted…but will back off slightly if he's assured that he will be heard.

•The Saccharine Snake. This coworker says friendly, sweet things to your face…while undermining and manipulating you behind your back. *Effective response:*

•Confrontation. If possible, gather five or six other people who are also being manipulated. Together, take the person out to lunch. Script the encounter so that each person has a chance to say some version of this message… *We really want to improve the work environment. We need you to stop playing games with us.*

The person will probably deny any game-playing, make excuses and false promises, and say sweet things. But if you keep repeating the above two sentences, the person will get the message that these people at lunch are not the ones he should try to manipulate—and he will look for more compliant targets.

If you can't find any allies, you may have to initiate this conversation yourself. Be sure to maintain eye contact and stay unemotional—use the same tone you would use with your seven-year-old child who has been stealing from your purse. Your calm demeanor will make it clear that the game-playing isn't going to work anymore.

•The Space Case. This person always seems distracted and oblivious to the task at hand. He is obsessed with the crisis of the minute—his car has broken down…his best friend's marriage is in trouble, etc. Your job is to become that crisis of the minute.

Effective response: Understand that these people are focused—however, they are not focused on the project you want them to focus on.

Sit down with the Space Case and explain just how desperately you need him to come through for you on this task. With as much drama as possible, describe how terrified you are that you or the department might get into trouble if the project isn't done correctly and on time.

Important: Make your tone collegial—as one coworker to another—not critical. Otherwise, the person will feel rejected and incompetent—and preoccupation with those feelings will be another distraction from the work to be done.

Don't be surprised if you have to keep using this technique for every project. These people only respond to the most recent alarm bell.

•The Invalidator. Invalidators live to find fault. They do not explode like Angry Screamers, but their incessant criticism can undermine your confidence just as severely.

Effective response: Recover your self-esteem by recognizing that these people criticize themselves as brutally as they criticize others. Because they're such perfectionists, one small mistake feels to them as though everything is wrong—so ask for specifics.

Example: Your boss, who falls into this category, says, *This report is a piece of garbage.* Take a few deep breaths and remind yourself that you did good work on the report. Then sit down with your boss—or write a memo—and say, *Can you identify the point at which you started to feel that this wasn't working?* This will force your boss to single out the genuine problem so you can fix it.

•The Cold Shoulder. This person excludes you from the "in" group—by failing to invite you to important meetings and withholding information that you need. These people like to feel powerful. By excluding others, they feel they're improving their own status.

Effective response: Find an ally. Identify someone who's on your side but whom the Cold Shoulder also respects. Ask that person to make sure you're kept informed and included in discussions on relevant projects. You may not even need to mention the freeze-out you're getting.

Keep a record…

Whenever you're undermined by an office troublemaker, be sure to document the experience in a journal or notebook. Your documentation should describe each unpleasant situation and list other people who were present.

Having something in writing can boost your confidence by reminding you that you're not imagining things and by giving you something concrete to analyze.

Even more important, a written record of these problems will make you more credible if you need to raise the issue with a supervisor …may help convince a squeamish personnel officer to take action…and can back you up if a termination decision is challenged.

Source: Leonard Felder, PhD, therapist and management consultant in private practice, 2566 Overland Ave., Suite 500, Los Angeles 90064. He is author of several best-selling books, most recently *Does Someone at Work Treat You Badly?* The Berkley Publishing Group.

Choosing Between Family and Career

Choosing between family and career is unavoidable. You may want to be Supermom or Superdad, but in the real world it's impossible to be a successful corporate leader and *always* be there for your family. If you're determined to be the best at whatever you do, you won't be the best at anything.

Source: Fred A. Krehbiel III, chairman and CEO, Molex, Inc., a family-run business based in Lisle, IL, that makes electronic connectors.

Determine Your Legacy

Determine your legacy—*while you're still alive*. Make a list of the accomplishments and qualities for which you think you'll be remembered if you were to die tomorrow. *Ask yourself:* Is my legacy a positive or a negative one? Am I leaving something for others or taking only for myself? Where have I taken chances? If you don't like the answers, consider making changes now, before it is too late.

Source: *Change Your Life Now: Get Out of Your Head, Get Into Your Life* by Gary Null, PhD, award-winning journalist, author of more than 50 books and host of a nationally syndicated radio show. Health Communications.

How to Be a Much More Effective Person

An effective person is one who is both successful and personally happy. The ability to achieve both of those aims must be based on inner character, not just learning a set of techniques to make you popular.

You must develop seven habits of character to use your knowledge, skills and desires in a truly effective way and maximize your own potential as well as your ability to interact positively with others.

Three habits are needed to develop mastery over yourself.

Three more help you master teamwork, co-operation and communications with others.

The other crucial habit is a commitment to continuous self-improvement that creates an upward spiral of growth.

Three habits of self-mastery…

• *Proactivity:* Effective people recognize that they are free. No matter how good or bad the circumstances in which you find yourself, you possess the freedom to decide your response. You don't have to simply react automatically. When you take the initiative yourself, not just drift with the tide, positive things happen.

How to be proactive: When faced with a problem, think what you can do about it yourself. Begin by replacing reactive language with proactive language.

Examples: Don't say, "There's nothing I can do"…say, "What are my alternatives?"

Don't say, "That's just the way I am"…say, "I can choose a different approach."

Don't say, "He makes me so mad"… say, "I control my own feelings."

Don't say, "I must"…say, "I prefer."

• *Begin with the end in mind:* To achieve a meaningful goal in life, you must know in advance what that goal is.

How to identify your goals: Visualize the eulogies you would like people to deliver at your funeral.

Think of the summary of your life and achievements, deeds and personal relationships you would like to hear from a close family member…a friend…a coworker…a fellow member of an organization you belong to. Then, think about what you are doing today to leave those memories behind.

Exercise: Write a personal mission statement summarizing who you want to be…what you want to do…your basic values and principles.

This will force you to think through your priorities and align your behavior with your beliefs.

• *Put first things first:* Define your priorities and act accordingly.

All your activities can be divided into four classes…

*I. Important and urgent…*crises, projects with deadlines.

*II. Important but not urgent…*building relationships, planning, preventing problems.

*III. Urgent but not important…*many phone calls, some meetings, popular activities.

*IV. Neither urgent nor important…*busy work, some phone calls, pleasant and time-wasting activities.

An exclusive focus on group I crisis-management activities leads to stress and burnout.

Spending too much time on groups III and IV activities, which are not important, demonstrates irresponsibility.

Truly effective people keep as much attention as possible on group II activities—those that are important but not urgent. Time spent on planning and preventive maintenance reduces the number of crises and maximizes their ability to find new opportunities.

Secret of time management…

Don't be afraid to say "no" when asked to do something of low priority. That will let you say "yes" to a more important task instead.

After you have mastered yourself, you must develop three habits for effective relationships with others…

• *Think win-win:* Life's true winners don't make everyone else a loser. They know how to cooperate so that no one is a loser.

When negotiating with other people, don't think that your choice is limited to doing it your way or doing it their way—look instead for a better way for everyone involved.

Best strategy: If you can't find a solution that everyone regards as a win, then agree to disagree amicably. That will leave the relationship intact for making better deals in the future.

• *Seek first to understand—then to be understood:* The key to effective communications is to listen to other people empathetically—not to agree with them, but to understand them emotionally and intellectually.

When they see that you are truly tuned in to what they are feeling and saying, not trying to manipulate or condescend to them, they will listen when you reply. And understanding their point of view will make it easier for you to make a case they can accept.

• *Synergize:* Synergy means putting together a whole that is greater than the sum of its parts. People who communicate respectfully and value each other's contributions come up with creative solutions to problems.

Example: Fred wanted to take his wife Wilma and sons on a fishing vacation for a week during the summer. She thought they should visit her ailing mother, 250 miles away. If either one had given in grudgingly to the other…or they had taken separate vacations…both would have been resentful.

Solution: Fred and Wilma listened to each other's concerns and talked until they came up with a third way—that was finding a lakeside cabin close to Wilma's mother.

• *Sharpen the saw:* If you have to cut down a thick tree with a saw, you will get the job done faster and easier if you stop periodically to sharpen the saw. In the same way, you can magnify your personal effectiveness by taking time out periodically to keep yourself in shape in all four dimensions of your life—physical, spiritual, mental and emotional.

How to do it: Set aside time every week to exercise…review values…learn something new …and improve relationships.

Source: Stephen R. Covey, PhD, chairman of the Covey Leadership Center in Provo, UT. He is the author of *The 7 Habits of Highly Effective People: Restoring the Character Ethic, Principle-Centered Leadership,* and most recently *First Things First,* Simon & Schuster.

Anxiety Disorder

Anxiety disorder is our nation's most prevalent psychiatric problem. At some point in their lives, nearly 15% of the population will suffer from panic attacks, obsessive-compulsive disorder or some other anxiety disorder.

Source: Steve Dager, MD, associate professor of psychiatry and bioengineering, University of Washington, Seattle.

New Treatment for Manic-Depression

Two drugs long used to treat epilepsy—*divalproex sodium* (Depakote) and *carbamazepine* (Tegretol)—control manic episodes without the weight gain, grogginess and memory impairment often caused by lithium, the standard treatment. New treatments for manic-depression are needed because about one-third of individuals with manic-depression fail to respond to lithium...and 60% who take it regularly will have another manic episode.

Source: Charles L. Bowden, MD, professor of psychiatry, University of Texas, San Antonio. His three-week study of Depakote use in 179 manic patients was published in the *Journal of the American Medical Association*, 515 N. State St., Chicago 60610.

Inside Psychotherapy

Psychotherapy is the general name for a variety of psychological approaches to help people resolve emotional, behavioral or interpersonal problems. The goal isn't to advise, direct or tell people what to do but to assist them in taking more active and effective charge of their lives.

There are three broad areas of living where therapy can help:

•Personal growth. You needn't be in the throes of great distress to consider therapy. You may have reached a point at which you're dissatisfied and want more out of life. Or you may simply wish to fulfill your potential—to grow through self-exploration.

•Problems of everyday living. You may be experiencing distress over something specific—relationship trouble, parent-child conflict, serious illness or a major life transition such as having a baby, changing jobs, entering middle age or losing a parent.

•Emotional and behavioral disorders. More severe mental or behavioral disturbances can produce symptoms of a psychiatric disorder. *Examples:* Symptoms of depression like feeling so hopeless that you can't get out of bed...being unable to stop after you've had your first drink...inexplicable panic attacks... or repetitive nightmares and flashbacks reliving a traumatic event.

•*For what kinds of problems is psychotherapy most helpful?*

In deciding whether you might benefit from psychotherapy, ask yourself...

•*Am I distressed enough that I want to do something about it?*

•*Am I able to handle my problems on my own or do I need more support?*

•*How much is my distress affecting my personal and business lives?*

•*Are my problems getting in the way of my daily functioning?*

• *Which therapy approach is best for my problem?*

There are five basic categories of psychotherapy.

The *psychodynamic* approach focuses on the psychological issues and conflicts that underlie emotional problems. This type of therapy requires an ability to put your thoughts and feelings into words, a genuine interest in understanding yourself better and a desire to use your relationship with your therapist as a vehicle for understanding and working through your problems. It's best suited for issues arising from long-standing internal or interpersonal conflicts.

The *behavioral* approach involves modifying specific behaviors and self-defeating habits. *Underlying assumption:* Emotional problems are learned responses to the environment that can be modified or unlearned. You must be willing to carry out "homework" between sessions and to accept focused and limited goals.

The behavioral approach is best for treating phobias, obsessions, shyness, faulty social skills, hostility, anxiety or loneliness and other problems with clear, definable symptoms.

The *cognitive* approach focuses on self-defeating or negative thoughts. If you're comfortable thinking things through rationally and reflectively, cognitive therapy may be appropriate for you. It's particularly helpful with panic attacks and agoraphobia. It's also effective for depression, anxiety, obsessive-compulsive disorder, psychosomatic illness, paranoia, eating disorders and chronic pain problems.

The *family systems* approach focuses on the couple or family rather than the individual. *Aim:* To change dysfunctional patterns of communication and interaction within the couple or family. It's the right approach whenever a couple or family agrees it has mutual problems.

The *supportive* approach aims to provide support rather than facilitate change. It's designed to help individuals through acute turmoil that undermines their ability to function —the loss of a job, death of a loved one, a divorce or a serious illness or disability.

• *How do I find the right therapist?*
Follow these six steps:

1. Acknowledge your need for help.

2. Have a working idea of what you want help with.

3. Know what to look for. Although no license is required to practice psychotherapy, it's best to find someone who *is* a licensed professional—a licensed psychologist, psychiatrist, social worker, psychiatric nurse or marriage and family therapist, etc. Such a practitioner is held accountable to a state regulatory agency as well as professional and ethical standards of conduct.

Get the names of potential therapists from other therapists or mental health professionals, community mental health centers or local professional associations for psychiatry, psychology, social work and nursing.

Caution: Be wary of recommendations from current or former clients. They're often too close to their therapists to have an objective view.

4. Check the therapist's credentials. Call your state licensing board or professional associations. Phone the therapist and say you'd like to ask some questions about his/her areas of specialization and professional qualifications before making an appointment.

Psychiatrists should have completed a residency in psychiatry, including training in psychotherapy...be board-certified...have full membership in the American Psychiatric Association...and have graduated from a psychotherapy institute.

Psychologists should have a doctorate in psychology or a related field...be licensed or certified in your state...have full membership in the American Psychological Association... and be registered in the national Register of Health Service Providers.

Social workers should have a master's in social work with a clinical concentration...be licensed or certified in your state...have full membership in the National Association of Social Workers.

5. Make an appointment for a consultation. Make it clear that you're not starting therapy but *discussing* starting therapy. If a therapist resists the idea of an initial consultation, thank him/her, then say good-bye.

A consultation is a mutual interview. The therapist wants to know about you and what you're looking for. You want to know how the therapist works, what kind of therapy he/she will recommend—and why. Expect to pay for this consultation.

6. Assess the consultation. Was it favorable, questionable—or unacceptable? Your impressions of the therapist and how he interacted with you are just as important as his credentials and what kind of therapy he does. Whatever your initial impression of the therapist, defer any final decision until after the consultation. Don't let the therapist pressure you into making an on-the-spot decision.

• *What questions should I ask during the first meeting?*

While a good match is critical, therapy is also a professional relationship. Since you're contracting for a service, it's important to work out an explicit set of agreements.

Agree on...

• the goals that you want to work toward.

•the format (individual, group, couple or family therapy).

•the therapeutic approach.

•the setting (usually the therapist's office).

•how frequently you'll meet.

•session length. The standard is 50 minutes for individual and couples therapy, 75 to 90 minutes for group and family therapy.

•roughly how long it should take you to reach the goals you've set.

•the therapist's stance on medication to help you psychologically.

• *How can I afford therapy?*

The standard fee is based upon an hourly rate, but many therapists use sliding fee scales or reduced fees for clients who can't afford their regular fee.

If you like the therapist and feel the fee is more than you can afford, don't be afraid to ask if you can be seen for less.

Major health insurers, including health maintenance organizations and managed-care programs, generally include both inpatient and outpatient mental health benefits. Most policies that allow you to choose your own therapist offer a certain dollar amount of coverage per year, irrespective of the therapist's fee. Other policies pay a portion of the fee per session, generally from 50% to 80%. There is often an annual deductible.

• *How can I tell if therapy is really working?*

Periodically evaluate—with your therapist—how your therapy is going. Review your focus and goals, your progress and your working relationship with your therapist.

Ask yourself how safe the therapeutic relationship feels, whether your therapist has your best interests at heart, whether you feel appreciated and believed in and whether you have a sense of increased competence and self-mastery.

If you're in doubt about how therapy is going or if you and your therapist disagree after talking it over, ask for a second opinion from another therapist. If your therapist tries to dissuade you, that should raise serious ethical questions about your therapist's relationship with you.

Important: Bear in mind that as you work on your problems, you may have to feel a little worse before you can feel better.

• *How will I know when to end treatment?*

Ending therapy is often the most important phase of treatment. That's when the work you've done either comes together—or doesn't.

You'll know it's time to end therapy when you feel you've developed the ability to manage on your own and you're confident that you can tackle this next period of your life with your own resources.

Talking about ending therapy can be uncomfortable for you and your therapist. But if you put off this discussion until you're 100% certain that you're ready to leave, there will never be a right moment.

Instead, discuss the issue over time. Set a date so that your remaining work can be done with a definite end in sight.

Review your therapy. Acknowledge what you accomplished and what you didn't, and allow yourself to mourn.

Important: Recognize the anxiety caused by ending therapy for what it is. You always have the option of going back to therapy if you find you can't make it on your own.

Source: Jack Engler, PhD, an instructor in psychology at Harvard Medical School, Boston. He is coauthor, with Daniel Goleman, PhD, of *The Consumer's Guide to Psychotherapy*, Simon & Schuster.

All About Electroconvulsive Therapy

If even the thought of electroconvulsive therapy (ECT) makes you shudder, you've probably been misled by inaccurate portrayals of "shock therapy" such as that appearing in the 1975 movie *One Flew Over the Cuckoo's Nest*.

That depiction of ECT as a terrifying, primitive procedure forced on an unwilling patient was at least 20 years out of date even then… and ECT has been further refined in the intervening years.

Today's "refined" ECT causes neither pain nor convulsions. It's fast, safe and more effective than drugs or psychotherapy for certain mental disorders, including...

•Immobilizing depression, especially the severe form accompanied by psychosis.

•Severe mania.

•Acute schizophrenia or another form of psychosis.

•Psychoses associated with systemic disorders such as lupus.

Even for these limited forms of mental illness, ECT is usually administered after drug therapy and psychotherapy have proven ineffective.

Exception: When an individual is in a vegetative state (suffering from catatonia) or is delusional, trying drugs or therapy first is often a waste of time. In such cases, psychiatrists often go straight to ECT.

What's involved...

Although a few private hospitals now offer ECT, it's usually given in teaching hospitals. It is not generally available in state, municipal or federal hospitals.

In most cases, ECT is administered by a team made up of a psychiatrist, anesthetist and two nurses—one with special ECT training, another to oversee the brief recovery process.

Before the electrical current is administered, the patient undergoing ECT receives...

•A short-acting anesthetic, given intravenously, to put the patient to sleep. This keeps the patient from remembering the seizure caused by the electrical current.

•A muscle relaxant to prevent thrashing during the seizure (as in the old movies).

Once the patient is asleep, electrodes are applied to the head, and a brief electrical pulse is applied (from 0.2 to 4.0 seconds with modern ECT devices and less than one second with older devices).

This current causes a "storm" of electrical impulses in the brain. Somehow—we don't yet know precisely—this storm helps lift the depression or other symptoms. The patient feels nothing.

The patient spends up to 30 minutes in the recovery room, then showers and goes home (or back to the hospital room). *Time elapsed:* About an hour.

Driving and other activities requiring mental alertness are forbidden that day—not because of the ECT but because of the effects of the anesthetic. ECT may cause memory loss—usually affecting the events during the period of mental illness or the ECT treatment.

Most patients undergoing ECT receive six to nine treatments over a two- to three-week period. In some cases, this period is followed by six to eight more treatments given once a week or once every other week.

How effective is ECT? When administered appropriately and by experienced professionals, 90% to 95% of patients experience marked improvement.

To locate a psychiatrist qualified to administer ECT, contact the psychiatry department at the nearest teaching or private psychiatric hospital. Or contact the Association for Convulsive Therapy, 1221 S. Grand Blvd., St. Louis 63104. *Attention:* Donald P. Hay, MD, executive director.

Source: Max Fink, MD, professor of psychiatry and neurology, State University of New York at Stony Brook. Since 1953, Dr. Fink has written more than 250 articles on electroconvulsive therapy. In 1978 and 1990, he served on the American Psychiatric Association's ECT task force.

The Healing Power Of Plants

You've probably heard that keeping a pet is good for your health. Close contact with animals has been shown to lower blood pressure, ease feelings of depression, boost feelings of self-esteem—and more.

Now we know that you can get many of the same health benefits by tending a garden. *Recent studies have demonstrated that plants...*

•Reduce stress. A study of college students worried after taking an exam found that the simple act of viewing plants increased positive feelings and reduced fear and anger. Other studies showed that viewing plants lowers blood pressure and reduces muscle tension.

• Boost self-esteem. As plants grow, so do their owners' feelings of self-worth. That's why plants are often used in psychiatric rehabilitation. Plants are also used in physical therapy. Caring for them requires balance, flexibility and coordination.

• Raise job performance. Studies have shown that workers whose offices afforded a view of trees and flowers experienced less job stress, enjoyed greater job satisfaction and experienced fewer ailments and headaches than those who could see only man-made elements from their windows.

• Speed recovery. In another study, gallbladder surgery patients whose rooms looked out on greenery had shorter post-operative hospital stays than patients without a view. Those with the view also used less painkilling medication, suggesting they were in less pain.

If you're intrigued by the idea of using plants for therapy, I recommend filling your home with plants. Just be sure not to buy more than you can comfortably care for. Neglected, sick plants are depressing.

Beware: Plants sold at discount stores tend to have more problems than those bought at a reputable nursery.

To derive maximum health benefits from your plants, I recommend caring for them yourself. If you don't have the time, consider hiring someone else to care for them for you. Simply being around plants is better than not being around them—even if you're not the gardener.

If you're a novice gardener, choose easy-to-raise plants, such as pothos, philodendron, cactus or dracaena marginate.

Rosemary, basil and thyme also do well inside, but they need more light.

Despite their popularity, ficus trees, scheffleras and corn plants are often tricky to care for.

If you'd like to derive physical as well as psychic nourishment from your plants, plant tomatoes, lettuce, etc., in pots on your patio—where you can enjoy watching them grow.

Source: Diane Relf, PhD, assistant professor of horticulture, Virginia Polytechnic Institute and State University, Blacksburg. She is the former president of the American Horticultural Therapy Association, 362A Christopher Ave., Gaithersburg, MD 20879.

9

Secrets of Success

Living Life to the Fullest... In the Later Years

Aging is so often thought of in our society as an entirely negative experience. So—we spoke with 40 people over the age of sixty about their experiences in aging.

We asked each person: "What can you say in praise of age?" Their answers were inspiring...

Maturity turns out to give us a chance to do many new things and to develop ourselves in new ways. Suggestions from the people we interviewed...

Develop a new avocation...

It's important to develop a vital, challenging interest that you can take up when you retire. This is especially important for people who, after years of work, have grown tired of their jobs. They look forward to retirement and then find themselves bored, with too much time on their hands, and they become depressed or even ill.

If you develop an avocational interest that's an alternative to your work well in advance of retirement, you will be able to make the transition with much less stress and sense of loss.

Example: Radio and television broadcaster Art Linkletter has used his "retirement years" to start a new career as a writer, using his personal experiences of aging as the basis for his work. His most recent book, *Old Age is Not for Sissies*, which focuses on the joys and pains of late life, has become a national best-seller.

Retirement is a full-time job...

A regular job consumes 35 or 40 hours a week—more if you factor in commuting. But if you're retired, you're retired 24 hours a day, seven days a week. And you alone have the responsibility for how your day turns out. Structuring your own time is a skill that has to be learned. That's particularly so if you've spent your life in a corporation, where a lot of structure was provided. Some retired people can't find enough activities they enjoy to fill their time, while others, like former Time Warner executive

Dick Munroe, find retirement to be busier than full-time work. "I love what I'm doing. I love not doing what I used to do," explains Munroe, "I'm just doing too many things and I should fix that!"

So find things you love to do and learn to say no to anything else.

Value your own experience...

Americans undervalue experience. We're so hooked on youth that we haven't yet recognized that inexperience isn't always a virtue, and knowing what you're doing isn't a handicap.

For people who stay open to change and growth throughout their lives, the mature years can prove to be unexpectedly rewarding.

Writer May Sarton told us she was glad to be old. She had solved a lot of problems that are very anguishing for young people, and she had come to terms with her own life in ways that made life much easier.

The late Norman Cousins spoke very specifically about being in the harvest years. He told us that he was using everything he had ever learned, everything he had ever done or known, and using it better than he ever had before. He could accomplish things with greater economy of effort than when he was younger.

The more you learn, the more you will ultimately be able to do. In a long life, you will have time to develop skills you don't have now but would like to. And when you have assembled them you will be able to use and truly enjoy them.

Become wise...

You don't necessarily grow wise as you grow old. Wisdom isn't a part of the biological process of aging. But you can work to develop it. Wisdom comes from wrestling with our experiences, making sense out of them...enjoying life's pleasures, letting go of its sorrows and mistakes, and moving forward.

Many of the people that we interviewed found great security in the knowledge gained through aging of what their moral values were and what's valuable in life. *Dancer and choreographer Bella Lewitsky told us:* "As I've aged I've grown more confident in my own values and at the same time more tolerant of differences."

Take time to enjoy the simple things in life...

We have the idea as we come into the later years that if we do nothing, or very simple things, we're not using our time very well.

But even the very famous people that we interviewed found pleasure in simple things, like *Peanuts* creator Charles Schulz. "I'm great for doing nothing," he said. He still draws his comic strip several hours a day, but he also likes to just sit, watch television, and play with his dog. He likes the feeling of comfort that he receives from simple and quiet activities.

Writer Eve Merriam—who died only recently—talked about how she relished the change of seasons, particularly the coming of spring, finding what she called daily joy in the colors and fragrances of the trees and flowers.

Explore your inner life...

Young adulthood and middle age don't leave us much time to explore the heart and spirit deeply. As the outer life shrinks, there's room for a great deal of inner growth for most people. Although we continue to need the nourishment of other human beings of all ages in our lives, we also need quiet and solitude to explore the inner self.

Through this self-exploration, many of the people we interviewed developed a strong spiritual sense as they grew older—and found that to be one of the richest aspects of aging. This spirituality was often connected with a reverence for nature.

Clarinetist Rosario Mazzeo finds his spiritual connection in nature and takes long walks in the woods every day.

The challenge of physical changes...

There's general agreement that the worst thing about aging is the physical erosion that often accompanies the later years—the slowing up of the body.

The attitude that you take toward your physical aging is extremely important. *Actor Hume Cronyn spoke about the lines on his face:* "Let them get deeper—particularly the laugh lines!"

Important: Deal with physical limitations and needs to care for yourself. Then move past them and focus on the many satisfactions that are possible out there.

While the body is subject to deterioration, the person inside has a continued capacity for growth, whatever the body's age.

Understand the value of life...

The best way to get the most out of life is to come to terms with mortality. Actor Jason Robards told us that to him, life is like a hotel—everybody checks in and everybody checks out. Once he fully grasped this, he was able to truly savor each day.

It is in fact the sense of the preciousness of time that we acquire as we get older which should fill our later years with a new richness and intensity.

Songwriter and singer Burl Ives finds that contemplating death gives him a renewed sense of joy in life.

Forget the myths...

If we want a richer later life, we have to take responsibility for achieving it. We can't accept the myths that "old is over," and that only youth matters. We must learn to appreciate and give thanks for the many gifts that aging brings us.

Source: Phillip Berman and Connie Goldman, authors of *The Ageless Spirit: Reflections on Living Life to the Fullest in Our Later Years*, Ballantine Books.

Positive Thinking For Tricky Times

Positive thinking is the belief in our *own* self-worth—and in the value of everyone else. That belief leads to self-confidence, respect for others and a lifestyle based on strong values.

A *value* is a principle that reflects an ideal moral standard by which individuals guide their own thoughts and actions...and from which society as a whole benefits.

Many people slip into the habit of negative thinking because they feel discouraged, depressed, lonely, isolated or stressed. They want results fast and easy.

But life isn't like that. Life is meant to be a challenge. When our minds are full of fear, doubt and clutter, good ideas can't get through. We get our best ideas and make our best decisions when we're relaxed, open to impressions and responsive to them. *Steps to thinking more positively...*

• *Talk about values with family and friends.* There are seven master values that make up the core principles in people's lives—*honesty, courage, enthusiasm, service, faith, hope* and *love.* You can improve your life by identifying behaviors associated with each master value and by talking about them with family and friends.

Unless we clarify our values by talking about them, we focus on the negative self-centered values of our culture. As a society, if we do not live by our positive values, we aren't likely to support one another.

Becoming *value-centered* counteracts the common tendency we have to be self-centered and negative. We can continue thinking everything is going wrong—or we can get into the habit of thinking we can make things turn out right.

• *See—and seize—opportunity.* Many people *see* opportunity...but they don't *seize* it. Seizing opportunity takes a greater step of faith. It also requires a plan because opportunity often is more illusive than the tasks you face at the moment.

You have to find a way to link the present situation with the opportunity that is before you. You can't just sit at a desk and think positively about something and expect it to happen. *You have to make it happen—or help make it happen.* Keeping alive a plan...a marriage...or even hope requires action.

If you have a positive, upbeat frame of mind, you will exercise your initiative, resourcefulness, creativity and judgment. You will devise a plan—a clear idea of what you can do—and fill in more and more details every day. Positive thinking is reinforced when you begin to see results.

Many people ask us, *Why think positively? What difference can I make? Things are beyond my control.* This is dangerous thinking. I urge people to have goals. Without goals, any direction *might* work. But *with* goals, you can choose the best course of action.

To learn how to set and achieve goals, start with one that is easy to measure. Perhaps you want to lose five pounds. List the steps—diet, exercise, calorie counting, etc.—and make a simple chart to record your progress. Mark the chart every day. Once you master a simple task, focus on more complex areas of your life.

It's hard to be positive if you live in a vacuum. You need to be doing important things that overcome negative feelings and fears.

• *Look for good news—ignore negative news.* Positive thinking encourages people to live by the values that have endured and held societies together over time. Many people today are looking for those values again. People want something positive to counteract all the bad news they hear in the media every day.

The best way to focus on the positive is to reach outside yourself and help another person. Drive an elderly person to the grocery store, visit a friend in the hospital or help a coworker finish a job that isn't your responsibility. Then you will *feel* the difference you are making in individual lives and the problems of the world get smaller.

• *Make decisions based on your positive values.* If parents are going to raise their children properly, they've got to have a value base upon which to make decisions. How might positive thinking help? When you look at a problem, your attitude is very important. For most problems, there is a right and a wrong decision—or at least *good, better* and *best* options.

You're more likely to reach the best decision by thinking positively, because positive thinking opens up new options.

Positive thinking begins by a process of thought replacement. Find a few affirmations like, *You can if you think you can…*or *Evil only triumphs when good men do nothing.* Fill your mind with them, and displace the tendency to be negative.

• *Take it one step—and one day—at a time.* Nothing important can be accomplished overnight. It takes time to set your goals—and to reach them. There will be plenty of opposition, frustration and disappointment along the way. The key is to concentrate on your short-term victories rather than on the overall goal. We can't always see the end when we start out. The best way to do this is to build a solid foundation. Start where you are, and go step by step.

• *Lead a good life.* Money can buy many things, but it can't buy love, trust, joy and peace. A person needs the power of positive thinking and living to experience the best in life and to find happiness and fulfillment both at home and at work.

There are some simple things you can do that will make a qualitative difference in your life. If you want to lead a good life, be a good person. Many people are confused by those who have lives full of comfort. That is a very superficial expression of the good life. The good life is one in which you are at peace with your inner soul…at peace with yourself and with others.

If you have habits of positive thinking and living, you can make each day better. Some people are naturally positive, but all of us can learn to be more positive. Even people who are born into and raised in terrible conditions can overcome those conditions once they have a sense of who they are and what they need to do.

Source: Ruth Stafford Peale, chairman, and Eric Fellman, president and chief executive, Center for Positive Thinking, 66 E. Main St., Pawling, NY 12564. The Center provides programs and published materials to help people embrace the principles of positive thinking. It was founded in 1940 by Mrs. Peale and her late husband, the Reverend Dr. Norman Vincent Peale, author of more than 45 books, including *The Power of Positive Thinking.* Fawcett Books.

How to Live More Healthfully

A quick cup of coffee, a doughnut, a harried commute—then hours in an "airless," artificially lighted office…topped off by an evening of TV. Given this daily ritual, is it any wonder Americans get sick so often?

It's possible to live a healthier life—to make life-affirming choices about what we eat, how we spend our time, what we feel. For starters, consider replacing your alarm clock with a cassette player on a timer. That way, you can wake to the sounds of a nature tape—surf, waterfalls, birds, etc. If you're a heavy sleeper, use an alarm clock as a backup—just in case.

You might skip the morning paper and morning TV shows, too. Most of us can benefit by limiting ourselves to one paper a day.

You can use your time before work to get in touch with your spiritual side. Listen to soothing music. *My favorite:* Any recording by clarinetist Tony Scott. Meditate, stretch and perform deep-breathing exercises. If possible, do 30 minutes of aerobic exercise. Then shower, finishing up with a blast of cold water—the perfect caffeine-free pick-me-up.

Dress comfortably—no tight belts or collars. Have a real breakfast, with fresh fruit, a high-fiber, whole-wheat, fat-free cereal and a spicy caffeine-free tea. Coffee provides a brief boost …but you'll pay the price with increased sluggishness later in the day. I also suggest for my patients a daily multivitamin containing at least 75 milligrams of vitamin B. I take Solgar VM75 vitamins.

Don't rush your commute. Forty percent of heart attacks occur before—or during—travel. Baby yourself on the way to work. If someone cuts you off or your train is late, take a few deep breaths—or even try singing.

While at work, try to maintain a sense of connection to the natural world. Position your desk so you can look out the window. Hang nature photos on the wall and keep a tape or CD player on hand to play nature sounds. Decorate with naturally soothing textures and colors—wood and stone, greens, blues and browns. Use bright colors as accents.

Take frequent work breaks. Drink spring water. Tap water is full of chlorine and other harmful chemicals. Lunch outdoors whenever possible. Keep a basket of fruit and fat-free crackers on hand to avoid nibbling candy and other sugary, fatty foods.

Surround yourself with plants. They give off oxygen, which helps make you feel more alert, and water vapor, which helps moisturize your skin and prevent breathing problems. And they're soothing to look at. *Also soothing:* Miniature waterfalls, such as those sold by the Nature Company (Call 800-227-1114 for a store nearest you).

I also urge you to be more open about your feelings at work. That might seem a little odd at first, but it's worth the effort. If you feel hurt or discouraged, say so. If you're happy, express your joy. Encourage others to do the same.

Open, honest expression of feelings is one of the best antidotes to stress.

After work, fight the temptation to plop down in front of the television. TV distracts you from exercise and other health-promoting activities. And because the sense of intimacy it provides is false, it can cause a subtle form of depression. You are made to feel as if you are connecting with the characters in your favorite sitcom. Of course, you're not. Your emotional and creative energy go to people whose caring about you can't be felt back.

Better: Draw…paint…make something with your hands…go for a walk…listen to music …sit in a café and watch people go by. Or do volunteer work. Volunteers live longer with less illness than their more isolated peers.

Remember to get—and give—at least three hugs a day.

Source: Sandra McLanahan, MD, directs the stress-management training program at Dr. Dean Ornish's Preventive Medicine Research Institute in Sausalito, CA. She is also executive medical director of the Integral Health Center and Spa in Buckingham, VA. She also teaches at the Integral Yoga Institute in New York City.

Stress/Cancer Connection

Long-term psychological stress can cause cancer of the colon and rectum. Patients who had serious job problems in the previous 10 or more years were 5.5 times more likely to develop colorectal cancer than adults without such problems.

Theory: Stress-induced hormonal changes boost production of tissue-damaging substances called *free radicals*. The higher the concentration of free radicals, the greater the cancer risk. *Also:* Stress weakens the immune system. This limits the body's ability to kill cancer cells, allowing them to grow into tumors. Further, stressful life events may lead to poorer diets and reduced levels of physical activity, also raising risk.

Source: Joseph G. Courtney, PhD, research epidemiologist, University of California, Los Angeles, School of Public Health.

Your Imagination And Your Health

One key to better health lies not with proper nutrition or regular doctor's visits…but with your imagination.

More than a tool for daydreaming or creativity, your imagination can affect your body as well as your mind.

See for yourself: Imagine quartering a lemon. See the bright yellow. Smell the citrus. Now imagine biting into a piece and swallowing the juice.

By now, you're probably starting to salivate. Your jaw may ache. Clearly, what you think affects your body as well as your mind—and this demonstration gives only the tiniest inkling of the vast potential of the mind/body link.

Imagination is powerful…

With practice, you'll be conjuring up images that help you ease psychological stress and alleviate the symptoms of many disorders. Imagery may even be able to heal these disorders.

Mental imagery can also help you change destructive habits or behavior patterns.

Imagery is how we represent things to ourselves—mentally. It's the natural way our nervous system processes information. Memories, dreams, daydreams, planning and creativity are most readily available to us through images—essentially thoughts that you can see, taste, smell and/or feel.

Imagery for relaxation…

The most basic use of imagery is for relaxation…

The imagery used in relaxation and stress reduction is really a directed daydream. In fact, it's the reverse of creating tension by worrying and imaging all the things that frighten you—and make you anxious.

What to do: Close your eyes. Breathe deeply and focus on each body part from head to toe. Invite each one to relax. Then imagine a place that's beautiful and serene—a stress-free "hideaway."

Some people imagine a windswept mountaintop. Others see a field full of wildflowers… or a warm, sunny beach.

Whatever you imagine, immerse yourself in the sights, sounds, aromas and feelings of being in this hideaway. After doing this for five to 15 minutes, you'll probably feel very peaceful and relaxed. Practiced regularly, this technique can be used to help alleviate a variety of medical problems—pain, allergies, high blood pressure, etc.

Caution: Imagery can change your body's need for—and tolerance of—certain medications. So if you're taking medications, make sure you're closely monitored by your doctor.

Help helps…

Most people can master simple visualization techniques on their own. Others do best when they use a guided-imagery audio- or videotape.

For especially complex problems, it may be necessary to seek the guidance of a professional "guide"—a psychotherapist experienced in the use of guided imagery.*

Such a guide can quickly lead you into a "quiet place" where it's possible to create an identity for the particular problem that's troubling you…and to confront this identity.

How imagery helped beat stomach pain…

One of my patients asked me to help her overcome the chronic pain in her chest and abdomen.

This woman—who had already received treatment for an ulcer—had been imagining her pain as a fire burning inside her stomach. She had visualized dousing this fire with water. That worked for a while, but the pain always came back.

I suggested that she let another image come to mind, and she saw a little hand pinching her stomach. She asked the hand why it was doing that. It angrily shook a fist at her.

She didn't understand what this meant. So I told her to ask. When she did, the fist opened up and a finger pointed directly at her heart.

Then she got an image of her heart encased in a burlap sack filled with sharp objects. These objects were piercing her heart. The hand, she concluded, wanted to protect her heart.

*While many hypnotists, psychotherapists and social workers may be able to help you apply visualization techniques, few professionals are trained in guided imagery. For more information, and to locate guides in your area, call the Academy for Guided Imagery, 800-726-2070.

With my help, she went on to visualize opening the sack and releasing each object. One of the first images to emerge was of her stepfather, who had been very violent. We eventually discovered that her current pain flared up in situations where she was treated abusively by her employer and where she felt powerless.

Creating awareness of this relationship between her emotions and her pain helped her develop assertiveness and ultimately relieved her pain.

So working with receptive imagery as above can be a form of education or psychotherapy that can help teach us about ourselves, expand our problem-solving abilities and train our minds to promote healthy bodies.

Like any other skill, guided imagery can be mastered only after considerable practice. Also, some people are more gifted at it than others. But almost anyone who pursues imagery derives deep relaxation and comfort. Most people also gain spiritual and possibly physical healing.

Source: Martin L. Rossman, MD, clinical associate professor of medicine, University of California, San Francisco, and codirector of the Academy for Guided Imagery, Mill Valley, CA. He is the author of *Healing Yourself: A Step-by-Step Program to Better Health* by Imagery, Pocket Books.

Live Much Longer...and Much, Much Better

Having watched many friends and loved ones grow old, fall ill and die, most of us operate under the assumption that the same lies in store for us.

In fact, while there's no way to stop the aging process, we can dramatically reduce the toll the years take on us. We can lead active, vital lives well into our 80s, 90s—and beyond.

Believe it or not, all it takes is a change in the way we see ourselves and the world.

If that claim sounds too strong to you, consider this dramatic but little-known study, conducted by Harvard researchers in 1979...

Two groups of healthy men age 75 and older spent a week at a country resort. Members of the first group were simply told to enjoy themselves.

The second group was told to "make believe" they were living in 1959. For this group, all references to the modern world were eliminated. On the reading table were issues of *Life* and *The Saturday Evening Post* from 1959. The only music played was at least 20 years old. And all talk had to refer to events and people of 1959.

The results of this play-acting were remarkable. Compared with the first group, the *make-believe* group showed significant improvements in memory and manual dexterity.

They became more active and self-sufficient. Stiff joints became flexible, and muscle strength, hearing and vision improved. Their faces even looked younger.

What did this study demonstrate? That through psychological intervention, virtually all the so-called "irreversible" signs of aging can be reversed.

That study and several others conducted since then have convinced me that each of us has the power to influence—to a remarkable degree—how quickly we age. I've decided to make the most of this awareness by eating lots of fresh fruits and vegetables, by performing yoga and running for an hour a day, by taking vitamin supplements—and by following several anti-aging strategies...

• *I try to be flexible.* Psychological studies on people who have made it to 100 suggest that one reason for their extreme longevity is that they are extremely adaptable in the face of stress. They respond creatively to change, are largely free of anxiety and have a capacity to integrate new things into their lives. To ensure that you'll be adaptable in old age, you must work on being that way well before you get there. That's why I'm always on the lookout for ways to reduce conflict, anxiety and worry in my life.

I also try not to have impossibly high expectations. I'm convinced that by making my life easier, I'm making myself less vulnerable to disease and the other common aspects of aging.

• *I try to be aware of my body.* To gain some control of the aging process, we must first have some awareness of it. Sadly, most of us are

159

blind and deaf to the subtle cues our bodies keep giving us.

No matter what I'm doing, I try to be aware of what's going on with my body. Each time I experience a minor ache or pain or even a feeling that something's not right, I take a few moments to focus my attention on the painful part of my body. Doing this helps initiate the healing process.

Here's an awareness-promoting technique I've found useful...

Sit quietly and relax your body. Envision a goal that's very important to you—greater energy and alertness or more youthful enthusiasm, for example. Expect and believe that you will achieve that goal. Try not to give in to doubt or worry—they only interfere with success. Just know that the message was delivered and that your result is on its way.

• *I acknowledge psychological pain.* Too many of us are victims of our own emotions. We fail to confront and "work through" the inevitable hurts we all suffer...and the pain gets locked up inside.

I used to be like that. Not any more. *What I do now:*

• *I pay attention to my pain—and the sensations it causes in my body.*

• *I keep a diary.* Each day, I record arguments, disappointments, failures and other causes of emotional pain—as well as my responses to these painful stimuli.

I might write down something like, "I felt angry or irritated because of ___." Then I consider whether anger or irritation really was an appropriate response.

• *I release my pain through ritual.* I might go so far as to jot down the source of my pain on a piece of paper—and then bury the paper or flush it down a toilet. Or I might simply go for a long run.

• *I share my painful experiences with a loved one.* I try not to blame anyone. I just let my loved one know how I feel. The simple act of describing my emotions to someone else helps me get rid of the bad feelings...and it trains me to choose my emotions, rather than simply let them happen to me.

• *I live a balanced life.* Living in harmony with the body's rhythms means not going to extremes. If we push the cycle of rest and activity in the wrong direction, we hasten the aging process.

The most striking example of how our bodies reflect an unbalanced lifestyle is heart disease. It's a major affliction of the elderly. And it's the cause of more deaths than all other diseases combined. As we all know by now, heart problems usually stem from too much fatty food and too little exercise.

I believe that to be truly balanced, a life must be split into thirds...

• One-third should be spent sleeping.

• One-third should be spent working. I believe our life's work should not only be pleasurable, but also should give us some spiritual fulfillment and serve humanity in some way.

• One-third should be spent in recreation —reading, seeing a movie, making love, going swimming, watching a sunset, etc.

This morning, I got up at 4:30, meditated until 5:30 and wrote until 6:30. Between 6:30 and 8:00, I went running. Right now it's only 8:30 am, and already I've had a lot of fun. In a few minutes I have a meeting, and then I'll go see a few patients in the afternoon. This evening, I'll meditate again and then have a nice dinner. By 10:00 pm I'll be in bed.

• *I try not to overreact to problems or annoyances.* If I miss a plane, I say to myself, "This moment is as it should be." I accept things as they are. You may not be able to change this moment and you certainly can't change the past, but you can influence the future. The best way to do that is to live totally in the present. After all, certainty would be so boring.

• *I don't take myself too seriously.* Seriousness arises from fear, or from an impulse to impress or manipulate people. I prefer to be carefree and lighthearted.

That doesn't mean that I am irresponsible. "Responsibility" means having the ability to respond. The measure of our responsibility is how creatively we respond to the challenges we're given. You don't have to be serious to do that.

• *I meditate*. Each day, I spend two hours meditating. I'm convinced that this is the real key to slowing down the aging process. Not everyone needs to meditate as long as I do—15 to 20 minutes is probably enough.

The connection between aging and the body's release of stress hormones such as cortisol and adrenaline has been strongly demonstrated. Daily meditation is perhaps the best way to reduce the levels of stress hormones.

Recent studies have shown that people who've been meditating for several years have remarkably low levels of cortisol and adrenaline in their bloodstream…and their abilities to cope with difficult situations are very strong.

There is simply no substitute for the creative inspiration, knowledge and stability that come from knowing how to contact your core of inner silence.

Source: Deepak Chopra, MD, director of the Institute for Mind/Body Medicine and Human Potential at Sharp Health Care in San Diego. Dr. Chopra is former chief of staff at New England Memorial Hospital in Boston. He is the author of several books, including *Ageless Body, Timeless Mind*, Random House.

Beating Procrastination

Problem: You have more to do than you can handle.

Solution: Prioritize responsibilities—put the most important ones first.

Problem: You put off a difficult task until you're "in the mood."

Solution: Remind yourself that the sooner you begin, the sooner it will be over.

Problem: You think you work best under pressure and put off projects until the last minute.

Solution: Set an earlier deadline, and challenge yourself to meet it.

Problem: You're a perfectionist.

Solution: Realize we make mistakes. Demanding perfection adds undue stress.

Problem: You convince yourself that if you put off doing something long enough, somebody else will do it.

Solution: Remind yourself that the one who does it receives the credit.

Problem: You feel so overwhelmed that you don't know where to begin.

Solution: Do *something*. Finishing one task could snowball into getting even more accomplished.

Source: Warren Huberman, PhD, clinical psychologist, Institute for Behavior Therapy, 137 E. 36 St., New York 10016.

The Art and Politics Of Getting the Best Second Opinion

A second opinion offers you a different—and invaluable—perspective on a medical problem…but it can also be confusing.

How do you know when you need a second opinion?

Whom should you consult for that second opinion?

And what should you do with the information—especially if it is vastly different from the first opinion?

To obtain optimal care today, it's vital that you not be intimidated by physicians. Patients are often *too* respectful of doctors and thus reluctant to ask questions or voice concerns for fear of offending them or sounding ignorant.

Reality: You have a right—and an obligation—to be assertive when gathering information about your condition. It's the only way you can make an informed, intelligent decision about your treatment.

Actually, the first step when a doctor makes a diagnosis or recommends a treatment *isn't* to seek a second opinion. The first step is to thoroughly question your primary doctor about his/her reasons for suggesting the course of action.

If you're not sure what to ask, try saying, *This is a bit overwhelming. If you were in my position, Doctor, what questions would you ask to understand the situation better?*

Push for specifics—for example, statistics on the *exact* percentage of sufferers who respond to the proposed treatment. *Also ask about…*

• The risks and side effects of the treatment

...and the odds that you'll experience a bad outcome.

•The benefits and how much you are likely to gain from the treatment.

•Any alternative treatments that you should consider—and the reasons why they are—or are not—recommended for you by the doctor.

•The costs and how fully they are reimbursed typically by health insurance.

When to get a second opinion...

There are several appropriate reasons why you may want a second opinion...

•If, after talking things through with your doctor, you're unsure about a treatment.

•If the treatment is so major that it will irrevocably change your life.

•If you have a condition about which experts disagree on the best treatment.

Example: Some doctors believe one-third to one-half of all cardiac surgeries are unnecessary and that drug therapy may offer equal benefit. If your case falls into an area where medical opinions differ, your personal judgments about the risks and benefits various therapies may hold for you should ultimately decide your course of action.

•If your insurer *requires* a second opinion before it will pay for treatment.

In all scenarios, be up front with your primary physician about seeking a second opinion. You may need him to talk with the other doctor, and you'll want copies of your records. *Appropriate phrasing...*

I respect your opinion, but I'm obligated to myself to get a second opinion and gather all the information I can. This doesn't mean I don't have confidence in you.

The doctor shouldn't be offended by this approach.

Finding a second-opinion doctor...

When you seek your second opinion, it is critical that you obtain one that is independent of your first doctor's opinion. *Suggestions...*

•*Don't see a doctor who practices in the same office*—or even the same hospital—as your first consulting specialist. Colleagues tend to agree with the first opinion rather than risk offending one another or jeopardizing a lucrative referral

source. Make sure your first- and second-opinion doctors are financially and socially independent of each other.

•*Take with a "grain of salt" the first doctor's recommendation of a physician.* Inquire about his relationship with that physician and exactly why he's recommending him. If the second-opinion doctor is a buddy of your first doctor, he will likely agree with the first opinion, and it won't be worth your time to see him.

•*Go to a hospital across town*—or even to a hospital in another town. That's often the best way to find someone who doesn't know the first doctor you saw and has no financial or personal ties to him.

•*Go to a physician who practices in a different type of institution* than the first doctor you consulted.

Reason: Because of their diverse practice settings and exposures, they're most likely to give you different perspectives on your problem.

Example: If, for your first opinion, you saw a physician affiliated with a community hospital, find a physician who has privileges at a medical school hospital for the second.

•*Ask your family doctor—your general doctor, not the specialist whose opinion you are trying to verify—for a recommendation.* He may know the top specialists in town.

•*Contact the American Board of Specialists* (800-776-2378) for names of board-certified physicians in your area. Call each doctor's office and ask for his credentials, training, affiliations and track record with the treatment you're considering. Call the hospital each is affiliated with or the Board of Specialists to verify information. An academic affiliation is usually a good sign.

Information to bring with you...

Advise the second doctor that you've seen another physician already and that you're seeking a second opinion on a proposed course of action.

Be sure to bring all medical records and originals or copies of X rays and lab reports with you. That way, the second physician will quickly be brought up to speed on your case and won't need to repeat a lot of tests. By moral obligation—and law, in many states—these materials are available to you, although the physician may charge a nominal fee for reproducing them.

What to make of the second opinion…

• *Be on the alert for any subtle signals* that indicate the second doctor disagrees with the first doctor—and be sure to follow up these signals with pointed questions.

Example: While reviewing your chart, the doctor says, *I wonder…* or *That's unusual.*

Don't let such seemingly innocuous comments slide. Press the doctor for details. What exactly does he wonder about? What is unusual? Would he have a different approach to your problem?

• *Encourage the first- and second-opinion doctors to discuss your case.* There is nothing wrong with the two doctors you've consulted discussing your case—provided their assessments are not clouded by professional or personal friendships or other nonrelated biases. Together, they may arrive at a joint decision about the best treatment for you.

Example: For early breast cancer, one surgeon may recommend mastectomy (removal of the whole breast)…whereas another may suggest a lumpectomy (removal of just the malignant tissue) followed by radiation therapy. The treatments are equally effective for many—but not for all—women. The two surgeons may find a common ground for a recommendation on whether a lumpectomy or mastectomy will be better for you. Or if they continue to disagree, they should isolate the basis of their disagreement so you and perhaps another consultant can decide what to do.

Third opinion…

If the two doctors can't reach a consensus, seek a third opinion. Then—armed with the information you've gathered—go with your gut feelings and personal preferences about which treatment will bring you the most benefit and the least harm.

Source: Richard N. Podell, MD, clinical professor of family medicine, University of Medicine and Dentistry of New Jersey–Robert Wood Johnson Medical School in New Brunswick, NJ. He is author of *When Your Doctor Doesn't Know Best.* Simon & Schuster.

Setting Goals… The Basics

Search for your life's meaning by asking who you are…where you are going…how you can prevent your life from being a series of accidents…what you want to be when you have fully grown up…how it might be possible for you to experience real community…how you can envision yourself dying happy.

Source: Thomas H. Naylor, PhD, professor of economics, Duke University, Durham, NC, and author of *The Search for Meaning.* Abingdon Press.

 # Tai Chi Helpful for Older People

Tai chi improves balance and may help reduce the risk of falls in elderly people. The ancient Chinese exercise—which involves gentle turning and pivoting—teaches participants to focus on how their weight is distributed. Older women who did tai chi three times a week for six months, along with leg presses and brisk walking, experienced a 17% improvement in their ability to balance on one leg. Those who only stretched and practiced tai chi once a week had no significant improvement.

Source: James Judge, MD, assistant professor of medicine, University of Connecticut School of Medicine, Farmington. His study of 21 women was reported in *Physical Therapy,* American Physical Therapy Association, 1111 N. Fairfax St., Alexandria, VA 22314.

Five-Day Plan for Overcoming Insomnia

One in every three adults has trouble falling or staying asleep. If you're one of them, you're probably all too familiar with the *anti-insomnia basics…*

• Avoid alcohol for two hours before bedtime.

• Avoid caffeine and tobacco for six hours before bedtime.

• Use your bed only for sleeping and sex, not for reading, eating, etc.

• Don't exercise, have heated discussions or engage in other stimulating activities close to bedtime.

If you've tried those steps to no avail, a shift in how you *think* about sleep—plus a few specific techniques—should pave the way to more restful slumber. Apply them faithfully, and you're likely to see a difference in just five nights.

• Don't *try* to sleep. The more you pursue a good night's rest, the more elusive that rest becomes. So stop trying so hard. Be more passive. *Think of sleep as...*

...a *gentle force* that will overcome you if you let it.

...an *ocean wave*. You're a surfer. Get into position and wait.

...a *friend* who will soon visit. If you make the proper preparations, she's sure to drop in —perhaps unexpectedly.

• Eliminate muscle tension. When you climb into bed, your muscles should be totally relaxed, your breathing slow, rhythmic and deep. If not, use deep breathing to promote relaxation. *What to do:*

1. Inhale slowly through your nose. Count to five as you feel the air inflate first your abdomen, then your chest. Breathe out just as slowly.

2. As you inhale, become aware of tension in your upper chest, arms, neck and head. As you exhale, feel the tension go.

3. As you breathe in again, feel the tension in your abdomen and lower chest. Breathe out and let it go.

4. Feel the tension in your legs and lower body, and release it.

Practice relaxation on a daily basis—outside of bed. If you make the mistake of trying it out when you're anxious about sleep, you're likely to stay tense...and to associate the technique itself with muscular tension.

• Relax your mind. If racing thoughts or intrusive worries keep you awake, a calming mental image will help drive them away.

Image I: You're lying on an air mattress in a tropical sea. The waves are lapping softly all around you, and you can feel the light, warm breeze on your skin.

Image II: You're walking down a curving staircase or riding down an escalator. As you descend, you sink deeper and deeper into relaxation. When you reach the bottom, doors open and you walk into a beautiful, sunlit garden.

• Rethink your attitude toward noise. It's not so much blaring sirens, loud music and other sounds that disrupt your sleep—it's your own sense of anger and irritation at being exposed to these sounds when you're trying to sleep. If your bedroom is noisy, you must contend with two enemies—the noise itself, and the emotional turmoil it can cause.

Self-defense: Substitute calming thoughts for the negative ones you usually experience.

Example I: Instead of *The traffic here is so noisy. I hate it!...*think *It's a loud, lively neighborhood all right. But I can get used to a little noise.*

Example II: Instead of *Why do the neighbors —those inconsiderate fools—play music so late? ...*think *This is just one night. I'll switch on a fan to cover up the noise.*

Earplugs not only block out noise, they give you a *sense of control* that lowers your anxiety level—whether you choose to use them or not.

• Buy a bigger bed. The average person shifts position a dozen times during the course of a night. Your bed partner may disturb your sleep without your being aware of it. A double bed is too small for two adults. *Better:* Two twin beds, pushed together...or two twin mattresses on one box spring. If all else fails, get separate beds.

• Get regular exercise. Try to work out for at least 30 minutes, four times a week. *Best time:* Late afternoon or early evening, five to six hours before bedtime.

Payoff: A workout that boosts your heart rate also raises your body temperature. Five or six hours later, your temperature will rebound to a level *below* normal. This slight reduction in body temperature is very conducive to sleep.

A hot bath produces the same temperature-lowering effect. However, it works best two to three hours before bedtime.

Caution: If you go to bed within two hours of exercising, your body temperature will still be above normal when you close your eyes. That makes falling asleep more difficult.

•Consider sleep restriction. Paradoxically, one of the best ways to get good sleep is to restrict the amount of time you spend in bed. Spend fewer hours in bed, and you will fall asleep faster and awaken less during the night. You'll spend more time in the deep, restorative stages of sleep and less in the lighter stages.

•Keep a "sleep log" to figure out how long you actually sleep. Note when you fall asleep, how long you're awake during the night, and when you awaken in the morning.

If you're getting about six hours of sleep right now, count back six hours from when you plan to get up, and *don't go to bed before then*. If you have to get up at 6 am, for example, go to bed at midnight.

Gradually extend your time in bed. Go to bed at 11:30, and see if your sleep remains sound. Then go to bed earlier, if you want. Experiment to learn what bedtime works best for you.

•Use your new-found time. Use the hour or more that you formerly spent tossing and turning to clean out a drawer, read a book, watch a video, etc. Doing so puts a positive spin on sleep restriction. Instead of lying there wishing you could sleep, you make productive use of the time.

Caution: Avoid activities that are physically or emotionally arousing. Tackling a career project just before bedtime usually isn't a good idea.

•Relax about sleeping less. Many people assume that if they don't get a full night's sleep, they'll make themselves vulnerable to illness or unable to do their job.

In fact, losing an hour or two of sleep has virtually no negative consequences. If you're alert during the day, you're getting enough sleep at night.

But if you feel chronically sleepy in the daytime, then ask your doctor to refer you to a sleep disorders center at a good hospital. Daytime drowsiness may be caused by a potentially serious sleep disorder such as sleep apnea, a form of disturbed breathing.

As long as you keep from becoming anxious or depressed over your sleep loss, it will harm neither your job performance nor your health.

•Every day, get out of bed at the same time. Other than avoiding caffeine, alcohol and nicotine before bedtime, waking up at the same time each day will do more to improve the quality of sleep than any other step you can take. Establishing a regular daily pattern strengthens your sleep-wake rhythms.

Common mistake: Sleeping late on weekends. Appealing as this may be, it can perpetuate problems by disrupting your sleep rhythm. If you get up late Saturday and Sunday mornings, you won't be sleepy at your usual bedtime on Sunday night. Even people who usually sleep easily are often plagued by "Sunday night insomnia."

If you really want to sleep in on Sunday morning, stay up Sunday night until you're sleepy. If you sleep less than usual, it won't hurt you.

If you find it hard to get up and stay up at the appointed hour, *lighten up*—literally. Exposing your retinas to bright light cues your body to make the transition from sleep to waking. Interior lights generally aren't bright enough to do the trick. Instead, go outside into daylight…or spend 20 to 30 minutes next to a sunny window.

What about naps? Some people find that daytime napping disrupts the sleep-wake rhythm, exacerbating their nighttime problems. But for about 20% of people, knowing that they can count on an extra 30 minutes of sleep helps reduce their anxiety about insomnia.

If you nap now, try skipping it for a day or two. If you've been avoiding naps, try one.

Source: James Perl, PhD, a psychologist in private practice in Boulder, CO. Dr. Perl is the author of *Sleep Right in Five Nights: A Clear and Effective Guide for Conquering Insomnia*, William Morrow & Company, Inc.

Helping Yourself to Sleep Better

As the stress of doing business under unsettled conditions continues month after month, the sleeping patterns of executives with top responsibilities become more and more unraveled. Late meetings, travel, and racing thoughts that produce late-night or morning insomnia result in irritability, poor work performance, and lethargy at times when key decisions must be made.

Improving sleep quality:

Researchers cannot easily determine how much sleep is optimum for a specific person. But they have determined that on average, people need seven or eight hours of sleep a day.

The evidence is clear, however, that psychological and physical health improves as the quality of sleep is enhanced. *To sleep better, you should:*

• Determine the right amount of sleep. *How:* Keep a diary of sleeping patterns for at least 10–14 days. If you feel productive and alert, the average sleep time during that period is probably the amount you need.

• Establish a regular bedtime and wakeup schedule, then stick to it even on weekends and holidays.

• Avoid trying to make up for loss of sleep one night by sleeping more the next. Sleep deprivation of two to four hours does not severely affect performance. Having the normal amount of sleep the next night compensates for the loss without changing the regular sleep pattern. And that has long-term benefits.

• Relax before bedtime. *Good ways to unwind:* Take a bath, read, have a snack (milk is ideal for many people), engage in sex. Avoid late-night exercise, work, arguments, and activities that cause tension.

Fighting insomnia:

Knowing the reason for insomnia is the only way to start overcoming it. If the cause is not quickly obvious, see a doctor. Many emotional and physical disorders express themselves as sleep disturbances.

Avoid sleeping pills. On a long-term basis, they are useless and sometimes dangerous. And when taken infrequently, they may produce a drug hangover the next day.

Catnaps:

Avoid naps in the middle of the day to compensate for lack of sleep the previous night. Take them only if you do so regularly and feel refreshed instead of groggy after a nap. *Test:* If you dream during a catnap, it is likely to delay sleep that evening or cause insomnia.

Tampering with nature:

Deliberate attempts to reduce the total amount of sleep you need have a dangerous appeal to hard-pressed executives who think they never have enough time to work. *Fact:* Carefully researched evidence from monitoring subjects in sleep laboratories indicates that these schemes are not only ineffective but unhealthful. *Why:* The daily biological cycle cannot be changed by gradually cutting back sleep over a period of months. Older persons apparently need slightly less sleep, but even here the exact difference is not yet known.

Hard-to-take but essential advice: Do not cut down on sleep in order to meet the clamoring and sometimes conflicting demands of a job, family, and friends. You may pay a penalty of spending less time with family and friends or losing the edge at work that compulsive workaholism may provide. But the payoff is better health performance.

Source: Dr. Charles P. Pollak, codirector, Sleep-Wake Disorders Center, Montefiore Hospital, New York.

How to Beat Insomnia

Do you take too long to fall asleep…toss and turn all night…wake up often or much too early?

More than 100 million Americans have trouble sleeping. During the day, they feel tired and irritable, doze off at inappropriate times or can't concentrate. Their problem is insomnia—*nonsleep.*

Lack of sleep qualifies as insomnia only if a person wants to sleep more but is unable to fall asleep or stay asleep…and if lack of sleep regularly disturbs a person's daytime mood and energy level.

For some people, three hours of sleep a night is enough, while others need 10. *Average sleep per night:* Seven and a half hours.

Like pain, insomnia is a *symptom*—not a disease. *Possible causes:*

• *Psychological problems.* Anxiety and depression top the list. Psychological stress causes more than half of the cases of chronic insomnia.

• *Medical problems.* Arthritis, back pain, indigestion, etc., can keep you awake. So can breathing difficulties, from allergies and asthma to a nonstop cough. *Other health considerations...*

• *Drugs.* Prescription or nonprescription medications containing caffeine, ephedrine, aminophylline, norepinephrine or amphetamine frequently disturb sleep.

Examples: Some antidepressants...high blood pressure medications...muscle relaxants....diet pills...bronchodilators (for asthma)...diuretics (to increase urination)...painkillers (Excedrin, Anacin, Midol, others)...steroids...thyroid preparations...cancer chemotherapy drugs.

Some medications that don't cause insomnia by themselves may do so when taken in combination with others. Make sure all your doctors —and your pharmacist—know all the drugs you're taking.

Important: Don't stop taking any prescription drug without first discussing your insomnia with your doctor.

• *Apnea.* During sleep, some people stop breathing for 10 to 90 seconds at a time, then jerk awake—many times a night. This potentially dangerous condition is called *apnea.* If you think this may be happening to you, get an evaluation at a sleep disorders center. Snoring is often associated with apnea. *Ways to relieve snoring:* Lose weight...sleep with your head elevated on pillows...never sleep on your back. More than 300 patented antisnoring devices are on the market, but these suggested steps are usually enough to alleviate snoring.

• *Restless-legs syndrome.* This is a powerful urge to move the legs all night. You may suffer from this if your sheets and blankets are all over the place in the morning or if your partner complains that you're kicking all night.

Often helpful: Avoid caffeine...exercise... with your doctor's approval, take iron, calcium, folic acid and vitamin E supplements—but usually prescription drugs are necessary to suppress restless legs.

• *Lifestyle factors.* Any of these can disturb your sleep...

• Drinking more than two cocktails, beers or glasses of wine a day.

• Abusing narcotics.

• Drinking coffee, tea or cola in the afternoon or evening.

• Smoking cigarettes.

• Severe stress at home or at work.

• Taking life too seriously.

• Not exercising.

• *Poor sleep habits.* It's easy to get in a rut and perpetuate habits that fight sleep. Bed can become a sexual battlefield—or a symbol of the frustrating failure to sleep. Some people sleep well only on weekends or anywhere *except* in their own beds.

Curing your own insomnia...

More than 80% of insomniacs can overcome their problems by identifying the causes and taking steps to eliminate them.

• *Keep a daily sleep log and day log.* In the *sleep log,* write the length of any naps you take, sleeping medications taken, what time you turned out the lights, how long you think it took you to fall asleep, total minutes awake all night, how often you woke, when you got up, total hours slept and how refreshing your sleep was.

In the *day log,* indicate the amount and type of exercise you did, any incidents—or thought of those incidents—that have upset you. Also record what and when you ate and drank— particularly high-sugar foods and caffeine—as well as medications taken.

After a week or two, choose your two best and two worst nights. Think about why you identified them that way. Can you make any changes to repair the situation?

• *Reduce caffeine.* Drinking a can of cola or cup of coffee in the late afternoon may keep you awake at midnight. Sensitivity to caffeine can increase with age. Anyone's sleep can be disturbed by having more than three cups of coffee or cola or several pain pills containing caffeine a day. Those amounts can be addictive, too.

• *Limit alcohol.* Late-night drinking will cause your sleep to be troubled and fragmented. Reliance on alcohol could also lead to dependency. And never mix alcohol with sleeping pills.

• *Don't smoke.* Nicotine is a stimulant. Insomnia is among smokers' greatest complaints. Cigarettes raise blood pressure, speed up heart rate and stimulate brain-wave activity, making it hard to relax. Smokers tend to wake up in the middle of the night, possibly experiencing nicotine withdrawal.

Sleeping hints...

• *Avoid sleeping pills.* They can be habit-forming. When you stop taking them, withdrawal may worsen your problem.

• *Spend less time in bed.* You'll end up with *more* hours of satisfactory sleep. Try the Bootzin technique for a few weeks: Whenever you are in the bed worrying about sleeping, get out of bed and do something else until you feel sleepy again. You'll be conditioning yourself to associate your bed with sleep rather than with nonsleep.

• *Find interesting things to do.* It's necessary to have at least a moderately exciting day in order to sleep soundly. Join a social group, do volunteer work or get involved in a community project.

• *Allow time to wind down.* Trade massages with a family member. Work on a crossword puzzle. Make love.

• *Keep a regular schedule.* Try to go to bed at roughly the same time each night. Then no matter how long you slept, get up at your usual time in the morning.

• *Exercise.* Aim for 20 minutes of exercise that increases your heart rate at least three times a week. Late afternoon is best.

• *Try napping.* Short naps (up to 30 minutes in the afternoon) help about one in five insomniacs. At night, they are less anxious since they've already slept some.

Caution: For four out of five insomniacs, naps are a mistake. Experiment. You'll know in about a week whether naps help or hinder your sleep at night.

• *Set yourself up for sleep.* Success may be as simple as buying a new mattress, installing room-darkening shades, creating "white noise" (by turning the radio dial between two FM stations), taking a warm bath before bedtime or having a light snack before bed.

Sleep disorders centers...

Although sleep disorders are among the most common problems that doctors encounter, few know how to treat them—most have spent only about two hours on the subject in medical school. Insomnia is often misinterpreted as anemia, a thyroid disorder or laziness. For many people, a sleep disorders center is the answer.

Sleep disorders centers can provide the competent staff, advanced testing equipment and helpful counseling techniques needed to find the root of your problem. Such centers help four out of five people with sleeping problems in general and three out of four with insomnia.

Anyone can open a sleep lab. Some are run by quacks, but many are excellent. The American Sleep Disorders Association (1610 14 St. NW, Rochester, Minnesota 55901, 507-287-6006) has accredited hundreds of centers nationwide. Ask the association to recommend a center near you.

Source: Peter Hauri, PhD, director of the insomnia program and codirector of the Sleep Disorders Center, both at the Mayo Clinic, Rochester, MN. Dr. Hauri established one of the first clinical sleep disorders centers in the US and was a cofounder of the American Sleep Disorders Association. He is coauthor of *No More Sleepless Nights.* John Wiley & Sons, Inc..

What Nourishes and What Poisons Friendship

Key nourishing qualities:

• Authenticity. Inauthentic behavior is contrived and false. Authentic behavior is spontaneous and unpremeditated. Being freely and deeply oneself is important to friendship.

• Acceptance. A sound friendship permits the expression of anger, childishness and silliness. It allows us to express the various facets of our personality without fear of harsh judgment. A feeling of being valued promotes our fullest functioning with other people.

• Direct expression. Coaxing, cajoling, dropping "cute" hints, manipulating and beating around the bush are all barriers to clear communications. When people know what they want from each other, they establish clear communication and contact. They're in a position to attempt an agreement regarding their desires. They may also realize they're too different to get long and that they may be less frustrated if their relationship is more casual.

• Empathy. This involves an effort to understand another's beliefs, practices and feelings (not necessarily agreeing with them). Empathy means listening, trying to understand, and communicating this understanding to the speaker.

What poisons friendships:

• Blame. Blame shifts responsibility and also can be a way of avoiding self-examination. The antithesis of blame and defensiveness is to assume responsibility for one's own feelings. If a person is honest enough to admit his mistakes and finds he's forgiven, he can then be tolerant of his friends' foibles.

• Excess dependency. Some people have lost touch with their values and their strength and need other people to lean on. This kind of person feels unable to be alone. In the dependent friendship, growth and development are stifled rather than enhanced.

Source: Dr. Joel D. Block, clinical psychologist and author of *Friendship: How to Give It, How to Get It*, Macmillan,.

Decision Making Made Easier

When you are facing too many decisions that are tough to make, you are probably suffering from poor-quality information. *Important resources to get you started:* More detailed call reports on customers…schedule a listening skills review for all employees, to help make their input more constructive.

Source: Alan Lakein, leading expert on time management and author of the classic self-help book *How to Gain Control of Your Time and Your Life*. Signet.

Learning Not to Smoke

Will power has less to do with kicking the cigarette habit than acquiring the skills to stop smoking. One widely successful treatment uses a gradual, self-directed learning program.

First, plan to stop smoking during a relatively stable period in your work and social life. Understand your smoking habits by keeping a simple diary that records how many cigarettes you smoke daily and how badly you want each one. Score the craving on a scale of one (automatic, boredom) to four (powerful desire). Firm up your commitment by enlisting a nonsmoking buddy to call up and encourage you several times a week.

Phase out the cigarettes in three stages:

1. Taper. Heavy smokers should reduce to 12 to 15 cigarettes daily. If that's your present level, then reduce to eight or nine a day. Use a smoke suppression drill, a mental learning process, each time you have an urge to smoke. Begin by focusing on the craving; then immediately associate it with a negative effect of smoking, such as filthy lung passages, clogged, fatty arteries, or skin wrinkled and aged by carbon monoxide and nicotine. *Next:* Relax and imagine a peaceful scene. Follow up with a pleasant image associated with nonsmoking (smooth skin, or greater vitality).

2. How to withdraw. One week before your scheduled quitting date, smoke only four cigarettes a day. Smoke two cigarettes in a 15-minute period. Wait at least an hour, and then smoke the other two. While gulping down the cigarettes, concentrate on the negative sensations: Scratchy throat and lungs, foul breath. Keep up negative thoughts for at least five minutes after finishing the last cigarette.

3. Quit. When a smoking urge arises, conjure up the negative image, relax, and follow it with a pleasing fantasy. Also, call your nonsmoking buddy for moral support.

Note: Never label yourself a failure. If you have a relapse, return to the tapering phase, and try the procedure again.

Source: *The American Way of Life Need Not Be Hazardous to Your Health* by John Farquhar, MD, W.W. Norton & Co.

Kicking the Smoking Habit

Kicking the smoking habit may be easier with the help of the antidepressant drug *bupropion* (Wellbutrin). In a recent study of 190 nondepressed heavy smokers, those who had previously tried and failed to quit received 300 milligrams of bupropion per day, along with education and support therapy. Four weeks later, 40% were still not smoking—compared with 24% who received a placebo. After 12 weeks, 28% taking the drug had not smoked, compared with 21% with the placebo.

Source: Linda Hyder Ferry, MD, MPH, assistant professor of public health and preventive medicine, Loma Linda University School of Medicine, Loma Linda, CA.

How to Help Your Child Get a World-Class Education

Many American parents continue to believe that their children are getting good-to-excellent educations. This is *particularly* true of parents whose children attend fine public or private schools.

Reality: Nothing could be further from the truth. American students consistently rank near the bottom in international comparisons. In one recent study, US students ranked 14th out of 20 nations in math and science achievement.

More shocking is that the situation is *worse* in the upper percentiles. When testing was limited to the top 1% of each country, our best and brightest finished last.

In math achievement, it's not until you get to our top 5% that we even approach the *average* level of Asian students.

Why the system fails...

•Rampant grade inflation. This is a more common occurrence today than most parents realize. Across the country, public and private school teachers are pressured by administrators to hand out B's to any student who "tries." Indeed, anything less is often grounds for lawsuits by outraged parents.

Twenty years ago, the average high school student graduated with twice as many C's as A's on his/her report card. That's what you would expect from a normal distribution of grades.

Today the average senior graduates with more A's than C's. This creates a false sense of accomplishment and encourages students to coast once they achieve grades that make their parents happy.

•Lack of a solid academic curriculum. International comparisons often focus on Asian superstudents. But the average French student spends twice as much class time studying core subjects—such as math, science, history and geography—as does the average American student. In Germany, the figure is two-and-a-half times.

As educators in these countries know only too well, without a thorough mastery of the basics, students will be unable to grasp more complex issues.

•Schools are based on an outmoded industrial factory model. Today, at most schools, a teacher still tells students what to do and students are expected to do it without asking questions.

To succeed in such a school system, students need only to develop a superficial facility for memorization, following orders and taking tests.

Problem: This system does not encourage students to think analytically or creatively. Nor does it help them develop new solutions. It's a dangerous and costly strategy in a highly competitive world.

How to help your child...

If you want to be sure your children are getting a world-class education, you must do more than merely help them with their homework. *Some suggestions...*

•Don't focus on grades. The scene is an American ritual worthy of a Norman Rockwell painting—children returning home at the end of a term clutching their report cards to show their parents. Knowing what you know now about grade inflation, you'll need other ways to evaluate the quality of your children's education.

Strategy: Instead of waiting for the report card or test score, try asking your children some of these questions at the dinner table:

• *What did you learn today?* Don't let them off the hook if they respond, *Oh, nothing much.*

• *Did you read or hear anything today that surprised you?*

• *Which of your beliefs or assumptions about the world changed today?*

• Insist that they read more than they do now. Computers and on-line services have made it much easier to access information. But by no means will this technology replace reading skills. Reading books and reflecting on the information they contain will help your children develop the thinking skills they will need in the electronic information age.

Shocking: The average American student reads 12 pages a day—*including* the reading done in school and at home.

• Encourage your children to pursue their passions. The point of an education is to help your children make sense of their lives…and to equip them with the tools, skills and habits they'll need to make significant contributions to society. But it is not easy for young people to see the connection between many of their academic subjects and their interests.

The habits and enthusiasm they develop now will spill over into other areas and new interests. *Examples:*

• Does your son love baseball and hate to read? Give him biographies of ball players. A discussion of batting averages can lead to a lesson in statistics.

• Does your daughter love English literature but hate history? Suggest historical novels. Spend a day with her at the library researching the society and era of her favorite piece of fiction.

• Teach your children the value of hard work in school. In another recent study, researchers asked students, parents and teachers which factor was most important to academic success.

The universal response in Asian countries was *hard work*—so they work hard.

By contrast, American students, parents and teachers replied *intelligence.* In other words, if you're intelligent, you shouldn't have to work hard. If you're not, there's no point in trying.

Let your children know that their success and satisfaction in any field or endeavor is achieved only by diligence and hard work.

• Make sure your children can write detailed and persuasive essays. According to a Department of Education report, fewer than 2% of American students have this ability.

Being able to develop an opinion, back it up with facts and reasons, and consider opposing viewpoints is a crucial skill both on the job and in life…as well as in high school and college.

Strategy: The next time your children ask for something, have them persuade you by writing an essay explaining their reasons. They should also try to anticipate and counter your possible objections.

Older children can put it in writing. A child who wants to stay up late or a teenager who wants to borrow your car will swiftly develop remarkably persuasive writing skills.

• Insist that your children take challenging courses. In an effort to get students motivated, high schools and even colleges abound in trivial courses such as *The Comic Book as Literature.*

In light of our abysmal education standards, these classes are expensive luxuries that result in lost learning opportunities.

Take an active role in helping your children plan their curriculums. Not every course needs to be rigorous and demanding—students should have fun. But most courses should be intellectually challenging and/or practical.

• Help your children set their own realistic standards—and continually raise their standards. Far too many students accept A's as the point at which they can coast, though we've seen that even at "elite" schools, A's are often easy to come by.

Those who excel in any field do so by continually reaching for the next level—by challenging their talents and abilities. It doesn't take much—they just have to get a little better each day.

• Teach them the art of asking questions. As we enter the Information Age, accessing data of any kind is becoming increasingly easy. The challenge is not being able to answer specific questions, but knowing what the important questions are in the first place.

Unfortunately, our education system is built on the opposite premise. Teachers ask the questions, and students are graded on how well they can answer them. Why not grade students on the quality of their questions?

Have fun: Over the dinner table, the classic game of *20 Questions* is an excellent way to teach deductive reasoning.

• Teach them to find the answers themselves. It's important for your children to cultivate resourcefulness in answering their own questions. Asking for help from the teacher should be their last resort. *Three strategies...*

• *Teach them to look beyond their textbooks.* Most students view their teachers and their textbooks as their only sources of information.

• *Introduce them to the Internet.* The one area in which American children excel far beyond those from any other country is computer literacy. Being able to access the global computer network will open up worlds for them.

According to an MIT study, the median age of Internet users—now 26—is expected to drop to 15 within the next five years. The Internet is open to anyone, and through it your child can communicate with many of the best minds in the country, if not the world.

• *Buy a CD-ROM player for your children's computer.* The non-game offerings are getting better by the week. Your best bet is to take your children to any large, well-stocked computer store. Ask what the best-selling titles are for your children. Better stores will let your children try them out there.

Example: Your children are far more likely to browse through a multimedia encyclopedia than through the traditional, heavy multivolume book versions.

Source: Adam Robinson, cofounder of the Princeton Review, a program that helps students do well on standardized tests. Robinson is currently working on a new system to transform American education and is speaking to educators on how to teach better. He is author of seven books on education, most recently *What Smart Students Know: Maximum Grades, Optimum Learning, Minimum Time.* Crown Publishers Inc.

Benefits of Learning The Basics

Learning the basics should be part of installing every new software program and every piece of hardware. Personal computers are not easy to use without instruction. Employees who do not get training will waste many hours trying to teach themselves—or asking other, more knowledgeable workers for help. *Bottom line:* Employees get as much from 12 hours in a computer classroom as from 72 hours of learning on their own. *Even more beneficial:* Personalized training for individuals.

Source: William Kirwin, analyst, The Gartner Group, business consultants, Stamford, CT.

How to Be a Better Grandparent

Those of us who are grandparents grew up in a world far different from today's world.

It was a world of stable families...strict rules of behavior...conventional ideas about the roles of men and women...little concern about crime and environmental destruction. As children, we led a slower paced and far less-stressed life than our grandchildren.

With a more complex world full of more choices, only one thing has not changed...the unconditional love and support grandparents can give their grandchildren.

Parents and grandparents...

To be good grandparents, we need to accept that our experience bringing up our own children does not entitle us to second-guess them in their current adult role as parents. They have the right to decide how to run their household and bring up their children.

When your children raise their children differently from the way you raised them, it is because they think their ways are better.

If you are uneasy about their choices, make sure you make any suggestions in a diplomatic fashion...and if they still think their way is right, accept it.

Example: Edna insisted her daughter Gloria follow formal rules of behavior from a very early age. Gloria did not want to be so strict with her own child, Antoinette. Edna feels that Gloria has gone too far in the other direction.

She should not say, "Antoinette is never going to learn how to behave herself unless you teach her some manners!"

A better approach…"Do you feel she's too young to learn to say 'please' and 'thank you'? I know there's a difference of opinion whether to teach children by example or by reminding them."

When you "take out" your grandchildren, don't be afraid to spoil them a little bit. Most parents fondly remember similar experiences with their own grandparents and regard it as part of the grandparents' role.

Exception: Be very strict about following health and safety rules set by your children. Grandchildren have to learn that their parents set the rules to protect them and that unconditional love does not mean dangerous permissiveness.

How much help?…

A basic fact of life is that grandparents are older than their children. It is often hard to cope with the demands of lively grandchildren, but it is well worth making an effort to find creative ways to help.

Example: When Eric's wife had to go to the hospital, he called his mother to ask her if he could bring his three young children to stay in her house. Grandma agreed on the spot…and immediately called a nanny agency and hired a full-time babysitter.

Later, she told me, "I love the children, they're very cute. I played with them 10 minutes here, 10 minutes there—and it worked out just fine!"

A developing relationship…

If you live close to your children, they may expect you always to be ready to drop everything and baby-sit at a moment's notice. Don't feel guilty to say no if it's too much for you.

The most exciting part of being a grandparent is watching a new generation grow up, without all the worries and responsibility you had with your own children. What to expect at different stages…

Infancy: Small babies need lots of attention …and the new parents need relief. Grandparents can give some by baby-sitting or providing financial aid and moral support.

Preschool: The years from two to five are critical to children's development. Grandparents can help them learn to cope with the complexities of language, feelings and relationships. *Key*

message to communicate: Accept feelings, but learn to control of behavior.

Example: If your three-year-old grandson calls you a dope, don't just tell him, "It's naughty and rude to say that!" *Better:* "If you're angry at me, you can tell me, but calling me 'dope' hurts my feelings."

School age: Children become more interested in their peers than their grandparents…but they still enjoy educational adventures. You can read to them…take them to museums and zoos…go on special trips. Show interest in their everyday activities…celebrate their birthdays…express joy at their successes but not disappointment at their failures.

Teenagers: At 12 or 13 they are likely to feel they have outgrown you and may refuse to come along with the family to visit you. Don't despair…they will come back later. You can provide sympathetic reactions to their problems and gently give advice they will accept more easily than their parents'.

At all ages: Tell your grandchildren tales about how you grew up. They will be fascinated to learn what the world was like in a different era …and develop a sense of where they came from.

Grandchildren with divorced parents…

With divorce more prevalent than ever before —grandparents can provide emotional support that their grandchildren need to cope with the emotional damage.

Your grandchildren love both their parents. It is best to avoid taking sides in front of the children, regardless of your opinion of who is at fault.

Try to do your best to maintain a good relationship with your child's ex-spouse, particularly if he/she has custody of your grandchildren.

When divorce is followed by remarriage, you may find yourself with a new set of step-grandchildren. You will help keep the new family stronger if you don't demonstrate favoritism to your own grandchildren.

The most important thing you can teach your grandchildren…

According to a Puerto Rican saying: "If someone has to boast about himself, other people say, 'I guess he has no grandmother.' "

By providing unconditional love to our grand-children just because they were born, we give them a sense of high self-esteem, the key to a worthwhile life.

Source: Eda LeShan, educator and family counselor. The latest of her 25 books is *Grandparenting in a Changing World*. Newmarket Press.

How to Organize a Family Reunion

You want to reunite with relatives you haven't seen in years, and meet some you've never even heard about.

You want to have a chance to re-establish relationships—even mend some bridges—and make new friendships. That's what a family re-union is all about…and it's worth the effort to organize one.

Keep it simple…

Since putting together a reunion takes lots of time and you must pay attention to detail, it is important that you start off right at the beginning with the motto: *Keep it simple*. In order to keep it simple, you need a plan and must be organized. Here's how to begin.

Goal: A big turnout…

One of the easiest ways to generate enthusi-asm for a family reunion is to plan it around a 50th wedding anniversary or the 75th (or 100th) birthday of an older, much-loved family member. Knowing that a great-grandmother or grandfather or the family's oldest living great-aunt will be holding court at the reunion adds excitement to the event and attracts the mature —and the younger—family members to be part of what will be a historic family event.

Pulling your team together…

Once you have selected the family relative whom you will fete and a date for the reunion, you'll need to plan three initial mailings:

First mailing: Write to every family member and announce the date and occasion for the re-union…and ask for nominations for chair-person, secretary and treasurer for a Family Reunion Executive Committee.

Enclose a form for each position that includes full name, address, date of birth, phone number and qualifications of nominees.

Request that the form be returned within two weeks so a decision can be made quickly. Don't be surprised if you, as the driving force behind the reunion, wind up as chairperson.

Second mailing: Send everyone the names of the nominees, and include a ballot due back in two weeks. This democratic process will imbue the newly elected with legitimate authority.

Third mailing: Announce the names of the Executive Committee, and begin to get the entire family involved by calling for volunteers for the following committees:

• *Communications Committee.* Develops the mailing list. Keeps track of all the correspon-dence and forms that will be sent to and re-ceived from a growing list of family members, including the introductory letter, mailing list, family address and telephone numbers, birth-day list and reservation forms.

• *Host Committee.* Chooses the ideal location for the reunion, such as an inn, dude ranch, spa, resort or family home.

• *Travel Committee.* Works with a travel agent to coordinate travel and accommodations… and gets the best price.

• *Welcoming Committee.* Greets and directs family members upon arrival in the host town.

• *Events Committee.* Plans raffles, scholarship awards, family member achievement awards.

• *Meals Committee.* Organizes the food for formal and informal indoor and outdoor events such as picnics, lunches and dances.

Source: Harry McKinzie, author of *Family Reunions: How to Plan Yours*. McKinzie Publishing Co.

10

Medical Problems and Solutions

How to Avoid Colds and Flu

If you're looking for a surefire way to avoid a runny nose and sore throat…sorry, I can't give you one. But there are ways to cut your risk of cold and influenza—and there are ways to hasten your recovery should you fall ill.

One thing that *doesn't* work is avoiding cold, wet weather. Colds and flu are caused by viruses. You catch them by coming into contact with them—not by going outside with wet hair. *These strategies will work…*

•Consider an annual flu shot. The vaccine prevents influenza only—its high fever and the feeling of having been "hit by a truck." It does not protect you against the score of viruses that cause the common cold.

Flu shots are essential for people older than 65, smokers, people with chronic diseases like diabetes or asthma…and those who tend to get lots of colds.

•Don't smoke. Colds and flu are not only more common among smokers, but also are more severe and longer lasting. *Also:* Smokers are more likely than nonsmokers to develop secondary bacterial infections like pneumonia, sinusitis or ear infections.

•Practice good hygiene. Wash your hands frequently. If you touch someone or something that might harbor a cold or flu virus (a telephone, for example), try not to touch your face. *Reason:* Cold and flu viruses enter the body via the mucous membranes of your mouth, eyes and nose. If no virus makes contact with these membranes, infection won't occur.

•Drink lots of fluids. That helps moisturize your mucous membranes—which, in turn, boosts their resistance to viruses. Drink at least four 8-ounce glasses of water a day.

•Eat crackers, soups and other salty foods. These foods aren't usually considered healthful, but during cold and flu season they can help your body retain water. That helps keep your mucous membranes moist.

•Use a hot-steam vaporizer. That's another way to keep your mucous membranes moist. *Caution:* Cool-mist units can become contaminated with fungus.

•Take vitamin C. I recommend 1,000 milligrams a day for my patients.

If you do get sick…

•Gargle with salt water or mouthwash. That relieves sore throat pain and kills the virus.

•Use over-the-counter remedies. Aspirin, ibuprofen and acetaminophen provide temporary relief of fever and other symptoms.

At night, take a nighttime cold remedy like NyQuil. During the day, use an antihistamine like Sudafed.

Nose drops work better than nasal sprays for relieving nasal congestion. *Caution:* Nose drops can be habit-forming. Don't use them for more than five days at a time.

For coughs, I tell my patients to take Robitussin DM.

If your symptoms are severe enough that you suspect influenza, ask your doctor about amantadine or rimantadine. These drugs significantly shorten the duration of influenza, although they're not effective against colds.

•Use antibiotics with extreme caution. They're great for treating bacterial infections—but ineffective against viral infections like colds or flu. Even worse, taking antibiotics for a cold or flu can make a secondary bacterial infection harder to treat. *Reason:* By killing off relatively benign throat bacteria, you encourage the growth of virulent strains. If your doctor doesn't prescribe antibiotics, don't encourage him/her to do so.

Cold and flu symptoms usually disappear within a week or two in nonsmokers but can last up to a month in smokers.

If your symptoms persist, or if you have an unusually high fever or white spots at the back of your throat (a symptom of strep throat), see a doctor.

Source: Bruce H. Yaffe, MD, an internist and gastroenterologist in private practice, 121 E. 84 St., New York 10028.

Healing Back Pain

Most back pain stems not from herniated disks or other structural problems, but from an inappropriate response to anger and other negative emotions.

As Snoopy once said, "There's nothing like a little physical pain to keep your mind off your emotional problems."

This kind of back pain is called *tension myositis syndrome* (TMS). It starts when unpleasant, repressed emotions—anger in particular—threaten to bubble up.

Oxygen deprivation…

If you're unable to deal with these emotions on a conscious level, your mind responds by creating a distraction. It instructs the autonomic nervous system to restrict blood flow to the postural muscles and underlying nerves.

Result: A state of mild oxygen deprivation called *ischemia.* It leads to a host of symptoms, including pain, numbness, tingling and sometimes weakness—in the neck, shoulders, back and limbs. Although the pain is often severe, it doesn't actually damage the body. That's very important to remember.

It's not that people with stress-induced back pain can't cope with their emotions. It is quite the opposite—TMS occurs because they cope too well. They keep a lid on emotions that threaten to interfere with their daily lives.

Many people suffering from back pain are perfectionists. These individuals generate a lot of subconscious anger and anxiety in response to the pressures of everyday life. Intensely competitive, they're accustomed to putting a great deal of pressure on themselves. They often feel as if they have not done enough.

In the 21 years I've been treating back pain, I've found that the key to a speedy recovery is a willingness to accept the idea that the pain is caused by emotional factors—both conscious and unconscious. That's something many patients are unwilling or unable to do.

Caution: Don't simply assume that you have TMS. See a doctor for a thorough exam to rule out legitimate physical causes of back pain. *Examples:* Tumors, cancer, certain bone diseases.

If the doctor can find no physical explanation for your pain, you probably have TMS. Even in many cases where there is a structural abnormality, TMS may be responsible for your pain.

The good news for TMS sufferers is that they needn't change their personalities, solve all their problems or stop repressing their feelings. Most patients get better—often in as little as four weeks—simply by learning about TMS…and changing their perceptions about their backs.

Pain-relief strategies…

Here's the advice I give my patients with back pain…

•Disregard familiar back pain warnings. Most of us have been warned about "incorrect" ways to bend, lift, sit, stand, lie in bed, etc. Believe it or not, these are all giant myths.

Reality: The back is not a fragile, delicate structure that must be pampered. It is immensely strong. And in most cases—including those involving severe pain—the back is anatomically normal. Yes, you may have pain. But it's not necessarily a back abnormality.

•Think psychological—not physical. Anytime you experience pain, shift your attention away from the physical—and onto the psychological. *Questions:* Are you worried about a family or financial problem? Is there a recurrent source of irritation in your life? Are you putting yourself under too much pressure? Are you perfectionistic? Do you feel the need to please everyone around you?

If you answer "yes" to any of these questions, you're filling yourself with resentment and possibly rage—two hallmarks of the TMS personality.

When you accept that the pain is simply your mind's attempt to mask these emotional factors, the pain usually stops.

•Avoid perfectionism. Since I wrote *Healing Back Pain,* I've become increasingly aware of the role that high expectations—of ourselves and of others—play in back pain.

Also, when we try too hard to be "people-pleasers," to help others, to do things for others, we create in ourselves severe psychological pressure. The internal self resents this enormously. That's where the anger comes from.

•"Talk" to your brain. This sounds silly, but it works. Let your brain know that you're not going to put up with this state of affairs, and you'll find that your back pain quickly dissipates. Many of my patients tell me that by doing this, they can abort an episode of back pain almost immediately.

•Discontinue all physical treatment. Anti-inflammatory drugs, heat, massage, specific exercise, acupuncture, physical therapy, learning to relax—all these presuppose a physical disorder. They may offer temporary relief, but unless you get to the root cause—psychological problems—the pain will keep coming back.

•Don't assume the worst. Individuals often panic during an acute attack, assuming they will be laid up for days or even weeks. But this attitude only prolongs the pain.

Better: If necessary, remain in bed and take a strong painkiller. But even if temporarily bedridden, keep testing your ability to move around. Resume physical activity as soon as possible. I mean not only walking and other gentle activities, but also bending, lifting, jogging, playing tennis, etc.

One success story…

One patient whom I had successfully treated for low back pain two years previously called recently to say she had developed pain in her neck, shoulder and arms. She blamed this pain on an emotional problem involving her husband and teenage stepdaughter…but she was unwilling to address the matter directly. *Result:* Her pain gradually worsened until it was difficult to move her arms.

One day she decided to face the problem squarely and confront her husband. When she did, they found a quick and surprisingly easy solution. *Result:* The situation was defused… and her pain eliminated.

Most of my back pain patients are able to sort through their emotional problems on their own in a matter of days or weeks. Others need the help of a psychologist. In general, I recommend counseling for back pain sufferers whose symptoms fail to improve after six weeks.

To stay focused...

I remind my patients that staying focused on their goal of eliminating back pain is crucial to their ultimate success. *A few reminders:*

- The pain is due to TMS, not to a structural abnormality.

- The direct reason for the pain is mild oxygen deprivation (ischemia).

- TMS is a harmless condition, caused by my repressed emotions.

- The principal emotion is repressed anger.

- TMS exists only to distract my attention from the emotions.

- Since my back is basically normal there is nothing to fear.

- Physical activity is not dangerous.

- I must resume all normal physical activity.

- I will not be concerned or intimidated by the pain.

- I will shift my attention from the pain to emotional issues.

- I intend to be in control—and not let my subconscious mind control me.

- I must think *psychological* at all times, not *physical.*

Source: John Sarno, MD, professor of clinical rehabilitative medicine, New York University School of Medicine, New York City. He is the author of *Healing Back Pain.* Warner Books.

Aspirin to the Rescue

Not all painkillers help prevent heart attacks as well as aspirin does. Aspirin cuts heart attack risk by keeping blood platelets from sticking together and blocking arteries. Acetaminophen (Tylenol) has no effect on platelets. The effect of ibuprofen (Motrin) is only short-lived.

Source: J. Michael Gaziano, MD, MPH, director of cardiovascular epidemiology, Brigham and Women's Hospital, Boston.

Heart Attacks: US vs. France

Heart attacks are rarer in France than in the US. *Possible reasons:* The French drink more wine, which raises levels of HDL (good) cholesterol...and they eat earlier in the day. The French eat about 57% of their daily calories before 2 pm, working for at least five hours afterward. Americans consume only about 38% of their calories by 2 pm, getting most of their calories at supper, before pursuing sedentary activities like watching TV and going to bed. This habit causes calories to turn to fat. *More:* Americans eat three snacks a day...compared to one snack for the French.

Source: R. Curtis Ellison, MD, professor of medicine and public health, Boston University School of Medicine. His study of 100 people in France and the US was reported in the *Medical Tribune,* 257 Park Ave. S., New York 10010.

Heart Attack Self-Defense

Before using CPR, call 911—if an adult is having a heart attack. Doctors used to recommend that trained rescuers give one minute of cardiopulmonary resuscitation before calling the emergency number. *New finding:* Survival and recovery rates are better if 911 is called first. *Important exception:* For children under age eight, a trained rescuer should use proper techniques before calling 911. All untrained rescuers should call 911 immediately.

Source: Emergency Cardiac Care Committee and subcommittee, American Heart Association, guidelines for cardiopulmonary resuscitation and emergency cardiac care, reported in *Journal of American Medical Association,* 515 N. State St., Chicago 60610.

Stroke News

Stroke, which afflicts 750,000 people in the US each year...and kills 250,000, ranks as the third-leading cause of death, after heart disease and cancer.

Although the number of strokes declined through the 1960s and 1970s, data from the 1980s shows that this decline has leveled off.

The number of strokes declined because doctors developed new ways to treat high blood pressure—a common cause of stroke—and people became more aware of the dangers of smoking and the importance of exercising.

Now, however, as the population ages, the incidence of stroke is increasing. *Reason:* Although strokes can affect people of any age, most occur in people over age 60.

New goal: To find new ways to prevent strokes…or at least to make them less severe if they do occur.

What happens…

A stroke is a sudden decrease in the blood supply to a portion of the brain. That portion of the brain which is affected dies.

Most strokes are caused by blocked arteries or high blood pressure. *What happens:* Blood flow to the brain is blocked by a narrow or closed artery…a small blood clot travels to the brain…a blood vessel in the brain ruptures…or an aneurysm—a bulge in an artery—ruptures.

Getting help…

People should seek emergency medical care and a complete neurological exam if they experience any of the following symptoms:

•Sudden paralysis or numbness on one side of the body.

•Difficulty speaking.

•Difficulty seeing.

•A severe headache—either the worst headache ever or a bad headache in someone who never gets headaches.

One of the biggest problems with stroke is that people who are having one often don't seek treatment right away. And delays can make the problem much, much worse.

Some people have so-called mini-strokes—they only suffer symptoms for a few minutes…and then they feel better. *Trap:* These people may be at increased risk for a major stroke.

Even people who experience very serious symptoms that don't go away take between three and six hours to go to the hospital after a stroke. Although part of the delay may be attributed to confusion or to difficulty communicating or moving, the person is usually just denying that something so terrible could really be happening.

Warning: A person who experiences any symptoms of a stroke should immediately call his/her doctor or go to the nearest emergency room.

Emergency treatment…

At the emergency room, a doctor will take the person's history and perform a physical examination to determine the urgency of the situation. Vital signs will be checked, including blood pressure.

A CAT scan of the brain can show signs of stroke and allow the doctor to investigate the small chance that the symptoms may be caused by another problem, like a tumor. The patient will be given oxygen and intravenous feeding in order to prevent dehydration.

Drug therapy…

Standard therapies:

•Aspirin. Many doctors are now recommending that some patients over age 50 with risk factors for stroke take one aspirin a day as a preventive measure. Aspirin thins the blood, making it less likely for a clot to form in the brain. *Note:* Aspirin is not recommended immediately after a stroke. *Reason:* It may result in bleeding into the brain around the area of the stroke.

Drawbacks: Although aspirin is cheap and reliable, it can cause a peptic ulcer or bleeding from the gastrointestinal tract. For this reason, patients should consult their doctors before starting aspirin therapy.

Doctors may prescribe specially coated aspirin to prevent ulcers from developing. Anyone taking aspirin every day who develops stomach pain, vomits blood or finds blood in his stools should be screened for ulcers.

•Heparin. This anti-coagulant can be used to prevent stroke and occasionally to treat an acute stroke.

Drawbacks: This type of therapy is much riskier than aspirin in terms of consequences from bleeding and may not be any better in preventing a stroke. Heparin is generally given only in hospitals because it requires intravenous (IV) administration.

Some patients who need to be on chronic anti-coagulant therapy are also prescribed an oral medication, warfarin (trade name: Coumadin).

This chronic medical therapy is reserved for patients with certain heart conditions—chronic irregularities of the heart rhythm or artificial mechanical heart valves—that predispose them to strokes.

•Nimodipine. Has been successfully used to treat strokes in which a blood vessel bursts—approximately 10% of all strokes. Nimodipine prevents spasm of the blood vessels in the brain region of the stroke—a significant problem after an aneurysm ruptures.

Drawbacks: Nimodipine may cause a significant drop in blood pressure, which may bring on a stroke, or make a stroke worse. There is not yet enough research data to recommend the use of nimodipine in the majority of stroke patients who do not have rupture of an aneurysm. In the future, this medication may be used on a broader range of stroke victims.

Experimental therapies:

•Ticlopidine. A new agent that works like aspirin but may or may not be any better than aspirin in preventing strokes.

Drawbacks: Adverse side effects that aspirin does not have—low white blood cell counts in some patients and elevated cholesterol levels. Considering its adverse effects, ticlopidine cannot yet be recommended as a replacement for aspirin.

•Rt-PA and streptokinase. Researchers are trying to determine if patients with strokes can be helped by these blood-thinning agents, now used during heart attacks to dissolve clots in the coronary artery. *Assumption:* If we can immediately dissolve the clot causing the stroke, we can reduce the damage. Rt-PA and streptokinase take only about a minute to work.

Drawback: 1% of heart attack patients given rt-PA or streptokinase will develop a stroke. Because it may cause worsening of the stroke from bleeding, this type of therapy cannot yet be recommended for stroke patients except under certain experimental protocols.

•Ancrod—an enzyme extracted from the Malaysian pit viper, which may enhance blood flow to areas of the brain that are affected by stroke. It is currently available only through experimental research protocols. Ancrod may herald the event of a number of other similar types of therapies in an area of research that's known as biorheological therapy. This involves methods to enhance cerebral blood flow by reducing blood viscosity. *Other similar measures now being investigated:*

•Expanding blood volume to increase cerebral blood flow using certain IV fluids.

•Pentoxifylline (trade name: Trental), which increases the ability of red blood cells that carry oxygen to reach distant parts of the brain despite narrowed blood vessels. Trental has been used for years to treat patients with circulation problems in the legs, but its efficacy in treating strokes has yet to be proven.

•Prostacyclin, a medication that is a prostaglandin. Prostaglandins—fatty acids found in virtually all body tissues—have numerous and often contradictory effects upon many bodily functions. *Example:* They can both increase and decrease blood flow to the brain through many mechanisms. This type of therapy is still in early experimental stages, but may one day be useful in affecting the basic underlying mechanisms causing strokes.

Prevention...

Of course, the best way to minimize damage from strokes is to prevent them in the first place. *Best:*

•Eat a diet that is low in fat.

•Exercise regularly.

•Eliminate risk factors such as being overweight and smoking.

•See a doctor on a routine basis for blood-pressure checks. Seek regular treatment if you have medical risk factors, such as diabetes or heart disease.

•Don't take oral contraceptives if you smoke. If you live with a smoker, consult your doctor to determine whether or not contraceptives are safe for you.

•Avoid over-the-counter diet pills. Most contain ingredients that increase the risk of stroke.

Finally, people who have aneurysms can elect to have surgical treatment that can prevent stroke.

What happens: Blood flow to the aneurysm is prevented with the placement of a permanent metal clip at the base of the aneurysm that allows blood to flow normally through the rest of the artery.

Source: Gary P. Young, MD, FACEP, FACP, director, emergency department, Veterans Affairs Medical Center, US Veterans Hospital Road, Portland, OR 97207. Dr. Young recently edited a special report on strokes for the medical journal, *Emergency Medicine Reports.*

 # Prostate News

The prostate has been called the gland that always goes wrong—at least after age 50 or so when prostate problems rise dramatically.

Yet new diagnostic and treatment techniques mean that more and more prostate problems can be caught early—and cured or successfully controlled. Certain lifestyle changes may even help to prevent prostate problems in the first place.

The prostate gland is located behind a man's pubic bone, at the mouth of the bladder. It is normally walnut-sized but tends to become larger with age. The gland is important during a man's prime reproductive years: It produces prostatic fluid, which makes up about 80% of semen and helps sperm to survive in the vagina after intercourse.

From men's 20s through their early 40s, prostate problems are usually limited to occasional infections. After the late 40s, however, problems may become more chronic or serious. But even prostate cancer, which strikes one in 11 American men, is treatable—the success rates are highest when the disease is diagnosed early.

The most common prostate problems and what can be done about them…

Prostate infection…

Symptoms of prostate infection, or prostatitis, include frequent and/or painful urination. The most common cause is bacteria spread through sexual activity…The more sex partners you have, the greater your chance of getting a prostate infection. The condition can usually be cured by antibiotics.

Prostate infections take longer to clear up than many other kinds of infections—patients must sometimes stay on antibiotics for several weeks—or even months. If your doctor prescribes antibiotics, be sure to keep taking the medication as long as your doctor advises—even if your symptoms have subsided.

Benign prostate enlargement…

Also called Benign Prostatic Hyperplasia, or BPH, this condition occurs when a mass of tissue begins to grow on the prostate. This benign tumor may cause pressure on the urethra, leading to an increased need to urinate (especially at night), a weak urine stream and the feeling that the bladder is never completely empty.

Not everyone with BPH has these symptoms. We don't know what causes BPH, but it seems to be related to testosterone production and to age. Nine out of 10 men who reach the age of 80 experience some form of BPH, usually mild.

BPH is not a cancerous condition —a benign tumor doesn't spread—but that doesn't mean it should be left alone. Uncontrolled prostate growth can lead to kidney or bladder damage —as it did for Howard Hughes, who died of complications brought on by benign prostate enlargement for which he had refused to seek treatment.

There are a number of options for treating BPH:

•Surgery. Since the 1940s, the surgical treatment of choice for BPH has been transurethral prostatectomy/TURP. The excess tissue is removed by means of a resectoscope, a narrow device inserted through the opening of the penis. The procedure takes less than an hour and has a very high success rate.

Disadvantages: TURP can lead to infertility …and fewer than one in five men may be impotent after the surgery. However, many new techniques are available to overcome impotence (see below).

Promising…laser surgery. It is also performed via a scope inserted through the penis.

Last year, lasers accounted for 10% of prostate surgeries performed in the US. Whereas TURP requires several days in the hospital and up to eight weeks of recovery time, laser surgery can be performed on an outpatient basis under local anesthesia…with the patient back at work after a few days.

Losing popularity: Balloon dilatation, a technique that received a great deal of publicity several years ago. In this nonsurgical procedure, a balloon is inserted through the penis via a catheter, inflated to widen the urethral channel, then withdrawn. Although many patients report temporary relief of discomfort related to urination after this procedure, long-term follow-up suggests that symptoms tend to recur.

A number of other treatments, including one using heat from microwave radiation, are undergoing experimental trials.

• Medication. Finestride (trade name: Proscar) received FDA approval in 1992. It shrinks the prostate by acting on an enzyme involved in the production of testosterone—without affecting testosterone levels elsewhere in the body. The drug must be taken for six months before the prostate begins to shrink. Finestride can be very effective but should not be prescribed blindly— it doesn't work for about 50% of patients.

Certain alpha adrenergic blockers, normally prescribed for high blood pressure, have also been shown to provide relief from prostate enlargement. One of these, terazosin (trade name: Hytrin), just received FDA approval as a BPH treatment. Terazosin works not by shrinking the prostate but by relaxing muscles at the neck of the bladder, making urination easier.

Prostate cancer…

A spate of recent celebrity deaths from prostate cancer—including rock musician Frank Zappa and actor Bill Bixby—have made many more Americans aware of this disease. About 165,000 new cases of prostate cancer occur each year, but by no means is it always fatal.

Because early detection is so important to successful treatment, every man over age 50 (over 40 for a man whose father, grandfather or brother had prostate cancer) should see a urolo-gist at least once a year. The annual visit should include both a rectal exam, and a relatively new test called the Prostate Specific Antigen (PSA).

This simple test measures the level of a chemical produced only in the prostate. If the level is higher than normal, it may be a sign of prostate enlargement and/or cancer.

Though the PSA test was a real breakthrough in early diagnosis, it's no panacea. It's estimated that 20% of men with elevated PSA readings do not have prostate cancer while 20% with low PSAs do have prostate cancer. That's why the rectal exam is so important. The doctor may be able to feel an abnormality not detected by the test. If either method suggests possible cancer, ultrasound should be performed to confirm the diagnosis.

The traditional treatment for prostate cancer is radical prostatectomy—surgical removal of the prostate. In many cases, this method allows the patient to live a long and full life. However, it is a drastic treatment that can result in impotence and incontinence.

One promising new treatment, known as "seeding," involves surgically implanting tiny radioactive capsules in the prostate. Radiation from the capsules kills cancer cells for about a year, with few side effects.

A study I've participated in for the past four years has found normal PSA levels in 93% of early-stage cancer patients after seed implantation treatment, using Palladium 103 as the radioactive source. The treatment is not generally effective for later-stage cancers, however.

In the past, castration was often recommended as part of prostate cancer treatment, in order to reduce testosterone production. A more recent alternative is hormonal therapy. Leuprolide (trade name: Lupron) is one of the newer medications. Injected by the urologist once a month, it blocks the action of testosterone, with fewer side effects than would result from taking female hormones such as estrogen.

Source: Steven Morganstern, MD, director of urologic services at Metropolitan Hospital in Atlanta. He is coauthor of *The Prostate Sourcebook* (Lowell House) and *Love Again, Live Again* (Prentice Hall).

New Treatment for Ulcerative Colitis

Ulcerative colitis that fails to respond to steroids may respond to *cyclosporine*, a drug long used to prevent organ rejection.

Study: Nine of 11 patients taking the drug had relief from bloody diarrhea and other symptoms—within a week. The drug was so effective that researchers cut the study short—they felt it would be unethical not to treat those subjects taking placebos.

Payoff: Cyclosporine therapy may eliminate the need for intestinal surgery.

Source: Simon Lichtiger, MD, assistant professor of medicine, Mount Sinai School of Medicine, New York City.

New Treatment for Hot Flashes

New treatment for hot flashes works for women—*and men.* It's no surprise that many postmenopausal women experience hot flashes. But hot flashes also afflict some men being treated for prostate cancer. In a recent study, the drug *megestrol acetate* (Megace) cut symptoms by 80%. Some women experienced menstrual bleeding one to three weeks after the medication had been discontinued…but that was the only side effect.

Source: Charles L. Loprinzi, MD, associate professor of medical oncology, Mayo Clinic, Rochester, MN.

Most Common Cause Of Gum Recession

Brushing too hard is the most common cause of gum recession. The front six top and bottom teeth are most vulnerable.

Self-defense: Use a soft-bristled brush. Hold it gently with your thumb and index finger as if gripping a pencil. Ask your dentist to show you how hard to brush.

Source: Robert Pick, DDS, MS, associate clinical professor of periodontics, Northwestern University Dental School, Chicago, speaking at a recent meeting of the American Academy of General Dentistry, 211 E. Chicago Ave., Suite 1200, Chicago 60611.

Migraine/Low Back Pain Connection

Migraines are far more common among women with low back pain than among the general female population.

Possible explanation: Migraines are triggered by back pain sufferers' incorrect use of their upper back and neck muscles…by psychological depression associated with long-term back pain…and by overuse of nonprescription painkillers against back pain.

Source: Paul N. Duckro, PhD, professor of psychiatry and human behavior and director of the Chronic Headache Program, St. Louis University Health Sciences Center, St. Louis.

Annette Funicello Tells How She Copes with Multiple Sclerosis

Close to 10 years ago, I was diagnosed with multiple sclerosis—an often debilitating neurological disorder that causes vision problems, muscle weakness and poor coordination.

At the time, I knew *nothing* about the illness —and I decided to keep it that way. For several years, I avoided thinking and talking about MS —and kept my diagnosis a secret from everyone but my mother, husband and children. I didn't even tell my father. I thought I could beat MS on my own and no one would ever have to know.

Looking back, I can see that my refusal to learn about my illness and my need to hide it were attempts to fend off fear. Unfortunately, the ignorance and secrecy only fueled my anxiety.

Since then, I've found far more effective ways of coping with MS…and with chronic illness in general. *Here's what I wish I'd known earlier…*

•Educate yourself. Learn as much about your illness—whether it's MS or another chronic ailment.

There are still many unanswered questions about MS—including what causes it, how best to treat it and what any individual's prognosis will be. Yet the more I've learned about MS, the more I realize that there is plenty of good news…

•MS is not fatal, contagious or hereditary. That's why I always use the term *illness* rather than the more frightening word *disease* when speaking about MS.

•MS is not always progressive. The damaged nerve cells that are characteristic of MS sometimes heal on their own, although we're still not sure under what conditions. Roughly three-quarters of people with MS experience spontaneous remissions during the course of their illness—and, in some cases, complete relief of symptoms. And researchers are getting close to finding a cure.

Sources of information: Your doctor, your local library and nonprofit organizations such as the National MS Society, 733 Third Ave., Sixth Floor, New York 10017. 800-344-4867. These organizations can put you in touch with support groups and other local resources.

•Admit you have a problem—and ask for the help and understanding you need. To convince family and friends that nothing was seriously wrong with me, I became a good liar. When I started having trouble with my balance, for example, I blamed it on tendinitis and a bad knee. Being dishonest with people I cared about sapped my self-esteem.

When you lie, you have to work hard to keep your stories straight. That takes a great deal of energy. It also creates a lot of psychological stress. As someone coping with the symptoms of MS, I certainly didn't need more of that.

I kept my illness secret partly because I didn't want to hurt anyone. But by avoiding people, making excuses and hiding the truth, I suspect I caused them—and myself—even more pain.

I "went public" with my diagnosis in 1992. I wasn't trying to be noble. Reporters from the tabloids had started knocking on neighbors' doors, trying to confirm rumors that my unsteady balance stemmed from a drinking problem. I realized I had to tell the truth—in public—before someone created an ugly story.

Once I did, a huge weight was lifted off my shoulders. There was an outpouring of support from friends and strangers alike. The calls, cards and letters made me realize how much I'd been cheating myself by trying to bear this burden alone.

My family has been wonderful, too. On bad days, when my symptoms flare up, they understand and aren't frightened—and I don't need to hide it.

Having MS has changed the way I view other people's disabilities. I used to feel sorry for wheelchair-bound people and those with other disabilities. Not anymore. I know that *I* don't want pity…and that people who cope with disability every day are tough. We learn to live with our challenges. We do our best with what we have.

•Keep busy—but know your limits. The busier I am, the less time I have to think about my illness. That helps me avoid the temptation of self-pity.

Since my diagnosis, I've launched several business ventures. More important, I started the Annette Funicello Research Fund for Neurological Diseases, which will help finance research into MS and related illnesses.

As busy as I am, I'm careful not to get overtired. In the beginning, I pushed myself too hard. I thought that by refusing to slow down, I could prove that my illness didn't really exist.

Now I rest when I need to. I hold most of my business meetings at home. When I travel, I keep my schedule as light as possible.

What's important is balance. Resting doesn't mean retiring from life.

•Find ways to cope that work for you. While I would not presume to tell anyone else how to deal with a chronic illness, I think that sharing information is important. So here are three things I've discovered that help me. Maybe they'll help you or someone close to you, too.

1. Stay cool. Because heat exacerbates MS symptoms, it's important to keep body temperature down—especially in summer. My favorite way to keep cool is to suck on crushed ice.

2. Elevate the legs. I've found that 10 minutes of lying down with a pillow under my knees and lower legs seems to make walking easier. I might do this several times a day.

3. Follow a healthy lifestyle. I firmly believe that anything that reduces stress helps fight illness. I feel much better now that I've given up smoking and drinking alcohol. I've also noticed that my symptoms are less bothersome when I eat a low-fat diet.

• Stay optimistic. I've tried more than two dozen treatments for MS, from acupuncture to vitamins to various prescription drugs. I discuss everything with my doctor and make sure I understand the risks and side effects of each treatment I try.

I must say that I'm very skeptical of "fad" treatments such as hyperbaric chambers...removing fillings from the teeth...chelation therapy. I keep my spirits up by making the most of my good days, and by remembering how many people are working to solve the puzzle of MS. I take one day at a time, and if one treatment doesn't work, I go on to the next.

So far, nothing has led to a remission. Although that's a little discouraging, I haven't stopped fighting—far from it.

I've always been religious, and my faith has been a great help. I know that my illness has a purpose, even though I don't yet know what that purpose might be.

I take comfort in knowing that the prayers of many loved ones are behind me. I keep a smile on my face—and I never give up hope.

Source: Annette Funicello, star of the popular 1950s television series *The Mickey Mouse Club*. She also starred in the motion pictures *Babes in Toyland* and *The Shaggy Dog*, as well as several beach party movies with Frankie Avalon. Ms. Funicello is the recipient of numerous awards, including the Helen Hayes Award, given by Saint Clare's Hospital and Health Center in New York City, in recognition of her professional accomplishments and her efforts to raise public awareness about MS. Her autobiography, *A Dream Is a Wish Your Heart Makes*, was published by Hyperion.

Hidden Stroke Danger

Bending the neck sharply to the back or side can pinch the arteries leading to the brain. *Result:* Increased risk of stroke. *At risk:* The elderly...anyone who has experienced dizziness or loss of balance after extreme or prolonged neck bending...anyone with certain deformities of the spine.

Self-defense: At-risk individuals should avoid bending their neck in this way...and should ask their doctors about wearing a cervical collar while sleeping.

Source: Michael I. Weintraub, MD, chief of neurology, Phelps Memorial Hospital, North Tarrytown, NY, and clinical professor of neurology, New York Medical College, Valhalla.

Multiple Chemical Sensitivity

Multiple chemical sensitivity is *not* a physical disease. It's a form of *agoraphobia* (abnormal fear of open or crowded spaces) or other anxiety reactions that people often blame on exposure to chemicals found in perfume, tap water, etc.

Implication: MCS sufferers should be treated not with injections, sublingual drops or diets, but by a psychiatrist with expertise in anxiety disorders.

Source: Arthur Leznoff, MD, head, department of immunology, University of Toronto, quoted in *The Medical Post*, 777 Bay St., Toronto, Ontario M5W 1A7.

Nearsightedness Danger

Extreme nearsightedness can lead to retinal detachment and glaucoma if allowed to progress. *Self-defense:* If you're becoming more nearsighted, ask your eye doctor about wearing rigid gas-permeable contact lenses. They exert pressure on the cornea, helping the eye keep its shape and preventing the progressive elongation of the eyeball that increases the risk of such eye-related medical problems.

Source: Martin Birnbaum, OD, professor of optometry, State University of New York College of Optometry, New York City.

Arthritis and Acupuncture

Arthritis pain in the knee can often be controlled by acupuncture. Following an eight-week course of twice-weekly treatments, 60% of patients with moderate to severe osteoarthritis reported feeling less pain and improved walking ability…and 70% got around better. Benefits continued for up to four weeks after treatment.

Source: Madalene Green, MD, former postdoctoral fellow, division of rheumatology and clinical immunology, University of Maryland Medical Center, Baltimore, now in private practice in Bowie, MD. Her study of 12 patients with moderate to severe osteoarthritis of the knee was presented at a recent meeting of the American College of Rheumatology, 60 Executive Park S., Atlanta 30324.

Pneumococcal Pneumonia

Vaccine for pneumococcal pneumonia is effective—but underused. Pneumonia is one of the deadliest complications of heart and lung disease. And because the vaccine is covered by Medicare, cost should not deter people age 65 and older from getting vaccinated. *At greatest risk:* Anyone who is 65 or older—and younger people who have heart or lung disease, diabetes, HIV infection or other immune system problems.

Source: Philip R. Lee, MD, director, US Public Health Service, Washington, DC.

New Treatment For Asthma

New allergy shot is far more effective than the old one at reducing asthma symptoms caused by dust mite allergies. *Study:* Compared to patients receiving the old shot (consisting of allergens alone), patients receiving the new *allergen-antibody* shot had far fewer attacks and were less likely to need oral or inhaled corticosteroids. Some patients experienced no allergy-induced asthma attacks after receiving the new shot.

Note: More research is needed to confirm results on a larger sample…and to test effectiveness of similar shots on asthma caused by allergic reactions to pollen, mold and animal dander.

Source: Gary Hunninghake, MD, president of the American Thoracic Society, commenting on a recent study by Jacques J. Machiels, MD, Clinique Saint-Pierre, Ottignies, Belgium, published in the *American Review of Respiratory Disease*, American Lung Association, 1740 Broadway, New York 10019.

Controlling Tinnitus

Ringing in the ears (tinnitus) can in many cases be controlled with the antianxiety drug *alprazolam* (Xanax). After three months on the drug, 75% of tinnitus sufferers reported a lessening of symptoms. *Caution:* See a doctor to rule out any underlying problems.

Source: Robert M. Johnson, PhD, professor of otolaryngology, Oregon Health Sciences University, Portland.

Bright Light/Sleep Connection

Exposure to bright light during the evening promotes better sleep at night. For some people, especially the elderly, *staying* asleep is a bigger problem than *falling* asleep. These individuals awaken earlier than they'd like…and feel drowsy the next day. *Finding:* Individuals who spent two hours exposed to a light box (a portable unit containing special full-spectrum fluorescent lights) spent less time lying awake in bed…and awoke less often during the night. If you're not sleeping well, discuss light box therapy with a sleep disorders specialist.

Source: Scott S. Campbell, PhD, associate professor of psychiatry, Cornell University Medical College, White Plains, NY. For help in locating a specialist, contact the National Sleep Foundation, 122 S. Robertson Blvd., Third Floor, Los Angeles 90048.

All About Minerals

Although minerals *are* essential nutrients, a number of untested claims have been made recently about the power of mineral supplements to bring about dramatic improvements in health.

Encouraged by news reports that a particular mineral may protect against heart disease or cancer, some people are attempting to self-medicate by taking supplements for specific disorders.

Problem: Ingested in large quantities or in the wrong proportions, mineral supplements can cause everything from minor chemical imbalances to severe—and potentially deadly —toxic reactions.

Vitamins vs. minerals…

Like vitamins, minerals are needed to maintain optimum cellular structure and function. How do vitamins and minerals differ? Vitamins are complex organic (carbon-containing) molecules. Minerals are simpler, inorganic molecules.

Although researchers have shown that several different minerals are necessary for good health, there's still a great deal to learn about exactly what these minerals do and how they interact in the body. The recommended daily dose has not yet been established for many minerals.

Some researchers argue that we can get adequate amounts of essential minerals from a well-rounded diet. This may well be the case. But not all of us eat as well as we should—and

modern processing techniques often reduce the nutritional value of foods.

In addition, some individuals need higher levels of vitamins and minerals than others— especially children, pregnant or nursing women and the elderly. This is where mineral supplements may be helpful—not as a *substitute* for a healthy diet, but as a kind of "insurance" for people concerned about getting the right combination of nutrients.

I avoid recommending specific "doses" of mineral supplements. There are two reasons for this. First, few people take time to calculate the mineral content of every food they eat, so they don't know their total mineral intake from foods. Second, the greatest danger in taking mineral supplements is the misguided notion, *If a little is good, a lot is better.*

Example: Risk related to excess buildup of potassium or selenium is worse than risk of a deficit.

Taking too much of one mineral can create imbalances that lead to deficiency in another.

To avoid this problem, a multivitamin-multimineral supplement is probably safer and just as effective as one or more single-mineral supplements taken in combination. In any case, do not exceed the recommended dose printed on the label of commercially prepared supplements.

We're still learning about the relationship between minerals and human health. *What we've learned so far…*

Major minerals…

Minerals are classified as major or minor— referring *not* to their importance, but to the amounts in which they're present in the body.

Major minerals (*macronutrients*) are found in relatively high concentrations. Minor elements (*micronutrients*, or trace elements) occur only in tiny amounts—yet deficiencies still occur.

Three of the macronutrients—chlorine, sodium and phosphorus—are abundant in nearly all diets. (In the case of chlorine and sodium, which are present in table salt, we're much more likely to get too much than too little.)

However, our diets are often deficient in certain minerals, including…

•Calcium. It's essential for building strong teeth and bones, as practically everyone knows —and it ensures proper functioning of nerve and muscle cells.

Calcium is especially important for children, whose bones are growing, and for postmenopausal women, who are prone to osteoporosis, which causes weak, brittle bones.

Dietary sources: Milk products, dark green and leafy vegetables, canned fish (such as salmon or sardines) normally eaten with bones.

•Magnesium. It plays a key role in the conversion of food into energy…as well as in the formation of tooth enamel and in nerve and muscle function. Some research suggests that too little magnesium causes weakness, poor coordination and gastrointestinal problems. Such deficiencies are uncommon among healthy individuals, but heavy drinkers may be at greater risk.

Excessive magnesium intake has been shown in animal experiments to cause temporary muscle weakness—even paralysis.

Dietary sources: Nuts, beans, whole grains, green leafy vegetables, seafood.

•Potassium. Another mineral involved in the function of all cells, potassium is especially important for proper muscle and nervous system activity.

Although most people get enough potassium from the foods they eat, excessive urination, vomiting and heavy exercise, especially in high heat, can deplete the body of potassium. *At greatest risk:* People with uncontrolled diabetes (who tend to produce a high volume of urine)…people taking thiazide-type diuretics…and those who are bulimic.

Dietary sources: Meats, beans, peas, milk, vegetables, fruits—especially bananas.

Trace minerals…

•Chromium. By enhancing the effect of insulin, chromium plays a role in the metabolism of glucose.

Dietary sources: Animal fats (including those in cheese and meats), barley and other whole grains, brewer's yeast, brown sugar.

•Cobalt. It's a component of vitamin B-12, which is required for formation of healthy red blood cells and for nerve cell function. Lack of B-12 can lead to anemia and possibly brain disorders. But it's not a good idea to take cobalt supplements, because the body can't simply convert it into B-12. People concerned about a possible deficiency should take vitamin B-12 instead.

Dietary sources (of vitamin B-12): Meats. Vegetarians may be able to get small amounts of the vitamin from legumes—although they may wish to discuss B-12 supplements with their doctors.

•Copper. This mineral keeps bone marrow healthy. A deficiency can disrupt marrow function, resulting in insufficient production of red and white blood cells.

Because zinc interferes with copper absorption, taking too much zinc can lead to copper-deficiency anemia. An excess of copper, however, irritates the stomach, causing nausea and vomiting. Acute copper poisoning—quite rare—can be fatal.

Dietary sources: Shellfish, mushrooms, nuts, leafy vegetables, tap water (if your home's plumbing system contains copper pipe).

•Iodine. This mineral is needed for synthesis of the thyroid hormone *thyroxine.* Without iodine, the thyroid gland can't produce this hormone. It compensates by enlarging—leading to a characteristic swelling of the neck known as *iodine-deficiency goiter.*

Because soil near the ocean is richer in iodine, iodine deficiency is more common in the interiors of continents than in coastal areas. Fortunately, the use of iodized table salt has virtually eliminated iodine deficiency in this country.

Dietary sources: Ocean fish, iodized salt.

•Iron. This mineral is an essential component of *hemoglobin,* the oxygen-carrying molecule inside red blood cells. It's also essential for proper metabolism in a variety of cells.

Women's need for iron increases during pregnancy and while nursing. Pregnancy is one of the factors that can cause iron-deficiency anemia, which is characterized by fatigue, listlessness and pallor. Chronic internal bleeding and excessive menstrual flow month after month can also deplete the body's iron stores.

Caution: If you think you have iron-deficiency anemia, avoid the temptation to self-medicate with iron pills. The blood loss that probably underlies your anemia could be pathological (from a peptic ulcer or even colorectal cancer) rather than from a normal physiological process (like menstruation). See a doctor to rule out serious conditions.

It's also possible to have too *much* iron in the body—a potentially dangerous condition. Excess iron can irritate the stomach...and an extreme overdose (as when a child eats a bottle of iron pills) floods the bloodstream with iron—a life-threatening condition.

Some researchers have found an apparent link between excessive iron in the bloodstream and heart disease. For this reason, iron supplements shouldn't be taken casually—especially by men and postmenopausal women, who are at greater risk for heart trouble.

Some scientists have also suggested that premenopausal women are protected against heart disease because their monthly cycles help maintain their body iron at safe levels. These researchers have gone so far as to recommend that men donate blood in order to keep their iron levels at a healthy level.

Dietary sources: Red meats, liver, whole-grain or enriched bread.

•Selenium. When absorbed in combination with the amino acid *methionine*, selenium acts as an antioxidant. It guards cells against damage caused by *free radicals*, the destructive byproducts of normal metabolism and some diseases. Selenium and other antioxidants—including beta-carotene and vitamins C and E—are thought to reduce the risk of heart disease and cancer. But megadoses can have toxic effects, including anemia...chronic "garlic" breath...and liver and spleen damage.

Dietary sources: Grains, meats, poultry, fish and other seafood, especially shrimp.

•Zinc. Unlike minerals that have only a few known roles, zinc is seemingly *everywhere* in the body. It's a vital component of more than 100 different natural proteins, including insulin. There may even be a link between zinc deficiency and certain mental illnesses, including schizophrenia—but research so far has not provided conclusive scientific evidence for this claim.

Zinc speeds wound healing and helps boosts immunity. That doesn't mean it's a good idea to take megadoses of zinc when you're injured or coming down with a cold—as mentioned earlier, zinc interferes with the absorption of copper and possibly iron.

Dietary sources: Meats, oysters and other seafood, nuts, beans and peas, whole grains, dairy products. (Zinc derived from animal sources seems to be more easily absorbed than zinc from vegetable sources.)

•Fluorine. This mineral helps produce strong, healthy, cavity-free teeth. In addition, a recent study found that areas where water was fluoridated had a lower incidence of Alzheimer's disease. While it hasn't been proven that fluoridation protects against Alzheimer's, the hypothesis is that fluorine blocks absorption of aluminum by the brain.

Recent rat data indicate that use of alcoholic beverages can increase the uptake of aluminum. Thus, heavier drinkers should avoid extra intake of aluminum, as in antacids or the antiulcer drug *sucralfate*. Some scientists reject the aluminum hypothesis of Alzheimer's disease, but others do not.

Excessively fluoridated water—such as that generated by accidents at water-fluoridation plants—can cause headache, nausea, dizziness, cramps and diarrhea. Chronic overdoses of fluorine damage tooth enamel and promote arthritis.

Dietary sources: Fluoridated (naturally or artificially) drinking water, vegetables grown in areas with fluoride-containing water.

Finally, recent research involving animals suggests that *manganese*, which is found in liver, red meats, nuts, whole grains and produce, and *molybdenum*, which can be found in meats, grains and legumes, are necessary trace elements for normal growth and development. However, their role in human health is unknown.

Source: W. Marvin Davis, PhD, professor of pharmacology and toxicology, University of Mississippi School of Pharmacy, Oxford.

How to Avoid Colon Cancer

Colon cancer is the second-deadliest form of cancer. Each year it strikes 158,000 Americans and kills 61,000. Only lung cancer is deadlier.

Three years ago, researchers identified the gene that causes *familial adenomatous polyposis* colon cancer. This rare form of the disease accounts for less than 1% of all cases of colon cancer.

Within the last year, two genes were found for another rare form of the disease, *hereditary nonpolyposis* colon cancer. It's believed to account for up to 15% of all colon cancers—roughly 20,000 cases a year.

As a result of these discoveries, scientists may soon be able to determine who will inherit these forms of colon cancer. Yet even if such a test does become available, it will not eliminate colon cancer. *Reason:* Most cases of the disease are *not* inherited. They're caused by the accumulation of spontaneous genetic mutations that occur in individual body cells throughout each person's lifetime.

Bottom line: No one knows the exact causes underlying most cases of colon cancer.

Who's at risk?

Colon cancer is very common. Anyone can get it. In fact, roughly one of every 20 Americans will develop the disease at some point in their life.

Of course, some people are at greater risk than others—specifically anyone with a sibling or parent who has or had colon cancer...or with a personal or family history of colon polyps—small nodules along the colon wall that sometimes turn cancerous.

Colon cancer risk rises with age. The disease is rare in people under 40. After age 50, the risk doubles every seven years.

The growth of cancer cells is a multistep process that takes place over a period of years. The earlier the cancer is detected, the better the chance of a cure.

Overall, the cure rate is about 50%. That means that roughly half of those people with colon cancer are still alive five years after their diagnosis. For early-stage cancer, the cure rate rises to 80%. But less than 10% of people with advanced colon cancer survive for five years.

In some cases, colon cancer produces symptoms only *after* the disease has progressed to a stage where successful treatment is difficult or impossible. But some people may notice certain "red flag" symptoms that may signal the presence of cancer early in the disease's progression—when effective treatment is still possible.

Warning signs: Rectal bleeding, recurrent abdominal cramps, bloating and/or abdominal pain or altered bowel habits.

If you have one or more of these symptoms, see a doctor at once. But don't panic at the first sign of symptoms. They do not necessarily mean that you have colon cancer or that you will develop it. These problems can be symptomatic of other, less severe conditions, including hemorrhoids, hiatal hernia or anal fissures.

The American Cancer Society recommends three different screening tests for the early detection of colon cancer. These tests are recommended for normal, healthy individuals in order to detect cancer in its earliest possible stage—when simple curative treatment is still possible.

Digital rectal exam...

A doctor inserts a gloved finger into the rectum to feel for abnormalities.

Accuracy: Relatively poor. Only about 10% of colon tumors develop within the part of the rectum that can be felt with a finger, so many tumors are missed.

Cost: Usually part of a routine physical exam.

Safety: Risk-free.

Discomfort: Minimal.

Recommended frequency: Once a year, starting at age 40.

Fecal occult blood test...

Small samples of your stool—collected at home—are smeared on special chemical-impregnated slides. A color change signals the presence of hidden (occult) blood, suggesting the possibility of colon cancer.

Accuracy: Relatively poor. "False positive" readings can be caused by bleeding ulcers, fissures, hemorrhoids—or just from eating red meat. "False negatives" can occur, too, because not all tumors bleed. *Bottom line:* The fecal occult blood test (FOBT) misses roughly half of all colon tumors. For this reason, FOBT could fall out of favor unless ways are found to increase its accuracy.

Cost: $20 to $40.

Safety: Risk-free.

Discomfort: Painless.

Recommended frequency: Once a year, starting at age 50.

Sigmoidoscopy...

Using a thin, lighted viewing tube inserted into the rectum, a doctor examines the last 23 inches of the colon. More than half of all cancers develop in this region—but not all. Sigmoidoscopy cannot detect tumors higher up in the colon.

Accuracy: Excellent. Picks up more than 95% of one-centimeter polyps or tumors appearing in the lower colon. Early detection by sigmoidoscopy can reduce colon cancer mortality by 30%.

Cost: $160 to $200.

Safety: One out of every 2,500 people undergoing sigmoidoscopy suffers colon perforation. If this happens, emergency surgery may be necessary.

Discomfort: Quite uncomfortable, although sedatives help. The test must be preceded by a series of enemas, administered at home.

Recommended frequency: The current consensus is that everyone should undergo sigmoidoscopy once every three to five years after age 50. But new studies suggest that once every 10 years may be sufficient.

Exception: Individuals with a family history of colon cancer should ask their doctor about beginning periodic screenings at an earlier age.

In addition, there are two diagnostic tests—colonoscopy and barium enema. These are used to follow up suspicious results on any of the screening tests. In addition, anyone with a significant family history of colon cancer or a personal history of inflammatory bowel disease or polyps should consider using colonoscopy as a screening test.

Colonoscopy...

Similar to sigmoidoscopy except that a much longer, flexible viewing instrument is used. Thus the *entire* colon can be examined.

Accuracy: This test identifies up to 95% of one-centimeter polyps or tumors appearing anywhere in the colon.

Cost: $700 to $900.

Safety: One in 1,000 chance of colon perforation.

Discomfort: This procedure generally causes some cramping—although liberal use of sedatives helps ease the discomfort. Colonoscopy requires thorough cleansing of the colon with laxatives and enemas—which some people find unpleasant.

Barium enema...

This procedure involves taking a series of X rays of the entire colon following the administration of laxatives and an enema containing chalky barium—and in some cases an inert gas.

Accuracy: Detects up to 95% of one-centimeter polyps and tumors.

Cost: $180 to $240.

Safety: There's a one-in-5,000 chance of colon perforation. There is also some exposure to X rays—although this is so low as to pose minimal risk.

Discomfort: Quite uncomfortable. In addition to requiring the use of enemas and laxatives, the test involves holding the barium in the colon without expelling it.

Fat and fiber...

While diet alone cannot cure colon cancer, recent evidence suggests that a low-fat diet can help prevent the disease. In fact, limiting your intake of fat to 30% or less of your total calories may reduce your risk of colon cancer by 50%. The typical American diet is 40% fat.

No one knows exactly why a fatty diet promotes colon cancer. Scientists believe, however, that fat stimulates the proliferation of colon cells, thus promoting development of cancer cells.

Boosting your consumption of fruits and vegetables not only reduces your intake of dietary fat but also raises your intake of beta-carotene and vitamins A, C and E. These nutrients may also help prevent the development of cancer.

Dietary fiber also plays a beneficial role—by speeding the passage of food through the gastrointestinal tract. A shorter "transit time" means carcinogens spend less time in contact with the colon lining.

Transit time might also be reduced by exercise—although scientists aren't sure what role, if any, exercise plays in cancer development.

An aspirin a day?

Recent studies—including one of more than 660,000 adults—suggest that regular consumption of aspirin and other nonsteroidal anti-inflammatory drugs (NSAIDs) may help prevent colon cancer.

It's thought that NSAIDs block cancer by inhibiting the body's synthesis of *prostaglandins*, natural substances that raise cancer risk by stimulating cell growth.

Caution: Although the results of aspirin studies are provocative, they're also preliminary. Further research is needed. And it is important to realize that stomach bleeding and other serious gastrointestinal ailments can result from regular aspirin use. The potential risks and benefits of aspirin therapy are not yet clear.

Source: Geoffrey M. Cooper, PhD, professor of pathology at Harvard Medical School and a member of the division of molecular genetics at the Dana-Farber Cancer Institute. He is the author of *The Cancer Book: A Guide to Understanding the Causes, Prevention, and Treatment of Cancer.* Jones and Bartlett Publishers.

Natural Allergy Relief

Good news for allergy sufferers: Sneezing, congestion, itchy eyes and other symptoms common this time of year can be stopped without harsh, costly and possibly addictive drugs.

Seasonal allergies result when a sensitive person inhales an allergen—pollen or mold, for example. This allergen causes cells lining the nose to release *histamine*, a compound that dilates small blood vessels in the nose, causing swelling and other allergy symptoms. There are several ways to interrupt this cascade of events...

Vitamin C, in very high doses, acts as a safe, natural antihistamine. *Best: Buffered* vitamin C, taken in several divided doses totaling 3,000 to 4,000 milligrams (mg) a day.

Quercetin and *hesperidin* also act as natural antihistamines. These compounds—members of a class of nutrients called *bioflavonoids*—work more slowly than conventional antihistamines but cause fewer side effects.

Fish oil contains essential fatty acids (polyunsaturates) that help make the body less allergy-prone. Be sure to follow directions on the label.

The herb *Ephedra* also offers effective allergy relief. It comes in tea, tincture (drops) or capsule form. Follow label directions.

If your allergy symptoms persist despite these measures, allergy testing and periodic injections may be necessary.

To pinpoint the offending allergen, most doctors use the familiar scratch test. But I've been having much greater success using an alternative technique called *serial dilution endpoint titration and optimal dose immunotherapy.*

In this method, I inject the patient's skin with a solution containing a suspected allergen. The injection raises a small bump (wheal) and—if the person is allergic to the allergen—frequently triggers allergic symptoms.

Over the next hour or so, I inject increasingly dilute solutions of this allergen—until there's no swelling and no allergic symptoms. This *neutralizing dose* is then administered twice a week to desensitize the patient.

Motion sickness and dehydration...

With many of you traveling during the coming months, I'd like you to know about some natural approaches for treating motion sickness...

Ginger tea can help alleviate nausea. So can the bioflavonoid *ginkgo*. And some people beat motion sickness by using acupressure wrist bands. Available at drugstores, these bands contain protuberances that press against an acupressure point on the wrist, thereby altering the flow of energy through the body and preventing nausea. If no bands are handy, you can use a finger to press against the nausea point.

And nausea isn't the only malady that acupressure can help…

•Pain can be relieved by massaging the web of skin between the thumb and index finger.

•Menstrual cramps can be relieved by rubbing the area just below and behind the ankle bone on the outside of the foot.

•Some allergies can be eased by pressing the sides of the nose where the nostrils connect to the cheek—or rubbing the base of the toes on the sole side of the foot.

Finally—I'm happy to see people toting around their own water bottles. Frequent sipping prevents dehydration and heat cramps during hot weather. And if your bottle contains spring or mineral water, you'll avoid chlorine and other toxins often found in tap water.

Source: Robban Sica-Cohen, MD, director of The Center for the Healing Arts in Orange, CT.

Green Tea Fights Disease

Green tea fights heart disease, cancer, flu—even tooth decay. It's rich in a class of natural antioxidant compounds called *polyphenols*. Green tea is derived from the same plant as the more common black tea, but it's processed differently. Black tea is fermented before drying—green tea is not. The fermentation process reduces the levels of polyphenols.

Source: Hasan Muktar, PhD, professor and director of research, Case Western Reserve University School of Medicine, Cleveland.

Chili Pepper Danger

Eating too many hot peppers may boost your risk of stomach cancer. Those who identified themselves as "heavy" consumers of chili peppers were 17 times more likely to develop stomach cancer than those who did not consume chilies. *Possible culprit:* Capsaicin, the hot-tasting component in chili peppers.

Source: Robert Dubrow, MD, PhD, associate professor of epidemiology and public health, Yale University School of Medicine, New Haven, CT. His study of 220 stomach cancer patients and 752 healthy individuals was published in the *American Journal of Epidemiology*, 2007 E. Monument St., Baltimore 21205.

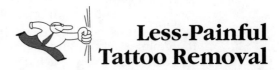

Less-Painful Tattoo Removal

Tattoos can be removed with less pain and little scarring, thanks to a recently approved laser called *Tatulazr*. It penetrates the skin, shattering the pigment that makes up the tattoo. White blood cells then attack the tiny pieces of pigment and eliminate them from the body. The treatment feels like a rubber band snapping against the skin. *Cost:* $275 and up, depending on tattoo size.

Source: Claude S. Burton, MD, assistant professor of medicine, Duke University School of Medicine, Durham, NC.

Wrinkled Skin Solution

Wrinkled skin can be smoothed via injections of botulinum toxin (Botox), a refined version of the toxin that causes food poisoning. When injected into the small muscle above the nose, Botox paralyzes the muscle, making it impossible to furrow the brow or frown. Injected into the muscles around the eyes, it helps eliminate crow's feet. The effect usually lasts three to six months. *Cost:* $175 to $300, depending upon the size of the wrinkle.

Source: Alastair Carruthers, FRCPC (Fellow of the Royal College of Physicians in Canada), clinical professor of dermatology, University of British Columbia, Vancouver.

Hidden Cause of Dry Eyes

Dry, red eyes aren't always caused by irritation or lack of sleep. *Another possibility:* Rosacea, a progressive skin disease marked not only by facial redness, but occasionally by burning, stinging or a feeling that there's something in the eye. *Danger:* Severe cases of ocular rosacea can cause scarring and even vision loss. Although the condition cannot be cured, it can be managed and controlled with oral antibiotics and possibly corticosteroid eye drops. See an ophthalmologist about any eye rash associated with redness, burning or itching that lasts for more than a couple of days.

Source: Jerome Z. Litt, MD, assistant clinical professor of dermatology, Case Western Reserve University School of Medicine, Cleveland.

Alzheimer's Preventive

Anti-inflammatory drugs used to treat arthritis may also help prevent Alzheimer's disease. In a recent study, Alzheimer's was four times less common among individuals who used steroids, aspirin, ibuprofen or other anti-inflammatory drugs for arthritis pain than individuals who did not use anti-inflammatory drugs. *Caution:* Do not begin self-medicating in an effort to avoid Alzheimer's. These drugs can cause serious side effects and should be taken regularly only on the advice of a physician.

Source: John Breitner, MD, MPH, associate professor of psychiatry, Duke University School of Medicine, Durham, NC. His study of 50 pairs of identical and fraternal twins was published in *Neurology*, 7500 Old Oak Blvd., Cleveland 44130.

Multiple Sclerosis Relief

New "cool suit" lowers body temperature, improving the function of nerve cells and helping to alleviate fatigue, labored breathing, slurred speech and other MS symptoms. Developed by NASA to cool astronauts during space walks, the microclimate cool suit consists of a vest and cap lined with tubing that circulates a water-based fluid chilled to 50° F. *Cost:* $500 to $2,000. Suits can also be borrowed from certain charitable organizations.

Source: Multiple Sclerosis Association of America, 601 White Horse Pike, Oaklyn, NJ 08107. For information about buying or borrowing a cool suit, call 800-833-4672.

Newborn Jaundice Treatment

An experimental drug called *tin mesoporphyrin* (SnMP) is just as effective as phototherapy (exposure to bright lights) in treating jaundice—and it's far more convenient to use. SnMP works by blocking production of *bilirubin*, the pigment that causes jaundice. It may become the treatment of choice once it's approved by the FDA.

Source: Attallah Kappas, MD, professor of medicine, The Rockefeller University, New York City. His four-year study of 517 babies born in a large maternity center in Greece was published in *Pediatrics*, 141 Northwest Point Blvd., Elk Grove Village, IL 60009.

New Shingles Treatment

A new drug called *valacyclovir* relieves shingle pain far more effectively than the current treatment, *acyclovir* (Zovirax). Patients given the new drug got rid of their pain on average within 38 days. Patients given acyclovir took an average of 51 days to recover. *Important:* For maximum effectiveness, valacyclovir therapy must be initiated within 72 hours of the appearance of the first shingles blister. Pending FDA approval, valacyclovir should be available later this year.

Source: Karl R. Beutner, MD, PhD, clinical associate professor of dermatology, University of California, San Francisco Medical School.

Children and Asthma: What You Need to Know

Children with intractable asthma may actually be suffering from panic disorder as well.

Problem: Kids are often prescribed unnecessary drugs—including steroids—when what they need is antipanic medication and psychotherapy to alleviate the conditions that trigger the panic. The misdiagnosis occurs because panic attacks and asthma attacks are so similar. Both are sudden, intense and often accompanied by a sensation of suffocation and fear.

Source: Chantal Baron, MD, associate professor of psychiatry, University of Montreal, Canada.

For the Million Lupus Sufferers... And Their Families

An occasional ache, pain, rash or infection is no cause for alarm—in most cases. Sometimes, however, such complaints are the first signs of a painful, debilitating and potentially life-threatening condition known as *systemic lupus erythematosus.*

An autoimmune disease, lupus occurs when renegade antibodies attack not disease-causing germs, but healthy body cells.

Roughly one million Americans have lupus. Most cases are diagnosed when patients are between 15 and 30 years of age. But the disorder also strikes younger children and senior citizens.

We don't understand what causes lupus, nor do we have a cure. But patients who are vigilant and who work closely with their doctors can "establish a truce" with this chronic disorder.

What does lupus feel like?

Lupus symptoms vary tremendously. *Most common:* Fever...hair loss...mouth sores... seizures...joint pain and swelling...mental confusion...overwhelming fatigue...a butterfly-shaped rash across the nose and cheeks...

fingers and toes that become painful and turn pale, blue or red in the cold.

Occasionally, lupus affects the tissues surrounding the heart and lungs. Nearly all lupus patients have blood abnormalities. About half have kidney problems.

Lupus symptoms may wax and wane. Often a bout with symptoms—called a *flare*—is followed by a period of remission lasting several weeks to years.

This on-again/off-again pattern can be a source of great frustration. Just when a patient feels she's beaten lupus, she experiences another flare...and the disease cycle starts anew.

Cause and diagnosis...

Although there is evidence that lupus may be caused by a virus, it's also clear that a viral infection isn't the sole explanation. *Other factors:*

•Sex. Lupus affects about nine times more women than men. This suggests that estrogen may play a key role in the disease.

•Race. Lupus is three times more common among African-American women than among whites.

•Family history. Lupus seems to run in families. About 20% of lupus patients have a close relative with lupus, rheumatoid arthritis, multiple sclerosis or some other autoimmune disorder.

Because lupus symptoms are so varied and because they come and go unpredictably, the disease is notoriously difficult to diagnose.

Many patients bounce from doctor to doctor for several years before finding a specialist—usually a rheumatologist—who makes the diagnosis.

There's no one specific test for lupus. Diagnoses are pieced together from the patient's symptoms and from blood, urine and immune system tests.

After confirming that the patient has lupus, the doctor must tailor therapy to the individual. What works for one person may not work for another.

Treating lupus...

A wide variety of drugs are used to treat lupus. *Most common:*

•Corticosteroids. These are usually given regularly, in low doses, to control inflammation. Higher doses are given when there's a flare. Very large doses are prescribed to counter deteriorating kidney function and other lupus-related crises.

Corticosteroids are effective. Used too long or in excessive doses, however, they can cause serious side effects—increased susceptibility to infection...unusual hair growth...cataracts... coronary artery disease...facial swelling...high blood pressure and osteoporosis.

•Nonsteroidal anti-inflammatory drugs (NSAIDs), such as aspirin and ibuprofen. While these are often highly effective against joint and muscle pain, they, too, can cause troublesome side effects. *Examples:* Stomach irritation, ulcers and ringing in the ears. These drugs may cause kidney impairment, high blood pressure, anemia, liver disease and blood abnormalities.

•Antimalarials. These medications help counter rashes, fever and swollen joints. Like other drugs, they can cause rashes and stomach upset. Antimalarials may also affect the eyes. This is often not noticed by the patient. *Self-defense:* People taking antimalarials should have their eyes examined by an ophthalmologist at least once every four to six months.

The take-charge patient...

Although a doctor's care is very important, it's ultimately the lupus patient who determines how well she'll cope with her illness on a day-to-day basis. *To minimize your symptoms:*

•Take your medications on schedule. Lupus patients are often on a complex drug regimen. Since fatigue and emotional swings can cloud thinking, it's a good idea to write down how and when to take each medication.

•Take steps to avoid osteoporosis. Because steroids taken over a long period of time and/ or at high doses can cause brittle bones, it's important to eat more calcium-rich foods, like yogurt and sardines, and to take calcium supplements.

•Exercise regularly. Many lupus patients are so fatigued that they can barely imagine physical activity. But exercise is very important. Besides strengthening the muscles, heart and bones, it's energizing—and it helps prevent osteoporosis.

If you haven't exercised in some time, start by walking around the block once a day. Gradually increase the distance until you can walk a mile a day. Stair-climbing and biking are also excellent exercises for people with lupus. Swimming is good for relieving achy joints.

•Minimize exposure to chemicals. Hydrazine and amines contained in certain foods and consumer products may exacerbate lupus symptoms in some patients.

Avoid hair dyes, photographic supplies, pesticides and tobacco smoke. Switch to hypoallergenic cosmetics—and use them sparingly. Also, skip alfalfa seeds or tablets, sprouts, beans and other legumes, smoked foods and artificial food coloring.

•Eat a "heart-healthy" diet. Because lupus often goes hand in hand with high cholesterol, lupus patients should minimize their consumption of fat and cholesterol and should boost their intake of grains, cereals, fruits and vegetables.

•Minimize exposure to sunlight. Sunlight causes rashes and flares in about a third of all cases of lupus. *Self-defense:* Wear protective clothing when outdoors. Use sunscreen.

Also: Avoid foods that increase your sensitivity to sunlight—lemons, limes, celery, parsnips, parsley and figs, all of which contain sensitivity-boosting compounds called *psoralens.*

Be especially careful of sunlight if you're taking medication that boosts your sun sensitivity. *Example:* Tetracycline, sulfa drugs, some antiseizure medications and some antidepressants.

•Take steps to avoid infections. Some lupus patients are susceptible to bacterial infections of the heart. Such infections can occur when bacteria from the mouth slip into the bloodstream during dental work. *Self-defense:* Before undergoing any dental work, ask your doctor if you should take antibiotics.

•Take precautions before becoming pregnant. Women with lupus often have difficulty becoming pregnant and are more likely to miscarry or deliver prematurely...although a period of remission at conception and during the previous six months or so reduces the odds of such complications. Women with lupus should make sure symptoms are under control before trying to conceive.

•Think twice about taking hormones. Oral contraceptives and other hormone-containing drugs can boost the risk of high blood pressure and blood clots in lupus patients.

Estrogen-replacement therapy (ERT) can make symptoms worse in severe cases of lupus. However, ERT is often a good idea for menopausal women with mild cases of lupus —it helps ward off osteoporosis.

Bottom line: Menopausal women with lupus should discuss the pros and cons of ERT carefully with their doctors.

•Get plenty of rest. If you suffer from lupus-induced fatigue, don't be embarrassed about sleeping longer at night...or taking frequent naps during the day. If necessary, curtail your daily activities or work schedule.

Source: Sheldon Paul Blau, MD, clinical professor of medicine, State University of New York, Stony Brook. He is coauthor of *Living with Lupus: All the Knowledge You Need to Help Yourself,* Addison-Wesley.

Hidden Cause of Stomach Problems

Bloating and stomach pain may be caused by *tight pants syndrome.* The "condition" was named by a doctor who treated a male patient who complained of mysterious abdominal pains. After a series of tests proved negative, the doctor discovered that the man's waist size was at least three inches greater than his pants size.

Source: Octavio Bessa, Jr., MD, clinical assistant professor of medicine, New York Medical College, Valhalla, and an internist practicing in Stamford, CT.

Pepper Cream Relief

Pepper cream helps relieve pain from backache, headache, arthritis, shingles and more. *Key ingredient:* Capsaicin, a chemical derived from hot chili peppers. It blocks the body's release of Substance P, a chemical that mediates the sensation of pain. Some patients experience a temporary burning sensation at the site of application, but this usually lessens with regular use. The cream is sold under the brand name Zostrix.

Source: Roy Altman, MD, chief of the arthritis division, and professor of medicine, University of Miami School of Medicine, and chief of the arthritis section, Miami VA Medical Center.

Eye Dryness Relief

Custom eyeglasses offer relief for severe eye dryness (Sjögren's syndrome). This condition can be very painful, particularly when outdoors. The custom glasses have plastic "moisture chambers" that hug the wearer's face to slow the evaporation of tears from the eye surface. Customizing a pair of eyeglasses takes at least three visits to the optometrist. The work is covered by some insurance plans. For more information on moisture-chamber glasses, write Dr. Dean Hart at 185 Woodbury Rd., Hicksville, New York 11801.

Source: Dean E. Hart, OD, associate research scientist, Harkness Eye Institute, Columbia University, New York City. His report on moisture-chamber eyeglasses was published in the *Journal of the American Optometric Association,* 243 N. Lindbergh Blvd., St. Louis 63141.

Acupuncture Strengthens Hands

Acupuncture helps treat hand paresis (weak, clumsy hands) in mild stroke patients—even when the treatment begins six to eight years after the stroke. In a recent study, patients whose hands were paralyzed following stroke received 20 to 40 acupuncture treatments over a two- or three-month period. All 11 patients in the study experienced improvement, including stronger grips, improved dexterity—even the ability to write more legibly. *To find a good acupuncturist:* Contact the American

Association of Acupuncture and Oriental Medicine, 433 Front St., Catasauqua, Pennsylvania 18032. 610-433-2448.

Source: Margaret A. Naeser, PhD, associate research professor of neurology, Boston University School of Medicine. Her study of partial paralysis in 11 stroke patients between 30 and 70 years of age was published in *Clinical Rehabilitation*, Mill Road, Dunton Green, Sevenoaks, Kent, England TN13 2YA.

Angioplasty Follow-Up

Coronary arteries stay clear longer following angioplasty if patients take calcium antagonists, including diltiazem, verapamil and nifedipine. These drugs reduced the renarrowing of the artery blockages for at least six months after the initial procedure. Coronary angioplasty involves opening clogged heart arteries with a balloon-tipped catheter. *Self-defense:* If you've had or are planning to have angioplasty, ask your cardiologist about calcium antagonists.

Source: William B. Hillegass, MD, MPH, fellow, cardiology department, Duke University Medical Center, Durham, NC. His review of five studies of calcium antagonist use in 919 angioplasty patients was published in *The American Journal of Cardiology*, 105 Raider Blvd., Belle Mead, NJ 08502.

New Pacemaker Surgery For Women

New pacemaker surgery for women allows the device to be implanted *beneath* the breast tissue. The technique leaves only small scars near the shoulder and under the breast, hidden from view. *Result:* Patients can wear low-cut dresses or bikinis without the stigma of having a long scar along the neckline. Surgery takes about two hours and is performed under local anesthesia. Recovery takes less than a week.

Source: Marc Roelke, MD, attending physician in cardiac pacing and electrophysiology, Beth Israel Hospital, Newark, NJ. His report on the use of the new surgery on 11 patients was presented at a recent meeting of the North American Society for Pacing and Electrophysiology, Upper Newton Falls, MA.

Gum Disease Can Be Spread By Kissing

In a recent study of 20 couples, both partners in each of four couples were found to harbor *identical* strains of the bacterium that causes gum disease. This suggests that the partners infected one another via oral contact. To ensure long-lasting treatment for gum disease, *both* partners may need to be checked for oral bacteria—even if only one partner has gum problems.

Source: Myron Bromberg, DDS, Academy of General Dentistry, 211 E. Chicago Ave., Chicago 60611.

Glaucoma—Prevention And Treatment

A leading cause of blindness,* glaucoma afflicts approximately two million Americans—half of whom may not even know that they have the disease.

Glaucoma occurs when the *optic nerve*—the nerve in the back of the eye that transmits visual information to the brain—is damaged by an abnormal rise in the pressure of the fluid filling the eyeball.

Normally, this fluid—called *aqueous humor*—drains out of the eye as new fluid is produced. In some individuals, however, the drainage system can become blocked.

Result: Increased intraocular pressure (pressure inside the eye).

Some people think that abnormal pressure itself constitutes glaucoma. But a patient is usually considered to have the disease only once the optic nerve is damaged.

Some people with high intraocular pressure, as measured by eye exams, have no nerve damage. Other patients with normal pressure readings but a more vulnerable optic nerve suffer vision loss.

There are two major types of glaucoma...

• Closed-angle glaucoma occurs when drainage becomes blocked. This can happen suddenly or gradually. Sudden (acute) closed-angle glaucoma is usually accompanied by eye pain or redness, seeing colored halos around lights and/or nausea. With this type of glaucoma, permanent vision damage can occur within a few days. See an ophthalmologist immediately if you notice any combination of these symptoms. The disease is usually treated with laser surgery. Gradual (chronic) closed-angle glaucoma is usually asymptomatic.

• Open-angle glaucoma is much more common. Unlike the acute closed-angle type, open-angle glaucoma rarely causes symptoms until the disease has caused a significant amount of damage to the optic nerve. Loss of peripheral vision may occur during the early stages of open-angle glaucoma—but so gradually that the person fails to notice it.

Risk factors...

People in their 60s are six times more likely to develop glaucoma than those younger than 60. But the elderly aren't the only ones at increased risk for the disease. *Also at risk:*

• People with a family history of glaucoma.
• African-Americans.
• People who use steroids in any form—including drops, creams and inhalers.
• Nearsighted people.
• Those with a past eye injury.
• Migraine sufferers.
• Diabetics.

Detecting glaucoma...

By the time glaucoma starts to produce symptoms, it may already be in an advanced stage. For this reason, every adult at increased risk for glaucoma should have annual eye exams.

A thorough glaucoma exam will include...

• Intraocular pressure measurement. Some doctors still measure pressure using a device called an air-puff tonometer. More accurate, however, is the *applanation tonometer*. It touches the eye directly, after it has been numbed with anesthetic drops.

• Visual field testing. This procedure checks for loss of peripheral vision, which is often an early sign of glaucoma. Usually, patients are asked to spot tiny lights as they appear on a screen.

• Optic disk exam. The most important part of the three-part exam because it can detect glaucoma in the earliest possible stages. The ophthalmologist uses a special lamp or viewing scope to peer into the back of the eye. The instrument does not actually come in contact with the eye.

Treatment...

Although glaucoma has no known cure, it can be arrested—usually with drug therapy. *Essential:* Early treatment.

Glaucoma medications—taken in drop form or as pills—are designed either to decrease the rate of aqueous humor production or improve the flow of the fluid out of the eye. A combination of drugs may be needed to achieve the correct fluid balance. In most cases, the medication must be taken indefinitely.

If drug therapy fails, laser surgery may be required to open up the eye's drainage system. A third treatment alternative—incisional surgery—involves creating a completely new drainage system. This system bypasses the eye's own blocked system. This treatment is now quite effective, thanks to newly developed medications that prevent scar formation.

The other two leading causes of blindness in the US are age-related macular degeneration and diabetic retinopathy.

Source: Martha Motuz Leen, MD, assistant professor of ophthalmology, glaucoma specialist, University of Washington, Seattle.

Better Bladder Cancer Therapy

Conventional surgery for bladder cancer that invades surrounding muscle tissue calls for removing the entire bladder along with the tumor. Without a bladder, patients who undergo this treatment must—for the rest of their lives—use an uncomfortable and inefficient urine-collection bag.

Now: An experimental treatment spares the bladder. The surgeon simply cuts out the tumor using instruments attached to a slender fiber-optic scope that's passed through the urethra.

The operation is followed by chemotherapy and radiation.

Outlook: Half of patients who underwent this procedure were still alive after four years with no signs of the cancer spreading. That's the same cure rate as obtained via the old method.

Source: Donald S. Kaufman, MD, associate clinical professor of medicine, Harvard University Medical School, and oncologist, Massachusetts General Hospital, Boston. His study of 53 bladder cancer patients was published in *The New England Journal of Medicine*, 10 Shattuck St., Boston 02115.

Treating Urinary Incontinence

Urinary incontinence can now be successfully treated without major surgery. New treatment—recently approved by the FDA—involves injecting collagen into the tissue surrounding the urethra. Collagen strengthens the tissue, helping prevent leakage of urine. In a recent study, the injections reduced incontinence symptoms in 93% of patients, with 62% of patients returning to complete continence. One to three shots are usually necessary. They are generally administered on an outpatient basis—no hospitalization needed.

Source: Rodney Appell, MD, head of urodynamics and female urology, Cleveland Clinic, Cleveland.

Cancer Pain Problem

One-fourth of all cancer patients fail to get adequate pain relief. *Reason:* They assume that pain is inevitable…they don't complain because they want to be "good" patients…they fear addiction…and they are afraid that pain management will distract the doctor from treating the disease. *Reality:* Pain management is an integral part of cancer treatment. Patients should not hesitate to communicate their needs.

Source: Jamie H. Von Roenn, MD, associate professor of medicine, section of medical oncology, Northwestern University Medical School, Chicago. Her survey of 897 cancer doctors was published in *Annals of Internal Medicine*, Independence Mall West, Sixth Street at Race, Philadelphia 19106.

Bee Sting Treatment

Don't squeeze a stinger out—that only injects more venom under the skin. Instead, scrape it out with a fingernail or the edge of a credit card. *For multiple stings:* Seek medical attention immediately. *If bees start to attack:* Cover your head with a jacket or sweater and run for the nearest house or car.

Source: Agricultural Research Service, US Department of Agriculture, Greenbelt, MD.

Music Soothes Alzheimer's Patients

Familiar tunes made them sing along and dance gracefully—despite their memory loss and lack of coordination. *Theory:* Appreciation of music remains even after other mental abilities have declined. Music also reduces the need for tranquilizers in disturbed people living in institutions.

Source: David Aldridge, PhD, associate clinical professor for clinical research methods, University of Witten Herdecke, Germany. His study of Alzheimer's patients was published in the *Journal of the Royal Society of Medicine*, 1 Wimpole St., London W1M 8AE, England.

Most Effective Treatment For Stroke

Treatment for stroke is most effective when administered within six hours of the onset of symptoms. Seek help immediately if you experience unexplained weakness on one side of the body…loss of vision or double vision…difficulty speaking…numbness on either side of the body…severe dizziness or loss of balance.

Source: David Sherman, MD, professor and chief, department of medicine/neurology, University of Texas Health Science Center, San Antonio.

Retin-A Repairs Damaged Skin

Retin-A doesn't just smooth wrinkles—it repairs damaged skin. In a recent study, 29 people with sun-damaged skin applied either 0.1% tretinoin (Retin-A) or a placebo cream once a day. After one year, those using tretinoin showed an 80% increase in formation of collagen, the protein that gives skin its elasticity. Those receiving the placebo cream had a 14% *decrease* in collagen synthesis.

Source: Albert M. Kligman, MD, PhD, professor of dermatology, University of Pennsylvania, Philadelphia. His study was published in *The New England Journal of Medicine*, 10 Shattuck St., Boston 02115.

Better Asthma Treatment

Daily monitoring and management—and regular use of anti-inflammatory drugs, in conjunction with beta-agonist bronchodilators. *First line of defense:* Inhaled corticosteroids, which don't have steroid side effects. *Also effective:* Cromolyn sodium (Intal) and nedocromil (Tilade) and anti-inflammatory agents. *Important:* Asthma sufferers should avoid asthma triggers...should request written medication plans for chronic management—and for handling attacks...and should check their lung capacity at least once a day with a peak-flow meter.

Source: Francis Adams, MD, assistant clinical professor of pulmonary medicine, New York University Medical Center, New York City. He maintains a private practice at 650 First Ave., New York City 10016.

Unnecessary Tests for Migraine Sufferers

Migraine sufferers do not benefit from routine MRIs and CAT scans—although many physicians continue to order these costly and potentially frightening tests for their migraine patients. *Exceptions:* To rule out brain tumors, these scans may be appropriate for individuals whose headache patterns change...who have a history of seizures...or who are experiencing numbness, weakness, changes in vision, difficulty maintaining balance or other neurological problems.

Source: B.M. Frishberg, MD, clinical assistant professor of neurology, Georgetown University School of Medicine, Washington, DC, and a neurologist in private practice in Bethesda, Maryland. His review of 17 studies involving 2,722 headache sufferers was published in the *American College of Physicians Journal Club*, Independence Mall West, Sixth Street at Race, Philadelphia 19106.

Silent Heart Disease

Five and a half million Americans have been formally diagnosed with coronary artery disease. And another 12 million have heart disease but don't know it—because they have had no symptoms...yet.

"Silent" heart disease is now the leading cause of sudden death in the US. Fortunately, there are ways to defend yourself against this insidious and often lethal illness.

Heart disease occurs when there is a reduction in blood flow to the heart—which, in turn, is usually caused by the accumulation of fatty material in one or more coronary arteries. This process of oxygen starvation is known as *myocardial ischemia.*

At one time, doctors believed that a coronary artery had to be almost completely occluded before the heart sustained any damage. Now it's clear that significant damage can occur even with partial blockage.

A blockage in the coronary arteries can cause a variety of symptoms—from simple angina (chest pain) and palpitations to a full-blown heart attack. But up to 80% of these episodes of ischemia are *silent*—that is, they produce no pain or any other symptoms. For every chest pain a person experiences, he/she may have four periods of *silent myocardial ischemia* (SMI).

SMI can occur at any time. It can last just a few seconds, or go on for several hours.

Who gets silent ischemia?

There are four key risk factors...

1. Cigarette smoking. Smokers are 10 times more likely than nonsmokers to suffer a heart attack.

2. High blood pressure. Sixty million Americans have it.

3. Elevated blood cholesterol.

4. Family history of premature heart disease.

Other, less significant risk factors for SMI include being over 40...being male...being obese ...having diabetes...being under severe psychological stress...not getting regular exercise. The more risk factors you have, the greater your risk.

Although he loved to exercise, the well-known runner and author Jim Fixx was at very high risk for silent ischemia. He was a 52-year-old former smoker with high cholesterol and a family history of heart disease.

Self-defense strategies...

•If you smoke, stop.

•Keep blood pressure and cholesterol in check. If they're elevated, make an effort to lose weight, get regular exercise, avoid excessive intake of alcohol and use meditation or another form of stress relief.

In some cases, cutting back on your intake of salt lowers blood pressure. Cutting out fatty, cholesterol-rich foods is good for your cholesterol levels, too. In fact, many scientists strongly recommend becoming a vegetarian to prevent or even reverse coronary artery disease. Your total cholesterol level should be below 200. Your LDL (bad) cholesterol should be no higher than 130.

If these measures fail, you'll probably need to take antihypertensive and/or cholesterol-lowering medication.

•Reduce psychological stress. Try to maintain your sense of humor. Learn to delegate responsibility, and take comfort from friends and family.

Helpful exercise: Close your door, disconnect the phone and sit quietly. Visualize a color...or repeat a mantra. Do this once or twice a day for five or 10 minutes each time.

•If you're diabetic, keep your blood sugar under strict control. Use diet, follow a weight reduction plan and take medication.

Screening for silent ischemia...

If you're 40 or older and have one or more risk factors for SMI, see your doctor for a complete physical examination. *Also:* Request a treadmill stress test.

This test—in which an electrocardiogram is taken as the patient runs at increasing speeds on a treadmill—is the single most reliable nonsurgical screening procedure for diagnosing coronary artery disease.

If the stress test reveals heart disease, your doctor will probably prescribe nitrates, beta-blockers or calcium-channel blockers. Depending on how many risk factors you have, you may want to get tested every few years.

Stress tests are offered by most cardiologists and many primary care doctors. Unless you're already experiencing symptoms of heart disease, they are usually *not* covered by health insurance plans. *Cost:* $175 to $300.

Source: Harold L. Karpman, MD, clinical professor of medicine and a cardiologist at the University of California, Los Angeles School of Medicine. He is the author of *Preventing Silent Heart Disease: How to Protect Yourself from America's #1 Killer.* Henry Holt.

Treating Chronic Coughs

Chronic coughs should *not* be treated with over-the-counter remedies. Most short-term coughs clear up on their own within a week or two. A chronic cough may signal an allergy, asthma or another more serious condition—which should be evaluated by a doctor.

Source: Steven Lamm, MD, clinical assistant professor of medicine, New York University School of Medicine, New York City.

New Relief for Eczema

Chronic itching caused by eczema can now be controlled by the prescription drug *doxepin* (Zonalon). In a recent test, a 5% doxepin cream applied four times a day for seven days produced a significant drop in itching. Side effects were limited to stinging, burning and mild drowsiness.

Source: Arthur Sober, MD, a dermatologist at Massachusetts General Hospital, Boston. His study of 270 eczema patients was published in the *Journal of the American Academy of Dermatology*, 171 Ashley Ave., Charleston, SC 29425.

New Hope for Multiple Sclerosis Sufferers

Multiple sclerosis patients can be helped by the antileukemia drug *cladribine* (Leustatin). In a recent study, it slowed the progression of chronic MS in nearly all patients tested. In some, it actually *reversed* the disease. Several patients who had been unable to walk before taking the medication were able to walk afterward.

Source: J.C. Sipe, MD, head, department of molecular and experimental medicine, Scripps Research Institute, La Jolla, CA. His study of 49 MS patients was published in *The Lancet*, 42 Bedford Square, London WC1B 3SL, England.

Ear Infection Advance

Children with chronic ear infections *(otitis media)* often are treated by having tubes inserted into their eardrums. About 10% of the million or so kids who get these *tympanostomy tubes* develop additional ear infections while the tubes are in place. *Better:* Coating the tubes with the antimicrobial agent *silver oxide* reduces the rate of ear infections by half. Coated tubes should be commercially available by this fall.

Source: Richard A. Chole, MD, PhD, professor and chairman, department of otolaryngology, University of California, Davis.

Leg Cramp Reliever

Nighttime leg-cramp relief: "Acupinch." *How it works:* With thumb and forefinger, pinch your upper lip—yes, lip—just below the nose for 20 to 30 seconds. This works about 80% of the time.

Source: Donald Cooper, former US Olympic team doctor, quoted in *Minute Health Tips: Medical Advice and Facts at a Glance* by Thomas G. Welch, MD, DCI/Chronimed Publishing, 13911 Ridgedale Dr., Suite 250, Minnetonka, MN 55343.

Smoking and Alzheimer's

In a health study conducted by Harvard University, it was observed that individuals who smoked more than one pack of cigarettes a day were four times as likely to develop Alzheimer's disease as those who smoked less. *Reason:* Unknown.

Source: Stuart L. Shalat, ScD, assistant professor of epidemiology and medicine, Yale University School of Medicine.

Misdiagnosed Alzheimer's Disease

•Pernicious anemia, a vitamin B_{12} deficiency that can cause memory loss, paranoia, dementia, and paralysis, is sometimes thought to be Alzheimer's. *Trap:* People over 65 can have it without even knowing. *Reason:* The usual test for the condition—a blood test—identifies the vitamin deficiency only after neurological damage has occurred. A new urine test, however, detects it before it can do any damage. *Cost:* $30. *Availability:* Only through the test's developer, Eric J. Norman, PhD, Norman Clinical Laboratory, 1044 Sunwood Ct., Cincinnati, OH 45231, 513-872-4233.

•Signs of senility caused by hypothyroidism (low hormone output by the thyroid gland) are treatable. *Problem:* The disorder is often confused with Alzheimer's disease. *Symptoms* include memory loss, depression, deafness, weight loss, weakness, constipation, and incontinence.

Source: *Healthwise.*

Tranquilizers and Hip Fractures

Elderly people who take tranquilizers that remain in the body for more than 24 hours are 70% more likely to fracture their hips in falls than those taking tranquilizers that remain in the body for less than 24 hours or those who don't take any at all. *Long-acting:* Diazepam, Flurazepam, chlordiazepoxide. *Short-acting:* Alprazolam, lorazepam, oxazepam.

Source: T. Franklin Williams, MD, director, National Institute on Aging, Bethesda, MD.

Unnecessary Cataract Surgery

Unless cataracts interfere with normal activities, surgery isn't recommended. *Trap:* Many doctors routinely remove cataracts before it's truly necessary. Because cataracts vary in size, density and location in the lens, they can exist for a lifetime without creating major vision problems. *Time for surgery:* When you can't read a newspaper because of cataracts.

Source: Dr. Stephen Bloomfield, associate professor of ophthalmology at Cornell University Medical School.

Pneumonia Self-Defense

Pneumonia/hospital connection. About two-thirds of all elderly pneumonia patients studied had been hospitalized within the past four years—for one illness or another. *Recommended:* Because many of these pneumonias are caused by pneumococcal infection, all people older than the age of 65 should have a pneumococcal vaccine following a hospital stay to protect against pneumonia. *Advantage:* The cost of a vaccination is approximately one-third the cost of hospital care for unvaccinated patients who are readmitted suffering from pneumonia.

Source: David S. Fedson, MD, professor of internal medicine, University of Virginia School of Medicine, Charlottesville.

Relieving Arthritis Pain

•Vegetable and fish oils can reduce arthritis pain. Polyunsaturated (vegetable) fats and eicosapentanoic acid (found in fish oil) relieve arthritis pain by producing a less inflammatory hormone than saturated (animal) fats.

Source: Albany Medical College, State University of New York, Albany, NY 12246.

•A fat-rich diet makes arthritis patients feel worse. When the patients in a recent study avoided red meat and other foods high in polyunsaturated fats, they reported less joint pain and morning stiffness.

Also helpful: Fish oil supplements.

Source: *The Lancet.*

Silent Heart Attacks

Many victims of heart disease are unaware of their problem because they suffer painless heart attacks. *Most vulnerable:* People who smoke or have high blood pressure or a high cholesterol level. *Protection:* People with one or more of these traits should undergo tests that detect susceptibility to painless attacks. If the potential is there, preventive drugs can be prescribed.

Source: Dr. Peter F. Cohn, chief of cardiology, State University of New York Health Sciences Center, quoted in *Venture.*

Estrogen/Cholesterol Connection

Women taking estrogen replacement have dramatically lower cholesterol levels than those not on treatment, sharply reducing their risk of heart disease. Women taking estrogen in a recent study had lower LDL, the "bad" cholesterol, and higher HDL, the "good" cholesterol. The same women showed less thickening of their carotid arteries than nonestrogen takers. Since getting even a late start on estrogen helps prevent bone loss, anyone who starts now may have a chance to derive at least some heart-attack prevention benefit.

Source: Teri A. Manolio, MD, the lead author of the National Heart, Lung and Blood Institute's Cardiovascular Heart Study.

Giving the Gift of Sight

Donate outdated eyeglasses to be distributed to the needy in the United States and around the world. *Also needed:* Metal eyeglass frames in any condition…reusable plastic-framed glasses …cataract glasses…nonprescription sunglasses …soft eyeglass cases.

Source: *Send old eyeglasses to:* New Eyes for the Needy, 549 Millburn Ave., Short Hills, NJ 07078.

Telephone Counseling

Telephone counseling helps heart attack survivors change their unhealthy habits. In a recent study, nurses phoned discharged heart patients once a month to check on their progress, answer questions and provide positive feedback. They also instructed the patients on how to quit smoking, exercise, eat more healthfully and take their medications. *Result:* Patients counseled repeatedly during the year after their heart attack were much more successful at reducing their risk factors than those who weren't. *Cost:* $500 to $700 a patient per year—much less than traditional rehabilitation or medical care in the event of a second heart attack.

Source: Robert DeBusk, MD, professor of medicine, Stanford University School of Medicine, Palo Alto, CA.

Bugging Out for Good Health

Leeches and maggots are two icky but effective medical therapies now making a come-

back. Leeches are helping reattach severed fingers, toes and limbs. Their saliva has anticoagulant, antibiotic and anesthetic properties. Maggots, applied to wounds, consume dead tissue while leaving healthy tissue alone. They also excrete an infection-fighting antibacterial substance.

Source: Jane Petro, MD, professor of surgery, New York Medical College, Valhalla.

Stroke-Prevention Strategy

Vitamin E helps prevent second strokes. In a recent study, patients who had suffered a small stroke—called a *transient ischemic attack*—were put on a regimen of either one aspirin a day or aspirin plus a vitamin E capsule. *Result:* Within 18 months, eight members of the aspirin-only group suffered a second stroke, compared with only two of the aspirin-and-vitamin E group. *Explanation:* Aspirin and vitamin E are thought to inhibit different steps leading to blood vessel blockage. Taking them in combination may confer additional protection. *Caution:* Together, the two may raise the risk of hemorrhage. Don't put yourself on a vitamin E-and-aspirin regimen without first consulting your doctor.

Source: Manfred Steiner, MD, PhD, professor of medicine, hematology and oncology, East Carolina University School of Medicine, Greenville, NC. His study of 100 patients who'd had transient ischemic attacks was reported at the second International Conference on Antioxidant Vitamins and Beta-Carotene in Disease Prevention held in Berlin, Germany.

New Drug for Cystic Fibrosis

New drug for cystic fibrosis gives CF patients fewer respiratory infections, improved lung function and an increased sense of well-being. Administered once or twice a day, dornase alpha (Pulmozyme) improved lung function significantly and reduced the risk of respiratory problems requiring antibiotics by 28% to 37%. Patients also spent less time in the hospital and fewer days at home. When inhaled, Pulmozyme acts like "molecular scissors," cutting up the thick mucus that builds up in the lungs of CF patients. Although not a cure, the medication has been approved by the FDA for use in patients older than age five.

Source: Bonnie W. Ramsey, MS, associate professor of medicine, University of Washington School of Medicine, Seattle. Her study of 900 CF patients at 51 US medical centers was published in *The New England Journal of Medicine,* 10 Shattuck St., Boston 02115.

Safer Gallstone Surgery

The new *laparoscopic* technique reduces the likelihood of death by 80%, compared with the traditional "open" surgical technique. In laparoscopic surgery, stones are removed via a narrow "telescope" inserted through four small incisions in the abdomen. Conventional "open" gallbladder surgery necessitates a much larger incision.

Source: Claudia A. Steiner, MD, MPH, senior fellow, Johns Hopkins University, Baltimore. Her review of discharge records at 54 Maryland hospitals was published in *The New England Journal of Medicine,* 10 Shattuck St., Boston 02115.

Birthmark Removal

Disfiguring birthmarks that change the skin's contour, causing thickness and bumps, can now be removed via a technique called sclerotherapy. Alcohol is injected directly into the birthmark, cutting off the blood supply and causing it to shrink or disappear. One to three treatments are generally necessary. The birthmarks —a type of *slow-flow hemangioma*—are made up of thick masses of blood vessels beneath the skin. Though generally harmless, they can cause deformity and severe psychological trauma, especially in children.

Source: Richard Towbin, MD, radiologist-in-chief, Children's Hospital of Pittsburgh.

11
Doctors, Hospitals and Medicines

How to Protect Yourself From Common Hospital Hazards

Although the word *hospital* has the same root as *hospitality*, being hospitalized can be far from a happy experience—if not outright hazardous to your health.

Hospital-caused infections, misdiagnosis, needless surgery, medication errors, sloppy nursing care and excessive X rays and laboratory testing are among the many pitfalls that can befall a hospitalized patient.

If you're ever hospitalized, remember…*You are not in custody. You alone are ultimately in charge of your well-being and comfort—not the doctor, nurse or administrator.*

Protect yourself by asking questions when you are not sure about something…and challenging any policy or practice you think might be detrimental or unnecessary. Taking a passive approach only increases the likelihood that you'll become a victim of medical negligence.

Experience…

Before consenting to any operation or diagnostic procedure, make sure the doctor performs the procedure on a regular basis—ideally at least 100 times *a year* for especially complex operations like coronary bypass surgery. Otherwise, he/she may lack important skills…or may be unable to respond effectively to complications.

Also make sure that the hospital staff is experienced at caring for patients undergoing your particular operation. If not, the staff—those who provide the bulk of your care—may lack the experience needed for quality care.

Ask specific questions. *Example:* "How many hysterectomies were performed here in 1993?" If you do not get a satisfactory answer, go elsewhere for care.

Nosocomial infections…

These are hospital-caused infections—potentially fatal—caused by microorganisms that thrive on some wards.

Examples: Pneumonia, urinary-tract infections, hepatitis B, staph infections.

Nosocomial infections add an average of four additional days of recovery time. They account for 15% of all hospital charges. Collectively, they add at least $2.5 billion to America's medical bills. Some experts say the true figure is double this amount because 25% of all nosocomial infections show up only *after* patients have been discharged.

Guarding against infection...

•Find a hospital with a good track record regarding nosocomial infections. Ask your doctor and contact your local department of health for their recommendations.

Ideal: An institution with an active infection-control committee...staff members who belong to the Association for Practitioners in Infection Control...at least one nurse-epidemiologist responsible for maintaining good infection-surveillance standards.

•Watch to make sure that all hospital personnel wash their hands before examining or treating you. Ask them to do so *in your room.*

•If you discover that your roommate has an infection that can be transmitted through the air or through the use of a common bathroom— bring this up with your doctor or nurse-epidemiologist. If there's any risk of your becoming infected, ask to be moved to another room.

•For any surgical procedure requiring the removal of hair, refuse to be shaven. In one study, people who were shaved had a nosocomial infection rate of 5.6%. Those whose hair was removed via chemical depilatories had a nosocomial infection rate of just 0.6%.

•To avoid urinary-tract infections, make sure your nurse regularly checks to see that any catheter is draining properly.

Doctor-induced illness...

Iatrogenic illnesses or injuries are those caused directly by a doctor who makes mistakes in judgment or handiwork.

In a study conducted at Boston University Medical Center, 36% of 815 consecutive hospital admissions were for treatment of iatrogenic problems.

Iatrogenic illnesses have many causes, including...

•Dangerous diagnostic tests or faulty diagnoses. Diagnostic tests themselves can be invasive and potentially dangerous.

Examples: Cardiac catheterizations, myelograms or any test involving radiation exposure.

Fancy diagnostic tools sometimes lead doctors astray. A recent Harvard study showed that 10% of all patients who had died while hospitalized *might have lived* had they been properly diagnosed. In some categories of disease, the misdiagnosis figure was greater than 20%.

What underlies these dismal figures? An over-reliance on sophisticated diagnostic tests, statistics and lab results, and not enough use of common sense and medical knowledge.

•Needless surgery. Twenty percent or more of all surgery performed in the US may be unnecessary.

In an *R.N.* magazine survey of nurses, 46% of the respondents estimated that at least 30% of operations were unnecessary. Another 20% of the nurses put the figure closer to 50%.

Two of the most frequently performed unnecessary procedures are *cesarean section* and *hysterectomy.*

Up to 80% of all C-sections are unnecessary. Since 1970, there's been a 500% increase in the rate at which this procedure is performed— with no discernible payoff.

And 50% to 75% of all hysterectomies are unnecessary—especially those involving removal of the ovaries. Hysterectomy is necessary for two conditions only—uterine cancer and irreparable damage to the uterus.

As for coronary bypass surgery, up to 33% of these procedures are unnecessary. In most of those cases it's possible to achieve the same results without surgery—via medication, lifestyle changes and/or angioplasty.

Another troubling trend: With the advent of more sensitive tests for prostate cancer, increasing numbers of men are undergoing radical prostatectomy. This operation can cause permanent impotence and incontinence. In many cases, it's not advisable or helpful to treat prostate cancer with surgery. Only rarely is it justified in men older than 70.

Other operations in the largely needless category: Knee and back surgery, tonsillectomy.

• **Drug mistakes.** Prescription drugs are another common cause of iatrogenic illness. *Reason:* Doctors aren't as savvy about drugs or their side effects as they should be. In many cases, they're guilty of overprescribing.

Guarding against iatrogenic illness...

• Before agreeing to an X ray or any other diagnostic test, ask your doctor to explain why the test is necessary. Ask him/her, "What will the results of this test tell you?" This key question makes you a participant in your diagnosis and treatment...and prevents you from being tested needlessly. If the doctor responds, "We won't know until we look," *call a halt.* Doctors should *always* know what a test is expected to reveal.

• Ask whether any recommended test or surgical procedure will be painful, dangerous or costly—and whether its benefits outweigh its drawbacks. Get a rundown of *all* options. Is there a less risky procedure? What would happen if you *didn't* have a certain procedure?

• To confirm the findings of a test, get a second opinion. Ask your doctor to recommend an *independent* expert—one not affiliated with the hospital. Otherwise—especially if the test is analyzed at the hospital—the second opinion might come from the same person who gave the first report...or a co-worker reluctant to contradict a colleague.

• If you'll be heavily dependent on medications during your hospital stay, try to choose a hospital with a pharmacy on each patient floor. This arrangement helps assure efficient, quality care—and minimizes prescription mistakes and other drug-related errors.

• If you're hooked up to an intravenous (IV) line, insist that the IV solution be mixed by the hospital pharmacist—not your nurse. IV bags opened by nurses tend to become contaminated with microorganisms circulating in the hospital. If these "bugs" enter your bloodstream, they can cause serious complications.

For complete sterility: Ask that the mixture be prepared under a *laminar flow hood.* This device keeps microbes at bay using a constant stream of sterile air over the pharmacist's hands and the IV bag.

• Make sure the pharmacy obtains a copy of your doctor's drug orders. If a nurse phones in the orders, there's a chance he/she will mispronounce a drug name or misinterpret the doctor's wishes. *Danger:* Different drugs often have similar spellings and pronunciations—though they have dramatically different effects on the body.

• Learn as much as you can about your ailment and the drugs and procedures used to treat it. Find out not only the names of the drugs you need to take, but also their doses, sizes—*even their shapes and colors.* Doing so may enable you to spot a mistake.

• Never tolerate discourtesy from any hospital personnel. If you're treated rudely or without respect, it's within your rights to get yourself off a table and leave an examination room.

If you and your nurse aren't getting along, talk things over first. If this approach fails, call in a mediator—your doctor, the nurse's superior or the hospital's patient representative. Explore various options, including being cared for by another nurse.

• Have a family member or friend with you as much as possible during your hospital stay. Trying to cope with an illness while staying alert to possible mistakes can be tough to handle on your own. Your ally can help you ask questions and make sure that hospital personnel are doing the right things at the right times, such as taking blood when they're supposed to, giving you the right medication, etc.

• Don't tolerate needless pain. Doctors often *undermedicate* their patients' pain for fear of turning them into addicts—a largely groundless fear.

Key question: Does your pain medication keep you reasonably comfortable between doses, or does pain return before the next dose? If you'd like this medication upped, tell your nurse. If he/she doesn't respond, ask for the head nurse or contact your doctor or another doctor.

Be sure to ask about alternative methods of pain relief, including biofeedback, relaxation and acupuncture. If you have a living will, be sure that it specifies that you'd like to be given enough painkillers to be as pain-free as possible.

• Before giving the go-ahead for any form of treatment, make sure the benefits outweigh the potential hazards. Don't be talked into "fad" operations. Get second—and third—opinions. When in doubt, don't proceed—especially when considering elective surgery.

Tell your doctor, nurse or patient representative about hospital procedures that you find intrusive or unnecessary, such as frequent awakenings during the night for blood samples or temperature readings. Above all, never take anything for granted—and question, question, question.

Source: Charles B. Inlander, president of the People's Medical Society, Allentown, PA, and a lecturer at Yale University School of Medicine, New Haven, CT. Mr. Inlander is coauthor of more than a dozen books on health topics, including *Take This Book to the Hospital with You.* People's Medical Society.

How to Protect Yourself From Your Doctor

The best doctors are sometimes the ones with the poorest personalities. Bedside manner is not necessarily a relevant criterion. *The prime dos and don'ts:*

• Do ask questions. Many patients are intimidated by the doctor's professional status. Don't be. Ask your prospective doctor about his medical philosophy. Pose specific questions—for example, does he believe in taking heroic measures in terminal cases? Look for a doctor who is attuned to the patient/doctor relationship. Be wary of a doctor who puts you off, who takes a question as a personal affront, or who says things like, "Don't worry, I'll take care of it."

• Don't be impressed by the diplomas on the wall. Many are probably from organizations that the doctor joined for a fee. *What you should know:* Is the doctor board-certified in his specialty?

• Do find out about the doctor's hospital affiliation. Is he on the medical staff of a hospital? Is it a local hospital of good reputation?

• Don't go straight to a specialist when you're having a problem. Specialists can be blind to any ailment that doesn't fall into their specialty. Have a generalist or internist assess your problem and send you to the appropriate specialist.

What else to consider…

A doctor should be willing to reevaluate and reassess. Too many doctors are ready to write off a patient as neurotic. I've had any number of cases in which people judged neurotic had something physically wrong with them.

A patient has an absolute right to a second opinion. The mere fact that the doctor doesn't suggest it is no reason to assume you don't need one. Many doctors become unpleasant when a patient mentions getting a second opinion. Ignore that and get one anyway if you have any questions as to a doctor's evaluation or if surgery is recommended.

You have a right to your medical records. You'll need them for the second opinion. Most states have statutes that make it mandatory to give patients a copy (not the original) of their records.

Obstetric malpractice…

Since obstetrics is the most common area of malpractice today, there are certain points that pregnant women should be aware of:

• The doctor, not the nurse, should give the care. Nurses can take a blood pressure or pulse reading, but the doctor should do the internal examinations.

• Any woman in a high-risk group should get special attention. Women over 35 with their first baby need that special attention. So do women with a history of toxemia in the family and women with a cardiac, renal, or diabetic condition.

• Make sure your obstetrician does all the basics—asks a lot of questions, does regular urine tests, and pays attention to your weight and changes in uterine height. Special attention should be given to swelling, headaches, and post-term pregnancy.

Hospital malpractice…

In a hospital you can't interview everyone who will be giving you care. But there are some things you can do:

•Voice your complaints…and I don't mean about the tasteless food. Complain about things like an IV bottle that's been empty for an hour, or a catheter left in, or a doctor who says he'll be back in 10 minutes and instead returns the next day. Make friends with the nurses. Be polite but firm about what you need.

•Make sure the doctors and nurses know what you're allergic to. Be sure the allergies are adequately documented in the health records.

•Find out, especially in a teaching hospital, who is giving you care. Not everyone in a white coat is automatically qualified. You have a right to know how much training the doctor administering your treatment has received.

•Make sure you have given informed consent to any invasive procedure. The biggest issue in my office is patients who routinely sign anything that's put in front of them. Find out the risks and alternatives to any invasive procedure. Request an oral explanation in layman's terms. Make sure you totally understand anything you sign.

•Learn the names of the drugs you're getting. Find out what they're for and what their side effects are. Then, if someone hands you a drug you don't recognize, question it. If you're taking drugs from more than one doctor, be sure each knows what the other has prescribed, including over-the-counter medications.

•Ask the reason for each test you're given.

•Tell the doctor or nurse your full health history. Should malpractice occur, you won't have a leg to stand on in court if you've withheld vital information.

•Before you're discharged from the hospital, get full instructions about what you should do after you leave. Write down your questions about diet, bed rest, exercise, medication, or anything else that concerns you.

•If you believe that you have been injured by the hospital or the doctor, consult a lawyer who specializes in malpractice. Don't wait too long. There are different statutes of limitation in various jurisdictions.

Source: Leonard C. Arnold, MD, JD, Chicago.

Assessing Your Doctor

1. Do I have the chance to express comfortably all that I feel?

2. Does the doctor really listen to me?

3. After communicating with my doctor, do I feel relieved or frustrated?

4. Do I share with my doctor the responsibility for my own well being?

5. Am I given the freedom of choice among different treatment plans?

6. When in doubt, do I feel comfortable in voicing my need for a second opinion?

7. Does the doctor share his/her knowledge without intimidation?

8. Do I follow my doctor's instructions, or do I use my own judgment?

9. Do I perceive that my doctor is doing everything possible to help me?

10. Does the relationship with my doctor fulfill my expectations and needs?

Source: *Holistic Medicine*, 4101 Lake Boone Trail, Raleigh, NC 27607.

Questionable Doctors

Discipline of doctors remains spotty at best. In 1992, only 1,974 *serious* disciplinary actions were taken against physicians. Yet each year, 150,000 to 300,000 Americans die in hospitals as a result of medical malpractice. A new report lists 10,289 doctors—1.7% of all doctors—disciplined by state or federal authorities for negligence, misprescribing drugs, substance abuse, sexual abuse, defaulting on loans or letting licenses lapse. *Scary:* Of the physicians listed for the most serious offenses, only one-third lost practice privileges.

Source: Sidney Wolfe, MD, director, Public Citizen Health Research Group, Washington, DC.

How to Get Doctors To Talk to You On the Phone

It's generally very hard to find out whether a doctor treats your particular problem or uses the procedure you need until you visit the office—a waste of your time and money, since you'll probably have to wait for the appointment and pay for the visit.

Instead: Try to get the information on the telephone. *Obstacle:* Most office staffs tend to overprotect doctors from such calls—even, on occasion, contrary to the doctor's inclination.

Trick: Refer to yourself on the phone as "doctor." It's amazing how that can open doors with medical professionals. Not all people feel comfortable with such deception, but given the payoff, it should be considered.

Source: Susan G. Cole, editor of *The Practical Guide to Cancer Care*, Health Improvement Research Corp., New York.

How to Get the Best From Your Doctor

Increasingly, patients are discovering they can no longer be passive in the doctor-patient relationship. They have to take an active interest to be sure they get not only the best care, but, in some instances, just adequate care—as the soaring number of medical malpractice suits seems to indicate.

Here is a valuable checklist of potential problems and advice for dealing with today's doctors…

• *Checkups:* The usual procedure is for a doctor to perform a physical checkup and do lab work-ups during the examination. Then, a few days later, the doctor's nurse calls and relates an oversimplified assessment of the lab results.

Instead: Arrange for a preliminary visit so that lab work can be done before the physical exam. That way, the doctor can go over the results of the tests in detail, answering any questions during the regular exam. If there is need for further lab work, it can be done later.

• *Medical records:* In most cases, your medical records are kept by the doctor. So if you move, decide to change doctors, or subsequently see a specialist, you have to go through a long procedure to get your records.

Instead: Ask for copies of all records and keep them in your own permanent file. *Especially useful:* Electrocardiograms, blood tests, and X rays. The doctor might charge you a nominal fee to make copies.

• *Doctor-patient relations:* Doctors usually prefer to be called "Doctor." Yet they frequently call patients by their first names.

That small difference helps to perpetuate the role of doctor as parent and patient as child—where the patient isn't expected to question the doctor's orders. This leaves the patient in a position of not sharing responsibility for his own health.

Instead: As a symbolic gesture, settle whether the two of you are on a first- or last-name basis.

More ways to win…

• If the doctor always keeps you waiting, call before you leave for your appointment. *Even better:* Ask someone else to call and explain that your professional duties make your schedule very tight.

• If the doctor diagnoses an illness and prescribes drugs, take notes on the name of the condition and the drugs being prescribed.

• If you're overcome by the news of the illness (which isn't unusual), call the doctor after you've had some time to calm down and frame any questions about the prognosis and the method of treatment. Also, arrange to bring a relative or friend with you to emotionally-charged doctor visits.

That'll give you the emotional space to "collapse" or to go temporarily "deaf" to bad news, while your companion is able to listen, ask questions, and interpret what the doctor says. The period right after serious illness is disclosed is hard to handle, so make arrangements to compensate for it.

Drugs…

Since even the "safest" drugs usually have some side effects, it's prudent to insist that you be included in any decisions about prescriptions.

Frequently, the decision isn't only which drug to take, but whether one should be taken at all. In some cases, there are alternatives to drugs…changes in diet, lifestyle, or exercise. Many doctors believe, perhaps correctly, that most patients don't feel that an office visit for an illness is complete unless a pill is prescribed. Make it clear that you don't feel that way.

• Insist that the druggist include the manufacturer's fact sheet with any prescription you're given. Read it. It's technical, but with the aid of a medical dictionary you may discover things about the drug you'll want to discuss with the doctor. It's hard, if not impossible, for doctors to know current information on all drugs. You may discover that the dose is excessive or that the medication is no longer considered effective for your condition.

• If you do take a drug that has side effects (dizziness, stomach distress, etc.), start taking it during a weekend or when you're home, so you'll be in a safer and more comfortable place when they hit.

Source: Susan G. Cole, editor of *The Practical Guide to Cancer Care*, Health Improvement Research Corp., New York.

Getting Fast Emergency Medical Care

Inside information: If you arrive at a hospital by ambulance, you usually will receive a higher priority…even if you could have gotten to the hospital without the ambulance. If your condition is serious enough that taking an ambulance isn't frivolous, it's a good strategy to call one. *Best:* Arriving in the hospital's own ambulance, because you automatically become one of the hospital's patients…and its patients receive priority.

For the same reason, the ambulance of a local volunteer unit or fire district is a good choice. These people know the local ER personnel, and they are your neighbors. *Recommended:* Contribute to their fund drives and post your contribution stickers.

If your condition is very serious: Call the police—always dial 911. Police response with an ambulance—or transport by the police themselves, if no ambulance is available—will help facilitate matters at the hospital. *Helpful:* Call the ambulance a "bus"—the inside term used by police. *Aim:* To get them to assume that you or a close relative is a cop and render service accordingly.

Source: Harry Alberts, MSW, certified social worker, Box 402, Commack, NY 11725, 718-353-HELP. Mr. Alberts was formerly with the New York State Department of Health.

How to Get VIP Treatment in a Hospital

The first thing an admitting clerk does when you're brought into a hospital is slip a plastic tag with an identity number onto your wrist. From that point on, like it or not, you are a number to most of the hospital staff.

Being a number instead of a name can be an awful shock. It means that you may be treated as if you have no identity—except for your symptoms, vital signs and medical treatment.

Fortunately, there are steps you can take to improve that treatment. And those steps, if successful, not only will make you feel more comfortable and human during your hospital visit, they could dramatically affect your state of health by the time you're ready to be discharged. In fact, it may be the issue that determines whether you leave alive or dead.

What you can do:

Think of a hospital as a sort of huge, complex hotel—however, one that dispenses more than food, entertainment and lodging.

As you obviously know, a hospital dispenses both life-saving and life-threatening services. A moment's inattention at a hospital can lead to tragedy.

So how do you get the hospital to treat you like a person instead of a number?

In general, you've got to use the same techniques you use in other aspects of your personal and business life. The key word is assertiveness. That's not to say you should complain and be demanding—although, as you'll see, that may be necessary under certain circumstances.

Finding the right doctor:

The first step in getting VIP treatment in a hospital should be taken long before you're admitted—and that's finding a doctor who can provide the leverage you'll need. You want someone with more than an M.D. after his name.

Every community has a clique of doctors who have "political" clout. Usually, these are physicians who serve on the local hospital's board of directors. Be aware, however, that a doctor with clout doesn't necessarily have the skills or any other attributes that make a physician a superior healer. Do you want such a person as your personal physician? Generally speaking, the answer is no, but there are exceptions. If you're satisfied that such a doctor can serve double-duty, so to speak, then you need go no farther.

The drawbacks:

Aside from the possibility that such a doctor may be more expert in a boardroom than an operating room there are other potential problems.

The most serious:

He may be more interested in keeping his professional calendar and the institution's beds filled than in your welfare. Of course, there are ways to get around that. If he wants to admit you to the hospital for treatment and there is any doubt in your mind about this decision, ask for a consultation.

Generally speaking, it's always wise to get a consultation for any complex medical procedure—and the likelihood is that the procedure he's recommending is relatively complex if he wants to hospitalize you. So by asking for a consultation, you're not showing lack of faith in your doctor.

Caveat: However, we've heard of many instances where doctors are annoyed when a patient announces that he would like a consulta- tion or second opinion. If you ever face a less-than-cooperative response to such a request, it would be prudent to seek out another doctor immediately. It's well within your rights to consult with as many physicians as you wish.

The personal touch:

To guarantee better attention once you know that you're going to spend time in the hospital, make a date with the hospital administrator. He may or may not be a doctor—but in any case, he is a businessman, so you can be sure he speaks the same language as you. Introduce yourself. Tell him that you're a little concerned about your hospital stay and that you'd appreciate it if he'd take a personal interest in your case.

He'll get the message, and in all likelihood, he'll take steps to be sure that you're well cared for. Now that you've made your presence known, he will probably, out of courtesy, call the head of nursing and the admitting office and tell them you are coming to the hospital and that they should be expecting you. It's just such words, without pressure, that may make all the difference in the way you're subsequently treated.

Once you're in the hospital:

Even if you've failed or haven't had the time to take the above steps, there are still things you can do to ensure good treatment, if not VIP treatment.

If you're not physically up to it, your spouse or a friend or relative may have to help you, but if you're feeling well enough, you can take the following steps yourself.

•During the admission procedure, ask what rooms are available. You may prefer a private room, or for the sake of company, you may want to share a room with someone else. If you do want to share, ask about your potential partner's medical status to be sure that you can deal with his illness.

•After settling into your room, ask to see the dietitian. Explain that you understand that the hospital is not a hotel, but within reasonable bounds, and limited by doctor's orders, there are foods that you do and do not like. Itemize them. If you present your request with tact, the dietitian will probably try to meet your reasonable requests.

•Go out of your way to be polite to the nursing staff. They are your lifeline—literally. If the nurses take a dislike to you, the recuperation period will not be smooth.

•It's not tacky to provide small favors, such as a box of candy, and even flowers, on each of the three nursing shifts: the 8 a.m. to 4 p.m., the 4 p.m. to midnight, and midnight to 8 a.m. Don't offer a gratuity until you're ready to be discharged. Nurses are professionals, and most would resent the offer. But if you received extra special care from a nurse during your stay, a tasteful gift isn't inappropriate.

•Make it clear that you'd like to know what medication or treatment is being given to you beforehand. That will require a discussion with your doctor. Most doctors work on the premise that patients don't want to know too much, and so only provide information as it's necessary or if the patient specifically requests it.

Why you should want this information:

Unfortunately, mistakes are made now and then, but if you ask the nurse, "What are these pills?" or, "What exactly will you be doing to me?", and she has orders from your doctor to provide that information on request, then it gives the staff the opportunity to double-check what they are doing and it gives you a chance to say, "Wait a minute!" if an obvious error is being committed.

How to complain:

If you're not happy with your care, explain your complaint firmly and politely to the nurse. If that gets you no place, ask to speak to the head nurse. And if that fails, you may have to speak to either your doctor or the hospital administrator. Usually, when you reach that level, and you're not being unreasonable, steps will be taken to satisfy your complaint and resolve your problem.

Fighting Premature Hospital Discharge

Patients are usually more than happy to leave the hospital following elective or emergency care. But some patients, mostly Medicare recipients, are being discharged before they've fully recovered.

Culprit: A pricing system established by Medicare that puts hospitals under pressure to discharge patients "quicker and sicker." Hospitals now have incentives to skimp on resources, and subtly devise ways to cut corners and increase their own profits. Medicare recipients include about 33 million people, mostly elderly.

You can fight an unjust early discharge. *Here's how:*

•Have your attending physician argue your case with the clinical director, who monitors length of stay. If the hospital still decides you must leave, appeal to your state's peer review organization, a government body that monitors hospital practices.

Although this may be a cumbersome process, the hospital will allow you a two-day grace period during the action. *Comforting:* Once you've begun an appeal process, chances are you will be allowed to stay longer. Hospitals know if a patient dies, they may face a malpractice suit.

•Contact the American Association of Retired Persons if you feel you've been mistreated. Few people realize the considerable power of this 28-million-member consumer organization. Write to the executive director of your local or regional chapter. The AARP can exert direct and indirect pressure on a hospital's chief executive officer.

The new pricing system resulted from Medicare's establishment of about 500 different groupings of inpatient and outpatient medical procedures, known as diagnostic related groups (DRGs).

Until five years ago, Medicare reimbursed a hospital for the cost of a procedure. Now Medicare uses DRGs to determine the average length of stay for a procedure and prices it accordingly. If the patient leaves before that "average period," the hospital makes money. If he stays longer, the hospital loses money. *Result:* Average length of stay in hospitals has dropped dramatically in the last few years.

On the positive side, DRGs have eliminated inefficiencies. Few patients need to stay longer than the designated period. Stays longer than necessary increase the chance of hospital-borne infections. However, no one should be discharged before it's medically wise

Source: Uwe Reinhardt, PhD, James Madison professor of political economy, Woodrow Wilson School, Princeton University.

Better Vocal Cord Repair

In the past, vocal cord implants had to be custom-carved to fit the larynx (voice box) as the patient lay on the operating table. New implants, made of the ceramic material *hydroxyapatite*, come in five sizes. The surgeon slips one into an opening cut into the patient's anesthetized throat and then asks the patient to recite the alphabet. If the patient doesn't like what he hears, the surgeon tries another size. More than 80% of those who have undergone this procedure report significant improvements in their ability to talk.

Source: Charles W. Cummings, MD, professor and director, division of otolaryngology and head and neck surgery, Johns Hopkins University School of Medicine, Baltimore. Results of his surgery on 39 patients were reported in *Annals of Otology, Rhinology and Otolaryngology*, 4507 Laclede Ave., St. Louis 63108.

Anticoagulant Danger

Anticoagulants taken to reduce risk of cardiovascular disease can lead to severe internal bleeding—if doses are too high. *Self-defense:* If you're on anticoagulants, ask your doctor about prescribing the lowest effective dose. Have periodic blood tests to check your anticoagulant levels. Avoid aspirin. Alert your doctor if there are any changes in your diet or use of alcohol.

Source: C. Seth Landefeld, MD, senior research associate, department of medicine, Cleveland Veterans Affairs Medical Center, and associate professor of medicine, Case Western Reserve University, Cleveland. His review of risks from anticoagulant-related bleeding was published in the *American Journal of Medicine*, Box 7722, Riverton, NJ 08077.

Which Painkiller Is Best for You?

With so many brightly colored boxes crowding drugstore shelves these days, choosing an over-the-counter painkiller can be a difficult and frustrating experience.

Just a few years ago, aspirin and acetaminophen (sold primarily under the Tylenol name) were the only choices. Ibuprofen (Advil, Motrin and Nuprin) came next. And now the painkiller naproxen (Aleve) is available over the counter, too.

Which painkiller is right for you? People differ in their response to these drugs, and a medication that works for one problem might not work for another.* It's a good idea to try several ones and see which works best for which conditions.

A look at what's available...

Aspirin...

Bayer aspirin, Bufferin, Excedrin, etc., are very effective for treating headache, fever and muscle pain resulting from overuse, sprains or mild cramps.

Problem: Aspirin can irritate the stomach—even cause it to bleed. It generally should be avoided by people with ulcers or inflammation of the stomach or esophagus.

Special danger: Aspirin can cause a potentially fatal inflammation of the brain called Reye's Syndrome when taken by children with a viral infection like chicken pox. Feverish children under age 16 should *never* be given aspirin—even baby aspirin. They should be given acetaminophen instead.

Acetaminophen...

It's good for headache and fever—but not so good for muscle or joint pain. It's less irritating to the stomach than any other nonprescription painkiller.

Caution: In higher-than-recommended daily doses, acetaminophen can damage or even destroy the liver. You should take no more than eight extra-strength (500 mg) or 12 regular (325 mg) tablets a day.

*Over-the-counter painkillers are appropriate only for minor aches, pains, fever and inflammation. If you're experiencing severe pain, see a doctor.

Ibuprofen...

Ibuprofen is highly effective against menstrual cramps and other forms of inflammation. It's less irritating to the stomach than aspirin—but more irritating than acetaminophen.

For maximum benefit, take ibuprofen before you start to feel pain. Obviously, you can't predict a headache. But if you always get cramps around the same time of the month, for instance, or if you're preparing for a tough tennis match, consider taking a precautionary dose.

Naproxen...

There's been a lot of hype about naproxen in recent weeks. Naproxen is a very effective painkiller. Like ibuprofen, it's much better at controlling toothache pain than aspirin or acetaminophen. And—it lasts for up to 12 hours, as compared with four hours for other nonprescription painkillers.

Naproxen may be a little more expensive than other painkillers. But when you take into account how long it lasts, it's not out of line.

Like aspirin and ibuprofen, naproxen belongs to a family of drugs called nonsteroidal anti-inflammatory drugs (NSAIDs). These drugs are very similar, so if you've had an allergic reaction to aspirin or ibuprofen, you should probably steer clear of naproxen, too.

More about painkillers...

• Never take more than one type of painkiller at a time. Doing so can cause severe reactions, including increased stomach irritation, ulcers and bleeding. If the first drug you try doesn't bring relief, wait four hours—or, in the case of naproxen, 12 hours—before trying something else.

• Avoid alcohol when taking painkillers. Combining aspirin, ibuprofen or naproxen with alcohol can irritate the stomach—or, in extreme cases, cause bleeding or ulcers. If you typically have more than three drinks a day, talk to your doctor before taking any over-the-counter painkiller.

• Beware of painkillers labeled "extra-strength." Such preparations can contain large amounts of caffeine, which can cause sleeplessness and other problems. Read labels carefully before buying.

• Don't be fooled by "buffered" products. Consumers often assume that these products—which contain an antacid—are easier on the stomach. Not so. Buffered aspirin is absorbed faster than regular or "enteric-coated" aspirin, but it's no easier on the stomach.

Enteric tablets *do* protect your stomach against irritation, because they're not absorbed until they reach the intestine. But they take longer to act. So, if you want quick relief for a headache, sprain or fever, nonenteric formulations are probably better.

• Buy generic. Generic forms of aspirin, acetaminophen and ibuprofen are just as effective—and much cheaper—than their brand-name counterparts. Naproxen isn't yet available in generic form.

• Watch out for marketing gimmicks. Some drug makers attempt to pass off a general-purpose painkiller as a remedy for a specific problem—back pain, for instance. Others claim that their remedy has been endorsed by an independent consumer's group, even though the remedy is identical to remedies that haven't been endorsed. Pain "powders," popular in the South, are nothing more than powdered aspirin or acetaminophen.

Source: Timothy Fagan, MD, associate professor of medicine and pharmacology, University of Arizona College of Medicine, Tucson. He works extensively with painkillers in clinical studies and in his private practice.

Intravenous Fluid Danger

Emergency intravenous fluids may do more harm than good when given to patients with severe bleeding. For decades, bleeding has been treated with an intravenous solution of saline or Ringer's lactate—given immediately, in an attempt to elevate the patient's blood pressure and to prevent organ damage and shock.

New finding: Among patients given intravenous fluids immediately, 62% survived. The survival rate among patients given intravenous fluids after the bleeding had stopped was 70%.

Also: Patients given fluids *after* the stoppage of bleeding left the hospital sooner and had fewer complications.

Theory: Fluids encourage bleeding both by keeping blood pressure high and by diluting coagulants in the blood.

Source: William H. Bickell, MD, director of research, St. Francis Hospital, Tulsa. His 37-month study of 289 trauma patients treated at Houston's Ben Taub General Hospital was published in *The New England Journal of Medicine*, 10 Shattuck St., Boston 02115.

Coal-Tar Treatment Warning

Coal-tar solutions used to treat psoriasis are highly flammable. For this reason, smoking is forbidden among patients undergoing coal-tar treatments. But, according to a recent article in *The New England Journal of Medicine*, one patient whose skin had just been treated with coal tar lit a cigarette—and burst into flame. Fortunately, he was able to extinguish the fire without serious injury.

Source: *Medical Abstracts Newsletter*, Box 2170, Teaneck, NJ 07666.

New Test for Prostate Cancer

The Reverse Transcriptase Polymerase Chain Reaction (RT-PCR) test is better at detecting the *spread* of prostate cancer than current diagnostic tests, including bone scan, CT scan, MRI or ultrasound. It uses DNA technology to detect even a single prostate cell in the bloodstream. The experimental test is not yet widely available.

Source: Aaron E. Katz, MD, assistant professor of urology, Columbia-Presbyterian Medical Center, New York City. His study of 65 men with localized prostate cancer and 18 men with metastatic prostate cancer was published in *Urology*, 105 Raider Blvd., Belle Meade, NJ 08502.

Doctors Do Not Eat Well

Most prefer red meat and chicken to fish… only 20% say they eat the recommended five servings of fruits and vegetables daily…and 55% are overweight.

Source: Nationwide study commissioned by Sudler & Hennessey, the health care and pharmaceuticals advertising division of Young & Rubicam, reported in *Adweek*, 1515 Broadway, New York 10036.

Drugs that Work Best When Taken on an Empty Stomach

Food slows the absorption of certain drugs, so they are best taken without food. If nausea or stomach upset results, discuss it with your physician or pharmacist. Common drugs that fall into this category include:

- Acetaminophen* (Tylenol, etc.)
- Enteric-coated aspirin
- Ampicillin
- Erythromycin
- Epsom salts
- Levodopa
- Mineral oil
- Magnesium hydroxide (milk of magnesia)
- Penicillin G and V
- Tetracycline
- Procainamide

Source: *50+: The Graedon's People's Pharmacy for Older Adults* by Joe and Teresa Graedon. Bantam Books.

Retin-A—Will It Make Skin Look Younger?

Retin-A can rectify, and may even prevent, the effects of chronic sun exposure on your skin—roughness, loss of elasticity, coarseness,

*Generic names are given.

brown spots, sallowness, precancerous lesions, blackheads around the eyes, etc.

Retin-A cannot, however, prevent the effects of the normal aging process, which are usually less severe than those caused by the sun and include roughness, laxity, and benign tumors.

It can:

• Improve skin color by increasing blood flow. Photoaging, which decreases blood flow, causes skin to become yellowish. As Retin-A increases blood flow, the complexion turns rosy again.

• Restore elasticity by boosting collagen production, which is usually retarded by photoaging.

• Thicken the epidermis by increasing cell turnover, which is also slowed by photoaging, and by stimulating the growth of the tiny blood vessels in the skin.

• Eliminate blotchiness and sun spots by improving the distribution of melanosomes (pigment granules) in the skin.

• Produce smoother, non-scaly skin by accelerating the shedding of the outer layer of dead cells. *Also:* The skin cells underneath, which then push their way to the surface, are more normal and look better than photoaged cells. *Result:* A smooth, more even skin color and texture.

• Correct sun-induced DNA damage by regulating abnormal cell reproduction. *Also:* Retin-A could lessen risk of skin cancer, but this hasn't been proven yet. Preliminary evidence shows that it reduces actinic keratoses—precancerous lesions.

None of the vitamin A products sold over-the-counter produce the same results as Retin-A. Although some of them may end up being converted to vitamin A acid in the skin, the effect is not significant.

Source: Dr. Alan Shalita, chairman, department of dermatology, State University of New York Health Science Center, Brooklyn.

Advantages of Buying Drugs Overseas

Many drugs that require a prescription in the US are sold over the counter in other countries. *Example:* Cough syrup with codeine.

Even when a medication requires a prescription overseas, most foreign doctors will give you one if you say you have a prescription in the US.

Prescription drugs that are commonly sold over the counter outside the US:

• Amoxicillin antibiotic
• Digoxin cardiac regulator
• Erythromycin antibiotic
• Lasix diuretic
• Megistrole codeine analgesic
• Metronidazole antifungal
• Motrin analgesic
• Penicillin antibiotic
• Prednisone steroid
• Propranolol cardiac regulator

Rules about prescriptions are much looser overseas. In Latin America, for instance, doctors commonly write large-quantity (100 tablets plus), refillable prescriptions for drugs that in the US require a new prescription each time the drug is dispensed.

Outside the US you can buy some medications that aren't available here, even with a prescription.

Also more readily available overseas: Experimental drugs.

Many people who suffer from fatal and very serious diseases are turned down for experimental treatment in the US. *Reasons:* There are manufacturers' restrictions on which patients are eligible for experimentation and there is potential for enormous losses from lawsuits.

The most publicized example is the use of AZT (azidothymidine) for the treatment of AIDS. Because AZT is a new treatment, not all AIDS patients can receive AZT therapy in the US. Treatment is more readily available in France, where researchers at the Pasteur Institute have studied AIDS extensively, and at

Caribbean and Mexican clinics set up solely to administer the drug.

Treatment using interferon for malignant forms of leukemia and melanoma are also available overseas.

The risks: Side effects and proper dosages of experimental medications aren't fully known. That's one of the reasons the Food and Drug Administration hasn't approved them for general use.

Source: Cynthia Ronan, MD, a pharmacologist at Griffin Hospital, 130 Division St., Derby, CT 06718.

How to Protect Yourself Against Disease Mongering

When it comes to treating cancer, heart disease, severe trauma, and other life-threatening ailments, the American health-care system is second to none. Our doctors are highly trained, our drugs carefully screened, our hospitals chockablock with sophisticated medical equipment.

Still, it pays to remember that a desire to aid the afflicted isn't the only motive driving our health-care system. *Also at work:* A powerful and unrelenting urge to maximize profits.

In order to remain in business, doctors, hospitals, diagnostic facilities, drug and medical equipment makers, insurance companies and other recipients of our health-care dollars all need one thing—patients with health insurance. The greater their number, the sicker they are, the more drugs they take, the more tests they undergo… the bigger the industry's profits.

Problem: To get more patients, the health-care industry often resorts to an insidious form of exploitation known as disease-mongering.

D*isease-mongering takes many forms…*

• It's the surgeon who insists upon treating a minor heart ailment with costly and often risky bypass surgery—just to earn more money.

• It's the drug maker that uses manipulative ads to portray the common cold as a debilitating ailment in need of drug therapy.

• It's the diagnostic clinic that sells mammograms even to women for whom there's no evidence that they work.

• It's also the medical journalist who earns his keep by hyping minor illnesses as plagues.

No matter what form disease-mongering takes, however, the result never varies—healthy people are led to believe they're ill or at risk of becoming ill…and persons suffering from minor ailments are led to believe they're seriously ill.

The health-care industry knows that once we're instilled with fear, we'll take action—scheduling costly medical checkups and diagnostic tests at the merest hint of trouble…using cold remedies, painkillers, and other drugs for conditions that clear up even without treatment …gobbling prescription drugs with nasty and potentially harmful side effects…and submitting to surgery that is risky and of questionable benefit.

Watch out for…

• Manipulative ads. Television, newspapers, and magazines are filled with ads for sinus remedies, arthritis pills, headache relievers—and, of course, even baldness cures.

The more often we encounter these ads, the more firmly we're convinced that we need the products they promote. *Reality:* Minor aches and pains, as well as occasional cold or flu symptoms, are a normal part of life. There's no good reason to visit the drugstore every time you sneeze.

To avoid being manipulated:

Each time you choose to read a health ad, ask yourself who really stands to benefit from its message—you or the makers of the product. Are there alternatives? What would happen if you took no action? Use only those products truly beneficial to you.

• "Man-made" diseases. While there's no doubt that broken bones and heart attacks need prompt treatment, not all medical conditions require treatment.

Example: Mild hypertension. The cutoff between "normal" and "high" blood pressure has been set arbitrarily low in this country—as a result, inflating the ranks of the "ill" and maximizing the profit potential for doctors and companies selling antihypertensive drugs. In fact, a blood pressure reading treated in this country with an aggressive drug regimen might be considered normal in England.

Blood pressure isn't the only such "man-made" disease. Elevated cholesterol level is considered a heart-disease risk factor—and rightly so. But often even mildly elevated cholesterol is treated as a disease in its own right. *Result:* People who feel perfectly fine are urged to take harsh and costly drugs, even though evidence of their value is controversial.

And in an effort to sell more estrogen, drug makers are now trying to turn menopause from a natural process into a deficiency disease that needs treatment. The list goes on and on.

To avoid trouble: If a doctor says you're at risk for or already have a particular disease and urges aggressive treatment, follow the advice only if there's solid evidence that the treatment will cut your risk. Get a second opinion, and do your own research.

•Needless diagnostic tests. Doctors order far too many diagnostic tests. Each time you have a mammogram, stress test, cholesterol test, AIDS test, etc., you're taking a risk. Not only that you'll hear bad news, but your test results could be wrong. The test might indicate you're okay when you're really sick, for instance, or that you're sick when you're healthy.

Danger: A "false positive" causes not only needless anxiety, but also labels you as "sick" and thereby jeopardizes your insurability. It can even lead you to seek risky treatments.

Example: There have been cases in which people died during heart surgery scheduled after stress tests mistakenly indicated that they had heart disease. Similarly, mammograms are often urged for women under 40—even though young breasts are usually too dense for accurate X ray readings.

To avoid trouble: For anyone already at reasonably high risk for a particular condition, the potential benefits of being tested generally outweigh the risk of inaccurate results. But if your risk for the ailment is very low, avoid being tested. Ask your doctor to explain your level of risk when making the decision.

Make sure the doctors with whom you discuss your case have no financial stake in performing the test.

Scandalous: Though the conflict of interest in such an arrangement is obvious, many doctors now own their own CT scanners, MRI scanners, and other diagnostic equipment. The more tests they schedule, the more money they make.

•Free screening clinics. These days, free screening is being offered for everything from prostate cancer to high blood pressure. It sounds like a good idea. But in many cases these clinics are set up to bring in more patients …and are more beneficial to their sponsors than to the general public.

Problem: Unreliable readings. Some serious medical problems are missed entirely, while problems are diagnosed in persons who are actually perfectly healthy.

To avoid trouble: Be tested in a doctor's office or a diagnostic facility specializing in medical tests. Make sure the person who interprets the test results is highly experienced.

•Needless surgery. A surprisingly large percentage of operations in this country are performed needlessly—up to 25% by some respectable estimates. Certain procedures are especially likely to be performed inappropriately, including hysterectomy, back surgery, Cesarean sections, and bypass surgery. *Result:* Needless expense, discomfort, and even the risk of fatal complications—all because a surgeon was eager to operate.

To avoid trouble: Always get a second opinion before agreeing to surgery. Many problems frequently treated with surgery can be resolved more cheaply and safely via exercise, changes in diet, physical therapy, and other nonsurgical methods.

•Overbearing doctors. Americans tend to be much more deferential toward doctors than toward lawyers, accountants, and other professionals we employ—and doctors rarely do anything to stop us.

Explanation: Most of us started seeing doctors when we were kids, and we still behave like kids in the presence of them.

Better way: Instead of blindly accepting your doctor's advice, make it a point to discuss all your available options.

Helpful: Calling your doctor by his/her first name—especially if the doctor calls you by yours. Doing so reminds you that you're on an equal footing with one another—that you're hiring the doctor, not the other way around.

•Overly aggressive treatment. Every good doctor knows that too much medical care is just as deleterious as too little. Unfortunately, patients often demand aggressive treatment.

Problem: While such treatment might be warranted for serious ailments, most conditions do just as well with minimal or no treatment. In fact, few medical conditions call for urgent intervention of any kind.

Certainly you should see a doctor right away for obvious injuries, severe pain, or high fever. In many cases, however, it's not only safe to wait a few weeks before seeking medical care, it's the smartest course of action.

Reason: Many conditions improve or disappear without treatment, saving you money, aggravation and more.

Source: Lynn Payer, former editor of *The New York Times Good Health Magazine* and author of several books on medical topics, including *Disease-Mongers: How Doctors, Drug Companies, and Insurers Are Making You Feel Sick.* John Wiley & Sons.

Cosmetic Surgery Do's and Don'ts

These days with so many people undergoing some kind of cosmetic surgery—whether it's a facelift, a nose job or a tummy tuck—it's important to remember that plastic surgery is, after all, surgery. It is not to be taken lightly. Here are my do's and don'ts for people now considering a cosmetic-surgery procedure…

•Choose a doctor you trust. First, you want a surgeon who's competent—he/she should be board-certified or at least board-eligible. If you're not sure, ask the surgeon directly—or check with your local medical society. But equally important is the way you feel about this doctor.

•Ask the surgeon for references—former patients who can testify to his competence. Choose a doctor you feel comfortable with. If you know former patients, talk to them. If you are uncomfortable with your doctor, it may affect your willingness to approach him with questions.

•Ask questions. Informed patients make good patients. You're paying good money to talk with an expert, so get your money's worth by asking everything you want to know about the procedure—the anticipated outcome, recovery time, costs…

If you don't understand something, ask to have it explained again. Write down the responses. During an initial consultation there's usually so much technical information discussed that the average patient retains only about 50% of it. Having written answers in hand will be a tremendous plus after you leave the office.

•Keep an open mind. People often come in to see the surgeon already loaded down with information—so many statistics and anecdotes from friends, relatives and magazine articles that they don't tune in to what the doctor is saying.

It's okay to challenge the surgeon's remarks with something you may have read or heard, but remember that everyone responds to procedures differently—your neighbor's experiences may not be the same as yours. Put aside your own beliefs and preconceptions long enough to really focus on what the doctor is telling you.

•Don't ignore the risks. Too many people assume that a nose job, say, or liposuction is so common that it's risk-free. All surgery carries risk.

Examples: It's very rare, but it's possible for a facial nerve to be damaged during a facelift and result in partial paralysis of the face. And TV talk-show host Jenny Jones went public with the serious problems she experienced with her breast implants, which she subsequently had removed.

The doctor should explain what your risks are—and if he doesn't, you should ask.

•Be wary of doctors who recommend procedures you didn't ask for. It's quite possible that a surgeon will give you a good suggestion you never considered. For instance, you might come in for a nose job, and the doctor might suggest that you also have a chin implant, to better balance your entire face.

But be alert to someone who suddenly tries to encourage you to have, say, breast implants when you're there for a facelift.

•Answer all questions honestly. During the initial consultation, the surgeon will—and should—ask you a lot of questions involving your health, your habits and even your personal life that may seem irrelevant or nosy…but they're not. They will help him assess whether you're a good candidate for surgery, as well as how well the procedure will turn out.

These questions may include:

•Do you smoke?

•Do you take any medications?

•Do you have a heart condition?

For whatever reason you may not want to answer the questions, but it's critical that you do so.

Examples: You might not want to admit that you smoke or when you had your last cigarette. But smoking can compromise the circulation to the skin, and smokers who have facelifts have a higher incidence of complications, so I generally tell patients to stop smoking six to eight weeks prior to surgery.

Or, a doctor may tell you to stop taking aspirin for a week before surgery, because aspirin has a blood-thinning effect—and you want your blood to clot properly during the operation. If the surgeon doesn't ask, volunteer any information you think might be important.

•Don't assume you know the best solution to your particular problem. The surgeon should, of course, consider any procedure you request, but he might recommend an alternative that may work better for you.

Example: You want surgery done on your eyelids to help correct a tired look, but what you might actually need is a forehead lift to raise your eyebrows.

Or you believe that liposuction will "cure" your obesity, but liposuction is not a weight reduction operation—it's a procedure designed to improve certain parts of the body that can't be trimmed any other way, such as "saddlebags" on an otherwise slim person.

The professional doctor will steer you in the right direction.

•Don't assume you can't have plastic surgery because you're "too old." The age of the patients coming to the operating table these days is getting older and older. Although the optimum age for a first facelift is from about 48 to 60 years old, people in their 80s are having them now.

The state of your health is more important to a plastic surgeon than your age, and if you're in generally good health, you may be a fine candidate for surgery.

•Examine your reasons for having surgery. During the initial consultation the doctor will probably ask, "Why are you having this surgery done?" If you're having a facelift because you think it'll enhance your chances to get a job, or simply because you want to like what you see in the mirror better, those are valid reasons.

But if you're doing it to win back a wife who left you for a younger man or because your new girlfriend wishes you would, those are poor reasons.

Plastic surgery should never be done to solve an emotional crisis or because you expect it to make you a different person. If you're doing it for someone else, rather than for yourself… reconsider.

Source: Stephen Cotlar, MD, a Houston-based plastic surgeon certified by the American Board of Plastic Surgery.

Smart Ways to Cut Your Medical Bills

In the 10 years between 1980 and 1990, US expenditures on health care more than doubled.

In 1990, each citizen's share of the bill was $2,566. By the year 2000, just five years from now, the Health Care Financing Administration predicts that each share will soar to $5,712. That's $22,848 for a family of four.

Here's how to stretch your health care dollar right now—without sacrificing top-quality care...

1. Stay well. The cheapest illness to treat is the one you never get. Adjust your lifestyle to reduce your risk of serious (and expensive) ailments—particularly cancer and heart disease.

What to do: Exercise for at least 30 minutes three times a week (see a doctor first if you're older than 35 or have a medical condition)... eat a low-fat, high-fiber diet...have no more than two drinks a day...and don't smoke.

2. Take advantage of free health care. In many parts of the country, shopping malls and drugstores offer everything from eye exams and flu shots to screenings for high blood pressure, diabetes and cancer.

These services are not scams. Yes, they publicize the store or hospital offering them. But they also provide free valuable care. The same tests can cost upward of $200 in a doctor's office.

3. Pick the highest deductible you can afford. Health insurance policies with high deductibles charge lower premiums. If you're young and in good health, for instance, pushing your deductible to $5,000 saves you up to 40% on premiums.

4. Read your insurance policy very carefully. Find out exactly what's covered, and be sure to submit claims for *everything* for which you can expect reimbursement.

People often assume they can't get reimbursed for incidental items—the small lancets diabetics use to obtain blood samples, for instance. Many policies do cover such items. But you have to submit a claim for them before you can be reimbursed.

5. Ask your doctor if he/she "accepts assignment." That means he accepts the portion that the health insurance company pays as full payment for your bill. More doctors take assignment than you might think, because collecting from nonpaying patients is such a hassle.

6. Avoid emergency rooms. In a true emergency, of course, a visit to the ER can save your life. But using the ER for nonemergency care is very expensive. You'll pay up to 10 times more than if you got the same treatment in your doc-

tor's office.

If your child has an earache Saturday night, phone your doctor. He should be able to give you an idea of how serious the problem is—and may be able to treat the illness swiftly and cheaply by writing a prescription...or by recommending simple at-home care.

7. Scrutinize your hospital bills. Hospital bills are notoriously inaccurate, and in cases where inaccuracies occur, they favor the hospital 80% of the time.

Before surgery, many items are placed in the operating room just in case the doctor needs them. Patients are mistakenly billed for them even if the doctor never uses them.

Check with the surgeon after surgery. Did he use all the equipment and supplies you were billed for? Was medication ordered that you never needed? If you find discrepancies, call the hospital billing department. Ask that your bill be reduced.

8. Ask your pharmacist about cost-cutting measures. Pharmacists are often knowledgeable about simple but effective ways to cut prescription costs.

Example I: Buying a 90-day supply of drugs rather than three 30-day supplies. That way, you pay only one co-payment instead of three.

Example II: Buying generic drugs. They cost significantly less than brand names.

Some insurance companies have special arrangements with mail-order pharmacies. Making use of such an arrangement can lower your drug bills even more.

If your insurance company does not offer such an arrangement, a discount pharmacy in your community is likely to have lower prices than most mail-order pharmacies.

Source: Rich Gulling, RPh, MBA, a registered pharmacist and adjunct professor of finance at Wright State University, Dayton, OH. He is coauthor of *Stay Well Without Going Broke: Winning the War Over Medical Bills.* Starburst Publishers.

Salt/Osteoporosis Trap

Too much salt can deplete the body of calcium, which can lead to osteoporosis. The amount of calcium needed to keep bones healthy is directly related to salt intake. Those on a low-salt diet may need only 450 to 500 milligrams (mg) of calcium daily—far lower than the recommended dietary allowance of 1,000 mg for adult women. If you consume a great deal of processed or fast foods, which usually contain a lot of salt, however, you might need as much as 2,000 mg of calcium a day.

Source: Robert P. Heaney, MD, a researcher and specialist in disorders of the bone at Creighton University, Omaha, NB.

Late-Night Eating

Late-night eating disturbs your sleep and can cause you to gain weight. *Better:* Eat equal, modest portions at all three meals, perhaps with small between-meal snacks. *If you must snack after hours:* Foods high in carbohydrates help induce sleep, while those high in protein increase alertness.

Source: Eunsook T. Koh, PhD, professor of nutritional sciences, University of Oklahoma Health Sciences Center, Oklahoma City.

Chronic Sinusitis

Chronic sinusitis may require up to six weeks of antibiotic therapy to be completely cured. *Also:* Because the condition may be caused by multiple strains of bacteria, combination treatment with two antibiotics may be useful for infections that fail to respond to a single antibiotic.

Source: Mark Dykewicz, MD, associate professor of internal medicine, allergy and immunology division, St. Louis University School of Medicine, quoted in *Internal Medicine News & Cardiology News,* 12230 Wilkins Ave., Rockville, MD 20852.

Excess Iron and Colorectal Cancer

Excess iron in the diet—from meat, iron-fortified cereal, etc.—may increase risk of colorectal cancer. Rats given iron injections had an almost twofold increase in colon tumors compared with control rats. *Theory:* Iron increases the body's sensitivity to radiation, gene mutations, etc. *Also:* Too much iron may nurture tumor cells by inhibiting the body's natural defenses and by stimulating tumor growth. *Caution:* Long-term studies are needed before such a link in humans can be confirmed.

Source: Eugene P. Weinberg, PhD, professor of microbiology, Indiana University, Bloomington. His 10-year review of studies on the link between excessive iron and cancer in animals and humans was published in *BioMetals,* Old Malt House, Paradise Street, Oxford, England OX1 1LD.

Better Hospital Recuperation

Patients whose rooms contained water-dominated nature photographs reported substantially less postoperative anxiety than those whose rooms contained photos of trees, abstract paintings...or a blank wall. Those exposed to the water photo also needed the least-strong pain medications. *Self-defense:* Bring your own pictures for the hospital wall—ones that you like and find relaxing to look at.

Source: Study of 160 Swedish cardiac patients, led by Roger Ulrich, PhD, professor, College of Architecture, Texas A&M University, College Station.

Diet and Exercise

Cancer-Fighters

Vitamin C isn't the only cancer-inhibiting substance found in fruits and vegetables. Produce also contains *p-coumaric* and *chlorogenic* acids, both of which fight cancer by blocking formation of powerful carcinogens called N-nitroso compounds. While these cancer-fighting acids are found in many different fruits and vegetables, the common garden tomato seems to have the highest concentrations.

Source: Joseph Hotchkiss, PhD, professor of food science, Cornell University, Ithaca, NY. His study of N-nitroso compound formation in 16 men was published in the *Journal of Agricultural and Food Chemistry*, Box 3337, Columbus, OH 43210.

Best Heart-Healthy Nutrient

Vitamin E works better than the other two natural antioxidants—vitamin C and beta-caro-tene—at clearing arteries of fatty plaque. Taken together, vitamins E and C and beta-carotene inhibited oxidation of LDL (bad) cholesterol—the process that initiates plaque formation—by 50%. But vitamin E taken alone had the same effect.

Source: Ishwarlal "Kenny" Jailal, MD, associate professor of pathology and internal medicine and a senior investigator in the Center for Human Nutrition, University of Texas Southwestern Medical Center, Dallas. His study of 36 men with and without heart disease, 25 to 65 years of age, was published in *Circulation*, St. Luke's Episcopal Hospital, Texas Heart Institute, MC 1-267, 6720 Bertner St., Houston 77030.

Vitamin Supplements And Cancer

A recent study conducted in Finland—refuting theories that vitamin supplements help prevent cancer—is suspect for two reasons. One, it involved only very long-term smokers. Whatever beneficial effect the supplements had was probably counteracted by decades of smoke-induced cellular damage. Two, it dealt with supplements of only two vitamins—vitamin E and beta-carotene. But vitamin E cuts cancer risk only when taken in conjunction with vitamin C. Until the vitamin question is settled conclusively, eat lots of fruits and vegetables…avoid smoking…eat less dietary fat…and consider daily supplements—vitamins C and E and beta-carotene. (For more on this study, see page 229.)

Source: Bruce N. Ames, PhD, professor of biochemistry and molecular biology, and director, National Institute of Environmental Health Sciences Center, University of California, Berkeley.

Vitamin C and Dental Healing

Nine out of 10 patients given daily doses of vitamin C for one week following tooth extraction exhibited rapid healing. Only six out of 10 patients who received a placebo exhibited rapid healing. If you're having a tooth pulled, start taking 1,500 milligrams of vitamin C per day one week before and continue for one week after.

Source: R.A. Halberstein, PhD, associate professor of epidemiology and public health, University of Miami School of Medicine, Coral Gables, FL. His study of 161 patients who had tooth extractions was published in *General Dentistry*, 211 E. Chicago Ave., Chicago 60611.

Breast Cancer and Eating Meat

Dietary fat has long been linked to breast cancer. *Latest finding:* Women who ate beef, veal, lamb, pork and luncheon meats each day had twice the risk of breast cancer as women who rarely ate these foods. *Self-defense:* Limit intake of meat and animal products to cut risk of heart ailments and breast and colon cancers.

Source: Paolo Toniolo, MD, professor of environmental medicine, New York University School of Medicine, New York City.

Certain Aromas Promote Weight Loss

Certain aromas, including banana, peppermint and green apple, "fool" the brain into thinking the stomach is full. *Result:* Diminished appetite and significant weight loss. *To promote weight loss:* Sniff food before eating…chew food thoroughly…and if your table mates can tolerate it, blow air through your carefully chewed food before swallowing. Hot food produces more odor—and therefore is more filling—than the same food eaten cold.

Source: Alan R. Hirsch, MD, neurologic director, Smell and Taste Treatment and Research Foundation, 845 N. Michigan Ave., Chicago 60611.

All About Antioxidants

"Antioxidants" may be the new health catchword, but many people are confused about what antioxidants are and what the conflicting data imply about their usefulness.

To clear up the confusion, we spoke to Dr. Kenneth H. Cooper, whose book *Aerobics* revolutionized America's attitude toward fitness 25 years ago.* He continues to direct research into exercise, diet, health and fitness at The Cooper Aerobics Center in Dallas.

• *What are antioxidants, and why are they important?*

To understand antioxidants, you must first understand the concept of free radicals.

A free radical is an unstable type of oxygen molecule. It lacks one of its electrons, and must therefore "steal" an electron from another molecule. When that unstable oxygen molecule seeks to replace its missing electron, it causes a chain reaction that can damage cell membranes and DNA.

Free radicals are unavoidable. They're a by-product of normal metabolism, as well as a response to environmental factors like air pollution, cigarette smoke, radiation, pesticide residues and other food contaminants, physi-

*Published by Bantam.

cal injury, excessive exercise and possibly emotional stress.

Another source of free radicals is *ischemia*, the cutoff of oxygen to cells, such as during surgery, followed by *reperfusion*, when blood rushes back into the deprived organ.

Free radicals aren't all bad. They're thought to help the immune system and are necessary for the proper function of organs and blood vessels. But when these renegade molecules get out of control, they can be very destructive…

•Free radicals promote cancer.

•Free radicals change LDL (bad) cholesterol into the harmful form that clogs arteries.

•Free radicals promote signs of aging, such as deterioration of the skin and other organs.

•Free radicals have also been linked to a variety of medical problems, from cataracts to stroke to rheumatoid arthritis and Parkinson's disease.

Fortunately, the body has weapons to keep free radicals under control—the antioxidants. These molecules prevent and repair free radical damage by sacrificing their own electrons …and by "mopping up" unstable molecules before they do damage.

Some antioxidants are endogenous, meaning they are produced within the body. The most important of these are superoxide dismutase, catalase and GSH. Others are exogenous, or taken from outside in the form of nutrients.

The primary exogenous antioxidants are vitamin C, vitamin E and beta-carotene.

• *Can you get enough of these exogenous antioxidants from food?*

Researchers are still trying to answer this question. A diet high in vitamin-rich fruits and vegetables—especially greens and cruciferous vegetables like cabbage and broccoli—is associated with a lower incidence of cancer and many other diseases. This may well be due to the foods' antioxidant properties, although the connection has yet to be proven.

Theoretically, it's possible to get all the vitamin C and beta-carotene you need from your diet—if you consume seven to nine servings of fruits and vegetables a day, prepared with minimal cutting, peeling, trimming and cooking so as to minimize vitamin loss.

But most Americans simply don't eat that many fruits and vegetables every day.

As for vitamin E, it's found primarily in fatty foods like nuts and seeds—making it virtually impossible to get enough of this vitamin through diet alone and still keep calories and fat under control.

Vitamin supplements are not a substitute for a healthful diet, regular exercise or controlled weight. But they probably enhance what we're getting from other sources—and at very little financial cost or physical risk. Think of them as a kind of insurance policy in our stress- and pollution-filled world.

• *Didn't a recent Finnish study find that taking vitamins increases health risk?*

This study did find that subjects who took beta-carotene supplements were more likely to develop lung cancer—a result trumpeted in the media around the world.

Since then, however, a number of experts have pointed out flaws in the research. The subjects had all smoked heavily for many years. The cases of lung cancer and heart disease that occurred might well have already been present—undiagnosed—before the study began. (Antioxidants are thought to have a protective, not a curative, effect.) The effects of supplements on nonsmokers weren't studied at all.

To say that beta-carotene is dangerous based on that one study is irresponsible. Far more research suggests that beta-carotene supplements protect against lung and other types of cancer.

Example: A recent study in China found a 13% reduction in all cancers, and a 9% reduction in overall mortality, among subjects who took supplements of beta-carotene, selenium and vitamin E.

The Finnish study did find that even minimal doses of vitamin E—50 international units (IU) per day—were linked to a 34% reduction in death from prostate cancer, a 16% reduction in death from colon cancer and a 5% reduction in death from heart attack. Yet the press ignored these encouraging findings.

• *What doses of vitamin supplements do you recommend?*

Based on the existing research, I believe that most adults should take a daily antioxidant "cocktail" containing...

•1,000 milligrams (mg) vitamin C. That's 500 mg taken twice a day. Costly sustained-release capsules seem to be no more effective than regular tablets.

•400 IU vitamin E. The natural form—d-alpha tocopherol—is preferable to synthetic dl-alpha tocopherol.

•25,000 IU beta-carotene. Beta-carotene is a precursor of vitamin A, which can be toxic in large doses.

• *What role does exercise play in the free radical/antioxidant equation?*

Moderate exercise appears to enhance the activity of the body's own antioxidants. However, excessive exercise—such as training for a marathon—seems to increase free radical production.

While I wouldn't presume to tell a marathon runner to stop training, I do think it makes sense to take higher levels of antioxidant supplements.

•3,000 mg vitamin C.

•1,200 IU vitamin E.

•50,000 IU beta-carotene.

• *Can these vitamins have toxic side effects?*

Not at the above doses, in most cases. *Exceptions:*

•Don't take beta-carotene within four hours of drinking an alcoholic beverage. The interaction of alcohol and beta-carotene can cause liver damage. Heavy drinkers probably shouldn't take beta-carotene at all.

•People on anticoagulant therapy should avoid vitamin E, since it can cause excessive bleeding.

•People with kidney stones should avoid large doses of vitamin C.

•Pregnant women should check with their doctors before taking vitamin supplements or any other type of medication.

Even if you are not in any of the above categories—but especially if you are—check with your doctor before beginning a vitamin regi-

men. And whenever you're asked about the kinds of medications you're taking, remember to include the supplements on your list.

• *Do you recommend any other antioxidant supplements?*

The compound Coenzyme Q10 and the mineral selenium help neutralize free radicals. However, Coenzyme Q10 hasn't yet been studied extensively. And excess selenium can cause hair loss, fatigue and other toxic effects. I need more data before I can recommend either of these as supplements.

• *What else can I do to head off free radical damage?*

Avoid sources of environmental stress. If you exercise outdoors, do so early in the morning or after sundown, when pollution levels are low. Stay away from major highways.

Limit your exposure to sunlight. Give some thought to the other environmental hazards you're likely to encounter—then think of ways to minimize them.

Don't try to change your whole life all at once, however. Pick one factor, address it—and once you've got it under control, start on another.

• *What about aspirin?*

Aspirin is not an antioxidant, but it has been recommended as protection against heart attacks. Yet most of the research indicates that aspirin is most beneficial to individuals who already have cardiovascular disease...and it may sightly increase the risk of hemorrhagic stroke.

Consequently, for healthy people with no known history of heart disease, I do not recommend taking aspirin regularly.

Source: Kenneth H. Cooper, MD, founder of the Cooper Aerobics Center, 12200 Preston Rd., Dallas 75230. His most recent book is *Dr. Kenneth H. Cooper's Antioxidant Revolution.* Thomas Nelson, Inc.

 # Obesity on the Rise

One in three American adults is overweight. This alarming increase follows decades during which one in four Americans was considered overweight. *Annual cost of illness associated with obesity:* $39 billion. This does not include money spent on diet programs or formulations or other weight-loss efforts.

Source: Robert J. Kuczmarski, MD, nutritionist, National Center for Health Statistics, Hyattsville, MD. His three-year study of 8,260 adults was published in the *Journal of the American Medical Association*, 515 N. State St., Chicago 60610.

Vitamins vs. Cataracts

Regular vitamin supplements may reduce the risk of cataracts. Patients who took a daily multivitamin were 27% less likely to develop cataracts and required 21% fewer operations to remove cataracts than those who did not take vitamins.

Source: Johanna M. Seddon, MD, associate professor of ophthalmology, Harvard Medical School, Boston. Her 60-month follow-up of a 1982 study of 17,744 participants 40 to 84 years of age was published in the *American Journal of Public Health*, 1015 15 St. NW, Washington, DC 20005.

Prostate Cancer Risk

In a recent study of 48,000 men, those who ate the most red meat, butter and chicken with skin were two and a half times more likely to develop late-stage prostate cancer than men who ate the least of these foods. By age 80, two-thirds of men have prostate cancer. But whether the cancer lies dormant for years or quickly becomes life-threatening may depend upon the amount of animal fat in the diet.

Source: Edward Giovannucci, MD, ScD, instructor of medicine, Harvard Medical School, Boston.

Healthy Eating Habits On the Decline

Americans eat worse today than 10 years ago. The percentage of those trying to avoid dietary fat dropped 4% between 1983 and 1993. Over the same time period, declines were also seen in those avoiding salt (-7%) and in those boosting intake of fiber (-6%) and calcium (-2%).

Source: Survey of American Health Habits, Baxter International, One Baxter Pkwy., Deerfield, IL 60015.

Vitamin E Helps Prevent Strokes

Vitamin E is still a good—and safe—stroke preventive. It's one of several dietary antioxidants—others are vitamins A and C, beta-carotene and selenium—that guard body tissues against deterioration due to age and pollution. While vitamin E is usually safe even at fairly high levels, large doses of vitamin A can be toxic. Before taking any antioxidant in pill form, check with your doctor. *The leading natural sources of vitamin E:* Walnuts, almonds, sunflower seeds …wheat germ…sweet potatoes…spinach.

Source: Arthur Winter, MD, assistant professor of neurosurgery, University of Medicine and Dentistry of New Jersey, Livingston. He is also director of the New Jersey Neurological Institute, Newark.

Breast Milk and Allergies

While breast-feeding helps protect infants from food allergies, it can sometimes cause allergic reactions in them. *Problem:* The mother herself may show no signs of the allergy.

Most common infant allergies: Milk, egg or peanut products. Breast-feeding mothers should avoid these foods if they notice signs of eczema—red, itchy blotches—on their baby's skin. If the rash continues, blood tests can help identify the problem food.

Prenatal protection: If food allergies run in your family, avoidance of these foods in the last trimester may be beneficial.

Source: Richard B. Moss, MD, associate professor of pediatrics, Stanford University Medical Center, Stanford, CA.

Fish-Dish Danger

Ciguatera fish poisoning is a hard-to-diagnose illness caused by consumption of fish that carry a hard-to-detect toxin. *Symptoms:* Nausea …vomiting…diarrhea…cramps…numbness or tingling of the lips, tongue and throat…reversal of hot and cold sensations…blurred vision… low blood pressure…labored breathing… depression.

Danger: There is no diagnostic test for the toxin, and symptoms are easily confused with those of other ailments. The only known remedy—large doses of the sugar *mannitol*—must be administered within 48 hours.

Self-defense: When traveling in tropical areas, avoid grouper, red snapper or any dish containing unspecified fish…*never* eat barracuda… avoid fish liver, where the toxin is most concentrated. *Usually safe:* Yellowtail snapper and mahimahi.

Source: Donna Blythe, MD, a ciguatera expert from Coral Gables, FL.

Poor Nutrition In the Elderly

Eating alone is the leading factor behind poor nutrition among old people. Women who eat alone tend to eat too few calories…while men who eat alone tend to eat too much fat.

Other contributors to poor nutrition: Low education level…belonging to a racial minority …living in a low-income neighborhood… smoking…wearing dentures…taking multiple medications.

Source: Katherine Tucker, PhD, assistant professor, Tufts School of Nutrition, Boston. Her study of 700 people ages 60 to 89 was published in *Food & Nutrition Research Briefs*, US Department of Agriculture, 6303 Ivy Lane, Fourth Floor, Greenbelt, MD 20770.

Citrus Juice vs. Kidney Stones

Citrus juice may help prevent kidney stones. Orange, grapefruit and cranberry juices all contain high levels of *citrate*, a natural inhibitor of stone formation. Kidney stone risk can also be cut by reducing consumption of salt. A low-salt diet that contains citrus juices is especially helpful for kidney stone patients who can't tolerate potassium citrate—the drug usually prescribed to treat the condition.

Source: Charles Y.C. Pak, MD, director, Robert T. Hayes Center for Mineral Metabolism Research, University of Texas Southwestern Medical Center, Dallas. His study of eight healthy men and three men with a history of kidney stones was published in the *Journal of Urology*, 428 E. Preston St., Baltimore 21202.

Margarine Problem

Semisolid, hydrogenated fats are less healthful than the oils they're made from. A group of people with high cholesterol went on a cholesterol-lowering diet that contained corn oil… and their LDL (bad) cholesterol fell an average of 17%. But LDL fell only 10% when researchers replaced the corn oil with corn oil margarine in stick form.

Source: Alice Lichtenstein, DSc, assistant professor of nutrition, lipid metabolism group, Human Nutrition Research Center on Aging, Tufts University, Boston. Her study of 14 men and women ranging in age from 44 to 78 was published in *Arteriosclerosis and Thrombosis*, 7272 Greenville Ave., Dallas 75231.

Canker Sore Prevention

Eat at least four tablespoons of plain yogurt a day…and avoid eating nuts, especially walnuts. *To treat an existing sore:* Apply a warm, moist tea bag directly to the sore. The tannin in regular black tea acts as an astringent. *Ineffective:* Herbal or decaffeinated tea. *Also:* Open and empty a 250-milligram capsule of tetracycline (available by prescription) into one and a half ounces of warm water. Shake very well—the tetracycline won't dissolve. Dip a cotton ball into the mixture. Apply it to the canker sore for three to four minutes. Repeat three to four times daily. *For multiple sores:* Gargle with the mixture.

Source: Jerome Z. Litt, MD, assistant clinical professor of dermatology, Case Western Reserve University School of Medicine, Cleveland.

Children and Vitamin Supplements

There's no evidence that children need supplements—or that vitamin megadoses will protect them from cancer and other diseases later in life. Even picky eaters almost always get all the nutrients they need from their diet. *Exception:* Kids with cystic fibrosis, liver disease, HIV infection or other illnesses that interfere with the body's use of vitamins may need supplements—under a doctor's supervision.

Source: Frederick Suchy, MD, professor of pediatrics, pediatric gastrointestinal medicine and hepatology, Yale University, New Haven, CT.

How to Take Weight Off And Keep It Off

Each year, Americans spend $33 billion on commercial diet programs—and much of that vast sum is essentially wasted.

Reason: The premise on which these programs are based—cut calories, and you'll lose weight—is at least 20 years out of date. In study after study, it's been thoroughly discredited.

Weight loss just isn't that simple. As we all know, the hard part isn't losing weight, but *keeping* it off. Unless you're willing to eat frozen dinners and drink low-cal shakes for the rest of your life, that is almost impossible on most of the commercial weight-loss programs.

Not surprising, then, that many dieters shuffle unsuccessfully from one diet plan to the next—losing weight on one program, putting it back on, and then moving on to another plan.

In fact, counselors working for the leading commercial diet plans freely admit that perhaps nine of 10 people who try one commercial diet program wind up trying two or three or more.

Weight-loss principles...

How do you take weight off and keep it off—once and for all? *There are three fundamental principles for effective and lasting weight loss...*

Principle #1: Take control of your life and your weight. Turning responsibility for what you eat and what you do over to anyone else is deadly. You need to design a program for yourself. You also need to open up your life to self-inspection.

Often, eating is a survival skill. It's a way of coping with frustrations and disappointments. Life can be very difficult. Eating can get you through it.

Overeating becomes a way to maintain emotional health—although, of course, physical health is jeopardized as a result.

To overcome this self-destructive approach to food, you must learn to separate food itself from its emotional symbolism. You may need the help of a psychologist specializing in weight problems. *Fee:* $50 to $75 an hour.

For referrals to a psychologist in your area, contact the National Association of Anorexia Nervosa and Associated Disorders, Box 7, Highland Park, Illinois 60035. 708-831-3438.

Principle #2: Accept your body. Focus not upon how your body looks, but on what it enables you to do. And don't compare yourself with the ideal body put forth in sexy movies or magazine ads. After all, body shape is determined largely by heredity. We tend to look like our mothers and fathers—and that persists even if we're successful at losing weight.

Principle #3: Make food a pleasure. Avoid thinking of food as a moral issue. "Good" foods are those you think you should be eating—fruits, vegetables, beans, pasta, etc. "Bad" foods taste good but are fattening—cakes, candy, sugary soft drinks, etc.

Substituting good foods for bad *sounds* like a good idea, but odds are it's just setting you up for failure. *Problem:* Even if you could steer clear of "bad" foods for several months, you'd give in to temptation—possibly by going on an eating binge.

Better way: If you like cheesecake, allow yourself the freedom to eat it on occasion. By removing this cheesecake "taboo," you reduce your obsession with it.

Dieting vs. your setpoint...

The only way to ensure lasting weight loss is to lower your set-point. That's the weight your body "thinks" it should weigh.

When people overeat, they generally gain weight only temporarily, returning to their usual weight, or "set-point" when they resume their previous eating habits.

Similarly, when you go on a low-calorie diet, your body wants to keep you from starving. As a result, your metabolism slows to maintain your set-point. *Result:* Weight loss occurs *very* slowly. When you resume your normal eating patterns, your weight quickly rises to its former level.

To lower your set-point, you must reduce your intake of dietary fat *and* increase your lean muscle mass. In other words, lighten up your eating habits and get enough exercise to build muscle.

Cutting out dietary fat...

•Start small. You're not going on a diet—you're changing the way you eat for the rest of your life. So there's no need to cut out dietary fat all at once.

You might start by switching to milk instead of cream in your coffee, then switching to low-fat mayonnaise on your sandwiches, etc.

•Eat what you like. If you already enjoy certain low-fat foods, make them staples of your diet. Make a list of your favorite high-fat foods, and find a way to substitute low-fat versions for some of them.

•Keep track of your fat intake. Buy a nutritional guide that lists the fat content of each food. Use it to calculate how many grams of fat you consume each day.

The maximum number of grams of fat you can eat each day and still lose weight is determined by your age, sex (men burn fat faster than women) and medical condition, among other things.

A woman over 30 should probably consume no more than 20% of her calories in the form of fat. A man over 30 can probably get away with up to 25%. (One gram of fat equals about nine calories.)

•Make sure the whole family adopts healthful eating habits. If your spouse has an ice cream sundae for dessert, you probably won't feel satisfied with a pear. But if everyone in the family starts eating healthfully, there's less temptation.

The importance of exercise...

The more you exercise, the more muscle you build. And because muscle cells burn dietary fat more efficiently than fat cells do, gaining muscle mass speeds your metabolism. *Payoff:* A thin person can eat much more fat than a fat person without gaining weight.

If you've been inactive for a long time, begin by exercising just five or 10 minutes a day. Gradually build until you're exercising at least 20 minutes a day, three to four days a week.

The point is to do what you like. Otherwise, you'll quickly give up exercising. If you used to thrive on volleyball or softball, for example, try to work these activities back into your schedule. If you're joining a gym, look for one where you feel comfortable. One reason people stop going to the gym is that they feel they don't measure up. If you feel intimidated by a chic club, try the local "Y" instead.

Consider hiring a personal trainer (for $15 to $50 per session). If you can't afford one, pool your money with a few friends and hire a trainer to come to one of your homes. Invest in headphones and a few good exercise tapes.

Source: Kathleen Thompson, coauthor of *Feeding on Dreams: Why America's Diet Industry Doesn't Work & What Will Work for You.* Macmillan.

The Truth About Wheat Bran

Wheat bran does *not* ease diarrhea and pain associated with irritable bowel syndrome (IBS)—although bran has long been recommended for this chronic gastrointestinal disorder. In fact, recent evidence suggests that eating more bran may actually make some cases worse. If a doctor recommends increased consumption of fiber, psyllium (found in Metamucil) may be a better choice.

Source: C.Y. Francis, MRCP, research registrar, department of medicine, University Hospital of South Manchester, Manchester, England. Her study of bran consumption by 100 IBS patients was published in *The Lancet,* 42 Bedford Square, London WC1B 3SL, England.

One More Reason to Eat Green Leafy Vegetables

They seem to help prevent *age-related macular degeneration*, the leading cause of blindness among elderly people. People who eat the most of certain types of carotenoids—found in spinach and other dark, leafy greens —had a 43% lower risk of developing the eye disorder than those who ate the least.

Source: Johanna M. Seddon, MD, associate professor of ophthalmology, Harvard Medical School and Harvard School of Public Health, and director, epidemiology unit, Massachusetts Eye and Ear Infirmary, all in Boston. Her study of 356 men and women, age 55 to 80, with age-related macular degeneration and 520 healthy people with normal vision was published in the *Journal of the American Medical Association*, 515 N. State St., Chicago 60610.

Motion Sickness and Diet

High-fat meals may exacerbate motion sickness. In a recent study, volunteers were placed in a rotating drum after eating either a low-fat or a high-fat meal. When the volunteers got in the drum *immediately* after eating, those who ate the high-fat meal were no more or less likely to experience nausea than those who ate the low-fat meal. But when they got in the drum a short time after eating—long enough for the meal to be partially digested—those who ate the high-fat meal were far more likely to experience nausea than those who ate the low-fat meal.

Lesson: Avoid fatty foods before airplane flights or car or train trips—particularly if you're prone to motion sickness.

Source: Christine Feinle, PhD candidate and research assistant, Centre for Human Nutrition, Northern General Hospital, Sheffield, England. Her study of motion sickness in healthy men was published in *Gastroenterology*, Curtis Center, Independence Square West, Philadelphia 19106.

New Diet Advice For Diabetics

People with adult-onset diabetes have long been urged to eat a high-carbohydrate diet with less than 30% of calories from fat. *Now:* A new study suggests that they'd fare better by cutting their intake of carbohydrates…and limiting intake of saturated fats (meats and dairy products) to 10% of calories, replacing anything over that amount with monounsaturated fats like peanut and canola oils. Diabetics on such a low-carb, high-mono diet had better control of their condition—lower blood levels of glucose, insulin and triglycerides. In response to this finding, the American Diabetes Association has issued revised dietary guidelines. These guidelines allow for varying proportions of carbs to fats, including a diet with more than 30% of calories from fat—particularly for those with high triglyceride levels.

Source: Ann Coulston, MS, RD, senior research dietitian, Stanford University School of Medicine, Palo Alto, CA.

Good News for Dieters

Yo-yo dieting does *not* increase overall body fat or permanently slow the body's metabolism …so it doesn't make future weight loss more difficult. Previous studies had suggested just the opposite.

Lesson: If you are overweight, it's a good idea to lose weight—even if there's a chance you'll gain it back. Of course, it's better to maintain a healthy weight via regular exercise and a balanced diet.

Source: Susan Yanofsky, executive secretary, National Task Force on the Prevention and Treatment of Obesity, Bethesda, MD. For more information, write to Weight Control Information Network, One Win Way, Bethesda, MD 20892.

The Minerals in Our Food

Thanks to everything we've read and heard lately about fat, fiber, and food additives, we've all become much smarter about what we're eating—and that's great.

However—a surprising number of myths remain concerning the minerals we take in, both in our daily diets and in the form of supplements. And that misinformation can be dangerous...even deadly.

What we do know for certain is that minerals are essential for life. To a large extent, the body is composed of minerals. For example, our blood carries significant amounts of sodium, potassium, and chloride. And our bones and teeth are rich in calcium, phosphorous, and magnesium.

The news about minerals is generally good: If you eat a healthy, varied diet—including adequate amounts of milk, fruits, and vegetables—your body should get all the minerals it requires. Special needs do arise, however.

Example: As people age, calcium is less well utilized, and extra amounts are recommended, especially for women. Prolonged gastrointestinal illness, and certain drugs, may also change requirements.

Minerals are an often-misunderstood category of nutrients, and you may do well to let go of some of the myths:

• *Myth:* A salty taste is a reliable indicator of salt content.

Truth: Food-content labels must be read very carefully—some items that you would never suspect to be high in sodium are. For example, ounce for ounce, certain dry cereals contain more salt than potato chips.

As most of us now know, too much salt in the diet can promote high blood pressure—and possibly strokes in susceptible individuals. We require only a tiny amount of salt to maintain good health—just 500 milligrams daily, or the equivalent of a quarter-teaspoon. Chances are you're getting more than that amount naturally from the foods you eat each day—you need never go near a salt shaker. In fact, the average American consumes closer to 4,000 to 5,000 milligrams per day—10 times what's needed, and in some ethnic groups, it can be twice that amount.

If you're a salt-lover, you'd be wise to wean yourself off it. Our taste for salt (or any other flavor) is acquired and thus can be unlearned at any age.

To keep your kids from getting hooked on salt, don't serve them salty food or snacks.

• *Myth:* Calcium deficiency is really only of concern to women approaching menopause.

Truth: Women are never too young to step up their calcium intake to help ward off future osteoporosis. Even teenage girls should start taking calcium supplements to build bone strength, especially if they don't drink milk. Bones that are strong at an early age are less likely to leach out calcium, a process that leads to fractures and other problems later on.

Between the ages of 19 and 24, women (and men) should be sure to get 1,200 milligrams of calcium per day—the amount provided by approximately a quart of milk. If you know you're not taking in sufficient quantities of calcium from your food—and most people's diets are imperfect—by all means take a calcium supplement.

• *Myth:* "Health" foods are better sources of minerals than ordinary foods.

Truth: Some so-called "health" or "natural" foods can in fact be harmful.

Example: Health-food fans will often buy "natural" calcium supplements. These supplements are generally produced from limestone and are rich in calcium and magnesium, but they can also contain dangerous impurities, including lead.

In general, it's unwise to buy foods that haven't been carefully inspected and analyzed by government agencies. *Problem:* Many products found in health-food stores have not undergone rigorous inspection. If you choose a food or a supplement that hasn't been government-approved, you run the risk of ingesting impurities. While some of them are harmless, others are not.

• *Myth:* Minerals lost through sweat during strenuous exercise should be replaced via a mineral-rich drink such as Gatorade or by taking salt tablets.

Truth: Gatorade, a dilute solution of some of the minerals found in the body, is a perfectly fine product, but you rarely need it. Your body will restore its lost minerals on its own.

It's far more important to replenish the water your body has lost in sweat.

As for salt tablets, athletes used to rely on them, but nowadays we know that these tablets can do more harm than good. Again, it's best to stick to plain water after your workout, unless the salt loss was truly excessive.

Exception: Pedialyte is a solution that pediatricians may give to children who've become dehydrated from excessive vomiting or diarrhea. That's because youngsters have a much more delicate constitution than adults, and so their water and mineral levels must be restored quickly and completely.

Minimum daily requirements...

•Sodium. 500 mg. (¼ teaspoon of table salt). *Sodium-rich foods:* Those that have been pickled, canned, smoked, or cured...soy sauce... luncheon meats...salted snack foods.

•Potassium. 2,000 mg. *Some potassium-rich foods include:* Bananas (four)...orange juice (four 8-ounce glasses)...carrots (six).

•Chloride. 750 mg. (or ¼ teaspoon of table salt). *Chloride-rich foods:* Most processed foods.

•Calcium. 1,200 mg. (ages 19 to 24)...800 mg. (age 25 and over). *Some calcium-rich foods:* Milk (three 8-ounce glasses)...plain yogurt (three 8-ounce cups)...cheddar cheese (6 ounces).

•Phosphorus. 1,200 mg. (ages 19 to 24)... 800 mg. (age 25 and over). *Phosphorus-rich foods:* Same as those rich in calcium.

•Magnesium. 350 mg. (men), 280 mg. (women). *Some magnesium-rich foods:* Green beans (five cups)...Brazil nuts (12).

•Sulfur. A daily requirement has not been established. *Sulfur-rich foods:* Cheese, eggs, milk, meat, nuts, vegetables.

Some essential trace elements—needed by the body in miniscule amounts...

•Iron. Daily requirement: 10 mg. (men)...15 mg. (women ages 19 to 50)...10 mg. (women 51 and over). *Some iron-rich foods:* Liver (4 ounces)... breakfast cereal, such as Cheerios or Raisin Bran (2 ounces).

•Selenium. *Daily requirement:* 70 micrograms (men)...55 micrograms (women). *Some selenium-rich foods:* Canned tuna (2½ ounces) ...molasses (2 ounces).

•Iodine. *Daily requirement:* 150 micrograms. *Some iodine-rich foods:* Iodized salt...haddock (4 ounces)...milk (8 ounces)...plain yogurt (two 8-ounce cups).

Source: Mia Parsonnet, MD, a member of the clinical faculty of the New Jersey College of Medicine and Dentistry. She is author of *What's Really in Our Food? Fact and Fiction about Fat and Fiber, Vitamins and Minerals, Nutrients, and Contaminants.* Shapolsky Publishers, Inc.

Seafood Savvy

Seafood and fish are an excellent protein source that is low in saturated fat, light on calories, and high in vitamins, minerals, and the omega-3 fatty acids that help reduce the risk of heart disease.

But there are risks. More than 80% of the seafood eaten in the US has not been inspected for chemical or microbial contaminants. Fortunately, there are things that you can do to enjoy maximum health and minimum risk...

•Avoid chemical contaminants. When you buy fish, choose younger, smaller ones, since they've accumulated fewer contaminants. Low-fat, offshore species like cod, haddock, and pollack are especially good choices. Always trim the skin, belly flap, and dark meat along the top or center, especially when it comes to fatty fish such as bluefish. Don't use the fatty parts to make sauce. Don't eat the green "tomalley" in lobsters or the "mustard" in crabs.

•Avoid natural toxins. When traveling in tropical climates, avoid reef fish such as amberjack, grouper, goatfish, or barracuda, which are more likely to be contaminated. Buy only seafood that has been kept continuously chilled, especially mahi-mahi, tuna, and bluefish, which produce an odorless toxin when they spoil.

•Avoid disease-causing microbes. Bite for bite, raw or undercooked shellfish is the riskiest food you can eat.

Self-defense: Don't eat shellfish whose shells remain closed after cooking. Do not eat raw fish or shellfish if you are over 60, HIV-positive, pregnant, have cancer or liver disease, or are vulnerable to infection. Cook all fish and shellfish thoroughly. Raw clams, oysters, and mussels should be steamed for six minutes.

•Don't buy fresh fish that has dull, sunken eyes, or fish that smells "fishy." Do not buy ready-to-eat seafood that is displayed too close to raw seafood.

Source: Lisa Y. Lefferts, an environmental-health consultant in Hyattsville, MD, who specializes in food safety, environmental policy, and risk assessment.

Hot-Flash Prevention

Japanese women have fewer hot flashes and other menopausal symptoms than American women. *Possible reason:* They eat about two ounces a day of foods made from soybeans, such as tofu (bean curd) and miso (soybean paste). Soybeans are rich in isoflavinoids, which are converted during digestion to estrogen-like substances that can help prevent hot flashes.

Sources: Barry Goldin, PhD, and Sherwood Gorbach, MD, Tufts University School of Medicine, and Herman Adlercreutz, MD, Helsinki University, Finland.

How You Cook Has a Lot to Do With Fiber Content

How much fiber a food gives you depends considerably on the method of preparation. Leaving the skins on vegetables and fruits enhances their fiber content. Browning bread increases its fiber (which is why crusts have more fiber than the interior of a loaf). Stir-frying or sautéing vegetables adds fiber more than boiling because less soluble fiber is removed. Deep-frying increases fiber, too, but at great cost in fat and calories. On the other hand, puréeing food decreases fiber, and reducing foods to juice almost completely destroys fiber content.

What to Eat to Prevent Cancer... And What Not to Eat

Although scientists continue to debate the role specific foods play in the development of cancer, there's now a consensus that Americans could dramatically lower their cancer risk by altering their eating habits—specifically, by eating less fat and more fiber.

The fat connection...

Most Americans consume 38% to 40% of their total calories in the form of fat—well above the 25% to 30% fat consumption considered desirable.

This makes us highly susceptible to cancer of the colon, breast, pancreas, and prostate.

No one knows exactly why eating too much fat promotes the development of cancer, but the evidence—drawn from studies on both animals and humans —is compelling.

Different foods contain different types and quantities of fat...

•Saturated fats are found in beef and other meats, fried foods, and poultry skin.

•Monounsaturated fats are found in peanuts, olives and a few other foods.

•Polyunsaturated fats are found in corn, safflower, and other cooking oils.

•Very unsaturated long-chain fatty acids are found in cold-water fish, such as herring and salmon.

It's important to keep track of what kinds of fats you eat because nutritionists now recommend that these fats be eaten in a 1:1:1 ratio. In other words, each day we should eat equal portions of polyunsaturated, monounsaturated, and saturated fats. For most of us, this means cutting down on saturated fats while increasing intake of monounsaturated and polyunsaturated fats.

To reduce your consumption of saturated fats, eat less fried foods, trim the fat off beef and other meats, and trim skin off poultry. These small sacrifices have big health payoffs.

About fish: Although fish contains oils that are highly unsaturated, it's still unclear what, if any, role this oil plays in preventing cancer. There is some early evidence, however, that eating large amounts of fish reduces cancer risk and lowers serum triglycerides—lipids that may be associated with heart disease.

The fiber connection...

While we're eating too much fat, we're also eating too little fiber. On the average, Americans consume only 10 to 12 grams of fiber a day. Instead, we should be eating 25 to 30 grams of fiber every day. (One gram is equivalent in weight to three pennies.)

Big problem: Our diet consists of highly refined, easy-to-chew foods instead of high-fiber fruits, vegetables, and grains.

There are two basic kinds of fiber:

•Insoluble fiber, found primarily in wheat bran, is fiber that is not broken down by bacteria in the intestine. By helping waste pass quickly through the colon, it helps prevent colon cancer, diverticulitis, and appendicitis.

•Soluble fiber, found in oat bran and in most fruits and vegetables, is fiber that is broken down by bacteria. It helps to prevent heart disease (by lowering cholesterol) and diabetes (by lowering the blood sugar).

Nutritionists now recommend that Americans should double their intake of dietary fiber ...fruits and vegetables as well as grains. Pears, for instance, at 4.6 grams of fiber each, contain more fiber than any other fruit. *Other good fiber sources:* Red kidney beans (7 grams), lentils (4 grams), apples (3.3 grams), bananas (2.7 grams), and grapefruit (1.5 grams per half).

Caution: Don't consume more than 40 grams of fiber a day. Too much can be almost as bad as too little. In animals, excessive consumption has been found to cause bulky stools that can result in a form of constipation.

There also is some early evidence that alfalfa and certain other grains may actually increase the risk of developing colon cancer. *Self-defense:* Until the final verdict is in, don't rely just on grains for your fiber...eat a wide variety of fiber-rich foods.

Beyond fat and fiber...

Other than increasing fiber and reducing fats, evidence linking dietary choices to cancer is less reliable.

Still, there are things to do that probably will help prevent cancer...and which won't hurt in any case.

•Eat a wide variety of foods. This limits your exposure to any carcinogens that might be found in a particular food...and eliminates the need for vitamin and mineral supplements.

•Increase your consumption of vitamin A. A powerful antioxidant, it keeps our cells from being attacked by oxygen, and thus prevents cancer. Vitamin A seems particularly effective in helping prevent lung cancer in smokers. To a lesser extent, it also seems to help stave off colon cancer, breast cancer, and lung cancer. *Best vitamin A sources:* Carrots, squash, and other orange and leafy vegetables.

•Increase your intake of selenium. Selenium is a trace element found in most vegetables. To get more into your diet, eat more vegetables. *Alternative:* Selenium supplements.

•Limit your consumption of smoked and pickled foods. They have been tied to stomach cancer. An occasional dill pickle won't hurt you, and neither will an occasional barbecued meal. But a daily regimen of pickled vegetables and smoked meats is imprudent.

•Avoid obesity. Obesity is clearly linked to cancer of both the endometrium (the lining of the uterus) and the breast. Also, obese women with breast cancer are far more likely to succumb to the disease than are normal-weight women diagnosed with similar breast cancer.

Keeping track of your diet is one step toward controlling your weight. *Also extremely helpful:* Exercise.

Watching TV, working in an office, and other aspects of a sedentary lifestyle all are associated with cancer.

Although it's not yet clear exactly how exercise helps prevent cancer, the incidence of colon cancer is much higher in men with sedentary occupations than men who are active. Women athletes have lower rates of reproductive-tract cancer than sedentary, out-of-shape women. And animal studies have demonstrated that moderate exercise cuts the risk of breast, pancreas, liver, and colon cancer.

Caution: Too much exercise may actually be almost as bad as too little. Several studies have indicated that extreme exertion (like that necessary to complete a marathon) temporarily weakens the immune system, opening the way for infectious bacteria and viruses—and possibly the development of cancer.

Evidence: At the turn of the century, stomach cancer was common in the US. Now that refrigeration is almost universal—and we rely less on pickling and smoking to preserve our foods—it is a rarity. In Japan, however, where pickled and smoked foods remain common, stomach cancer rates are among the highest in the world.

•Limit your consumption of simple carbohydrates (sugars). Evolving man ate very little sugar. As a result of this, our bodies are not set up to properly digest it.

Problem: Simple carbohydrates cause the pancreas to produce a large amount of insulin very rapidly, and there is now some evidence suggesting that this can have a harmful effect on the pancreas. *Better:* Complex carbohydrates —found in pastas and breads.

•Limit your caffeine consumption. Caffeine has been tied to a variety of cancers, including those of the pancreas and bladder. More recent data suggest caffeine does not cause cancer. Nonetheless, caffeine is very clearly a potent drug, and it makes sense to consume it in moderation.

•Limit your alcohol consumption. Drinking to excess (more than a couple of drinks a day) has been linked to cancer of the mouth and throat. People who drink and smoke are at high risk. Most patients with head or neck cancer are alcoholics or near-alcoholics with poor nutritional habits who smoke regularly.

Source: Leonard A. Cohen, PhD, head of the section of nutritional endocrinology, the American Health Foundation, One Dana Rd., Valhalla, NY 10595. Dr. Cohen's specialty is in the area of nutritional carcinogenesis.

Calcium vs. Memory

Memory impairment may be caused by too much calcium. Calcium is involved in the transmission of messages along brain neurons in the portion of the brain thought to direct memory functions.

As rats age, calcium flow into nerve cells increases, impairing the flow of messages. *Implications:* If similar results occur in humans, calcium-blocking drugs might be used to prevent memory loss…calcium supplements may contribute to memory loss.

Source: Philip Landfield, MD, professor of physiology, Bowman Gray School of Medicine, Wake Forest University, Winston-Salem, NC.

The Fiber/Calcium Connection

Dietary fiber can prevent the body from absorbing calcium. *Recommended:* Eat high-fiber and high-calcium foods at different times.

Source: *American Health*, New York.

Sugar and Cancer Risk

Biliary-tract cancer—including cancer of the gallbladder and bile ducts—is usually fatal within a year of diagnosis. Risk factors are poorly understood. *New finding:* High sugar intake may increase the chance of developing the disease. *Possibility:* Eating large quantities of sugar may make gallstones more likely to develop—and gallstones may increase biliary-cancer risk.

Source: Study of almost 600 patients by researchers at the National Institute of Public Health and Environmental Protection of the Netherlands, reported in *Nutrition Research Newsletter,* Box 700, Palisades, NY 10964.

Are Brand-Name Nutritional Supplements Better than Generics?

Supplements are pretty much the same no matter how much you pay for them. But some pills are too big to swallow easily…and some brands require you to take two or three pills a day rather than just one. So, when picking a supplement, try to check the size of the pills… and read the label to see how many pills you'll have to take each day. *Note:* While most individuals get all the nutrients they need from food, supplements are recommended for pregnant women (folic acid and iron), very low-calorie dieters (vitamin B6, iron and calcium), strict vegetarians (iron, calcium and vitamins B12 and D), elderly "shut-ins" (vitamin D) and for infants still being nursed after six months of age (iron and vitamin D).

Source: Johanna Dwyer, DSc, RD, professor of medicine at Tufts University School of Medicine and director of the Frances Stern Nutrition Center, both in Boston.

Caffeine Caution

People with high blood pressure should avoid caffeine for at least three hours before exercising. *Reason:* Exercise causes blood pressure to rise. Caffeine aggravates this rise, especially in those with hypertension. Coffee is not the only culprit. Watch out for caffeine in tea, chocolate, soft drinks, over-the-counter medications like cold and allergy pills, and appetite suppressants.

Source: Bong Hee Sung, PhD, research associate professor of medicine, State University of New York, Buffalo. Her study of 28 coffee drinkers 30 to 45 years of age was presented at the Second Congress of International Behavioral Medicine, Hamburg, Germany.

Antacid Danger

Orange juice should not be mixed with antacids like Maalox or Amphojel. *Reason:* Orange juice increases the body's absorption of the aluminum in these antacids by as much as tenfold. Consumed on a regular basis, even tiny amounts of aluminum can accumulate in the body and cause health problems. *Rule of thumb:* Wait at least three hours after taking aluminum-containing antacids before drinking orange juice.

Source: *Environmental Nutrition,* 52 Riverside Dr., New York 10024.

How Herbs Can Keep You Healthy

I never stop being amazed by the remarkable healing power of herbs. As a dedicated physician, I've been recommending them to my patients for more than 25 years. Unfortunately, herbal medicine isn't taught in US medical schools, and few physicians have taken the initiative to learn about herbs.

Herbs have several advantages over conventional drugs. They're inexpensive, potent and — if you take care not to overdose—far less likely to cause allergic reactions or other side effects. (Potentially dangerous herbs, including sassafras and chaparral, have been taken off the market.) Herbs are readily available without a prescription at health-food stores—although it's best to check with your doctor before using herbs.

Here are the herbal remedies I find most useful…

•Aloe vera is wonderful for soothing minor burns and preventing subsequent infection. Although it's available in gel form, recent research suggests that fresh aloe vera leaves are more potent in their anesthetic and antibacterial properties. I urge my friends, family and patients to keep an aloe vera plant in the kitchen and use its leaves to dab on minor burns.

•Chamomile tea contains oils that have antispasmodic and anti-inflammatory effects. It's good for indigestion, anxiety, insomnia and exhaustion. Babies given chamomile tea in their bottle fall asleep faster.

•Comfrey contains allantoin, a compound that speeds healing by promoting growth of muscle and connective tissue. It helps prevent bruising and swelling associated with muscle sprains and strains. Applied to the skin as a paste…not to be taken by mouth.

•Echinacea—sometimes blended with the natural antibiotic goldenseal—stimulates the body's production of the virus-fighting compound interferon and boosts the number and activity of white cells. That makes it a perfect all-around remedy for colds or flu. It's also good for urinary tract infections. Often taken as drops mixed in a glass of water.

•Garlic lowers cholesterol, boosts the immune system and kills disease-causing germs. People who eat lots of garlic get fewer colds. *Important:* Deodorized garlic preparations—used by individuals worried about bad breath—are somewhat less potent than fresh garlic. Parsley helps eliminate bad breath.

•Ginger tea relieves nausea caused by motion sickness, morning sickness, influenza or radiation therapy. In tincture form, ginger is also effective against flatulence and indigestion. It may also be useful for lowering serum cholesterol, although at this point the data are preliminary.

•Milk thistle is widely used in Japan to treat liver problems, including hepatitis A, B and C. It contains compounds that promote the flow of bile and stimulate production of new liver cells. Taken in capsule form.

•Nettle contains the compounds choline, acetylcholine and histamine. Together, they reduce inflammation, helping to relieve runny nose, watery eyes and other allergy symptoms. It also stimulates the immune system. Recent studies at the National College of Naturopathic Medicine in Portland, Oregon, demonstrated that two milk thistle capsules a day reduced symptoms of hay fever. Taken as capsules or brewed as a tea.

•Saw palmetto contains liposterol, a compound that inhibits action of the male hormone dihydrotestosterone. It's an extremely potent remedy for prostate problems, including frequent urination, groin pain, prostatitis (prostate inflammation) and benign prostatic hypertrophy (prostate enlargement).

•St. John's Wort contains an antibacterial oil. It's good for treating stubborn colds or coughs—and possibly flu and other viral infections. Taken as capsules or drops.

Source: Sandra McLanahan, MD, director of the stress-management training program at Dr. Dean Ornish's Preventive Medicine Research Institute in Sausalito, CA, and executive medical director of the Integral Health Center and Spa, Buckingham, VA. For more information on herbs, or for information on starting an herb garden, Dr. McLanahan recommends *The Healing Herbs,* by Michael Castleman. St. Martin's Press.

Cola and Bone Fractures

Girls who drink cola face an increased risk of bone fractures. *Theory:* The phosphoric acid contained in colas makes bones more brittle. Noncola soft drinks do not contain phosphoric acid.

Source: Grace Wyshak, PhD, lecturer, Center for Population and International Studies, Harvard School of Public Health, Boston. Her study of 76 girls and 51 boys eight to 16 years of age was published in the *Journal of Adolescent Health,* 655 Avenue of the Americas, New York 10010.

Breast Cancer Danger

Women who gain 15 pounds or more between 16 and 30 years of age face an increased risk of breast cancer. In a recent study, half of women diagnosed with breast cancer had gained more than 15 pounds between these ages. At age 30, women who went on to get breast cancer weighed an average of 131 pounds...while women who remained healthy weighed an average of 120 pounds.

Source: Nagi B. Kumar, PhD, RD, director of nutrition, H. Lee Moffitt Cancer Center and Research Institute, Tampa, FL. Her study of 218 women with breast cancer and 436 healthy women was presented at a recent meeting of the Society of Clinical Oncology, 435 N. Michigan Ave., Chicago 60611.

Body-Fat/Breast Cancer Debate

Previous studies suggested that breast cancer is more common in women with upper-body fat than in those whose fat is mostly in the buttocks. *Latest study:* Waist-to-hip ratios (WHRs) were calculated for more than 300 women having breast biopsies. *Result:* There was no difference in the fat distribution of women diagnosed with breast cancer...and those who proved to be cancer-free. Family history and unknown factors are still considered key factors in breast cancer risk.

Source: Jeanne Petrek, MD, attending surgeon, Memorial Sloan-Kettering Cancer Center, New York City. Her study was reported in *The Medical Post,* 777 Bay St., Toronto, Ontario M5W 1A7.

Thin Isn't Always In

Being thin is not a guarantee against the effects of high blood pressure. In fact, thin hypertensives are more likely to die of heart disease than obese hypertensives. People with high blood pressure should be carefully monitored and treated—*regardless of weight.*

Source: Wendy Carman, MPH, senior research associate, University of Michigan School of Public Health, Ann Arbor. Her study of 2,197 men and women was presented at a recent meeting of the American Heart Association, 7272 Greenville Ave., Dallas 75231.

Elderly and Weight-Lifting

Frailty in the elderly is often blamed on lack of exercise and poor nutrition. *Reality:* Weight-lifting exercise boosts muscle strength and size and mobility in the elderly, while nutritional supplements have no benefit on these outcomes —either alone or in conjunction with exercise.

Source: Maria A. Fiatarone, MD, chief of the human physiology laboratory, Human Nutrition Research Center on Aging, Tufts University, Boston. Her 10-week study of 100 frail nursing home residents was published in *The New England Journal of Medicine,* 10 Shattuck St., Boston 02115.

Obesity Research

Researchers are studying body fat and its role in the development of heart disease, diabetes and other chronic health problems. They're also seeking to explain why African-Americans tend to have a higher percentage of body fat and a greater risk of heart disease than whites.

Eligible: Fraternal and identical twins of both sexes and of all ages, weights and ethnic backgrounds.

Source: David Allison, MD, St. Luke's/Roosevelt Hospital, Obesity Research Center, 411 W. 114 St., New York 10025.

Shoe-Buying Basics

• Pay attention only to the shoe's fit, not its size.

• Match the shoe to the shape of your foot.

• Measure feet each time you buy shoes.

• Buy shoes to match the larger of your feet. Almost everyone has one foot slightly larger than the other.

• Shop for shoes late in the day, when your feet are slightly swollen.

• Avoid nonleather shoes. They don't stretch well.

• Stand up when trying on shoes. Make sure there's a ⅛- to ½-inch space between your longest toe and the front of the shoe.

• Make sure the ball of the foot fits into the widest part of the shoe.

• Don't assume tight shoes will stretch. Buy shoes only if they feel comfortable.

• If you have bunions, hammertoe or any other foot problem, have the shoes stretched by a shoemaker to make more room.

• Walk in the shoes to make sure the heel doesn't slip.

Source: Saul Trevino, MD, associate professor of clinical orthopedic surgery, Baylor College of Medicine, Houston.

Foot Pain Relief

To relieve foot pain from high arches, a protruding bone or a nerve or tendon injury, try leaving a space in your shoelaces. Skip the eyelets at the painful point and draw the laces to the next set of eyelets.

Source: Carol Frey, MD, chief, foot and ankle clinic, University of Southern California, Los Angeles.

Running Shoe Self-Defense

Running shoes should be "rested" for at least 24 hours before reuse. *Reason:* The material in shoe insteps and soles needs about a day to relax back into its original shape. *Helpful:* Keep an extra pair of shoes for times when you run two or more days in a row.

Source: Thomas Branch, MD, chief, Emory Clinic Sports Medicine Center, Atlanta.

Don't Think Diet

People *do* lose weight on trendy diets. But most of them gain back the pounds—and then some. Successful weight loss occurs only when you make a permanent commitment to replacing refined, calorie-dense foods with foods that are natural and unrefined. It's not that difficult.

Typical American dinner: A big piece of steak, a heap of fries and a tiny pile of vegetables. You can slash fat and calories simply by shifting the proportions. Eat one-half or one-third the portion of meat (or substitute fish) plus two big piles of veggies—and brown rice or another whole grain. You'll still feel satisfied.

To cut fat even more, replace the meat with lentils or beans. *Caution:* If you don't feel well on a vegetarian diet, do *not* force yourself. I'd estimate that one-third of the population has trouble metabolizing grains, fruits, vegetables and other carbohydrates. For these people, a carbohydrate-intensive diet can cause big trouble—including heart disease or a cholesterol or blood sugar problem.

The mineral chromium is a great weight-loss aid. It burns fat, builds muscle and helps reduce cravings for sweets. And chromium may lower levels of LDL (bad) cholesterol and raise levels of HDL (good) cholesterol.

It's hard to get enough chromium from food. Vegetables are poor sources—most are grown in chromium-depleted soil. Organ meats and dairy products contain chromium—but they're too fatty. Whole grains are chromium-rich, too, but they contain phytates—compounds that block the body's absorption of chromium and other trace elements.

Solution: Supplements of *chromium picolinate.* I recommend 200 micrograms (mcg)—three times a day, with meals—for any overweight adult, especially those who crave sweets or who have a blood sugar or cholesterol/triglyceride problem. *Caution:* Chromium can cause glucose levels to drop in diabetics, requiring a reduction in dosage of insulin. Even if you don't have diabetes, talk to your doctor before taking chromium.

To further boost your fat-burning power, team chromium with the amino acid *L-carnitine. Recommended:* 250 milligrams (mg) three times a day, with meals.

Source: Robban Sica-Cohen, MD, director of the Center for the Healing Arts, Orange, CT. She specializes in environmental and nutritional medicine.

A Safer, Gentler Estrogen

Most women are familiar with ERT, which is used to prevent menopause-related problems—hot flashes, vaginal dryness, heart disease and osteoporosis. However, not all women are aware that there are two kinds of estrogen. Most doctors prescribe *estradiol* even though some studies have linked this form of estrogen to breast cancer. Another, less frequently prescribed form—called *estriol*—fights symptoms of menopause without promoting breast cancer.

Most women on ERT also take a synthetic hormone called *medroxy-progesterone* to offset some of the increased risk caused by estrogen. But the natural form of this drug—*progesterone*—not only reduces these risks but also stimulates bone growth, helping prevent and treat osteoporosis.

In my practice, I use estriol and progesterone exclusively. Although they cost a bit more, they cause fewer side effects, including bloating, irritability and breast tenderness. Both substances are available by prescription at compounding pharmacists. These "old-fashioned" practitioners can mix and encapsulate the hormones and other medications not widely marketed.

Source: Robban Sica-Cohen, MD, director of the Center for the Healing Arts, Orange, CT. She specializes in environmental and nutritional medicine.

Physical Inactivity Causes Heart Disease

Physical inactivity is just as likely to cause heart disease as smoking. *Alarming:* About 65% of American men and 85% of American women are unfit, while only about 26% of us continue to smoke. *Self-defense:* Even a small amount of regular physical activity—gardening, walking, etc.—helps curb heart disease.

Source: Lars-Goran Ekelund, MD, PhD, associate professor of medicine, Duke University, Durham, NC. His 12-year study of almost 6,000 men and women was reported in The Medical Post, 777 Bay St., Toronto, Ontario M5W 1A7.

New Exercise— Lateral Training

Lateral training—the new exercise in which participants wearing nylon boots slide from side to side on a plastic sheet—burns three times as many calories as walking at an equivalent pace. *Drawback:* The squatting position required to do the exercise can cause back soreness and tendinitis in the knee and Achilles tendon. *To avoid problems:* Alternate five minutes of sliding with five minutes of some other aerobic activity, such as cycling. Continue for 30 minutes at least three times weekly. Slides and boots are available at sporting goods stores.

Source: Susan A. Frodge, MA, exercise physiologist, Human Performance Laboratory, Adelphi University, Garden City, NY. Her study of lateral training was reported in *American Health*, 28 W. 23 St., New York 10001.

Avoiding Knee Injuries

Avoid knee injuries by developing strong, flexible quadriceps and hamstrings—the muscles that support the knee. *Helpful exercise:* Stand with your feet together and your back 18 to 24 inches from a wall. Leaning against the wall, slide down to a "chair" position. Initially hold for 15 to 30 seconds and work up to one to two minutes. *Also beneficial:* Ride a stationary exercise bike for 20 minutes three or four times a week. *And:* Knee curls. Attach ankle weights and lie face-down on a weightlifting bench (or the floor). Bend your legs until your heels touch your buttocks. Avoid knee extensions and deep knee bends. They place too much pressure on the knees.

Source: James Garrick, MD, director, Center for Sports Medicine, St. Francis Memorial Hospital, San Francisco.

Exercise and Lactic Acid

Lactic acid builds up during exercise and may contribute to the uncomfortable burning sensation that many exercisers feel. *To remove lactic acid faster:* Have an active recovery period after a workout, like walking after running…instead of a passive one, like lying down.

Source: Karen Segal, PhD, associate professor of physiology in pediatrics, director of exercise physiology lab, Cornell University Medical College and New York Hospital, New York City.

Are Athletes Healthier Emotionally?

High school athletes are less likely than non-athletes to suffer depression, smoke cigarettes or marijuana or consider suicide.

Source: Michael J. Oler, MD, director, family practice residency program, St. Elizabeth Medical Center, Dayton, OH. His survey of 823 high school athletes was published in *Archives of Family Medicine*, 515 N. State St., Chicago 60610.

Exercise and Your Immune System

Brisk walks strengthen your immune system—but too-strenuous workouts can lower immunity to colds and flu. Exercising near your maximum capacity for just 45 minutes—or more—produces a six-hour "window" of vulnerability afterward. *Better:* Exercise at a moderate level—the equivalent of a brisk walk—if not training for competition.

Source: David Nieman, DrPH, professor of health, department of health and exercise science, Appalachian State University, Boone, NC.

Improved Backswings For Older Golfers

Backswings get shorter as golfers get older. When the swing gets too short, you'll lose distance, accuracy, and consistency.

Remedies: Hold the club lightly. *Reason:* Too tight a grip tenses the arm and shoulder muscles and restricts the backswing.

Put more weight on your right foot, especially on full swings with woods and longer irons. *Result:* A head start on your swing and less weight to shift.

Turn your chin to the right (or to the left, if you're a southpaw) as you start your backswing. If it throws your timing off, cock your chin in the direction of the backswing before you swing.

Exercises to Do In the Car

(1) *Double chin:* Lift chin slightly and open and close mouth as though chewing. (2) *Flabby neck:* Move head toward right shoulder while looking straight ahead at the road. Return head to center, then toward left shoulder. (3) *Pot belly:* Sit straight with spine against back seat. Pull stomach in and hold breath for count of 5. Relax, then repeat. The exercise also relieves tension and helps fight sleepiness.

Spotting Fraudulent Weight-Loss Programs

Avoid weight-loss programs that:

•Promise rapid weight loss (substantially more than 1% of total body weight per week).

•Try to make clients dependent on special products rather than teaching how to make good choices from conventional foods.

•Do not encourage permanent, realistic lifestyle changes.

•Misrepresent salespeople as "counselors" supposedly qualified to give guidance in nutrition and/or general health.

•Require a large sum of money at the start, or require clients to sign a contract for an expensive, long-term program.

•Fail to inform clients about the various health risks associated with weight loss.

•Promote unproven or spurious weight-loss aids.

•Claim that "cellulite" exists in the body.

•Claim that the use of an appetite suppressant or bulking agent enables a person to lose fat without restricting caloric intake.

•Claim that a weight-control product contains a unique ingredient or component, unless that component really is not available in other weight-loss products.

Source: William T. Jarvis, PhD, president of the National Council Against Health Fraud, quoted in *Nutrition Forum,* George F. Stickley Co., Philadelphia 19106.

How Men Can Lose 10 to 75 Pounds... For Good

From everything we read and hear, it may seem as though weight were primarily a woman's problem.

In fact, there are more overweight men than overweight women. There are now approximately 25 million men in the United States who are considered clinically obese (more than 20% above their ideal weight).

And there are another 10 to 15 million men who are heavier than they would like to be. For men, weight-gain frequently accompanies middle age and a higher-than-average socio-economic status.

Four basic steps...

•Control stress-eating. Uncontrolled, unplanned nibbling tends to involve high-fat, snack-type foods.

If you find yourself eating from stress or other emotions, such as anger or frustration, seek out enjoyable alternatives, which can include reading a mystery or going out to a movie.

If you're at your job, try to leave the building for a 10-minute walk or do some deep breathing while sitting at your desk.

•Avoid alcohol. Alcohol is high in calories and impairs judgment. In addition, it tends to work against your self-restraint when you're eating out.

Example: Drinking a glass or two of wine before ordering an entrée can lower your guard when the waiter shows up. Alcohol improves the chances that you'll switch from the plain green salad and broiled fish you intended to order to prime rib and salad drenched in bleu-cheese dressing. Further, alcohol in the system slows down the body's fat-burning process.

•Decrease the amount of fat you consume. This one basic nutritional change can make a big difference in your weight.

Reduce dietary fat, found in red meat, fried and greasy foods, cheese, chips and ice cream, to name but a few. You'll lose weight even if you eat the same quantity of food as before.

That's because eliminating high-fat items automatically means replacing them with low-fat, low-calorie carbohydrates (fruits and vegetables, breads and grains) and protein (fish, poultry, beans and low-fat milk products).

•Increase exercise. Exercise reduces stress, helps burn more calories and produces a "post-exercise burn"—so that your metabolic rate remains at a higher-than-normal level, even hours after your workout.

Exercise also raises the levels of endorphins, resulting in a nice, drug-free "high." Sustained weight loss is virtually impossible without an ongoing exercise program. If you don't continue to exercise, any weight that is lost will almost certainly return.

Start slowly. Unlike out-of-shape women, out-of-shape men tend to plunge right into a new fitness program, attempting to accomplish too much too soon.

First, get your doctor's OK. Then, begin a brisk-walking program five to six days a week, 20 to 25 minutes a day.

If necessary, break up your exercise into two sessions—morning and afternoon. Increase your time by five minutes per week until you're up to 45 minutes a day. You may want to eventually graduate to slow jogging or a stationary bicycle.

Smart food choices...

After 15 years of working with both male and female dieters, I've discovered that smart men are nutritionally ignorant—they just don't know what's in the food they're eating and why it can be harmful.

Example: A chef's salad and a diet soft drink is many men's idea of a healthy, low-calorie lunch...but they couldn't be more wrong. A chef's salad is a 750- to 1,000-calorie, high-fat meal, usually containing cheese and luncheon meat (each approximately 100 calories per ounce) and about 80% to 90% fat—all smothered in two or three ladles of dressing (200 to 250 calories).

A man will wash down his chef's salad with a diet drink—and feel virtuous because the soda has no calories. But, in fact, he may have just consumed more than half his caloric and fat limits for the entire day.

Healthy, long-term weight control means making smart choices. *Some simple food substitutions that will produce weight-loss without a feeling of deprivation:*

Instead of...	Have...
Half a pepperoni pizza	2 regular slices and a green salad
A bran or corn muffin	Bagel or English muffin
A handful of cashews	2 handfuls of popcorn
Chicken nuggets	Broiled chicken sandwich
Fettuccini Alfredo	Pasta with vegetables in tomato sauce
16 ounces of red meat	6 ounces of red meat with a baked potato and tossed green salad

Important: Don't let yourself feel deprived. While you will have to give up the notion that you can eat whatever you want whenever you want it, there is no reason you can't eat the foods you like and still slim down and improve your health. You should try to stick to the rules you have set, but you don't have to be perfect.

Source: Clinical psychologist Morton H. Shaevitz, PhD, director of the behavioral health programs at the Scripps Clinic and Research Foundation in La Jolla, CA. He is the author of *Lean & Mean: The No Hassle, Life-Extending Weight Loss Program for Men.* G. P. Putnam's Sons.

Guarding Against Skating Injuries

In-line skating, roller-skating and skate boarding cause an estimated 160,000 injuries a year. *Most common:* Wrist fractures. *Important:* Participants should wear wrist guards, approved helmets, and knee and elbow pads.

Source: Richard A. Schieber, MD, Division of Unintentional Injury Prevention, National Center for Injury Prevention and Control, Centers for Disease Control and Prevention, Atlanta. His study was published in *The Journal of the American Medical Association*, 515 N. State St., Chicago 60610.

Secrets of Exercise Stick-to-it-iveness

Seventy-five percent of people who start an exercise program quit within a year. *To be an exercise veteran...*

- Choose a program that is fun for you. *Best:* Lifetime sports—hiking, swimming, walking, dancing, gardening, volleyball, tennis, golf (no golf carts please). Add appropriate conditioning exercises once you are comfortable with the regime.
- Pick a motivating role model—someone you've seen on the tennis court or in your aerobics class.
- Join—or create—a team to add fun, competition and socializing.
- Treat exercise times like "appointments." Those who miss three consecutive exercise sessions are more likely to abandon the program altogether.

Source: Robert Hopper, PhD, gives seminars on health and fitness nationwide. He is based in Santa Barbara, CA.

Walking for Health

Walkers Club of America offers a free list of walking clinics and clubs. Send a self-addressed, stamped envelope to Box M, Livingston Manor, New York 12758. *More walking information:* National Association of Mall Walkers, Box 191, Hermann, Missouri 65041...Walkways Center, 1400 16 St. NW, Washington, DC 20036.

Source: *Freebies (& More) for Folks Over Fifty* by Linda Bowman, COM-OP Publishing, Box 6661, Malibu, CA 90265.

Real Cause of Flabby Muscles

Lack of exercise—not aging. Muscle mass does decline between ages 30 and 70. But isotonic—strength-building—exercises can reverse the decline. Half an hour of isotonics two or three times a week can increase strength within two weeks and double it in 12 weeks—by changing the ratio of muscle to fat. *Bonus:* Increased bone density—helping prevent fractures caused by osteoporosis.

Source: William J. Evans, PhD, Director of Noll Laboratories of Human Performance Research, Pennsylvania State University, University Park, and coauthor, *Biomarkers: The 10 Determinants of Aging You Can Control.* Simon & Schuster, Inc..

Treadmill Traps

Setting the speed too fast or the incline too steep... keeping your ankles too stiff, which can lead to shinsplints...flailing your arms, which can twist your torso and stress the back ...locking your arms in one position, which prevents your body from making subtle adjustments to better absorb impact. *Helpful:* Keep your gait smooth, upper body loose and arms close to your torso, moving them back and forth in a relatively straight line.

Source: Mike Motta, president, Plus One Fitness in New York City, quoted in *American Health,* 28 W. 23 St., New York 10010.

Best Exercise Videos

• *Best for dancers: Kicking With Country,* by Denise Austin. Learn to line dance to original hits from top country stars. Well taught and strenuous. 45 minutes.

• *Best for stress relief: Yoga Exercise Workout,* by Jane Fonda. The best information available on breathing and relaxing into the moves. Variations for people with limited flexibility. 56 minutes.

• *Best for strength training: TNT Workout,* by Troy DeMond. Comes with resistance tubing (a large rubber band) for upper- and lower-body conditioning. 65 minutes.

• *Best for die-hard exercisers: Energy Sprint,* by Karen Voight. Extremely demanding, full-body aerobic conditioning. Includes a "step" section. 85 minutes.

• *Best for older adults: Low Impact, High Comedy Workout,* by Milton Berle. Safe, effective and very funny. Carries the seal of approval of the Aerobics and Fitness Association of America. 61 minutes.

• *Best for kids: Let's Play Sports! Tips from the Pros.* Two-volume set covers 12 sports—soccer, tennis, softball, more—presented by stars like Peggy Fleming and Bruce Jenner. 80 minutes.

• *Best for overweight people: Sweat and Shout,* by Richard Simmons. Humorous, effective weight-loss program—with original disco hits from the 1970s. 60 minutes.

• *Best for pregnant women: Pregnancy Program,* by Kathy Smith. Safe workouts for all stages of pregnancy and the postpartum period. Mixes low-impact aerobics with exercises for flexibility and good posture. 95 minutes.

• *Best for "step" aerobics enthusiasts: CherFitness: Body Confidence.* An excellent step program developed by Cher's personal trainer, Keli Roberts. With original hits from the 1980s. 88 minutes.

• *Best for disabled people:* Exercise tapes for paraplegics, quadriplegics, amputees and persons with cerebral palsy are available from National Handicapped Sports, 451 Hungerford Dr., Suite 100, Rockville, Maryland 20850. 30 minutes each.

Source: Peg Jordan, RN, author of several books on fitness and editor in chief of *American Fitness,* 1520 Ventura Blvd., Sherman Oaks, CA 91403. A good mail-order source for exercise tapes is Collage Video Specialties, 5390 Main St. NE, Minneapolis 55421.

Special-Order Food

You can special-order food at practically any fine restaurant. Dining out can be troublesome for people on special diets—to cut fat or salt... if you are a vegetarian...if you have a food allergy, etc. Most chefs will modify dishes at your request. If your needs are very specific or you want to be sure of getting what you need, call the chef. *Note:* If you're calling, remember that chefs are busiest from 12 pm to 2 pm and 6 pm to 9 pm. Call the restaurant during off hours prior to your reservation.

Source: Tim Zagat, president of Zagat Survey, which publishes the best-selling guides to restaurants in major US cities, 4 Columbus Circle, New York 10019.

Salt-Substitute Danger

Salt substitutes containing a mixture of sodium chloride and potassium chloride can be dangerous for those on sodium-restricted diets. *Danger:* Used liberally by such individuals, these products can result in a potassium build-up, leading to irregular heartbeat or even a fatal heart rhythm disturbance. *Better way:* Instead of salt substitutes, add flavor to food with garlic, onion, lemon juice or herbs. Salt substitutes are generally safe for healthy individuals.

Source: Randall Zusman, MD, associate professor of medicine, Harvard Medical School, and director, division of hypertension and vascular medicine, Massachusetts General Hospital, Boston.

13

Very, Very Personal

How to Get the Love You Want

There is hope: A deep and long-lasting love and companionship in marriage is possible…

The secret: Couples must change from an unconscious marriage to a conscious marriage.

Almost all couples start their relationship as an unconscious marriage just by falling in love. In this state of romantic love, infatuation or "love at first sight," you feel your union is "magical"—and that your beloved is "the perfect one"…"the answer to your dreams."

What you do not realize is that this "person of your dreams" has qualities—voice tone, posture, facial expression, mood and character traits—that match an "image" in your unconscious mind of important people from your past (parents, other childhood caretakers). You actually fall in love with someone similar to those childhood caretakers.

More often we unconsciously choose mates who have similar negative rather than positive traits, that become obvious and disturbing after the "glow" of romance fades. They also have positive traits but the negative traits are more apparent.

Example: Picking a husband who ignores you like your father, or a wife who nags like your mother.

The marriage becomes "unconscious" because both people try to recreate—in order to repair—their childhood.

They feel more or less in love depending on their unconscious anticipation of getting early needs met in the marriage.

Problems emerge when the partner, similar to the past figure, does not repair the initial hurt or give them the love they never got from their parents, leading to disillusionment, distrust or divorce.

Instead of love notes, back rubs, avid listening and time together, now each "escapes" into separate interests, friends, activities.

This unconscious repetition of the past to satisfy unmet needs—wanting from your spouse what you did not get from your parents—explains why spouses sometimes get more furious at their partners than the situation warrants.

Example: If your husband isn't at the office when you call, you panic, fearing he's having an affair or will leave you, triggering old feelings of abandonment when mother left you with a baby-sitter, or was sick and unavailable —or worse—died.

Another common problem emerging from the unconscious marriage is the power struggle, where spouses react like children toward each other or as their parents reacted toward them.

While couples may panic over such conflicts, there is a hidden gain: The end of romantic love and being numb to each other's negative traits can be the beginning of more realistic reappraisals and growing up.

This is where "Imago Relationship Therapy" comes in (imago means image). This is a synthesis and expansion of ideas and techniques from other schools—including psychoanalysis, social learning theory, transactional analysis, gestalt and systems theory—to help couples move from repetitions in an unconscious marriage to a constructively conscious marriage.

The conscious marriage brings an end to romantic attachment and power struggles. The couple makes a commitment to uncover the unconscious needs that ignited their initial attraction, to heal their wounds, and to move to a more evolved relationship based on personal wholeness and accepting and appreciating each other as separate beings. The spouse goes from being a surrogate parent to a passionate friend.

The steps to create a conscious marriage can be done alone—or with the professional help of a therapist. *Important:*

• Learn the dialogue—an essential communications skill that enables couples to heal each other's emotional wounds by…

Mirroring—repeating back what each other says about needs.

Validating—telling your partner you understand the logic of his/her needs given his/her childhood frustrations.

Empathy—experiencing your partner's feelings.

• Use the dialogue process, mutually identifying unmet needs and the corresponding specific request underlying a complaint.

Example: "You come home late" reveals "I need to feel loved" and the resulting request, "I would like you to come home by 7 pm on Tuesday nights."

• Identify the unmet agenda, the one from childhood that repeats in the marriage (attention, praise, comfort, independence) and how it sabotages the current relationship.

Example: "Isolators" need "space" out of fear of being smothered by a spouse as they were by a parent. "Fusers," abandoned as children, want to merge with a spouse.

Helpful: Imagine addressing each important person in your childhood home, noting their positive and negative traits, what you liked and didn't like, wanted but didn't get. Ask then for what you want—and imagine them giving it. And—to separate yourself and your partner from parents, compare positive and negative traits, what you enjoy most, what you want and don't get.

• Develop personal wholeness— instead of seeking a mate to fill in your "holes." Find your "lost self."

Example: Because your father drank, you learned to ignore feelings of shame and sadness.

Drop the facade or "false self" that protects you from hurt. Reclaim your "disowned self" that was criticized and denied.

Example: Your mother always said you're not as smart as your brother so you don't act smart even if you are.

Change your own negative traits without projecting them onto a partner (complaining "He's bitter, not me" when you are really bitter) or acting them out.

• Validate and support each other's efforts.

• Communicate your needs instead of clinging to the childhood belief that your partner instinctively knows your needs. Fulfill some needs on your own.

• Meet your partner's needs more often than putting yourself first—in healing his/her wounds, you heal your own.

Example: When an emotionally unavailable man marries a woman with a similar type father, the husband heals her wound and his own by becoming more sensitive to her needs.

Stretching exercise: Do something that your partner wants that is difficult for you to do.

Make a verbal or written commitment to stop "exits"—escapes from intimacy like overworking, over-involvement with children, shopping, drinking, lying, picking fights—and to work together for a defined time. Set aside an hour of uninterrupted time together for a defined time.

Write a personal and joint relationship vision —"we are affectionate with each other," "we are loving parents," "we have fun."

Communicate better by taking turns as deliverer who describes a thought, feeling, anger or complaint, starting with "I" ("I felt anxious today at work")—and as receiver who paraphrases the message and asks for clarification. ("This morning you woke up wanting to stay home. Did I understand you right?").

"Reromanticize" by sharing what pleases you now—("I feel loved when you call me from work…and when you massage my back…and when you listen when I'm upset"—what once pleased you—"I used to feel loved when you held my hand, wrote love notes, whispered sexy things in my ear.").

What would please you—("I would feel loved if you took a shower with me, watched my favorite TV show, slept in the nude.").

Do two each day for the next two months—and keep adding to the list.

Surprise each other with one new pleasure each week and one fun activity—walking, tennis, dancing, showering.

Visualize your love healing your partner—visualize your partner's love healing you.

This new conscious love will create a stable and passionate bond between the two of you, and improve physical and emotional health. This new conscious love will also help you strengthen your immune system. It will flower into broader concern for others and the environment and a spiritual union with the universe.

Source: Harville Hendrix, PhD, educator and therapist who is the founder and director of the Institute for Relationship Therapy in New York. He is the author of the best-selling book *Getting the Love You Want: A Guide for Couples* (Harper/Perennial), and *Keeping the Love You Find: A Guide for Singles* (Pocket Books).

How to be Prepared When Your Spouse Retires

One of the greatest mistakes a couple can make is to assume that retirement will simply be a continuation of married life as they have known it.

Retirement has its own rhythm, just as the honeymoon years, child-rearing years and empty-nest years had theirs.

Most likely change: You will spend much more time together. *Result:* Trouble spots may arise in the smallest areas of daily life. Many newly retired couples, even those who agree on the major issues of their retirement—where to live, how to handle the finances—are surprised by how infuriating they may suddenly find their comfortable, cherished mate.

Most common trouble spots…

• Lack of retirement planning. Many a husband has been shocked to learn that his wife has no desire to move to the fishing village he always pictured as a retirement home. Failure to communicate expectations about retirement, or to do the pre-planning necessary to make your plans a reality, can cause terrible conflict in retiring couples.

To offset clashes over major issues: Attend a retirement planning workshop at your local Chamber of Commerce, community college or senior center.

• Failure to appreciate the psychological impact of retirement. Couples must realize that retirement can be a traumatic passage, particularly for men. Even men who look forward to retirement may feel fearful and "lost" when they no longer have a routine and the familiar identity of their working selves. Concerns with mortality and self-worth may loom large for the first time.

Best course for women: Respect the grieving period. Don't crowd or smother your husband with suggestions, opinions, questions or demands or push him into a full schedule before he is ready. But do let him know that you are there. This is a good time for extra cuddling, affection and reassurance. Let him percolate a bit, and shift the focus to your own feelings.

Many women feel that they have spent their entire lives deferring to the needs of their husbands and families. They expect retirement to be "their turn," and fear being trapped again by their husbands' needs.

Best course: Have compassion for your husband's feelings, but be very firm regarding your own needs.

Once the transitional period passes, women can help their husbands back into active life. Men are badly needed as community volunteers. Some may just want to "play" a while, others may enjoy part-time work or a second career.

•Alcoholism/clinical depression. Alcoholism is under-recognized and badly under-treated in seniors, even though treatment has a high likelihood of success in this age group.

Depression, with or without alcohol, can afflict either sex, but is especially common among those forced to take "early retirement." Depression can also be triggered by many medications. If you suspect either problem in your family, don't hesitate to seek professional help.

Small stuff—but major gripes...

•Grocery shopping. It sounds hilarious—but this is a top area of conflict cited by retired couples. Often the wife has been shopping for years, and finds it insulting when her husband suddenly questions every choice and examines every tomato.

I have met many couples who have had bitter arguments over who gets to push the cart!

Solution: Decide that one of you will do all the shopping. Or shop with two lists. He can select the produce, while she does the rest.

•Territorial strife. With two people in one house, problems often arise over rooms and routines.

Examples: She wants the spare room as a sewing room, he wants a den. He used to leave for work, so she could drink coffee and watch *Good Morning, America,* before starting her chores. Now he wants to watch CNN and complains when she starts the housework.

Solution: Communication, compassion and compromise. It's your retirement as well as your spouse's. Wives must be willing to cede some

domestic territory—it's his kitchen, too. Husbands must face the necessity to "get a life," and not expect their wives to provide one.

•Comings and goings. Insecurity often manifests as controlling behavior... *Where are you going? When will you be home? Who's on the phone?*

Solution: Stay calm and considerate. Reassure your mate, but don't be bullied. *Essential:* Keep your sense of humor.

•Division of labor. He expects her to perform the same chores she always has, even if she's still working part-time. She expects that now he's retired, he'll take on some household chores.

Solutions: It's time to be fair.

Men: You may have retired from work, but not from the partnership of a marriage. Offer to take on the vacuuming. Don't force her to ask.

Women: Acknowledge the work he does do—caring for the yard, garbage, car, etc. Then ask for the help you need from your spouse. But if you ask him to vacuum, let him do it his way. *Helpful:* List chores you each hate, and negotiate for the other to take them on. Hire help for chores you both hate.

•Sex. Many men find sex a means of self-proof as well as pleasure. So a pleasant side effect of the anxieties retirement can produce is that many men discover a renewed enthusiasm for sex. Older men often have a stronger sex drive in the morning—so don't be too quick to leap out of bed. You don't have to—you're retired!

Wives: Enjoy it, buy some new lingerie, be willing to try new things.

Caution: Some couples experience the opposite, and shy away from intimacy after retirement. If your sex life is unhealthy, this is a problem that needs to be resolved through frank discussion or counseling.

•Television. Get two!

Source: Gloria Bledsoe Goodman, author of *Keys to Living With a Retired Husband.* Barron's Educational Series, Inc.

How to Handle Trouble

There is no way to solve all life's problems. The best we can do is to use our inner intellectual, emotional and spiritual resources to face them squarely. If we do that, we can grow from the confrontation...and then we will find ourselves better able to cope with future troubles.

Example: As a young boy, I experienced the pain and embarrassment of growing up with an alcoholic father who was unable to provide an emotionally stable and financially secure home life for his family. The difficulties I endured then, the ways I learned to cope, and later the knowledge that I had survived, strengthened me emotionally and prepared me for later travails, most recently the diagnosis that I have terminal cancer of the bone marrow.

Your resources for handling trouble can be summarized as thinking, feeling, sharing, deciding and praying. Let me discuss them in turn.

Thinking...

The more effectively you are able to use your mind, the more success you are likely to have in dealing with your troubles. Set out to guide your actions by reason, a realistic understanding of the facts of your problem—not by illusions or fantasies.

Find out the basic facts you need to know.

Example: If the bank tells you that one of your checks bounced, it indicates some kind of financial problem. How big a problem and what you have to do depends on knowing some other facts. If it is the first time this ever happened and came after you unknowingly deposited a bad check from someone else, it is just a minor annoyance. If you never balance your checkbook and it is the fourth time it has happened this month, then you may do well to change your habits.

When faced with more complicated trouble than this...like a legal or medical problem...be prepared both to do your own research and to consult experts to acquire all the information you need to study the options and make an informed decision.

Use your imagination to create a vivid mental picture of what you want to achieve...that will encourage you to find ways to do it.

After exercising your mind, you will develop a deeper understanding of your problem, and become better at judging. Finally, when you put your individual problems in perspective with the larger amount of suffering in this world, you develop the peace of mind that comes from knowing you have done whatever you can.

Feeling...

Your thoughts and feelings are intimately related. Try to understand the hidden inner feelings that may be preventing you from taking effective action.

In times of trouble, negative feelings like pain, fear, anxiety and helplessness make us doubt our own value. If you are able to look into yourself and recognize your different emotional responses and needs, you can stop being a victim and start to exert control over your life despite your troubles.

Sharing...

We need to find ways to develop our inner strength to deal with troubles, but we can't always do it on our own. Don't be afraid to connect with others. When your troubles have you down, family and friends can give you the emotional help you need to recover your self-confidence. You will also find many other people who can give you assistance...if you are prepared to take the first step.

Look to others for both emotional support and practical advice. You cannot be objective about yourself, and can get a better sense of perspective if you break out of your isolation. Talk to a variety of advisers whose wisdom and friendship you trust. Start with your spouse, parents, other family members and friends.

Then consider professional counselors, clergy, teachers you respect. Even young children can be a rich source of emotional honesty.

If a number of these people tell you the same thing about your problems and the way you should handle them, you can probably believe them.

Deciding...

After you have learned about your thoughts, your feelings and your friends, it is time to decide what you should do...then actually do it.

Before you make your decision, picture the consequences in as much imaginative detail as you can. Weigh the advice you have received from different sources and your own instincts… be as objective as possible. Write down the pluses and minuses of each option…uncover any buried fears within yourself that make the choice hard for you.

Important: Don't try to make important decisions unless your emotions are settled. If you are feeling euphoric—or depressed—your judgment is not likely to be very good.

Praying…

The last most basic resource for handling your trouble is praying—surrendering yourself to the mysteriousness of life. You are bound to die. Your life will never be certain or tidy. Accept pain with hope and joy, if you can.

Source: John Carmody, PhD, senior research fellow in religion at the University of Tulsa, who has written more than 40 books. His latest is *How to Handle Trouble.* Doubleday.

Lessons from Widowhood

My husband, Dr. Milton Brothers, died four years ago. As a psychologist, I knew that bereaved people pass through a predictable series of stages in the normal course of grieving, but this knowledge did not make my personal emotional turmoil any less.

Emotional recovery…

For months after losing Milton, after almost 40 years of an intensely happy marriage, I was in a state of despair…even though I was financially secure and my career kept me constantly busy. All my lecturing, writing and traveling seemed meaningless without my husband to share it. I was overcome by agonizing loneliness.

Today, the loneliness is still there, but it is much less intense. Life has recovered its meaning. Once again, I am able to look forward to new experiences and when I think of my husband, most of the time it brings not tears but smiles because of the legacy of happy memories he left me.

Stages of grief…

British psychiatrist Dr. Colin Parkes discovered the predictable stages of grief following the loss of a spouse or other close relative.

First stage: Immediately following the death is shock…followed by numbness.

Even though Milt had been struggling for 18 months with terminal cancer, his death still came as a dramatic shock to me.

In the immediate aftermath, I was kept so busy notifying relatives and friends and arranging the details of the funeral that I was essentially operating on autopilot, feeling nothing.

To this day, I still cannot remember the details of those days immediately following Milt's death…not even what I wore to the funeral.

Second stage: Suffering. When the numbness wears off, the pain begins.

Every person's pain is different…a different blend of emotions…a different period of time needed to recover.

The pain seems to be least for those who have suffered a lot in life and learned to accept the vicissitudes it brings.

I was not one of those people, because my life had been full of love, happiness and achievement…all shared with Milt.

Now I recognize that my major emotional problem was self-pity. I cried…

•When someone asked how I was.

•When I reached out for Milton—and once again—I remembered him in his absence.

•Whenever I passed our favorite restaurant.

•When I saw Milt's car.

•When I recognized Milton's signature.

Value of tears: When someone cries, it makes others uncomfortable and they usually try to make the person crying feel better. But research has shown that crying fulfills a valuable physiological function.

Tears of sadness or anger contain leucine-enkephalin, a natural pain reliever, and prolactin, a hormone that encourages the secretion of tears. These chemicals are produced in the brain at times of stress. This has led biochemists to suggest that crying is an emotionally helpful process that relieves stress by washing out the chemicals that stress builds up.

So I believe that tears are really a widow's friend, helping her deal with the frustrations and difficulties of life without her helpmate.

As I began to emerge from the stage of intense suffering, the nature of my tears began to change. One day, on the farm where my husband and I had spent so many of our favorite hours together, I noticed the coffee pot. I touched it, remembering how much pride Milt always took in the coffee he made, and I cried.

But this time, I realized that I was not shedding tears for myself and my constant loneliness...they were for Milt, dead at only 62, missing out on decades of vibrant life he should have continued to enjoy. I was emerging from the depths.

Other reactions...

Anger: Along with sadness, I was full of anger, like many widows. I was angry at Milt for leaving me alone to deal with many unfamiliar aspects of life. I was angry at him for continuing to smoke even though he, a physician, certainly knew the association between smoking and disease, including the cancer that killed him. And I was angry whenever I saw couples together, enjoying what I had lost.

It is natural for widows to be angry. The loss of emotional security accompanied by loneliness produces tremendous stress. Stress, say experts like Dr. John Larson of the Institute of Stress Medicine at Norwalk Hospital, deprives brain cells of essential nutrients and leaves the victim irritable and angry.

Insecurity: Widowhood lowers a woman's social status and leaves her feeling insecure in many different ways.

Even though I am something of a celebrity, professionally successful and financially comfortable, I was not immune from insecurity.

One afternoon, a major talk show failed to call me back to confirm the date I was tentatively scheduled for. Normally, I would not have been concerned. But, just six months after Milt's death, I felt they didn't want me on their show...and nobody else would, ever again.

I was only reassured when the scheduler called me again the next morning, explaining that she hadn't been able to speak to the producer earlier.

Coping with loss...

My experience has taught me that nothing can prepare you for the devastating experience of the loss of a loved one. I was not able to manage my grief better than anyone else.

But I have learned first-hand a number of ways a widow can help herself...

• Stay in control of your life. It is very helpful if a child or other close relative offers to take care of all your bills, taxes and financial matters...but don't let the person do it for more than a month or two.

It shouldn't take long to learn how to take care of basic bill paying and check balancing yourself. For tax expertise, you may want to hire an accountant or other professional...but you make the decisions.

• Avoid hasty decisions. If possible, a widow should not make any major decisions for at least a year after her husband's death. If you cannot avoid it, get the best advice you can from a variety of sources.

I regret that a few weeks after Milt died I sold his big farm tractor to a neighbor, thinking I would never need it. Now I regret that I didn't keep it and learn to operate it, so that every time I used it, Milt's memory would have ridden along with me.

• Maintain your regular routine. Losing a husband is such a shock that it seems hard to do anything. If you succumb to that, you may end up in a long-term state of depression. Pushing yourself to continue your regular activities serves as an early therapy for grief. Later, when the grief has eased, you will find it easier to make changes.

• Plan anniversaries and holidays—they are more painful because of the memories they evoke.

Helpful: Surround yourself with people. The first Thanksgiving after Milt's death, I invited 18 people to the farm for Thanksgiving weekend. I was far too busy to feel miserable. If you can't do it with your own family, invite people you know who will be alone otherwise. You will do good for them as well as yourself... always a rewarding experience. Weekends are also times of potential loneliness, so be sure to plan ahead so you have something worthwhile to do...religious services...sports or hobbies.

• Be good to yourself. Widows need coddling...so coddle yourself. Get your hair done ...have a facial or massage...and be sure to exercise.

•Check your progress. Every three months, see how you have progressed. Do you feel better? Are you less depressed? The answer will not always be yes. But as the months pass, you will notice signs of improvement. There is no timetable, but if you see no progress after a year, it may be a good idea to consult your doctor or therapist for advice and reassurance. You will always feel your loss, but with time you should be able to smile once again. I know that I do, especially when the many happy hours I spend with our grandchildren remind me what a joyous legacy Milton left behind.

Source: Dr. Joyce Brothers, noted psychologist and author of *Widowed.* Ballantine Books.

How to Find a Missing Person

When a private investigator is hired to trace a missing person, he/she doesn't immediately put on his trench coat and head for the closest seedy waterfront bar.

The first move is to do some simple research into easily accessible public records. If you want to find your long-lost uncle...old college roommate...someone who owes you money...runaway spouse...childhood sweetheart...or anyone else, you can do the same.

Here are the most useful sources of information...

Motor vehicle records...

Write to the Commissioner of Motor Vehicles of the state where the missing person last lived and ask for his/her driving record. First call the driving record division to ask the fee for this service—it's usually about $3 to $7.

In your letter, give the subject's date of birth ...or the year you guess is closest to it. If the Department of Motor Vehicles (DMV) informs you that many people in their file share that name and age, write back specifying which part of the state the subject lived in.

If you still get back driving records for a number of individuals, don't give up...these records list valuable information that may help

you pin down your target, including some or all of the following:

•Address
•Social Security number
•Height
•Date of birth
•Weight
•Dates and locations of accidents
•Eye color
•Dates and locations of traffic tickets
•Hair color
•Restrictions (eyeglasses, etc.)

Disadvantage: Driver's licenses may be renewed as infrequently as once in eight years, so you may find that the address on the record is outdated. If that happens, write again for the motor vehicle registrations on file for your subject's name and date of birth. The address will be more current, because registrations must be renewed annually. Don't forget to enclose a check for the service.

If you still don't track down a current address, you may find more clues by writing to the tag department of the DMV. Quote the title number and vehicle identification number from the registration of a vehicle he previously owned, and request the vehicle history (sometimes called body file).

This is a packet of up to 30 pages that includes paper work with the subject's signature, as well as previous addresses listed on yearly registrations. The people who live at those addresses now...and/or the current owner of the subject's old car...may be able to give you more current information about your missing person.

Records of vital statistics...

State departments of vital statistics will provide records of birth, death, marriage and divorce. In some states, divorce records must be obtained from the clerk of the court in the jurisdiction that granted the divorce.

Birth records contain much valuable information, including:

•Complete name
•Exact date of birth
•Parents' names

- Place of birth
- Parents' ages
- Parents' occupations
- Parents' address
- Mother's maiden name
- Parents' places of birth

Using your knowledge of the family names of both parents of the missing person, you can try to contact relatives who may be in touch with him. Start looking for relatives near the subject's place of birth.

Master death file: This file kept by the Social Security Administration lists all deaths since 1962…including Social Security number, first and last names, dates of birth and death and place of death (by zip code).

How to use it: From the death record of the missing person's parent, find the place of death and write there for a copy of the death certificate.

Contact the funeral home listed on the certificate and ask for the next-of-kin of the deceased, who will be your subject or a close relative. You can obtain access to information on the Master Death File from private companies. The one I use is Research Is Company, 7907 NW 53 St., Suite 420, Miami 33166. *Cost:* $45.

Running someone's Social Security number: The Research Is Company will put through their computers any Social Security number you provide to give you addresses that someone has used for the past several years. *Cost:* $35—and if they do not give you at least one address from that Social Security number it will be refunded.

Federal Parent Locator Service: If you have a child support order against a missing person, this government agency will search through government records to find him/her at no cost to you.

Important: You must first approach your state's Child Support Enforcement Division to contact the state's Parent Locator Service. *Other sources:*

- Abandoned property files
- Bankruptcy records
- College records
- Military records
- Corporation records
- Small claims court
- Boat registrations
- National cemeteries
- Bar associations
- Medical boards
- Foreign embassies
- Passport records
- Workers' comp. records
- US Postal Service

Good hunting!

Source: Joseph J. Culligan, licensed private investigator. He is the author of *You, Too, Can Find Anybody: A Reference Manual.* Available in book or video from the author at 4995 NW 79 Ave., Miami 33166.

Prostate Problems Self-Defense

The good news about prostate cancer is that the disease is almost 100% curable—if it's caught early.

The bad news: Because most men fail to get regular checkups, and because they often ignore the telltale symptoms—chiefly frequent urination, especially at night, and a weak urine stream—most cases of prostate cancer are spotted far too late for successful treatment. *Result:* Prostate cancer now kills more men than all other forms of cancer except lung cancer.

Prostate cancer strikes men of all ages, but it is remarkably common among men in their fifties and sixties. Recent statistics suggest that roughly one of every 20 men age 50 or older has prostate cancer, even though few are aware of the problem. *At special risk:* African-Americans and those with a family history of prostate cancer…

- Having one primary relative (father, brother, or son) with prostate cancer doubles your risk of having the disease.
- Having two increases your risk three to four times.
- Having three raises your risk by a factor of eight to 10.

Recent reports suggesting that having a vasectomy promotes prostate cancer are inconclusive. Men who have had vasectomies do seem to have a higher incidence of prostate cancer. But it's simply not clear yet whether this additional risk stems from the vasectomy itself or merely from the fact that men who get vasectomies tend to see a urologist more frequently than men who do not. In any case, this apparent increase in risk is extremely slight.

Bottom line: Men who have already undergone a vasectomy need not take any special precautions—beyond regular checkups.

To prevent prostate trouble...

•Eat less fat. As with heart disease and many other forms of cancer, prostate cancer is more common among men who eat a fatty diet than among those who don't. *Especially dangerous:* Saturated fat, found primarily in meat and dairy products. It seems to be particularly effective at promoting tumor growth. To protect yourself, eat less meat and dairy products. Increase your intake of fruits, vegetables, grains, and non-fat dairy products.

•Don't smoke. Recent studies show clearly that men who smoke face an increased risk of prostate cancer. While this additional risk is small, it's best not to smoke at all—especially if you're elderly, African-American, or if you have a family history of prostate cancer. Try also to avoid exposure to second-hand smoke.

•Have regular checkups. All men should have an annual prostate exam starting at age 50 —age 40 for men at risk. This exam should be conducted by a board-certified urologist or radiologist. It should include not only the familiar digital rectal exam, in which the doctor inserts a gloved finger into the rectum to feel for prostate tumors, but also the recently developed blood test for prostate specific antigen (PSA). *Cost:* $30 to $75.

An elevated PSA level does not necessarily mean prostate cancer. *Other possibilities:* Enlargement of the prostate (benign prostatic hypertrophy or hyperplasia) or prostate inflammation (prostatitis).

Like prostate cancer, these conditions raise PSA levels. And they cause the same symptoms. Yet unlike prostate cancer, these conditions are generally benign. They can often be controlled with drug therapy.

To pinpoint the cause of an elevated PSA level, the doctor must conduct an ultrasound examination of the prostate. In this procedure, performed without anesthesia on an outpatient basis, the doctor inserts a needle-tipped fiberoptic probe into the rectum.

If any suspicious areas are found, the doctor uses this same probe to take tiny tissue samples. These samples are then biopsied. *Cost:* $300 to $500.

If the biopsy confirms the presence of cancer, your doctor will likely recommend surgical removal of the prostate or radiation therapy. The best treatment for advanced prostate cancer is hormone therapy. Chemotherapy is usually ineffective against prostate cancer.

Source: William J. Catalona, MD, chief of urologic surgery, Washington University Medical Center, St. Louis. He is also urologist-in-chief at Barnes and Allied hospitals in St. Louis. Ninety-five percent of Dr. Catalona's practice is devoted to the treatment of prostate cancer.

Impotence Cure

A device that corrects psychogenic (psychologically based) impotence is now in clinical trials. *The goal:* To free men from lengthy psychoanalysis or the surgery required for implanting a prosthesis. *How it works:* A small plastic unit (about 7/8" x 3") is inserted into the rectum, where it is positioned near the nerve center responsible for initiating erections. Next, a tiny transmitter hidden in a piece of jewelry signals the battery-powered insert to generate an electrical field. This prompts a "natural" erection. The device is completely portable, requires no surgery, and can be inserted and removed at will by the user.

Source: Biosonics, Inc.

Seasonal Decline

Semen quality deteriorates during summer. *Theory:* Sperm production is impaired by longer periods of daylight—or possibly hotter temperatures. No way has yet been found to counteract this seasonal decline.

Source: Richard J. LeVine, MD, epidemiology branch, National Institute of Child Health and Human Development, Bethesda, MD.

Declining Sperm Counts

The decline in sperm counts, which has been reported recently in the media following several studies worldwide, is real. *Possible factor:* Increased exposure to estrogen and estrogen-like substances, which inhibit testosterone production. Until about 15 years ago, estrogen-like substances were given to beef cattle. Estrogen in urine of women on birth control pills could be contaminating the water supply. Estrogenic substances are by-products of gasoline combustion. Soy-based foods contain weak estrogens. *Exposure to toxic chemicals*, such as pesticides, may also be a factor. *Lifestyle factors may include:* Having children later —sperm count declines with age…sitting too much, which causes testicles to get too warm …regular use of steam rooms and saunas… obesity…use of cigarettes, alcohol or marijuana …varicose veins in the scrotum (varicoceles). *Important:* There is little evidence that fertility is declining. Increased awareness of infertility may, though, make it seem so.

Source: Marc Goldstein, MD, professor of urology and director, Center for Male Reproductive Medicine & Microsurgery, New York Hospital–Cornell Medical Center, New York.

 Testosterone Tablets

Testosterone tablets deliver the hormone into the bloodstream without the roller-coaster effect of traditional injections. Men who get testosterone shots often complain of emotional swings following a shot and energy lulls between shots. The new experimental delivery system resembles a small tablet. It's held be-

tween the upper lip and front teeth and contains a 24-hour dose of the hormone.

Source: Adrian Dobs, MD, associate professor of medicine and director of clinical studies, The Johns Hopkins Medical Institutions, Baltimore.

AIDS Update

AIDS patients diagnosed in 1991 are living twice as long as those diagnosed in 1984. *Reasons:* Better drugs…and better prevention and treatment of pneumonia and other opportunistic infections.

Source: Lisa Jacobson, ScM, coordinator, Multicenter AIDS Cohort Study Center, Johns Hopkins School of Public Health, Baltimore.

Should You Be Worried About Getting AIDS?

The risk of being exposed to the AIDS virus is greater than many people think. If a woman starts having sex at age 18 and has sex with a different man each year, she winds up having nine sex partners by age 27. But if each of these men behaves the same way—adding one new partner each year between the ages of 18 and 27—the woman winds up with 502 "phantom" partners. If any of these direct or phantom partners is infected with the AIDS virus, the woman is at risk of contracting the disease.

Source: Laura Brannon, PhD, assistant professor of psychology, Ohio State University, Lima.

Statistically Speaking

The average erect penis is 5.72 inches long.

Source: Claudio Teloken, MD, PhD, adjunct professor of urology, Santa Casa and FFFCM-PA Medical School, Porto Alegre, Brazil. His study of 150 male Caucasians was presented at a recent meeting of the American Urological Association, 1120 N. Charles St., Baltimore 21201.

Overcoming Premature Ejaculation

Premature ejaculation can now be overcome with *clomipramine* (Anafranil)—a drug long used to treat depression and obsessive-compulsive disorder. A dose of 50 milligrams (mg) increased time before ejaculation from an average of 81 to 409 seconds. At 25 mg, ejaculation was delayed to an average of 202 seconds. *Side effects:* Dry mouth and constipation.

Source: Stanley Althof, PhD, psychologist in sexual disorders, Case Western Reserve University, Cleveland. His study of 15 monogamous couples 21 to 65 years of age was presented at a recent meeting of the American Urological Association, 1120 N. Charles St., Baltimore 21202.

Hidden Cause of Memory Problems

Memory problems in elderly men may be caused by loss of testosterone. Healthy men older than 50 who received testosterone injections had improved performance on memory tests. These men also experienced greater grip strength, lower LDL (bad) cholesterol levels—and increased libido.

Source: John E. Morley, MB, BCH, professor of gerontology, St. Louis University School of Medicine. His study of 32 healthy men was reported in *Internal Medicine News & Cardiology News*, 12230 Wilkins Ave., Rockville, MD 20852.

Genital Bites

Treatment of genital bites is often delayed because victims are embarrassed. Men bitten by dogs typically go to an emergency room within an hour. But men whose penises are bitten or scraped during oral sex often ignore the injury even after infection sets in—and may not seek help for 24 hours to six weeks. *Danger:* Infected human bites can be more serious than dog bites. Bitten men need to be treated for infection and tested for sexually transmitted diseases.

Source: J. Stuart Wolf, Jr., MD, chief urology resident, University of California, San Francisco, Hospital.

Music vs. Rectal Exam Pain

Colorectal cancer is the second-leading cause of death by cancer in the US, but many patients are reluctant to undergo a sigmoidoscopy because the exam can be embarrassing and uncomfortable. *Good news:* 88% of patients who listened to music during a sigmoidoscopy reported reduced levels of anxiety and pain. Their blood pressure and heart rates were also lower than those of people who didn't listen to music.

Source: Brian Sweeney, MD, assistant professor of surgery, University of Massachusetts Medical Center, Worcester. His study of 50 men and women 20 to 76 years of age was presented at a recent meeting of the American Society of Colon and Rectal Surgeons, 85 W. Algonquin Rd., Arlington Heights, IL 60005.

Vasectomy vs. Testicular Cancer

Vasectomy does not cause testicular cancer, although several recent studies suggested that it did. *Latest evidence:* In a recent study of 73,917 vasectomized men, testicular cancer rates were no higher among men who had undergone the procedure than among men who had not. *However:* This study neither proved nor refuted the apparent link between vasectomy and prostate cancer. Earlier studies found evidence of such a link—but only after about 15 years following the surgery.

Source: Lisbeth Knudsen, MD, and Elsebeth Lynge, MD, epidemiologists, Danish Cancer Society, Copenhagen.

All About Men with Enlarged Breasts

Breast cancer is extremely rare among men, accounting for only about 1% of all cases of the disease. But *gynecomastia*, a benign form of breast enlargement that is sometimes painful and often embarrassing, is common—especially among teenagers and men older than 60.

The precise cause of gynecomastia is unknown. Most cases seem to stem from a hormone imbalance or simply from obesity... although long-term use of heart medications or diuretics and abuse of alcohol or marijuana is sometimes to blame.

To make sure that the enlargement is benign, any man with an enlarged breast or breasts should consult a doctor right away—especially if he notices any of the three warning signs of breast cancer...

• A discharge from the nipple.

• A lump.

• An ulceration or retraction of the nipple or skin around the breast.

Mild cases of gynecomastia rarely warrant treatment. To mask the enlargement, some men choose loose-fitting or oversized clothing.

But when the breast becomes painful or tender—or when men are embarrassed by their appearance—plastic surgery to remove the extra tissue is recommended.

Depending upon the consistency of the tissue to be removed, the surgeon may use liposuction, in which fat is sucked out of the body through a hollow tube inserted into the body —or conventional surgery.

The operation, which can be performed on an outpatient basis, is covered by most insurance policies. *Cost:* About $2,500.

Scarring is minimal when the surgery is performed by an experienced plastic surgeon. The incisions are usually made in the armpit or the dark skin of the nipple (areola), where they're less visible. Side effects—including infection, asymmetry of the breasts and adverse reactions to the anesthesia—are quite rare. Most patients are quite satisfied with the results.

Following surgery, patients can usually return to work within three days, although swelling of the chest may persist for several weeks.

Source: Richard A. Cooper, MD, associate professor of radiology and anatomy, and Juan Angelats, MD, professor of clinical surgery, both at Loyola University Medical Center, Maywood, IL.

New Treatment for Penis Curvature

Severe penis curvature *(Peyronie's disease)* can now be minimized via injections of *verapamil*, a calcium channel blocker. Peyronie's is caused by scar tissue resulting from injury to the erectile bodies, the two long chambers within the penis that fill with blood to form an erection. If severe enough, this curvature can make intercourse impossible. *Now:* Regular injections of verapamil into the scar resulted in better erectile function in 80% of the men who received treatment. Seventy percent of the men noted a reduction in the curvature. All the men reported a significant decrease in the narrowing of the penis, another common result of Peyronie's. If you have a curved penis, ask a urologist about verapamil.

Source: Laurence Levine, MD, director of the male sexual function and fertility program, Rush–Presbyterian/St. Luke's Medical Center, Chicago. His study of 14 men with Peyronie's disease was published in the *Journal of Urology,* 1120 N. Charles St., Baltimore 21202.

Best Time for Older Men to Have Sex

Older men who have trouble attaining erections at night can do better with morning sex. Testosterone levels are higher earlier in the day.

Source: *Medical Aspects of Human Sexuality.*

Sexual Side Effects of Commonly Prescribed Drugs

In the past, doctors attributed most sexual disorders to psychological causes. But there is a growing awareness—fueled by a growing number of studies—that more than half these conditions are triggered by physical ailments or, more surprisingly, the drugs used to treat these ailments.

Many commonly prescribed drugs produce sexual side effects that most patients—no matter how frightened or delighted they are by the effects—are too embarrassed to discuss with their doctors. Knowing about these drugs ahead of time can help to alleviate the problems.

Drugs that enhance sexual performance and enjoyment...

• *Amphetamines,* once widely used as diet aids, are now used mainly to treat narcolepsy (a condition characterized by uncontrollable attacks of deep sleep) and hyperactivity and attention-span disorders in children. They can cause heightened sexual awareness in both sexes and prolonged erection in males. But, if taken in high doses, they can have the reverse effects—decreased sex drive, inhibited male and female orgasm...and impotence.

• *Amyl nitrate* is a vasodilator (opening up the circulatory blood vessels) prescribed to relieve chest pain brought on by coronary artery spasms. But when crushed under the nose and inhaled (the way it's supposed to be used) just before orgasm, the drug's vapor increases blood flow to the genital area, enhancing and prolonging the feeling of orgasm. In some cases, however, this drug can inhibit orgasm and cause erectile difficulties.

• *Labetalol* is an antihypertensive drug. But unlike most drugs of its kind, which are notorious for causing impotence, this one may actually delay loss of erection after intercourse.

• *Levodopa,* used to treat patients with Parkinson's disease, increases the body's level of dopamine (a natural sexual stimulant) and causes patients to feel sexually aroused. As a result, the drug has been used to treat impotence in otherwise healthy subjects. *Success rate in one study:* 70%.

• *Mazindol,* an appetite-suppressant, can greatly increase female sexual desire.

• *Nitroglycerin* is a vasodilator used to treat patients with angina. It may also increase blood flow to the genitals, thereby facilitating erections in men who have trouble achieving them.

• *Oral contraceptives* can work both positively and negatively. Many women experience a decreased sexual drive when taking the Pill, while others report an increased sex drive. Researchers are still unclear as to why these contradictory effects occur.

• *Papaverine* is another vasodilator which increases the flow of blood to the genitals and is often prescribed to treat impotence. The patient simply injects the drug at the base of his penis immediately prior to intercourse. An erection is almost instantaneous.

• *Phenoxybenzamine* and *phentolamine* are alpha-blockers that are most commonly used to lower blood pressure. But since they prevent the constriction of blood vessels, they are also being used to treat impotence.

• *Valium* and valium-like drugs inhibit sexual performance when taken in high doses. But when given in very low doses to patients with psychologically caused sexual problems, they enable these patients to relax and become sexually aroused. These drugs can also delay ejaculation and orgasm.

• *Yohimbine* is designed specifically to enhance sexual performance and enjoyment. As a result, it has been touted as the ultimate aphrodisiac. It's especially effective in treating diabetic impotence, which results when the nerves leading to the genital area degenerate.

Drugs that inhibit sexual performance and enjoyment...

• *Alcohol,* ingested alone or in liquid medications (cough, medicine, etc.), can cause inhibited erection, decreased sexual desire, delayed ejaculation, male infertility, and gynecomastia (painful breast growth in men).

• *Anabolic steroids* are analogs of testosterone that are prescribed to build muscle tissue in malnourished patients. While they are not widely prescribed, they are widely abused by athletes, especially body-builders. In males these drugs can cause reduced sex drive, impotence, decreased testicle size, and decreased sperm production, gynecomastia, and priapism (prolonged, painful erections). In females, they can cause male-type hair growth and balding, deepening of the voice, reduction in breast size, clitoral enlargement, decreased uterine size, irregular menstruation, and cessation of ovulation.

• *Digoxin* is prescribed to regulate heart beat. It very closely resembles the female hormone estrogen, and can cause decreased sex drive, impotence, and gynecomastia.

• *Estrogen*, used to treat women with certain kinds of cancer and to reduce the unpleasant symptoms of menopause (including vaginal dryness and hot flashes), can cause problems for an older woman's sexual partner. *Reason:* As men age, they may require more and more friction during intercourse to achieve orgasm. But the vaginal lubrication resulting from estrogen supplements decreases this friction.

• *Isotretinoin* (Accutane) is a marvelous drug that has received a lot of attention for its successful treatment of severe cases of acne. It can, however, cause impotence, decreased sex drive, menstrual irregularities, galactorrhea (discharge from the female breasts), and vaginal dryness.

• *Lithium*, prescribed for the treatment of manic depressive disorder, can cause decreased sex drive, inhibited erection, male infertility, and the discharge of milk from female breasts.

• *Nicotine* is a vasoconstrictor that often blocks blood flow to the genitals. As a result, it can cause impotence, vaginal dryness, and even early menopause.

• *Penicillin-derived antibiotics* can accumulate in the semen, triggering allergic reactions in susceptible partners.

• *Thiazide diuretics*, which account for about 90% of diuretics, cause a loss of zinc through the urine. Since zinc is vital to male potency, men using this drug often become impotent.

• *Timolol*, a beta-blocker, is the only eye-drop that has been associated with impotence and decreased sex drive.

Source: M. Laurence Lieberman, a pharmacist in New York and author of *The Sexual Pharmacy*. New American Library. His book lists a total of 226 drugs that are known to influence sexual performance or enjoyment.

Older Men and Sex

It is a myth that older men are dissatisfied with the quality of their sex lives, according to the largest research study on impotence since the famous Kinsey report. It is true that more than half of men between 40 and 70 experience some difficulty in obtaining and maintaining erections. But they expect a decline in performance to occur as they age, so their level of satisfaction with sex remains the same as when they were younger.

Source: John McKinlay, PhD, is an epidemiologist with the New England Research Institute, Nine Galen St., Watertown, MA 02172.

Testicle Injuries

A blow to the testicles during boyhood may cause infertility later in life. In a study of infertile men, 16.8% reported at least one childhood incident involving a severe blow to the testicles. The average age at which these injuries occurred was 15. Most were sports-related. These men had 25% higher blood levels of the female hormone estradiol and lower sperm counts than did fertile men. *Theory:* Trauma to the testicles causes irreversible tissue damage and increased production of estradiol, which, in turn, impairs sperm production. *Self-defense:* To avoid injury, boys should wear protective cups during contact sports and be careful when riding a bike on uneven terrain. Any boy who does experience a blow to the testicles should rest, use an ice pack and seek medical treatment.

Source: Wolfram E. Nolten, MD, associate professor of medicine, University of Wisconsin–Madison Medical School.

Premature Graying

Gray hair is considered premature if it begins before age 20 in Caucasians...age 30 in African-Americans. The rate at which you go gray has nothing to do with your hair color.

Source: Eileen Lambroza, MD, clinical instructor of dermatology, New York Hospital–Cornell University Medical Center, New York City. Her remarks were reported in *American Health*, 28 W. 23 St., New York 10010.

Surprising Cause Of Impotence

Penises can "fracture" during sex or masturbation. In fact, such fractures—actually a rupture of the blood-filled chambers inside the penis—account for three to four million cases of impotence.

Self-defense: Use lubricants, if necessary. Avoid sudden twists or striking of the penis. Alert your partner right away at the first sign of pain...and avoid sex if you or your partner feels "out of control" from alcohol or drugs.

Source: Irwin Goldstein, MD, professor of urology, Boston University School of Medicine.

Don't Learn to Live with Urinary Incontinence— Control It

Whether it involves an occasional drip or daily puddles, urinary incontinence is messy, uncomfortable, embarrassing—and more common than one might expect. Half of all women and one of every five men experience incontinence at some time.

Sadly, the prospect of a public accident leads many people to limit their activities outside the home. So what starts out as an occasional embarrassment turns into a debilitating condition.

Good news: Incontinence can usually be corrected or significantly improved—via special exercises, behavioral training, drugs or surgery. Behavior treatments alone are beneficial for most adults.

Types of urinary incontinence...

•Urge incontinence. This type makes it hard to get to the bathroom in time.

Usual causes: Infection of the bladder or urethra...prostate enlargement (common in men older than 50)...thinning of urethral tissues (common in postmenopausal women).

•Stress incontinence. Urine is accidentally released when you cough, sneeze, lift something heavy, exercise or do anything else that applies a sudden force to the lower body. Stress incontinence is far more common among women than among men.

Usual causes: Weakness in the tissues that surround and support the bladder and urethra. The urinary sphincter can be weakened by pregnancy—the fetus presses down on the pelvis, causing stretching and sagging...or by childbirth, when tissues are stretched or torn as the baby passes through the vagina. In men, stress incontinence often stems from damage to pelvic tissues caused by prostate surgery.

In a misguided attempt to solve their problem, incontinence sufferers make many mistakes. *Examples:*

•Turning to sanitary napkins or adult diapers prematurely, when the problem could be treatable.

•Reducing intake of water and other fluids. Cutting back on fluids can cause dehydration. And doing so is pointless anyway, because there's always enough urine in the body for an accident—even if you've avoided drinking for hours.

Reducing your intake of caffeine and alcohol might help, since these beverages act as diuretics. But many antihypertensive medications are diuretics as well. Individuals taking these drugs should not stop taking them without first consulting their physician.

To help determine what triggers your accidents, keep a detailed bladder diary for at least a week. For every accident, describe the time and place, the extent of the urine leakage and the situation in which it occurred. List any possible triggers—coughing, lifting, running water, arriving home. Once you've pinpointed your triggers, the following techniques often prove helpful with both kinds of incontinence…

•Kegel exercises. They strengthen the urinary sphincter and other pelvic muscles, boosting your ability to "hold it in."

What to do: Squeeze your pelvic muscles. Go to the toilet and start to void. Once the stream of urine has started, try to stop it. If you can slow the stream of urine even slightly, you are using the right muscle. You should feel a "pulling" sensation in your anus, but your buttocks and abdomen shouldn't move. Hold the tension for three counts, then release and rest for three counts.

This squeeze-release pair counts as a single Kegel exercise. Do 15 exercises a day while lying down, 15 while sitting (at your desk, in your car, on the bus, etc.) and 15 while standing (brushing your teeth, waiting in line at the bank or supermarket). Improvement usually begins in two weeks.

•Behavioral training for urge incontinence. When you feel the urge to urinate, don't rush to the bathroom. The jiggling motion of your bladder increases the likelihood that urine will be released accidentally. Instead, sit or stand quietly for a few moments until the urgency subsides. Squeeze your pelvic muscles quickly several times, pausing briefly in between. Breathe deeply. Concentrate on suppressing the urge to urinate.

When the urge has diminished, walk to the bathroom at a normal pace, repeatedly squeezing those muscles. This technique is particularly helpful in case the urge to urinate strikes while you're on the highway or another place without ready access to a bathroom.

•Behavioral training for stress incontinence. Refer frequently to your bladder diary. If you find that your incontinence occurs with coughing, sneezing or other physical activity, squeeze your muscles just before and during these activities. This helps to keep the urethra closed holding the urine in.

Whether or not you consider your urine loss a problem and whether or not you want treatment, you should see your doctor for an evaluation. Incontinence is a sign that something isn't right. Don't ignore it. A visit to your doctor will reveal any easily reversible cause of incontinence as well as any type that requires immediate treatment. Consult an internist, urologist, gynecologist or geriatrician. Or ask a local hospital or medical school for the name of an incontinence clinic. Wherever you get help for your problem, be sure to take along your bladder diary.

In some cases, individuals seeking medical help for incontinence must undergo urodynamic testing. *Procedure:* Special equipment measures physical conditions such as pelvic muscle tone and how much urine your bladder can hold.

Health-care providers use a variety of techniques to control incontinence, including…

•Biofeedback. A type of behavioral training, biofeedback uses special equipment to help you learn how to control your pelvic muscles and bladder. It is especially useful in helping people to identify the proper muscles and contract them correctly. Some people can learn to control pelvic muscles without biofeedback. However, many exercise the wrong muscles and could benefit from biofeedback.

With this training, a probe is usually inserted into the vagina or rectum. Measurements taken from the probe are displayed so that you can watch what your muscles are doing.

With this immediate feedback, you can learn quickly and be assured that you are exercising properly.

•Bladder training. Another type of behavioral training, this therapy alters your voiding habits. You go to the bathroom on a regular schedule and the time between voids is gradually increased. Bladder training helps both stress and urge incontinence.

•Drug therapy. Prescription drugs are available both to prevent bladder spasms (urge incontinence) and to strengthen the urethral sphincter (stress incontinence).

Some who take these drugs have side effects. Dry mouth is the most common side effect of the drugs that prevent bladder spasms. Older women, especially prone to incontinence, should ask a doctor about taking estrogen to reduce irritation of and thicken the tissues of the urethra.

• Collagen injections. This therapy—widely reported in recent weeks—is useful only for patients with a type of stress incontinence called urethral insufficiency. Bovine collagen, a viscous substance derived from cattle bones, is injected into tissue surrounding the urethra. This helps keep it closed except for urination.

• Electrical stimulation. In this therapy, an electrical probe inserted into the vagina or rectum emits a low-intensity current that stimulates the muscles supporting the bladder and urethra.

• Surgery. For some types of incontinence, surgery is the best and only appropriate treatment. Certain physical conditions, such as a urethral obstruction or a hole in the bladder (fistula), can be corrected only via surgery.

Helpful organizations...

• Help for Incontinent People (HIP), Box 544, Union, South Carolina 29379. 800-252-3337.

• The Simon Foundation, 3621 Thayer St., Evanston, Illinois 60201. 800-237-4666.

Source: Kathryn L. Burgio, PhD, director of the continence program at the University of Alabama at Birmingham, and associate professor of medicine at the university's medical school. She is coauthor of *Staying Dry: A Practical Guide to Bladder Control.* Johns Hopkins University Press.

Sexual Satisfaction Dos and Don'ts

Only 5.3% of married men are dissatisfied with their sex lives—compared with 10.1% of women. *Factors that influence a wife's sexual satisfaction:* Amount of foreplay...when and if she has an orgasm... her husband's sexual satisfaction...who initiates the sex...whether she agrees to sex if her husband was the initiator. *Factors that influence a husband's sexual satisfaction:* Frequency of sex...successful ejaculation ...his wife's sexual satisfaction...his attitude toward his wife's choice of contraceptive.

Source: Survey of 1,800 married women of reproductive age in Shanghai, by researchers at Lu Wan Maternity and Child Health Hospital, People's Republic of China. Published in *Journal of Psychology and Human Sexuality,* 1300 S. Second St., Minneapolis 55454.

Men and Menopause

Not enough men understand what menopause is. As a result, even the most sympathetic man may be thrown completely off balance when the woman in his life begins to exhibit the physiological and emotional symptoms of menopause. Sadly, his ignorance will prevent him from helping the woman he loves...and may even cause him to inadvertently do and say things that make matters worse.

Thanks to books like Gail Sheehy's *The Silent Passage* and Germaine Greer's *The Change,* magazine articles, and TV talk shows, the whole subject of menopause is coming out of the closet. But plenty of myths and misconceptions remain—and they often lead to problems between men—who see in menopause their own mortality—and their menopausal wives'. Answers to basic questions:

What is menopause? Menopause occurs when the ovaries stop producing the female hormone estrogen and menstruation ceases.

When does menopause typically occur? Menopause is actually a prolonged series of events that occur over years. On average, menopause starts at around age 51, but the symptoms are the most intense during perimenopause— approximately two years before and two years afterward.

What's causing my wife's physical and emotional changes? The hot flashes, the thinning of the vaginal tissues, the decreased vaginal lubrication, the mood swings are all the result of the ovaries producing little or no estrogen now. Any or all of these changes are perfectly normal and to be expected.

Why is my wife less interested in sex now? We've always had a good sex life before. A couple of reasons: The changes in the reproductive tract may make intercourse painful. And hormonal changes may cause a decrease in her sexual desire—even though she probably loves you as much as ever.

Is there any good news? Definitely! Most of the worst symptoms of menopause can be alleviated with hormone-replacement therapy. If she chooses to take hormones, she'll be able to see and feel relief within a matter of weeks. Even if she doesn't take hormones, some of the troublesome symptoms may naturally wane in time. She should discuss her course of action with her gynecologist. *Advantages of hormone therapy:* Control of hot flashes...restoration of integrity of genital tissues... women generally feel better. *Long-term bonus:* Hormonal therapy helps protect against osteoporosis and coronary heart disease. *Disadvantages:* Women with an intact uterus also receive progestin to prevent endometrial cancer, and this can cause resumption of menstruation. *Long-term risk:* Estrogen therapy for more than 15 years can cause a slightly increased risk of breast cancer.

How can I be more supportive of my wife now? Visit the gynecologist with her, so that you can show your support and get your own questions about menopause answered—just as more and more husbands are going to prenatal classes to learn about pregnancy and labor and to be there for their wives.

Give your wife a break. If she's more tired than usual these days, tell her you won't mind if she isn't up to attending the theater or going out after work. *Better:* Make dinner for the two of you, order in...or take her out to eat more often. Don't gripe when she wants to fling open the windows in mid-December—just get yourself another blanket. Offer to rub her feet or bring her a cup of tea. You get the idea.

Anything else? Avoid such inflammatory comments as:

"It's all in your mind!"..."There's nothing wrong with you!"..."You look perfectly fine to me!"

We have to be careful not to make menopause sound like an illness. Without the fear of pregnancy now...with the children perhaps grown and out of the house...with greater time for recreation and for each other, many couples report that this is the happiest time in their life ...and that sex is better than ever. Menopause can actually be the start of a wonderful new phase for you both.

Bottom line...

Educated, informed couples are finally starting to treat menopause as the normal, natural life event it is—and less and less as a crisis. Menopause means that a woman is middle-

aged, not that it's all over or that she's dying. The current life expectancy for women is 84 years...so there's a lot of life left to be enjoyed —for both of you—after menopause.

Source: Barbara Sherwin, PhD, co-director of the McGill University Menopause Clinic in Montreal and associate professor of psychology and obstetrics and gynecology at McGill University.

Surgery Preventive For Women

Precancerous lesions of the cervix may not always require treatment with surgery or lasers. Repeated topical application of the acne drug *retinoic acid* (Retin-A) reversed early (stage 2) lesions. However, retinoic acid was ineffective against stage 3 lesions. *Side effect:* Mild vaginal inflammation.

Source: Frank L. Meyskens, Jr., MD, director, Clinical Cancer Center, University of California, Irvine. His five-year study of more than 300 women with cervical lesions was reported in *The Medical Post*, 777 Bay St., Toronto, Ontario, M5W 1A7, Canada.

Cancer Warning

Vaginal bleeding or "spotting" following menopause can signal cancer of the cervix, uterus or vulva. Postmenopausal women too often disregard such bleeding, but a doctor's exam is important to rule out these serious ailments. Cervical, uterine and vulvar cancer kill nearly 12,000 American women a year.

Source: Katherine O'Hanlan, MD, associate director of the gynecologic cancer service, Stanford University Medical Center, Palo Alto, CA.

Women Continue to Get Shockingly Substandard Medical Care

For the past several decades, American women have been systematically excluded from most research on new drugs, medical treatments and surgical techniques. As a result of this neglect, women are often denied the life-saving and life-extending treatments routinely offered to men.

Example I: Women are less likely than men to be referred for angioplasty, a surgical technique proven to clear blocked coronary arteries.

Example II: Women with AIDS are less likely than men to be prescribed the drug AZT.

Example III: Among sufferers of kidney failure, women are 30% less likely than men to receive kidney transplants.

This sex bias pervades medicine, directly undermining the treatment women receive in clinics, hospitals and doctors' offices across the country.

Common problems women face when seeking medical care...

• *Having your symptoms dismissed as being "all in your head."* Medical mythology has it that women are "complainers" whose symptoms often stem from emotional stress. This insidious attitude among doctors keeps women from getting the diagnostic tests they need.

In a recent study, only 4% of women with abnormal stress tests received follow-up tests necessary for pinpointing arterial blockages. But these important tests were ordered for 40% of men with abnormal stress tests.

Similarly, because women's physical complaints are often viewed as evidence of psychological problems, women are more likely than men to receive prescriptions for psychiatric drugs.

Women make up 66% of those diagnosed with depression, yet they receive 73% of prescriptions for psychiatric medication—and 90% when the prescribing doctor is not a psychiatrist.

Self-defense: Communicate your problem to your doctor as clearly and concisely as possible.

Before your office visit, make a list of the questions you want to ask—in order of importance. If you get interrupted before you're through, at least you'll have covered the most crucial information.

If you feel your doctor is being dismissive, say so. If he/she still refuses to take your problem seriously, find another doctor.

• *Having your symptoms of heart disease go unrecognized.* Unlike men, women experiencing a heart attack often do not experience the classic symptoms—pain radiating down the arm or the elephant-sitting-on-your-chest type of pain.

Self-defense: Women should realize that vague abdominal discomfort, nausea, vomiting and shortness of breath can all be signs of heart attack. Take these symptoms very seriously. Make sure your doctor does, too.

• *Not being told to have routine mammograms and Pap smears.* Women over 65 account for almost half of the deaths from cervical cancer and are at greater risk of breast cancer than women of other age groups. But these older women are less likely than younger women to get the appropriate screening tests, often because their doctors fail to refer them for testing.

Self-defense: Annual mammograms, clinical breast exams and pelvic exams are recommended for all women 50 to 64 years of age.

The National Cancer Society recommends mammograms every one to two years for women 40 to 49 years of age.

A panel convened by the National Cancer Institute and the National Institute on Aging urges women 65 to 74 to have a clinical breast exam annually and a mammogram every two years, and women 75 and older to have both tests every two years. After three consecutive Pap smears with normal results, older women should have a Pap at least every three years. Younger women also need routine Pap smears.

• *Not being told that lumpectomy is a safe alternative to mastectomy.* Ninety percent of women with breast cancer are eligible for lumpectomy (removal of the tumor and a small margin of tissue), yet more than half undergo mastectomy (removal of the entire breast). The type of surgery a woman receives depends on such nonmedical factors as where she lives, her age, income and race.

Most likely to have a mastectomy: Black women, Medicare recipients, older women and women who live in the Midwest or South.

Self-defense: If your doctor says you need a mastectomy, get a second opinion—from a surgeon unaffiliated with your doctor's institution. Ask your doctor if he/she is aware of studies showing that lumpectomy followed by radiation is just as effective as mastectomy in treating early-stage breast tumors.

For more information on lumpectomy, call the National Cancer Institute at 800-4-CANCER.

• *Not having your early warning signs of AIDS recognized in time for effective treatment.* AIDS is now the fifth-leading killer of reproductive-age women. Yet many doctors continue to operate under the mistaken belief that "women don't get AIDS." As a result, women with clear signs of AIDS often fail to get tested for the disease.

Self-defense: If you're involved in a new sexual relationship or if you're in a relationship with a man who may be unfaithful, insist that he wear a condom.

If you have recurrent vaginal yeast infections, genital herpes or cervical dysplasia, get tested for the AIDS virus. These conditions may be an early sign of infection.

• *Being subjected to a needless hysterectomy.* More than half of the 500,000 hysterectomies performed annually in the US are medically unjustified.

Self-defense: Women should know about the proven alternatives to hysterectomy. *Example:* Uterine fibroid tumors, which are usually benign, can often be shrunk with medication, then removed in a comparatively minor surgical procedure called myomectomy.

Women should also ask about subtotal hysterectomy—a procedure in which only the top of the uterus is removed and the cervix is left intact. This method, which is common in Europe, helps women maintain sexual responsiveness.

• *Being prescribed drugs that were never properly tested in women.* Women may suffer more or different side effects than men who take the same medication. *Example:* Doctors are often unaware that some drugs cause adverse reactions when combined with estrogen-replacement therapy and oral contraceptives.

Self-defense: If you're experiencing troublesome side effects, ask your doctor if you can switch to another medication. Realize that anti-anxiety drugs and postmenopausal estrogen taken together increase the risk of seizures and reduce the effectiveness of estrogen in treating hot flashes and other symptoms of menopause.

Hormone-replacement therapy (HRT) and oral contraceptives decrease the liver's metabolism of tricyclic antidepressants, leading to a greater risk of toxicity in women. For some women, doses of antidepressants may also need to be increased premenstrually.

• *Being urged to go on hormone-replacement therapy despite the continuing debate over its long-term safety.* Estrogen must be used continuously to maintain its benefits on the bones and heart. But most women—fearful of the link between estrogen and breast cancer—take HRT for a few years to relieve hot flashes and other menopausal symptoms and then stop.

Self-defense: Women may get almost as much protection if they take HRT to relieve short-term symptoms, discontinue it and start up again in their 70s. It's something to discuss with your doctor.

• *Being overmedicated.* Many common medical complaints of older women—including confusion and incontinence—may be caused by overmedication. Older women take drugs at twice the rate of older men, and are more apt to take multiple medications, increasing their risk of toxic side effects.

Self-defense: Older women should be aware that they metabolize many drugs differently than men. In women older than 65, for example, psychotropic drugs have a longer half-life, meaning that they remain in the body longer. To reduce the risk of side effects, physicians may need to reduce the doses of these drugs by one-third.

Elderly women also need to know that high doses of antipsychotic medication may increase their risk for chronic side effects such as tardive dyskinesia, a neurological disorder that results in abnormal movement of the mouth and tongue. Dextroamphetamine—a drug that tends to induce euphoria and increased alertness in men—sedates postmenopausal women.

• *Receiving medical care that is haphazard or fragmented.* While men may see one doctor for all their health-care needs, women must see a gynecologist for a Pap smear and pelvic exam, an internist for a general physical exam and a radiologist for a mammogram.

Typically, one doctor doesn't know what the other is doing. Services often overlap, wasting time and money—and leading to inadequate care.

Self-defense: Find an internist with training in gynecology, qualifying him/her to perform pelvic exams and Pap smears. Find out whether there's a comprehensive women's health center in your community. These centers, generally affiliated with a major teaching hospital, offer one-stop medical care. Practitioners with training in gynecology, general medicine, cardiology, menopause care, oncology, infectious diseases, endocrinology and bone metabolism make themselves available to you during a single appointment.

With this trend toward women-centered care, women may finally be seen by the medical establishment not as a collection of reproductive organs but as human beings with hearts and lungs and colons and kidneys—just like men.

Source: Leslie Laurence, author of the nationally syndicated newspaper column "Her Health" and coauthor of *Outrageous Practices: The Alarming Truth about How Medicine Mistreats Women.* Fawcett Columbine.

Trichomoniasis and Infertility in Women

Gonorrhea isn't the only sexually transmitted disease that causes infertility in women. *Trichomoniasis*—infection with the *Trichomonas* protozoan—can also cause the problem. Compared with healthy women, those with trichomoniasis were 1.9 times more likely to have tubal infertility...while those with gonorrhea were 2.4 times as likely to be infertile.

Source: Francine Grodstein, ScD, research fellow, department of epidemiology, Harvard School of Public Health, Boston. Her study of more than 4,000 women was reported in *Family Planning Perspectives*, 111 Fifth Ave., New York 10003.

Endometrial Biopsies Not Always Necessary

Routine endometrial biopsies aren't always necessary before women begin hormone-replacement therapy (HRT) for menopause. For years, gynecologists have initiated HRT only after performing such a biopsy—a $300 procedure in which a tissue sample is removed for evaluation. *New view:* Unless a woman has had uterine bleeding or abnormal growth of uterine tissue, she can safely begin HRT with only routine surveillance by a gynecologist.

Source: Daniel H. Belsky, DO, MSC, professor and chair of obstetrics and gynecology, School of Osteopathic Medicine, University of Medicine and Dentistry of New Jersey, Stratford. His survey of case histories of 100 menopausal women was published in *Contemporary OB/GYN*, 5 Paragon Dr., Montvale, NJ 07645.

Better Vaginal Exams

To help your gynecologist obtain the most accurate results possible, do not douche or use vaginal medication or spermicide for at least 48 hours before a pelvic exam. *Also:* Refrain from intercourse both the morning of the exam and the night before.

Source: Hee Ok Park, MD, clinical associate professor of obstetrics and gynecology, Thomas Jefferson University Hospital, Philadelphia.

Frequently Misdiagnosed: Vaginal Infections

Most women being treated for chronic yeast infections—either by their internists or by themselves with over-the-counter preparations — actually have a different condition. *Other causes of symptoms:* Bacterial vaginosis or herpes infections, which require different treatments than that for yeast infections. *Caution:* Never diagnose yourself. Over-the-counter treatments could make your symptoms worse. If you think you have a vaginal infection, ask your doctor to perform a complete physical examination and comprehensive medical history.

Source: Karen Carroll, MD, departments of pathology and infectious diseases, and Paul Summers, MD, department of obstetrics and gynecology, both at the University of Utah Medical Center in Salt Lake City.

Benign Breast Lumps

Benign breast lumps occur in more than half of all women at some point in their lives. For 97% of these women, such lumps represent no significant increase in their risk of developing breast cancer. But some breast lumps are cancerous. Any woman who notices a lump should see her doctor right away.

Source: James R. Dolan, MD, assistant professor of obstetrics, gynecology and gynecologic oncology, and co-director of the Breast Care Center, Loyola University Medical Center, Maywood, IL.

Possible Pitfalls of Gene Therapy

Within the span of just a few years, "gene therapy" has changed from a distant goal into an exciting here-and-now reality.

Having pinpointed many defective, disease-causing genes, geneticists are now devising ways of reintroducing healthy versions of these genes into the body.

Payoff: Effective treatments—and possibly cures—for cancer, cystic fibrosis, high blood cholesterol, hemophilia, AIDS and more.

Genetic testing...

Inside the nucleus of almost every cell in the human body are 46 chromosomes—long, coiled strands of deoxyribonucleic acid (DNA). The 100,000 or so genes contained inside this "master molecule" direct the synthesis of the hormones, enzymes and all the other vital building blocks that keep our bodies running smoothly.

As with any complex device, the body's genetic machinery sometimes breaks down.

This breakdown can be triggered by environmental toxins (including tobacco smoke, contaminated water, etc.), viruses, radiation, inherited defects—or some combination of these factors.

Scientists have recently learned that cancer is, in fact, a *genetic* disease, resulting when key genes fail to "brake" uncontrolled, abnormal growth of certain cells. The cells of some liver, lung and breast cancer patients, for example, may have defects in a tumor-suppressing gene called p53.

When healthy, p53 ensures that all chromosomes within a cell remain intact during cell division. If any chromosomal damage occurs, the gene creates a protein that stops the cell from dividing out of control...and causing a malignancy.

Blood tests for the defective P53 gene may soon be in widespread use. In many cases, these tests may predict the likelihood of cancer years before it develops in people with a family history of this genetic aberration.

Likewise, a diagnostic test to identify family members carrying the BRCA1 gene (for breast cancer) will be available in the future. This gene is believed to cause at least half of the 18,000 cases of breast cancer stemming from hereditary defects.

Examples: Telltale genes detectable in cells floating in saliva may be red flags for throat cancer. Similar genes lurking in stool samples may mean colon cancer.

Other genes now being pinpointed may allow doctors to identify patients likely to develop certain forms of heart disease, diabetes or Alzheimer's disease—years beforehand.

Potential risks...

While such predictive genetic testing can be considered a medical marvel, it also has potential drawbacks...

•The awareness that one carries a disease-causing gene may cause great psychological distress—especially true for those suspected of having genes for Huntington's chorea, Alzheimer's disease or other incurable diseases.

•Genetic tests are costly and may not be covered by your health insurance. Thus poor people may have limited access to these tests.

• The ready availability of genetic testing may force people to divulge their test results to employers, health insurance companies, adoption agencies and other organizations. These organizations might use this information to discriminate against individuals carrying defective genes—by denying employment, insurance coverage, etc.*

Genetic tests are open to interpretation. They do not offer a simple "yes" or "no" answer. Great care is needed in administering and interpreting them.

Healing with genes...

In addition to testing for faulty genes, scientists are exploring ways of preventing or undoing the damage these genes inflict upon the body.

Especially promising: Somatic cell gene therapy. In this technique, healthy versions of defective genes are inserted into a patient's cells.

One major focus of somatic cell therapy is cancer, with a particular emphasis on genetically modifying immune system cells to combat malignant growths.

One landmark study, conducted recently by University of Michigan scientists, involved mimicking the process of rejection that often occurs with organ transplants.

When a new organ is transplanted, the recipient's immune system quickly recognizes the transplanted tissue as "foreign." Next, the immune system mounts an attack against this "invader." Left unchecked by drugs, this process of rejection gradually destroys the transplanted tissue...a process that can also kill the transplant recipient.

The rejection process is triggered by the presence of certain proteins on the cell membranes of transplanted tissue. The scientists realized that if they could tag melanoma cells with similar foreign proteins (called transplant antigens), they could persuade the body to launch an immune response against these melanoma cells.

The scientists inserted copies of a gene for transplant antigens inside tiny globules of fat,

then injected the globules into the melanoma tumors of lab animals. The newly inserted genes began to synthesize the telltale protein. As a result, the lab animals' immune systems promptly began to recognize these melanoma cells as foreign...and quickly destroyed them. Ongoing clinical trials are testing the safety of the technology and the proper dosages.

Another new form of gene therapy involves use of genetically altered viruses to transfer new genes into body cells. In a recent experiment, melanoma patients improved dramatically when infected with viruses altered to contain copies of a gene that produced a powerful anti-tumor protein called *tumor necrosis factor* (TNF).

In another study, ovarian tumor cells were removed from patients and grown in the lab. By infecting these cells with a safe, genetically modified herpes virus, researchers incorporated into the tumor cells a gene that produced a protein sensitive to the antiviral drug *acyclovir.* When these genetically altered tumor cells were reinserted into the bodies of mice, administration of acyclovir killed these cells.

By early 1994, dozens of clinical trials around the country were under way for gene therapy for malignant melanoma, ovarian, brain, kidney and lung cancer.

Coming...

Other diseases that are likely candidates for gene therapy include...

• Cystic fibrosis. Caused by a defective gene on chromosome 7, CF is the most common inherited disorder among Caucasians. It causes excessive and ultimately fatal buildup of mucus in the lungs. Until recently, individuals with CF rarely survived beyond their early 20s.

In one recent—and highly promising—study, researchers injected the lungs of animals and people with viruses "remodeled" to contain healthy versions of the gene that causes CF. The genetic defect was pronounced corrected in a small patch of cells lining the nasal passages of three patients.

• Heart disease. Through gene therapy, scientists are inserting genetically modified liver cell genes into the lining of blood vessels of

---

*One goal of the Human Genome Project—an ongoing 15-year, $3-billion effort to map all the genes that play a role in human disease—is to find ways to ensure that all confidential genetic information remains confidential.

people with familial hypercholesterolemia—an inherited disorder that interferes with the body's removal of "bad" cholesterol from the body. Inserted into the body, the altered genes make a protein that acts as a receptor for the undesirable cholesterol, transporting it to cells for processing and ultimately removal from the body.

In a dramatic breakthrough in April 1994, scientists at the University of Pennsylvania Medical Center announced that they had partly corrected hypercholesterolemia in a 30-year-old woman. They had removed a small portion of her liver, added to the liver cells a harmless virus carrying genes for removing blood cholesterol and returned the cells to her body. Her harmful cholesterol levels were lowered by 20%.

Researchers are also exploring delivery of genes that produce a clot-busting protein called tissue *plasminogen activator* (tPA).

In mid-September, scientists at St. Elizabeth's Hospital in Boston obtained permission to begin testing a gene therapy technique aimed at providing new blood circulation in patients with blocked arteries. Slender tubes will be threaded into the leg arteries of 12 patients, providing a means of delivering genes shown to produce a chemical factor that stimulates growth of new blood vessels.

The researchers hope that the genes will take root in some of the cells lining the blocked blood vessel walls and begin to churn out enough of the factor to make new arteries sprout, forming bypass around the obstruction.

•Muscular dystrophy. A variety of strategies are being explored to ferry into diseased muscles genes that make normal muscle protein.

If these methods prove successful, scientists may be able to implant insulin-releasing muscle cells (to control diabetes) or muscle cells that generate the blood-clotting agent Factor VIII (to control hemophilia).

•AIDS. Several anti-AIDS strategies are under investigation. Some experiments involve triggering a person's cells to make HIV proteins—which might activate the body's immune response and slow the progression of the disease. Others aim to express in certain body cells a gene that deters HIV by making destructive enzyme-like molecules.

Controversial techniques...

Two other forms of genetic manipulation—not yet tested in humans but on the drawing board for future studies—are attracting considerable controversy...

•Germ-line gene therapy. It involves correcting a gene-related defect in an individual's reproductive cells so that it can no longer be passed on to his/her offspring. If performed early in the individual's life, perhaps even at the embryonic stage, the disorder might be corrected in the person being treated as well.

Germ-line therapy has sparked intense debate. *Reason:* Any alteration of egg, sperm or early embryonic cells would have an irrevocable impact on future generations. Many scientists object to this in principle, pointing out the possibility not only of unforeseen risks, but also noting that the rights of newborns would be violated.

•Enhancement genetic engineering. It involves inserting a gene at a pertinent stage in a person's development so that a specific characteristic would be improved or enhanced. For example, it might be possible to introduce a gene to boost the body's production of growth hormone, resulting in a taller individual.

While the jury is still out on both germ-line and enhancement therapy, some scientists argue that these options should be explored—provided that they are preceded by years of experience with somatic cell gene therapy and animal studies, and that they are accepted by an informed public.

Potential risks...

Somatic cell gene therapy has enormous potential to control or even cure a range of diseases. But it also poses a possible drawback—namely that putting genes into people is not a precise or predictable process. There is a slight but real chance the new "upstart" gene might settle inside a healthy one and interfere with its function.

However, for those with a terminal or otherwise incurable illness, that small risk may be outweighed by the therapy's potential benefits.

Many researchers feel that gene therapy is now a safe and ethical option for treating serious disease. In fact, gene therapy is often compared to an organ transplant—the difference being that genes are transplanted rather than entire organs.

Staying well-informed about the ongoing developments in gene therapy is one way to help determine whether this new medical technology is appropriate for you, a friend or a member of your family.

For more information: Contact The National Center for Human Genome Research, National Institutes of Health, 9000 Rockville Pike, Building 38A, Bethesda, Maryland 20892. 301-496-0844.

Source: Thomas F. Lee, PhD, professor of microbiology at St. Anselm College, Manchester, NH. He is the author of *The Human Genome Project: Cracking the Genetic Code of Life* and *Gene Future: The Promise and Perils of the New Biology.* Plenum.

Zinc/Alzheimer's Connection

Alzheimer's disease may be caused by excessive consumption of zinc. In a recent test-tube study, zinc added to a chemical normally found in the brain caused formation of *amyloid plaques*—gluelike clumps that gum up the brains of Alzheimer's sufferers and which are considered a hallmark of the disease.

Danger: Zinc supplements are often recommended to the elderly to treat slow healing, loss of appetite and other symptoms of zinc deficiency.

Self-defense: Although the zinc-Alzheimer's link has not yet been proven, and there are valid reasons for taking the mineral, *taking megadoses of zinc may be unwise.* Discuss the matter with your doctor.

Good news: In the same set of experiments, aluminum and other minerals sometimes linked to Alzheimer's caused *little* clumping.

Source: Rudolph Tanzi, PhD, associate professor of neurology, Harvard Medical School, and director of the laboratory on genetics and aging, Massachusetts General Hospital, both in Boston.

Are You Worried About Alzheimer's?

Since Ronald Reagan disclosed that he has Alzheimer's disease, many of my patients have expressed fear that they, too, are suffering from this devastating form of dementia.

Bad news: Alzheimer's is very common. Four million Americans have it, including one in 12 over age 65. And despite some promising research suggesting a genetic basis for the disease, we still don't know what causes Alzheimer's (I'm not convinced that exposure to aluminum or electromagnetic fields is to blame). The disease remains both incurable and largely untreatable.

Good news: Most memory problems are evidence not of Alzheimer's, but of less serious, treatable conditions.

As we age, most of us suffer a subtle decline in our memory—occasionally forgetting words or names, misplacing our keys, etc. (Alzheimer's brings on a much more profound type of memory loss—not simply misplacing your keys, for instance, but forgetting what keys are for.)

Aging-related memory loss often stems from a sort of "mental slackness." That's why it's so important to keep exercising our minds as we grow older—seeking out new friends and experiences, taking classes, reading, etc.

Other treatable causes of memory loss include...

•Depression or anxiety.

•Heavy drinking.

•Lack of sleep.

•Certain drugs, including antidepressants, beta-blockers and even over-the-counter antihistamines. In many cases, simply switching to another drug is all that's needed.

•Vitamin B12 deficiency. This problem can usually be corrected via supplements.

•Thyroid disease. It can be treated via drug therapy or surgery.

•Stroke. Although stroke-induced brain damage is irreversible, it may be possible to halt additional memory loss via drug therapy or changes in diet.

Alzheimer's is diagnosed by ruling out these treatable causes of dementia via blood and psychological tests, EKGs, CAT scans, etc. A fast, apparently accurate "eyedrop test" for Alzheimer's has shown promise in early tests, but it probably won't be available for some time.

What if Alzheimer's is diagnosed? Some doctors prescribe the recently approved memory-enhancing drug tacrine (Cognex). *Problem:* Tacrine is very costly, and people taking it must be carefully watched for liver problems and other side effects. Only one in three persons taking tacrine seems to benefit...and the benefit is invariably small.

Sedatives are helpful in easing the agitation, frustration and other emotional problems that often accompany Alzheimer's.

If you're caring for someone with Alzheimer's, simplify the living environment as much as possible. Avoid excessive noise, loud conversation, too many "comings and goings," etc. Other caregiving strategies include...

•Being supportive. Don't point out mistakes in the person's speaking or writing. Use gentle encouragement to keep the person's spirits up.

•Legal and financial planning. Consider setting up a living will and/or a power of attorney. Make plans to pay for nursing home care, when that becomes necessary.

•Making use of all available caregiving resources—other family members, friends, Meals-on-Wheels, visiting nurses, respite programs, etc.

•Not neglecting your own needs. Take an occasional vacation to avoid excessive stress or feelings of guilt. Be realistic about what will happen.

Eventually, the patient's thinking becomes so disrupted that he/she will probably have to enter a nursing home. Most Alzheimer's patients die of their disease within eight years of diagnosis.

For more information, contact the Alzheimer's Association, 919 N. Michigan Ave., Suite 1000, Chicago 60611. 800-272-3900.

Source: Bruce H. Yaffe, MD, an internist and gastroenterologist in private practice, 121 E. 84 St., New York 10028.

Prescription Nation

American doctors wrote 2.3 billion prescriptions last year. That's about eight for every man, woman and child in the country.

Source: Richard L. Keller, MD, staff physician, emergency department, St. Therese Medical Center, Waukegan, Illinois, writing in *Emergency Medicine,* 3525 Piedmont Rd., Atlanta 30305.

14

Home Smarts

Healthy Supermarket Strategies

Every year, 3,000 new products appear on US supermarket shelves. They're all produced and packaged to appeal to our senses, and a lot are fattening and unhealthful.

But—if you know what to look for and how to shop, you'll bring home groceries that are both inexpensive and nutritious.

Your first line of defense against supermarket mistakes is your shopping list. Having a small notebook in your purse or a list on the refrigerator will save you time—and calories.

As accurately as possible, calculate one week's food needs for your family. Use the food pyramid as your guide. Each day, every member of your family should consume:

•Six to 11 servings of bread, cereal, rice or pasta. One serving equals one slice of bread… ½ cup cooked rice, pasta or cooked cereal… one ounce ready-to-eat cereal.

•Three to five servings of vegetables. One serving equals ½ cup chopped, raw or cooked vegetables…one cup leafy raw vegetables.

•Two to four servings of fruit. One serving equals one piece of fruit or melon wedge…¾ cup juice…½ cup canned fruit…¼ cup dried fruit.

•Two to three servings of dairy. One serving equals 1 cup milk or yogurt…1½ to 2 ounces cheese.

•Two to three servings of meat, poultry, fish, beans, eggs or nuts. One serving equals 2½ to 3 ounces of cooked lean meat, poultry or fish (½ cup cooked beans, 1 egg or 2 tablespoons peanut butter equals 1 ounce lean meat).

Shopping basics…

Most people are already familiar with the peril of shopping on an empty stomach—you're tempted to forage. But having a meal before grocery shopping is just one of several helpful shopping strategies. *Others include…*

•Set a tight budget. After making your shopping list, estimate the cost of your groceries.

Take enough cash to cover your purchases, plus a little extra as a cushion. If you take too much cash, you might be tempted to buy items not on your list.

•Shop alone. If you take along someone who's not as conscientious as you are, you'll be more likely to make unplanned purchases.

•Set a shopping schedule—and stick to it. That way, you leave yourself no extra time to browse or buy things you don't really need.

•Familiarize yourself with food labels. They give more realistic serving sizes, so it's easier to figure out the nutritional content of products.

Key values: The total number of grams of fat, cholesterol and sodium. The "percent daily values" section of the label shows how a food fits into a daily diet of 2,000 calories. Women and older adults generally need about 1,600 calories...children, teenage girls, active women and most men about 2,200 calories...teenage boys and active men about 2,800 calories.

•Learn how to work the aisles. Save time and reduce your exposure to tempting high-fat foods by avoiding crisscrossing and backtracking.

Pick up nonfood items first. A cart filled with detergent, paper towels, soap and floor wax will prevent you from loading up on high-calorie goodies.

Next, head for the produce section. Fresh fruits and vegetables are high in nutritional value and low in calories, so select whatever your family enjoys.

To prevent spoilage: Buy no more than a week's supply of produce. Stick to fresh fruits and vegetables as much as possible. If fresh produce isn't available, opt for frozen or canned —but avoid products with added sugar.

Beware: Produce departments are often stocked with "cross-merchandised" items— salad dressings, croutons and other nonplant foods. While these items are complementary to fruits and vegetables, they're much more fattening. Just because an item is shelved alongside produce doesn't mean that it's good for you.

Freezer cases should be your last stop—so that, of course, frozen foods don't begin to de-frost in your cart. As a rule, you'll spend most of your time on the store's perimeter, where most staples are stocked.

Soft drinks and snacks...

Be careful when you go through the aisle marked "nuts, snacks and cocktail mixes." Many of these foods are high in fat and low in protein, vitamins and minerals. If you absolutely insist on snacks, get unflavored popcorn. Air-pop it, and flavor with butter-flavored granules or cooking spray—not real butter.

Alternative: "Light" microwave popcorn. Most brands have much less fat than regular popcorn.

Soft drinks have no nutritional value, and many are high in sodium and caffeine. *More healthful:* Plain or lightly flavored sparkling water. If you must have soft drinks, pick a one-calorie version.

Breads and cereals...

Breads and cereals should be the foundation of your daily diet. If you're watching your weight, stick with packaged breads. Their wrappers provide complete nutritional information. Unlabeled breads from the in-store bakery are often high in fat. Of course, it's best to steer clear of cakes, cookies, pastries, muffins, etc.

Cereals are filling and generally nutritious, but there are exceptions. Granola, for instance, is often full of fat—even though many people consider it to be very healthful.

Self-defense: Pick a cereal without added sugar or sweeteners. Some labels make it easy to make this distinction. Others require a bit of deduction.

Most boxes of ready-to-eat cereals base their nutritional information on a one-ounce serving ...while we tend to measure our cereal by "eyeballing" the bowl. *Problem:* One bowl of a dense brand like Grape Nuts can contain a vastly different amount of cereal than another (like puffed rice). Keep that in mind when you make your selection.

Pasta...

Pasta deserves a premier position in your diet. It's very satisfying...and properly prepared, it can qualify as a low-fat food. One cup of cooked pasta has only 210 calories and one gram of fat.

If you drench your pasta in an oil-based sauce, however, you add another 200 calories and more than 20 grams of fat.

With so many reduced-calorie pasta sauces on the market, this problem is easy to avoid. I recommend "solid" pastas such as spaghetti, linguini and fettuccini. "Hollow" varieties such as macaroni and rigatoni hold more sauce—and more calories.

A few words on fats...

All dietary fats are equally dense in calories, but some are less unhealthful than others. Minimize your intake of saturated fats, which are found in meat, poultry and dairy products. These fats increase levels of LDL (bad) cholesterol, boosting your risk of heart attack.

Monounsaturated oils such as canola, peanut and olive oils are generally more healthful than saturated fats.

Beware: One tablespoon of oil takes care of your total dietary need for fat—for the entire day.

If you like cheese, try the new "light" versions of many popular brands.

Select leaner cuts and grades of meat. Eat salami and other luncheon meats in moderation—or not at all.

By the way, switching to a mostly vegetarian diet will cut your food bill by 50%...and you'll probably lose weight as a result. Store brands are another great way to cut costs.

Source: Valerie A. George, PhD, a nutritionist who heads the Healthy Women's Program at the University of Miami School of Medicine. Dr. George and Richard N. Nathanson are coauthors of *The Supermarket Diet*. Health Communications.

Food Additives Appear Safe for Most People... But Not All

Although food additives are safer than many people imagine them to be, certain additives can cause allergic reactions, including hives, childhood hyperactivity—and worse.

Most common culprits...

•Antimicrobials, including benzoates like sodium benzoate and benzoic acid, are used to fight growth of yeasts and bacteria in many canned or pickled foods and some cereals.

Problem I: Benzoates can cause asthma and hives.

Problem II: They may cause hypersensitivity in some children. Other problems, including joint pain and diarrhea, have also been reported.

•Antioxidants, such as BHA and BHT, are used to retard spoilage of cereal, margarine, potato chips, pastries and other packaged foods.

Problem I: Some people have developed contact dermatitis after handling products treated with antioxidants. In rare cases, people sensitized through skin contact with antioxidants later become sensitive to these additives in foods.

Problem II: Like benzoates, antioxidants may cause hives.

•Azo dyes are colorfast dyes used in pills, foods and clothing. One azo dye—tartrazine (FD&C yellow #5)—was dubbed the *yellow peril* 20 years ago when it was suspected of causing asthmatic reactions, hives and hyperactivity.

In fact, tartrazine and other azo dyes, such as sunset yellow (FD&C yellow #6), *do* cause hives in susceptible people—but not asthma as previously thought.

Azo dyes, including tartrazine, can cause hyperactivity but not as commonly as once suspected.

Most vulnerable: Children of preschool age—especially boys.

•Monosodium glutamate (MSG) is used as a flavor enhancer in Chinese and Japanese cooking, soup bases and convenience foods. It has been linked to *Chinese restaurant syndrome*.

This ailment—marked by flushing, headache, nausea and a feeling of warmth across the shoulders—typically occurs an hour or so after eating food that contains MSG. Chinese restaurant syndrome is not thought to be dangerous.

Recently, MSG has been blamed for full-blown asthma attacks, which have occurred up to 12 hours after eating MSG. We don't yet know what percentage of the asthmatic population is affected by this susceptibility...but it is thought to be quite small.

•Sulfites are used to prevent food from dis coloring—and to retard growth of mold and bacteria.

Sulfites are often found in dried fruits, wines, some beers and shrimp. At one time they were sprayed on the produce in salad bars. In most localities, however, legislation now restricts this use.

At highest risk: Asthmatics. For them, ingesting sulfites can cause shortness of breath—and in very sensitive people, a potentially fatal asthma attack.

Inhaling sulfites—which might occur when sulfur dioxide gas is released upon opening a bag of dried fruit—can temporarily irritate the mouth and nose of asthmatics and nonasthmatics alike.

Do restricted diets help?

Asthmatics should avoid sulfites and possibly MSG. For others, however, there is no good evidence that dietary restrictions are necessary or helpful.

Some people susceptible to hives have shown improvement after several months on a diet free of dyes and preservatives as well as natural salicylates (the active ingredient in aspirin, which also occurs naturally in apples and lingonberries).

But we don't know whether the diets themselves helped these patients or whether the symptoms stemmed from another cause, such as a virus that simply ran its course.

Important: Because drastically restricted diets may be deficient in key nutrients, check with a doctor or nutritionist before attempting to eliminate additives from your diet.

Source: Richard W. Weber, MD, staff allergist, Allergy Respiratory Institute of Colorado, 5800 E. Evans Ave., Denver 80222. Dr. Weber has also served as director of allergy training programs for the US Army and the University of Michigan.

Too Many Dangerous Chemicals Are in Too Many of Our Homes

According to the Environmental Protection Agency's estimates, the average household contains between three and 10 gallons of hazardous chemicals—and many of them are organic compounds that vaporize at room temperature.

In the effort to save money by sealing our homes to reduce heating and air-conditioning bills, and by becoming do-it-yourselfers for many tasks once left to professionals, we expose ourselves and our families to high levels of these toxic substances.

Read the label...

"We are all guilty of not thoroughly reading labels," according to Charles Jacobson, compliance officer, US Consumer Products Safety Commission.

If vapors may be harmful, it doesn't do much good to read the label after you have used the product and inhaled the vapors.

Important: Read the labels before buying a product to select the safest in a category. If you find any of the 11 ingredients listed below on a container, avoid buying it. If you must buy it, use extreme caution when working with...

Dangerous chemicals...

1. *Methylene chloride.* A widely used solvent, it is in pesticide aerosols, refrigeration and air-conditioning equipment, cleansing creams, and in paint and varnish removers. Some paint strippers are 80% methylene chloride. Its toxic effects include damage to liver, kidneys, and central nervous system. It increases the carbon monoxide level in the blood, and people with angina (chest pains) are extremely sensitive to the chemical. Methylene chloride has been linked to heart attacks and cancer.

2. *Dichlorvos (DDVP).* An investigation by the National Toxicology Program of the Department of Health and Human Services revealed a significant leukemia hazard from this common household pesticide. It's been widely used in pet, house, and yard aerosol products since the 1950S. The EPA has had DDVP in special review since February, 1988, and it has been considering banning it from food packaging.

3. *2,4-D.* A weed killer related to Agent Orange—which allegedly caused health problems in exposed Vietnam veterans, 2,4-D is widely used by home gardeners and farmers.

It does not cause acute toxicity, but its long term effects are scary—much higher incidence of cancer—and non-Hodgkin's lymphoma has been associated with its use among farmers. The National Cancer Institute also reports that dogs whose owners use 2,4-D on their lawns have an increased rate of a type of cancer closely related to human non-Hodgkin's lymphoma.

4. *Perchlorethylene.* The main solvent employed in the dry-cleaning process, metal degreasing, and in some adhesives, aerosols, paints, and coatings, it can be absorbed through your lungs or your skin. The most common effects of overexposure are irritation of the eyes, nose, throat, or skin. Effects on the nervous system include dizziness, headache, nausea, fatigue, confusion, and loss of balance. At very high exposure it can cause death.

5. *Formaldehyde.* An inexpensive and effective preservative used in more than 3,000 household products. They include disinfectants, cosmetics, fungicides, preservatives, and adhesives. It is also used in pressed-wood products —wall paneling, fiberboard, and furniture, and in some papers. There are serious questions about its safety. It is estimated that 4% to 8% of the population is sensitive to it. Vapors are intensely irritating to mucous membranes and can cause nasal, lung, and eye problems.

6. *Benzene.* Among the top five organic chemicals produced in the United States, this petroleum derivative's use in consumer products has, in recent years, been greatly reduced. However, it is still employed as a solvent for waxes, resins, and oils and is in varnish and lacquer. It is also an "antiknock" additive in gasoline—thus, make sure your house is well ventilated and insulated from vapors that arise from an attached garage.

Benzene is highly flammable, poisonous when ingested, and irritating to mucous membranes. Amounts that are harmful may be absorbed through the skin. *Possible results:* Blood, brain, and nerve damage.

7. *Cyanide.* One of the most rapid poisons known, it is used to kill fungus, insects, and rats. It is in metal polishes (especially silver), in art materials, and photographic solutions.

8. *Naphthalene.* Derived from coal, it is used in solvents, fungicides, in toilet bowl deodorizers, and as a moth repellent. It can be absorbed through the skin and eyes as well as through the lungs. It may damage the eyes, liver, kidneys, skin, red blood cells, and the central nervous system. It has reportedly caused anemia in infants exposed to clothing and blankets stored in naphthalene mothballs. This chemical can cause allergic skin rashes in adults and children.

9. *Paradichlorobenzene (PDB).* Made from chlorine and benzene, it is in metal polishes, in moth repellents, general insecticides, germicides, spray deodorants, and fumigants. PDB is also commonly found in room deodorizers. Vapors may cause irritation to the skin, throat, and eyes. Prolonged exposure to high concentrations may cause weakness, dizziness, loss of weight, and liver damage. A well-known animal cancer-causing agent, the chemical can linger in the home for months or even years.

10. *Trichloroethylene (TCE).* A solvent used in waxes, paint thinners, fumigants, metal polishes, shoe polish, and rug cleaners. Tests conducted by the National Cancer Institute showed TCE caused cancer of the liver. A combination of alcohol ingestion with exposure to trichloroethylene can cause flushing of the skin, nausea, and vomiting.

11. *Hydroxides/lye products.* These include automatic dishwasher detergents, toilet-bowl cleaners, fire proofing, paint remover, and drain cleaners. Ingestion causes vomiting, prostration, and collapse. Inhalation causes lung damage. Prolonged contact with dilute solutions can have a destructive effect upon tissue, leading to skin irritations and eruptions.

Source: Ruth Winter, author of *A Consumer's Dictionary of Household, Yard, and Office Chemicals.* Crown Publishers.

Is that House Environmentally Safe?

• Does the neighborhood in which the property is located appear on any government hazards lists? This is not something that the owner of the property is likely to know. The information is available by calling your regional Environmental Protection Agency (EPA) Superfund office. It will tell you whether the EPA has targeted the area for cleanup.

In some cases, you must rely on the Freedom of Information Act,* a process that often takes six weeks or more. If the EPA is unable to help you, there are several fee-based information groups. *They include:*

• *Environmental Risk Information and Imaging Service (ERIIS).* Located in Alexandria, Virginia, it can provide current and prior-use information on registered federal and state hazardous sites. *Cost:* $75 to $295. *Information:* 800-989-0403.

• *Vista Environmental Information Inc.* This fee-based firm in San Diego has developed residential reports that are available by mail and overnight delivery. *Information:* 619-450-6100.

•How has the property been used during the past 40 or 50 years? Not all hazardous sites are listed in state or federal records. Check with the city's or town's zoning records. Speak with people who have lived there for a long time.

Harmful: Was the property ever used as an auto-repair facility...a pottery, art or photo studio...a dry cleaner...a printer...a farm...or a junkyard? The chemicals used by these businesses may have leached into the ground, raising the chances of health hazards from contaminated soil.

•Is the property—or adjoining properties—built on a former landfill? Landfill dirt can contain asbestos and other outlawed substances. Over time, these substances can create harmful gases or contaminate the surrounding land. Check with your state's Solid Waste Management Office or Landfill Office.

•Is there, or was there ever, a gas station, chemical plant or factory within one-quarter mile of the property? The underground storage tanks for facilities built in the 1950s and 1960s are prone to leakage. There have been cases in which leaks went undetected for years and gasoline or chemicals permeated the soil of entire neighborhoods.

*Contact your local EPA office for more information.

The locations of such facilities will appear on a Fire Insurance Map—available at most public and university libraries, at your fire department, in the databases of ERIIS and Vista, in city or county site records or on the federal government's Leaking Underground Storage Tanks list.

•Has a radon screen been performed on the property? Many states require the seller to do a radon test on behalf of the buyer. Your state or regional radon office will tell you if radon is a problem in your area. Home test kits, available in hardware stores, are adequate. *Cost for a kit:* $10 to $50. Or hire an EPA-certified radon inspector. The EPA will send you a free list of all certified radon inspectors in your state. *Cost for an inspection:* $100 to $300.

Source: Gary T. Deane, EdD, executive director of the National Society of Environmental Consultants, a fee-based group that trains realtors, bankers and appraisers to detect environmental hazards of commercial and residential properties, 303 W. Cypress St., San Antonio 78212.

Smoke Detector Warning

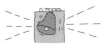

One in five home smoke detectors doesn't work—usually because of dead or missing batteries. Nearly half of home fires and three-fifths of home fire deaths in 1993 occurred in homes without working detectors. A fire department responds to a fire every 16 seconds somewhere in the US...a home fire occurs every 67 seconds ...someone is injured in a fire every 17 minutes ...someone dies in a fire every 113 minutes.

Source: National Fire Protection Association, One Batterymarch Park, Quincy, MA 02269.

Contact Lens Storage

Contact lens storage cases are best disinfected by rinsing them in hot water and then leaving the lens wells open to air-dry after each use. *Also:* Cases should be replaced every two to three months. Dirty lens cases can result in infectious keratitis, a potentially blinding in-flammation of the cornea. *Symptoms:* Contact lens intolerance…eye irritation…blurry vision.

Source: Noemi D. Larragoiti, OD, Southern California College of Optometry, Fullerton. Her study of contact lens storage case cleaning methods was published in the *Journal of the American Optometric Association*, 243 Lindbergh Blvd., St. Louis 63141.

Garlic Danger

Fresh garlic mixes can cause botulism if stored at room temperature. The preservatives found in *commercial* garlic preparations retard spoilage only when refrigerated. Because they lack preservatives, *homemade* garlic mixes may spoil even if stored in the refrigerator. After two weeks, throw them out.

Source Joseph M. Madden, PhD, strategic manager for microbiology, Center for Food Safety and Applied Nutrition, Food and Drug Administration, Washington, DC.

Living Better With Arthritis

Many of the 37 million Americans with ar-thritis have learned to be remarkably creative in overcoming their physical limitations.

If pain and stiffness are making daily life hard for you or someone you know, look into the amazing array of "assistive" devices that are now available.

Some can be easily made at home…

•A wooden pizza paddle can be used to tuck sheets under a mattress.

•A cloth or leather loop tied to knobs and handles makes it easier to open drawers, cabi-nets, refrigerators, etc.

•Velcro—sold at sewing shops and hardware stores—makes a good replacement for hard-to-use buttons, zippers, shoelaces and more.

•A carpenter's apron can be worn around the house to carry cleaning supplies or other items in its big pockets.

Handy items for daily tasks…

There is also a wealth of catalog products. Some are designed specifically for people with disabilities. Others do the trick serendipitously. *A modest sampling:*

•Battery-operated jar opener. Up to five times stronger than a human hand, this opener works on caps as small as one-half inch and as large as four inches. Mounts on wall or under a cabinet.

OpenUp jar opener/#41013W, $29.95.* Four D batteries included. Hammacher Schlemmer.

•Dressing aid. Wire buttoning aid at one end and a brass zipper-puller at the other. Built-up wood and rubber handle.

Button Aid & Zipper Pull/#16564, $9.99.* Sears Health Care Catalog.

•Easily turned faucets. Large, easy-to-grasp knobs attach to existing sink or shower faucets.

Gripper Knob Turner/#NC28266, $15.00.* Tap Turner for acrylic taps/#NC28276, $25.50.* Allied Medical.

•Easy-to-handle eating utensils. Lightweight handles built up with soft foam etched with "gripper waves." Not dishwasher-safe.

Teaspoon/#19990…soup spoon/#l9991…fork/#19992, each $5.82.* Knife/#19993, $6.47.* Vandenberg Aids for Daily Living.

•Easy-to-hold ballpoint pen. Thick barrel with suedelike covering makes writing easier for people with arthritic fingers.

Biocurve #D15, three for $14.50.* Aids for Arthritis.

•Grasping tool. Lightweight aluminum pole with trigger-action jaws and a combination pulling lug/magnet. Eliminates stretching for hard-to-reach items.

The Reacher, 26-inch model/#4109, $18.95.* 32-inch model/#4107, $19.95.* Fred Sammons Company.

•Pain-free "scissors." Rolls like a pizza cutter. For right or left hands.

Rolling Scissors/#PJ00010, $15.88.* Reliable Office Supply.

•Remote control for electrical appliances. Plug the lamp, TV set, etc., into this 2½" x 3½" unit, then plug the unit into a wall outlet. Works with small hand-held remote control unit to turn appliances on and off.

Remote Switch/#132332, $25.* Brookstone.

*Additional tax, shipping and handling charges usually apply. Call to determine total price.

•Telephone headset. Replaces the handset for more comfortable calls.

Model S Plug-In Headset, $99.99. AT&T Accessible Communications Product Center.

•Velcro clothes. No hard-to-operate zippers, buttons, hooks, etc.

JC Penney Easy Dressing Fashions.

Most complete catalogs…

The most complete catalogs are those from Sears Health Care and Fred Sammons.

Other excellent resources for arthritis-related products:

• *Guide to Independent Living for People with Arthritis*, published by the Arthritis Foundation and the Arthritis Health Professions Association. This heavily illustrated, 415-page, spiral-bound book lists an astonishing 537 companies that sell arthritis products. Also explains how to make arthritis products at home.

Arthritis Foundation, Box 19000, Atlanta 30326. $11.95. (Call 800-283-7800 to get the address of the Arthritis Foundation chapter in your area.)

• *Rheumatrex Sharing Innovations* booklet, Lederle Laboratories. Presents creative coping ideas for people with arthritis.

Sharing Innovations, Box 585, Summit, NJ 07902. Free (one booklet per request).

Source: Earl J. Brewer, Jr., MD, former head of pediatric rheumatology at Texas Children's Hospital and Baylor College of Medicine, Houston. Founder and first chairman of the rheumatology section of the American Academy of Pediatrics, Dr. Brewer is coauthor of *The Arthritis Sourcebook*. Lowell House.

Better Carpet Cleaning

Find out how long a cleaning company has been in business. Check last year's phone directory to be sure it has been around for at least a year. Check the firm's complaint history with the Better Business Bureau. Pick a firm based on recommendations from people you trust. Find out from the maker or retailer of your carpet how it should be cleaned—do not leave it up to the service. Pay by credit card in case problems arise after the cleaning service leaves.

Source: Carrie Getty, vice president, Better Business Bureau, New York.

Energy-Saving Compact Fluorescent Lights

Energy-saving compact fluorescent lights can interfere with the signals from remote controls that are used to operate TVs, VCRs and stereos. *If you seem to have a problem:* Move the lamps away from where you use the remote…replace the remote's batteries so its signal is stronger.

Source: Arnold Buddenberg, lighting-systems specialist at Rensselaer Polytechnic Institute, Troy, NY.

Simple Secrets of a Chemical-Free Lawn

There is no doubt that Americans love their lawns—all of our five million acres of lawns. And so we spend $6 billion a year on lawn care and cultivation.

Problem: The excessive—and largely unnecessary—use of pesticides, herbicides and fertilizers could be avoided. They are damaging our soil, contaminating our water systems and exposing our families to hazardous chemicals.

A healthy lawn has no need for chemicals. It can keep out weeds, disease and insects by itself. Think of your lawn as a garden of grass, and simply follow the principles of good gardening. Consider climate, soil and available light. And—select plant varieties with care… and learn to feed, mow and water correctly.

Grass gardening made easy…

•*If you are planting a new lawn:* Consult a reputable garden center for recommendations on grass varieties and advice on sowing or sodding. Many new grasses are resistant to insects and disease.

Grasses are bred to thrive in specific climates and conditions. You may want to have a soil sample analyzed by your state's agricultural college or cooperative extension service. When choosing a grass, consider how you use your lawn. Color is important for perfect vistas, whereas toughness (the ability to bounce back from wear) is crucial in heavy traffic areas such as children's play areas.

• *To convert to and maintain a chemical-free lawn:*

Fertilizers. Use a slowly soluble organic fertilizer, with no more than two pounds of nitrogen per 1,000 feet per year.

Fertilize only once a year, in the fall. Then you won't be fertilizing your weeds…they are not programmed to germinate and grow strongly in the fall. But grass leaves and roots both grow vigorously well into the fall. Fertilizing before winter sets in allows the roots to build up carbon reserves that carry over to spring.

Weeds. Weeds are crowded out by healthy turf. They appear only when a lawn is suffering. *Usual culprit:* Wrong type of grass in the wrong place. *Best approach:* To avoid damage to the surrounding turf, weed by hand. Many of the new, long-handled weeding tools are excellent. Then go back to the bare spots and reseed.

Note: Just because it doesn't look like a blade of grass doesn't mean it's a weed. Enjoy the many plants, such as violets and speedwell that were brought to this country as ornamentals. They add color and attract beneficial insects.

Mowing. Most people mow too often—and too low. *Problem:* When grass is cut too short the roots stop growing. Longer grass shades out weeds—and has deeper roots. *Best:* Raise mower blades to maintain grass at three to four inches high. Never cut more than 40% of the height of grass at one time. Keep mower blades sharp to avoid shredding the grass. Mow higher and less often in hot, dry weather. Let grass grow one inch higher in the shade for increased photosynthesis. To cut back on mowing, plant ground cover around trees, on banks, etc.

Watering. Most people water too often—and too lightly. Sprinkling induces roots to stay near the surface. *Best:* Allow water to soak six to 10 inches deep into the soil. Hold off watering again until the grass begins to wilt. This forces roots to grow deeper, for a healthier lawn. Too much water on the surface can encourage disease. So water in the morning after dew has dried, or in the afternoon—not at night.

Insects. Insects are rarely troublesome when turf and soil are healthy. *Best:* Add shrubs and trees to encourage grub-eating birds. Plant wildflowers and herbs to encourage beneficial insects. If your lawn is actually being damaged by a specific pest, consider reseeding with a resistant strain of grass. *Last resort:* Apply an organic pesticide at the risk of also killing useful bugs.

Diseases. Diseases are usually a symptom of grass that has been overwatered and overfertilized. Most are caused by fungi. *Solutions:* Improve drainage, overseed with resistant strains of grass, stop using chemicals.

Lawn care companies…

Negotiate with your lawn service to do less. Ask them to set mower blades higher. Look for an organic fertilizer program. Discontinue routine weed-spraying, pest treatments, etc. Then, tell your neighbors how you got your lawn to thrive.

Source: Warren Schultz, author of *The Chemical-Free Lawn*. Rodale.

When Buying a New Condominium

Buying a condominium is more complicated than buying a house. *Reason:* The purchase is really for two separate pieces of property—your unit and the property held in common. Before signing any contract for a new condominium, which is harder to check out than an established condominium, buyers should study the prospectus for any of these pitfalls:

•The prospectus includes a plan of the unit you are buying, showing rooms of specific dimensions. But the plan omits closet space. *Result:* The living space you are buying is probably smaller than you think.

•The prospectus includes this clause: "The interior design shall be substantially similar."

Result: The developer can alter both the size and design of your unit.

• The common charges set forth in the prospectus are unrealistically low. Buyers should never rely on a developer's estimate of common charges. *Instead:* They should find out the charges at similarly functioning condominiums.

• *Common charges include:* Electricity for hallways and outside areas, water, cleaning, garbage disposal, insurance for common areas, pool maintenance, groundskeeping, legal and accounting fees, reserves for future repairs.

• *Variation on the common-charge trap:* The developer is paying common charges on unsold units. But these charges are unrealistically low. *Reason:* The developer has either under insured or underestimated the taxes due, omitted security expenses, or failed to set up a reserve fund.

• *The prospectus includes this clause:* "The seller will not be obligated to pay monthly charges for unsold units." *Result:* The owners of a partially occupied condominium have to pay for all operating expenses.

• The prospectus warns about the seller's limited liability. But an unsuspecting buyer may still purchase a condominium unit on which back monthly charges are due, or even on which there's a lien for failure to pay back carrying charges.

• The prospectus makes no mention of parking spaces. *Result:* You must lease from the developer.

• The prospectus is imprecise about the total number of units to be built. *Result:* Facilities are inadequate for the number of residents.

• *The prospectus includes this clause:* "Transfer of ownership (of the common property from the developer to the homeowners' association) will take place 60 days after the last unit is sold." *Trap:* The developer deliberately does not sell one unit, keeps on managing the condominium, and awards sweetheart maintenance and operating contracts to his subcontractors.

• The prospectus specifies that the developer will become the property manager of the functioning condominium. But the language spelling out monthly common charges and management fees is imprecise. *Result:* The owners cannot control monthly charges and fees.

Source: Dorothy Tymon, author, *The Condominium: A Guide for The Alert Buyer.* Golden Lee Books.

The Big Home Remodeling Mistakes... And How to Avoid Them

Making major changes in your home's design and structure can add thousands of dollars to its sale price. In other cases, fixing up your home is more cost-efficient and practical than moving.

As more and more people take on the tasks of designing new rooms, choosing materials and hiring labor for the first time, they are more likely to fall into traps that cost them time and money.

Here are the most common errors to avoid when renovating your home...

Mistake: Not seeing the big picture. When planning major structural changes, such as adding a room, many people do not take the architectural integrity of their homes into consideration. They need additional space or want their homes to look new, so their main concerns are that the work be done quickly and at a cost that is within their budgets.

Problems: Renovation work that is out of character with the rest of the home sticks out and will be a big turnoff to potential buyers if you decide to sell in the future.

In addition, many people try to do too much without having enough money to do it right. The result is shoddy work.

Example: Redoing the basement may be less important—and ultimately less financially rewarding when selling your home—than adding a high-quality den or family room.

Strategy: First determine how much you can afford to spend on renovating. Then draw up a wish list of what you want done, in order of preference. To find out what your money might realistically buy, invite two architects *and* two contractors to look around your home and provide you with ballpark estimates. They should do this for free.

Then plan on striking a proper balance between solving your needs and achieving an appropriate level of quality for your type of home while working within your budget. If you can't get to it all, postpone renovations on other parts of the house until next year or the year after.

Trap: Spending too much on the renovation project and making your home the most expensive one on the street, thereby pricing it out of competition.

Choose work that will truly improve your lifestyle and make your home more attractive —without putting it beyond the reach of a potential buyer. *Doing too much* is also a problem. You may be left with a home whose parts no longer work together.

Example: Add three bedrooms, and you may find your dining room seems small.

Mistake: Being excessively trendy. As the number of colorful home-improvement magazines and TV shows increases, so do home owners' wishes for the fancy things they see.

Examples: Heavy terra-cotta floor tiles in the kitchen…fancy opaque glass walls…geometric fireplaces…trendy colors and finishes.

While many of these features may look great for a few years, you'll probably outgrow them faster than you think. In all likelihood, you'll also have to live with them—since the expense of redoing what you have done will be higher in the future.

Before you commit to the latest design fad or put a Jacuzzi in the family room, consider the long-term consequences. Ask yourself if you will be comfortable with this new style for the next 20 years. When it comes to resale, conservative, timeless work—such as elegant, functional spaces and generally neutral colors in kitchens and bathrooms—always holds up best.

Mistake: Assuming that you will pay what your neighbors did for the same work. When home owners go looking for architects, contractors, carpenters, electricians, etc., they usually call their friends for recommendations. They also frequently ask what their friends paid for remodeling or renovation work that was done a few years ago.

With those estimates in mind, they are often shocked when they hear what the work will cost today. During the 1990-1991 recession, business was terrible for architects and contractors. They often worked at distress prices. In addition, the cost of lumber has soared in the last four years.

Be prepared to pay 5% to 15% more.

Mistake: Not spending enough time hiring the right people. Most home owners who set out to hire people to design or build for them wish the job were already finished. It's only natural to want your renovations completed shortly after you imagine them. But it's important to be practical and take the project one step at a time.

Once you've talked to a few architects and contractors, ask three of each for bids—no matter how inexpensive the project. Of course, the contractors' bids are solicited after the architect completes documents for bidding. The contractor will hire electricians, plumbers, etc.

Ask each for three references, and be sure to contact all of them. *Key questions…*

•Were you happy with the work and the working relationship?

•How long did it take to complete the job?

•Was the job completed within the estimated time?

•Did the contractor ask for many change orders that boosted the cost of the work well past the estimate?

•Did the architect handle the smaller details (electrical, lighting, etc.)?

Important: Don't automatically choose the lowest bid. This is a major temptation, but beware—a low price may result in low-quality work, either because the caliber of the person is low or because the person did not understand the actual scope of the work and bid too low.

A bid is probably too low if it is very different from other quotes. Most people who get three bids accept the middle one, if it is reasonable.

Exception: If the three bids are vastly different—say, $20,000, $40,000 and $60,000. In these cases, you're probably not comparing similar types of work.

Strategy: Eliminate much of this confusion by having contractors bid after seeing a complete set of the construction documents prepared by the architect.

Another mistake people make is hiring a design professional whose skills are appropriate for a different type of work.

Example: If you're planning an addition to an elegant Tudor-style house, you should find an architect who has done work in the Tudor style. Request photos of his work, or visit a home on which he has worked.

Strategy: To find someone with the right skills, ask owners of similar homes, look in magazines or contact a historical society.

Mistake: Not deciding on the details early enough. Many delays are the fault of the contractor. But some are caused by home owners who haven't selected fixtures, colors, etc. Avoid delays by selecting your faucets, tiles and stones early and making sure everything the contractor needs is in place. Holding up a project for a few days because you have changed your mind about some element can add weeks to the timetable.

Example: The contractor may have budgeted only two months to complete your job, after which he must move onto another project. A two-day delay may cause him to stop working on your house for several weeks.

You may save money by ordering and picking up finish materials yourself. Get a list of what you need from the contractor. Bring samples home to make sure the new tiles work with the rest of the room. Ripping up newly laid tiles costs time and money.

Mistake: Assuming you can live in your home while work is being done. If possible, home owners should move out while extensive interior work is being done. It's not just a question of noise and workmen underfoot. There will be dust, debris and furniture out of place. There may even be hazardous materials around.

Strategy: Arrange alternate accommodations at a residence hotel, which offers lower weekly and monthly rates than commercial hotels… or sublet an apartment. If you do continue to live in your home, be willing to make certain sacrifices.

Example: Don't make a fuss if you hate the music the workers play on the job. You'll have a happier crew that does better work.

Mistake: Not overseeing the work properly. It's important to keep tabs on how the work is progressing. It's your house, and there is a certain joy in seeing your plans come to fruition.

Avoid being bossy and looking over the contractor's shoulder 10 times a day. On the other hand, don't be aloof or inaccessible. If you're not there to raise an important issue or answer questions, the contractor may not bring it up or the project may be delayed.

Strategy: Check on the progress every day or every other day. Raise any issues as soon as possible with the contractor.

If there are enormous conceptual issues involved, call the architect first and have him help you discuss matters with the contractor. If you need to talk with the contractor about a serious problem, do it away from the crew so you don't undermine his/her authority. It's also a problem if you *and* your spouse communicate different opinions and information to the contractor. Couples should agree on their wants and needs in advance.

Strategy: Determine who will speak with the contractor and workers. Generally, the same person should handle this task throughout the job.

Whenever possible, hash out your and your spouse's aesthetic disagreements *before* talking to the professionals who are working on your home. If your spouse has a question that you can't answer or are uncomfortable asking, both of you should sit down with the contractor and calmly go over the problem.

Source: James Paragano, RA, AIA, a registered architect specializing in custom residential work, 37 Kings Rd., Ste. 202, Madison, NJ 07940. He has remodeled about 150 homes.

Home Repair Grants

Home owners age 62 and over can qualify for up to $5,000 to repair their homes. *Other requirements:* The home must be in a rural area—population under 10,000…applicants must show that they cannot repay the money.

Source: Farmers Home Administration, Washington, DC.

Is Your Property's Assessed Value Too High?

The effective real-estate tax is the tax rate multiplied by the assessed value. There's not much an individual can do about the tax rate, but assessment can often be challenged successfully. *Requirements:* Proof that either the property is overvalued or the assessment is higher than on comparable property in the same area. *When to ask for a reduction:*

• Just before making necessary repairs of damages that have lowered the value.

• Local tax records err in description by overstating size or income.

• Net income drops due to factors beyond owner's control.

• When the price paid for the building in an arm's length transaction is lower than the assessed value.

What to do:

• Determine the ratio of the assessed value to the present market value. Compare against average ratios of similar properties recently sold in the same area. *Sources:* Ratios available to public in tax districts. Real-estate brokers, professional assessors can also be consulted.

• Check tax records for a description of the property, income.

• Consult a lawyer on the strength of the case, whether it can be handled by an informal talk with the assessor, and how much it will cost if a formal proceeding and appeal are necessary.

When the New House Is a Lemon

A home buyer may be able to get out of the entire purchase contract if the seller has misrepresented a house with many serious defects.

Normally, when defects show up after the buyers move in, they can sue for damages. Some state courts have ruled that two reasons for suing may void the entire sale: (1) Misrepresentation of an important aspect of the house. (2) The presence of many serious defects.

One case: The builder had assured the buyer that there would be no water problem. But the house was flooded soon after the closing. The court said the related damage would be impossible to repair.

Source: *Chastain v. Billings,* 570 SW2d 866.

Best Opportunity Yet To Buy a Home From the RTC

It's not too late to buy a house at a bargain price from the Resolution Trust Corporation (RTC)—the agency organized to dispose of the assets of failed banks and savings & loans.

While institutional investors have been snapping up many of the RTC properties, there are a large number of residential properties available for individual investors and first-time buyers.

In fact, the RTC has scheduled a surge of property auctions for 1993. It currently has $35 billion of property to dispose of and will obtain much more from the 150 banks and S&Ls expected to fail during 1993—double the failure rate of 1992.

Bargains abound. Discounts of two-thirds off are being reported. And special programs exist to help middle-income property buyers. *Important:* You have to know how to find the property you want.

Finding out...

To help prospective property buyers, the RTC has beefed up its promotion department.

You can receive educational brochures explaining various RTC programs free by calling 800-431-0600...or by writing to the RTC National Sale Center, 1133 21 St. NW, Washington, DC 20036.

The RTC also provides listings of properties that are available in your zip code. This service is free if you request a list of fewer than 50 properties. Larger listings will cost a small fee, which you can put on your credit card. *To use this service:* Call the RTC at 800-RTC-3006.

Opportunity: Before being auctioned off, properties are listed by brokers who often have a "make me an offer" attitude toward these properties. You may be able to buy the property you want before it is auctioned simply by making a reasonable offer to a broker who is eager to dispose of it.

Bargain: Under a special program designed to help middle-class buyers, the Affordable Housing Disposition Program (AHDP), the RTC will accept a down payment of as little as 3% and provide financing for auctioned property.

The AHDP is available to buyers who fall under certain income limits, which vary by region. *Example:* In New York, $48,000. In addition, the property sales price must fall in the following range:

Type	up to
One-unit dwelling	$67,500
Two-unit dwelling	$76,000
Three-unit dwelling	$93,000
Four-unit dwelling	$107,000

For details about the AHDP, and to learn if you qualify, call 800-533-8951.

Be prepared...

While great bargains are available, the quality of RTC-held properties varies greatly.

Look over several properties, to become informed of the quality of RTC offerings in your area. Then focus on the ones that are most attractive, and give them a thorough inspection before making any offer to a broker or auction bid.

Properties are sold on an "as is" basis...so what you buy, for better or worse, will be what you keep.

Source: George Chekelis, author of *The Official Government Auction Guide.* Crown Publishers.

When to Watch Your Broker Closely

A company or individual listing property for sale with a real estate agent may find it's no longer listed after an offer is turned down. *Reason:* The agent is trying to make the commission by temporarily taking the property off the active list in the hope the owner will give up and accept the offer. The agent may keep other agents from sending around prospects by removing the file or spreading word that the property has been sold.

Lemon Law vs. Manufacturer's Responsibility

If your new car is a lemon, first give the dealer a chance to fix it and keep copies of all the repair orders. After the second unsuccessful repair attempt—or after the car has been out of service for 15 days—contact the manufacturer's regional office and ask for assistance in getting the car repaired. After three repair attempts—or after the car has been out of service for 20 days—write to the manufacturer's headquarters and explain that you will invoke your lemon law right to a refund or replacement unless repairs are successful. After four repair attempts or 30 days out of service, demand a refund or replacement. If the manufacturer refuses, go to court or arbitration—attorney fees can be re deemed under federal or state lemon laws.

Source: Clarence Ditlow, executive director of the Center for Auto Safety. For a lemon-lawyer referral, write to Center for Auto Safety, 2001 S St. NW, Washington, DC 20009. Include a self-addressed, stamped, business-sized envelope.

15

Enjoying Your Travel and Leisure

Secrets of Flying Safely In Unsafe Times

Despite new technology, there's no evidence that airlines are appreciably safer than they were a decade ago. Over the last 10 years, US airlines have averaged one fatal accident for every 2,000,000 departures.

Part of the problem is an unintentional consequence of deregulation. During the era of federal control, many airlines exceeded minimum safety requirements. But today, fewer airlines exceed the standards because deregulation has toughened competition, thereby creating financial problems that have forced some airlines to divert resources away from safety.

But…more information about airline performance is now available, and it gives passengers new ways to choose safer airlines and increase their chances of surviving a crash.

How to choose safer airlines…

Rule #1: If possible, don't fly an airline that's in financial difficulty. There's no certainty that

a money-troubled airline will be less safe. But the FAA itself increases safety surveillance of such airlines on the assumption that they're under pressure to cut corners on safety and maintenance.

For similar reasons, think twice about flying an airline with severe labor problems, especially those that disrupt maintenance operations.

Rule #2: Avoid small regional airlines whenever possible. While some regionals have good safety records, statistics show that you're three times more likely to die in a crash on a plane with 30 seats or fewer than a larger craft. Among other problems, regionals often use small airports that aren't as well-equipped to guide planes in at night and in bad weather as larger airports are. Also, small airplanes often lack the more sophisticated instrumentation for bad-weather flying, and regional pilots are generally not as experienced as those who fly for major carriers.

Trap: Airlines don't always tell passengers that they're routed on a regional carrier for a particular leg of their trip. For that reason, al-

293

ways ask which airline you'll be flying on each leg. You may find that another major airline will fly directly to your destination or that you can rent a car and drive from a nearby major city.

Safest planes…safest seats…

The National Transportation Safety Board* keeps records on accidents of specific planes, and these are available to the public. *Challenge:* The accident data are difficult to interpret because problems may originate with the different kinds of engines that a single type of aircraft may use. And some aircraft that are flown over more dangerous routes may appear statistically less safe than others when they're really not.

Nevertheless, if for no other reason than peace of mind, travelers can avoid specific types of planes, particularly the DC-10 that's been involved in several recent disasters. And, avoiding a certain type of plane is easier than most passengers realize.

When you make reservations, ask the ticket agents or travel agents what kind of plane is scheduled on your flight. If they balk, be insistent. Agents virtually always have that information. If you have qualms about the plane, ask for another flight or make reservations with another airline.

Before you leave for the airport, check again with the airline to see if there's been a change in planes. If there has been, and if you don't want to fly on the craft, you again have the option of making other travel arrangements (unless you have a nonrefundable ticket).

Even with a nonrefundable ticket, don't give up. Go to the airport and use persuasion on the ticket agent. Unfortunately, you have no other power to ask him to switch your flight.

Agents are under no obligation to help travelers in that situation. But if you make it clear that the only reason you want to switch is to fly on another type of aircraft, the agent may accommodate you to earn goodwill for the airline.

Choosing the safest seats…

Myth: That the safest seats on all commercial aircraft are those next to emergency exits.

Reality: Aisle seats close to the overwing emergency exits are safer. These seats are commonly in the mid-front section of the plane. If

*800 Independence Ave. SW, Washington, DC 20594.

you sit in the window seat next to an emergency exit, you may be worse off in the event of a crash that jams the exit. Aisle seats near several exits give you more escape options in the event of a crash.

Lifesaving precaution. When you take your seat in the plane, count and memorize the number of rows to the nearest exits. *Reason:* If smoke fills the cabin after a crash, you may have to feel your way in the dark to an exit. This precaution is based on the tactics that crash survivors actually have used to get out of a plane.

Other lifesavers…

• For some protection against fire, wear full-length clothing, suits or dresses, made of wool or cotton, sturdy shoes and eyeglasses with an attachable lanyard. Avoid wearing shorts or clothing made of synthetics like polyester which can melt to your body in a fire.

• Women should not wear high-heeled shoes on a plane. They can cause you to trip, and they can snag on the emergency exit slide.

• If the plane fills with smoke, stay low, even if you have to crawl. Two or three breaths of toxic smoke can kill you. If there's enough warning before a crash, place a damp cloth over your mouth in order to breathe through smoke.

• Get as far away from the plane as possible if you're lucky enough to escape it after a crash. People on the ground are often killed when a downed plane explodes.

• Learn how to open the exits by reading the emergency instructions soon after you get on the plane. That's something you don't want to learn as the aircraft bursts into flames.

Source: Geraldine Fankowski, director, Aviation Consumer Action Project, an advocacy group for airline safety and passenger rights, 2000 P St. NW, Washington, DC 20036.

How to Fly Free

Big bargains are available on air travel and are easy to get. The hard part is getting someone to tell you what these deals are and how you can take advantage of them. *Examples:*

• If you fly to a nearby "secondary" airport, you may be able to save 10% to 34% on your ticket, and avoid many of the hassles associated with overcrowded primary airports.

• If you fly on Thanksgiving, Christmas or New Year's day, you can save up to 70% on your ticket—and still arrive in plenty of time for dinner.

• If you fly as a senior citizen, you can save 10% to 100% on your ticket. The older you get the more you save. George Burns at 99 can get 99% off his ticket on some airlines. When he reaches 100, he'll be eligible for a 100% discount.

Research pays...

If you take the time to do the research and analyze your options, you will be able to take advantage of special fares and money-saving situations. *Examples:*

Hidden city flights...

The trick here is to get off or on in the connecting city, rather than take the plane to its final destination.

Example: A one-way fare for the nonstop, direct flight from Dallas/Ft. Worth to Phoenix might cost $393, but if you booked a nondirect flight from Houston to Phoenix where you changed planes in Ft. Worth, you might pay as little as $207 and beat the higher fare. You would get on the plane in Ft. Worth and only use that part of your ticket.

Split ticketing...

Beat the mandatory Saturday night stay on excursion fares to cities you'll visit more than once by buying two round-trip discount tickets.

Here's how to do it...

• Ticket A from your home town to your destination and back again.

• Ticket B from your destination to your home, and back to your destination.

You use the outbound part of your ticket A to get you to your destination, but use the outbound ticket from ticket B to get home. The airline will not realize that you didn't stay over on a Saturday. Use the remaining portions of your two round-trip tickets for your next trip.

Special member discounts...

Members of the clergy, Red Cross workers, military personnel, medical students, children, job corps trainees and seamen all can qualify for as much as a 50% discount on air travel.

Consolidator fares...

Independent discount travel brokers buy blocks of surplus seats on international flights and sell these seats at fares far less than those a retail travel agent or the airline can offer you directly.

Check the travel sections of major metropolitan newspapers or ask your travel agent if he/she uses consolidators or wholesalers.

Bumping from an overbooked flight...

Some people hope to be bumped from flights so that they can receive a free flight voucher as compensation. To help make this happen, book your flight during a time when there is a great likelihood that there will be bumping. Take only carry-on luggage. Seat yourself very near the check-in clerk so that you can be the first to volunteer when volunteers are called for.

You'll have lost a few hours in travel time, but gained a free ticket for your next adventure.

The flexible traveler...

If you've always got your bags packed, and you are ready to go, but are interested in the best deals to the best places, subscribe to *Best Fares* (800-635-3033)—*Travel Smart* (800-FARE-OFF) or *Consumer Reports Travel Letter* (800-234-1970).

These are very thorough monthly publications specializing in the latest information about travel promotions and discounts being offered by cruise lines, airlines, hotel chains, car rental agencies and frequent flyer programs.

Traveling absolutely free...

Group leader: Organize your entire extended family for a trip, or get together a group of friends with similar interests.

If you can put together a big enough tour group—sometimes six is big enough—you can go free.

If you can recruit 12 fellow travelers, you may be able to bring a friend free, too.

Work with your travel agent or directly with an airline group travel representative to set it up.

Tour escort: If you are fluent in a foreign language, you can become a tour escort. Check with large travel agencies or tour operators.

Courier: Volunteer your services as an air courier and escort freight (usually documents) to a distant client. Air couriers fly free to exotic spots all over the world. Check the *Yellow Pages* or metropolitan papers for advertisements.

Know it all...

The key to traveling inexpensively is to do the research yourself by creating a file of cheap flight advertisements, subscribing to travel publications, scouring the travel sections of the Sunday newspapers and comparing all your options before you pick up the phone to book your trip.

Bottom line: Always use a charge card to pay for your trip so you'll have some recourse if your trip doesn't go as planned.

And if you're hoping to sleep en route, bring along a U-shaped, blow-up pillow—they're great.

Source: Linda Bowman, author of *Freebies (and More) for Folks Over 50.* COM-OP Publishing.

Hepatitis A Self-Defense

Travelers to developing countries should be vaccinated for hepatitis A. If the vaccine is unavailable, they should receive a shot of immune globulin.

Reason: Each month, as many as three in 1,000 travelers staying in a developing country are infected with the disease, making it the most frequent vaccine-preventable infection in travelers.

Added danger: People born after 1945 have limited natural immunity—and so are even more susceptible to infection.

Source: Robert Steffen, MD, division of epidemiology and prevention of communicable diseases, Institute of Social and Preventive Medicine, University of Zurich, Switzerland.

How to Travel Free

Instead of traveling cheap, you could be traveling free—from transportation by air—or sea—to lodgings, meals, and entertainment. Most free travel requires no special skills, credentials, or contacts. And it can be just as luxurious—and often more pleasurable—than the most expensive paid vacation.

Cruise lines generally offer a free passage to anyone who recruits 10 to 15 paying passengers. (Many airlines offer similar deals.) If you can't lure that many customers, you can get a prorated reduction on your fare.

You can also cruise free as an expert in a pertinent subject. Historians, anthropologists, naturalists, and ornithologists are in especially high demand. Your job on the cruise would be to present a series of lectures and to be available for informal questioning. It helps to have a PhD (or at least a Master's) and to have published articles on the subject, but an affable personality and a willingness to share your knowledge with others can stretch your credentials. After your first cruise in this capacity, a good reference will ease the way at other lines.

Free cruises are available to doctors and nurses who are willing to be on 24-hour call (here a salary is an added inducement)...to athletic directors and coaches who can help organize recreational activities...to musicians and entertainers willing to perform—to cosmetologists who can barter their services for a ride.

There is also a strong demand for "hosts"—distinguished single gentlemen who are usually 55 years old and up. They serve by dining and dancing with the many unattached older women taking these vacation cruises. Besides free room and board, hosts are encouraged to make use of an unlimited bar tab available for themselves and their new female friends.

Source: Robert William Kirk, author of *You Can Travel Free.* Pelican Publishing Co.

Senior-Citizen Discounts

Offered by most airlines, these discounts are applicable for one companion, regardless of the companion's age—a great travel opportunity for grandparents and grandchildren.

Source: *Bill & Pam Bryan's Off the Beaten Path,* 109 E. Main St., Bozeman, MT 59715.

Frequent Flyers

Flying frequently increases cancer risk because of the higher level of radiation at higher altitudes. *Among frequently flying passengers and crew:* There are 1,000 more cancer-related deaths per 100,000 people who fly cross country 98 times per year over a 20-year period. Flyers who take 54 cross-country flights each year for 20 years have 500 more deaths from cancer per 100,000. There are 1,200 more cancer deaths per 100,000 among flyers who take 74 flights per year over the North Pole between New York and Tokyo for 10 years.

Source: Study conducted by the Department of Transportation, reported in *International Living,* 824 E. Baltimore St., Baltimore 21202.

Traveling Is Not as Simple as It Used to Be

The best way to protect yourself from today's airlines is to know how to beat them at their own game. *Common questions…uncommon advice:*

With all the turmoil in the industry, I'm worried that the airline I've made my vacation reservations with may go bankrupt. What's the best way to protect myself?

•Pay for your tickets with a charge card. That way you can charge back the tickets if you don't receive the service for which you've paid. *Trap:* Sometimes an airline will continue to operate on a reduced schedule while in bankruptcy. And even though you suffer great inconvenience, it will be difficult for you to charge back the tickets because the airline is still providing service.

•Have the travel agent who made your reservations cancel the tickets. This may be possible if the airline goes bankrupt just a day or two after you make your reservations…and before the travel agent has forwarded the money to the airline.

•Buy trip-cancellation insurance. This will enable you to recover at least part of your expense. *Drawback:* This insurance is quite expensive (usually $5 for each $100 of protection). And it will not protect you against fraud or failure involving the travel organization that sold you the insurance. *Self-defense:* Don't buy this insurance from your travel agent or trip coordinator. Purchase it directly from an insurance company.

Protecting your travel plans is more difficult than protecting yourself financially. If your airline does go bankrupt, other airlines will sometimes honor your original tickets…but on a low-priority basis. That generally means you must fly standby.

Is it true that the airlines have improved their on-time arrival records?

Sort of. The nominal improvements are not from operating more efficiently, but from relaxed standards. What used to be described as, say, a three-hour trip is now listed as three and a half hours. *Trap:* The new schedules are much less precise than the old ones. If your plane is supposed to land at 3 pm, you can expect to arrive between 2:30 and 3:30.

If you don't travel very often, does it still pay to join an airline's frequent-flyer program?

Yes. It costs nothing to join, and it takes surprisingly little to earn a free trip.

Example: In most cases, 20,000 miles of travel gets you a free trip, coach class, anywhere in the US (except Alaska and Hawaii). To earn that 20,000 miles, you need only two transcontinental trips.

And even if you don't fly enough to qualify for a free trip, just joining the plan puts you on the program's mailing list…you'll learn about cut-rate promotional fares not advertised to the public.

Example: Earlier this year, Northwest and Continental both offered members of their frequent-flyer plans the chance to fly anywhere in the US for $200 (one-way).

How can I be sure I'm getting the lowest price available at a hotel?

To get the best deal: Don't automatically accept the rack rate—the one that's posted in the room, quoted over the phone, and listed on the computer. *Better:* Ask if there are any special rates for the period in which you are interested.

If the hotel is not fully booked (or doesn't expect to be), it may offer promotional rates that are 25% less than the rack rate. *Note:* This is good advice whenever you make a hotel reservation anywhere.

Source: Ed Perkins, editor of *Consumer Reports Travel Letter*, 246 Washington St., Mt. Vernon, NY 10550.

Second Passports: The State Department's Best-Kept Secret

Some countries won't permit entry to travelers whose passports show that they've previously visited certain other countries. Most Arab countries, for example, won't allow entry to people whose passports have a stamp showing that they've visited Israel. A similar situation confronts people traveling among some African countries. Traveling freely among these countries is a matter of carrying two passports and knowing when to use them.

You can get a second passport—a restricted passport. It looks just like a regular US passport, with one exception...it clearly states that it is limited to use for travel to specific countries. The restricted passport can't be substituted for a regular passport. It can't be used to enter every country, only the ones that are specified on the application. And it isn't issued for countries with which the United States has no diplomatic relations.

Apply for one at your regional passport office, but be prepared to document your legitimate need...itinerary, assignment from your employer specifying that you need to do business in a particular country, etc. Take two signed passport-sized photos.

To find out if you'll need a restricted passport, check the "Visa Information Sheet" available from any passport office. That document will help you to determine if there are visa or passport conflicts among the countries on your itinerary. *Extra protection:* Check with the consulate or embassy of each country you plan to visit.

Reason: Customs regulations of foreign governments change so quickly that even the State Department is unable to keep its information on these regulations absolutely up-to-date.

Avoid relying on information from travel agencies. They use the *Travel Information Manual* put out by an airline organization. Because the compiling, distribution, etc., can take a long time, the manual can be out-of-date as soon as it's issued.

While traveling, be sure to stay on top of possible entry-rule changes at borders you plan to cross. If entrance to a country depends on the restricted passport, show only that document. Put away your regular passport. Using two passports is officially frowned upon by most governments, so there could be repercussions.

If you use the wrong passport on arrival, you'll probably be refused entry. If you're caught with the wrong document when leaving, on the other hand, chances are the border guards will let you depart.

Very, very important: The restricted passport may not be honored by some countries. If it isn't, contact the nearest US embassy or consulate for emergency assistance.

Source: Information from our insiders at the US State Department.

Travel Savvy

Senior-citizen discounts offered by most airlines are applicable for one companion, regardless of the companion's age—a great travel opportunity for grandparents and grandchildren.

Source: *Bill & Pam Bryan's Off the Beaten Path,* 109 E. Main St., Bozeman, MT 59715.

The Most Dangerous Airlines in the World

Based on the number of fatal accidents per million flights, the five airlines with the worst records over a 20-year period (excluding terrorist-related fatalities) are: Aeroflot (USSR)... China Airlines (Taiwan)...Turkish Airlines... Egypt-Air...CAAC (China).

Based on the number of fatalities per million passengers, the airlines with the worst records over a 20-year period (excluding terrorist-related deaths) are…Turkish Airlines (124.48 fatalities per million passengers)…Air India (21.48 fatalities)…Avianca (5.93 fatalities)… Nigeria Airways (5.53 fatalities)…LOT Polish Airlines (4.54 fatalities).

Source: *Condé Nast Traveler,* 350 Madison Ave., New York 10017.

How to Save Time… Money…Hassle at Disney World

Plan ahead. Walt Disney World in Florida is no place to "wing it." Plan what you want to do before you go. The less time you spend waiting in lines and the more you are able to see, the more value you get for your money. Call in advance to see if any rides are closed for repair. *Also…*

• *Get going early.* The theme parks open about one-half hour earlier than the "official" opening time. The same four rides you can enjoy in one hour early in the day could take up to three hours after 11:30 am. *Recommended:* Arrive 50 minutes before the official opening time, an hour and a half on major holidays.

• *Avoid major holidays.* Disney World is busiest from Christmas Day through New Year's Day, the week of Washington's Birthday, and during spring break and Easter weeks.

Least busy times: After Thanksgiving weekend until Christmas, September until the weekend before Thanksgiving, January 4th through the first half of February, the week after Easter until early June.

Lightest days: Friday, Sunday.

• *Buy tickets in advance by mail from Disney World or a Disney store.* Do not buy tickets at non-Disney hotels, because you'll have to pay up to 10% more.

Admissions options: 1 Park/1 Day, about $40 for an adult. 4-Day/3 Parks Pass, about $132. 5-Day Pass, about $198. Annual Passport, $243. Florida-resident pass, $222.*

*All prices are subject to change.

Best bets: For one- or two-day visits, one day tickets. For longer visits, the 4- and 5-Day Passes.

Caution: The 5-Day Super Pass provides admission to Discovery Island, Pleasure Island, Typhoon Lagoon, and River Country for seven days only from the date of purchase. If you do not plan to visit the smaller attractions, don't pay for the Super Pass.

• *Save the Magic Kingdom for last,* especially if you are traveling with children who may not appreciate the more serious parks. Its rides and attractions are highly rewarding for kids and adults. *Recommended:* See EPCOT first, then MGM, then the Magic Kingdom. Allow a full day for each park.

• *Consider a non-Disney World hotel.* Some hotels near the main gate entrance on US 192 are closer to MGM and the Magic Kingdom than many on-site hotels. Staying off-site can cut your lodging costs by 40% to 60%. Savings on food off-site, especially breakfast and lunch, can be tremendous.

Trade-off: Luxury, convenience. The Disney hotels are much nicer than off-site hotels, and provide certain advantages.

Examples: Child-care options, preferential treatment at the theme parks, transportation independence for teenage children. Most of the expensive Disney hotels provide transportation to the various Disney parks. You do not need a car unless you want to visit attractions outside of Disney.

Best bets: Stay on-site during busy seasons. Join the Magic Kingdom Club ($49) for Disney hotel and admissions discounts. During the off-season, there is little impact on convenience staying off-site, and off-site may be more convenient if you plan to visit Universal Studios or other area attractions.

• *Evaluate travel packages carefully.* Choose a package with features you'll use. Compare package prices with what you would pay booking the trip yourself. If you don't intend to rent a car, choose a package that includes transportation from the airport. Cab fare to Disney World can run up to $42 one way.

• *Limit on-site snacks.* It is easy to spend $40 a day on popcorn, ice cream, etc. *Helpful:* Bring snacks, and set an itinerary before entering the park: "We're going to go like crazy until 11:30, have a snack break, then go to a show, and then sit down and have lunch."

• *Watch out for souvenir-madness.* Even the most jaded visitors to Disney World find themselves wanting a Mickey T-shirt. Prepare your kids to stay within a budget and set limits for yourself, too.

• *Remember that you will be in Florida.* Bring sunscreen, sunglasses, hats, cool, comfortable shoes, aspirin, etc. Drink plenty of fluids. If you suffer from motion sickness, stay off the wilder rides.

Source: Bob Sehlinger, author of *The Unofficial Guide to Walt Disney World & EPCOT.* Prentice-Hall Travel.

Ex-Jeopardy People Picker Tells How You, Too, Can be a Game Show Contestant

After years of watching game shows and knowing most of the answers, you may want to become a contestant.

More than 650,000 potential contestants audition every year, so if you want to be a winner you must master your game...and develop your personality.

Select your game...

Every TV game is different, so for the best chance target the one for which you are most suited. Spend time watching as many game shows as possible. Determine which of the four types most interests you...which game most closely fits your skills and personality...

• Trivia/quiz games test your knowledge of topics including people, current events, history, religion, business, sports, entertainment, products...and how quickly you can recall your knowledge.

• Word/puzzle games test your vocabulary and language skills.

• Personality games test your spontaneous responses and emotional reactions to your personal experiences and real-life situations.

• Kids/teens game shows feature contestants who are less than 18 years old.

Focusing...

If you can't decide immediately, try playing board/computer/video games that duplicate the shows you think you might want to try for. See which you enjoy most...are quickest at... win most often.

Choose a particular game: After watching all the shows of that type, study their formats.

Zero in on your final choice by asking yourself what you want in a game show. Do you want money? Goods? A great date? Do you want to play individually or with teammates? Other contestants? Celebrities? How fast-paced is the game? How far are you willing to travel for the audition?

Know your game...

Become an expert: If you want to win...or even to get through the audition...you must be thoroughly familiar with your chosen game. You need to know the playing format.

Example: On *Jeopardy!*, contestants provide a question to the host's answer.

You must know the rules cold.

Example: On *Wheel of Fortune*, after spinning the wheel, you must supply a consonant to put in the puzzle.

Learn your game's jargon...the particular phrases favored by the game show. If you don't use them at the audition, you're unlikely to get on the show.

Practice, practice, practice...until the game becomes second nature. Play along while watching it...cover up the answers on the screen or turn your chair around while you answer...write down your answers and check your score...use the game's language and expressions...talk and act like the contestants.

Sharpen your skills with board games or videos...broaden your knowledge of a subject by reading books, magazines and newspapers ...compete with family members and friends who play the game well.

Helpful: Set up a mock game show set in your own home using your own furniture... simulate studio distractions with bright lamps and a noisy radio in the background.

Develop your personality…

Imagine you were auditioning yourself… what would you notice about your appearance and personality? What have other people told you are your five strongest points?

Examples: Winning smile…quick wit.

Those strong points will show in your audition if you have spent hours practicing the game in front of the TV so it feels natural to you.

Work on your verbal skills…enunciate clearly and loudly…speak in complete sentences using words you are comfortable with…maintain eye contact…always show enthusiasm… and smile.

When you feel you have practiced enough, call or send a postcard to the show to say you want to be a contestant. Ask if you can audition in your own area. If you must travel to the show's home town, schedule it when you have time.

When audition day arrives, make sure you look your best…let your sparkling personality shine through. Be prepared to fill in forms and take a written puzzle test.

Those who pass go on to a second audition where the game is actually played in competition with others. If you do well enough, you will be one of the chosen few.

Important: Shows have many legal restrictions. *Example:* Knowing anyone who works at the studio will disqualify you.

The show…

If you are chosen, you will get about a month's notice, with instructions on where to go and what to bring.

Example: Five shows are typically taped in one day…so take five outfits in case you are a multiple winner.

How well you do depends on your skills, practice, competitors…you may win big money and/or valuable merchandise. Even if you end up with only a consolation prize, you'll have a memorable experience and lifetime recollections of your few moments of fame.

Source: Greg Muntean, a former contestant coordinator for *Jeopardy!* He is the co-author of *How to Be a Game Show Contestant*. Ballantine Books.

The Secrets of Better Vacations In the Caribbean

Wonderful vacations and the Caribbean just seem to go together. But spending a few days or longer at some balmy island getaway can be a pretty expensive affair. So—here are some ways to trim costs without sacrificing romance.

Of course, planning a Caribbean vacation can be a daunting task given the number of diverse islands spread across thousands of square miles of sea.

The cost of a vacation can vary widely from each island, or group of islands. There are some approaches and general rules to follow that will help you find that romantic vacation without breaking the bank.

The Caribbean is just like any other vacation destination. It is always cheaper to go in the off-season. That runs from mid-April to mid-November. Vacation prices across the board can be as much as 30% to 40% cheaper in the off-season than during the height of the season.

Prices begin to rise as the high season approaches, but in general there are deals to be had throughout the region right up to the beginning of the high season. What makes the Caribbean different from a lot of vacation spots is the consistency of the weather. There is, in fact, little difference in weather between the the high season and the middle of the off-season when temperatures are, at most, 5 to 10 degrees warmer.

Even during the height of the season, there are opportunities to get a price break. There is a three-week period between January 10 and early February when demand slackens somewhat and hoteliers are willing to cut rates by as much as a third.

Watch the headlines…

Another way to tap into a great vacation at an affordable price is to think about going to the Caribbean immediately following a hurricane, storm or some international crisis.

Demand always falls off at these times and hotels and resorts trim prices to encourage vacationers to return. *Catch:* Make sure that the hurricane or storm you're following hasn't disrupted your target island's infrastructure.

The best deals to the Caribbean are usually found on the larger islands with the greatest number of hotels and resorts, particularly Jamaica and the US Virgin Islands. The reason is simple. The greater number of vacation choices provides competition that helps keep prices down. Conversely, smaller, less developed islands, such as St. Barts, Grenada, the Grenadines and Anguilla, are generally more expensive.

Honeymooners forever...

Ask if there are special rates for honeymooners. They are regularly offered special deals, sometimes cutting as much as 50%—but at least 10% to 20% off the price of a stay. Hotels and resorts do this in hopes that honeymooners will come back repeatedly in future years.

Quality price...

If you're traveling with other couples it may be worth contacting several hotels to see if they'll give you a special rate for booking at least three rooms at a time.

Villas...

Some of the best deals in the Caribbean don't involve hotels or resorts—but villas. These range in size from one or two bedrooms to small mansions. Depending on the price, they include pools, maid service, cooks, private beaches, tennis courts and other amenities. The cost can be quite reasonable. A small one or two bedroom villa might rent for $1,000 a week during the high season, while the larger villas can go for $5,000 a week.

Even at the upper end of the market, the price can still be reasonable if it's split between three or four couples. Villas are available on most islands. *Good source to check:* Villas and Apartments Abroad Ltd., 212-759-1025 or 800-433-3020.

Floating feast...

Another option, particularly for the more adventurous, is renting a sailboat for a few days or a week. Again, it is an affordable option, especially if several couples are involved. These boats range from 50-footers up. They can come with a crew, including a cook. Sailboats give vacationers the chance to see several islands instead of just one. The only limitations are time

and weather. Prices start at $3,000 a week during the high season. There are dozens of chartering services.

A few good ones...
- Bahamas Yachting, 800-327-2276.
- Boat US Travel, 800-477-4427.
- Cruise One, 800-227-8633.

One price for all...

All-inclusive packages (where a single price covers everything) are increasingly popular throughout the Caribbean. Some are offered as an alternative pricing structure at certain resorts, while other resorts are exclusively all-in-one. These packages offer simple yet affordable vacations where one price covers everything from rooms to meals, drinks, entertainment and even sporting activities. The cost of these packages ranges from $1,000 to $3,000 a week. Their value is often determined by how much a guest may eat or drink during a week.

Country retreats...

Puerto Rico leads the way in offering simple yet generally inviting country inns that are extremely affordable. The price for a room for two ranges from $30 to $80 a night. Meals are not included—unless noted. *Good ones in Puerto Rico include:*
- Parador Banos de Coamo, 809-825-2186.
- Parador Hacienda Gripinas, 809-721-2400.
- Parador Oasis, 809-892-1175.

For information and reservations on other paradores call 800-443-0266 or 809-721-2884.

Source: Larry Fox, a *Washington Post* reporter and Barbara Radin-Fox, a social worker and photographer. They are co-authors of several books including *Romantic Island Getaways, The Caribbean, Bermuda and the Bahamas.* John Wiley & Sons.

Vacation Traps...and Wonderful Alternatives

It's a shame to waste money on a vacation that fails to meet your expectations. *Overrated destinations:*

- *Trap:* Hawaiian "fantasy" resorts. In both architecture and amenities, these multi-million dollar resorts completely lack any feel for the culture of Hawaii. Guest activities include Clydesdale horse riding and gondola sailing on man-made lakes. If fantasy is what you're looking for, go to Disney World instead.

Better: The island of Lanai. Once home to pineapple plantations, the island has recently seen the opening of its first major resorts. *Result:* It still retains the atmosphere of early Hawaii.

• *Trap:* Bermuda in winter. Many vacationers don't realize that this island is located in the Atlantic Ocean, not the Caribbean—at about the same latitude as North Carolina. Winter weather is often rainy and chilly.

Better: Cancun or Cozumel on the Mexican Caribbean. Both offer good winter rates.

• *Trap:* Venice in the summer. Poor sanitation, hordes of tourists, and heat and humidity combine to make Venice smelly and unpleasant in the summer. Visit at another time of year.

Better: If you want both art and canals, try Amsterdam.

• *Trap:* Miami Beach. The city lost its luster long ago. Hotel Row has become crowded and expensive.

Better: Fort Morgan Island on the Alabama Gulf Coast. This 25-mile breaker island is quiet and offers a pleasing southern atmosphere. *Drawback:* Winter weather isn't as mild as in South Florida.

• *Trap:* The overbuilt Caribbean islands. These include Nassau/Paradise Islands in the Bahamas, the Montego Bay area in Jamaica, and the Dutch side of St. Maarten.

Better: The quieter Bahamian islands of Eleuthera and Exuma. If you want quiet and excitement, Anguilla is only a 20-minute ferry ride from the shopping and casinos of St. Maarten.

Great Vacation Retreats

United States...

• *Blantyre.* America's consummate estate sanctuary offering refined service amid the baronial salons of an elegant Berkshire mansion. Lenox, MA 01240.

• *Elk Canyon Ranch.* Appealing to discerning families of all ages, this handsome outpost caps the sweeping ridge of a far-flung western spread.
1151 Smith River Rd., White Sulphur Springs, MT 59645.

• *Lodge at Koele.* Framed by stately trees and gardens and a glorious championship golf course, Hawaii's most captivating and evocative manorial resort is located in the magical highlands of Lanai.
Box L, Island of Lanaí, HI 96763.

• *Meadowood.* Exuding a casual country club ambience, the Napa Valley's most exclusive resort veils its cottage lodgings within a 250-acre parkland estate.
900 Meadowood Lane, St. Helena, CA 94574.

• *The Old Tavern.* Delightfully nostalgic, deftly restored 18th-century inn set along the idyllic maple-lined street of a fetching New England hamlet.
Grafton, VT 05146.

• *The Point.* Formerly a Rockefeller lakefront retreat, now a splendidly restored and atmospheric Adirondack lodge evoking the gracious North Woods lifestyle of a bygone era.
HCR#1, Box 65, Saranac Lake, NY 12983.

• *Safety Harbor Club.* An agreeable cottage enclave fronting a remote shell-strewn beach on undiscovered, car-free Upper Captiva Island.
Box 2276, Pineland, FL 33945.

• *Triple Creek.* Romantic couples-only ranch resort redefining wilderness living with posh custom log cabins and a remarkably caring staff.
West Fork Stage Rte., Darby, MT 59829.

• *Twin Farms.* A fascinating and luxuriously intimate hideaway with the highest standards, secluded in a scenic valley near the village of Woodstock.
Stage Rd., Barnard, VT 05031.

• *Ventana.* A sensuous bluff-top gem artfully blended against a backdrop of grassy meadows, deep canyons and towering redwoods along the rugged Pacific coast.
Highway One, Big Sur, CA 93920.

Source: An expert who has been writing about travel for more than two decades.

Fishing a New Lake

If you know where to start looking, you can fish any lake successfully.

Where bass congregate:

• Near trees that have recently fallen into the water.

• *In hot weather:* Under lily pads, especially in the only shallow spots around.

• *In consistently mild weather:* In backwater ponds and coves off the main lake. *Best:* Good weed or brush cover, with a creek running in.

• *Any time at all:* In sunken moss beds near the shore.

Source: *Outdoor Life.*

Hotel-Room-Rate Trap

Paying the rack rate—the price listed in the hotel brochure—for a night's lodging. Call the hotel directly and ask for the best possible rate —weekend packages, seasonal specials, or senior discounts. These will likely be lower than the rate quoted by travel agents and 800-number reservation operators. *Also helpful:* Ask for the corporate rate—available even to individual travelers—which is usually 10% to 15% off the rack rate.

Source: Herb Teison, editor, *Travel Smart*, 40 Beechdale Rd., Dobbs Ferry, NY 10522.

The Best Slot Machines

Vegas rules are most chaotic for slot machines. In Atlantic City, all machines must return at least 83% of the amount wagered… and a few return even more than 83%. But in Nevada, one machine might pay back 99%, while the one right next to it pays back only 60%. The bettor's problem is that it's impossible to identify the hot machines. Their placement is the casino's closely guarded secret.

The best-paying machines are usually found third or fourth from the end of a busy aisle, where the most people will see and hear the payoffs.

Worst payoffs: Any machine near the door of a casino showroom.

Among Atlantic City's casinos, the variations are narrower than in Vegas, but they can still be worked for or against you.

Source: Lee Pantano, Box 47, Atlantic Highlands, NJ 07716.

Bingo Never Was a Game of Chance

Most people play bingo as if it were a game of sheer chance—as if any set of cards had just as good a chance of winning as any other. They are mistaken. If you correctly choose the cards you play, you can significantly improve your odds of winning any bingo game.

The following system works with straight bingo (where you must cover five squares in a row—vertically, horizontally, or diagonally), coverall (a jackpot game, in which you must cover every square on your card), or any other variation.

Key strategy: To get as many of the 75 numbers as possible on a given set of cards. There are 24 numbers printed on every bingo card. (There are 25 squares, but the center square is a non-numbered free space.) If you chose three cards at random, their 72 numbered spaces would represent only 49 different numbers—the other 23 spaces would have duplicate numbers.

It is possible, however, to find sets of three cards with no duplicates—with 72 different numbers. (Time permitting, players can choose their cards freely at the beginning of any session.) If you were to play such a set, you would be 25% more likely to win a given game than a player with a random set. Depending on the size of the prizes, that edge can translate into hundreds—or even thousands—of dollars of winnings within a few weeks.

The truth about "lucky" cards:

Ironically, most players choose sets that are worse than random. They look for cards with one or two "lucky" numbers—7 or 11, for example. And they are especially drawn to cards where those lucky numbers are at the corners.

The results are devastating. In an average straight game with 1,000 cards in play, a bingo will occur after 15 numbers are called. That means that any given number—regardless of whether it is "lucky" or not—will be called in only one of five games. In those other four games, any set of cards with an uncalled "lucky" number is 25% less likely to win. (When a number is at a corner, it affects three lines—one vertical, one horizontal, one diagonal.)

Another advantage of choosing non-duplicating cards is that it makes it easier to keep track of the numbers you're covering—and harder to miss one by accident.

There are countless statistical systems favored by bingo players, but this is the only one I've found that generates consistent profits.

Where to play:

The only live variable in bingo is the proportion of money collected that is returned to the players. Most operators hold back at least 50% for overhead and revenue. (The percentage is usually posted on the bingo sheets or somewhere in the hall.)

Other games, however, return as much as 75% to the players. The more money that comes back, of course, the better your chances of coming out ahead.

Source: John "Dee" Wyrick, author of *Complete Authoritative Guide to Bingo.* Gambler's Book Club.

Radio Contests: More than Luck

Almost every popular radio station uses giveaways. Rewards include cash, cars, vacations, and other prizes, ranging from record albums to TV sets. Playing the contests won't make you rich, but there's nothing like the thrill of hearing your name announced over the radio—as a winner.

Although chance plays the major role, you can greatly increase your odds of winning by understanding how call-in contests are run.

To begin: Pick a few stations that have entertaining contests and good prizes. Listen to each closely for a few hours, and phone in several times to get a feel for how the game is played.

The more contests you enter, the greater your chance of winning. The trick is to do this without spending your life on the phone. *The key:* Each program's disk jockey has a format that he follows closely.

Example: My prime listening time is from 11 pm to 1 am. By monitoring four stations, I have found that one holds regular contests at 42 minutes after the hour, another at either 15 or 45 minutes after the hour, another at either 5 or 35 minutes after the hour, and another at 5 of the hour. I tune into those stations only at those times.

After the contest has been announced, several factors determine how quickly you should place your call:

• *The winning number.* The number of the winning call often corresponds to the station's location on the dial. For example, one station, at 95.5 FM, always rewards the 95th caller. If you dial right away, you'll be about number 20 (stations generally tell you your number when your call is answered). So wait 35 seconds before dialing. By the time the call goes through and the phone rings a few times (at least five seconds per ring), you'll be pretty close to call number 95. It usually takes the station 70–75 seconds to reach that call.

• *The number of lines at the station.* This helps determine how quickly they get to the winning number. A station with only two phone lines moves more slowly than one with 22. If you ask, most stations will tell you how many lines they use for contests.

• *The number of people answering the phones.* Stations that have two or more people handling the calls move more quickly than those where it's left up to the DJ. After you've played the contests a few times, you'll get to know the voices —and the number of phone answerers at each station.

• *Individual speeds.* Some DJs get the contest rolling quickly; others are slower. Get to know their habits.

There's always an element of chance. The difference between being caller number 94 and caller number 95 is a split second, and there's no way you can control that. But you can greatly increase the odds of winning.

Don't give up. If you get a call through and you're five or more numbers away from winning, hang up and try again. And don't let a busy signal discourage you. *Hint:* Many stations have a recording that says "Please try again later" if all the lines are busy. Stay on the line. Your call will be answered...sometimes in the middle of the recording, sometimes soon after it is completed.

Some DJs award the prize at random rather than counting through the calls to, say, number 95. Others announce that caller number two will win, so they don't have to answer 95 calls (and with such a low number, it's really no contest at all). Your only recourse in such a situation is to complain to the station's management. If lazy DJs know they've been caught, they'll improve.

Source: Bob Gross, who has won more than $10,500 in cash and prizes in radio contests over the past five years.

Credit-Card Calling

When you have more than one phone call to make from a hotel or pay phone, don't hang up after each call. Push the # button between calls. This will allow you to stay connected with your chosen long-distance carrier. *Added benefit:* Most hotel computers will register several calls made this way as a single local call, saving you surcharges.

Source: *Travel and Leisure,* 1120 Ave. of the Americas, New York 10036.

Choosing the Safest Seats On an Airplane

Myth: That the safest seats on all commercial aircraft are those next to emergency exits.

Reality: Aisle seats close to the overwing emergency exits are safer. These seats are commonly in the mid-front section of the plane. If you sit in the window seat next to an emergency exit, you may be worse off in the event of a crash that jams the exit. Aisle seats near several exits give you more escape options in the event of a crash.

Lifesaving precaution: When you take your seat in the plane, count and memorize the number of rows to the nearest exits. *Reason:* If smoke fills the cabin after a crash, you may have to feel your way in the dark to an exit. This precaution is based on the tactics that crash survivors actually have used to get out of a plane.

Source: Geraldine Frankowski, director, Aviation Consumer Action Project, an advocacy group for airline safety and passenger rights, 2000 P St. NW, Washington, DC 20036.

Airline-Ticket Buying Savvy

When ordering airline tickets, pay for them with credit cards. Along with attractive sale prices as airlines try to lure flyers, the industry is experiencing a spate of bankruptcies. People who pay cash are in danger of losing their money if a carrier goes under. Credit-card customers usually can get a refund.

Source: *New Choices for the Best Years,* 28 W. 23 St., New York 10010.

Combating Air-Travel Fatigue

• *Before takeoff:* Food and beverages. Eat and drink lightly for 24 hours before a flight. *Recommended:* Salads, fish, chicken, wine. *Avoid:* Liquor, bon-voyage parties.

Forty-eight hours before departure: Ask the airline for a special severe hypoglycemia (low blood sugar) in-flight meal. You will probably get a nice seafood salad from the first-class galley, even if you have an economy ticket. On boarding, remind the chief flight attendant about the special meal you ordered.

Clothes: Wear loose-fitting clothing. Bring slip-on shoes. *Reason:* Long hours of sitting can cause swelling of the legs and, especially, of the feet.

Women: If possible, plan a plane trip within 7 to 10 days after the onset of the menstrual cycle.

Medication: Take an adequate supply and a copy of your prescriptions. A note from your doctor can often avoid hassles with overzealous customs officials.

• *In the air:* Avoid consuming all the food and drink offered. Alcohol, nuts, soft drinks, and other foods that have empty calories can cause a swing from high to low blood sugar. You go from feeling great to feeling tired, cramped, and headachy.

Don't do important business work while flying. *Reason:* Decision-making and complicated paperwork add to an already increased stress level. *Better:* Accomplish as much as you can before departure. *Aboard:* Read nondemanding work-related material. *Preferred:* Relax by reading an absorbing book.

• *At your destination:* Changes of time, space, and place can cause a feeling of dislocation. Continue following the airborne guidelines of moderation suggested. Realize that your tolerance level for everything from decision-making to dining are below average while on a short trip abroad.

Source: Warren Levin, MD, and Howard Bezow, MD, World Health Group, 5 World Trade Center, New York 10048.

Smarter Trip Planning

Save big on airfares by studying a map before you purchase tickets. Make a list of cities within driving distance of your destination and ask about the fares to those cities. *Example:* A recent round-trip fare from Chicago to Cincinnati for a family of four was $1,028. By flying to Louisville, a route with a "friends fly free" program to a city that is one hour's drive from Cincinnati, the round-trip fare was $196.

Source: Tom Parsons, editor of *Best Fares Discount Travel,* 1111 W. Arkansas Lane, Arlington, TX 76013.

Lost Luggage Self-Defense

Report the loss before leaving the airport… keep your baggage ticket—it's the only evidence that you checked the bag with the airline …make sure the airline attendant processes your claim correctly. *Future help:* International Airline Passengers Association. It offers a lost luggage retrieval service as part of its $90 annual membership. IAPA, Box 70188, Dallas 75787. 214-404-9980.

Source: *The Safe Travel Book* by Peter Savage, director of Capital Trading International, a crisis management consulting firm, Lexington Books, New York.

How to Get More from Frequent Guest Programs

Virtually all hotel chains now have frequent guest programs. And in recent months these programs have gone through a fundamental shift. Unlike the past where guests were awarded both frequent flyer miles and points in the hotel's own program, almost all the chains are now making their guests choose one or the other.

While this "either/or" approach may now be an industry standard, hotel programs still vary widely, making them difficult to compare.

Example: Rewards range from free rooms to free upgrades and services to merchandise. Hotels also take different approaches to issuing points.

Rewards…

Hotel schemes have some advantages over airline plans.

Example: They rarely impose blackout dates or space limitations on guests trying to claim their awards.

In general, rewards come fairly quickly. Most chains begin offering free weekend night stays after as few as three paid visits. Even free airline tickets can come with booking as few as 10 nights in some chains.

Regardless, the greatest rewards still go to travelers who know how to take advantage of the differences between the programs.

Guidelines...

It is best to concentrate on participating in only one or two programs instead of a dozen or more. This allows a traveler to claim rewards more quickly.

In line with this, it is best to choose a chain or two that has hotels in the cities a traveler most regularly visits. It also pays to understand how points are awarded. They are given by the number of stays, the total hotel bill or the type of room rented.

Major chains' programs...

• Marriott...the granddaddy of these...has two programs.

One is tied to awarding free rooms and the other offers frequent flyer mileage points in conjunction with five different partners—Continental, Northwest, USAir, TWA and British Airways.

The hotel guest program's biggest advantage is that it offers lots of ways to gain bonus points. If, for example, you use one of Marriott's airline partners, you receive an automatic 25% bonus on hotel points. In addition, renting a car from Hertz gives Marriott's guests another 20% bonus.

Marriott's award of frequent flyer miles is simple and lucrative. Guests earn 1,000 miles for every night they stay, regardless of the rate they pay. Marriott also awards guests frequent flyer miles if they stay five consecutive nights. As a result, a five-night stay will yield 10,000 miles. With this in mind, in as few as 10 nights (20,000 miles) a guest can claim a free airline ticket on Continental.

• Hilton has a program that lets guests earn both miles and points simultaneously. It also guarantees that its rewards are as good as any of its competitors and the chain is willing to back up its guarantee. This program does have some restrictions, however. Guests are awarded no more than 500 points regardless of their bill if they stay in a resort or pay discounted rates. Otherwise, the points garnered are based on a guest's total bill.

• Hyatt has switched over to the "either miles *or* hotel points" plan. Points are given on the basis of a guest's total bill. Beyond the quality of the chain's properties, one advantage Hyatt offers is that guests can accumulate points on booking more than one room at the same time. Marriott also follows this rule. Other chains may award points for multiple bookings, but it is often up to the discretion of the hotel's general manager.

• Ritz-Carlton, like many upmarket chains, participates in guest programs. But given its clientele, it offers more free service rewards rather than free rooms. So, participants can get free upgrades to junior suites or limousine service.

• Holiday Inn offers miles or points. It is also one of the most flexible programs, offering merchandise and gift certificates in addition to free rooms. There are drawbacks, however...

Points are not given for discount rates. They only come into play for corporate rates and above. There is also an initial $10 entry fee to join the program.

• Sheraton offers either frequent flyer miles or hotel program points. Its major plus-points are awarded on the basis of a guest's entire hotel bill. In fact, you don't even have to stay at a Sheraton to get points. They can be collected by renting an Avis car or by using any of the hotel's facilities—the bar or restaurant, for example. Beyond this, Sheraton probably offers more promotions than any other chain in the country, allowing guests to claim bonus points during certain periods. *Drawback:* It costs $25 a year to join Sheraton's program.

Source: Randy Petersen, editor of *Inside Flyer,* a magazine written for frequent travelers. Petersen logs up to 400,000 miles a year. *Inside Flyer,* Colorado Springs.

Fanny Pack Trap

Thieves cut off belt bags and fanny packs strapped around travelers' waists. The bags advertise to a thief where you keep your valuables. *Best:* Carry only small change, a pen or sunglasses in the packs—things you can afford to lose. Put valuables in more hidden places, such as an under-the-arm shoulder holster.

Source: *Travel Companions,* Box 833, Amityville, NY 11701.

16

Self-Defense

The Ultimate Guide to Avoiding Violent Crime

The first rule of avoiding violent crime on the street or in the home is to understand this —*it can happen to you.* These days, no neighborhood is immune.

You can improve your odds that the bad guy won't pick you. How? Make yourself a tough target.

Just as the lion chooses the weakest antelope to pick off from the pack, the bad guy chooses the easiest victim—the weak one, the one who isn't paying attention, the one least likely to resist.

But there's a trick to this game. It's not how tough you really are—it's how tough you *look.*

Psychologists use the term, "displaying the weapons of aggression." Dogs bare their teeth, cats show their claws and you should show the bad guys you have something to fight back with, too.

Example: A woman who jogs with a dog might be no tougher than one without a dog, but she looks tougher. The dog is an unknown quantity to any would-be muggers—and muggers don't like to take unnecessary chances.

Pepper sprays and personal alarms…

Another weapon of aggression you should consider is pepper spray. It's easy to use. Pressing the button sprays a stream of oleoresin capsicum more than 1,000 times more powerful than Tabasco sauce. Unlike tear gas, pepper spray deters even crazed drug users and vicious animals. That's why mail carriers use it.

If you're afraid you wouldn't be able to use pepper spray on someone, consider a personal alarm. Pull out the pin, and it emits a piercing alarm until you reinsert the pin. They're better than whistles, because whistles stop making noise the moment you stop blowing.

Important: To scare off potential attackers, keep the spray in your hand, ready for fire. Keep the alarm attached to your waistband or in a jacket pocket.

Personal alarms and pepper sprays are available in hardware stores and gun shops. If you have trouble finding them, call your local police department and ask where they get theirs.

People often ask me whether it's a good idea to own a gun. It's always a personal choice, but I don't recommend it. A gun in the home is far more likely to be fired by accident, during a domestic dispute or in a suicide, than used to protect the family from an intruder. Any situation that reaches the point where you need to use a gun has already gone too far. Prevention is much better.

Avoiding sexual assault...

To keep a date from turning into date rape, a woman should resist unwanted sexual advances strongly and clearly, or she runs the risk of being misunderstood.

If a man kisses you against your will, bite down on his lower lip...or grab his scrotum and wring it like a towel.

Teach your children that it's okay to say no to adults—especially in the area of forced affection. Never insist that a child must allow Grandpa to kiss her—give her the choice. Otherwise, you'll be giving her the message that it's okay for adults to force themselves on her.

When kids go somewhere together, remind them never to leave one another behind. If they have to run, the faster one should always wait for the slower one.

Bank machine self-defense...

Automatic teller machines (ATMs) are certainly convenient, but they can leave you exposed to muggers.

To minimize risk: Use a drive-through ATM whenever possible. If anyone approaches, drive away. Failing that, stick to an ATM in an enclosed kiosk—one that requires a magnetic card for entry and which is equipped with a security camera. ATM kiosks inside a building or store are safer than stand-alone kiosks.

Avoid ATMs located directly on the street—especially if it's a deserted street at night. If the ATM is next to an alley, where someone can pop out with no warning, that's even worse.

If you must use a street ATM, do so during the day or with a friend—in an area with people around.

Special problem: ATMs with vertical keypads. They allow a robber to watch as you punch in your personal identification number—increasing the odds that he'll try to steal your card. Try to use an ATM with a horizontal keypad—one that's parallel with the ground.

On the street...

Don't make things easy on muggers by wearing headphones and listening to loud music. Headphones prevent you from hearing someone coming up behind you—making you an easy target.

Don't flash jewelry on the street, subway or bus either—even if it's fake.

Women: Carry your purse in front of you, not bouncing on your hip.

Men: Keep your wallet in your front pants pocket or in the vest pocket inside your coat. Using the back pants pocket only invites pickpockets.

If you're approached by a suspicious-looking character, cross the street or walk in the middle of the street to maintain your distance. Don't worry about appearing overly cautious.

Helpful: Wrap two $1 bills inside a $5 bill and put them in a money clip. If a robber demands your money, toss the clip in one direction, say "That's all I've got," and run as fast as you can in the other direction.

In your home...

There's no doubt about it—good locks and bright lighting are your best bet against a break-in. Keep shrubs pruned so that they don't hide your windows from neighbors' view.

The best alarm systems are those monitored by the company that sells them. Typically, these alarm systems call the police or fire department when a signal goes off.

You're provided with code numbers to use in case you set it off accidentally...and a "hostage code" to secretly alert police that you're being held.

At the first sound of an intruder, dial 911. If you own a cellular phone, keep the recharger near your bed. That way, if an intruder cuts your phone lines, you can still call 911.

Thwarting carjackers...

A car phone is a great investment in safety. You can use it to dial 911 in any emergency.

And just the sight of it is often enough to deter would-be attackers.

Some motorists are now equipping their cars with electronic homing devices that automatically alert the police if their car is stolen—and lead them to it. These devices are effective—but expensive for many people.

Every car is already equipped with the best possible anti-carjacking device—the door locks. Use them even when you're inside the car. It's hard for a carjacker to be successful if he cannot get inside your car.

If someone does get in—get out. No car is worth dying for.

If someone orders you into a car—his or yours—don't do it. Odds are you'll never come back. *Instead:* Run for it. Statistics show that 95% of people who run from an armed kidnapper survive. Most kidnappers won't shoot. The few who do usually miss.

Source: J.J. Bittenbinder, a retired detective with the Chicago Police and a frequent lecturer on personal safety. For a free copy of Det. Bittenbinder's booklet *Tough Target: Guide to Staying Safe,* call Speakers International at 800-345-8255.

Protecting Yourself Against Muggers

The best defense against becoming a crime victim is to avoid a setup. Muggers, like most people, don't take more risks or work harder than they have to. *Point:* They choose victims who seem easy to handle. And they create situations that make the attack simpler.

Chief defense: Don't allow yourself to be distracted, isolated, or simply stopped on the street by a stranger. Muggers prefer victims who have stopped moving. *They use every technique to accomplish that:* Asking for directions, a match, or a handout.

First and most important rule: When spoken to by a suspicious stranger, don't stop. Move away quickly. Don't slow down to watch an argument or any other commotion on the street. Fake street fights are a favorite way to set up a robbery.

Defensive tactics:

Walk down the middle of the sidewalk near the street. Be wary of corners and doorways. Reduce the possibility of being grabbed from the shadows. Hugging the curb permits you to see around the corner while at a distance. Be alert to someone hiding between or behind parked cars.

Walk a couple of extra blocks to take a safe route, especially late at night. Keep to known neighborhoods. Identify in advance where the places of refuge are, in the event of trouble.

Look ahead up the street (not down) to see what's happening. Be alert, especially to people loitering or moving suspiciously. *Example:* Two men up ahead who suddenly separate and begin walking apart. They could be preparing to set you up.

However foolish or rude it may seem, don't get on any self-service elevator if there's somebody at all suspicious on it. Never let an elevator you are on go to the basement. *How to avoid it:* When entering an open elevator, keep a foot in the door while pressing the floor number. Keep your eyes on the elevator indicator. If the arrow is pointing down, don't get in.

Don't get into a self-service elevator late at night without making sure nobody is waiting on an upper floor to intercept you. *How to do it:* Push the top floor elevator button, but don't get in. If the elevator does not stop on any floor on the way up or down, it's safe.

Avoid places where gangs of juveniles congregate. They can be more dangerous than professional muggers because they will often hurt a victim rather than take the money and run.

Get into the habit of automatically saying *excuse me* when you bump into someone on the street. Say it no matter whose fault it is.

Never show money in public, whether at a newsstand, market, bank, or getting out of a cab. Muggers are watching.

If you are mugged: Cooperate. Above all, communicate the willingness to cooperate. Keep calm. It can help relax the mugger, too, which is crucial. *Reason:* If a mugger is pointing a cocked revolver, nervousness on his part could be fatal to you. *Ways to calm the situation:*

Say something reassuring, or ask a distracting question that establishes the mugging as a businesslike transaction. *Example:* "You can have anything you want. Do you mind if I just keep my driver's license?"

Never move suddenly. *Tell the mugger where your wallet is and ask:* "Do you want me to get it or do you want to get it?"

A woman mugger with a knife or gun can kill just as easily as a man. Letting macho feelings interfere with cooperating is suicidal.

Don't show the slightest condescension or hostility. Be careful of your tone of voice. Cooperating with disdain can set off violence. *Best attitude to project:* You've got to earn a living, too. *Or:* I don't hold this against you at all; times are tough.

Don't make jokes. They are too risky, and the chance for misinterpretation is too great.

Avoid direct or steady eye contact.

If a mugger is particularly hostile, be supercooperative. Offer money or possessions he has overlooked.

Bottom line: Always carry mugger money. Keep $25 to $100 in your pocket as insurance. A happy mugger is much less likely to do harm than one who comes away empty-handed.

Source: Ken Glickman, coordinator of Educational Services, Greenwich Institute for American Education, Greenwich, CT 06830.

Dangerous Drug Mix

Anticoagulants such as warfarin (Coumadin), taken in combination with aspirin, ibuprofen or another nonsteroidal anti-inflammatory drug (NSAID). Those who combine both drugs have a 13-fold risk of developing a bleeding peptic ulcer, compared with those who use neither drug. Patients taking anticoagulants should ask their doctors about substituting an NSAID alternative, such as acetaminophen.

Source: Ronald I. Shorr, MD, assistant professor of pharmacoepidemiology, Vanderbilt University School of Medicine, Nashville. His study of anticoagulant use was published in *Archives of Internal Medicine*, 515 N. State St., Chicago 60610.

Alzheimer's Care Basics

Establish a daily routine for the person suffering from Alzheimer's…*remove items that might encourage the person to wander, such as a coat rack near the door*…have the person wear an ID bracelet in case he/she does leave home unattended…*plan at least one regular daily outing, such as a walk or trip to the grocery store*…reduce clutter so that misplaced items can be more easily found…*respond to agitation by distracting and reassuring rather than arguing or correcting the person*…make others a part of the regular care routine.

Source: Rebecca Logsdon, PhD, clinical psychologist, University of Washington, Seattle.

Day-Care Center Alert

Toys, water fountains, water-play tables, telephones and toilets are often contaminated with a virus that causes diarrhea and other health problems. Virus contamination was found in 19% of the samples taken from two day-care centers. *Self-defense:* Frequent hand-washing and disinfection of contaminated surfaces.

Source: Arlene M. Butz, RN, ScD, associate professor, department of pediatrics, Johns Hopkins University School of Nursing, Baltimore. Her six-month study of two day-care centers was published in *Pediatrics*, 141 NW Point Rd., Elk Grove Village, IL.

Breast Cancer Scandal

Women who've had a lumpectomy (removal of the breast tumor alone) should *not* be alarmed by recent reports of falsified data in breast cancer studies. Thousands of breast cancer patients opted for lumpectomy after several studies concluded that this procedure was just as safe and effective as the more disfiguring procedure *mastectomy* (removal of the entire breast). The fact that one of these studies has been questioned does not affect the validity of the others.

Lumpectomy was—and still is—a valid option for many women with breast cancer.

Source: Harmon Eyre, MD, chief medical officer, American Cancer Society, 1599 Clifton Rd. NE, Atlanta 30329.

Health Scams

If you think quacks are sleazy-looking characters whom you can spot a mile away—think again.

Many of today's medical hucksters have so much medical knowledge and are so familiar with medical jargon that they're capable of fooling doctors. In fact, some quacks are themselves doctors who believe in the ill-conceived treatments they offer. *The trendiest and most dangerous health scams now...*

• *False memory syndrome (FMS).* The darling topic of afternoon talk shows, FMS involves adults undergoing psychotherapy who suddenly recall long-repressed cases of physical and/or emotional abuse. As a result, many FMS "victims" falsely accuse, disown or sue once-loved relatives.

Recovered memories may be legitimate in rare cases. But I'm convinced that many of these people—with the help of misguided or incompetent psychotherapists—are "recalling" past events that never occurred.

These therapists—some of whom call themselves "traumatists"—often misuse hypnosis, meditation or guided imagery to help patients regress to their childhood or even to "past lives." Or the patient may be inspired by FMS books or talk show guests, and the therapist fails to help the patient distinguish fact from fantasy.

As someone who practiced psychiatry for more than 35 years, I find it very hard to believe that a person could forget such abuse. Indeed, it's much more common for victims of abuse to have trouble putting memories of abuse out of their minds.

• *Diet hocus-pocus.* Beware of any weight-loss product or program that purports to melt off pounds by suppressing appetite through hormonal manipulation or by blocking the absorption of fats, carbohydrates, sugar or calories. Such products are always phony.

And while very-low-calorie diets can help obese people under medical supervision, do-it-yourself starvation plans are dangerous. They force the body to burn lean body mass—muscles and major organs—for fuel. These plans can also cause anemia, liver damage, kidney stones and mineral imbalances. In some cases they are fatal.

Some diets—including many of those spelled out in popular diet books—are pure nonsense. Authors of these hugely profitable books, who often have no training in nutrition, claim they've discovered weight-control secrets.

For example, one popular book says that when certain foods are combined in the body, they rot, poison the system and make a person fat. To avoid this, dieters are urged to eat fats, carbohydrates and protein at separate meals, concentrating on fruits in the morning and vegetables in the afternoon. The premise is utter nonsense.

In recent years, commercial weight-loss programs and diets have become very popular. While these programs may help people lose weight, they don't teach dieters how to maintain their weight loss with proper eating and exercise. *Result:* The weight comes right back on.

The only sensible way to lose weight is to exercise more and eat less. Bringing about these changes may require help from a registered dietitian or another professional.

• *Chelation therapy.* This treatment involves intravenous injections of EDTA, a synthetic amino acid.

While chelation therapy is a legitimate treatment for lead poisoning, some advocates maintain that it can prevent or even reverse the accumulation of fatty deposits along artery walls (a process known as atherosclerosis).

Duped by this claim, some patients with badly blocked coronary arteries are forgoing the bypass surgery that they so desperately need, opting instead for worthless chelation injections. At least one person suffered a heart attack while on chelation therapy. Others undergoing the treatments have died of kidney failure (EDTA can be very toxic to kidneys if not properly administered).

Some proponents of chelation therapy also claim that it is effective against arthritis, Parkinson's disease, emphysema, multiple sclerosis, gangrene and psoriasis. But there's absolutely no scientific evidence to back up these contentions.

• *"Environmental illness."* Certain practitioners called clinical ecologists say the immune system can become overloaded by constant exposure to toxins in the environment.

As a result of being exposed to these toxins, these practitioners claim, certain people develop a host of ailments ranging from depression, irritability, inability to concentrate and poor memory to fatigue, respiratory problems, rashes, headache and muscle and joint pain.

Clinical ecologists "diagnose" their patients by injecting them with suspected chemical culprits and then observing their reactions—even though careful research has invalidated this provocation and neutralization test. And scientific panels have deemed the entire field of clinical ecology speculative and unproven.

Still, desperate patients agree to treatment. Some go so far as to move to the desert or rip apart their houses to get rid of synthetic chemicals…or even avoid contact with certain people suspected of giving off irritating odors.

Some patients ultimately become hermits in their own homes—afraid to venture out into a toxin-tainted world.

In fact, the symptoms these people suffer are real. But the origin of these symptoms is usually psychological, not chemical. Once patients understand this, psychotherapy may help them.

Spotting a quack…

While it's essential to maintain a healthy level of skepticism when discussing medical treatments, skepticism alone is not enough to protect yourself against quacks. *I also recommend avoiding any doctor who…*

• Claims that *everyone* needs to take vitamin supplements. There's simply no evidence for this.

• Recommends vitamins for a large number of ailments. In fact, vitamin supplements are useful only against a very limited number of conditions.

• Uses anecdotes and testimonials to support his/her claims. Look instead for carefully controlled clinical studies.

• Says that most diseases are caused by hidden allergies. This is untrue.

• Claims that large numbers of Americans suffer from low blood sugar (hypoglycemia) or hidden yeast infections. Again, not true.

Source: Stephen Barrett, MD, a retired psychiatrist, consumer advocate and board member of the National Council Against Health Fraud, Box 1276, Loma Linda, CA 92354. He is coauthor of *The Health Robbers: A Close Look at Quackery in America*, Prometheus Books.

Unnecessary Chest X-Rays

Half of all chest X rays performed prior to surgery are unnecessary. Doctors often order them anyway out of habit or because they fear being sued for failing to diagnose a problem that an X ray might have revealed.

Source: Perry G. Pernicano, MD, assistant chief, radiology service, Veterans Affairs Medical Center, Ann Arbor, MI. His study of 108 pre-op chest X rays was presented at a recent meeting of the Radiological Society of North America, 2021 Spring Rd., Oak Brook, IL 60521.

Less-Stressful MRI

10% of all magnetic resonance imaging (MRI) scans must be stopped prematurely because patients become claustrophobic and panic. *To reduce anxiety:* Have your doctor or your doctor's assistant explain the procedure to you in detail. *Also:* Ask to be taken out of the tunnel-like MRI machine between scans. Close your eyes and let your mind wander, visualizing peaceful scenes. Ask to lie on your stomach instead of your back so you can see out of the machine. Bring along a supportive friend or family member. If necessary, ask for a mild sedative beforehand. Some facilities use "open" MRI scanners, although the opening may be too small to prevent claustrophobia.

Source: E. McCrank, MD, chief of psychiatry, University Hospital, Ontario, Canada.

Hair/Dye Cancer Connections

Black hair dye may boost risk of some cancers. In a recent study, women who used black dye for 20 years or longer faced an increased risk of death from non-Hodgkin's lymphoma and multiple myeloma. Other colors were found to be safe—even with long-term use. *Good news:* Less than 1% of hair-dye users have used black dye for more than 20 years.

Source: Michael J. Thun, MD, MS, director of analytic epidemiology, American Cancer Society, 1599 Clifton Rd. NE, Atlanta. His study of hair dye use among 570,000 American women was published in the *Journal of the National Cancer Institute*, 9030 Old Georgetown Rd., Building 82, Room 209, Bethesda, MD 20814.

Depression and The Elderly

Because today's elderly grew up at a time when psychological depression was considered a sign of weakness, many old people are too embarrassed to seek treatment. Be on the lookout for symptoms of depression among elderly friends and relatives—frequent crying …periods of hopelessness or worthlessness… missed church events, family outings or other social events. Also, depression may masquerade as general complaints, such as backache, headache or insomnia. Anyone experiencing these problems should see a doctor.

Source: Martiece Carson, MD, assistant professor of psychiatry, University of Oklahoma Health Sciences Center, Oklahoma City.

New Drinking Water Threat: Cryptosporidium

The threat posed by this microbe is smaller than recent media reports have suggested. There's no need to boil tap water or drink bottled water unless your water utility issues an alert. Utilities have been extremely vigilant since the outbreak of crypto-related illness in Milwaukee last year. If there is an alert, boil *all* the water you ingest—that used for brushing your teeth, washing produce, etc., as well as for drinking. If you were to ingest crypto, you'd experience diarrhea and nausea lasting one to two weeks. *Exception:* Crypto may be fatal to AIDS patients and others with weak immunities. Several experts now urge *these* individuals to boil their water even in the absence of a crypto alert, although there's really not enough evidence to say that this precaution is necessary.

Source: Rosemary Soave, MD, associate professor of medicine and public health, New York Hospital-Cornell Medical Center, New York City.

What Causes Teeth to Become Yellowed

Yellowed teeth are usually caused by coffee, tobacco or *gastroesophageal reflux disease* (GERD). In this condition, corrosive stomach acids back up into the esophagus and mouth …eroding teeth and eventually causing them to break off. GERD can often be controlled with *omeprazole* (Prilosec) or other prescription medications.

Source: Pat Schroeder, MD, gastroenterology fellow, University of Alabama School of Medicine, Birmingham.

Bypass Surgery: Who Really Needs It?

The number of heart bypass operations performed in the US is soaring—from 20,000 in 1971…to 200,000 in 1987…to an estimated 400,000 this year.

For individuals whose heart vessels are so blocked that they feel chest pain (angina) even while resting, bypass surgery can be a lifesaver. But estimates are that up to half of bypass operations may be unnecessary—exposing patients to needless expense and risk of death.

Self-defense: If a doctor recommends bypass surgery for you, be sure to get a second opinion if…

…you feel no chest pain while resting.

…you feel slight chest pain *only* when you exert yourself—when running to catch a bus or taking a hike up a hill, for instance.

In these instances, medications and lifestyle changes—quitting smoking, exercising more and eating less fat—are better.

Why? Because although generally safe, bypass surgery is not without risk. Two percent of patients younger than 70 who undergo bypass die from the surgery, and 3% to 4% of people older than 70 die.

And bypass surgery is only a quick fix. Heart vessels can clog up again—especially if lifestyle changes aren't made.

Don't get a second opinion from another doctor in your own doctor's practice or HMO. *Better:* A doctor who practices at a local hospital—especially one that's affiliated with the cardiology department of a university.

If bypass surgery is necessary, shop around. Surgeons and hos-pitals that do the most bypass surgery procedures have the best survival rates.

Helpful: US News & World Report's annual guide to the best hospitals in America, published in the magazine each July. For a reprint of the most recent guide, send a $2 check or money order to *US News & World Report* reprints, 2400 N St. NW, Washington, DC 20037. 202-955-2398.

Source: Thomas B. Graboys, MD, associate professor of medicine at Harvard Medical School and director of the Lown Cardiovascular Center at Brigham and Women's Hospital, both in Boston.

What You Can Do to Protect Your Privacy

Nothing is more sensitive than your medical records. They detail everything from what illnesses you've been treated for…to what drugs you've been prescribed…to whether you've ever seen a psychiatrist.

For the past decade or so, medical records, along with credit card and bank account records, have been stored in vast computer databases. Not surprisingly, this sensitive information often falls into the hands of people who really have no business knowing the details of your private life.

Example: A doctor at a Chicago hospital recently counted the people who had access to patient records. He stopped when he reached 75…and that number included only individuals able to obtain the records without breaking hospital rules. Many of those counted were secretaries, file clerks, auditors and others with no meaningful role in patient treatment.

Your private medical information is also routinely made available to direct marketing firms, health insurance companies and other organizations. Yet the information contained in these records is often irrelevant—or inaccurate.

Self-defense strategies…

• *Check your medical records for accuracy.* Many doctors prefer not to show patients their records, because they feel that the medical jargon contained in the records might be misleading or upsetting.

If your doctor is hesitant about showing you your medical records, ask that they be sent to another doctor of your choice who can interpret them for you.

A comprehensive set of your medical records is probably on file at the Medical Information Bureau (MIB), an insurance industry association that collects and disseminates data relating to the insurance policies of more than 12 million people.

The MIB not only allows individuals access to their records but also has a procedure for correcting these records.

If you've been rejected by an insurer or just want to see if the MIB has a report on you, request a report from MIB at Box 105, Essex Station, Boston 02112 (617-426-3660). If a report exists, it should arrive about a month after you mail in your request. There is no fee.

• *Never volunteer information to an employer, insurer, etc.* You gain nothing by giving more. It can only come back to haunt you. When filling out forms, give as little information as is acceptable.

• *Ask your doctor not to disclose information about you.* Insist that he/she get your written permission before disclosing information to anyone else. If your doctor asks to forward information about you, ask what exactly is being disclosed, and for what purpose. Insist that he follow the same rule you do—give out only relevant information.

• *Check your employer's policy regarding medical records.* Companies that manufacture or distribute dangerous substances (such as toxic chemicals) must maintain such records. Other companies that administer their own medical programs may also maintain such records.

Ask your company's personnel director whether your medical records are included in your personnel file. If so, ask to see them. If you notice any mistakes, ask that they be corrected.*

If there's a written policy regarding medical records, ask to see it. Don't worry about appearing paranoid. Companies now expect employees (and prospective employees) to ask. It's not an uncommon request.

Special problem: Company-sponsored employee-assistance programs. Such programs— designed to help employees deal with depression and other personal or financial problems —may pledge to keep whatever you disclose confidential. However, no federal law requires them to do so.

If you're thinking of participating in such a program, find out the circumstances under which information about you might be released to your employer—and be sure to get it in writing.

• *Consider paying medical bills in cash.* This approach is taken by many executives, politicians, military personnel and others who want to protect their careers from the stigma of psychotherapy or other potentially embarrassing treatment. You'll have to forgo reimbursement by your health insurance company, but your medical information will have less exposure.

• *Think twice before signing insurance releases.* When you apply for health or life insurance or submit an insurance claim, you may

*A recent survey of 126 Fortune 500 companies found that half of these firms use medical records when making key decisions regarding personnel.

be asked to sign a release granting the insurer access to your medical records.

If the release seems too broad, strike out portions that permit unlimited access to information not directly relevant to the service. Check to make sure the insurer permits such deletions.

• *Be wary of magazine or TV ads offering free medical information.* When you respond to such offers by filling out a form or placing a phone call, a marketer somewhere links your name with at least the possibility of a certain health problem.

And since marketers buy mailing lists from one other, the data may be joined with other personal information you disclose to another marketer down the line.

Source: David F. Linowes, professor of political economy and public policy at the University of Illinois, Urbana-Champaign. A former chairman of both the Presidential Commission on Privatization and the US Privacy Protection Commission, he is the author of *Privacy in America.* University of Illinois Press.

Condoms Do Help Prevent AIDS

In the most definitive study yet, not one of the 124 couples who used latex condoms every time they had vaginal or anal sex transmitted the AIDS virus—even though one partner in each couple was already infected. Of 121 couples who used latex condoms inconsistently, transmission occurred 12 times.

Source: Isabelle de Vincenzi, MD, MPH, staff epidemiologist, European Centre for the Epidemiological Monitoring of AIDS, Paris.

Jumping vs. Osteoporosis

Premenopausal women who performed 50 two-legged jumps daily for six months increased their hip-bone density by four percent —presumably lowering their risk of osteoporosis-related fractures. *Essential:* The jumping routine must be performed at least three times a week—preferably daily. There is no need to get out of breath. Jumps can be done 10 at a time. Fifty jumps take one minute to perform. Anything longer risks injury. To avoid fractures, women older than 45 and those whose bones may already be weakened should perform jumping exercises only under a doctor's supervision.

Source: Joan Bassey, PhD, senior lecturer, department of physiology and pharmacology, University of Nottingham School of Medicine, England. Her study of bone density among women 20 to 45 years of age was published in *Osteoporosis International*, 8 Alexandra Rd., London SW197J2 England.

Blood Test Rules Out Heart Attacks

New blood test quickly determines whether chest pain is caused by a heart attack—or something less serious. The test, which compares two forms of a blood enzyme, determines within six hours whether a heart attack has occurred. Current tests take 12 to 24 hours. *Payoff:* Seven of 10 people treated for chest pain in coronary care units have not had a heart attack. The new test will keep these people from needlessly receiving scary and very costly care—saving an estimated $3 billion to $4 billion a year. For those whose chest pain is caused by a heart attack, the new test will speed the delivery of appropriate care. A commercial version of the test was recently released to hospitals. It should be widely available soon.

Source: Peter R. Puleo, MD, staff physician, department of medicine, section of cardiology, Christ Hospital, Cincinnati. His evaluation of 1,110 chest pain patients was published in *The New England Journal of Medicine*, 10 Shattuck St., Boston 02115.

Mammogram Advice

Annual mammograms are still a good idea for all women 40 or older, even though the National Cancer Institute now recommends routine mam-

mography only for women 50 or older. Annual screening permits detection of tumors at the earliest possible time. Early detection means better chances for survival, more treatment options and less disruption of daily life.

Source: Christine E. Williamson, MD, director of breast imaging, Providence Medical Center, Seattle, and a member of the American Cancer Society's breast cancer task force.

The Importance of Washing Your Hands

Inadequate hand-washing is responsible for most cases of diarrhea and vomiting. *Self-defense:* Always wash your hands before eating or handling food. Always wash after handling uncooked food—especially meat...after handling money or garbage...after using a bathroom or changing a diaper...after blowing your nose, sneezing or coughing into your hand... after playing with a pet. *Most effective:* Apply soap to hands, rub vigorously for at least 10 seconds in warm water, then rinse thoroughly. Be sure not to miss your cuticles and underneath your fingernails.

Source: *Mayo Clinic Health Letter*, 200 First St. SW, Rochester, MN 55905.

Acne/Telephone Connection

Frequent telephone use can cause acne. *Self-defense:* Clean the telephone receiver each morning with alcohol...and hold it away from your face as you talk. If you use the telephone for more than two hours a day, use a headset.

Source: Amit Pandya, MD, assistant professor of dermatology, University of Texas Southwestern Medical Center, Dallas.

The Return of Tuberculosis: Self-Defense Strategies

Tuberculosis (TB) is no longer the scourge it was earlier in this century—but TB is on the rise again after a long decline.

In 1989 and 1990, according to published reports, more than 400 workers in a Maine shipyard were infected with TB. The problem was traced to a single worker.

In 1992, more than 100 children in Arkansas became infected with TB—after they had been cared for by a woman with TB.

There are many more similar stories.

AIDS and immigration...

What underlies this resurgence of TB? *There are two primary explanations...*

•The AIDS epidemic. Infection with the AIDS virus compromises the immune system, making a person more vulnerable to TB bacteria...and allowing a latent TB infection to become activated.

•Increasing immigration to the US from areas where tuberculosis is still rampant.

New danger: Antibiotic-resistant strains of TB, created by spontaneous mutations of ordinary TB. Normally, drug-resistant strains can be wiped out by a combination of several different drugs taken over a long period of time. But if a patient doesn't take all the drugs prescribed or takes them in smaller doses or for shorter periods, the mutant bacteria may multiply and escape destruction.

Unfortunately, because TB is treated in sanitariums or other institutional settings only rarely now...and because the disease spreads rapidly among disadvantaged populations, incomplete or improper use of TB medication is increasingly common. This increases the prevalence of drug-resistant strains.

This doesn't mean that Americans should panic. In 1992, only about 27,000 cases—a fairly small number—were reported in the US, mostly in urban areas.

In addition, TB has a long latency period. Only one in 10 newly infected people will ever develop active TB. (Skin tests can detect a latent infection, but only the active form of the disease is contagious.)

TB is common in nursing homes, where longstanding TB infections and weakened immune systems are common. But family members living in the same household as people with active TB have less than a 50% chance of becoming infected themselves.

Theoretically, you could get TB from someone coughing near you on the bus or even from airborne particles that have lingered for several hours. But the odds of this ever happening are very, very small. However, repeated exposure to people with TB raises your chances of contracting the infection. This explains the high prevalence of TB among health-care workers...and the scattered reports of TB outbreaks among people working in the same office building.

Self-defense...

There is still no effective TB vaccine. Wearing a surgical mask won't protect you either—the infectious particles are small enough to pass through all but the most sophisticated filtration masks.

Because the incidence of TB is still relatively low, however, normal, healthy adults need not take drastic steps to avoid the disease. *But two precautions are sensible...*

•Before checking into a hospital for any reason, find out whether the hospital has taken any steps to reduce the transmission of TB between patients and staff.

Example: Improving ventilation systems to circulate more fresh air and less recycled, possibly contaminated, air.

•If you think you may have been exposed to the disease, take a skin test to find out if you have a latent infection. I recommend the Mantoux test. It's more accurate than the four-pronged tine test. Latent TB can be cured—by taking one of the standard TB drugs for six to 12 months.

Source: Michael Iseman, MD, professor of pulmonary medicine and infectious diseases at the University of Colorado School of Medicine, and chief of the mycobacterial disease service at the National Jewish Center for Immunology and Respiratory Medicine, Denver.

Fluorescent Lighting And Skin Cancer

Skin cancer risk is boosted by exposure to fluorescent lighting—but only slightly. Eight hours under an unshielded fluorescent light is equal to 1.2 minutes of July sunlight in Washington, DC. To eliminate this slight risk, cover lights with *acrylic transmission diffusers*—plastic covers.

Source: W. Howard Cyr, PhD, senior biophysicist, office of science and technology, Center for Devices and Radiological Health, Food and Drug Administration, Rockville, MD.

Quitting Smoking: Never Too Late

Lung cancer patients who kept smoking after diagnosis were three times more likely to get a second primary lung cancer than ones who quit after diagnosis. Stopping smoking benefits anyone, no matter how long he/she has smoked and no matter what the state of his/her health.

Source: Bruce Johnson, MD, chief of the lung cancer biology section, National Cancer Institute, Bethesda, MD. His study of more than 450 lung cancer patients was published in *Annals of Internal Medicine*, Independence Mall West, Sixth Street at Race, Philadelphia 19106.

Smoking and Asthmatic Children

Parents who smoke can significantly reduce asthma attacks in their children—by stopping. Asthmatic children of smokers average four serious asthma attacks per year...compared with only two attacks per year for asthmatic children of nonsmokers.

Source: James E. Haddow, MD, medical director, Foundation for Blood Research, Scarborough, ME. His study of the effects of passive smoking on asthmatic children was published in *The New England Journal of Medicine*, 10 Shattuck St., Boston 02115.

What You Need To Know About Blood Pressure Drugs

Blood pressure drugs should not be prescribed solely on the basis of only one or two blood pressure readings. Additional readings—taken over a period of weeks or months—are necessary to accurately gauge a patient's blood pressure...and to compensate for the "white coat" effect, in which anxiety caused by being in the doctor's office brings on a temporary spike in blood pressure.

Helpful: Home blood pressure monitoring kits to compare readings taken at home with those taken in a doctor's office. For a truly accurate gauge of your blood pressure, take two home readings a day, three days a week for two weeks.

Source: Thomas G. Pickering, MD, professor of medicine, New York Hospital–Cornell University Medical Center, New York City.

When You Need a Tetanus Shot

Get a tetanus shot at least once every decade. If you sustain a serious puncture wound five or more years after your last shot, ask your doctor about getting another booster. *Also:* Be sure to thoroughly wash any cut, abrasion or puncture wound—no matter how minor—with soap and water. You may wish to apply an over-the-counter antibiotic ointment...and keep the wound clean and dry with a bandage. If redness surrounding the wound extends more than one-quarter inch, see a doctor right away. It may be infected.

Source: James Brand, MD, assistant professor of medicine, University of Oklahoma Health Sciences Center, Oklahoma City.

To Avoid Hip Trouble

• *Avoid smoking and excessive drinking.* Both tobacco and alcohol promote the bone loss that is characteristic of osteoporosis—the leading risk factor for hip fracture.

• *Beware of cortisone.* Long-term use of this drug—commonly prescribed for asthma and certain skin conditions—raises the risk of osteoporosis. Cortisone should never be taken casually.

If your doctor prescribes cortisone, ask if the benefits of the treatment outweigh the risks.

For severe asthma, the answer is probably yes. For poison ivy or another minor skin problem, the answer is probably no. (Poison ivy usually requires nothing more than calamine lotion.)

• *Get plenty of calcium.* It's essential for building and maintaining strong, healthy bones. How much calcium you need each day depends upon your age and other factors. *The National Institutes of Health recommends...*

...1,200–1,500 mg/day for adolescents and young adults (11–24 years).

...1,000 mg/day for women ages 25–50.

...1,200–1,500 mg/day for pregnant or lactating women.

...1,000 mg/day for postmenopausal women on estrogen replacement therapy and 1,500 mg/day for postmenopausal women not on estrogen therapy.

...1,000 mg/day for men ages 25–65.

...1,500 mg/day for all men and women older than 65.

Each serving of a dairy product provides about 300 milligrams of calcium.

• *Get regular exercise.* The familiar maxim "use it or lose it" applies to bones as well as muscles. That's why weak bones are such a problem for individuals who have been bedridden for a long period of time.

The exercises most beneficial to the hip are those that force the skeleton to bear your full weight. *Examples:* Walking, jogging, stair-climbing and weight lifting. Nonweight-bearing exercises, like isometrics or swimming, are not as helpful.

Caution: If you haven't been physically active recently, start slowly. Build up gradually until you're working out for 30 minutes three to four times per week. Working out more frequently may cause premature wear of the hip joints.

• *Eliminate hazards in your home.* The first step is to place a rubber mat underneath throw rugs to keep them from slipping. Do not use dark or patterned carpeting on stairs. *Other important precautions...*

•Keep telephone and electrical cords up and out of the way. Keep stairways and floors free of clutter.

•Keep coffee tables and plants out of the way.

•Install a rubber mat in your tub and a slip-resistant rug on the floor beside it.

•Replace loose stairway boards or rugs.

•Install night-lights.

• *Consider hormone-replacement therapy.* When a woman undergoes menopause, her body stops synthesizing the female hormone estrogen. The loss of estrogen accelerates the loss of bone.

Supplemental estrogen helps protect the bones. However, because it has side effects (including an increased risk for uterine cancer), hormone-replacement therapy should be undertaken only *after* you've consulted your gynecologist or family doctor.

• *Watch out for signs of hip problems in young children.* If you have a newborn baby, ask the doctor to check him/her for hip instability (dysplasia) before he/she comes home from the hospital—especially if the condition runs in your family. Dysplasia can usually be corrected simply by "double-diapering." Left untreated, however, it can lead to severe osteoarthritis of the hips later on.

Between the ages of five and 10, boys are at risk for *Legg Perthes disease*, a condition in which the hip bone begins to degenerate.

Early warning sign: Pain in the hip or groin. If

your son complains of such pain, consult a doctor. The disease is treated with bed rest, sometimes combined with the use of a cast or special brace. The earlier Legg Perthes is treated, the better.

If your son is heavy-set, help him lose weight. Heavy-set boys between the ages of 10 and 14 are at increased risk of *slipped capital femoral epiphyses (SCFE)*—a condition in which the head of the thigh bone (femur) separates from the shaft.

Caught early, SCFE can be treated with relatively simply surgery. If it is discovered late, it can be a major problem and the prognosis is poor.

Source: Richard Welch, MD, chief of orthopedic surgery at St. Mary's Hospital in San Francisco and president of the Hip Society, a group of board-certified orthopedists who specialize in hip study, care and surgery. For more information about hip surgery, contact the American Academy of Orthopaedic Surgeons, 6300 N. River Rd., Rosemont, IL 60018.

Herbal Remedy Danger

Herbal remedies can be risky—even deadly. Although most remedies on the market are safe, comfrey, borage and coltsfoot contain *pyrrolizidine alkaloids*, toxic chemicals that can cause liver disease...*chaparral* has been linked to liver disease...*Ma huang*, touted as a weight loss aid, can cause a rise in blood pressure that is particularly unsafe for those with heart or thyroid disease or diabetes...*germanium* can damage kidneys when used over the long-term ...*yohimbé* can cause tremors, anxiety, high blood pressure and rapid heart rate.

Source: *Mayo Clinic Health Letter*, Mayo Foundation for Medical Education and Research, 200 First St. SW, Rochester, MN 55905.

Car Battery Danger

Exploding vehicle batteries injure 6,000 people a year. *Jump-start precautions:* Make sure that the vehicle with the dead battery isn't touching the car providing the jump...turn off the ignition on both vehicles...set the emergency brakes...turn off the radio, lights and all other accessories in both cars...set vehicles in neutral or park...make sure battery vent caps, if any, are tight and level. *For additional safety:* Keep a pair of splash-proof safety goggles in your trunk.

Source: Tod Turriff, safety director, Prevent Blindness America, 500 E. Remington Rd., Schaumburg, IL 60173.

Still Smoking?

One in two smokers will eventually be killed by their habit. Researchers used to believe that long-term, middle-aged smokers had twice the risk of premature death as nonsmokers of the same age. *Reality:* A recent study found that the rate is almost *three times* as high. Smoking has been linked not only to lung cancer, but also to heart disease, stroke and cancer of the mouth, throat, stomach, pancreas, bladder and rectum.

Source: Richard Doll, MD, FRS, honorary consultant, Imperial Cancer Research Fund Cancer Studies Unit, Radcliffe Infirmary, Oxford, England. His review of a 40-year study of 34,439 male doctors was published in the *British Medical Journal*, Tavistock Square, London WCIH 9JR, England.

Contact Lens Infection Danger

Putting contact lenses in your mouth can cause a bacterial or viral infection of the cornea. *Also dangerous:* Cleaning contact lenses with tap water. *Reason:* Tap water often contains *Acanthamoeba*, an organism that can cause a potentially blinding infection. *Self-defense:* Clean lenses only with a sterile solution sold for that purpose. If no solution is handy, leave the lenses out.

Source: R. Wayne Bowman, MD, associate professor of ophthalmology, University of Texas Southwestern Medical Center, Dallas.

Transdermal Patch Warning

Transdermal patches should be applied only to skin that is dry, clean, free of cuts, scratches or irritation, and hairless. If you can't find a hairless spot, clip the hair rather than shaving it. *Reason:* Shaving alters the skin surface, letting the drug from the transdermal patch penetrate into the bloodstream too quickly.

Source: Neil Schultz, MD, a dermatologist in private practice in New York City.

Free Hearing Test

Free hearing test identifies hearing problems in your own home. *How it works:* Call 800-222-3277 from 9 am to 5 pm, EST, Monday through Friday. Request your local Dial-A-Hearing-Screening-Test number. Call that number from a quiet room using a corded telephone (not a cordless or cellular phone). A recording will play four tones for each ear. If you don't hear all eight, see a doctor or audiologist.

Source: Occupational Hearing Services, Box 1880, Media, PA 19063.

Police-Impersonator Self-Defense

The color of the flashing lights atop police cars are not standardized across the United States. While red flashers are common, many police forces use combinations on their vehicles, such as blue-and-red and blue-and-white. Other police forces use just blue lights. *Self-defense:* To protect yourself from criminals impersonating highway police—without violating the law—turn on emergency flashers when an unmarked vehicle signals you from behind...stay on the road...slow down...then stop at the first well-lighted, populated area, such as a gas station.

Source: Phil Lynn, manager, National Law Enforcement Policy Center, International Association of Chiefs of Police, Alexandria, VA.

Social Security Ripoff

There are now four million illegal users of fake Social Security numbers. *Result:* Someone else may be receiving your benefits. *Self-defense:* Call the Social Security Administration (800-772-1213) to request your summary statement of earnings. Compare it with your past W-2 statements. Lower annual figures may mean benefits are being misdirected. Higher figures could mean your number has been stolen and could attract the IRS, which scans this data to uncover hidden income. Statute of limitations for an appeal: Three years, three months, and three days from the contested year.

Source: Mark Nestmann, editor of *Low Profile*, a financial-privacy newsletter, Box 84910, Phoenix 85071.

Snow-Shoveling Self-Defense

Do not hold your breath and strain when lifting a shovelful—this slows blood flow to the heart. When breath is released, blood pressure suddenly rebounds and becomes significantly elevated—which can create a dangerous heart overload. *Correct way to shovel:* Breathe out as you lift the shovel and toss the snow off to the side.

Source: *Cardiac Alert*, 7811 Montrose Rd., Potomac, MD 20854.

Bathroom Danger

Dirty hotel bathtubs can transmit athlete's foot, skin rashes and other infections. Make sure your tub is dry, smooth and free of cracks. When in doubt, clean it with Comet or a similar product.

Source: Yehudi M. Felman, MD, clinical professor of dermatology, Downstate Medical School, Brooklyn, NY.

How to Protect Yourself From a Package Bomb

Package bombs and letter bombs often have clues to alert recipients to possible trouble. *Danger signs:*

- Excessive weight for the size.
- Too much postage.
- No return address.
- Mailed from a foreign country, or via airmail or special delivery.
- A rigid or lopsided envelope.
- Common words are misspelled.
- Restrictive markings, such as Confidential or Personal.
- Incorrect title for the addressee, or a title without a person's name.
- Handwritten or poorly typed address.
- Protruding wires or tinfoil.
- Excessive securing material, such as tape or string.
- Oily stains or discoloration on the outside of the package.

If you're suspicious: Don't touch the package —not even to move it out of the way…immediately call your local FBI office, or police or fire department…or call the FBI's Bomb Data Center at 202-FBI-BOMB.

Source: William Carter is with the Federal Bureau of Investigation at their headquarters in Washington, DC.

Age-Discrimination Traps

Age discrimination laws can be circumvented with employment contracts. A federal court recently approved the firing of a man who had an employment contract that expired on his 70th birthday. The man was kept on for six more months, without a contract, then let go. *Court:* The action did not constitute manda-tory retirement, which is illegal, but merely the legal termination of the services of someone whose contract had expired.

Source: *Harrington v. Aetna-Bearing,* USCD No. Ill, 1/30.

Most Frequent Hospital Bill Mistake

97% of hospital bills are wrong, and less than 2% of those errors are in the patient's favor. *Average error:* $1,400.

Frequent mistake: Billing for items or services never delivered (lab work, medication, thermometers, wheelchairs, etc.).

Self-defense: Insist on completely itemized bills…and review them carefully.

Source: Harvey Rosenfield, head of watchdog group Bills Project.

How to Decide Whether to Accept Your Company's Buyout Offer

As more companies resort to cutting their staffs to boost profitability and competitiveness, more and more people are offered early retirement or voluntary separation. When to accept? It depends. *Consider these questions…*

- *Where do you stand in your career?* If you have reached a plateau …your job is no longer satisfying…or you have been waiting for a chance to start your own company but lacked the necessary capital…a buyout may be ideal.

- *How healthy is your company?* If you believe the company's problems are temporary— and a smaller staff will create new opportunities for advancement—consider staying. But if you believe that layoffs will follow the offer, it makes sense to accept the offer and leave.

Types of plans…

- *Early-retirement plans* offer benefits similar to those provided for the company's retirees. Though companies cannot legally target workers by age when offering early retirement, they can structure plans so they are more attractive to people who are nearing retirement. This can be done by adding years to your age and service, which in some cases makes you eligible for greater benefits. By law, though, early-retirement plans are not negotiable.

• *Voluntary-separation plans* are structured to appeal to workers regardless of age and length of service. In theory these offers are negotiable, but in practice they are usually take-it-or-leave-it deals. Management does not want to offer one employee greater incentives for fear that others will find out and demand identical treatment.

Typical scenarios...

• *Simple case:* The company offers you one month's pay for every year of service. You have been employed for 12 years and therefore get one year's pay. You'll make out well if you find another job in less than a year.

Trap: Medical-insurance costs can reduce a lump-sum buyout significantly. By law, you must be retained in the firm's medical plan for up to 18 months after you leave. But you must pay all costs of the insurance unless the voluntary-separation program provides otherwise.

• *More complex case:* In addition to compensation based on years of service, your company may sweeten the deal by offering to add five years to your age and five years to your length of service. This may make you eligible for benefits you might not otherwise receive.

Opportunity: If you are nearing retirement and are unsure of the company's future, the offer may be perfect.

However, if you intend to find another job and your medical coverage runs out before you're hired, you may be completely uninsurable as an individual in the current marketplace.

Trap: Even if you do find a new job, illnesses covered by your old policy may be excluded by your new one.

Bottom line...

Make medical coverage a priority when deciding whether to accept a buyout deal. If you have any leverage in the negotiation, focus on health benefits rather than on the amount of the lump sum.

Ideally, you want the company to keep paying premiums during the full buyout term. If the company added five years of service to your package, it should consider adding five years of coverage.

At the very least, see if your company will pay for your health insurance during the 18-month period following your departure.

Source: Jim Klein, vice president, Towers Perrin, an international employee-benefits consultant, 245 Park Ave., New York 10167.

Warning Signs Of a Stroke

• Numbness, weakness or paralysis of face, arm or leg, especially on one side of the body.

• Difficulty speaking or understanding simple statements.

• Sudden blurred or decreased vision in one or both eyes.

• Loss of balance or coordination, when combined with other warning signs.

What to do: Immediately call your physician, who will contact the appropriate ambulance for emergency treatment.

Source: National Stroke Association, 8480 E. Orchard Rd., Englewood, CO 80111.

Beware of Nutritionists Who Advertise

Fewer than half of the so-called professionals listed in the Yellow Pages in 32 states were reliable sources of sound, scientifically based nutrition information. Seventy percent of those who claimed to be PhDs had phony degrees or delivered fraudulent information. Others boasted nonexistent degrees—certified nutritionist (CN), doctor of nutrimedicine (NMD) and nutrition counselor (NC). Still others had "degrees" from nonaccredited schools.

Bottom line: Don't trust nutritionists who cannot show their credentials from an accredited college or university. For a directory of accredited schools, see the *Accredited Institutions of Postsecondary Education* in your local library.

Source: Survey by the National Council Against Health Fraud, reported in *Tufts University Diet & Nutrition Letter*, 203 Harrison Ave., Boston 02111.

Family-Business Trap to Avoid

Family-business members *who are not members of the family:* Avoid taking sides in family arguments. Try to be liked by everyone. Listen to the grapevine but do not spread rumors. Demonstrate loyalty. Become an important source of information for family members by learning the business thoroughly. Accept the fact that family members, as the firm's owners, are likely to be paid more than you—the extra amounts represent return on the family's investment.

Source: Robert Half, founder, Robert Half International and Accountemps Worldwide, executive recruiters, Menlo Park, CA.

How Not to Be Swindled

To help you steer clear of swindlers...

•If any offer sounds too good to be true, you can be virtually certain that it is.

•Never rush or impulse buy. Swindlers don't want to give you any time to think the deal over because your common sense might prevail.

•Responses to help separate the good guys from the bad guys: "Well, let me talk this over with my attorney."..."I'll check this out with the Better Business Bureau and get back to you."

•If an offer is in person or by phone, insist on getting details in writing before making a decision.

•Check out any offer or recommendation thoroughly. Call your local Area Agency on Aging or Better Business Bureau.

•Investigate and comparison shop as you would with any major purchase. Check it out

with knowledgeable people.

•Don't sign anything until you've done your investigation.

•Use credit cards, or at least checks—never cash. With credit cards and checks there is a legal record of your payment.

•Never give out your credit card, Medicare, Social Security, telephone calling card or bank account numbers to solicitors.

•The fact that an offer appears on network TV or in a respected magazine or major newspaper means nothing. Acceptance standards for ads are notoriously lax and virtually anyone can buy advertising.

•Beware of anyone touting "little or no risk."

•If you get taken, don't be too embarrassed to report it to the police, your local attorney general, the Better Business Bureau and any relevant professional association. You might help save others from being hurt.

Source: J. L. Simmons, PhD, author of *67 Ways to Protect Seniors From Crime,* Henry Holt and Co. Inc.

Warning Signs to Heed

Reasons to call a doctor no matter what time it is: Severe headaches, vomiting, diarrhea, nausea, dizziness or sweating...chest pains or feelings of pressure or tightness in the chest... breathing difficulty...severe earaches or vision problems...high fever...difficulty urinating... any significant pain you can't explain.

Source: *Men's Health,* Emmaus, PA.

Self-Defense for Older Drivers

Older drivers need to take precautions to compensate for the physical and perceptual changes associated with aging. *Self-defense:* Plan your trips—and drive your plan. Knowing your route lets you concentrate on driving, not navigating…choose less demanding routes, such as intersections with safer left-turn arrows …drive with a large "anticipation zone," giving yourself room to react.

Source: For a copy of AARP's handbook, *Older Driver Skill Assessment and Resource Guide: Creating Mobility Choices,* send a postcard to AARP(EE0620), stock # D14957, Box 22796, Long Beach, CA 90801.

Before You Give To Charity…

Check on how a charity spends its money before you donate. Send the name of the charity and a self-addressed, stamped envelope to the National Charities Information Bureau (NCIB), 19 Union Square W., Sixth Floor, New York 10003. You can also request a free copy of the NCIB's *Wise Giving Guide,* which evaluates 300 charitable organizations. *Also:* You can request free information on up to three charities by sending a letter accompanied by a self-addressed, stamped envelope to the Philanthropic Advisory Service of the Council of Better Business Bureaus, 4200 Wilson Blvd., Arlington, VA 22203.

Source: Nancy Dunnan, financial columnist, writing in *Your Money,* 5705 N. Lincoln Ave., Chicago 60659.

Painkiller Danger

Taken in high doses and for long periods of time, Advil, Nuprin, Motrin, Aleve, Naprosyn, Indocin and other non-steroidal anti-inflammatory drugs (NSAIDs) may cause elevated blood pressure. Often used to treat arthritis, gout and other painful conditions, NSAIDs have long been known to cause small increases in blood pressure. *Now:* A recent study links these drugs to an increased need for antihypertensive therapy, particularly among the elderly. Although the link was found with prescription NSAIDs, users of over-the-counter versions of these drugs often take more—sometimes much more —than the label recommends. *Self-defense:*

Take only as much of any NSAID as is prescribed or indicated on the label, or switch to Tylenol or another pain reliever containing acetaminophen. Aspirin in low doses has not been linked to increases in blood pressure.

Source: Jerry H. Gurwitz, MD, assistant professor of medicine, Harvard Medical School, Boston. His study of NSAID use among 9,411 Medicaid patients was published in the *Journal of the American Medical Association,* 515 N. State St., Chicago 60610.

Ear-Cleaning Danger

Cotton-tipped swabs used to clean a child's ears of wax can cause blockage, pain—even temporary hearing loss. In a recent study, kids whose parents used swabs to clean their ears were far more likely to have their ear canals blocked by wax. There's rarely reason to clean wax from a child's ear. A little wax is good—it protects against infection and foreign bodies. Left alone, it eventually drops out of the ear by itself.

Source: Michael Macknin, MD, associate professor of pediatrics, Ohio State University School of Medicine, and section head, department of general pediatrics, Cleveland Clinic Foundation. His survey of 651 patients between the ages of two weeks and 20 years was published in *Clinical Pediatrics,* 500 Executive Blvd., Ossining, NY 10562.

Dementia Predictors

Dementia—including that caused by Alzheimer's disease—can now be predicted up to four years in advance. Subjects are asked to memorize and then recall a series of words and objects. Each subject must rapidly name objects within a category, such as vegetables, and quickly find and copy a series of symbols. Given to those in their 70s and 80s, these neurological tests are better at predicting who will *not* develop dementia, rather than identifying those who will.

Source: David Masur, PhD, associate clinical professor of neurology, Albert Einstein College of Medicine and Montefiore Medical Center, New York City.

Prostate Cancer— How to Outsmart the #2 Cancer Killer of Men

Prostate cancer is the second-leading cause of cancer death in men (after lung cancer). It kills an estimated 38,000 men a year.

Experts disagree on how to fight the disease. Should men take the blood test to detect prostate cancer? And how should they treat the cancer if it's detected? We asked Gerald Chodak, MD, to clear up the confusion…

Dr. Chodak, what causes prostate cancer?

We don't yet know the precise causes, but we have identified several factors that put men at increased risk…

• being African-American

• having a father, grandfather or uncle who had the disease

• eating a diet high in fat, especially animal fat

• possibly infrequent sexual activity.

Exposure to sunlight seems to help prevent prostate cancer, although the reason for this protective effect is unknown. But it's possible to get prostate cancer even in the absence of these risk factors. Any man can get prostate cancer.

What's the best way to detect prostate cancer?

In the past few years, doctors have begun to rely on the prostate-specific antigen (PSA) test. This test measures the blood level of PSA, a protein released in microscopic amounts by the prostate gland. The digital rectal exam is also an important diagnostic tool.

But I've heard that the PSA test isn't always accurate.

That's true. A high PSA reading may be a sign of cancer. But high readings sometimes occur in men who are cancer-free—causing needless alarm and the expense of additional tests.

Even if prostate cancer is accurately detected, it may grow so slowly that the man dies of an unrelated ailment long before the cancer has a chance to harm him.

Prostate cancer experts still don't know whether aggressive treatment of these slow-growing tumors is beneficial—especially since surgery and radiation have severe side effects, including incontinence and impotence. Some doctors think it's better to do nothing—to try "watchful waiting" instead.

Even if surgery or radiation is performed, there's no guarantee that the cancer won't spread to other areas of the body. Men who take the PSA test might be setting themselves up for needless expense, worry and treatment-related complications, without gaining any survival benefit.

What's your view of the PSA test?

I tell my patients that if their desire to minimize their risk of prostate cancer outweighs their concern about being subjected to possibly unnecessary, possibly harmful medical care, then they should get tested. You can discuss the matter with your own doctor, but ultimately it's your decision.

What role does a man's age play in determining whether he should be tested?

For men younger than 50, there's not much to be gained by getting tested. *Reason:* Prostate cancer is very rare in men that young. If you have a family history of the disease or if you're African-American, however, you might benefit from getting the test before age 50. That's something to discuss with your doctor.

If you are older than 70, or if other ailments have cut your life expectancy to 10 years or less, odds are you won't benefit much from the test, either. Even if you did have prostate cancer, you'd probably die of another cause. There would be no reason to treat the cancer.

Men between the ages of 50 and 70 are most likely to benefit from PSA testing. Men at the lower end of that age range are especially likely to benefit.

Have you had a PSA test?

I'm 47 now, so I haven't yet felt the need to be tested. But I probably will get tested when I'm 50. I'd like to reach 80. I'd prefer to reach 90, and I don't want prostate cancer to get in the way.

How often should men get tested?

Men who are especially concerned about prostate cancer can get a PSA test once a year. Even once every six months is not too often. That way you'll know what's normal for you—and be able to see if the numbers shoot up, signaling cancer growth.

What do the test results mean?

The traditional view has been that any PSA level over 4.0 suggests trouble. But recent evidence suggests that numbers well below 4.0 might be risky for younger men…while higher numbers might be normal in elderly men.

New standard: For a 40-year-old man, a PSA above 2.5 is now considered abnormal. But among 60-year-olds, a reading as high as 6.5 might be normal.

What if my PSA reading is suspiciously high?

Your doctor should refer you to a urologist, who will perform an ultrasound exam to try to locate a tumor site. If a tumor is found, you'll have a biopsy to determine whether it is malignant. Don't worry—a biopsy does not spread the cancer.

What if cancer is found?

The decision about treatment is about trade-offs. The older the patient and the shorter his life expectancy, the smaller a chance of benefitting from aggressive treatment. But at any age, some of the treated men will probably benefit. The question is whether the benefit is worth the risk.

For younger men who are otherwise healthy, the benefits of treatment outweigh the risks. If the cancer were to remain untreated, your risk of dying of prostate cancer in the next 20 years would be about 60%.

What's the best treatment for prostate cancer?

Complete surgical removal of the prostate (a procedure called radical prostatectomy) offers the best chance for a cure. But surgery has drawbacks. Recent studies of Medicare patients have shown that up to 70% of men experience impotence following surgery. Of course, many older men are already impotent due to other diseases.

Good news: It's often possible to remove the prostate without injuring the nerves to the penis. Ask your surgeon if you're a candidate for nerve-sparing surgery.

About 18% of men will experience at least minor incontinence after surgery. But only 2% to 4% say that post-surgical incontinence is a serious problem.

What about radiation therapy?

Radiation is roughly comparable to surgery in terms of its ability to prolong life. And radia-tion controls the cancer while avoiding some of the complications of surgery.

Problem: For at least two years following the treatment, it's hard to tell whether radiation therapy has worked. In cases where radiation therapy does not work, it becomes very difficult to find a cure. And when incontinence and impotence occur following radiation, they're often harder to treat than the same problems caused by surgery.

Bottom line: Either surgery or radiation is a reasonable alternative, depending on your own preferences.

I read that it's possible to treat prostate cancer with radioactive "seeds." Is that effective?

Studies of radioactive pellets have been inconclusive. Some suggest that the pellets are effective, others that they're not. For this reason, I don't recommend them. We'll have to wait several years before we know the results of current tests.

Source: Gerald W. Chodak, MD, professor of surgery at the University of Chicago Hospitals, and director of the prostate and urology center at the Louis A. Weiss Memorial Hospital in Chicago.

Child-Proof Your Dog

Before acquiring the dog…

Both the age of your child and the dog's breed are important considerations when buying a new pet.

• *Age.* It is not advisable to introduce a dog into a household if your child is younger than four years old.

Neither the baby nor the dog can call for help if the other misbehaves or becomes aggressive.

All dogs must be trained. And it is difficult to raise a puppy at the same time you're raising a baby.

• *Breed.* While virtually all dogs can be trained, handling some dogs requires more effort and experience.

Breeds to avoid: Chows, rottweilers and akitas. These dogs can be aggressive and very protective and generally require experienced handlers.

Better: Retrievers and most spaniels, which are less aggressive and have a people-loving disposition.

Of course, there are exceptions with any breed. That's why it's important to determine if the dog you've chosen is attracted to people and how it responds to loud noises and discomfort.

Strategy: One way to check a dog's discomfort level is to pinch the dog slightly between its toes. Avoid pups that immediately scream and bite. Select the one that only whines a bit.

Once the dog is home...

• *Neutering your dog—male or female—is important.* It will make the dog easier to handle and less likely to fight with other dogs. An unneutered dog is usually more aggressive, moody and more likely to develop aggression problems in the future. Neutering doesn't meaningfully alter a dog's personality or make it fat and lazy.

• *Manners are extremely important.* Children should leave a dog alone when it is eating. But interruptions do occur. For this reason, dogs need to be taught not to lunge at food and to be passive around their food bowls. This is taught through a gradual process of intervention. Once or twice a day, while the dog is eating, add a treat to his bowl. This will teach the dog to look forward to your arrival and to not react aggressively.

It is also important that dogs learn to respond immediately to certain fundamental commands. They must sit, lie down, stay and move—*on command.*

• *Some dogs change as children become older and more active.* If a dog suddenly stops obeying commands or begins showing signs of aggression, get professional dog-handling advice *immediately.*

Usually a local vet or dog shelter can supply you with the name of reputable trainers.

Children and dog training...

• *Teach children about a dog's body language.* If a dog is inflating its body, trying to hold its tail erect or its ears are up, it is in an aggressive mode. The dog should be left alone.

If the dog is crouching down with its head and ears low, it may be afraid and could act aggressively if approached.

• *Never move quickly or shout around a dog, especially another person's dog.* Children must be taught to stroke a dog, not grab it. They should also learn not to surprise a dog when it's sleeping or to play too roughly with it.

A child should only pet a dog if it has shown interest in being petted and if an adult is present. Good places to pet a dog are on the sides of the neck, shoulders or chest and underside of his neck.

• *When it comes to dogs and children—think S-A-F-E.* This acronym should remind you of the basics...

Supervise a child with a dog at all times. Even the kindest dog can react aggressively if cornered or inadvertently hurt by a child.

Anticipate problems. If a dog is backing away from your child, hiding under a table or hopping up on a piece of furniture, it wants to be alone. Prevent the child from pursuing the dog.

Follow through. Make sure both your dog and your child obey your commands, whether it is having the dog sit or stopping the child from bothering your pet.

Educate your child to treat the dog with care and respect.

Source: Brian Kilcommons, a professional dog trainer with The Family Dog, Inc., RD #2, Box 398, Prospect Rd., Middletown, NY 10940. He is author of *Child-Proofing Your Dog.* Warner Books.

17

Retirement Options

How to Start Your Own Business with Almost No Money Down

You don't need a fortune to start your own business. In fact, many types of enterprises can get off the ground for less than $1,000, particularly those that require little more than your own know-how, a telephone and a bare-bones marketing campaign.

Examples: Selling products that you can make in your home or providing any of a wide variety of services, from pet care to consulting.

The risk is small, and once in a great, great while you'll strike it rich, like the shoestring entrepreneurs who started Pepperidge Farms, Celestial Seasonings and Subway sandwiches.

What you'll need...

To start a minibusiness, the only equipment that's absolutely necessary is a telephone and an answering machine. *Cost:* About $30 a month for the phone and $35 and up for an answering machine.

The need for other equipment, such as a computer, fax machine, etc., will depend on the type of business you intend to start. If you have equipment, fine. But don't rush to buy anything unless you are sure your business really needs it.

Other requirements...

Business cards ($10 and up) and a simple brochure or flier ($30 and up depending on quality/quantity).

Sales ability. This simply means projecting the faith you have in your idea and your enthusiasm for it. Not all businesses require excellent selling skills. But if yours does, consider taking a Dale Carnegie course or a short course in sales offered at many community colleges.

Choosing a business...

Keys to success: Select a business that you know a lot about...and for which there's a market. As the owner of a minibusiness, you obviously can't afford to do extensive market research. But it's not costly to talk with as many potential customers as you can. This is what big companies call field research. It pays off.

Example: If you're thinking about going into the landscaping business, talk directly with home owners. Ask what they like and dislike about their current landscaping service. Inquire about price and about problems they've experienced. Also ask how they found out about the service they're now using.

Answers give you a wealth of information—which neighborhoods have the most potential customers, how to reach them, how to price your service and how to do a better job than the competition.

Or you may discover that the real market isn't in landscaping but in caring for indoor plants while owners are away. In many cases, field research is tantamount to lining up customers before you commit yourself to starting the business. If you find a dozen or so home owners who are dissatisfied with their current service you can simply ask them if they'd switch to the service you plan to offer. Attaching flyers to the outside of mailboxes is another inexpensive way to test the market. (*Note:* It is illegal to put anything but mail into someone's mailbox.) If you distribute 1,000 inexpensive fliers and don't have any inquiries, you can be sure there's a problem with the product or service, its price or the neighborhood you've targeted. Don't rely on friends or family to tell you whether your business idea has potential. They're all too eager to give you encouragement, but what you really need is hard, practical information.

Start-up traps...

Trap: Overestimating sales. Some of the world's best-known companies have made this mistake, and the error can be fatal for a small business with little capital to fall back on.

Even after you've identified potential customers, it's easy to convince yourself that they'll soon be clamoring for your product or service. In reality, it may take time to develop a market. And without much capital, you can often come up short if customers are slow in paying.

Safeguard: Once you estimate sales, cut the figure by 30%. Don't start your business unless you can break even on the 70% that remains.

Trap: Underestimating long-term expenses. It's fairly easy to gauge the money you'll need to get a business off the ground, but it's harder to estimate working capital for the next six to 12 months.

Example: Operating expenses, such as telephone, utilities and advertising.

Safeguard: Talk with others who have started similar businesses...especially those located outside the area in which you intend to do business. Ask about their operating expenses. And don't underestimate demands on your time. Even the simplest, least expensive businesses require time to answer phone calls, fill orders, do a minimum amount of marketing and take care of paperwork. And all of these compete with your personal schedule, including doctor appointments, shopping, social events and vacations.

Budget-conscious marketing...

For small, home-based businesses, the most efficient ways to reach potential customers are by personal contact, flyers, weekly shopper advertising and signs on trucks and cars.

Supplement these with free publicity.

Join civic groups so you can meet people and tell them about your product or service ...and give out your business card!

Write articles about your field of expertise.

Example: If you go into the business of making desserts for local restaurants, write articles for the food page of your local papers.

Do free work or donate samples of your product to religious or charitable organizations. It often leads to jobs that pay, and you may be able to take a tax deduction for your efforts. (Check with your accountant about this first.)

Typical minibusinesses...

• *Caretaker (children, older people or pets).* All are growth businesses in many parts of the country. Religious institutions can often steer you to people who need help.

• *Consultant.* If you developed a special skill in business, you may now be able to sell that expertise as a consultant.

Market your skill by contacting companies and individuals that are likely to have a need for your service.

• *Home repair person.* There's an almost endless list of niches in this field, including fixing things, interior decorating and vinyl and furniture repair.

Community colleges and vocational schools often have courses in these areas, and correspondence courses in many fields are available through the International Correspondence Schools, 925 Oak St., Scranton, PA 18515, 717-342-7701, or the Foley-Belsaw Institute, 6301 Equitable Rd., Kansas City, MO 64120, 816-483-6400. *Cost:* $399 to $1,295.

• *Property tax reduction expert.* If you have experience in real estate, taxes or the law, this could be an option for you. Since many homes are assessed too high, owners will often pay an expert who can get the assessment lowered.

If you lack experience, consider taking a course in real estate that covers tax assessment. Offer to work for a percentage of the money you save your clients.

• *Specialty foods preparer.* Restaurants and gourmet retailers are often on the lookout for interesting food items, including fancy desserts and dehydrated fruits and vegetables. Making them in your home can produce substantial income.

Caution: You may need a license for food preparation. Consult your local government agencies or an attorney familiar with the requirements.

Helpful: Books and equipment available from the New England Cheesemaking Supply Co., 85 Main St., Ashfield, MA 01330. 413-628-3808.

• *T-shirt and bumper sticker printer.* These are made by the silk-screen printing process, which can cost less than $500 to set up at home. Schools, civic groups and clubs are good markets for products that carry a slogan. Art supply stores often carry silk-screen equipment or can recommend catalog companies that supply it.

Source: Will Davis, president of The Success Team, which offers seminars for small businesses. He is author of *Start Your Own Business for $1,000 or Less.* Upstart Publishing Co.

Businesses You Can Start for Under $500

Starting a business is not as hard as you think. You don't even need a great deal of money to launch one. Here are several businesses that you can run out of your home with an investment of $500 or less…

• *Credit-repair service.* Customers usually seek this service after being rejected for a home or car loan. You would resolve their credit disputes, set up payment schedules with credit-card companies, etc.

Key: Screen potential clients. You want those you can actually help. To be eligible for your services, problem accounts must have been paid off for at least one year, preferably three or four. Guarantee clients an overall improvement in their credit.

Cost: $500 for office expenses, placement of ads in area newspapers, research of credit recordkeeping and reporting laws. *Earning potential:* $100,000 a year.

• *Estate sales.* Visit estate sales and study the business before soliciting clients of your own. You will need to learn how to price antiques and how to draw up a contract with clients.

Key: Letting clients know that you will take care of everything.

Cost: $200 to $300 to advertise your service in daily and shoppers' newspapers. The clients pay to advertise sales. *Earning potential:* 25% of sales.

• *Meeting planner.* Put together events, meetings, and conventions for clients.

Key: Pay attention to details. Thoroughly research hotels, restaurants, meeting facilities, and travel arrangements you make for clients. Your business will grow through word-of-mouth referrals.

Cost: $500 for office expenses, yellow pages ad. Earning potential: $30,000+ a year.

Source: Stephen Wagner, associate publisher and editor of *Income Opportunities* magazine and author of *Mind Your Own Business: The Best Businesses You Can Start Today for Under $500.* Bob Adams, Inc.

How to Make Money As a Consultant

At one time or another, most executives consider selling their expertise on their own, as consultants. The majority are at least moderately successful, but many fail. Most commonly, they overestimate the salability of their services and underestimate the effort needed to sell them.

Pitfalls for new consultants...

•Not realizing that consultants, especially new ones, spend more time selling their services than performing them.

•Wasting time on unproductive prospects.

•Choosing too broad a field in which to consult.

•Not learning to talk the client's language. This is essential because many consultants sell a highly specialized service with its own vocabulary to an equally specialized customer who uses a completely different language. *Example:* A computer expert who is hired to automate market research for a diaper manufacturer.

To sell their services, successful consultants:

•Maintain pressure by keeping in touch with clients and prospects.

•Master such sales and marketing methods as the art of writing letters, making convincing phone calls, and developing presentations.

•Start at the top, contacting the chief executives of the Fortune 1000 companies.

Source: Charles Moldenhauer, VP, Lefkowith, Inc., marketing and corporate-communications consultants, New York.

Working After Retirement

Many retirees would like to keep working after retirement, at least part-time. But those who want to work for financial reasons should be aware of these drawbacks:

•You can work and still collect Social Security benefits, but for every $3 earned above a government-determined ceiling you lose $1 in benefits. When you add your commuting costs, job-related expenses, and payroll deductions, you may find part-time work doesn't pay off.

•If you continue working part-time for the same company, you may not be eligible to collect your pension. One way around this, if the company will go along, is to retire as an employee and return as a consultant or freelancer. Since you're now self-employed, your pension won't be affected.

•Although most employees can't legally be compelled to retire before age 70, companies still set up retirement ages of 65 or under. You can work past that age, but you won't earn further pension credits. And you lose Social Security and pension benefits while you continue to work.

A very attractive alternative to working part-time is to start your own business. Professionals such as lawyers can often set up a practice, setting their own hours. Or you might turn a hobby into a business.

Source: William W. Parrott, a chartered financial consultant at Merrill Lynch, Pierce, Fenner & Smith, Inc., 1185 Ave. of the Americas, New York 10036.

Index

335

G

Gallstones, safer surgery for, 205
Game show, tips for becoming contestant on, 300–301
Garlic
  benefits of, 242
  dangers of, 285
Gastroesophageal reflux disease (GERD) as cause of yellow teeth, 317
Gastrointestinal cancer, smoking as factor in, 119
General Agreement on Tariffs and Trade (GATT), 21
Gene therapy, pitfalls of, 273–76
Genital bites, treatment of, 262
Germ-line gene therapy, 275
Gifts, using, to cut estate, 29–30
Ginger tea, benefits of, 242
Ginkgo in alleviating motion sickness, 192–93
Glaucoma
  and nearsightedness, 185–86
  prevention and treatment of, 198–99
  risk for, 185–86
Goals, setting, 163
Goggles, vision-enhancement, 109
Golfers, improved backswings for older, 246
Government aid, getting, for health care, 16–18
Grandfather trust, 64
Grandparent, being better, 172–74
Grants, home repair, 291
Graying, premature, 266
  as early sign of osteoporosis, 127
Green tea in fighting disease, 193
Growth investments, investing in, 19, 23
Guaranteed investment contracts (GICs), getting out of, 30–32
Gum disease, spread by kissing, 198
Gum recession, causes of, 183
Gums, brushing, 112
Gynecomastia, 263

H

Hair conditioners, shopping for, 108
Hair dye, and cancer, 317
Hands, importance of washing, 320
Headaches, overcoming, 124–26
Healing
  and the mind-body connection, 131–32
  pets in, 132–35
Health care, 175–206. *See also* Cancer; Dental health; Emotional health; specific condition
  acupuncture in strengthening hands, 197–98
  for aging parents, 97
  aging process in, 103–6, 115–17, 123
  and air travel, 110
  Alzheimer's disease
    music in treating, 200
    preventing, 194
    and smoking, 203
  angioplasty, follow-up, 198
  arthritis
    and acupuncture, 186
    relieving pain from, 204

asthma
  in children, 195
  treating, 186, 201
avoiding colds and flu, 175–76
birthmark removal in, 206
caffeine in, 109
cataracts, unnecessary surgery for, 204
as catastrophic problem, 120–22
causes of death in, 109–10
causes of stomach problems, 197
chili pepper dangers in, 193
chronic pain in, 124–26
colds in, 124
connection between bright light and sleep, 186–87
connection between imagination and, 158–59
controlling tinnitus, 186
donating used eyeglasses, 205
ear infection advances in, 203
emergency treatment for, 179
estrogen and cholesterol connection in, 204–5
eye dryness, relief for, 197
gallstone surgery in, 206
getting government aid for, 16–18
getting relief from leg cramps, 203
green tea in, fighting disease, 193
gum recession in, 183
handling catastrophic problems in, 120–22
healing back pain, 176–78
heart attack
  aspirin in prevention, 178
  silent, 204
  telephone counseling for, 205
heartburn in, 109
heart disease in, 107, 110, 120
  silent, 201–2
hidden cause of dry eyes, 194
HMO traps in, 100–101
hot flashes in, 183
ingestion in, 109
leeches and maggots in, 205
leg pain in, 124
liposuction in, 122
and living healthier life, 156–57
living with arthritis, 285–86
medical research in, 110–12
menopause in, 113
migraines
  low back pain connection, 183
  unnecessary tests for, 201
minerals in, 187–90
misdiagnosed, 203
multiple chemical sensitivity, 185
multiple sclerosis
  coping with, 183–85
  new hope for, 203
  relief from, 194
natural relief for allergies, 192–93
nearsightedness, 185–86
and need for getting second opinion, 161–63
and need for living will, 23
and need for protein, 127
new relief for eczema, 202–3
and osteoporosis, 127
pacemaker surgery for, 198
pepper cream relief in, 197

pneumococcal pneumonia, 186
preventing and treating glaucoma, 198–99
and preventive medicine, 127–28
prostate in, 181–83
Retin-A in repairing damaged skin, 201
risks for, 185
saving money on, 8–9
scalding self-defense in, 113
scams in, 313–14
self-defense for, 178
self-defense for pneumonia, 204
shingles treatment, 194
shopping for toiletries in, 107–8
single shoes for amputees in, 109
smell in, 126–27
and smoking, 326
smoothing wrinkled skin, 193
spreading gum disease, 198
strokes in, 178–81
  prevention of, 205
  treating, 200
substandard medical care for women, 269–72
systemic lupus erythematosus in, 195–97
taking charge of your, 136
tattoo removal, 193
tax deductions for, 64, 68, 69
therapies for, 179–80
tobacco dangers in, 118–20, 126
tranquilizers and hip fractures, 204
treating bee stings, 200
treating chronic coughs, 202
treating cystic fibrosis, 205–6
treating jaundice in, 194
treating urinary incontinence, 200
ulcerative colitis in, 183
in U. S. versus France, 178
vaccines
  for pneumonia, 109
  for polio, 112
vision in, 109
ways to cut costs in, 223–24
Health insurance
  collecting claims from, 87–88
  considering, in retirement planning, 41
  determining adequate coverage in, 95–96
  saving on, 3
  as tax loophole, 66
Hearing, free tests for, 326
Heart, tips for having healthier, 117–18
Heart attack
  aspirin in preventing, 178
  blood test in ruling out, 320
  predicting time of occurrence, 107
  self-defense for, 178
  silent, 204
  telephone counseling for survivors of, 205
  in U. S. versus France, 178
Heartburn, treating, 109
Heart disease
  gene therapy for, 274–75
  physical inactivity as cause of, 245
  predicting death from, 110
  silent, 201–2
  smoking as factor in, 119
Help for Incontinent People (HIP), 268
Hemoglobin, 188

Heparin for strokes, 179–80
Hepatitis A, vaccine for, 296
Herbs
    dangers of, 325
    and health, 241–42
Hesperidin in allergy relief, 192
High blood pressure, and weight control, 243
Hip fractures, tranquilizers and, 204
Hip trouble, avoiding, 324–25
Histamine in allergy relief, 192
Hobby, classifying sidelines business as, 64
Home care under Medicare, 91
Home-equity loans, 49
    appraisals for, 78
    interest on as deductible, 68–69
Homeowner's insurance, saving money on, 2
Home repair grants, 291
Hormone replacement therapy (HRT), need
    for endometrial biopsies prior to, 272
Hospital
    better recuperation, 225
    fighting premature discharge from, 215–16
    frequent mistakes on bill, 328
    getting VIP treatment in, 213–15
    and malpractice, 210
    protecting yourself from common hazards
      at, 207–9
Hotels
    frequent guest programs for, 307–8
    rates for, 304
Hot flashes
    new treatment for, 183
    prevention of, 238
House
    buying from Resolution Trust Corporation,
      291–92
    chemicals in, 282–83
    defects in new, 291
    environmental safety of, 283–84
    remodeling mistakes, 288–90
Hybrid funds, investing in, 25
Hydroxides, safety of, 283
Hysterectomy, performance of unnecessary,
    208

I

Iatrogenic illnesses, 208
    causes of, 208–9
    guarding against, 209
Ibuprofen as painkiller, 217
Imagination, connection between health and,
    158–59
Immune system, exercise and, 246
Impotence
    cure for, 260
    surprising cause of, 266
Incentive stock options, as tax loophole, 66
Independent living as alternative to nursing
    home, 342
Indigestion, treating, 109
Infections, nosocomial, 207–8
Infectious keratitis, 285
Infertility
    smoking as factor in, 119
    in women, 272
Inner life, exploring, 154

Insomnia
    beating, 167–68
    fighting, 166
    five-day plan for overcoming, 163–65
Insurance, 87–101. *See also* Disability
    insurance; Health insurance; Homeowner's
    insurance; Life insurance
    mistakes when filing claims, 95
    savings on, 2, 3
Insurance companies
    collection claims from, 94–95
    safety of, 96
Internal Revenue Service (IRS)
    negotiating with, 52–54
    traps in dealing with, 54–55
International investment, retirement funds in,
    26
Intravenous fluid, dangers from, 217–18
Investments. *See also* Bonds; Stocks
    adapting retirement funds, to uncertain
      market, 339–41
    answers to commonly asked questions
      about, 22–24
    avoiding mistakes in, 28–30
    in bonds, 37
    lessons in, 32–33
    loopholes for, 34–35
    of lump-sum distribution, 84–85
    saving money with, 15–16
    shifting, from stocks to bonds, 36–37
    strategies under the new tax law, 19–20
Iodine, 188
    minimum daily requirements of, 237
Iodine-deficiency goiter, 188
IRAs, 24. *See also* Keogh plan; Keogh plans;
    Pension plans; Pensions; Retirement plans
    consolidation of, 45
    FDIC insurance on bank, 74
    investing in bank, 76–77
    investing maximum in, 20
    investments for, 24
    passing on to IRA, 79–81
    saving on inherited, 37–39
    short-term use of funds, 49
    taking money out of, 37, 58–59
    tax mistakes with, 56–58
    withdrawals, 58
Iron, 188–89
    excess, and colorectal cancer, 225
    minimum daily requirements of, 237
Iron-deficiency anemia, 189
Irritable bowel syndrome (IBS) and wheat
    bran, 234
Ischemia, 176
    as source of free radicals, 229
Isotretinoin (Accutane), sexual side effects
    from, 265

J

Japanese women versus American women,
    113
Jaundice, treatment for, 194
Jing, 128
Job performance, plants in raising, 152
Joint/separate returns, 65
Journal-writing, 129–31
Jumping versus osteoporosis, 319–20

K

Karaya gum, 122
Keogh plans, 48–49
    defined-benefit, 39–40
    defined-contribution plans, 48
    FDIC insurance on bank, 74
    money-purchase plans, 48
    terminating, and rolling money into IRA, 50
Kidney cancer, smoking as factor in, 119
Kidney disease, warning signs for, 333
Kidney stones versus citrus juice, 232
Kissing in spreading gum disease, 198
Knee injuries, avoiding, 245

L

Labetalol, sexual side effects from, 264
Lactic acid, exercise and, 245
Lake, fishing in new, 304
Laryngeal cancer, smoking as factor in, 119
Late-night eating, 225
Lateral training, as new exercise, 245
Lawn, secrets of chemical-free, 286–87
Leeches, medical therapies as, 205
Legacy, determining your, 146
Leg cramp, relief from, 203
Legg Perthes disease, 325
Leg pain, warning from, 124
Lemon law versus manufacturer's
    responsibility, 292
Leukemia, smoking as factor in, 119
Leuprolide for prostate cancer, 182
Levodopa, sexual side effects from, 264
Life
    living, to the fullest, 153–55
    understand the value of, 155
Life-care as alternative to nursing home, 342
Life insurance
    company-paid, 65–66
    determining needs in, 23–24
    making full use of company, 41
    passing physical for, 90
    term, 98–100
    variable universal, 20
    whole, 98
Life insurance companies, protecting yourself
    from, 88–90
Lifestyle
    improving, 156–57
    and insomnia, 167
Light, exposure to bright, and sleep, 186–87
Liposuction, 122
Lithium, sexual side effects from, 265
Living trust, establishing to avoid probate, 83
Living will, 23
Loan cosigners, cautions for, 77
Longevity
    and optimists, 142
    and pets, 133
    predicting, 107
Love, getting wanted, 251–53
Low birth weight, smoking as factor in, 119
Low-fat diet in preventing colon cancer,
    191–92
Low-Vision Enhancement System, 109
Luggage, self-defense for lost, 307
Lump-sum distributions, investing, 84–85
Lye products, safety of, 283

M

Macronutrients, 187
Maggots as medical therapies, 205
Magnesium, minimum daily requirements of, 237
Malpractice
    hospital, 210–11
    obstetric, 210
Mammogram, recommendation on, 320
Manganese, 189
Manic-depression, new treatment for, 148
Manufacturer's responsibility versus lemon laws, 292
Manufacturer's warranties, 13
Margarine, and cholesterol, 232
Marriage, delaying, until after year-end, 67–68
Master death file in finding mission persons, 259
Mazindol, sexual side effects from, 264
Measles, link between Crohn's disease and, 333
Meat, eating, and breast cancer, 228
Medical care. *See* Doctors; Health care; Hospitals; Medications
Medical databases, online, 112
Medical detective, becoming your own, 315–16
Medical research, doing your own, 110–12
Medicare
    coverages of, 90–92
    getting most from, 17–18
Medications. *See also* Drugs; *specific medication*
    advantages of buying overseas, 219–20
    on empty stomach, 218
    impact on brain function, 138
    and menopause, 244–45
    side effects from, 213
    statistics on prescriptions, 277
Medigap insurance, 121–22
    need for, 92
    shopping for, 18
Meditation, 161
    basics in, 174
Medroxyprogesterone and menopause, 244
Meeting planner, starting business as, 338
Megestrol acetate (Megace) for hot flashes, 183
Memory
    calcium versus, 240
    hidden cause of problems in, 262
Men
    and declining sperm counts, 261
    and enlarged breasts, 262, 263
    genital bites in, 262
    impotence in
        causes of, 266
        curing, 260
    length of penis, 261
    memory problems in, 262
    and menopause, 268–69
    premature ejaculation in, 262
    prostate cancer self-defense for, 259–60
    seasonal decline of semen quality, 260–61
    sex for older, 263, 265
    sexual satisfaction do's and don'ts, 268
    testicle injuries, 265

testosterone tablets for, 261
    and treating penis curvature, 262
    vasectomy versus testicular cancer, 262
    weight management for, 247–48
Menopause
    in American versus Japanese women, 113
    in men, 268–69
    and preventing hot flashes, 238
    preventing problems related to, 244–45
Mental fitness, 140–41
Merchandise, returning, to store, 12–14
Methionine, 189
Methylene chloride, safety of, 282
Micronutrients, 187
Migraines
    connection between low back pain and, 183
    unnecessary tests for, 201
Milk thistle, benefits of, 242
Mind-body connection in healing, 131–32
Minerals. *See also* Nutritional supplements
    major, 187–88
    in our food, 235–37
    trace, 188–90
    versus vitamins, 187
Minimum balance requirements, asking for waiver of, 71–72
Missing person, locating, 258–59
Moisturizing lotions, shopping for, 108
Molybdenum, 189
Money
    answers to commonly asked questions about, 22–24
    answers to the most-asked questions about, 26–28
    making as consultant, 338–39
    tips for saving, 1–18
        on banking, 3
        on car rentals, 7
        on catalog shopping, 10–12
        on clothing, 2–3, 4
        on college, 3
        on computers, 16
        on entertainment, 4
        on food, 1–2, 4, 7, 9–10
        on gasoline, 16
        on health care, 8–9, 16–18
        on insurance, 2, 3
        on personal finances, 14–15
        on restaurants, 10
        on utilities, 2, 3, 8
Money market fund, putting money in, 15
Monosodium glutamate (MSG), safety of, 281
Moods, mastering, 142–43
Mortgages
    approvals on, 78
    claiming interest on, as deduction for vacation home, 62–63
    escrow accounts for, 76
    paying down, 23
    reverse, 73
Motion sickness
    and diet, 234
    preventing, 192–93
Motor vehicle records in locating missing person, 258
Mouth cancer, smoking as factor in, 119
MRI, less-stressful, 314
Muggers, protecting yourself against, 311–12

Multiple chemical sensitivity, 185
Multiple myeloma, living with, 136–38
Multiple sclerosis
    coping with, 183–85
    new hope for, 203
    relief from, 194
Municipal bonds
    investing in, 23
    IRA investments in, 64–65
    as not proper investment for IRA, 24
Muscles, cause of flabby, 248–49
Muscular dystrophy, gene therapy for, 275
Music
    versus rectal exam pain, 262
    in soothing Alzheimer's patients, 200
Mutual fund
    bank-sponsored, 73–74
    determining to sell, 24
    getting money out of, 35
    for retirement planning, 27
    taxes paid by, to foreign government, 20
Myocardial ischemia, 201–2

N

Naphthalene, safety of, 283
Naproxen as painkiller, 217
National Kidney Foundation, donating old cars to, 70
National Odd Shoe Exchange (NOSE), 109
Nearsightedness, 185
Nedocromil (Tilade) in treating asthma, 201
Nettle, benefits of, 242
Newsletters
    on annuities, 44
    refunding, 5
Newspaper subscription, sharing, 4
Nicotine, sexual side effects from, 265
Nimodipine for strokes, 180
Nitroglycerin, sexual side effects from, 264
N-nitroso compounds in fighting cancer, 227
Nondeductible expenses, tax deduction for, 68–70
Nonsteroidal anti-inflammatory drugs (NSAIDs) in treating lupus, 196
North American Free Trade Agreement (NAFTA), 21
Nosocomial infections, 207–8
Nursing homes
    alternatives to, 341–43
    expenses in, 63
    health care problems in, 122
    under Medicare, 91
    picking, 343
Nutrition. *See* Diet
Nutritional supplements
    brand-name versus generic, 240–41
    and cancer, 227–28
    and children, 233
Nutritionists, being wary of advertising, 329

O

Obesity. *See also* Weight management
    increase in, 230–31
    research on, 243
Obstetric malpractice, 210

Occupational lung cancer, smoking as factor in, 119–20
Official Coupon Supplier Program, 7
Older people. *See* Elderly
Omeprazole (Prilosec) for gastroesophageal reflux disease (GERD), 317
On-line medical databases, 112
Optimists, and longevity, 142
Oral contraceptives, sexual side effects from, 264
Osteoporosis
  jumping versus, 319–20
  and premature gray hair, 127
  and salt, 224–25
  smoking as factor in, 120
Otitis media, 203
Overdraft service, 75
  avoiding charges for, 71
Oxygen deprivation and back pain, 176

P

Pacemaker surgery for women, 198
Package bomb, protecting yourself from, 327
Painkillers
  danger with, 330–31
  identifying best, 216–17
Papaverine, sexual side effects from, 264
Paradichlorobenzene (PDB), safety of, 283
Parents
  employing, in family business, 14–15
  health care for aging, 97
Passport, second, 298
P-coumaric in fighting cancer, 227
Penicillin-derived antibiotics, sexual side effects from, 265
Penis
  average length of erect, 261
  treatment for curvature of, 263
Pensions. *See also* IRAs; Keogh plans; Retirement plans
  annuity opportunities in, 43–45
  as benefit loophole, 65
  benefits from, 42
  borrowing from, 45
  safety of, 42–43
  taking advantage of, 14
  as taxable, 63
  taxes on, 63
Pentoxifylline for strokes, 180
Pepper cream, relief from, 197
Pepper sprays in avoiding violent crime, 309–10
Perchlorethylene, safety of, 283
Pernicious anemia, 203
Personal alarms in avoiding violent crime, 309–10
Personal concerns, 251–77
  getting love, 251–53
  handling trouble, 255–56
  lessons from widowhood, 256–58
  locating missing person, 258–59
  retirement of spouse, 253–54
Personal finances, saving money in, 14–15
Personality, self-talk link to, 142
Pets, healing power of, 132–35
Peyronie's disease, 263

Phantom stock as tax loophole, 66
Pharyngeal (throat) cancer, smoking as factor in, 120
Phenoxybenzamine, sexual side effects from, 264
Phentolamine, sexual side effects from, 264
Phosphorus, minimum daily requirements of, 237
Physical changes, challenge of, 154–55
Physical inactivity as cause of heart disease, 245
Plants
  benefits of, 157
  healing power of, 151–52
Plasminogen activator (tPA), 275
Plastic surgery, problems in, 113–15
Pneumococcal pneumonia, vaccine for, 186
Pneumonia
  self-defense for, 204
  vaccination for, 109
Police-impersonator, self-defense for, 326–27
Polio vaccinations, need for, 112
Positive thinking
  practicing, 137
  for tricky times, 155–56
Potassium, 188
  minimum daily requirements of, 237
Power of attorney, durable, 23, 86
Premature ejaculation, overcoming, 262
Premature graying, 266
  as early sign of osteoporosis, 127
Premier Dining Club, 10
Prescription, statistics on, 277
Preventive medicine, taoist principles of, 127–28
Price earnings ratios, 45
Privacy, protecting your, 318–19
Private foundations
  donating to, 52
  tax deduction for, 64
Probate, avoiding, 83
Procrastination, beating, 161
Profit-sharing plans as benefit loophole, 65
Progesterone, and menopause, 244
Property
  assessed value of, 291
  making gifts of appreciated, 52
Prostacyclin for strokes, 180
Prostate, 181–83
Prostate cancer, 182, 331
  new test for, 218
  risks from, 231
  self-defense for, 259–60
Prostatectomy, performance of unnecessary, 208
Prostate infection, symptoms of, 181
Prostate Specific Antigen (PSA), 182
Prostatitis, symptoms of, 181
Protein, need for, in elderly, 127
Psittacosis, 135
Psychological age, 103–4
Psychological problems, and insomnia, 167
Psychotherapy, inside, 148–50

Q

Quercetin in allergy relief, 192

R

Rabbi trust, 67
Radio contests, tips for, 305–6
Rainy-day fund, need for, 24
Real estate broker, watching closely, 292
Real Estate Investment Trusts (REITs), investing in, 27
Rebate receipt, requesting, for stores, 7
Recalculation method of calculating IRA withdrawals, 58
Recovery, plants in speeding, 152
Rectal exam pain, music versus, 262
Refunding newsletter, subscribing to, 7
Refundle Bundle, 5, 7
Relaxation, practicing and insomnia, 164
Reperfusion as source of free radicals, 229
Resolution Trust Corporation (RTC), buying house from, 291–92
Restaurants, saving money on, 10
Restless-legs syndrome, 167
Retin-A
  effect of on skin, 218–19
  for precancerous lesions of cervix, 269
  in repairing damaged skin, 201
Retinal detachment
  and nearsightedness, 185–86
  and risk for, 185–86
Retinoblastoma as hereditary, 333
Retirement
  benefits of early, 45
  as full-time job, 153–54
  healthiest places in USA, 335–36
  selecting best places for, 59–61
  of spouse, 253–54
  working after, 339
Retirement account
  using, to save money, 52
  zero-coupon bonds buying for, 22
Retirement funds
  adapting, to uncertain markets, 339–41
  bonds in, 27–28
  overall allocation of assets for, 26–27
  taking as lump sum versus annuity, 22
Retirement investments, crash-proofing, 24–26
Retirement plans. *See also* IRAs; Keogh plans; Pensions
  contributing maximum to your employer-sponsored, 20
  cutting tax on payouts, 67
  defined benefit keogh plan in, 39–40
  as means of cutting taxes, 47–49
  mutual fund for, 27
  as source of emergency cash, 49
  tax advantaged ways of tapping into, 49
  traps in, 40–42
  variable annuity in, 27
Reverse mortgages, 73
Reverse Transcriptase Polymerase Chain Reaction (RTPCR), 218
Risk capital, investing in speculative investments, 16
Rt-PA for strokes, 180
Running shoes, resting before reuse, 244

S

Safe-deposit-boxes, at bank, 76
Safety
    chemicals in homes, 282–83
    environmental, of house, 283–84
    of food additives, 281–82
    and scalding injuries, 113
St. John Wort, benefits of, 242
Salt
    danger of substitutes, 250
    and osteoporosis, 224–25
Saw palmetto, benefits of, 242
Scalding, self-defense, 113
Seafood, risks with, 237–38
Second opinion, getting best, 161–63
Second passports, 298
Section 1244 stock, deducting losses on sale of, 34–35
Secular trusts as tax loophole, 66–67
Securities
    giving appreciated, 34
    writing off worthless, 35
Select Coupon Program, 7
Selenium, 189
    minimum daily requirements of, 237
Self-esteem, plants in boosting, 152
Self-mastery in being more effective, 146–47
Self-promotion as career booster, 143–44
Self-talk, link to personality, 142
Self-worth, believing in own, 155–56
Semen quality, seasonal decline of, 260–61
Senior-citizen discounts, 296
Serial dilution endpoint titration and optimal dose immunotherapy, and allergy relief, 192
Setpoint, dieting versus your, 233–34
Sexual assault, avoiding, 310
Sexual issues
    curing impotence, 260
    and declining sperm counts, 261
    and enlarged breasts, 262
    and length of penis, 261
    premature ejaculation in, 262
    seasonal decline of semen quality, 260–61
    sex for older men, 263, 265
    testicle injuries, 265
    testosterone tablets for, 261
    and treating penis curvature, 262
    vasectomy versus testicular cancer, 262
Sexually transmitted disease. See AIDS
Sexual satisfaction, do's and don'ts of, 268
Sexual side effects of commonly prescribed drugs, 264–65
Shampoos, shopping for, 108
Shingles, treatment for, 194
Shoes
    basics in buying, 243
    buying single, for amputees, 109
    resting running, before reuse, 244
Sigmoidoscopy, 191
Silent myocardial ischemia (SMI), 201–2
Simon Foundation, 268
Skating injuries, guarding against, 248
Skin
    effect of Retin-A on, 218–19
    Retin-A in repairing, 201
    smoothing wrinkled, 193
Skin cancer, fluorescent lighting and, 323

Skin cleansers, shopping for, 107–8
Sleep
    exposure to bright light and, 186–87
    improving quality of, 166
    and late-night eating, 225
    restriction of, and insomnia, 164–65
Sleep disorders centers, 168
Sleep log, keeping, 165, 167–68
Slipped capital femoral epiphyses (SCFE), 325
Slot machines, best, 304
Slow-flow hemangioma, removal of, 206
Small-cap stocks, investing in, 36
Smell, measuring sense of, 126–27
Smoke detector, warning for, 284
Smoking
    and Alzheimer's disease, 203
    and asthmatic children, 324
    and cold and flu prevention, 175, 176
    dangers from, 118–20
    and death, 126
    and health problems, 326
    quitting, 170, 323
    saving on, 4
    and sleeping habits, 168
    tips for learning not to, 169–70
Snow-shoveling, self-defense in, 327
Social Security
    basic rights in, 92–93
    rip-off in, 327
    understanding, 41
Sodium, minimum daily requirements of, 237
Somatic cell gene therapy, 275
Spendthrift, identifying, 81
Sperm counts, declining, 261
Spouse, handling retirement of, 253–54
State taxes, overpayment of, 20
Steam, inhaling, in getting rid of cold, 124
Stock appreciation rights as tax loophole, 66
Stock market, playing, 21–22
Stock mutual funds, balancing stocks versus, 25
Stocks
    adding international, to your portfolio, 37
    balancing stock mutual funds versus, 25
    versus bonds, 23
    with cash in tandem as tax loophole, 66
    investing in, 23
    investing in small-cap, 36
    price earnings ratio on, 45
    shifting investments from, to bonds, 36–37
Stomach cancer, and chili pepper, 193
Stomach problems, hidden cause of, 197
Strawberry plants, growing, 358–59
Streptokinase, for strokes, 180
Stress
    in aging process, 104–5
    and cancer, 157–58
Stress management
    plants in, 151
    proper breathing in, 142
Stress tests, no-stress, 316
Strokes, 178–81
    prevention of, 180–81, 205
    risks for, 185
    treatment for, 200
    vitamin E in preventing, 231
    warning signs of, 329

Success, 153–74
    being better grandparent, 172–74
    and decision making, 169
    and education, 170–72
    friendship in, 169
    gaining, 159–61
    and getting second opinion, 161–63
    and healthier life, 156–57
    imagination in, 158–59
    and living life to fullest, 153–55
    and meditation, 174
    and overcoming insomnia, 163–65, 166–68
    and positive thinking, 155–56
    and procrastination, 161
    and quitting smoking, 169–70
    and setting goals, 163
    and stress/cancer connection, 157–58
    tai chi in, 165–66
Sucralfate, 189
Sugar, and cancer risk, 240
Sulfites, safety of, 282
Sulfur, minimum daily requirements of, 237
Sunscreens, shopping for, 108
Supermarket, healthy strategies at, 279–81
Support group, joining, 137
Surgery
    do's and don'ts for cosmetic, 222–23
    recovery from, and caffeine, 109
    for urinary incontinence, 268
Swindlers, steering clear of, 329–30
Synergy, 147
Systemic lupus erythematosus, 195
    causes and diagnosis of, 195
    symptoms of, 195
    treating, 195–97

T

Tai chi, benefits of, for older people, 165–66
Taoist principles of preventive medicine, 127–28
Tattoos, removal of, 193
Tatulazr in removing tattoos, 193
Tax Act of 1986, 42
Taxes
    and bankruptcy, 50
    cutting before year-end, 51–52
    cutting last year's, 47–49
    deductions
        for medical expenses, 64, 68
        for nursing-home expenses, 63
    deductions in, summertime, 61–63
    filing joint/separate returns, 65
    importance of planning, 49–50
    and investment strategies, 19–20
    mistakes made with IRAs, 56–58
Tax-exempt funds
    investing in, 20
    as not appropriate for IRAS, 24, 64–65
Teeth, yellowing of, 317
Telephone
    counseling on for heart attack survivors, 205
    credit card calling on, 306
    talking with doctor on, 212
    use of, as cause of acne, 320
Tension myositis syndrome (TMS), treating, 176–78